D1572316

ASTRONOMICAL PHOTOMETRY

ASTRONOMICAL PHOTOMETRY

A Text and Handbook
for the Advanced Amateur
and Professional Astronomer

Arne A. Henden
Ronald H. Kaitchuck

Department of Astronomy
The Ohio State University

Published by
Willmann–Bell, Inc.
P.O. Box 35025
Richmond, Virginia 23235 ☎ (804)
United States of America 320-7016

Publishers and Booksellers

Serving Astronomers Worldwide
Since 1973

Published by Willmann-Bell, Inc.
P.O. Box 35025, Richmond, Virginia 23235

First published 1982
Second printing, with corrections 1990

Printed in the United States of America

Library of Congress Cataloging-in-Publication Data
Henden, Arne A.
    Astronomical photometry : a text and handbook for the advanced amateur and professional astronomer / Arne A. Henden, Ronald H. Kaitchuck
        p.   cm.
    Includes bibliographical references.
    ISBN 0-943396-25-5
    1. Photometry, Astronomical. I. Kaitchuck, Ronald H.   II. Title.
QB135.H44 1990   90-11908
522'.62–dc20   CIP

PREFACE

Most people who do astronomical photometry have had to learn the hard way. Books for the newcomer to this field are almost totally lacking. We had to learn by word-of-mouth and searching libraries for what few references we could find.

The situation improved markedly after we began our graduate studies in astronomy at Indiana University. We then had access to professional astronomers with many years of experience in photometry. Indiana has a very good astronomical library, and the copy machine was used heavily by both of us. Nevertheless, information was still gleaned in a piecemeal fashion. It became obvious to us that, as tedious as our educational process had been, it must be a frustrating experience for those with more limited reference resources. We were also aware of the many "tricks" we had learned which somehow never found their way into print. With this in mind, we set out to write a reference text both to spare the beginner some of the hardships and mistakes we encountered, and to encourage others to share in the satisfaction of doing meaningful research.

Our basic approach was to create a self-contained book that could be used by the interested amateur with little or no college background, and by the astronomy major who is new to photometry. By self-contained, we mean the inclusion of sections on observational techniques, construction, and reference material such as standard stars. In addition, we added substantial theoretical background material. The more esoteric material was placed in appendices at the back of the book, thereby retaining the beginning level throughout the bulk of the manual yet providing heavier reading for the most advanced student.

Photoelectric photometry is a relatively small field of science, and therefore does not have the large commercial suppliers of instrumentation. We have tried wherever possible to indicate sources of equipment, not to recommend any particular brand but to indicate starting points for any equipment selection procedure. Any implied endorsement is unintentional.

Similarly, we advocate certain techniques in both the data acquisition and reduction. There are as many methods in photoelectric astronomy as there are observers and we will certainly have made some arguable statements. We have tried to only present techniques that we have used and found successful.

This book would not have been possible without the dedicated help of Professor Martin S. Burkhead, who instructed us in observational techniques and acquainted us with Indiana University facilities, and Professor R. Kent Honeycutt, who provided much of our theoretical background knowledge by course material and stimulating conversations. Both these professors, Russ Genet and Bob Cornett have proofread much of the text for which we are very grateful. We would also like to thank Thomas L. Mullikin for writing the section on occultation techniques. Our wives contributed more time and effort into proofreading and correcting than we would like to admit!

We hope that reading this book will instill in you the excitement and satisfaction that we have found in astronomical photometry. Good luck!

Arne A. Henden
Ronald H. Kaitchuck

CONTENTS

ASTRONOMICAL PHOTOMETRY

CHAPTER 1
AN INTRODUCTION TO ASTRONOMICAL PHOTOMETRY

1.1 AN INVITATION

In the direction of the constellation Lyra, at a distance of 26 light years, there is a star called Vega. Unknown to the ancients who named this star, its surface temperature is almost twice that of the sun and each square centimeter of its surface radiates over 175,000 watts in the visible portion of the spectrum. This is roughly 100 times the power of all the electric lights in a typical home, radiating from a spot a little smaller than a postage stamp. After traveling for 26 years, the light from Vega reaches the neighborhood of the sun diluted by a factor of 10^{-39}. Of this remaining light, approximately 20 percent is lost by absorption in passing through the earth's atmosphere. Approximately 30 percent is lost by scattering and absorption in the optics of a telescope. A 25-centimeter (10-inch) diameter telescope pointed at Vega will collect only one half-billionth of a watt at its focus. Of this, only a fraction is actually detected by a modern photoelectric detector. This incredibly small amount of energy corresponds to one of the brightest stars in the night sky. The amazing thing is that the stars can be seen at all! Perhaps even more amazing is that starlight can be accurately measured by a device which can be constructed at a cost of a few hundred dollars. Such is the nature of astronomical photometry.

The photometry of stars is of fundamental importance to astronomy. It gives the astronomer a direct measurement of the energy output of stars at several wavelengths and thus sets constraints on the models of stellar structure. The color of stars, as determined by measurements at two different spectral regions, leads to information on the star's temperature. Sometimes these same measurements are used as a probe of interstellar dust. Photometry is often needed to establish a star's distance and size. The Hertzsprung-Russell diagram, the key to understanding stellar evolution, is based on photometry and spectroscopy.

Finally, many stars are variable in their light output either due to internal changes or to an occasional eclipse by a binary partner. In both cases, the light curves obtained by photometry lead to important information about the structure and character of the stars. The photometry of stars, especially at several wavelengths, is one of the most important observational techniques in astronomy.

Astronomy differs from other modern sciences in an important aspect. Vast commercial laboratories or university facilities are not necessary to undertake important research. An amateur astronomer with a modest telescope or persons with access to a small college observatory equipped with a simple photoelectric photometer can make *a valuable and a needed contribution to science.* The number of stars, galaxies, and nebulae vastly outnumber the professional astronomers. As an example, there are less than 3000 professional astronomers in the United States and yet there are over 25,000 catalogued variable stars. On any given night, almost all of them go unobserved! Furthermore, an observer with a large telescope will concentrate on faint objects for which a large instrument was intended. Very little time is given to the brighter stars even though they are no better understood than the faint ones! A small telescope is well suited for these objects and even a simple photometer can produce first-class results in the hands of a careful observer. This book is, in part, an invitation and a guide to the amateur astronomer or persons with access to small college observatories to share in the satisfaction of astronomical research through photoelectric photometry. In Chapter 10, research projects for a small telescope are discussed. However, to give the reader a "feel" for what can be done, we cite two examples now. Figure 1.1 shows a light curve for the short-period eclipsing binary V566 Ophiuchi. This light curve was collected over several nights using a homemade photometer on a 30-centimeter (12-inch) telescope. One result of this study was the discovery of a change in the orbital period, the first such change seen for this binary in 13 years. These changes are believed to be related to mass transfer, from one of the two stars to the other, which in turn is related to changes in the stars. Thus, indirectly, photometry allows stellar evolution to be seen!

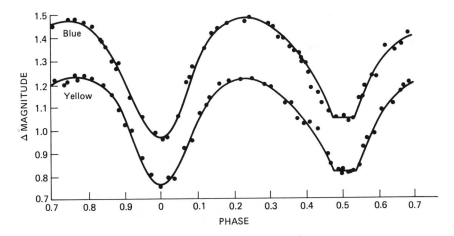

Figure 1.1 Light curve of an eclipsing binary.

Figure 1.2 shows the light curve of the double-mode cepheid TU Cassiopeiae taken with a 40-centimeter (16-inch) telescope. The scatter in the light curve is not due to poor photometry, but rather to the beating of two pulsations, with different periods, that are occurring in this star. Careful determination of both periods allows theorists to determine its mass, and the temporal variations in the light curve amplitude give constraints on its evolutionary behavior. Monitoring this type of star over long periods of time is essential, but difficult for the professional astronomer to do without preventing colleagues from using the telescope for their research.

This book is also directed toward a second type of reader. Often undergraduate or graduate students in astronomy are faced with the prospect of beginning their research only to discover that the "how-to"of photometry is lacking in textbooks. Much of the necessary information, such as lists and finding charts of standard stars, is scattered throughout the literature. Hopefully, this book will go a long way toward solving this problem. This reader will be more interested in the observing techniques and data reduction and less interested in construction details than the amateur astronomer. In like manner, there are theoretical sections that will be of less interest to the amateur. These sections have been either marked by an asterisk or placed in the appendices. The amateur astronomer may read or skip these sections as

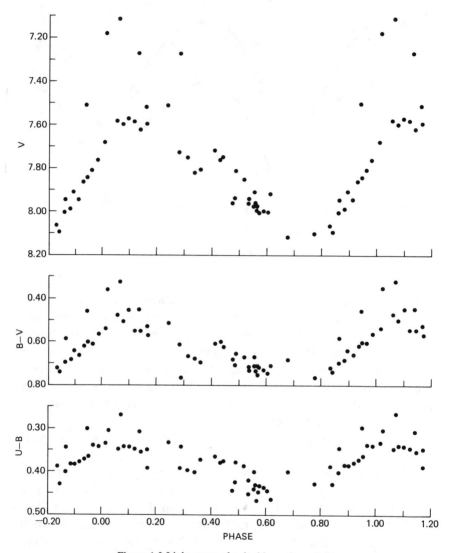

Figure 1.2 Light curve of a double-mode cepheid.

they are not mandatory for the construction and successful use of a photometer.

Overall, this book is intended to be a thorough guide from theory through practical circuits and construction hints to worked examples of data reduction. As a first step, we discuss the history of photometry and then consider a layout of a photoelectric photometer.

1.2 THE HISTORY OF PHOTOMETRY

A person need not own a telescope or a photometer to know that stars differ greatly in apparent brightness. It is therefore not surprising that the first attempt to categorize stars predates the telescope and was based solely on the human eye. Over 2000 years ago, the Greek astronomer Hipparchus divided the naked eye stars into six brightness classes. He produced a catalog of over 1000 stars ranking them by "magnitudes" one through six, from the brightest to the dimmest. In about A.D. 180, Claudius Ptolemy extended the work of Hipparchus, and from that time, the magnitude system became part of astronomical tradition. In 1856, N. R. Pogson confirmed Herchel's earlier discovery that a first magnitude star produces roughly 100 times the light flux[†] of a sixth magnitude star. The magnitude system had been based on the human eye, which has a nonlinear response to light. The eye is designed to suppress differences in brightness. It is this feature of the eye which allows it to go from a darkened room into broad daylight without damage. A photomultiplier tube or a television camera, which responds linearly, cannot handle such a change without precautionary steps. It is this same feature which makes the eye a poor discriminator of small brightness differences and the photomultiplier tube a good one. Pogson decided to redefine the magnitude scale so that a difference of five magnitudes was *exactly* a factor of 100 in light flux. The light flux ratio for a one-magnitude difference is $100^{1/5}$ or $10^{2/5}$ or 2.512. This definition is often referred to as a *Pogson scale*. The flux ratio for a two magnitude difference is $(10^{2/5})^2$ and a three magnitude difference is $(10^{2/5})^3$ and so on. In general,

$$F_1/F_2 = (10^{2/5})^{m_2 - m_1} \qquad (1.1)$$

where F_1, F_2 and m_1, m_2 refer to the fluxes and magnitudes of two stars. This can be rewritten as

$$\log (F_1/F_2) = \tfrac{2}{5}(m_2 - m_1) \qquad (1.2)$$

or

$$m_1 - m_2 = -2.5 \log F_1/F_2. \qquad (1.3)$$

[†]See Appendix J for a discussion of flux, intensity, luminosity, and blackbody radiation.

Note that the 2.5 is exact and not 2.512 rounded off. Equation 1.1 tells us that the eye responds in such a way that equal magnitude *differences* correspond to equal flux *ratios*. Pogson made his new magnitude scale roughly agree with the old one by defining the stars Aldebaran and Altair as having a magnitude of 1.0.

The human eye can generally interpolate the brightness of one star relative to nearby comparisons to about 0.2 magnitude. This is an acceptable error for certain programs such as the monitoring of long-period, large-amplitude variable stars. Because of the speed of measurement, visual photometry can be performed in sky conditions unsuitable for other forms of measurement. However, many problems exist with visual photometry, not the least of which are systematic errors such as color sensitivity differences between observers, difficulty in extrapolating to fainter stars, and lack of accuracy. The latter can be reduced somewhat by mechanical means introduced in the nineteenth century, so that the light from a variable artificial star visible to the observer can be adjusted to the same brightness as the object being measured. This type of photometer was invented by Zöllner and reduced the error to about 0.1 magnitude. A brief description of this device can be found in Miczaika and Sinton.[1]

Photography was quickly applied to photometry by Bond[2] and others at Harvard in the 1850s. The density and size of the image seemed to be directly related to the brightness of the star. However, the magnitudes determined by the photographic plate are not, in general, the same as those determined by the eye. The visual magnitudes are determined in the yellow-green portion of the spectrum where the sensitivity of the eye reaches a peak. The peak sensitivity of the basic photographic emulsion is in the blue portion of the spectrum. Magnitudes determined by this method are called *blue* or *photographic magnitudes*. The more recent panchromatic photographic plates can yield results which roughly agree with visual magnitudes by placing a yellow filter in front of the film. Magnitudes obtained in such manner are referred to as *photovisual*. Photographic photometry quickly showed that the old visual scale was not accurate enough for photographic work. What was needed was a new system, based on photographic photometry, and defined by a large number of standard stars. The unknown magnitude of a star could then be found by comparing it to the standards and applying Equation 1.1, where the flux ratio is determined by the image densities on the film. Because the brightest stars are not always well positioned for observation, a group of standard stars was defined in the vicinity of the north celestial pole. For a Northern Hemisphere observer, these stars would always be above the horizon. The group became known as the *North Polar Sequence*. Their magnitudes were defined so that the brightest stars in the sky would still be close to the photovisual magnitude of one. This system became known as the *International System*. At Mount Wilson Observatory, stars in 139 selected regions of the sky were established as secondary standards by comparison with the North Polar Sequence. Some of these stars were as faint as nineteenth magnitude. However, a large departure from Pogson's scale had occurred for the fainter stars because the nonlinearity of the photographic plate was not properly taken into account. Photographic photometry is still in use today, but primarily as a method of interpolating between nearby comparison stars, giving an error of about 0.02 magnitude. Photography offers a permanent record with a vast multiplexing advantage: thousands of images are recorded at one time.

Because of the difficulties inherent in visual and photographic methods, the application of the photoelectric method of measuring starlight in the late 1800s ushered in a new era in astronomy. Most early work such as that of Minchin[3] used selenium *photoconductive* cells which changed their resistance upon exposure to light. These cells are similar to the photocells found in some modern cameras. A constant voltage source was applied to the cell and the resulting variable current was measured with a galvanometer (a very sensitive current indicator.) A galvanometer is not used very often at present, primarily because of its bulk and its difficult calibration and operation. Joel Stebbins and F. C. Brown[4] were the first to use the selenium cell in the United States. Stebbins and his students were involved in most of the later development of photoelectric photometry (see Kron[5] for more details).

Some of the major disadvantages of the selenium cell were its low sensitivity (only bright stars and the moon were measured), narrow spectral response, and lack of commercial availability. Each cell had to be made individually, and it often took dozens of trials to produce a sensitive cell. Even so, in 1910 Stebbins[6] published a light curve of Algol of far greater precision than ever before, showing for the first time the shallow secondary eclipse that had eluded visual observers.

The discovery of the *photoelectric cell* in 1911 promised more sensitive measurements. These cells were similar to a tube-type diode using sodium, potassium, or other alkaline electrodes. A voltage of approximately 300 volts was applied, and when the cell was exposed to light, electrons liberated by the photoelectric process created a small current. This response was *linear,* that is, a source twice as bright gave twice the current. Schultz,[7] working with Stebbins, used the photoelectric cell to record light from Arcturus and Capella. Similar systems were being developed in Europe by Guthnick[8] and Rosenberg.[9] For many years, the problems associated with selenium cells plagued the newer design. Commercial photoelectric cells were not available until the 1930s. Galvanometers hung directly on the telescope and had to be kept level. The limit of detectability for the photoelectric cell-galvanometer combination was about a seventh magnitude star for a 40-centimeter (16-inch) telescope. The reader is referred to Stebbins[10] for details about these early measurements.

The electronic amplifier was introduced into astronomy by Whitford,[11] stepping up the feeble photocurrents to the point where less expensive meters and, more importantly, chart recorders could be used. At the same time, however, tube thermionic noise and amplifier instabilities were now problems and became the limiting component of a photoelectric system. The late 1920s and the 1930s also saw the advent of wide-band filters and the increasing adoption of the photoelectric photometer.

The invention of the electron multiplier tube or photomultiplier in the late 1930s was an important advance for astronomy. This tube is essentially a photocell with the addition of several cascaded secondary electron stages which allow noiseless amplification of the photocurrent. Whitford and Kron[12] used a prototype photomultiplier for automatic guiding. RCA introduced the 931 photomultiplier just prior to World War II and the 1P21 during the war. Kron[13] was the first to use these tubes for astronomical purposes. With the prototype tubes and a galvanometer, eleventh magnitude stars were measured on the Lick 36-inch refractor.

It became clear with the development of photoelectric techniques that the North Polar Sequence had not been established with enough accuracy. The new photoelectric magnitude systems are now defined by the choice of filters, photomultiplier tube and a network of standard stars. The definition of these systems are taken up in detail in Chapter 2.

Recent years have seen improvements on existing photometric systems, but no major changes. Various filter combinations and newer photocathode materials extending measurements from the near-ultraviolet to the near-infrared are being used. Less noisy amplifiers and pulse counting techniques have been developed to retrieve the feeble pulsed current. Innovative new designs that are in the prototype stage at this writing promise a bright future for the photoelectric measurement of starlight.

1.3 A TYPICAL PHOTOMETER

The heart of any photometer is the light detector. This device is explained in detail in Section 1.5. For now, it is sufficient to say it is a device that produces an electric current which is proportional to the light flux striking its surface. The output of the detector must be amplified before it can be measured and recorded by a device such as a strip-chart recorder. The detector is mounted in an enclosure on the telescope called the *head,* which allows only the light from a selected star to reach the light-sensitive element. Figure 1.3 shows the principal components of a photoelectric photometer, when the light detector is a photomultiplier tube. The telescope shown is a Cassegrain type, but any type may be used. The components enclosed by a dashed line are contained in the head, with its relative size exaggerated for clarity.

The first component is a circular diaphragm whose function is to exclude all light except that coming from a small area of sky surround-

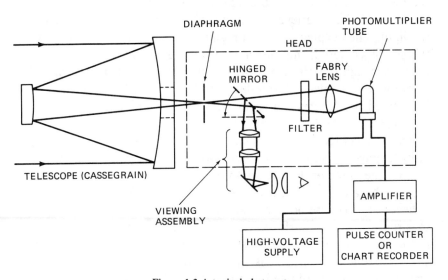

Figure 1.3 A typical photometer.

ing the star under study. The sky background between the stars is not totally dark for a number of reasons, not the least of which is city light scattered by dust particles in the atmosphere. Some of this background light also enters the diaphragm. The telescope must be offset from the star in order to make a separate measurement of the sky background, which can then be subtracted from the stellar measurement. The size of a stellar image at the focal plane of the telescope will vary with atmospheric conditions. Some nights it may seem nearly pinpoint in size while on other nights atmospheric turbulence may enlarge the image greatly. For this reason, a slide containing apertures of various sizes replaces the single diaphragm. To keep the effects of the sky background at a minimum, it is advantageous to use a small diaphragm. On the other hand, this puts great demands on the telescope's clock drive to track accurately for the duration of the measurement. On any given night, a few minutes of trial and error are necessary to determine the best diaphragm choice.

The next component is a diaphragm viewing assembly. This consists of a movable mirror, two lenses, and an eyepiece. Its purpose is to allow the astronomer to view the star in the diaphragm to achieve proper centering. When the mirror is swung into the light path, the diverging light cone is directed toward the first lens. The focal length of this lens is equal to its distance from the diaphragm (which is at the focal point of the telescope). This makes the light rays parallel after passing through the lens. The second lens is a small telescope objective that refocuses the light. The eyepiece gives a magnified view of the diaphragm. Once the star is centered, the mirror is swung out of the way and the light passes through the filter. As with the diaphragm, this is part of a slide assembly that allows different filters to be selected. The choice of filters is dictated by the spectral regions to be measured and is discussed in Chapter 6.

The next component is the *Fabry lens*. This simple lens is very important. Its purpose is to keep the light from the star projected on the same spot on the detector despite any motions the star may have in the diaphragm because of clock drive errors or atmospheric turbulence. This is necessary because no photocathode can be made with uniform light sensitivity across its surface. Without the Fabry lens, small variations in the star's position would cause false variations in the measurements. The focal length of this lens is chosen so that it projects an image of the primary mirror, illuminated by the light of the star, on the detector.

The final component in the photometer head is the photomultiplier tube. It is usually housed in its own subcompartment with a dark slide so that it can be made light-tight from the rest of the head. The tube is surrounded by a magnetic shield that prevents external fields from deviating the paths of the electrons and hence changing the output of the tube. Details on the construction of the photometer head are discussed in Chapter 6.

1.4 THE TELESCOPE

Before the reader rushes out to buy parts and start construction of that shiny new photometer, there is a very important practical consideration to be tackled. *Take a good, hard look at your telescope.* Most amateur-built telescopes, and even those commercially made for amateurs, are not directly suitable for photometry. The problem is usually not optical, but rather mechanical. These telescopes are seldom designed to carry the weight of a photometer head at the focal plane. Even the simplest head containing an uncooled detector weighs in the neighborhood of 4.5 kilograms (10 pounds). The telescope should be capable of being rebalanced to carry this load and the clock drive must still be capable of tracking smoothly. Furthermore, the mount must be sturdy enough so that small gusts of wind do not shake the telescope and move the star out of the diaphragm.

If your telescope has a portable mount, there should be some provision for attaining an equatorial alignment to better than 1°. There are several techniques of alignment that have been discussed in the literature.[14,15,16,17] The clock drive must have sufficient accuracy to keep a star centered in a diaphragm long enough to make a measurement. Typically, this means 5 minutes when using a diaphragm size of 20 arc seconds. Many clock drive systems have difficulty doing this. It is not uncommon for amateur drive systems to suffer from periodic tracking error. This is because of cutting errors in making the worm gear, and results in the telescope oscillating between tracking too slowly and too fast. The cure is to use a large worm gear of good quality. It is essential to have slow-motion controls on both axes. It is nearly impossible to center a star in a small diaphragm by hand. For right ascension, the slow-motion control can be the standard variable frequency drive corrector in common use today. The mechanical declination slow-motion controls supplied by most telescope manufacturers are far too coarse.

The declination motion should be as slow as the right ascension slow motion. It may be possible to gear down an existing system that is too coarse. An especially convenient method is to motorize the declination motion and then operate both axes by pushbuttons in a single hand control.

There are some requirements of the optical system as well. First of all, a large F-ratio is preferred. A small F-ratio produces a light cone that diverges very rapidly inside the head. This means that the components must be placed uncomfortably close together near the focal point. Photometers have been placed on telescopes with F-ratios as small as five. However, an F-ratio of eight or larger is recommended. A large F-ratio has a second advantage. It is highly desirable that the angular diameter of a diaphragm on the sky be kept as small as possible. This reduces the sky background light that enters the photometer. With a short F-ratio telescope, this becomes difficult since the diaphragm holes cannot be drilled small enough with a conventional drill press.

Another important consideration is the location of the focal point. Some telescopes are designed so that the prime focus never extends outside the drawtube. However, the diaphragm must be placed at the prime focus (see Figure 1.3). It may be necessary to move an optical element in the telescope to accomplish this.

Finally, the choice of the optical system itself is important. Refracting telescopes have very serious disadvantages. The glass of the objective lens does not transmit ultraviolet light. Hence, the U magnitude of the UBV system cannot be measured. Note that this problem also applies to Schmidt-Cassegrain telescopes (like the Celestron) though to a lesser extent, since the lens is very thin. A second problem with refractors is chromatic aberration. No matter how well the lens is made, not all wavelengths have a common focal point. The modern achromatic lens minimizes this effect, but perfect correction is not possible. When the diaphragm is at the focal point of blue light, some of the red light is excluded from the photometer, because the red light cone is too wide to pass through the diaphragm. The only solution is to use very large diaphragms that allow a large amount of sky background light to reach the detector. This makes the measurement of faint stars very difficult because the detector sees more sky background light than star light.

Thus, the Newtonian and Cassegrain telescopes are preferred. However, there is still a potential problem. Most small reflecting telescopes come with mirrors which have been overcoated with silicon monoxide.

As the coating ages, it converts to silicon dioxide, which does not transmit ultraviolet light as well. The solution is to keep the overcoating always fresh, or not to overcoat the mirrors, or simply plan not to do any ultraviolet measurements.

We recommend that you modify or improve your telescope before you spend a very frustrating night of attempting photometry with an inadequate telescope. Lest we end this section on too negative a note, it should be emphasized that these modifications are well worth the effort and will result in a much better telescope.

1.5 LIGHT DETECTORS

Since the late 1940s, the most commonly used light detector in astronomy has been the photomultiplier tube. However, a solid-state detector known as the photodiode may well become important in the near future. We discuss each of these devices in turn in this section.

1.5a Photomultiplier Tubes

The key to the operation of the photomultiplier tube is the *photoelectric effect,* discovered in 1887 by Heinrich Hertz. He found that when light struck a metal surface, electrons were released, with the number of electrons released each second being directly proportional to the light intensity. The photoelectric effect is perfectly linear in this regard. The kinetic energy of the released electrons depends on the frequency of the light source and not on its brightness. For a given metal, there is a certain minimum frequency below which no electrons are released no matter how intense the light source may be.

The explanation of the photoelectric effect was given by Albert Einstein in 1905 for which he was later awarded the Nobel Prize. He pictured light as a stream of energy "bullets" or *photons,* each containing an amount of energy directly proportional to the frequency and inversely proportional to the wavelength of the light. Because electrons are bound to the metal by electrical forces, a certain minimum energy is required to free an electron. When an electron absorbs a photon, it gains the photon's energy. However, unless the frequency is above a certain value, the energy is insufficient for the electron to escape the metal. For frequencies higher than this threshold value, the electron can escape and any excess energy above the threshold becomes the kinetic energy of the electron. For all frequencies above the threshold value, the number of electrons released is directly proportional to the number of photons striking the metal surface.

There are other ways of releasing electrons from a metal surface which are also of interest. *Thermionic emission* is essentially the same as the photoelectric effect except that the energy that releases the electrons comes from heating of the metal rather than from light. *Secondary emission* is the release of electrons because of the transfer of kinetic energy from particles that hit the metal surface. Finally, *field emission* is the removal of electrons from the metal by a strong external electric field. All of the above effects come into play in a photomultiplier tube.

Most photomultiplier (PM) tubes are about the size of the old-fashioned vacuum tubes used in radios and televisions. The components of the tube are contained by a glass envelope in a partial vacuum, so that the electrons can travel freely without colliding with air molecules. Figure 6.2 shows a photograph of an RCA 1P21 PM tube. The heart of the tube is the metal surface that releases the photoelectrons. Since this surface is at a large negative voltage with respect to ground, it is called the *photocathode.*

Photocathodes are not constructed of simple, common metals but rather a combination of metals (antimony and cesium in the case of the 1P21). The metals are chosen to give the desired spectral response and light sensitivity. For a typical photocathode material, the quantum efficiency is about 10 percent. (Of every 100 incident photons, only 10 will be successful in releasing a photoelectron. The energy from the remaining 90 photons is absorbed by the metal and dissipated in other ways.) The current produced by the photoelectrons is very weak and difficult to measure even for bright stars. For this reason, the early use of photocells met with limited success.

The PM tube differs from the photocell in that the PM tube amplifies this current internally. In order to accomplish this, the photoelectrons released by the photocathode are attracted to another metal surface by an electric potential. This metal surface is called a *dynode* and in the 1P21 it is at a potential 100 V less negative than the photocathode. As a result, this dynode looks positive compared to the photocathode. Photoelectrons are accelerated toward its surface, and the impact of each releases about five more electrons by the process of secondary emission. These electrons are in turn accelerated toward another dynode that is 100 V less negative than the previous dynode. Once again, the process of secondary emission releases about five electrons per incident electron.

This process is then repeated at other dynodes. The 1P21 has nine dynodes, so for each photoelectron emitted at the photocathode there are 5^9 or two million electrons emitted at the last dynode. This tube is said to have an internal gain of two million. These electrons are then collected at a final metal surface, called the *anode*, from which they flow through a wire to the external electronics.

Figure 1.4 shows the arrangement of the photocathode, dynodes, and anode inside a 1P21. The arrows show the paths of the electrons (for simplicity, not all the electron paths are shown). There are other PM tube designs and Figure 1.4 shows, schematically, the "venetian blind," and the "box-and-grid" types. The 1P21 is called a "squirrel-cage" design. Note that the 1P21 is a "side-window" design while the others pictured in Figure 1.4 are examples of "end-on" tubes.

The current amplification produced by the dynode chain is an extremely important characteristic of the PM tube. This amplification is essentially noise-free. Unlike the early photocells, far less external amplification is required. As a result, the external amplifier noise is relatively unimportant.

While the amplification process of a PM tube is noise-free, there are, unfortunately, noise sources within the tube. Noise is defined as any output current that is not the result of light striking the photocathode. With the PM tube sitting in total darkness, with the high voltage on, there is a so-called "dark current" which is produced by the tube. This current is a result of electrons released at the dynodes by thermionic and field emission. Even at room temperature, the dynodes are warm

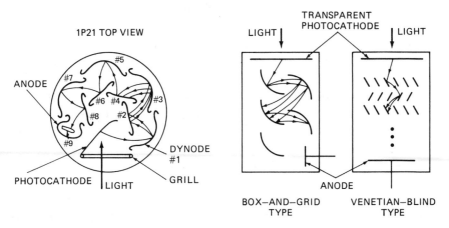

Figure 1.4 Photomultiplier tube designs.

enough for an electron to be released occasionally. When this happens, the electron is accelerated and amplified by the remaining dynode chain.

The obvious solution to large dark currents is to reduce the temperature of the tube. Most professional astronomers cool the PM tube with dry ice, almost totally eliminating thermionic emission. The amateur astronomer need not exert this much effort as an uncooled tube is still very useful. The only problem is that very faint stars are difficult to detect because the current they produce at the anode may be as small or smaller than the dark current. There is little that can be done to eliminate field emission because the tube must contain strong electric fields. However, in practice this noise source is very small compared to thermionic emission.

The current that leaves the anode is still very weak and requires amplification before it can be easily measured. There are two general ways to accomplish this. Because each photoelectron produces a burst of electrons at the anode, a pulse amplifier can be used to amplify each burst and convert it to a voltage pulse that can be counted electronically. The number of pulses counted in a given time interval is a measure of the number of photons that strike the photocathode in the same time interval. (We use the terms *pulse counting* and *photon counting* interchangeably whenever referring to the technique of counting individual photoelectron pulses caused by an incident photon on the photocathode of a photomultiplier tube.) The second technique is to use a DC amplifier and to smooth the bursts to look like a continuous current. This current is amplified and measured by a meter or a strip-chart recorder. Both techniques are discussed in detail in Chapters 7 and 8.

No photocathode material releases the same number of electrons at all wavelengths even when the light source is equally bright at all wavelengths. The spectral response of a photomultiplier is an important characteristic to know. Figure 1.5 shows the spectral responses of a few types of photocathode materials. The most common in astronomical use today is the cesium antimonide (Sb-Cs) surface, used in the first mass-produced photomultiplier, the RCA 931A. The RCA 1P21 is the successor to this tube and is used to define the *UBV* photometric system. The spectral response of this surface is labeled "S-4" in Figure 1.5 (the "S" numbers refer to different spectral responses). The light sensitivity peaks near 4000 Å, cutting off at the blue end near 3000 Å while on the red end there is a long tail to 6000 Å. Individual tubes vary and some-

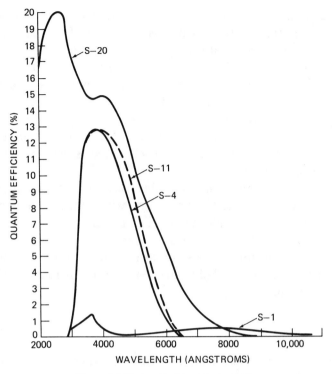

Figure 1.5 Photocathode spectral response.

times the response goes beyond 7000 Å, producing a problem when blue
or ultraviolet filters are used. These filters transmit some light in the
red and the tube detects red light passed by these filters. For red stars,
this "red leak" can cause an error in a blue magnitude of a few percent.
This problem is discussed later.

In Figure 1.4, two types of photocathodes are illustrated. The 1P21
is a side-window device. The light strikes the front surface of the photocathode and electrons are released from the same front surface. This
is called an opaque photocathode. With a semitransparent photocathode, used with "end-on" PM tubes, the light strikes the front surface
and the electrons are released from the *back* surface. These two types
of cathodes, even if made of the same material, have a slightly different
spectral response. The semitransparent photocathodes tend to be more
red-sensitive. For this reason, a semitransparent photocathode made of
Sb-Cs is designated S-11, not S-4.

Another important photocathode material is the so-called "tri-alkali" designated as S-20. Figure 1.5 shows that this material covers much the same spectral range as the S-4 but with much useful sensitivity in the near-infrared. This material is extremely sensitive in blue light and has a quantum efficiency of 20 percent. By contrast, the Ag-O-Cs, S-1 surface has a very low quantum efficiency of a few tenths of a percent. However, it has an extremely broad response up to 11,000 Å. There is a wide dip in its sensitivity centered at 4700 Å. The advantage of the S-1 photocathode is that a single tube can be used to measure from the blue to the infrared. The disadvantage, of course, is that you are limited to fairly bright objects.

Noise is a problem with PM tubes designed for infrared work. Infrared photons carry very little energy, which means the photocathode must be made of a material in which the electrons are bound very loosely. Unfortunately, this means they are very easy to release thermally. Hence all infrared tubes are cooled with dry ice, and detectors for the far-infrared are cooled to an even lower temperature with liquid nitrogen or liquid helium.

1.5b PIN Photodiodes

To date, very little experimentation with photodiodes for astronomical photometry has been published. However, these devices look very promising.[18,19,20,21,22,23] A well-designed photodiode photometer is now commercially available from Optec, Inc.[24] To understand the photodiode, we will review the operation of an ordinary diode briefly. More complete explanations can be found in most elementary electronics texts.

In an isolated atom, electrons are confined to orbits about the nucleus, which correspond to sharply defined energy levels. When atoms are linked in a crystal of a solid, the energy level structure is quite different. In a simplified view, the energy levels become two distinct bands. The lower band "contains" all the electrons (at least at very low temperatures) while the upper band is empty. There is a gap between the two energy bands that represents energy states unavailable to the electrons. If an electron somehow receives sufficient energy to reach the upper band, it can move freely through the crystal, unattached to any one atom. An external electric field easily can cause these electrons to move. For this reason, the upper band is called the *conduction band*. The electrons in the lower band are involved in the chemical bonds to neighboring atoms in the crystal, so this band is called the *valence band*. For solids that are insulators, the gap between the two bands is very large. It is very unlikely that an electron from the valence band will receive enough energy to promote it to the conduction band. Therefore, insulators are poor conductors of electric current. Likewise, a conductor is a material in which the two bands merge and electrons can easily move into the conduction band. Semiconductors have a small gap between energy bands. Germanium (Ge) and silicon (Si) are the two most commonly used semiconductor materials for making diodes and transistors.

Semiconductors without impurities are called *intrinsic semiconductors*. They have a rather low conductivity, but not as low as an insulator. If a semiconductor is "doped" with impurities, its conductivity can be increased markedly. Si and Ge each have four valence electrons per atom, which are used in bonding to four adjacent atoms when making a crystal. The process of doping involves replacing a few of these atoms with atoms that have one fewer (three) or one more (five) valence electrons. Suppose a Ge crystal is doped with arsenic, which has five valence electrons. Four of these electrons are used to bind the atom in the crystal with four neighboring Ge atoms. However, the fifth electron is loosely bound with an energy just below the conduction band. This electron cannot be in the valence band since this band is "full." A small amount of energy promotes this electron into the conduction band. Thus, doping has greatly increased the electrical conductivity. The impurity atom, arsenic, in this case is referred to as a *donor* because it supplied the extra electron. A semiconductor doped in this way is referred to as an *n-type* because a negative charge was donated.

The conduction of the crystal is also increased if it is doped with atoms that have only three valence electrons. These atoms are one short of completing their bonds with neighboring atoms. Thus, a "hole" exists. This atom has an unfilled energy level and a nearby valence electron can move into this location. Of course, this electron leaves a hole behind. In this way, it is possible for holes to migrate through the crystal. This impurity is labeled an *acceptor* because it accepts a valence electron from elsewhere in the crystal. Acceptor-doped crystals are referred to as *p-type* semiconductors because the current carriers are holes, or a lack of electrons, which look positive by comparison to the electrons.

A diode is made by bringing p-type and n-type material together. The

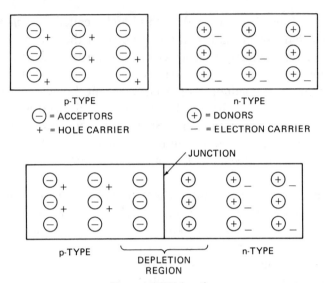

Figure 1.6 P-N junction.

surface of contact is referred to as the *junction*. Holes from the p-side and electrons from the n-side diffuse across the junction until an equilibrium is reached. The result is a region on either side of the junction where there are no charge carriers because the electrons and holes have combined to annihilate each other. This is called the *depletion region,* as shown in Figure 1.6. An electrostatic field is produced across the junction because the p-side now has an excess of electrons filling the holes and the n-side now has an excess of holes because it has lost electrons to the p-side. This results in a situation where an electron from the n-side is not likely to cross the junction because it is faced with an excess of electrons on the p-side that repel it. Similarly, a hole from the p-side will no longer cross to the n-side. If an external electric circuit is connected to the diode, such that the n-side is connected to a positive potential and the p-side to a negative potential (called *reversed biased*), no current will flow. This is because the external potential only increases the potential difference across the depletion layer. If the contacts are reversed, the current from the external circuit will tend to neutralize the charge difference across the junction. The potential difference drops and current flows. It is in this manner that alternating current can be converted into direct current, because during only one half of the cycle, when the diode is *forward biased,* will current be allowed to flow.

Normally, when electronics texts discuss the operation of a diode, as we have done above, they fail to mention one additional "complication." A graphic illustration of this is seen in the following experiment. Go to your local electronics store and find a glass-encapsulated diode. With a knife, scrape off the black paint that coats the glass. Connect a voltmeter capable of reading a few tenths of a volt across the diode. Shine a bright light on the diode and watch the meter. The added "complication" is just what makes diodes interesting to astronomers; they are highly light-sensitive. Light energy absorbed at the p-n junction raises an electron from the valence band to the conduction band. Such an electron is repelled by the p-side of the depletion region and attracted by the n-side. The opposite is true for the hole left behind. This process, when repeated over and over as light continues to strike the junction, results in the voltage detected in the above experiment. A diode used to measure light in this manner is said to be used in the *photovoltaic mode*.

In practice, diodes designed for light detection are constructed differently from ordinary diodes. In the so-called PIN photodiode a p-type layer (P) is separated from the n-type layer (N) by an intrinsic layer (I). The light is absorbed in the intrinsic layer, creating an electron-hole pair. The hole is attracted to the p-material and the electron to the n-material after drifting through the I layer. The function of the I layer is to reduce noise current produced by such effects as electron-hole pairs created by thermal processes. Nevertheless, this is still the major source of noise in a photodiode.

There are numerous advantages to a photodiode as a detector in a photometer. One advantage is seen in Figure 1.7, which shows that a blue-enhanced photodiode is an efficient detector from the ultraviolet to the infrared. Furthermore, the quantum efficiency of the photodiode is much better than the photomultiplier, reaching 90 percent in the near-infrared. Even though an S-1 photomultiplier can also span this range of wavelengths, it has a quantum efficiency of only a few tenths of a percent. Compared to photomultiplier tubes, photodiodes are also less expensive, much smaller, and do not require a high-voltage supply. It would thus appear that the professional astronomers should rush to replace the photomultipliers with photodiodes. The reason this has not occurred is that the photomultiplier tube still has one very important advantage. The dynode chain of the photomultiplier yields an internal current amplification (gain) of about 10^6. This is not the case for the photodiode. Therefore, the external electronics must amplify an addi-

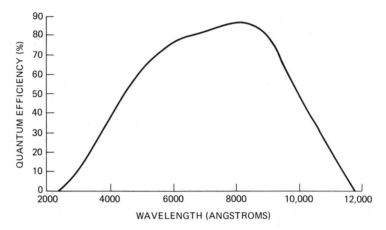

Figure 1.7 Approximate quantum efficiency of a blue-enhanced photodiode.

tional factor of 10^6 and this introduces noise. For a photodiode to be competitive with a photomultiplier tube, a well-designed amplifier is required and both the photodiode and the amplifier should be cooled. The internal gain of a photodiode is unity, which means that pulse-counting techniques cannot be used, so that DC photometry is required. In Appendix K, it is shown that DC is inferior to pulse counting when it comes to measuring faint stars, but for bright stars the photodiode works well. This fact, combined with its convenience, makes the photodiode a detector to be seriously considered. Also in Appendix K, a theoretical comparison of the photodiode and the photomultiplier is presented in order to help one decide on the best light detector for one's observing program and budget.

The size of the active area (light-sensitive area) of a photodiode should be kept fairly small to minimize the noise introduced by thermally produced electron-hole pairs. Thus, unlike the photomultiplier, the photodiode is placed at the focus of the telescope. This necessitates some design changes in the photometer head. Figure 1.8 illustrates the optical layout schematically when a photodiode is used. The first difference is that no diaphragms are used. The light-sensitive area of the photodiode is so small (typically 0.5 millimeter across) that it acts as its own diaphragm. It is not possible to place a viewing eyepiece behind the diaphragm. Instead, the eyepiece must be placed in front of the photodiode and equipped with a cross hair for centering the star on the photodiode. The placement of the photodiode as shown eliminates the need

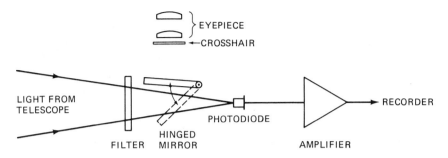

Figure 1.8 Photodiode photometer.

for a Fabry lens. The spectral response of the photodiode necessitates some special considerations when choosing filters. These are discussed in Chapter 6.

1.6 WHAT HAPPENS AT THE TELESCOPE

In later chapters, we discuss observing techniques and data reduction in detail. However, for the benefit of the novice, we now outline the observing procedure and define some terms. The actual observing pattern depends on the goal of the project and the form in which the final data are needed. In general, one of two techniques is followed. The simplest observing scheme, and the one highly recommended to the beginner, is *differential photometry*. In addition to its simplicity, it is the most accurate technique for measuring small variations in brightness. This technique is widely used on variable stars, especially short-period variables and eclipsing-binary systems.

In differential photometry, a second star of nearly the same color and brightness as the variable star is used as a *comparison star*. This star should be as near to the variable as possible, preferably within one degree. This allows the observer to switch rapidly between the two stars. Another extremely important reason for choosing a nearby comparison star is that the extinction correction (Section 1.8) can often be ignored, because both stars are seen through nearly identical atmospheric layers. All changes in the variable star are determined as magnitude differences between it and the comparison star. It is important that the comparison star be measured frequently because the altitude of these objects is continuously changing throughout the night. This type of photometry can be extremely accurate (0.005 magnitude) and is highly recommended where atmospheric conditions can be quite variable, such as the midwestern United States. Any star that meets the criteria can be a comparison star. However, it is a good idea to pick a second star, called the check star, as a test of the nonvariability of the comparison star. The check star need be measured only occasionally during the night.

The observational procedure is to alternate between the variable and comparison stars, measuring them a few times in each filter. A "measurement" consists of centering the star in the diaphragm and then moving the flip mirror out of the light path so that the light can fall on the detector. You then record the meter reading on your amplifier along with the time. If you are using pulse-counting equipment, you record the number displayed on your counter. If you are very lucky, your microcomputer can record it for you! Once this has been done for each filter, the star is moved out of the diaphragm and the sky background is recorded through each filter. This is necessary since the measurements of the star really include the star and the sky background.

The magnitude differences between the variable and comparison stars in each filter can then be calculated using the expression

$$m_x - m_c = -2.5 \log (d_x/d_c) \qquad (1.4)$$

where d_x and d_c represent the measurement of the variable and the comparison stars minus sky background, respectively. If different amplifier gains were used for the two stars, this must also be included. An advantage of differential photometry is that no calibration to the standard photometric system is necessary for many projects. The disadvantage is that your magnitude differences will not be exactly the same as those measured on the standard system. However, if you are using the specified detector and filters, and have matched the color of the comparison and variable stars, your results will not differ very much (see Section 2.6). A further disadvantage is that your final results will be in *differences*. You will not be able to specify the actual magnitudes or colors of the variable star unless you standardize the comparison star. However, these results are good enough for many projects such as determining light curve shapes or the times of minimum light of an eclipsing binary.

The second technique is the most general and commonly used by professional astronomers. It is also the most demanding on the quality of the sky conditions. In this scheme, numerous program stars, located in many different places in the sky, are to be measured to determine their magnitudes and colors. As before, each star and its sky background are measured through all filters. However, because each star is observed at a different altitude above the horizon, each is seen through a slightly different thickness of the earth's atmosphere. Therefore, observations must also be made of another set of stars of known magnitudes and colors to determine the atmospheric extinction corrections. Finally, a set of standard stars must be observed to determine the transformation coefficients so the measurements of the program stars can be transformed into magnitudes and colors of a standard system, such as the *UBV* system. This procedure often involves less observing time than it would appear at first glance. This is because it is often possible to use some of the same observations to determine the extinction corrections and the transformation coefficients. Furthermore, the transformation coefficients need only be determined occasionally. Details of the procedures are treated in Chapters 4 and 9.

1.7 INSTRUMENTAL MAGNITUDES AND COLORS

It would appear to the beginner that the determination of a star's magnitude is fairly simple and, furthermore, that magnitude can be simply related to the star's light flux. Unfortunately, the latter is far from true. To see this more clearly, we rewrite Equation 1.3 as

$$m_1 = m_2 - 2.5 \log F_1 + 2.5 \log F_2. \tag{1.5}$$

Suppose star "2" is a reference star of magnitude zero and star "1" is the unknown. Then

$$m_1 = q - 2.5 \log F_1 \tag{1.6}$$

where q is a constant. Since there is now only one star the subscript "1" can be dropped in favor of lambda (λ) to remind us that the magnitude depends on the wavelength of observation. Thus,

$$m_\lambda = q_\lambda - 2.5 \log F_\lambda. \tag{1.7}$$

Again, this equation only seems to verify the simple relationship between magnitude and flux. However, the above equation refers to the *observed* flux. The observed flux is related to the actual flux in a very complicated way. The problems can be broken into two groups: (1) extinction because of absorption or scattering of the stellar radiation on its way to the detector and (2) the departure of the detecting instrument from one with ideal characteristics. We now discuss these two problems in turn.

There are two sources of absorption of the stellar flux: interstellar absorption because of dust and absorption within the earth's atmosphere. The former is generally neglected for published observations, but the latter is usually taken into account. The earth's atmosphere does not transmit all wavelengths freely. For example, ultraviolet light is heavily absorbed. Human life can be thankful for that! Observatories at higher elevations have less of the absorbing material above them, while others located near large bodies of water have more water vapor above them. In addition, the atmosphere scatters blue light much more than red light.

Not all telescopes transmit light in the same manner and this can be a function of wavelength. For instance, glass absorbs ultraviolet light heavily, and various aluminum and silver coatings have different wavelength dependences of the reflectivity. Also, in practice it is not possible to measure the flux from a star at one wavelength. Any filter transmits light over an interval of wavelengths. Despite the best efforts of the manufacturers, no two filters or light detectors can be made with exactly the same wavelength characteristics. As a result, no two observatories measure the same observed flux for a given star.

A calibration process is necessary to enable instruments to yield the same results. The observed flux, F_λ, is related to the actual stellar flux, F^*_λ, outside the earth's atmosphere, by

$$F_\lambda = \int_0^\infty \phi_A(\lambda)\phi_T(\lambda)\phi_F(\lambda)\phi_D(\lambda) F^*_\lambda d\lambda$$

where

$\phi_A(\lambda)$ = fractional transmission of the earth's atmosphere
$\phi_T(\lambda)$ = fractional transmission of the telescope
$\phi_F(\lambda)$ = fractional transmission of the filter
$\phi_D(\lambda)$ = efficiency of the detector (1.0 corresponds to 100 percent).

This expression can be very complicated and the many factors are usually poorly known. It is for this reason that stellar fluxes are very difficult to measure accurately. Fortunately, the determination of stellar magnitudes does not require a knowledge of most of these factors, except in an indirect manner. The magnitude scheme requires only that certain stars be *defined* to have certain magnitudes, so that magnitudes of other stars can be determined from observed fluxes that are corrected only for atmospheric absorption. This is why the seemingly awkward magnitude system has survived so long.

The only remaining problem is to account for the individual differences among telescope, filter, and detector combinations. This is where the set of standard stars comes into use. By observing a set of known stars, it is possible for each observatory to determine the necessary transformation coefficients to transform their instrumental magnitudes to the common standard system.

In practice, a star is not measured in flux units. The detector produces an electrical output that is directly proportional to the observed stellar flux. In DC photometry, the amplified output current of the detector is measured, while in pulse-counting techniques the number of counts per second is recorded. In either case, the recorded quantity is only proportional to the observed flux. Symbolically,

$$F_\lambda = K d_\lambda \qquad (1.8)$$

where d_λ is the practical measurement (i.e., current or counts per second), and K is the constant of proportionality. Equation 1.7 can be written as

$$m_\lambda = q_\lambda - 2.5 \log K - 2.5 \log d_\lambda \qquad (1.9)$$

or

$$m_\lambda = q'_\lambda - 2.5 \log d_\lambda \qquad (1.10)$$

This then relates the actual measurement, d_λ, to the instrumental zero point constant q'_λ, and to the *instrumental magnitude, m_λ*. The *color index* of a star is defined as the magnitude difference between two different spectral regions. If the subscripts 1 and 2 refer to these two regions, then a color index is defined as

$$m_{\lambda 1} - m_{\lambda 2} = q'_{\lambda 1} - q'_{\lambda 2} - 2.5 \log d_{\lambda 1} + 2.5 \log d_{\lambda 2} \quad (1.11)$$

or

$$m_{\lambda 1} - m_{\lambda 2} = q_{\lambda 12} - 2.5 \log (d_{\lambda 1}/d_{\lambda 2}) \quad (1.12)$$

where the zero point constants have been collected into a single term, $q_{\lambda 12}$. Again the quantity $(m_{\lambda 1} - m_{\lambda 2})$ is in the instrumental system. The transformation from the instrumental system to the standard system is discussed shortly. Before that transformation can be made, it is necessary to correct for the absorption effects of the earth's atmosphere.

1.8 ATMOSPHERIC EXTINCTION CORRECTIONS

Even on the clearest of nights, the stars are dimmed significantly by absorption and scattering of their light by the earth's atmosphere. The amount of light loss depends on the height of the star above the horizon, the wavelength of observation and the current atmospheric conditions. Because of this complex behavior, the measured magnitudes and color indices are corrected to a location "above the earth's atmosphere." In other words, they are corrected to give the same values an observer in space would measure. In this way, measurements by two different observatories can be effectively compared.

A measured magnitude, m_λ, is corrected to the magnitude that would be measured above the earth's atmosphere, $m_{\lambda 0}$, by the following equation,

$$m_{\lambda 0} = m_\lambda - (k'_\lambda + k''_\lambda c)\, X, \quad (1.13)$$

where k'_λ is called the *principal extinction coefficient* and k''_λ is the *second-order extinction coeffcient*. This second-order term is often small enough to be ignored in practice. Here c is the observed color index and

X is called the *air mass*. At the zenith, X is 1.00 and it grows larger as the altitude above the horizon decreases. To a good approximation,

$$X = \sec z, \qquad (1.14)$$

where z is the zenith distance ($90° -$ altitude) of the star.

Just as the sun grows red in color as it sets, the atmospheric extinction process affects the color indices of stars. A measured color index, c, is transformed to a color index as seen from above the earth's atmosphere, c_0, by the following expression:

$$c_0 = c - k'_c X - k''_c X c. \qquad (1.15)$$

as above, k'_c and k''_c represent the principal and second-order extinction coefficients, respectively. The subscript c is a reminder that the value of the coefficient depends on the two wavelength regions measured. That is to say, the extinction coefficient for a color index based on a blue and a yellow filter is not the same as that based on a yellow and red filter. The extinction coefficients, k'_λ, k''_λ, k'_c and k''_c are determined observationally. The details of this technique will be discussed in Chapter 4. The derivation of the above extinction equations can be found in Appendix *J*.

1.9 TRANSFORMING TO A STANDARD SYSTEM

A system of magnitudes and colors, such as the *UBV* system, is defined by a set of standard stars measured by a particular detector and filter set. In order for observers at different observatories to be able to compare observations, the observations must be transformed from the instrumental systems (which are all different) to a standard system. It is important for the observers to match the equipment used to define the system of standard stars as closely as possible. However, no two filter sets or detectors are exactly the same. Hence, it is necessary for all observers to measure the standard stars in order to determine how to transform their observations to the standard system.

A derivation of the transformation equations can be found in Appendix J. Only the results are stated here. Once the observed magnitude has been corrected for atmospheric extinction, it can be transformed to a standardized magnitude (M_λ) by

$$M_\lambda = m_{\lambda 0} + \beta_\lambda C + \gamma_\lambda \qquad (1.16)$$

where C is the standard color index of the star, β_λ and γ_λ are the color coefficient and zero-point constant, respectively, of the instrument. The standardized color index is given by

$$C = \delta c_0 + \gamma_c \qquad (1.17)$$

where c_0 is the observed color index which has been corrected for atmospheric extinction. Again, δ is a color coefficient and γ_c is a zero-point constant. These coefficients and zero-point constants are determined for each photometer system by the observation of standard stars. The details of this are taken up in Chapter 4.

1.10 OTHER SOURCES ON PHOTOELECTRIC PHOTOMETRY

There are several sources relating to photoelectric photometry that are available in good astronomical libraries. Some of these are obscure and are difficult to locate. Most of the references listed below are out of print or are sections of expensive texts. However, if you are interested in more detail than can be found in this text, we recommend looking at those references available in your area.

- Irwin, J. B., ed. 1953. *Proceedings of the National Science Foundation Astronomical Photoelectric Conference.* Flagstaff, Arizona: Lowell Observatory. This book has considerable detail on sky conditions and site selections for observatories.
- Wood, F. B., ed. 1953. *Astronomical Photoelectric Photometry.* Washington, D.C.: AAAS. This is the proceedings of a symposium on December 31, 1951. Contains many references of early photometry and describes DC, AC, and pulse-counting techniques as practiced at that time.
- Hiltner, W. A., ed. 1962. *Astronomical Techniques.* Chicago: Univ. of Chicago Press. Three chapters of this book are of particular interest: Lallemand ("Photomultipliers"), Johnson ("Photoelectric Pho-

tometers and Amplifiers"), and Hardie ("Photoelectric Reductions").

- Whitford, A. E. 1962. "Photoelectric Techniques." In *Handbuch der Physik*. Berlin: Springer-Verlag Co. Edited by S. Flugge, p. 240. This chapter is a well-rounded description of photomultiplier tube photometry.
- Wood, F. B. 1963. *Photoelectric Astronomy for Amateurs*. New York: Macmillan. This text is low level and understandable, but is incomplete and contains out of date circuitry.
- *AAVSO*, 1967. *Manual for Astronomical Photoelectric Photometry*. Cambridge: AAVSO. The AAVSO has a short manual to start observers on photometry.
- Golay, M. 1974. *Introduction to Astronomical Photometry*. Holland: D. Reidel. For complete theoretical descriptions of wide-band photometry, this text is hard to beat. Requires extensive mathematics and astronomy background.
- Young, A. T. 1974. In *Methods of Experimental Physics: Astrophysics* **vol. 12A**. Edited by N. Carleton. New York: Academic Press. This is extremely complete in the problems arising in photometry and should be required reading.

In addition, some professional observatories have their own small manuals that can be obtained directly from them.

Amateur and professional astronomers interested in photometry are strongly encouraged to join the International Amateur-Professional Photoelectric Photometry (IAPPP) association. The goal of this group is to foster communication on the practical aspects of photometry. This is accomplished through annual IAPPP symposia and the IAPPP Communications. Interested persons should contact either of the following people:

Dr. Terry D. Oswalt
Dept. of Physics and Space Sciences
Florida Institute of Technology
Melbourne, FL 32901

Mr. Robert C. Reisenweber
Rolling Ridge Observatory
3621 Ridge Parkway
Erie, PA 16510
U. S. A.

Amateur astronomers are encouraged to coordinate their photometric observing programs with those of other amateurs by contacting one of the following organizations.

American Association of Variable Star Observers (AAVSO)
25 Birch Street
Cambridge, MA 02138

Royal Astronomical Society of New Zealand
Variable Star Section
P. O. Box 3093 Greenton
Tauranga, New Zealand

REFERENCES

1. Miczaika, C. R., and Sinton, W. M. 1961. *Tools of the Astronomer*. Cambridge, Mass.: Harvard Univ. Press, p. 156.
2. Bond, W. C. 1850. *Annals of the Harvard College Observatory,* I, 1, CXLIX.
3. Minchin, G. M. 1895. *Proc. Roy. Soc.* **58**, 142.
4. Stebbins, J., and Brown, F. C. 1907. *Ap. J.* **26**, 326.
5. Kron, G. E. 1966. *Pub. A.S.P.* **78**, 214.
6. Stebbins, J. 1910. *Ap. J.* **32**, 185.
7. Schultz, W. F. 1913. *AP. J.* **38**, 187.
8. Guthnick, P. 1913. *Ast. Nach.* **196**, 357.
9. Rosenberg, H. 1913. *Viert. der Ast. Gesell.* **48**, 210.
10. Stebbins, J. 1928. *Pub. Washburn Obs.* XV, 1.
11. Whitford, A. E. 1932. *Ap. J.* **76**, 213.
12. Whitford, A. E., and Kron, G. E., 1937. *Rev. Sci. Inst.* **8**, 78.
13. Kron, G. E. 1946, *Ap. J.* **103**, 326.
14. Davis, F. W., Jr. 1973. *Griffith Observer* (May), 8.
15. Custer, C. P. 1973. *Sky and Tel.* **46**, 329.
16. Souther, B. L. 1978. *Sky and Tel.* **55**, 78.
17. Souther, B. L. 1978. *Sky and Tel.* **55**, 173.
18. De Lara, E., Chavarria, K. C., Johnson, H. L. and Moreno, R. 1977. *Revistia Mexicana de Astron. y Astrof.* **2**, 65.
19. Schumann, J. D., 1977. In *Astronomical Applications of Image Detectors with Linear Response*, I. A. U. Colloquium No. 40, 31-1.
20. Fisher, R. 1968. *Appl Optics* **7**, 1079.
21. Masek, N. L. 1976. *South. Stars* **26**, 175.
22. Corney, A. C. 1976. *South. Stars* **26**, 177.
23. McFaul, T. G. 1979. *J. AAVSO* **8**, 64.
24. Optec Inc., 119 Smith, Lowell, MI 49331.

Chapter 2
Photometric Systems

The basic goal of astronomical photometry sounds simple enough: to measure the light flux from a celestial object. So it would seem that simply placing a light detector at the focus of a telescope is all that is needed. The problem begins when different observers using different light detectors and telescopes try to compare or combine their data. Even though they may have been observing the same star at exactly the same time, their measurements will not necessarily be the same. This difference is due to the different spectral response of the telescope and detector. To take an extreme example, suppose a detector is mostly sensitive to blue light while a second is mostly sensitive to red. Stars are not equally bright at all wavelengths so the two detectors cannot possibly give the same results for the same star.

The obvious first step toward a uniform data set would be to have all observers use the same kind of detector. It would also be extremely valuable to isolate and measure certain portions of the spectrum containing features that indicate physical conditions of the star. This can be achieved by using a detector with a broad spectral response with individual spectral regions isolated by filters transmitting only a limited wavelength interval to the detector. Every observer should match the detector and filters as closely as possible to a common system. However, even this is not enough to yield strict uniformity as it is impossible to manufacture identical light detectors and filters. Thus, a third and final component is necessary: standard stars. Observations of the same, nonvariable (hopefully!) stars, of known magnitudes and colors, will allow each observer to determine his own coefficients for Equations 1.16 and 1.17. It is then possible to measure any unknown star and use these equations to transform the results to a common photometric system.

This is how a photometric system is defined: by specifying the detector, filters, and a set of standard stars.

Photometric systems can be broken into three rough categories based on the size of the wavelength intervals transmitted by their filters. Wide-band systems (such as the *UBV* system) have filter widths of about 900 Å, while intermediate-band filter widths are about 200 Å. Narrow-band systems are used to isolate and measure a single spectral line and may have widths of 30 Å or less. While the narrow-band systems give very specific spectral information, they transmit only a small fraction of the light of the star. Unless a large telescope is used, their use is limited to very bright stars. A discussion of various photometric systems can be found in Golay.[1]

At the end of this chapter, an intermediate-band and a narrow-band system are considered. However, in what follows, and throughout the remainder of this book, the wide-band *UBV* system will be discussed. By adopting a single system, specific examples of observing techniques and data reduction can be used, avoiding a very general discussion that would be of much less benefit to the beginner. However, many of those procedures can be applied to any system. The choice of the *UBV* system as "the system" for this book is based on a number of considerations. The *UBV* system has become popular among astronomers, and there exists a considerable data base of *UBV* observations in the literature. Being a wide-band system makes it especially suitable for users of small telescopes. The photomultiplier tube and filters used to define the system are readily available and relatively inexpensive. There is also a fairly extensive set of standard stars. The reader should not assume that the choice of the *UBV* system for this book means that the other systems are less important or yield measurements that tell us less about the stars. As you will see later, the *UBV* system is not a perfect system, and for some research projects, other systems are preferred.

2.1 PROPERTIES OF THE *UBV* SYSTEM

The *UBV* system was defined and established by H. L. Johnson and W. W. Morgan.[2,3] They desired to establish a photoelectric system that would yield results comparable to the yellow and blue magnitudes of the International System (see Section 1.2), to have a third color for better discrimination of stellar attributes, and to be closely tied to the Morgan-Keenan (M-K) spectral classification system. The *UBV* system

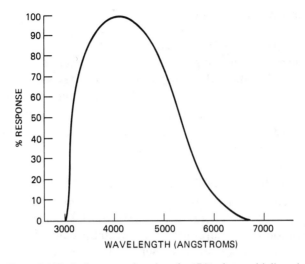

Figure 2.1 Typical response function of a 1P21 photomultiplier tube.

was developed around the RCA 1P21 photomultiplier tube and three broad-band filters that give a visual magnitude (V), a blue magnitude (B), and an ultraviolet magnitude (U). The response function of the 1P21 is shown in Figure 2.1 and the transmission curves of the filters are shown in Figure 2.2.

The V filter is yellow with a peak transmission around 5500 Å. This filter was chosen so that the V magnitude is almost identical to the pho-

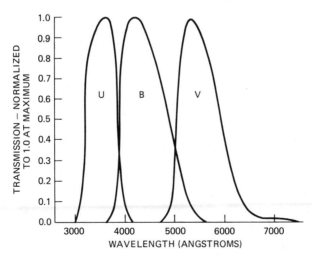

Figure 2.2 Normalized transmission function of the UBV filters.

tovisual magnitude of the International System. The long wavelength cutoff is determined by the response of the 1P21 and not the filter. The blue (*B*) filter is centered around 4300 Å but has some transmission over most of the sensitivity range of the 1P21. The *B* magnitude corresponds well with the earlier blue photographic magnitudes. This filter actually consists of two: a blue filter and an ultraviolet blocking filter. This latter filter prevents the *B* magnitude from being affected by the Balmer discontinuity, which is discussed later. The *U* filter is centered on 3500 Å and has two problems. This filter has a red "leak," that is, it transmits some light in the near infrared. This red light must be blocked by a second filter or the red leak must be measured and subtracted from the *U* measurement. The second problem is that the short wavelength cutoff is not set by either the filter or the photomultiplier, but instead by the earth's atmospheric ultraviolet transmission. This is a function of the observatory's altitude and can be variable depending on atmospheric conditions. Thus the *UBV* system is not totally filter-defined.

The *UBV* standard stars were measured by Johnson's original photometer without any transformation. In other words, except for some additive constants, the *UBV* system is the instrumental system of that photometer. The zero points of the color indices, (*B* − *V*) and (*U* − *B*), are defined by six A0 V stars. These stars are α Lyr, γ UMa, 109 Vir, α Crb, γ Oph, and HR 3314. The average color index of these stars is defined to be zero, that is

$$(B - V) = (U - B) = 0.$$

The system was originally defined with 10 primary standard stars. Just 10 stars, spaced over the entire sky, is an insufficient number to allow other observatories to calibrate their photometers. Johnson and Morgan established a more extensive list of secondary standards that are closely tied to the ten primary stars. Appendix C lists these stars. Secondary standards were also established within three open-star clusters. These clusters are especially valuable for *UBV* calibration since the uncertainties in atmospheric extinction are less important because of the proximity of the stars. The names of these clusters along with finder charts are found in Appendix D.

2.2 THE *UBV* TRANSFORMATION EQUATIONS

Through the observations of standard stars, an observer can take instrumental measurements of program stars and transform them to the standard *UBV* system. In Chapter 1, the transformation equations are presented in a general form to be applied to any photometric system. It is customary to change the symbols used in the transformation equations to indicate the use of the *UBV* system. Equation 1.10 is replaced by

$$v = -2.5 \log d_v \tag{2.1}$$
$$b = -2.5 \log d_b \tag{2.2}$$
$$u = -2.5 \log d_u \tag{2.3}$$

where v, b, u and d_v, d_b, d_u represent the instrumental magnitudes and measurements through the V, B, and U filters, respectively. The constants, q', have been dropped because they can be "absorbed" by the zero-point constant in the transformation equations. Equation 1.12 is replaced by

$$(b - v) = -2.5 \log d_b/d_v \tag{2.4}$$
$$(u - b) = -2.5 \log d_u/d_b \tag{2.5}$$

The lower case u, b, v refer to the instrumental system while U, B, V refer to the standard system. The magnitude and colors corrected for atmospheric extinction, Equations 1.13 and 1.15 become

$$v_0 = v - k'_v X \tag{2.6}$$
$$(b - v)_0 = (b - v)(1 - k''_{bv} X) - k'_{bv} X \tag{2.7}$$
$$(u - b)_0 = (u - b) - k'_{ub} X \tag{2.8}$$

In the *UBV* system, k''_{ub} is defined to be zero (more about this later), and experience has shown that k''_v is very small so it is not included in Equation 2.6. Equations 1.16 and 1.17 become

$$V = v_0 + \epsilon(B - V) + \zeta_v \tag{2.9}$$
$$(B - V) = \mu(b - v)_0 + \zeta_{bv} \tag{2.10}$$
$$(U - B) = \psi(u - b)_0 + \zeta_{ub} \tag{2.11}$$

where ϵ, μ, ψ are the transformation coefficients and ζ_v, ζ_{bv}, ζ_{ub} are the zero-point constants. These six values are found by observations of the standard stars in Appendices C and D. The details of this calibration are given in Chapter 4.

2.3 THE MORGAN-KEENAN SPECTRAL CLASSIFICATION SYSTEM

Spectral classification is a very important topic in stellar astronomy and the reader can find an elementary review of this topic in the books by Abell,[4] Swihart,[5] and Smith and Jacobs,[6] to name but a few. A more advanced discussion is given by Keenan.[7] A brief review is given here because of the close relationship of the *UBV* system to the Morgan-Keenan (M-K) spectral classification system.

The first large-scale classification of stellar spectra began in the 1920s at Harvard College Observatory and became known as the *Henry Draper Catalog*. Over 400,000 stellar spectra were classified. At first, the stars were broken into a few groups based on the strength of the hydrogen absorption lines. The groups were designated A through P, from strongest to the weakest lines. In time, it became clear that some of these classes did not exist but were a product of poor quality spectrograms. Furthermore, simply arranging the spectrograms so the hydrogen lines varied from strong to weak did not produce a continuous and logical pattern in the remaining lines. Consequently, some classes were dropped and the remainder were rearranged. The result was a scrambled alphabetic sequence (O, B, A, F, G, K, M) but a logical and continuous variation in strength of all spectral lines. Better quality spectrograms have led to the development of 10 subclasses indicated by a number (zero through nine) following the letter. The sun is designated as a G2 while Vega is an A0 star. Figure 2.3 shows several spectra of main sequence stars. At the bottom of the figure, a typical filter plus photomultiplier tube response function for the *UBV* system is shown. It is customary to refer to stars near the beginning of the sequence as *early type* and those near the end as *late type*. That is, an A0 star is an earlier type than an F5, and a K0 is earlier than a K5.

We now know that the spectral sequence is an ordering by stellar surface temperature. For instance, O stars are approximately 50,000 K while M stars are 3000 K. The changing pattern of spectral lines in Figure 2.3 is a direct result of the change in the stellar temperature. An O type star shows few lines because most atoms are totally ionized.

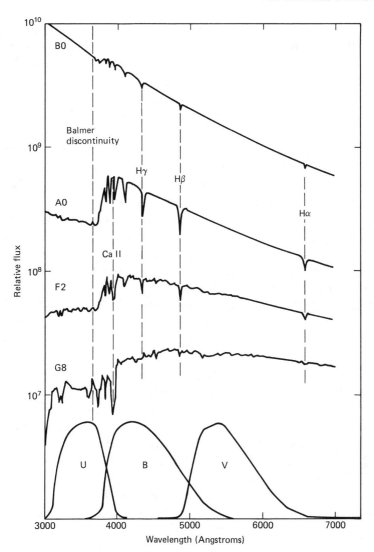

Figure 2.3 Spectra of some main sequence stars.

However, lines of He II (singly ionized helium) are fairly strong and are sometimes seen in emission. As one progresses towards the B class, the He II lines grow weaker and He I (neutral, un-ionized helium) and hydrogen lines grow stronger. By class B2, the He I lines dominate the spectrum. Hydrogen and ionized metal[†] lines grow stronger until early type A. Hydrogen and many ionized metals reach maximum strength at A0. By late A and into early F, the ionized metal lines grow while hydrogen lines decrease rapidly. Through classes F to G the spectral lines of Ca II strengthen reaching a peak at G2. Neutral metals continue to gain in strength as their ionized counterparts disappear. By late K, molecular bands appear and neutral metal lines dominate. The hydrogen lines are essentially gone and the calcium lines are still strong. By late K and into M, the bands of titanium oxide become prominent. Lines of the neutral metals are still stronger.

As stated earlier, the V filter was chosen to match the old visual magnitudes and the B filter to match the photographic magnitudes. The U filter was chosen to measure a spectral feature. In Figure 2.3, it is easy to see that the hydrogen lines dominate the early spectral types. The spacing between these lines becomes closer and closer until at the Balmer limit they merge and the absorption becomes continuous. Therefore, at the Balmer limit (3647 Å) there is a sharp drop in the continum level, called the *Balmer discontinuity*. Figure 2.3 also shows that the U filter straddles this discontinuity. Thus, the $(U - B)$ color index is sensitive to the strength of the discontinuity, which in turn is a function of the star's spectral type. Note that the effective wavelength of observation through the U filter depends on the strength of the Balmer discontinuity. If the discontinuity is strong, very little light is received shortward of 3647 Å. The light measured through the U filter is that which passes through the "red wing" of the filter, longward of 3647 Å. Thus, we are effectively looking at a wavelength that is longer than the middle of the filter bandpass. On the other hand, a star that has a very weak discontinuity supplies light roughly equally across the bandpass of the filter. Then the effective wavelength of observation is near the center of the bandpass. An important consequence of this effect is that the second-order atmospheric extinction coefficient for $U - B$ has a complicated behavior with spectral type. That is to say, unlike the behavior of

---

[†]Astronomers use the term "metal" in a very different sense than do chemists. The term is used to designate any element other than hydrogen or helium.

k''_{bv}, k''_{ub} does not vary smoothly with spectral type, but rather shows a double sawtoothed variation from type O to M. To avoid the time-consuming process of correcting k''_{ub}, Johnson and Morgan defined it to be zero. Since second-order terms are small, the error introduced by this definition is of the order of 0.03 in $U - B$. A more detailed discussion of this problem can be found in Section 4.9.

The Harvard System is a one-dimensional classification scheme. However, it was realized rather early that a second dimension might be necessary. Some stars showed narrower absorption lines than other stars of the same class even though the pattern of spectral lines matched well. Between 1914 and 1935, Mount Wilson Observatory ordered spectra of the same class by the strength of certain spectral features. In time, it was realized that narrower lines resulted from a lower density in the atmosphere of these stars. Because the temperatures are the same, their atmospheres are much larger than those of normal main sequence stars. Therefore, these narrow-line stars are brighter than their main sequence counterparts. (See Equation J.23.)

These spectral "anomalies" are in fact luminosity indicators. W. W. Morgan, P. C. Keenan, and E. Kellman[8] developed a second dimension to the spectral classification now in general use. This M-K system introduces luminosity classes as follows:

I:	Supergiants
II:	Bright giants
III:	Giants
IV:	Subgiants
V:	Main sequence (dwarfs)
VI:	Subdwarfs

The location of these groups in the Hertzsprung-Russell (H-R) diagram is shown in Figure 2.4. Classes I to V may be subdivided by using the suffix a (brightest), or ab, or b (dimmest). The luminosity criteria are based on line strengths, ratios of line strengths, and widths of hydrogen lines. The low density in the atmospheres of the larger stars alters the percentage of atoms that are ionized. This in turn alters the line strengths and makes the spectrum appear to belong to a hotter star, and therefore to an earlier spectral type. Note in Figure 2.4 that the spectral classes of the giants and supergiants occur to the right of the same classes for stars on the main sequence. However, the color index is

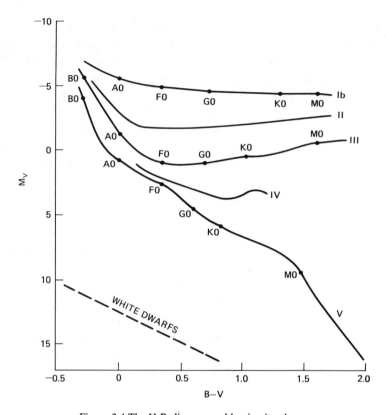

Figure 2.4 The H-R diagram and luminosity classes.

largely unaffected by the changes in the lines and therefore indicates a different temperature.

2.4 THE M-K SYSTEM AND *UBV* PHOTOMETRY

One of the most important aspects of the *UBV* system is its close ties to the M-K spectral classification system. As stated earlier, the zero points for the color indices were defined by stars classified as A0 V on the M-K system. This allows the colors of the *UBV* system to be related directly to an M-K spectral type and temperature. Figures 2.5a and b and Table 2.1 show these relationships for main sequence stars. These apply to stars that are not viewed through significant quantities of interstellar dust. This dust selectively absorbs more blue light than red light making a star appear redder than it actually is.

TABLE 2.1. Color Indices and Temperatures for Main Sequence Stars

Spectral Type	$(B - V)$	$(U - B)$	Effective Temperature ($^{\circ}$K)
O5	−0.32	−1.15	54,000
B0	−0.30	−1.08	29,200
B5	−0.16	−0.56	15,200
A0	0.00	0.00	9600
A5	+0.14	+0.11	8310
F0	0.31	0.06	7350
F5	0.43	0.00	6700
G0	0.59	0.11	6050
G5	0.66	0.20	5660
K0	0.82	0.47	5240
K5	1.15	1.03	4400
M0	1.41	1.26	3750
M5	1.61	1.19	3200

SOURCE: Novotny, E. 1973. *Introduction to Stellar Atmospheres and Interiors.* New York: Oxford University Press, p. 10.

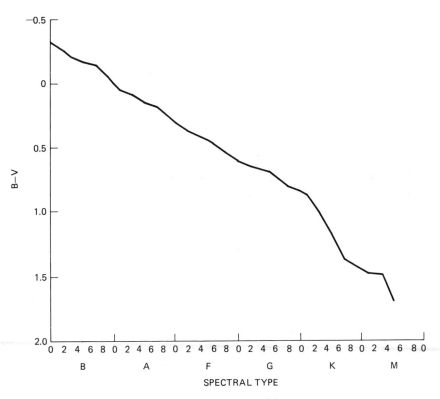

Figure 2.5a B-V versus spectral type.

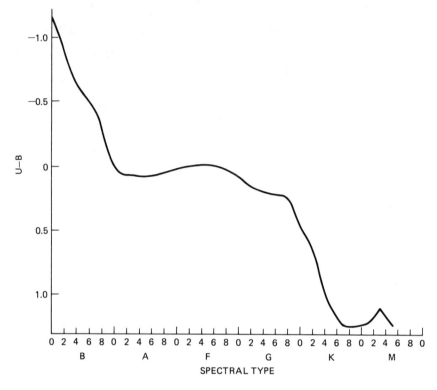

Figure 2.5b U-B versus spectral type.

Johnson and Morgan established the relationship between color indices and absolute magnitude by a two-step process. The first step was to measure the color indices of nearby stars with accurately known parallaxes. From the parallax and apparent magnitude, the absolute magnitude can be calculated directly. Unfortunately, there are very few early-type stars with accurately measured parallaxes because these stars are relatively rare. Even the A, F, and G stars are not as common as one would like for calibration purposes. The second step was to fill these gaps in spectral types using stars in nearby galactic clusters. A color versus *apparent* magnitude plot can be made for these clusters after correcting the magnitudes for interstellar absorption. Because all the stars within the cluster are nearly the same distance away, the apparent magnitude for each star differs from the absolute magnitude by some additive constant. If it is assumed that there is no difference between the main sequence of nearby field stars and that of a cluster, then the plot for the cluster can be slid vertically (in magnitude) on top of the plot for the field stars until the main sequences match. Then, the absolute magnitude of the cluster stars and the distance to the cluster is defined. The clusters used for this process were NGC 2362, the Pleiades, and the Praesepe. The completed diagram appears in Figure 2.6, which is an H-R diagram using a color index instead of the M-K type. Because of the effect discussed at the end of Section 2.3, the relation between color index and spectral class depends slightly on the luminosity class.

Figure 2.7 shows a plot of $(U - B)$ versus $(B - V)$, for (unreddened) main-sequence stars. This is a so-called *color-color diagram*. Note that the $(U - B)$ color gets smaller as you move upwards in the plot (the star is becoming brighter in U than in B). Blackbodies of various temperatures follow a nearly linear relation (upper curve). However, stars (lower curve) deviate significantly from a blackbody. These two curves differ because of the absorption lines in stellar spectra. From type O to A0, the hydrogen absorption lines increase in strength and so does the Balmer discontinuity. The flux seen in the U filter decreases causing $(U - B)$ to become larger. (Remember, magnitudes are larger if a star is fainter.) After A0, the Balmer lines (and the discontinuity) grow weaker and $(U - B)$ begins to decrease. After class F5, however, the metal lines and molecular bands become strong. Many of these

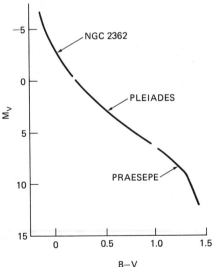

Figure 2.6 Main sequence matching.

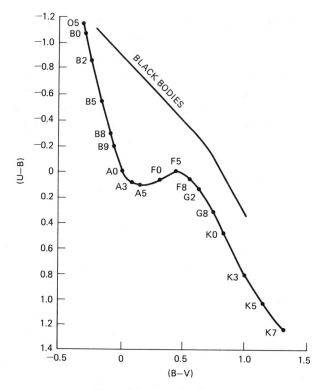

Figure 2.7 Color-color diagram.

absorption features are in the ultraviolet and cause the $(U - B)$ color to become large again. There is a complication for stars near the bump in the color-color plot at F5. Because the value of $(U - B)$ depends on the amount of absorption by metal lines, an abnormal metal abundance can have a significant effect on this color. A low metal abundance causes the star to plot higher than a normal star.

Figure 2.8 shows the color-color plot again, but this time to illustrate the effect of interstellar reddening. Reddening causes a star to move to the right nearly parallel to the reddening line in the figure. As an example, if an observed star plots at point A in the diagram, it can be assumed that extrapolating to the left, parallel to the reddening line, yields its intrinsic colors. The amount of color change produced by the dust is called the *color excess* and is denoted by $E(B - V)$ and $E(U - B)$, as labeled in Figure 2.8. The slope of the reddening line is given by

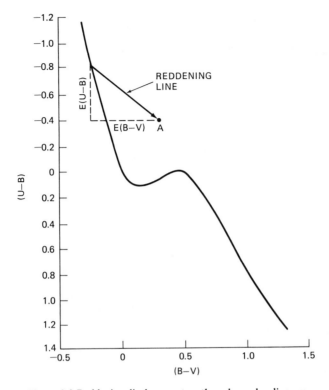

Figure 2.8 Reddening displacement on the color–color diagram.

$$\frac{E(U - B)}{E(B - V)} = 0.72 - 0.05(B - V) \qquad (2.12)$$

For early type stars $(B - V)$ is nearly zero, so the second term is very small and

$$\frac{E(U - B)}{E(B - V)} \simeq 0.72 \qquad (2.13)$$

For stars that are later than type A0, it is not possible to use a color-color plot to determine the intrinsic color unambiguously. This is true because the color-color curve turns upward at A0. Extrapolating to the left along the reddening line will result in two intersections of the color-color curve. For stars later than A0, the color excesses must be obtained by comparing the spectral class implied by the observed colors to that obtained by spectroscopy. The latter is not affected by the reddening because it is based on the pattern of spectral lines.

For stars from type B0 to A0, there is yet another way to deal with interstellar reddening. The quantity Q is defined as

$$Q = (U - B) - 0.72(B - V) \tag{2.14}$$

where $(U - B)$ and $(B - V)$ are the observed colors. Q is independent of reddening. To see this, note that

$$E(B - V) = (B - V) - (B - V)_i \tag{2.15}$$

and

$$E(U - B) = (U - B) - (U - B)_i \tag{2.16}$$

where $(B - V)_i$ and $(U - B)_i$ are the intrinsic colors of the star. Now we solve these two equations for $(B - V)$ and $(U - B)$, respectively, and substitute into Equation 2.14. Then,

$$Q = E(U - B) + (U - B)_i - 0.72 \left[E(B - V) + (B - V)_i \right] \tag{2.17}$$

$$Q = (U - B)_i - 0.72(B - V)_i + E(U - B) - 0.72E(B - V). \tag{2.18}$$

Now substitute Equation 2.13, which results in

$$Q = (U - B)_i - 0.72(B - V)_i, \tag{2.19}$$

independent of reddening. Equation 2.19 is then used to produce Figure 2.9. The observed colors of a reddened star can be used to calculate Q by Equation 2.14. Figure 2.9 then yields the intrinsic spectral type.

The total absorption in the visual magnitude can be estimated in the following way. Define a quantity R as

$$R = \frac{A_V}{A_B - A_V} \tag{2.20}$$

where A_V and A_B are the absorption, in magnitudes, in V and B, respec-

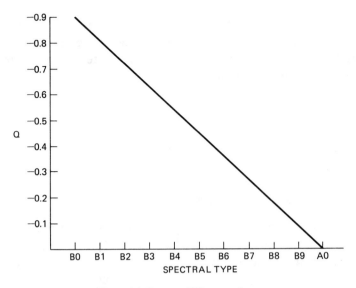

Figure 2.9 Q versus MK spectral type.

tively. The observed magnitudes are related to the intrinsic magnitudes by

$$B = B_i + A_B \qquad (2.21)$$
$$V = V_i + A_V. \qquad (2.22)$$

Substituting these two expressions into Equation 2.15 gives

$$E(B - V) = [(B_i + A_B) - (V_i + A_V)] - (B - V)_i \qquad (2.23)$$
$$E(B - V) = A_B - A_V. \qquad (2.24)$$

Thus, Equation 2.20 becomes

$$R = \frac{A_V}{E(B - V)} \qquad (2.25)$$

or

$$A_V = RE(B - V). \qquad (2.26)$$

The value of R has been found to be about 3.0 for most directions in our galaxy. However, there appear to be some regions where the nature of the interstellar dust is different and R may reach values as high as 12. If $E(B - V)$ is determined by one of the above methods and R is assumed to be 3.0, it is then possible to calculate A_V and correct the apparent visual magnitude by

$$V_i = V - A_V \qquad (2.27)$$

to obtain the intrinsic visual magnitude.

*2.5 ABSOLUTE CALIBRATION

It is sometimes helpful or necessary to convert a measured magnitude into an actual flux measurement. The process of absolute calibration is both difficult and tedious. The process has recently been discussed by Lockwood et al.[9] No attempt to explain the process is made here, but a means of approximately transforming UBV measurements into flux is shown. Recall Equation 1.7:

$$m_\lambda = q_\lambda - 2.5 \log F_\lambda.$$

Assume that the atmospheric extinction correction has been made. Denote this by an added subscript on m, that is,

$$m_{\lambda 0} = q_\lambda - 2.5 \log F_\lambda, \qquad (2.28)$$

or more explicitly,

$$V_0 = q_v - 2.5 \log F_v \qquad (2.29)$$
$$B_0 = q_b - 2.5 \log F_b \qquad (2.30)$$
$$U_0 = q_u - 2.5 \log F_u. \qquad (2.31)$$

Johnson[10] has determined the q's as they appear in Table 2.2. Thus, the flux can be determined by

$$F_V = 10^{-0.4(V_0 - q_v)} \qquad (2.32)$$
$$F_B = 10^{-0.4(B_0 - q_b)} \qquad (2.33)$$
$$F_U = 10^{-0.4(U_0 - q_u)} \qquad (2.34)$$

TABLE 2.2. Absolute Zero-Point Constants

Filter	Approximate Equivalent Wavelength (Angstroms)	q_λ
U	3600	−38.40
B	4400	−37.86
V	5500	−38.52
R	7000	−39.39
I	9000	−40.2
J	12,500	−41.2
K	22,000	−43.5
L	34,000	−45.2
M	50,000	−46.6
N	102,000	−49.8

NOTE: Filters I through N will be explained in Section 2.7a.

The constants that appear in Table 2.2 are simply 2.5 times the logarithm of the flux of a zero magnitude star, in watts per square centimeter per Angstrom. Because of the difficulties of the calibration process, these constants may contain errors between 10 and 20 percent.

Example: What is the flux reaching the earth from a star which has $V_0 = 3.0$? From Table 2.2, $q_v = -38.52$.

$$F_V = 10^{-0.4(3.0+38.52)}$$
$$F_V = 10^{-16.61}$$
$$F_V = 2.47 \times 10^{-17} \frac{\text{watts}}{\text{cm}^2 \text{ Angstrom}}$$

This is the flux at the equivalent wavelength of observation. (See Equation J.53.) The total flux measured in the V filter can be found, approximately, by multiplying this number by the width of the filter's bandpass (1000 Å). Thus,

$$F_V \approx 2.5 \times 10^{-14} \text{ watts/cm}^2.$$

The total power collected in the V filter by the telescope is obtained by multiplying by the collecting area, that is

$$P_V \approx 2.5 \times 10^{-14} (\pi R_t^2) \text{ watts,}$$

where R_t is the radius in centimeters of the primary mirror or lens of the telescope.

2.6 DIFFERENTIAL PHOTOMETRY

The concept of differential photometry is outlined in Section 1.6. We now proceed to a more detailed discussion. The actual observations consist of a series of measurements, which are given in counts per second (pulse counting) or percent of full-scale deflection (DC) through each filter of both the variable and the comparison star. We represent the measurements through the V, B, and U filters by d_v, d_b, and d_u, respectively. We add a second subscript to indicate the variable (x) or the comparison star (c). The magnitude difference between the variable and the comparison star in each filter is given by

$$\Delta v = -2.5 \log \frac{d_{vx}}{d_{vc}} \tag{2.35}$$

$$\Delta b = -2.5 \log \frac{d_{bx}}{d_{bc}} \tag{2.36}$$

$$\Delta u = -2.5 \log \frac{d_{ux}}{d_{uc}} \tag{2.37}$$

if pulse-counting electronics are used. If DC electronics are used, it is possible that the two stars may require a different amplifier gain. The above equations are then modified to read,

$$\Delta v = -2.5 \log \frac{d_{vx}}{d_{vc}} + G_{vx} - G_{vc} \tag{2.38}$$

$$\Delta b = -2.5 \log \frac{d_{bx}}{d_{bc}} + G_{bx} - G_{bc} \tag{2.39}$$

$$\Delta u = -2.5 \log \frac{d_{ux}}{d_{uc}} + G_{ux} - G_{uc} \tag{2.40}$$

The additional terms give the difference in amplifier gain (in magnitudes) between the variable and the comparison star. In Chapter 8, the procedure of gain calibration is discussed.

It is also possible to use these same measurements to form differences in color indices between the variable and the comparison star. To see this, note that

$$\begin{aligned}
\Delta(b - v) &= (b_x - v_x) - (b_c - v_c)\\
&= (b_x - b_c) - (v_x - v_c)\\
&= \Delta b - \Delta v.
\end{aligned} \tag{2.41}$$

Likewise,

$$\Delta(u - b) = \Delta u - \Delta b. \tag{2.42}$$

The beginner need not carry the data reduction beyond this point. There are many worthwhile observing projects that can be done with differential photometry, some of which are discussed in Chapter 10.

In rare circumstances, it might be necessary to apply a small extinction correction to differential photometry. This should seldom be necessary, because the variable and comparison star are close together in the sky and have been viewed through essentially the same air mass. However, in practice, this sometimes does not occur. It may be that a suitable comparison star was not found within 1° of the variable or that the comparison star was not observed frequently. In the latter case, the earth's diurnal motion causes the two stars to be viewed through significantly different air masses. Equations 2.35 through 2.37 (or 2.38 through 2.40) must be corrected to give the magnitude difference above the earth's atmosphere by making use of Equation 2.6. Thus,

$$(\Delta v)_0 = \Delta v - k_v'(X_x - X_c) \tag{2.43}$$
$$(\Delta b)_0 = \Delta b - k_b'(X_x - X_c) \tag{2.44}$$
$$(\Delta u)_0 = \Delta u - k_u'(X_x - X_c), \tag{2.45}$$

where X_x and X_c are the air masses of the variable and comparison star, respectively, at the time of observation. The color index differences can be corrected using Equations 2.7 and 2.8. That is,

$$\Delta(b - v)_0 = \Delta(b - v) - k_{bv}'(X_x - X_c) - k_{bv}'' \Delta(b - v)\overline{X} \tag{2.46}$$

and

$$\Delta(u - b)_0 = \Delta(u - b) - k'_{ub}(X_x - X_c), \qquad (2.47)$$

where $\overline{X}$ is the average air mass of the variable and comparison star.

It must be stressed that all of the above magnitude and color differences are on the instrumental system of the photometer in use. It is possible to do differential photometry on the standard UBV system. The procedure is to observe your comparison star along with some UBV standards. You can then determine V, $(B - V)$, and $(U - B)$ of the comparison star. This need only be done on one night if it is done well. On all other nights, you only need observe your variable and the comparison star. The magnitude and color differences between your variable and comparison star on the standard system can be found by rewriting Equations 2.9 through 2.11 to obtain

$$\Delta V = (\Delta v)_0 + \epsilon\Delta(B - V) \qquad (2.48)$$

$$\Delta(B - V) = \mu\Delta(b - v)_0 \qquad (2.49)$$

$$\Delta(U - B) = \psi\Delta(u - b)_0 \qquad (2.50)$$

Note that if the two stars have nearly the same color, the second term on the right of Equation 2.48 is nearly zero. Furthermore, μ and ψ are approximately equal to one for most photometers using the 1P21 photomultiplier tube and standard UBV filters. This justifies the earlier statement that an uncalibrated photometer gives nearly the same magnitude and color difference as a calibrated one. The real advantage of calibrating the comparison star is that you can use your observations to compute the actual standardized magnitude and colors of the variable star by

$$V_x = V_c + \Delta V \qquad (2.51)$$

$$(B - V)_x = (B - V)_c + \Delta(B - V) \qquad (2.52)$$

$$(U - \dot{B})_x = (U - B)_c + \Delta(U - B). \qquad (2.53)$$

2.7 OTHER PHOTOMETRIC SYSTEMS

By no means is the UBV system the only photometric system. There are many other valuable systems. A complete discussion of all these systems is beyond the scope of this text. However, we describe briefly an intermediate-band and a narrow-band system following the discussion of an extension to the *UBV* system.

2.7a The Infrared Extension of the *UBV* System

In order to expand the usefulness of the *UBV* system to the classification of cool stars, the system has been extended with bandpasses in the infrared. Table 2.2 lists the letter designation of each filter and its approximate effective wavelength. Photometry with filters *U, B, V, R, I* can be accomplished using an S-1, an extended-red S-20 photomultiplier,[11] or a photodiode as a detector. Wavelengths in the range of J through N require specialized detectors, such as those using lead sulfide, and cooling to liquid-helium temperatures. These techniques are beyond the scope of this text. Interested readers are referred to a review by Low and Rieke.[12]

2.7b The Strömgren Four-Color System

The Strömgren system[13] is an intermediate-band width system that overcomes many of the shortcomings of the *UBV* system and provides astrophysically important information. Table 2.3 contains the filter designations, central wavelengths, and bandwidths of the four filters.

Unlike the *UBV* system, the Strömgren system is almost totally filter-defined. The *y* (yellow) filter matches the visual magnitude and corresponds well with *V* magnitudes. This filter transmits no strong spectral features in early-type stars. The red limit is set by the filter and not by the detector as in the case of the *UBV* system. The *b* (blue) filter is centered about 300 Å to the red of the *B* filter of the UBV system to reduce the effects of "line blanketing." For stars of spectral types later

TABLE 2.3. Filters Used in the Strömgren System

Filter	Central Wavelength (Angstroms)	Full Width at Half Transmission (Angstroms)
y	5500	200
b	4700	100
v	4100	200
u	3500	400

than A0, absorption lines of metals become strong. A filter that is centered in a wavelength region where such lines are common transmits less flux than it would if the lines were absent. This blanketing effect is a temperature indicator in that it becomes strong in later spectral types. To get a clear measure of its strength, it is necessary to measure a star's flux in a region relatively free of blanketing and compare it to a region where blanketing is strong. For early type stars, the *b* and *y* filters are free from blanketing. In later type stars, the two filters are affected almost equally. The violet (*v*) filter is centered in a region of strong blanketing but longwards of the region where the hydrogen lines begin crowding together near the Balmer limit. The *u* (ultraviolet) filter measures both blanketing and the Balmer discontinuity. Unlike the *U* filter in the *UBV* system, this filter is completely to the short wavelength side of the Balmer discontinuity. Yet, it is centered far enough from the atmospheric limit near 3000 Å so that the observing site plays no role in defining the wavelength region observed. Hence, the system is nearly filter-defined and insensitive to the detector used. There are essentially no effects due to the filter's bandwidth. That is, there are no second-order color terms in the extinction corrections or the transformation equations. This is a simplification compared with the *UBV* system.

Figure 2.10 schematically illustrates a stellar spectrum and the placement of the four filters. The color indices in the Strömgren system are very useful quantities. Because both the *b* and *y* filters are relatively free from blanketing, the index (*b* − *y*) is a good indicator of color and

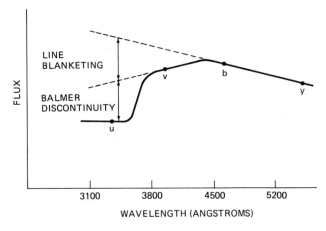

Figure 2.10 Placement of the Strömgren filters.
Note: For the sake of clarity, stellar absorption lines are not shown.

effective temperature. A color index is essentially the slope of the continuum. In the absence of blanketing, the continuum slope would be roughly constant and $(b - y)$ approximately equals $(v - b)$. Because $(v - b)$ is affected by blanketing, the difference between these two indices indicates the strength of blanketing. Hence a metal index, m_1, can be defined as

$$m_1 = (v - b) - (b - y). \qquad (2.54)$$

To determine how the continuum slope has been affected by the Balmer discontinuity, the index c_1 is defined as

$$c_1 = (u - v) - (v - b). \qquad (2.55)$$

This index measures the Balmer discontinuity, nearly free from the affects of line blanketing. To see this, note that the u measurement contains the effects of both blanketing and the Balmer discontinuity. The v filter contains only the effect of blanketing which is roughly one-half as strong as in the u filter. Further note that c_1 has been defined so that Equation 2.55 can be rewritten as

$$c_1 = (u - 2v + b). \qquad (2.56)$$

Subtraction of the $2v$ term essentially cancels the blanketing, leaving the effects of the Balmer discontinuity.

In summary, the Strömgren system provides a visual magnitude, a measure of the effective temperature, a measure of the strength of metal lines, and a measure of the Balmer discontinuity. Furthermore, it is filter-defined, independent of any one detector and requires no second-order terms in extinction or transformation equations. The only major drawback of the system is that the smaller bandpasses make faint stars more difficult to measure. *The Astronomical Almanac*[14] has a list of standard stars for the Strömgren system.

2.7c Narrow-Band Hβ Photometry

As our example of narrow-band photometry, we discuss briefly a frequently used extension of the four-color system, Hβ photometry. In this system, a narrow interference filter that is centered on the Hβ line is

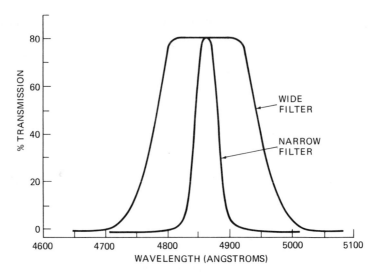

Figure 2.11 Filter responses, Hβ system.

used. In early type stars, this is a strong absorption line. The amount of light flux passed by the filter is heavily dependent on the line strength. The strength of Hβ is a luminosity indicator in stars of spectral type O to A and a temperature indicator in types A to G.

This system actually requires two filters since a small amount of detected flux could mean a strong Hβ absorption line or, simply, a faint star. Thus, a second, broader filter that measures much of the adjacent continuum is used. The ratio of the measurements through the two filters indicates the strength of Hβ with respect to the continuum. Figure 2.11 shows the response of the filters.

Obviously, effective narrow-band photometry requires a large telescope. Furthermore, interference filters are expensive and require thermostating at the telescope. It is for these reasons we do not go into further depth on this topic. The interested reader is referred to Chapter 5 in Golay.[1]

REFERENCES

1. Golay, M. 1974. *Introduction to Astronomical Photometry.* Boston: D. Reidel.
2. Johnson, H. L., and Morgan, W. W. 1951. *Ap. J.* **114**, 522.
3. Johnson, H. L., and Morgan, W. W. 1953. *Ap. J.* **117**, 313.
4. Abell, G. 1978. *Exploration of the Universe.* New York: Holt, Rinehart and Winston.

5. Swihart, T. L. 1968. *Astrophysics and Stellar Astronomy*. New York: John Wiley and Sons.
6. Smith, E., and Jacobs, K. 1973. *Introductory Astronomy and Astrophysics*. Philadelphia: W. B. Saunders Co.
7. Keenan, P. C. 1963. In *Basic Astronomical Data*. Edited by K. Aa Strand. Chicago: Univ. of Chicago Press, chapter 8.
8. Morgan, W. W., Keenan, P. C., and Kellman, E. 1943. *An Atlas of Stellar Spectra*. Chicago: Univ. of Chicago Press.
9. Lockwood, G. W., White, N. M., and Tüg, H. 1978. *Sky and Tel.* **56**, 286.
10. Johnson, H. L. 1965. *Comm. Lunar and Planetary Lab.* No. 53.
11. Fernie, J. D. 1974. *Pub. A.S.P.* **86**, 837.
12. Low, F. J., and Rieke, G. H. 1974. In *Methods of Experimental Physics*. New York: Academic Press **12**, chapter 9.
13. Strömgren, B., 1966. *Ann. Rev. Astr. Ap.* **4**, 433. Palo Alto: Annual Review Inc.
14. *The Astronomical Almanac*. Washington, D.C.: Government Printing Office. Issued annually.

CHAPTER 3
STATISTICS

If we measure 23,944 counts from a source in 10 seconds, will we measure the same number of counts in the next 10-second interval? How many counts are needed to achieve 1 percent accuracy for the measurement? How do I analyze my data for errors? These are but a few of the questions that need to be answered before any data reduction is complete.

Experimental observations always have inaccuracies. The role of the experimenter is to know the extent of these inaccuracies and to account for them in the best manner. You must know how to combine observations and errors to compute a result. If your observations are to be compared to theoretical predictions, it is necessary to know something about the accuracies of both calculations if you want to make an intelligent comparison of their agreement.

This chapter attempts to answer some questions about errors and the field of statistics in general. The derivations and advanced concepts can be found in Appendix K. The majority of the material presented in this chapter comes from texts by Young and Bevington (see Section 3.8), both of which are available in paperback and are highly recommended.

3.1 KINDS OF ERRORS

Errors come in different types. Most errors occur in three major categories: illegitimate, systematic, and random. These are discussed in turn.

Illegitimate errors are not directly concerned with the data itself. Instead, these include mistakes in recording numbers, setting up the equipment incorrectly, and blunders in arithmetic. They cannot be represented by any theoretical model and must be eliminated by the observer through careful work.

Systematic errors are errors associated with the equipment itself or with the technique of using the equipment. For instance, if an analog amplifier has an offset voltage, the resulting chart recorder deflection will be in error. Another example is not removing the U filter's red leak from your data. Red stars will then appear brighter in the U filter than they really are.

Very often in experimental work, systematic errors are more important than random errors. However, they are also much more difficult to deal with. Always compare your results with the standard system values and other observers whenever possible to calibrate your equipment and observing procedures.

Random or chance errors are produced by a large number of unpredictable and unknown variations in the experimental situation. They can result from small errors in judgment on the part of the observer, such as in reading a chart recorder record. Other causes are unpredictable fluctuations in conditions, such as nearly invisible cirrus clouds or variations in a photomultiplier tube's high-voltage power supply. It is found empirically that such random errors are frequently distributed according to a simple law. This makes it possible to use statistical methods to treat random errors.

Because random errors can be modeled, they form the basis for much of the remaining material in this chapter. Illegitimate and systematic errors must be eliminated by the experimentalist wherever possible.

3.2 MEAN AND MEDIAN

The actual value of what you are trying to measure is unknown. No one knows the exact magnitude of a star, just as the speed of light, although well measured, is not known exactly. If you determine the magnitude of a star on five separate occasions, you are likely to get five different values. Intuitively, you would suspect that the most reliable result for the star's magnitude would be obtained by using all five measurements rather than only one of them. You can approximate the true value by taking these measurements (a sample) and determining the *average* or *sample mean* by summing all of the measurements and dividing by the number of them. In a more general mathematical notation,

$$\bar{x} = \frac{1}{N} \sum_{i=1}^{N} x_i, \qquad (3.1)$$

where x_i are the values of the individual measurements and N is the total number of measurements taken. The summation sign in Equation 3.1 is just a shorthand way of saying "the sum of x values from $i = 1$ to N." All such summations in the rest of the chapter have similar limits, and we may drop the $i = 1$ and N from the summation sign at times.

Example: On five occasions, you measured the visual magnitude of Mizar to be 4.50, 4.65, 4.55, 4.45, and 4.60. What is Mizar's mean visual magnitude from this data?

$$\bar{x} = \frac{1}{5}(4.50 + 4.65 + 4.55 + 4.45 + 4.60)$$
$$\bar{x} = \frac{1}{5}(22.75)$$
$$\bar{x} = 4.55$$

Sometimes we want to compute the average of a set of values in which some of the numbers are more important than others. For instance, measurements taken on a cloudy night or at low altitudes are probably less important than those taken on a crystal-clear night near the zenith.

A procedure that suggests itself is to assume that the clear zenith observation was made more than once. Suppose we have a cloudy observation, a low observation, and the clear zenith value. We include the clear zenith value twice to account for its supposed better accuracy. Then, of course, we must divide by the total number of observations, which is now four. More generally, if we have several observations with different degrees of reliability, we can multiply each by an appropriate "weighting factor," and then divide the sum of these products by the sum of all of the weighting factors. This is the concept of the *weighted mean*, and can be represented mathematically by

$$\bar{x} = \frac{\sum\limits_{i=1}^{N} w_i x_i}{\sum\limits_{i=1}^{N} w_i}. \tag{3.2}$$

Note that if all of the weights are unity (or more generally, if they are all equal), the weighted mean reduces to the mean as previously defined by Equation 3.1. The problem with weighted means is determining the weights in a rigorous manner without any observer bias. That is, is an observation on a clear night two, three, or only one and a half times as good as a cloudy night observation? Unless you can decide on a consistent scheme, it is probably better to just take a straight mean and use as many observations as possible.

The *median* of a sample (or set of observations) is defined as that value for which half of the observations will be less than the median and half greater. For our five-observation example, we first order the observations in increasing order: 4.45, 4.50, 4.55, 4.60, and 4.65. The median is then the mid-value or 4.55. If we had six observations, the median would fall between the third and fourth values. To compute the median, we would average these two values.

Example: We now make a sixth observation of Mizar and obtain a visual magnitude of 4.90. What is the mean and median of our sample?

mean $= \dfrac{1}{6}$ (4.50 + 4.65 + 4.55 + 4.45 + 4.60 + 4.90)

mean $= \dfrac{1}{6}$ (27.65)

mean $= 4.61$

ordered values: 4.45, 4.50, 4.55, 4.60, 4.65, 4.90

median $= (4.55 + 4.60)/2$

median $= 4.57$

Note that the mean and median do not have to agree, as they are independent estimates of the best value for the sample. Usually the mean is used but there are cases in which the median is a better indicator of the sample.

3.3 DISPERSION AND STANDARD DEVIATION

Now that we have a method of determining the best value from our sample of observations, we need some indication of how much faith we have in that value.

The *deviation* (d_i) or *residual* of any measurement x_i from the mean $\bar{x}$ is defined as the difference between x_i and $\bar{x}$. Mathematically,

$$d_i = x_i - \bar{x} \qquad (3.3)$$

the deviation is a measure of the quality of the observations, so intuitively you would think that taking their sum and dividing by the number of values would give an average deviation. The problem is that some of the deviations are positive and others negative, and because of the way we defined the mean and the deviations, their sum is exactly equal to zero. One method to get around this problem is to use the absolute value of each deviation in the sum (i.e., all negative deviations are now positive). This defines the *average* or *mean deviation:*

$$\bar{d} = \frac{1}{N-1} \sum_{i=1}^{N} |x_i - \bar{x}| \qquad (3.4)$$

We divide by $N - 1$ rather than N because we use at least one measurement to determine the mean, $\bar{x}$, and therefore get an unrealistic deviation of zero for one measurement. The average deviation is a measure of the *dispersion* (or spread or scatter) of the observations around the mean. The presence of the absolute value sign makes the average deviation cumbersome to use in practice. It is not correct to call d_i the error in measurement x_i because $\bar{x}$ is only an approximation to the true value. However, this is a fine point that few observers obey.

A parameter that is easier to use analytically and is theoretically justified is the *standard deviation, σ*. It is obtained by first squaring each deviation, thereby removing any minus signs, and obtaining the mean squared, which is the *variance, σ^2*:

$$\sigma_x^2 = \frac{1}{N-1} \sum_{i=1}^{N} (x_i - \bar{x})^2. \tag{3.5}$$

The standard deviation (σ or s.d.) is just the square root of the variance:

$$\sigma_x = \sqrt{\frac{1}{N-1} \sum_{i=1}^{N} (x_i - \bar{x})^2}. \tag{3.6}$$

By rearranging, an easier computational form for σ_x can be obtained:

$$\sigma_x = \sqrt{\left[\frac{1}{N-1} \sum_{i=1}^{N} x_i^2 \right] - \bar{x}^2}. \tag{3.7}$$

Thus, the standard deviation is the *root mean square* of the deviations. Note that the standard deviation is always positive and has the same units as x_i.

The standard deviation defined in this manner tells us the amount of dispersion to be expected in any single measurement. Clearly, a single measurement in the sample has a larger deviation than the deviation of the mean of the sample. In other words, if you measure the magnitude of a star on five separate occasions, you have confidence that the mean of these five observations is accurate. If you make a *single* additional measurement, it may deviate significantly from the mean. However, the mean of five additional observations lies close to the first mean.

We can therefore define the standard deviation of the mean ($\sigma_{\bar{x}}$). It can be shown that $\sigma_{\bar{x}}$ is very closely related to σ_x, and is given by

$$\sigma_{\bar{x}} = \frac{1}{\sqrt{N}} \sigma_x \tag{3.8}$$

or

$$\sigma_{\bar{x}} = \sqrt{\frac{\sum_{i=1}^{N} (x_i - \bar{x})^2}{N(N-1)}}. \tag{3.9}$$

Authors often quote $\sigma_{\bar{x}}$ and thereby indicate greater accuracy in their results than is correct. In general, use σ_x unless you thoroughly understand the difference between these two values and know when to use $\sigma_{\bar{x}}$.

3.4 REJECTION OF DATA

To understand the significance of the standard deviation, we must first know the expected distribution of observations. The probability distribution is found by taking a large number of observations and seeing how probable it is to obtain any given value. This has been performed both experimentally and analytically and it has been found that most experiments have a common probability distribution, called the *normal* or *Gaussian distribution*. It is defined by the equation

$$f(x) = \frac{1}{\sigma\sqrt{2\pi}} \exp\left[\frac{-(x-\bar{x})^2}{2\sigma^2}\right] \tag{3.10}$$

and is shown in Figure 3.1. We are not going to describe this distribution in detail, but you should notice that it is symmetrical about the mean and that the width of the peak depends on σ, the standard deviation. A smaller σ will yield a sharper peak. It can be shown that if the data can be represented by a Gaussian distribution, then 68 percent of the data will fall within 1σ of the mean, 95 percent within 2σ, and 99.7 percent within 3σ. This says that if a data point falls more than 3σ from the mean, there is a 99.7 percent probability that it is faulty.

One other term, called the *most probable error* (*p.e.*), is frequently used. If the data can be represented by a Gaussian distribution, 50 percent of the data falls within one probable error of the mean. Expressed in terms of the standard deviation,

$$p.e. = 0.675\sigma. \tag{3.11}$$

Most scientific calculators are furnished with programs that calculate the mean and standard deviation of a set of numbers. *Learn always to quote an error when presenting data.* A number by itself is almost useless!

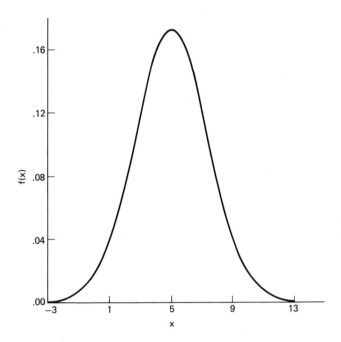

Figure 3.1 Gaussian distribution for $\bar{x} = 5.0, \sigma = 2.3$.

Example: Using our set of six measurements of Mizar, compute the standard deviation and present the mean.

$$\sigma_x^2 = \frac{1}{5} \ [(4.50 - 4.61)^2 + (4.65 - 4.61)^2 + (4.55 - 4.61)^2$$
$$+ (4.45 - 4.61)^2 + (4.60 - 4.61)^2 + (4.90 - 4.61)^2]$$
$$= \frac{1}{5} \ [0.0121 + 0.0016 + 0.0036 + 0.0256 + 0.0001$$
$$+ 0.0841]$$
$$\sigma_x^2 = 0.0254$$
$$\sigma_x = \sqrt{\sigma_x^2} = 0.16$$

visual magnitude of Mizar $= 4.61 \pm 0.16$ (s.d.)

All of the discussion in this section has been leading up to the question of the rejection of data. Our sixth data point of 4.90 deviates by

2σ from the mean. It is tempting to regard this large deviation as a blunder or mistake rather than a random error. Should we remove it from the sample?

This is a controversial question and has no simple answer. It could be that Mizar is an unknown eclipsing binary and you caught it during eclipse. Throwing out that data value throws away the eclipse information! In any event, removing measurements constitutes tampering with or "fudging" the data.

Unless you can confidently state that a given measure is in error because it was a cloudy night or some similar obvious problem, you will have to make some sort of decision on data obviously out of bounds. There are two differing points of view that should be considered. It is your choice as to what method should be employed.

At one extreme, there is the point of view that there is never any justification for throwing out data, and to do so is dishonest. If you adopt this point of view, there is nothing more to say. You can remove much of the effect of one bad point by taking additional data, or you could mention any extraneous points when you report your results.

The other point of view is to reject a measure if its occurrence is so improbable that it would not be reasonably expected to occur. The usual criterion is that data should be more than 2σ or 3σ from the mean. The best way may be not to use the errant value in your calculations but report it so others may make their own choice. In any case, never iterate, that is, remove data, calculate a new mean and standard deviation, and remove data again.

Of course, there is a third possibility. It is possible that the data are *not* represented by a simple Gaussian, and that the wings of the distribution are larger than those of the Gaussian that fits the peak. Thus, the measure may be correct after all. You must decide this either by theoretical considerations or by taking enough measures to map out the wings of the distribution.

3.5 LINEAR LEAST SQUARES

The method of *least squares* or *regression analysis* is almost exclusively used in fitting lines to experimental data. In examining a plot of experimental data, the human mind will "eyeball" a line that roughly splits half of the data above the line and half below. In a crude fashion, the mind is approximating a least-squares line.

*3.5a   Derivation of Linear Least Squares

If a straight line is to be fitted to data, then the line has the functional form

$$\hat{y} = a + bx \tag{3.12}$$

where $\hat{y}$ is the *calculated* y value for a given value of x. The fit is called *simple linear regression,* that is a linear function of only one variable, x. The deviations of the individual data points from this line can be defined as

$$\Delta y_i = (y_i - \hat{y}_i) \tag{3.13}$$

or

$$\Delta y_i = y_i - (a + bx_i) \tag{3.14}$$

Equation 3.14 is known as the *equation of condition.* Just as in the case of standard deviation, we square the deviations and try to minimize their sum. This yields the line with the least error, or the *least squared deviation.* If M is the sum of the squared deviations,

$$M = \sum_{i=1}^{N} (\Delta y_i)^2 \tag{3.15}$$

$$M = \Sigma\, y_i^2 + b^2\, \Sigma x_i^2 + Na^2 + 2ab\Sigma x_i \\ - 2b\Sigma x_i y_i - 2a\Sigma y_i. \tag{3.16}$$

How do we minimize the sum? Mathematically, this is accomplished by taking the partial derivative of the function M with respect to each variable of concern, and then setting these derivatives equal to zero. The reader must take care to realize that the variables in this problem are a and b (not x and y). So set

$$\frac{\partial M}{\partial a} = \frac{\partial M}{\partial b} = 0.$$

The equations derived in this manner are called the *normal equations*. For our simple linear-regression example,

$$\frac{\partial M}{\partial a} = 2Na + 2b\Sigma x_i - 2\Sigma y_i = 0$$

$$\frac{\partial M}{\partial b} = 2b\Sigma x_i^2 + 2a\Sigma x_i - 2\Sigma x_i y_i = 0$$

or, rearranging,

$$(N)a + (\sum_{i=1}^{N} x_i)b = \sum_{i=1}^{N} y_i \tag{3.17}$$

$$(\sum_{i=1}^{N} x_i)a + (\sum_{i=1}^{N} x_i^2)b = \sum_{i=1}^{N} x_i y_i. \tag{3.18}$$

3.5b Equations for Linear Least Squares

Equations 3.17 and 3.18 can be solved simultaneously to yield after using some identities:

$$\text{Slope: } b = \frac{N\Sigma x_i y_i - \Sigma x_i \Sigma y_i}{N\Sigma x_i^2 - (\Sigma x_i)^2} = \frac{\Sigma(x_i - \overline{x})(y_i - \overline{y})}{\Sigma(x_i - \overline{x})^2} \tag{3.19}$$

$$\text{Intercept: } a = \frac{-\Sigma x_i \Sigma x_i y_i + \Sigma x_i^2 \Sigma y_i}{N\Sigma x_i^2 - (\Sigma x_i)^2} = \overline{y} - b\overline{x} \tag{3.20}$$

Fitting a straight line to experimental data is the most common use of least squares. A FORTRAN routine to perform simple linear regression is given in Section I.4. This method can be generalized to any power of x or function M. For example,

$$\hat{y} = a_0 x^0 + a_1 x^1 + a_2 x^2 + \cdots$$

$$M = \Sigma[y_i - (a_0 x_i^0 + a_1 x_i^1 + a_2 x_i^2 + \cdots)]^2,$$

or

$$\hat{y} = a \cos(x)$$

$$M = \Sigma[y_i - a\cos(x_i)]^2.$$

Some comments are in order at this stage in the procedure. There are two basic reasons why the least-squares method is used rather than a freehand drawing. First, different people draw the freehand curve slightly differently because of observer bias. Second, the freehand method does not allow a quantitative measure of the goodness of the fit, an estimate of our confidence in the fitted line. The *standard error*, σ_e, of the least-squares estimate is given by

$$\sigma_e = \sqrt{\frac{1}{N-2}\sum_{i=1}^{N}(y_i - \hat{y})^2} \qquad (3.21)$$

This tells us the error expected at any point along the line. The *goodness of fit*, *r*, is given by

$$r = \frac{\dfrac{1}{N-1}\Sigma(x_1 - \bar{x})(y_i - \bar{y})}{\sqrt{\dfrac{1}{N-1}\Sigma(x_i - \bar{x})^2}\sqrt{\dfrac{1}{N-1}\Sigma(y_i - \bar{y})^2}} \qquad (3.22)$$

The four values determined in the least-squares analysis (slope, b; intercept, a; standard error, σ_e; goodness of fit, r) are used so commonly that several calculators are preprogrammed to perform the analysis. To be safe, always plot the data and draw the calculated line. Any significant deviations or a trend to the errors that may cause a lack of confidence in the fit then become obvious. A plot also serves as a check that all the data were entered correctly.

Example: We have just built a DC amplifier. Because it is transistorized, we suspect that its gain is temperature-sensitive. An experiment is devised, where a constant current is fed to the amplifier and the temperature of the amplifier is changed, with the chart-recorder reading recorded at various temperatures. The values obtained are listed below in the first two columns.

Temperature, °C(x)	Amplifier Gain (y)	$\hat{y}$
0	0.12	0.117
5	0.15	0.148
10	0.16	0.179
15	0.21	0.210
20	0.25	0.241
25	0.29	0.272
30	0.30	0.303
35	0.34	0.334
40	0.34	0.365
45	0.40	0.395
50	0.43	0.426

The data are shown in Figure 3.2. By visual inspection, it is obvious that the gain is increasing with increasing temperature. A linear least-squares line can be fit to the data and slope becomes the amplifier gain change per Celsius degree.

$$N = 11$$

$$\Sigma x_i = 275 \qquad \Sigma y_i = 2.99$$

$$\Sigma x_i y_i = 91.75 \qquad \Sigma x_i^2 = 9625$$

$$b = \frac{11 \times 91.75 - 275 \times 2.99}{11 \times 9625 - 275 \times 275} = 0.006182$$

$$a = \frac{1}{11}(2.99 - 0.006182 \times 275) = 0.1173$$

$$\Sigma(y_i - y)^2 = 0.001490$$

$$\sigma_e = \sqrt{\frac{1}{9}(0.001490)} = 0.013$$

The plotted straight line is the linear least-squares fit, whose numerical values are listed under $\hat{y}$ in the table above.

Multiple linear regression occurs when solving for more than one slope. That is the case where

$$y_i = a + b_1 x_i + b_2 w_i + b_3 z_i + \cdots$$

The solution to this problem is slightly more complicated because it involves putting the equation into matrix form and solving it by vector

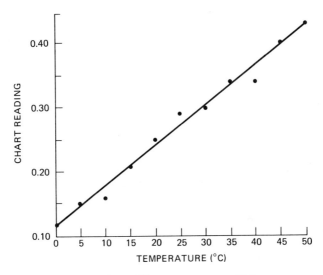

Figure 3.2 Amplifier temperature sensitivity.

differentiation and inversion. The solution is particularly useful in the least-squares solution of the standard *UBV* transformation equations and in the extinction calculation, but a discussion of this method is more involved than warranted for this chapter. Appendix K gives a complete discussion of the multivariate least-squares method. The average observer may find it more accurate to treat the transformation equation problem as a series of simple regression cases, thereby allowing better control over each step of the process.

3.6 INTERPOLATION AND EXTRAPOLATION

Often in photometry it is necessary to *interpolate,* that is, to find the value of some function between two base points. An example is when performing differential photometry in which several variable star observations are sandwiched between consecutive comparison star measures and you want the approximate comparison star reading at the time of each variable measure.

Consider the function in Figure 3.3. The solid line represents the true values of the function, with points identified at the base values x_0, x_1, x_2, and x_3. The function $y(x)$ might represent the star's intensity as it crosses the meridian, and x the time of the observation. We want to know its intensity between values x_1 and x_2. There are two usual approaches: exact and smoothed interpolation.

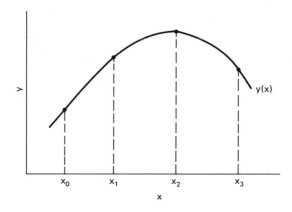

Figure 3.3 Interpolating between points.

3.6a Exact Interpolation

Exact interpolation makes use of the fact that there is one and only one polynomial of degree n or less which assumes the exact values $y(x_0)$, $y(x_1)$, ... , $y(x_n)$ at the $n + 1$ distinct base points $x_0, x_1, \ldots , x_n$. Therefore, to find $y(x)$ between x_1 and x_2, we could use a linear polynomial with points x_1 and x_2, a quadratic with x_0, x_1, and x_2, or a cubic with all four points. Exact only means that the polynomial fits the known data points exactly, not that it will interpolate exactly between those points. For example, consider linear interpolation for our desired value between x_1 and x_2. If we use a straight line between x_1 and x_2, we get a value reasonably close to the correct answer. If we use x_0 and x_3 instead as our end points and draw a straight line between them, the resultant answer lies considerably below the correct one.

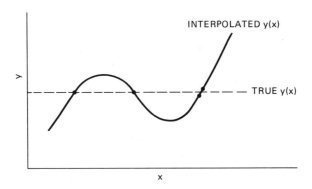

Figure 3.4 High-order interpolation.

Two problems arise in using high-order interpolating polynomials. First, increasing the order increases the number of "wiggles" between data values. This is shown in Figure 3.4, where we are using a cubic polynomial to fit data that essentially lie on a straight line. Second, interpolating polynomials using unequally spaced base points get very complicated with higher order. Therefore, unless you know that the answers should lie on a cubic or quartic line, use linear or at most quadratic interpolation.

To interpolate between points linearly, the function

$$y = a + bx \qquad (3.23)$$

is used, where b is the slope and a the intercept of the linear interpolating polynomial. To evaluate the slope and intercept:

$$b = \frac{y_2 - y_1}{x_2 - x_1} \qquad (3.24)$$

$$a = y_1 - bx_1 \qquad (3.25)$$

So,

$$y = a + bx$$
$$y = y_1 - bx_1 + bx$$
$$y = y_1 + b(x - x_1)$$
$$y = y_1 + \frac{y_2 - y_1}{x_2 - x_1}(x - x_1) \qquad (3.26)$$

Example: The count rate of Mizar was measured to be 200,000 counts per second at 03:00 UT and 300,000 counts per second at 04:00 UT. What is the best linear guess as to the count rate at 03:30 UT?

03:30 UT = 3.5 hours UT

$$y = 200,000 + \frac{(300,000 - 200,000)}{(4 - 3)}(3.5 - 3)$$

$$y = 200,000 + \frac{100,000}{1}(0.5)$$

$$y = 250,000 \text{ counts per second at } 03:30 \text{ UT.}$$

Working in a similar manner, we can derive the interpolating formula for the second-order or quadratic polynomial between points x_0, x_1, and x_2 as

$$y = y_0 + \left(\frac{y_1 - y_0}{x_1 - x_0}\right)(x - x_0) + \left[\left(\frac{y_2 - y_1}{x_2 - x_1}\right) - \left(\frac{y_1 - y_0}{x_1 - x_0}\right)\right]\left[\frac{(x - x_0)(x - x_1)}{(x_2 - x_0)}\right] \quad (3.27)$$

You can see that even the quadratic interpolating polynomial is getting complicated. Usually, higher-order polynomials are evaluated by computer. Note that Equation 3.27 looks like the linear form with an added term. This extra term can be considered the error that exists if linear interpolation were used instead, and can be used to give an approximate error when presenting the interpolated value.

3.6b Smoothed Interpolation

So far, we have investigated polynomials that passed exactly through the base values. As seen from Figure 3.4, this can cause large errors if the base values have some inaccuracies built into them. The best method of interpolating under these circumstances is to use some sort of least-squares polynomial through the base points, and interpolate with this approximate function. For photometric data, better accuracy can be achieved with smoothed interpolation, but with increased complexity. An example is to use several comparison star observations and fit a linear least-squares line to the observed count rate. Then this line can be used along with the variable star measurements to derive the intensity differences for differential photometry. You usually achieve greater accuracy than if you use the comparison star observation closest to the variable star measure because you are using the information contained in earlier and later measurements.

In general, we suggest that you use exact linear interpolation whenever interpolation is necessary. If you have a large number of base values, smoothed linear interpolation could be used. Remember however, that interpolation by nature is not exact, and requires data on either side of the value to be calculated.

3.6c Extrapolation

We have neglected the case of *extrapolation,* that is, the determination of $y(x)$ where x lies beyond any of the observed values. This is because extrapolation is very, very risky and should be avoided at all costs!

An example of the errors that can arise from extrapolation is the measurement of the atmospheric extinction. If you follow an extinction star from the zenith to, say 45° above the horizon, determine extinction from it, and use your values for an observation on the horizon, your results may be good. But there also may be a cloud bank or smoke layer on the horizon, making extinction there much different than near the zenith.

The rule of thumb for extrapolation is that if the data point is close to the last base value, you can extrapolate, but should consider this extrapolated value as having very low weight.

3.7 SIGNAL-TO-NOISE-RATIO

It is intuitively obvious that the longer we continue to gather data on a star during a single observation, the more accurate our results become. We would like a quantitative measure of this accuracy. Experimental scientists commonly use a quantity known as the *signal-to-noise ratio,* or S/N, which tells us the relative size of the desired signal to the underlying noise or background light. The noise is defined as the standard deviation of a single measurement from the mean of all of the measurements made on a star.

Astronomers typically consider a good photoelectric measurement as one that has a signal-to-noise ratio of 100, or in other words, the noise is 1 percent of the signal. For photon arrivals, the statistical noise fluctuation is represented by the Poisson distribution, and for bright sources where the sky background is negligible,

$$\frac{S}{N} = \frac{\text{total received counts}}{\sqrt{\text{total received counts}}}$$

$$\frac{S}{N} = \sqrt{\text{total received counts}} \qquad (3.28)$$

Therefore, for a *S/N* of 100, we must acquire 10,000 counts. A *S/N* of 100 means that the noise causes the counts to fluctuate about the mean by an amount equal to one hundredth of the mean value. To compute this error in magnitudes, we compare the mean number of counts, c, to the maximum or minimum values induced by the noise, that is

$$\Delta m = -2.5 \log \left(\frac{c \pm \dfrac{c}{100}}{c} \right)$$

$$\Delta m = -2.5 \log \left(1 \pm \frac{1}{100} \right)$$

$$= \pm 0.01 \text{ magnitude.}$$

In other words, a S/N of 100 implies an observational error of 0.01 magnitude. More detail on both the signal-to-noise ratio and the Poisson distribution can be found in Appendix K.

3.8 SOURCES ON STATISTICS

Listed below is a sample of statistics and numerical analysis texts that may be of interest to the reader. This list is by no means complete as we have not examined the dozens of available texts, but the sources listed do appear to present the material in a manner useful to the astronomer.

- Bevington, A. R. 1969. *Data Reduction and Error Analysis for The Physical Sciences.* New York: McGraw-Hill. Nice beginning college-level text with FORTRAN programs. Highly recommended.
- Bruning, J. L., and Kintz, B. L. 1977. *Computational Handbook of Statistics.* 2d ed. Glenview, Illinois: Scott, Foresman & Co. No least squares, but takes a computational approach. Includes FORTRAN programs.
- Carnahan, B., Luther, H. A., and Wilkes J. O. 1969. *Applied Numerical Methods.* New York: John Wiley and Sons. One of the best FORTRAN numerical analysis books. Explanation is at college level.
- Ehrenberg, A. S. C. 1975. *Data Reduction: Analyzing and Interpreting Statistical Data.* New York: John Wiley and Sons. Good beginning college text.
- Harnett, D. L. 1975. *Introduction to Statistical Methods.* 2d ed. Reading, Mass. Addison Wesley. Beginning college level.

- Meyer, S. L. 1975. *Data Analysis for Scientists and Engineers.* New York: John Wiley and Sons. Beginning college level.
- Young, H. D. 1962. *Statistical Treatment of Experimental Data.* New York: McGraw Hill. Very nice advanced high school level text with lots of explanations.

CHAPTER 4
DATA REDUCTION

There are three stages in the treatment of photoelectric data, which we call *acquisition, reduction,* and *analysis.* The techniques for data acquisition are presented in Chapter 9 and should be thoroughly studied before raw data are acquired. We treat data reduction now, rather than after Chapter 9, because intelligent data acquisition requires a knowledge of the types of observations necessary for the reduction process. The reduction of data from counts or meter deflections into magnitudes tied to the standard system can be a complicated process, but one that is required by many research projects. Careful reading of this material and the examples in the appendices will enable you to reduce any *UBV* observations and place them on the standard system. Most of the third stage, data analysis, is left up to the individual. Analysis involves the calculation of such quantities as periods, orbital elements, and in general all calculations beyond the determination of magnitudes and colors. The analysis depends greatly on the purpose of the investigation and should be obtained from other sources.

4.1 A DATA-REDUCTION OVERVIEW

You have some raw instrumental measurements of stars and sky background. What are the steps necessary to complete the reduction? There are many different ways that data reduction can proceed. A general outline that fits most situations follows:

1. If you are pulse counting, correct your values to one consistent set, that is, counts per second rather than counts per various arbitrary time intervals. The count rates should be corrected for dead time.

For DC photometry, the amplifier gain settings must be corrected to true gain using the gain table, which is discussed in Section 8.6.

2. Subtract the sky background from each stellar measurement. This must be done before the numbers are converted into logarithmic values (magnitudes).

3. Calculate the instrumental magnitude and colors. For differential photometry, calculate the magnitude differences between the variable and the comparison star.

4. Determine the extinction coefficients and apply the extinction correction. This step is often unnecessary for differential photometry. If you intend to leave your differential photometry on the instrumental system, skip to step 7.

5. Use the standard stars to determine the zero-point constants and, if necessary, the transformation coefficients.

6. Transform your instrumental measurements to the standard system.

7. Estimate the quality of the night by comparing the transformed standard-star magnitudes and colors with their accepted values. For differential photometry, check the reproducibility of the comparison star measurements after correcting them for extinction.

8. Perform any ancillary calculations such as time conversions that are necessary to make your observations useful and publishable.

Steps 1, 2, 3, 5, 6, and 7 are illustrated by a worked example in Appendix H. An example of step 4 is found in Appendix G. Step 8 is covered in detail in Chapter 5. In what follows, we review the concepts and difficulties of some of these steps and present a worked example of the data reduction associated with differential photometry.

4.2 DEAD-TIME CORRECTION

One of the major drawbacks of a pulse-counting system is its inability to count closely spaced pulses with accuracy. After the photomultiplier tube, preamp, or counter detects a pulse, there is a short time interval in which the device is unable to respond to an additional pulse. If two or more pulses arrive at any of the major components in an interval shorter than the so-called *dead time* of the component, these pulses will be detected as a single count. Incident photons from bright sources will on the average be more closely spaced in time than those from fainter sources. But these photons do not arrive in evenly spaced time intervals. From a bright source, four pulses may arrive in the first 10 nanoseconds, none in the next 10 nanoseconds, etc. The manufacturer's specifications on the photomultiplier tube, preamp, or counter dead times should not be relied upon, as those figures are based on evenly spaced, uniform pulses that are never found except in the testing laboratory.

The component with the longest dead time is the major contributor to the inaccuracy, so in general use a counter with at least a 100-MHz response and the fastest preamp possible. At Goethe Link Observatory, the Taylor preamp (see Chapter 7) is the slowest component. In general, the photomultiplier tube dead time is insignificant compared to that of the preamp or counter. The dead-time problem makes pulse counting nonlinear for bright sources.

The equation for the dead-time correction is simple in form, but difficult to solve. The equation can be written as

$$n = Ne^{-tN} \tag{4.1}$$

where

n = observed count rate in counts per second
N = "true" count rate for a perfect system in counts per second
t = dead-time coefficient defined as $t = 1/N$ when observed count rate falls to $1/e$ of the true count rate.

Equation 4.1 can be rearranged to yield

$$\frac{n}{N} = e^{-tN}. \tag{4.2}$$

Taking the natural logarithm of each side yields

$$\ln (n/N) = -tN$$

or

$$\ln (N/n) = tN. \tag{4.3}$$

If we graph $\ln (N/n)$ versus N, then t is the slope of the best-fitted line.

Our problem, though, is that we do not know N and therefore cannot solve for t.

The technique for finding t takes advantage of the fact that for low count rates, the dead-time correction is negligible. Suppose we have some device that can attenuate the light reaching the photomultiplier tube by a known factor, which we will designate as b. Then, when the attenuator is in place, only $1/b$ of the light reaches the photomultiplier tube. (The nature of the attenuator is discussed later.) If we observe a light source or star with the device in place, the observed count rate, n_L, will be low and will very nearly equal the true count rate, N_L. If the attenuator is removed, the *true* count rate, N_H, will increase b times. That is,

$$N_H = bN_L \simeq bn_L. \tag{4.3a}$$

However, the *observed* rate increases by some smaller factor because of dead-time losses. A comparison of the observed rate, n_H, to bn_L gives a measure of the dead-time coefficient. Equation 4.3 can now be rewritten as

$$\ln\left(\frac{bn_L}{n_H}\right) = tbn_L. \tag{4.4}$$

If several light sources of different brightnesses are observed both with and without the attenuator, a plot of $\ln(bn_L/n_H)$ versus bn_L yields a line with slope t.

There are three methods of attenuation commonly used. Each method is considered in turn.

1. *Using aperture stops.* In this method, the telescope is pointed at a bright star and the front of the tube is covered by a piece of cardboard with a small circular opening. The count rate recorded through this opening is n_L. The count rate recorded through a larger opening in a second piece of cardboard is n_H. The factor b is just the ratio of the areas of the two apertures. There is a disadvantage with this method if a reflecting telescope is used. In this case, the apertures must be made small enough to be placed off the optical axis so that the secondary mirror support does not

block incoming light. If this is not done, then one must be careful to account for the area of the secondary support in the calculation of b. This may not be difficult to do if the mirror cell has a circular cross section and the support vanes are thin enough to ignore.

2. *Using the photometer diaphragms.* In this method, the light source cannot be a star. It must be an extended object with uniform surface brightness. For this purpose, a uniformly illuminated white card can be placed in front of the telescope. The diaphragms in the photometer head can then be used, a small one to measure n_L and a large one to measure n_H. The ratio of the diaphragm areas is b. The problem with this method is that the card must be uniformly illuminated, the diaphragm sizes must be known accurately, and the light source must be variable if more than one observation is to be made with the available diaphragms. The daytime sky can be used as the light source if extreme care is used to prevent current overload of the photomultiplier tube.

3. *Using a "neutral" density filter.* This method uses a neutral density filter placed in the filter slide. The star need only be measured once with and once without the filter in the light path. The density of the filter is then b. The problem with this method is that no filter is truly "neutral." This means that the amount of light transmitted by the filter depends, at least weakly, on the color of the star. This would seem to make this method very cumbersome. However, once this color effect is calibrated, the neutral density filter offers a convenient way to find the dead-time coefficient. To calibrate the color dependence of the filter, several stars of widely different colors are observed both with and without the filter. The stars selected (see Appendix C) should be relatively faint so that the dead-time correction is negligible. For each star, a magnitude difference $(v_1 - v_0)$ is calculated by

$$v_1 - v_0 = -2.5 \log (n_1/n_0), \tag{4.5}$$

where n_1 is the count rate with the filter in place and n_0 is the rate without the filter. Then $(v_1 - v_0)$ is plotted versus $(B - V)$ for each star. The resultant graph should be a nearly horizontal line. In the case of a filter used at Indiana University, a least-squares fit resulted in

$$v_1 - v_0 = -0.008 (B - V) + 3.934.$$

It can be seen that this relation depends very weakly on color. The factor, b, is the ratio of light intensity without the filter to that transmitted. That is,

$$v_1 - v_0 = -2.5 \log (I_1/I_0) \qquad (4.6)$$

or

$$b = I_0/I_1 = 10^{0.4(v_1 - v_0)}. \qquad (4.7)$$

The dead-time coefficient can then be found using the observations of bright stars.

An example of a dead-time coefficient determination can be found in Appendix F. Even when t is known for a given count rate, an iterative technique is required to solve Equation 4.1. First substitute the observed count rate, n_0, for N and calculate a corrected count rate, n_1. This new value is then substituted for N and the process is repeated until n_k approaches n_{k+1} to the accuracy required. A FORTRAN subroutine to iterate this equation is given in Section I.1, in addition to an example shown in Appendix H.

4.3 CALCULATION OF INSTRUMENTAL MAGNITUDES AND COLORS

Section 1.7 derives the equations necessary to formulate instrumental magnitudes and colors, along with a physical understanding of the constants involved. Writing Equations 1.10 and 1.12 explicitly for the *UBV* system, we have

$$v = c_v - 2.5 \log d_v \qquad (4.8)$$
$$b - v = c_{bv} - 2.5 \log (d_b/d_v) \qquad (4.9)$$
$$u - b = c_{ub} - 2.5 \log (d_u/d_b), \qquad (4.10)$$

which relate the observed deflections or counts, d, to the instrumental magnitudes and colors. Because these instrumental values are used in Section 4.5 to evaluate the zero-point shifts in the transformation equations, the constants, the c's, are arbitrary. For DC work, the usual forms of Equations 4.8 through 4.10 are:

$$v = -2.5 \log (d_v) + G_v \qquad (4.11)$$
$$b - v = -2.5 \log (d_b/d_v) + G_b - G_v \qquad (4.12)$$
$$u - b = -2.5 \log (d_u/d_b) + G_u - G_b \qquad (4.13)$$

where G is the relative gain for each filter and d is the chart-recorder deflection at that gain setting. For pulse counting, the equations become:

$$v = -2.5 \log (\dot{C}_v) \qquad (4.14)$$
$$b - v = -2.5 \log (\dot{C}_b/\dot{C}_v) \qquad (4.15)$$
$$u - b = -2.5 \log (\dot{C}_u/\dot{C}_b) \qquad (4.16)$$

where $\dot{C}$ is the count rate in counts per second through each filter. Worked examples of both forms of magnitude calculations can be found in Appendix H.

4.4 EXTINCTION CORRECTIONS

Remember that extinction represents the loss of starlight while traversing the earth's atmosphere. All published photometric results correct for this and essentially give the apparent magnitude of the star outside of the earth's atmosphere, called the *extra-atmospheric magnitude*. The equations discussed in Section 1.8 and derived in Appendix J are the basis for the treatment of extinction. Much of the material in this section makes use of the results obtained by Hardie.[1] Most extinction corrections account for first-order extinction, along with the associated air mass calculation. For greater accuracy, second-order extinction should be taken into account.

4.4a Air Mass Calculations

At altitudes more than 30° above the horizon, the simple plane-parallel approximation, derived in Appendix J, for the amount of atmosphere between an observer and a star is accurate to within 0.2 percent. When a star's altitude is greater than 30° or correspondingly, the zenith distance, z, is less than 60°, this approximation gives

$$X = \sec z \qquad (4.17)$$

where

$$\sec z = (\sin \phi \sin \delta + \cos \phi \cos \delta \cos H)^{-1} \qquad (4.18)$$

where ϕ is the observer's latitude, δ the declination of the star, and H is its hour angle in degrees. The mass of the air traversed by the starlight is X. This quantity is at a minimum when a star is directly overhead, or

$$\sec z = \sec 0° = 1.$$

This amount of air is called one *air mass* for convenience, rather than trying to remember some large-numbered column density.

For zenith distances greater than 60°, the plane-parallel approximation breaks down. An equation that more closely approximates the effects of the spherical earth must be used. The most common polynomial approximation was made to data collected by Bemporad in 1904 and is given in Hardie[1] as:

$$X = \sec z - 0.0018167 (\sec z - 1) - 0.002875 (\sec z - 1)^2 \\ - 0.0008083 (\sec z - 1)^3 \qquad (4.19)$$

where z is the *apparent,* not true, zenith distance. Equation 4.19 fits Bemporad's data to better than 0.1 percent at an air mass of 6.8. That is only 10° from the horizon and closer than you would want to observe. Because these data represent only average sky conditions at one location at the turn of the century, we cannot expect that the actual accuracy of the air mass calculation is 0.1 percent.

Other methods of determining air mass involve the use of tables or nomographs and are not presented here because they are less practical than solving the equations above with a scientific calculator.

Example: An observer located at 40° north latitude locates Sigma Leo (RA = $11^h20^m6^s$, Dec. = $6°8'21''$) at an apparent hour angle of 3^h, which is 45°. What is the air mass between the observer and Sigma Leo?

From Equation 4.18, we have:

$$\sec z = [\sin (40°) \sin (6.1392°)$$
$$+ \cos (40°) \cos (6.1392°) \cos (45°)]^{-1}$$
$$\sec z = 1.6466$$

From Equation 4.17, we have:

$$X = \sec z = 1.6466$$

For comparison, we can now use Equation 4.19 to improve our accuracy:

$$X = 1.6466 - 0.0018167(0.6466) - 0.002875(0.6466)^2$$
$$- 0.0008083(0.6466)^3$$
$$X = 1.6440$$

Notice that the two methods agree to about 0.1 percent.

4.4b First-order Extinction

Extinction is very difficult to model exactly because of the many variables that play important roles in the absorption of light in the earth's atmosphere. To do a first-order approximation is to account for the largest contributor, the air mass variation. In this approximation, the following equations hold:

$$v_0 = v - k'_v X \tag{4.20}$$
$$(b - v)_0 = (b - v) - k'_{bv} X \tag{4.21}$$
$$(u - b)_0 = (u - b) - k'_{ub} X, \tag{4.22}$$

where k' is the principal extinction coefficient in units of magnitudes per air mass and the subscript 0 is used to denote an extra-atmospheric value. Rearranging these three equations, we obtain

$$v = k'_v X + v_0 \tag{4.23}$$
$$(b - v) = k'_{bv} X + (b - v)_0 \tag{4.24}$$
$$(u - b) = k'_{ub} X + (u - b)_0. \tag{4.25}$$

The values of the extinction coefficients can then be found by following one star through changing air masses and plotting the color index or magnitude versus X. The slope of the line is the extinction coefficient and the intercept the extra-atmosphere magnitude or color index.

What has been presented is an ideal case. In reality, by the time the air mass in the direction of a star has changed appreciably, the sky may have undergone considerable change. Even if the atmosphere is static, the extinction in various parts of the sky is not constant. The change may be due to a local fluctuation, giving rise to scatter about the mean curve, or it may be on a large scale, such as an east-west variation. Moreover, the atmosphere varies daily depending on its moisture and dust content. As is explained in Section 4.4c another complication arises as a result of the extinction itself being color-dependent.

Do not be discouraged by all of the problems discussed above. The accurate measurement of extinction is a tough problem and if determined to high precision would leave little time for the actual observations! Therefore, knowing the value of the extinction coefficients to an accuracy of 2 or 3 percent is considered acceptable by most professional astronomers. Observational recommendations for extinction can be found in Chapter 9. Several methods of determining the principal extinction coefficients are available. The two most common are using comparison stars, and using a sample of A0 stars near your variables. These are discussed below.

Because of the spatial variation possible in extinction, the best possible choice for your extinction star is the comparison star for the observed variable. This choice has two advantages: the extinction measurements are never far in time or space from the variable star values, and if you are using comparison stars of the same color as your variables, second-order effects become negligible. This method is only suited to observing programs in which a single variable is observed most of the night. This is the only way to collect enough measurements of the comparison star, over a wide range of air mass, in order to determine the extinction coefficients.

Another method of determining the principal extinction coefficients is to use a sample of A0 stars covering the region of the sky in which you are observing. The extinction can then be determined by using least-squares analysis directly. This technique has the advantage of requiring a smaller amount of observing time. However, the analysis is more complicated and if a computer program is used, there is a temptation not to plot the measurements. In which case, one bad measurement because of haze moving in during your observations may not be apparent, yet it can affect your results drastically.

*4.4c Second-order Extinction

If we include the color dependence of the extinction coefficients, as explained in Section J.3, then we can modify the principal coefficients to

$$k'_v \rightarrow k'_v + k''_v(b - v) \tag{4.26}$$
$$k'_{bv} \rightarrow k'_{bv} + k''_{bv}(b - v) \tag{4.27}$$

Equations 4.20 and 4.21 become

$$v_0 = v - k'_v X - k''_v(b - v)X \tag{4.28}$$
$$(b - v)_0 = (b - v) - k'_{bv}X - k''_{bv}(b - v)X. \tag{4.29}$$

Equation 4.22 remains the same because of the definition of k''_{ub} as zero. We can solve Equations 4.28 and 4.29 for the second-order coefficients by using a close optical pair having very different colors. Because of their proximity, the air mass remains constant between them and we can obtain

$$v_{01} - v_{02} = (v_1 - k'_v X - k''_v(b - v)_1 X) $$
$$- (v_2 - k'_v X - k''_v(b - v)_2 X)$$

or

$$\Delta v_0 = \Delta v - k''_v \, \Delta(b - v)X \tag{4.30}$$
$$\Delta v = k''_v \, \Delta(b - v)X + \Delta v_0.$$

Similarly,

$$\Delta(b - v) = k''_{bv} \, \Delta(b - v)X + \Delta(b - v)_0 \tag{4.31}$$

where Δ indicates the difference in colors or magnitudes of the two stars at each air mass. The solution of Equations 4.30 and 4.31 is performed easily by plotting Δv or $\Delta(b - v)$ versus $\Delta(b - v)X$; the slope is then the second-order extinction coefficient. Each pair so measured can also be used to determine the principal coefficients once the second-order values are known.

From experience and theory, the second-order coefficient for v is essentially negligible. In addition, the values found through the use of Equation 4.31 have been found to be relatively constant and probably do not need to be determined any more often than are the color transformation coefficients.

An extinction example for both principal and second-order extinction can be found in Appendix G. Suitable pairs of stars can be found in Appendix B. Most of these pairs are from a list prepared by Kitt Peak National Observatory and are near the equator. Note that the red stars are quite often faint and are more difficult to measure. Bright pairs are just hard to find!

4.5 ZERO-POINT VALUES

From Chapter 2, we have the equations

$$V = \epsilon(B - V) + v_0 + \zeta_v \qquad (4.32)$$
$$(B - V) = \mu(b - v)_0 + \zeta_{bv} \qquad (4.33)$$
$$(U - B) = \psi(u - b)_0 + \zeta_{ub}. \qquad (4.34)$$

These three equations are the working equations for this and the following sections. Rearranging,

$$\zeta_v = V - v_0 - \epsilon(B - V) \qquad (4.35)$$
$$\zeta_{bv} = (B - V) - \mu(b - v)_0 \qquad (4.36)$$
$$\zeta_{ub} = (U - B) - \psi(u - b)_0. \qquad (4.37)$$

In other words, the zero point is equal to the standard value minus the transformed extra-atmospheric value. The zero points are calculated by solving Equations 4.35 to 4.37 for each standard and then taking means.

Figure 4.1 plots the three zero points determined with pulse-counting equipment at Goethe Link Observatory over an 18-month period. The break in ζ_v occurred when the mirrors were realuminized. It indicates an approximate 0.5 magnitude gain in sensitivity. The scatter is caused

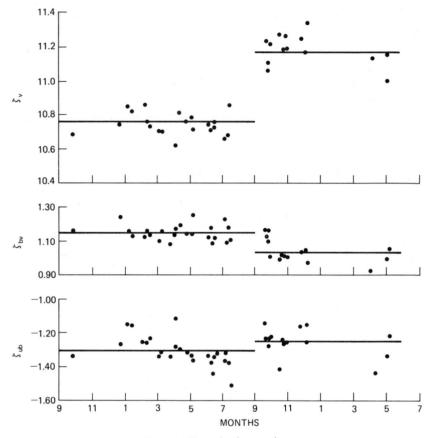

Figure 4.1 Example of zero points.

primarily by the small number of standard stars used in the zero-point calculation and by differing sky transparency. The zero-point values must be determined nightly.

4.6 STANDARD MAGNITUDES AND COLORS

Once the transformation coefficients have been determined, along with the nightly values of extinction and the zero-point shifts, Equations 4.28, 4.29, and 4.22 can be used to determine the extra-atmospheric instrumental magnitudes and colors. Substituting these values into Equations 4.32 through 4.34 yields the transformed standard magnitudes and colors. These values may not agree with accepted values for a constant star because of statistical scatter and the quality of the night, but means determined over several nights should yield good numbers.

4.7 TRANSFORMATION COEFFICIENTS

The transformation coefficients defined in Chapter 2 could be determined directly from Equations 4.32 to 4.34 by measuring several stars whose standard magnitudes and colors are known. In fact, that is the approach used for determining the V coefficient, ϵ:

$$V - v_0 = \epsilon(B - V) + \zeta_v. \tag{4.38}$$

The slope of the best-fitted line for a plot of $(V - v_0)$ versus $(B - V)$ will be the coefficient ϵ. Note that you are plotting the difference between the two magnitudes; this is more accurate than plotting V versus v_0 because it magnifies small variations in either number. For instance, the change in v from 8.79 to 8.80 is less than 1 percent. But if $V = 8.85$, then $V - v_0 = 0.06$ in one case and 0.05 in the other, a difference of 20 percent.

However, our two equations for the color indices are not in differential form. They can be converted to differential measurements by solving for the extra-atmospheric instrumental colors as shown for $(b - v)$:

$$(b - v)_0 = \frac{(B - V) - \zeta_{bv}}{\mu}. \tag{4.39}$$

Subtracting the extra-atmospheric instrumental value, $(b - v)_0$, from both sides of Equation 4.33;

$$(B - V) - (b - v)_0 = \mu(b - v)_0 - (b - v)_0 + \zeta_{bv}$$
$$= (\mu - 1)(b - v)_0 + \zeta_{bv}$$

and then substituting Equation 4.39 into the right-hand side, yielding

$$(B - V) - (b - v)_0 = \left(1 - \frac{1}{\mu}\right)(B - V) + \frac{\zeta_{bv}}{\mu}, \tag{4.40}$$

and similarly for $(U - B)$,

$$(U - B) - (u - b)_0 = \left(1 - \frac{1}{\psi}\right)(U - B) + \frac{\zeta_{ub}}{\psi}. \quad (4.41)$$

Equations 4.40 and 4.41 along with Equation 4.38 are our working equations for determining the transformation coefficients. Plots of the left-hand sides of these equations versus either $(B - V)$ for Equations 4.38 and 4.40, or $(U - B)$ for Equation 4.41, yield slopes that are related to the transformation coefficients.

In practice, there are two methods commonly used to solve for the transformation coefficients:

1. Choose several standards from the Johnson standard list in Appendix C, measure them, and determine the transformation coefficients. With this method, you are able to select bright stars of widely differing colors. It has the disadvantage of requiring accurate knowledge of the extinction coefficients. Select at least 10 and preferably 20 or more standard stars with a wide range of $(B - V)$ and $(U - B)$ colors and try to observe them when they are near the zenith. Note that the Johnson list has internal errors of $\pm 0^m02$, so do not expect to achieve results that are significantly more accurate.
2. Use one of the standard clusters from Appendix D for your standards. This eliminates the extinction problem, but adds the problem of faintness. Not only are most clusters fourth to sixth magnitude or fainter, but also the red stars are fainter than the hot blue stars of the cluster and add more error to the determination. Another problem is systematic errors in the cluster standard values that can make the coefficient determination from one cluster different from another. This is a minor effect, but it should be kept in mind.

We suggest that you use method 1 with a telescope aperture of 25 centimeters (10 inches) or less. For larger telescopes, use method 2. The normal procedure is to determine carefully the transformation coefficients at the beginning and end of your observing season, as well as once or twice in between. Resolve to spend half of a good night for each of these determinations. The coefficients change very slowly with time, and mean values are generally sufficient. For method 2, the different determinations should be made using different clusters, if possible. Transformation examples using method 1 for DC photometry and method 2 for pulse counting are given in Appendix H.

4.8 DIFFERENTIAL PHOTOMETRY

The reduction of differential photometry data is treated somewhat differently from the descriptions found in previous sections. Because differential photometry is the starting point for most newcomers to photometry, we explain the reduction process in detail. We assume that the observations were made in accordance with the recommendations of Section 9.3c. Variable star observations are bracketed by those of the comparison stars.

Table 4.1 contains a partial list of observations of the eclipsing binary UZ Leonis. In this example, a DC photometer was used. Columns 1, 2, and 3 contain the object's name, universal time of observation, and the filter designation. Column 4 contains the amplifier gain in magnitudes. Columns 5 and 6 contain the chart recorder pen deflection of the star and sky through each filter.

1. The first step is to subtract the sky background from each stellar measurement. The results appear on column 7. If a pulse-counting photometer had been used, and if the stars were fairly bright, a dead-time correction would be applied (Section 4.2) before subtracting the sky background.
2. The observations in column 7 follow a pattern such as

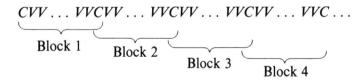

where C and V represent a measurement through each filter of the comparison and variable star, respectively. The data have a block structure where each string of several variable star measurements is sandwiched between two comparison star measurements. Each block is reduced separately by averaging the comparison star measurement at the beginning and end of the block. Equations 2.38 through 2.40 or 2.35 through 2.37 are used to pro-

TABLE 4.1. Differential Photometry Data

Block 1

Object	UT	Filter	Gain	Star	Sky	Net	Δv	Δb	Δu	ΔV	Δ(B − V)	Δ(U − B)
Comp.		V	10.505	40.2	12.0	28.2						
		B	10.505	50.0	12.0	38.0						
		U	11.938	44.3	24.0	20.3						
UZ Leo	2:40	V	11.034	41.2	15.1	26.1	0.628			0.628		
		B	11.034	48.4	15.1	33.3		0.689			0.057	
		U	12.432	50.7	33.6	17.1			0.717			0.033
	2:42	V	·	41.1	15.1	26.0	0.633			0.633		
		B	·	48.4	15.1	33.3		0.689			0.052	
		U	·	50.3	33.6	16.7			0.743			0.064
	2:45	V	·	41.5	15.1	26.4	0.616			0.616		
		B	·	48.8	15.1	33.7		0.676			0.056	
		U	·	51.0	33.6	17.4			0.698			0.026

Block 2

Object	UT	Filter	Gain	Star	Sky	Net	Δv	Δb	Δu	ΔV	Δ(B − V)	Δ(U − B)
Comp.		U	11.938	46.2	24.5	21.7						
		B	10.505	51.2	12.0	39.2						
		V	10.505	41.0	12.0	29.0						
UZ Leo	2:59	U	12.432	51.4	34.6	16.8			0.762			0.075
		B	11.034	49.2	15.3	33.9		0.687			0.049	
		V	11.034	41.8	15.3	26.5	0.634			0.634		
	3:01	U	·	52.5	34.6	17.9			0.693			0.016
		B	·	49.5	15.3	34.2		0.677			0.047	
		V	·	42.0	15.3	26.7	0.626			0.626		
	3:04	U	·	52.5	34.6	17.9			0.693			0.038
		B	·	50.0	15.3	34.7		0.661			0.036	
		V	·	42.1	15.3	26.8	0.622			0.622		
Comp.		V	10.505	41.2	11.8	29.4						
		B	10.505	51.0	11.8	39.2						
		U	11.938	45.3	24.0	21.3						

Average: $\Delta V = 0.626 \pm 0.007$ (s.d.)
$\Delta(B - V) = 0.049 \pm 0.007$
$\Delta(U - B) = 0.042 \pm 0.024$

duce a value of Δv, Δb, Δu for each variable star measurement within the block. The process is then repeated until all the blocks have been reduced. Note that each comparison star measurement does "double duty" because the last comparison star measurement in one block is also the first one in the next block. Columns 8, 9, and 10 contain the calculated magnitude differences. Check a few of these entries with your calculator.

In many cases, reduction stops at this point because extinction corrections are often ignored in differential photometry. Conversion to the standard photometric system is unnecessary for many types of research projects. However, if the variable and comparison are separated by more than a degree it may be wise to apply an extinction correction. A worked example of this correction to differential photometry can be found in Appendix G. The data in Table 4.1 do not require this correction.

If the transformation coefficients are known, it is possible to convert the magnitude differences from the instrumental to the standard system.

3. In this example, $\epsilon = -0.004$, $\mu = 0.927$, and $\psi = 1.178$. Equations 2.41 and 2.42 were used to compute $\Delta(b - v)$ and $\Delta(u - b)$ for each stellar measurement. Equation 2.49 and 2.50 can then be used to compute $\Delta(B - V)$ and $\Delta(U - B)$. Finally, Equation 2.48 can be used to compute ΔV. Check a few of the entries in columns 11 through 13. Note that the difference between the magnitude and colors in the instrumental and standard systems is practically negligible. This means that the detector and filters used match the standard system well.

If the comparison star has been standardized, Equations 2.51 through 2.53 can be used to calculate the actual magnitude and color of the variable. In this particular example, the comparison star was standardized on a previous night with the following results:

$$V = 8.950 \pm 0.038 \text{ (s.d.)}$$
$$(B - V) = 0.287 \pm 0.012$$
$$(U - B) = 0.039 \pm 0.058.$$

If we average the values of ΔV, $\Delta(B - V)$, and $\Delta(U - B)$ in columns 11, 12, and 13 we can compute the magnitude and colors of UZ Leonis to be

$$V = 8.95 + 0.63 = 9.58$$
$$(B - V) = 0.29 + 0.05 = 0.34$$
$$(U - B) = 0.04 + 0.04 = 0.08.$$

The probable errors for these values are found by adding the standard deviations of the comparison and variable star in quadrature, that is

$$\text{p.e.} = 0.675 \sqrt{\sigma_{comp}^2 + \sigma_{var}^2}.$$

The final quoted results are then

$$V = 9.58 \pm 0.03 \text{ (p.e.)}$$
$$(B - V) = 0.34 \pm 0.01$$
$$(U - B) = 0.08 \pm 0.04.$$

The larger error in $(U - B)$ reflects the fact that both the comparison star and UZ Leonis are very faint in the U filter.

*4.9   THE $(U - B)$ PROBLEM

In Chapter 2, the second-order extinction coefficient for $(U - B)$ was arbitrarily defined as zero. However, k_{ub}'' can be a larger correction than k_{bv}'', because the u extinction depends on:

1. the Balmer discontinuity
2. the second-order color term
3. systematic nonlinear deviations resulting from the assumption that k_{ub}'' was constant in the the original UBV data.

Because of these problems, the $(U - B)$ color term is inaccurate and poorly defined. Unfortunately, use of the existing system is so traditional that it would be extremely difficult to redefine the UBV system. The best solution is to calculate your $(u - b)_0$ values correctly, accounting for all first- and second-order effects, and then transform your ubv data to the existing, but nonideal, standard UBV system.

The remainder of this section presents one such method of transformation as derived by Moffat and Vogt.[2] This kind of correction is complicated and should only be attempted by those who are experienced in photometry.

Moffat and Vogt found that, for any given star, the residuals in $(U - B)$ vary linearly with air mass, X. That is,

$$\Delta[(U - B) - (u - b)] = \gamma_1 + \gamma_2 X. \qquad (4.42)$$

A plot of this equation indicates that γ_1 and γ_2 are linearly related. That is,

$$\gamma_2 = \beta\gamma_1$$

where

$$\beta \simeq -0.27.$$

We can therefore rewrite Equation 4.42 as

$$\Delta[(U - B) - (u - b)] = \gamma_1(1 + \beta X) \qquad (4.43)$$

where β is a constant and γ_1 is a function of spectral type or color. The problem of correcting for $(U - B)$ differences is then reduced to one of determining γ_1. However, γ_1 is a nonlinear function of $(U - B)$ and, in addition, is not a unique function of $(U - B)$. But it is a linear and unique function of another parameter, q, that is similar to the reddening-free parameter of Johnson and Morgan:[3]

$$\gamma_1 = \rho q \qquad (4.44)$$

where

$$q = (U - B) - 1.05(B - V). \qquad (4.45)$$

The procedure to follow in correcting $(U - B)$ is:

1. For each standard star, determine q from Equation 4.45.

2. For each standard, determine γ_1 from

$$\gamma_1 = \frac{(U - B) - (u - b)}{1 + \beta X} \qquad (4.46)$$

3. Plot γ_1 versus q and determine ρ from Equation 4.44.
4. For all future stars, correct $(U - B)$ by

$$(U - B) = \psi(u - b)_0 + \zeta_{ub} + \rho q (1 + \beta X) \qquad (4.47)$$

This procedure will reduce the mean external error in $(U - B)$ to about $0^m.02$. Without it, the mean error would be approximately three times higher. Include k''_{ub} in all equations in a similar manner as k''_{bv} is included in $(B - V)$ equations.

REFERENCES

1. Hardie, R. H. 1962. In *Astronomical Techniques*. Edited by W. A. Hiltner. Chicago: Univ. of Chicago Press, chapter 8.
2. Moffat, A. F. J., and Vogt, N. 1977. *Pub. A.S.P.* **89**, 323.
3. Johnson, H. L., and Morgan, W. W. 1953. *Ap. J.* **117**, 313.

CHAPTER 5
OBSERVATIONAL CALCULATIONS

There are a number of calculations that are useful for obtaining and reducing observational data. These include determining when an object appears above the horizon on a given night, precession of coordinates, and the calculation of date and time quantities. These and other calculations are discussed in this chapter. The subjects are recommended reading even if photometry is not attempted, as they are also involved in most visual observations.

5.1 CALCULATORS AND COMPUTERS

Observational calculations and data reduction are very tedious without the use of a calculator or computer. The scientific calculator has now been in existence for a decade. Since the introduction of the Hewlett-Packard HP-35, calculators have made great strides in capability with a reduction in cost. Programmable varieties are excellent and card-programmables are the ultimate, as programs and data can be stored for later recall. The mode of operation (whether reverse Polish notation (RPN), algebraic, or even a high-level language such as BASIC) is unimportant as long as you are comfortable with your choice. We suggest the use of a programmable calculator with seven to 10-digit accuracy and the capability of converting degrees-minutes-seconds into decimal degrees, a real blessing to astronomers! The well-known brands, such as Hewlett-Packard and Texas Instruments, should be your first choice. A review of calculators is given in *Sky and Telescope.*[1]

A calculator is all that is required to perform the data reduction. However, some people may prefer something more advanced. The next step up from a programmable scientific calculator is the microcomputer. Large-scale integration has advanced sufficiently that the purchase of a microcomputer should be considered if much data reduction or instrumentation control is anticipated. The 16-bit microcomputer is the industry standard at this time, though eight-bit and 32 bit systems are also available. As the industry seems to change with about a one-year time scale, only use this information as a general guide.

We strongly recommend the use of a bus-type computer. Examples of these are the Apple II, the IBM PC and the Macintosh II. These computers give you the easy ability to expand as your needs warrant. For example, you can add a pulse counting board or image processing capability of any of these computers. Other, non-expandable computers are usually cheaper and can be cost-effective if you know beforehand what your computer needs will be in the next few years.

At the time of this writing, the IBM PC is the industry standard computer. You can buy a better computer at lower cost with more peripherals and software programs for this system than any other. We recommend you look at a PC clone as your first choice.

Arithmetic operations used in data reduction can be performed in software at the expense of speed and space. Since most microprocessors do not include floating point operations in hardware, all such operations must be emulated in software. However, for many microprocessors, numeric coprocessor chips are available. For example, the Intel 8088 has the 8087 coprocessor, and Motorola 68000 has the 68881. Such chips perform floating-point operations a hundred times faster than can be accomplished in software. We highly recommend the purchase of a numeric coprocessor for your computer for astronomical data processing.

Hard disks are another useful peripheral. Only a few years ago the floppy disk was king of the mountain, and 360Kb of storage on one disk was thought to be enormous. Now 20Mb hard disks are so cheap that few computers are sold without at least this much on-line storage. You will still want to archive your data on removable media such as floppy disks or cartridge tape, but the hard disk gives you speed during processing and the ability to easily look at many data sets.

Some sort of graphics capability is essential. Most PC clones come with Hercules-compatible monochrome graphics, which is perfectly adequate. Color is useful to overlay several data sets on the same plot, for memos and windows in data reduction programs, and in general any place where feature separation or visibility is important. Keep in mind, however, that color systems cost more, and getting multicolored printouts can be difficult.

A printer is essential. Inexpensive dot-matrix printers can be purchased for a few hundred dollars. Often these printers have built-in bit-mapped graphics which enable you, with the proper software package, to incorportate drawings, and graphs directly into your final print-out. Other printer choices include color ink-jet printers (very nice for multicolored graphics) and laser printers which are both fast and have high-quality output. When first introduced, the H-P LaserJet was priced well over $3,500 but within several years, and several model changes, it is possible to purchase a 4 page per minute model for under $1,000.

A nice option is the modem. This device links your computer to the telephone line so that you can communicate with other computer systems. We use a modem to access database services such as CompuServe, where other users post messages, catalogs, data and computer programs that are of interest to astronomers. You should not only consider the purchase price when choosing a modem but the differential in connect time between it and a faster device. Almost every time you use a modem you will be either paying long distance or user fees which are based on time.

Equally as important as the computer hardware is the software necessary to run it. There are two approaches to computer software: buying commercial programs and developing your own. There are many astronomical software packages available, including star catalogs, astronomical utilities (time/date, rise/set, etc.), image processing and much more. For example, there is an optional companion suite of software for this book that requires no programming knowledge to do photoelectric data reduction. Look through the ads in major astronomical magazines or find reviews to give you more information on these commercial programs.

The other approach is to write your own programs. If you take this approach, we recommend using a high-level language like FORTRAN, BASIC, FORTH or C, preferably compiled rather than interpreted and with relocatable object code. There are many such compilers available, so look for reviews to help you decide which one to purchase. In addition, your computer should have the capability of being programmed in machine language for dedicated tasks or input/output operations. Often, the high-level language comes with assembly language programming capability built-in.

A very good microcomputer system built around an IBM-PC clone with 1Mb memory, 20Mb hard disk, numeric coprocessor, dot-matrix printer, 2400-baud modem, monochrome graphics and software can be purchased for around $2,500 (1990). This may seem expensive, but the cost is still decreasing and some of it is defrayed by the fact that the computer can replace considerable equipment, such as the counter and magnetic tape unit of the photon-counting system. Find a computer store and ask the dealer to help you in your computer selection.

Another approach to data reduction involves the use of a computing center found at many universities. Here all of the hardware is maintained for you, and high-speed, reliable, and efficient programming languages and equipment are available. In addition, computing centers may have programming support and plotting or graphics capabilities on hand. Some centers allow outsiders to use the system at minimal cost if it is being used for research. Approach the center directly, or talk to someone in the astronomy, physics, or computer science departments about your needs and desires.

5.2 ATMOSPHERIC REFRACTION AND DISPERSION

When we observe the sun and stars near the horizon, the atmosphere bends the rays and makes the object appear higher in the sky than it really is, as shown in Figure 5.1. This effect reaches a maximum on the horizon, where an object appears to be 35 arc minutes above its actual location. This means that when the sun appears to touch the horizon, in reality it has already set! Atmospheric refraction affects images in three ways: it changes the measured zenith angle and therefore the air mass, it disperses the image so that each star looks like a miniature spectrum, and it changes the apparent right ascension and declination of a star. These effects must be accounted for accurately when viewing objects near the horizon.

5.2a Calculating Refraction

The simplest method of calculating refraction is to assume a plane-parallel atmosphere made of layers, each with a differing index of refrac-

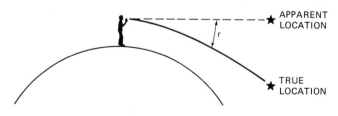

Figure 5.1 Refraction.

tion decreasing uniformly outward. Using Snell's law at each boundary, we find the angle of refraction, r, is approximately equal to

$$r = 60\rlap{.}''4 \tan z_{tr}, \qquad (5.1)$$

where z_{tr} is the true zenith distance.

This equation has an error of about 1 arc second at $z = 60°$. An empirical improvement was derived by Cassini and Bessel in the seventeenth century and is of the form

$$r = 60\rlap{.}''4 \tan z_{tr} - 0\rlap{.}''06688 \tan^3 z_{tr}. \qquad (5.2)$$

Equation 5.2 is accurate to better than 1 arc second at $z = 75°$, or $15°$ above the horizon. A more accurate equation which accounts for atmospheric pressure, temperature, and the observer's elevation is given by Doggett et al.[2] A short listing of the refraction correction is presented in Table 5.1. Remember that this correction is subtracted from the true zenith distance to get the apparent zenith distance, z_{ap}.

TABLE 5.1.   Atmospheric Refraction (760 mm Hg, 10°C, 5500 Å)

$z_{ap}°$	r''	$z_{ap}°$	r''	$z_{ap}°$	r''
5	5	58	93	75	214
10	10	59	97	76	229
15	16	60	101	77	247
20	21	61	105	78	267
25	27	62	109	79	291
30	34	63	114	80	319
35	41	64	119	81	353
40	49	65	124	82	393
45	59	66	130	83	444
46	60	67	136	84	508
48	65	68	143	85	592
50	69	69	151	86	704
52	74	70	159	87	865
54	80	71	168	88	1105
55	83	72	177	89	1494
56	86	73	188	89.5	1790
57	89	74	200	90	2189

Example: The true zenith distance of BX And was determined to be 69°. What is its apparent location?

1. From Equation 5.1 we have:

$$r = 60\overset{''}{.}4 \tan(69°)$$
$$= 157\overset{''}{.}3$$
$$r = 2'37''$$
$$z_{ap} = z_{tr} - r \qquad\qquad (5.2a)$$
$$= 69° - 2'37''$$
$$z_{ap} = 68°57'23''$$

2. From Equation 5.2:

$$r = 60\overset{''}{.}4 \tan(69°) - 0\overset{''}{.}06688 \tan^3(69°)$$
$$r = 156\overset{''}{.}2$$
$$z_{ap} = 68°57'24''$$

3. From Table 5.1:

$$r = 143''$$
$$z_{ap} = 68°57'37''$$

Because z_{ap} approximately equals z_{tr}, you can use either value in Equation 5.1 or 5.2 with minimal error.

5.2b Effect of Refraction on Air Mass

If you use the apparent zenith distance, the air mass calculated from either Equation 4.18 or 4.19 will be correct. However, you must assume that the hour angle setting circle is correct, or you must include the refraction numerically in the hour angle calculation. Table 5.2 shows the error involved in neglecting refraction at several zenith distances. For z greater than 60°, the error is significant enough that it cannot be ignored. Generally, you can neglect refraction above an altitude of 30°, but be sure to include the correction at lower altitudes.

TABLE 5.2.   Refraction Air Mass
Errors

z_{ap} °	X_{ap}	X_{tr}	%
0	1.000	1.000	0.00
30	1.154	1.154	0.00
60	1.994	1.996	0.10
65	2.356	2.359	0.13
70	2.904	2.910	0.21
75	3.816	3.830	0.37
80	5.598	5.645	0.83
85	10.211	10.468	2.46

5.2c Differential Refraction

The index of refraction for glass, air, or any material is not constant with wavelength. This spreads the light from a star into a miniature spectrum, as if the earth's atmosphere were a prism. This dispersion is obvious when looking at stars near the horizon, as they appear blue on the top and red below. It also gives rise to the "green flash" of the setting sun. Table 5.3 gives the separation angle of the red and blue images at various zenith distances. For z greater than 75°, the images are far enough apart that they are no longer centered in a small diaphragm. They cause erroneous measurements unless a correction is made. In other words, do not observe within 15° of the horizon unless it is absolutely necessary! A secondary effect of differential refraction is that the red and blue rays that make up the observed stellar image are separated by the earth's atmosphere and thus give rise to a color-dependent scintillation, manifested in red and blue flashes. More detail on various

TABLE 5.3.   Red and Blue Image
Separation

z	r''
0	0.00
30	0.35
45	0.60
60	1.04
75	2.24
90	29.00

refractive effects can be found in Tricker[3] or Humphreys.[4] Both make quite interesting reading.

5.3 TIME

Time is the most accurate piece of data the astronomer has and should be treated accordingly. A 1 percent error in the determination of the magnitude of a star is considered excellent, yet a digital watch has an accuracy of 1 second in a day (0.001 percent), or 1000 times more accurate.

Because astronomers are located worldwide and have been observing for centuries, certain conventions are observed in order that measurements made by two different observers can be correlated with minimal effort.

This section assumes some knowledge of the various time systems involved: solar time, sidereal time, and so on. More detail can be found in any good introductory astronomy text such as Abell.[5]

5.3a Solar Time

An *apparent solar day* is defined as the length of time between two successive transits of the sun, from astronomical noon until astronomical noon the following day. The length of time is dependent on three factors: the rotation of the earth on its axis, the obliquity of the ecliptic, and the speed of the earth in its revolution around the sun. Because the latter two items have effects which are variable throughout the year, the length of the apparent day is not constant. *Mean solar time,* the length of an average day, one year divided by 365¼ days, eliminates this problem. Apparent solar time is measured by sundials; mean solar time is the time measured by clocks, with which everyone is familiar.

Another problem exists because noon does not occur simultaneously at all places on earth. Time zones were created to eliminate this problem, with each zone being about 15° wide or approximately ¼₄ of the earth's daily rotation. Greenwich, England is defined as the arbitrary zero point; an observer located at 15° west longitude is one hour behind Greenwich, an observer at 30° west longitude is two hours behind Greenwich, and so forth. This is convenient for daily living but not for the astronomer. If an eclipse was observed at 3 p.m. local time in

Hawaii, what time was it where you live? *All astronomical observations must be recorded in Universal Time (UT), the local mean time in Greenwich, England.* For an observer in San Francisco, eight hours are added to Pacific Standard Time (PST) before recording data. UT is kept on a 24-hour clock to eliminate a.m.-p.m. ambiguities.

Example: A meteor is seen at 10:30 pm EST in New York on January 1, 1981. What UT should be recorded?

1. Convert EST to 24-hour time.

$$10:30 \text{ pm} = 22:30 \text{ EST}$$

2. Add 5 hours for time-zone difference.

$$22:30 \text{ EST} + 05:00 = 27:30 \text{ UT}$$

3. Subtract 24 hours (it is the next day in Greenwich).

$$27:30 - 24:00 = 03:30 \text{ UT}$$

4. Add 1 day to the date because of step 3.

$$\text{January } 1 + 1 = \text{January } 2$$

The observation was made on January 2, 1981 at 03:30 UT.

5.3b Universal Time

Observations should be recorded to within the nearest minute, or more precisely for rapidly varying objects. This accuracy cannot be reliably obtained from your AM radio or local bank sign. The best method is to use a shortwave receiver and listen to one of the national time signals broadcast by WWV in the United States, CHU in Canada, and similar services in other countries. A complete list is published by the British Astronomical Association.[6] WWV broadcasts at 2.5, 5, 10, and 15 MHz, and CHU broadcasts at 3.330, 7.335, and 14.670 MHz.

To receive these signals, buy a new portable multiband radio or a single-frequency radio such as the Radio Shack TIMEKUBE® or buy a used general-coverage receiver. Check local ads, amateur radio dealers and clubs, or the classified ads of a magazine such as *QST* or *Ham Radio*. If the radio you obtain works on batteries only, consider buying an AC adapter as batteries are adversely affected by cold weather and may become inoperative. A word of warning: if you intend to use a microcomputer with your system, the harmonics generated by its internal clock will interfere with the WWV frequencies, but generally not those of CHU.

A digital 24-hour clock is extremely convenient for the observatory, as no conversion is necessary to record the time. Several commercial clocks are available on the market at reasonable cost. Instructions for building your own can be found in back issues of many electronics magazines. Look for those using direct drive to each digit to eliminate RF multiplexing noise. Clocks with internal calendars, such as the CT7001 by Cal-Tex, or with BCD output, such as the MM5313 by National, may be used in microcomputer applications.

5.3c   Sidereal Time

Sidereal time (ST) is the time kept by the stars, or more precisely, the right ascension of a star currently on the meridian. The length of a *sidereal day* is defined as the time between successive transits of the vernal equinox. A sidereal day is about 4 minutes shorter than a solar day. Knowledge of this time is essential to be able to point your telescope to the right region of the sky.

For many telescopes, the normal setting circles measure declination and *hour angle,* the distance from the celestial meridian. Hour angle can be expressed as

Hour angle (HA) = Local sidereal time (LST)
$$- \text{ Right ascension (RA)}. \quad (5.3)$$

We use the terms *local sidereal time* and *sidereal time* interchangeably in this chapter. The RA of a star in this equation is for the *present* epoch, that is not 1900, 1950, and so forth. Given the HA of an object and its coordinates, you can then point your telescope to the correct direction in space. Correspondingly, given the ST and RA for an object, the hour angle can be calculated for use in computing air mass.

Calculation of sidereal time can be accomplished in four basic ways: (1) from the HA and RA of some easily found object such as a bright star; (2) from tables given in *The Astronomical Almanac;*[7] (3) through use of a programmable calculator if the UT and date are known; or (4) from a sidereal rate clock. These four methods are explained below.

1. *From HA and RA.* Pick some bright star and set your telescope on it. By reading the HA from the setting circles, set a solar rate clock to ST from the equation

$$ST = RA + HA \qquad (5.4)$$

This method is as accurate as your setting circles. The solar rate clock keeps nearly sidereal time for about a night's observations.

2. *From tables. The Astronomical Almanac*[7] gives the sidereal time at 0^h UT for every day of the year. Abell[5] includes a coarser table. Converting this time to the sidereal time at another location is a fairly complicated procedure. Examples are given in the *Almanac.* You need to know the day, UT, and your longitude, which can be found from Goode's World Atlas, or from a road atlas, a topographic map, or a plot survey of your observatory.

Example: What is the ST at 03:00 UT on July 7, 1973, for an observer at longitude 86°23′.7 west?

LST at Greenwich from the *Almanac*	$18^h\ 59^m\ 16^s$
− your longitude (86°23′.7 at 15° per hour	$-5^{\ h}\ 45^m\ 35^s$
+ UT difference from 0^h	$+3^{\ h}\ 00^m\ 00^s$
+ ST/UT difference over 3^h period at 10^s	$+\qquad 30^s$
per hour	
Sidereal Time at 03:00 UT:	$16^{\ h}\ 14^m\ 11^s$

3. *With a calculator.* Given the longitude, UT, and Julian date (see Section 5.3d), there is a simple equation to obtain sidereal time:

$$ST = 6.6460556 + 2400.0512617\ (JD - 2415020)/36525$$
$$+ 1.0027379\ (UT) - \text{longitude (hours).}\quad (5.5)$$

This equation takes into account the fact that there is approximately one extra sidereal day in a year, or 2400 extra hours in a century. We want $0 \leq ST \leq 24^h$, so after solving the above equation, we must subtract off that multiple of 24 hours (extra sidereal days) that leaves a remainder in this range. A FORTRAN subroutine that calculates sidereal time can be found in Section I.6.

Example: Calculate ST for 03:00 UT on July 7, 1973, from longitude 86° 23′.7 west ($5^h45^m35^s$).
The Julian date is 2441870.5 at 0^h UT from the *Almanac*. Then

$$ST = 6.6460556 + 2400.0512617(2441870.5$$
$$- 2415020)/36525 + 1.0027379(3) - 5.75972$$
$$= 1768.23611 \text{ hours } (73 \times 24 = 1752 \text{ hours})$$
$$= 1768.23611 - 1752.0$$
$$ST = 16^h14^m10^s$$

4. *From a sidereal rate clock.* There are two varieties of this specialized clock: an electric clock, with a sidereal rate motor that is very expensive, and an electronic digital clock. Both can be purchased commercially. The electronic version can also be built from plans published in *Sky and Telescope*.[8] It is basically the same as a pulse counter, counting one pulse per sidereal second. This can be achieved either by using a crystal oscillator or by adding extra pulses to a 60-Hz clock. Setting the sidereal rate clock should be performed using methods 2 or 3 above and should be checked often in case of power failures or oscillator drift.

5.3d Julian Date

Just as time zones cause problems between widely spaced observers, differing dates of observations can be a real headache when using the standard calendar. How many days have passed since you were born? The simplest approach is to use a running count of the number of elapsed days. This count was proposed by J. J. Scaliger in 1582 and is called the *Julian date* (JD) of an observation or event. The zero point was set far enough in the past that all recorded astronomical events have a positive JD. Scaliger suggested the use of Julian date $0 = 12^h$ UT on January 1, 4713 B.C. because several calendars were in phase on that day. The JD begins at noon because most active observers in the sixteenth century were in Europe and no date change would occur during a night's observations for them.

The Julian date for any given day can be found in the *Almanac* or through use of the following equation:

$$JD\ (0^h\ UT) = 2415020 + 365\ (year - 1900)$$
$$+ (days\ from\ start\ of\ year) + (no.\ of\ leap\ years\ since\ 1900) - 0.5.$$
$$(5.6)$$

A FORTRAN subroutine for this calculation can be found in Section I.2. Note that most observations are recorded in JD units including fractions of a day, instead of separate JD and UT.

Example: An observation was made on June 15, 1973, at 11:40 UT. What Julian date should be recorded?

$$JD\ (0^h\ UT) = 2415020 + 365\ (1973 - 1900) + 166 + 18 - 0.5$$

$$JD\ (0^h\ UT) = 2441848.5$$

$$11:40\ UT = 11.6667\ hours\ UT/24 = 0.4861\ day\ UT$$

$$JD = 2441848.5 + 0.4861$$

$$JD = 2441848.9861.$$

*5.3e Heliocentric Julian Date (HJD)

Any time recorded in the process of observing is *geocentric,* that is, made from a site on the earth. Because the earth revolves around the sun, an observer is closer to or further from a particular star at different times of the year. Six months after the earth's closest approach to the star, it is two astronomical units farther away (or less if the star is not on the ecliptic). Because of the finite speed of light, up to an additional 16 minutes are required for its light to traverse this extra distance. This light-travel-time effect causes scatter around the mean light curve of a variable, as compared with observations made from a relatively stationary object like the sun. Astronomers therefore prefer to record all observations as though made from the sun by adding or subtracting the light's travel time, depending on whether the earth is farther or closer, respectively, to the object than the sun is. The date derived in this manner is called the *heliocentric Julian date* (HJD).

Before the advent of the small computer, the heliocentric correction was made through the use of laboriously precomputed tables. Examples of these are Prager,[9] which is difficult to find, Landolt and Blondeau,[10] and Bateson,[11] which is coarser and less accurate than the others. It is now simpler to compute the correction than to use tables.

The most thorough description of the geometry involved is presented by Binnendijk,[12] and the reader is encouraged to glance at his figures and derivations. Basically, the problem is one of projection. There are two planes involved: the earth's equatorial plane, where right ascension, declination, and solar X, Y, Z Cartesian coordinates are defined; and the earth-sun-object plane, where we wish to know the projection of the earth's distance from the sun on the sun-object line. If the projections are carried through properly, one arrives at

$$HJD = JD + \Delta t \qquad (5.7)$$

where

$$\Delta t \text{ (days)} = -0.0057755[(\cos \delta \cos \alpha)X \\ + (\tan \epsilon \sin \delta + \cos \delta \sin \alpha)Y] \qquad (5.8)$$

and X, Y are the rectangular coordinates of the sun for the date in question; α, δ are the right ascension and declination of the star for that date, respectively; and ϵ is the *obliquity of the ecliptic,* $23°27'$. Equation 5.8 holds as long as epochs are consistent. The values of X and Y can be obtained from the *Almanac*[7] or by the trigonometric series given by Doggett et al.[2]

The method of Doggett et al.[2] is shown below because it is relatively easy to program on a small computer or programmable calculator. See Doggett et al. for definitions of the various terms used in this method.

1. Determine the relative Julian century by

$$T = (JD - 2415020)/36525 \qquad (5.9)$$

2. Obtain the mean solar longitude from

$$L = 279°696678 + 36000.76892T + 0.000303T^2 - p \quad (5.10)$$

where

$$p = [1.396041 + 0.000308(T + 0.5)][T - 0.499998] \quad (5.11)$$

The value p is the precession from 1950 to date and therefore is subtracted from the present epoch longitude in Equation 5.10 to obtain 1950.0 longitude.

3. Obtain the *mean solar anomaly* by

$$G = 358°475833 + 35999.04975T - 0.00015T^2 \quad (5.12)$$

4. Finally, obtain X and Y for 1950.0 through the expansions

$$
\begin{aligned}
X = {} & 0.99986 \cos L - 0.025127 \cos (G - L) \\
& + 0.008374 \cos (G + L) \\
& + 0.000105 \cos (2G + L) + 0.000063T \cos (G - L) \\
& + 0.000035 \cos (2G - L) \quad (5.13)
\end{aligned}
$$

$$
\begin{aligned}
Y = {} & 0.917308 \sin L + 0.023053 \sin (G - L) \\
& + 0.007683 \sin (G + L) \\
& + 0.000097 \sin (2G + L) - 0.000057T \sin (G - L) \\
& - 0.000032 \sin (2G - L). \quad (5.14)
\end{aligned}
$$

Only the first few terms of the X and Y expansions need to be kept for the accuracy required in this application. A slightly more accurate FOR-TRAN routine that calculates X, Y, and Z coordinates is presented in Section I.7.

Example: On June 15, 1973, at 11:40 UT, an observation was made of V402 Cygni. What is the appropriate heliocentric correction?

1. $T = (2441848.9861 - 2415020)/36525$
   $T = 0.7345376$ century

2. $L = 279°696678 + 36000.76892(0.7345376)$
   $+ 0.000303(0.7345376)^2 - [1.396041$
   $+ 0.000308(0.7345376 + 0.5)](0.7345376 - 0.499998)$
   $L = 26723°2879$ (subtract multiples of 360° to get 83°2879)
3. $G = 358°475833 + 35999.04975(0.7345376)$
   $- 0.00015(0.7345376)^2$
   $G = 26801°1315$ (subtract multiples of 360° to get 161°1315)
4. Compute X and Y from Equations 5.13 and 5.14

$$X = 0.108021$$
$$Y = 0.926683$$

5. Calculate coordinates

$$\delta = 37°0'33 = 37°00556 \ (1950.0)$$
$$\alpha = 20^h07^m15^s = 20^h12083 = 301°8125 \ (1950.0)$$

6. Finally, calculate Δt and the heliocentric date

$\Delta t = -0.0057755\{[\cos (37°00556) \cos (301°8125)]0.108021$
$+ [\tan (23°27') \sin (37°00556) + \cos (37°00556)$
$\sin (301°8125)] \times 0.926683\}$
$\Delta t = -0.0057755(0.045473 - 0.386915)$
$\Delta t = 0^d.00197$
$$HJD = 2441848.9861 + 0.00197$$
$$HJD = 2441848.9881$$

This calculation is much easier when programmed on a calculator or computer!

5.4 PRECESSION OF COORDINATES

The coordinates of a star or other celestial object do not remain constant with time. Listed below are some of the major contributing factors, along with their *maximum* values. This should give you an idea how difficult it is to set a telescope accurately.

1. *Precession:* 50 arc seconds per year.
2. *Nutation:* 9 arc seconds over 19 years.

3. *Aberration:* 20 arc seconds over 1 year.
4. *Heliocentric parallax:* 0.75 arc second over 1 year.
5. *Refraction:* 60.4 tan z arc seconds daily.
6. *Variation in latitude:* 0.3 arc second.
7. *Proper motion:* 10 arc seconds per year.
8. *Barycentric parallax of solar system:* a few arc seconds.
9. *Geocentric parallax:* at most a few arc seconds even for solar system objects.

Most of these are short-term, cyclic aberrations, except for precession and proper motion. Proper motion is not discussed because it has a significant effect only on the closest stars.

Precession is caused by the gravitational pull on the earth's equatorial bulge by the sun and planets. The coordinates go through a complete cycle in 26,000 years, so the change per year is small, but the effect is cumulative. Catalogs and atlases give the mean coordinates of stars, usually at the beginning of some year, such as Equinox 1950.0. However, to identify a star on the Bonner Durchmusterung (BD) atlas (see Section 9.1a), which is Equinox 1855.0, with 1950 coordinates can be difficult unless one precesses the coordinates to the equinox of the atlas. More importantly, a telescope measures the *present equinox coordinates* and not those of 1900.0, 1950.0, or any other equinox given in standard catalogs.

Because the precession of the earth's axis is well known, equations to precess the coordinates are available. Their basic form is

$$\Delta\alpha = (m + n^s \tan \delta_m \sin \alpha_m)(t_f - t_0) \qquad (5.15)$$
$$\Delta\delta = (n'' \cos \alpha_m)(t_f - t_0) \qquad (5.16)$$

where $\Delta\alpha$ is in seconds, $\Delta\delta$ is in arc seconds and

$t_o =$ equinox of the known coordinates (years)
$t_f =$ equinox to precess to (years)
$$m = 3^s.07234 + 0^s.00001863 t_m \qquad (5.17)$$
$$n^s = 1^s.336457 - 0^s.00000569 t_m \qquad (5.18)$$
$$n'' = 20''.04685 - 0''.0000853 t_m \qquad (5.19)$$

t_m = mean time with respect to 1900:

$$t_m = (t_f + t_0)/2 - 1900 \qquad (5.20)$$

This value is negative for equinoxes before 1900. The subscript m for α and δ indicate that the coordinates should be for the *midpoint* of the precession. That is, if you are precessing from 1950 to 1980, the coordinates on the right-hand side of the equations should be for 1965. Also, because you are taking the sine and cosine of right ascension, α should be converted to degrees.

For most calculations, the above equations will give reasonably good results, even if α_m and δ_m are replaced by α_0 and δ_0 (the original equinox).

Example: Precess γ Aql from 1953.0 to 1975.0.

γ Aql 1953.0: $\alpha = 19^h44^m01^s.458 = 19^h.733738 = 296°.00607$
$\qquad\qquad\quad \delta = 10°29'50''.83 = 10°.497453$

γ Aql 1975.0:

$t_f - t_0 = 1975 - 1953 = 22$ years

$t_m = (1975 + 1953)/2 - 1900 = 64$ years

$m = 3.07234 + 0.00001863(64) = 3^s.073532$

$n^s = 1.336457 - 0.00000569(64) = 1^s.3360928$

$n'' = 20.04685 - 0.0000853(64) = 20''.041391$

$\Delta\alpha = [3.073532 + 1.3360928 \tan(10.497453) \sin(296.00607)](22)$
$\Delta\alpha = 62^s.723$

$\Delta\delta = [20.041391 \cos(296.00607)](22)$
$\Delta\delta = 193''.32$

$$\alpha(1975) = \alpha(1953) + \Delta\alpha$$
$$= 19^h44^m01\overset{s}{.}458 + 62\overset{s}{.}723$$
$$\alpha(1975) = 19^h45^m04\overset{s}{.}181$$
$$\delta(1975) = \delta(1953) + \Delta\delta$$
$$= 10°29'50\overset{''}{.}83 + 193\overset{''}{.}325$$
$$\delta(1975) = 10°33'4\overset{''}{.}15$$

For comparison, here are the values from the 1975 *Almanac:*

$$\gamma \text{ Aql } (1975.0): \alpha = 19^h45^m4\overset{s}{.}2$$
$$\delta = 10°33'5''$$

Note that within the accuracy of the *Almanac,* our answers are correct even though the mean coordinates were not used.

When high accuracy is needed, an analytical method of obtaining the coordinates by integrating the precession equations is used rather than using the mean coordinates with iteration. This more rigorous method is presented in the explanation in the *Almanac,*[7] and a FORTRAN subroutine using it is given in Section I.3.

5.5 ALTITUDE AND AZIMUTH

One of the most common calculations made by astronomers is determining where an object is above the horizon and where along the horizon it lies. These two coordinates are called *altitude* and *azimuth,* and constitute the most natural coordinate system.

The equations for determining altitude and azimuth can be found in Smart,[13] who gives diagrams, and Doggett et al.,[2] who give the equations used in the *Almanac.* Neither source gives a complete explanation of how the equations are derived. Though these equations can be used by themselves, it is useful to know their derivation.

*5.5a Derivation of Equations

Figure 5.2 shows the situation where the altitude and azimuth of a star is unknown. This is a problem in spherical trigonometry because we are

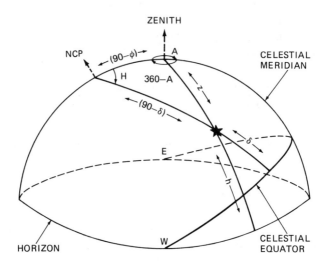

Figure 5.2 Altitude-azimuth sphere.

measuring angles on the celestial sphere. We are looking for h, the altitude above the horizon, and A, the azimuth measured east from due north. Three great circle lines are shown, one representing the celestial equator and two passing through the star from the zenith to the horizon and from the north celestial pole (NCP) to the celestial equator. The latter two lines and the celestial meridian define the spherical triangle needed to obtain h and A.

A spherical arc is defined by

$$D = R\theta \qquad (5.21)$$

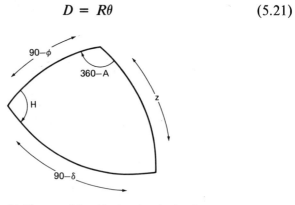

Figure 5.3 Close-up of the altitude-azimuth triangle.

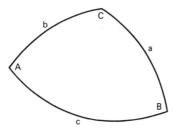

Figure 5.4 A general spherical triangle.

where θ is the angle subtended by the arc and R is the spherical radius. In the case of a *unit sphere* ($R = 1$), the sides of the spherical triangle are equal to the angle subtended by the arc. Therefore, the three sides are: (1) from the NCP to z, an angle of $90° - \phi$, ϕ = latitude; (2) from the zenith to the star, the zenith distance or $90° - h$; and (3) from the NCP to the star, an angle of $90° - \delta$, δ = declination. The enclosed angles of concern are the hour angle, H, measured from the celestial meridian to the star, and the coazimuth, $360° - A$. See Figure 5.3.

The solution of the triangle makes use of the law of cosines, and can be found in books such as the CRC tables.[14] Referring to Figure 5.4,

$$\cos a = \cos b \cos c + \sin b \sin c \cos A. \qquad (5.22)$$

This works with any appropriate permutation. For altitude, we note:

$$\cos (90° - h) = \cos (90° - \phi) \cos (90° - \delta) \\ + \sin (90° - \phi) \sin (90° - \delta) \cos H$$

or

$$\sin h = \sin \phi \sin \delta + \cos \phi \cos \delta \cos H \qquad (5.23)$$

where H is given in degrees by

$$H = 15(\text{LST} - \alpha). \qquad (5.24)$$

For azimuth, we use the other known enclosed angle:

$$\cos(90° - \delta) = \cos(90° - \phi)\cos(90° - h)$$
$$+ \sin(90° - \phi)\sin(90° - h)\cos(360° - A)$$

or

$$\sin\delta = \sin\phi\sin h + \cos\phi\cos h\cos A. \qquad (5.25)$$

Solving for the azimuth,

$$\cos A = (\sin\delta - \sin\phi\sin h)/(\cos\phi\cos h). \qquad (5.26)$$

5.5b General Considerations

Equations 5.23 and 5.26 are our working relations for altitude and azimuth. One problem exists in solving for A. All calculators and computers return values of cosines only between 0 and 180°, yet azimuth extends over the entire range of 0 to 360°. We can remove the ambiguity by noting that when H is greater than 0°, A is greater than 180°. Therefore, for $-180° \leq H \leq 180°$,

$$A = A \quad \text{when } H \leq 0, \text{ and}$$
$$A = 360° - A \quad \text{when } H > 0.$$

Another solution, by Doggett et al.[2] solves for $\tan A$. While this gives some computational simplicity in that the altitude is not needed, it adds the complexity that $\tan A$ is undefined at $+90°$ and $-90°$. It is suggested that Equation 5.26 be used, unless there is good reason to use another method.

Example: What is altitude and azimuth for AS Cas on February 5, 1979, at 01:00 UT from Goethe Link Observatory? For that date and time, $LST = 4^h12^m = 4^h.2000$.

$\alpha(1979) = 0^h24^m23^s = 0^h.4064$
$\delta(1979) = 64°6'.5 = 64°.1083$
$\phi = 39°18' = 39°.30$
$H = 15 (4.2000 - 0.4064) = 56°.9042)$

$$\sin h = \sin (39°3) \sin (64°1083)$$
$$+ \cos (39°3) \cos (64°1083) \cos (56°9042)$$
$$\sin h = 0.75432$$

$$h = 48°97$$

$$\cos A = [\sin (64°1083) - \sin (39°3) \sin (48°97)]/$$
$$[\cos (39°3) \cos (48°97)] = 0.83037$$

$$A = 33°86.$$

But, since $H = 56°$ $(H > 0)$,

$$A = 360° - 33°86$$

$$A = 326°14.$$

REFERENCES

1. Staff, 1979. *Sky and Tel.* **58**, 25.
2. Doggett, L. E., Kaplan, G. H., and Seidelmann, P. K. 1978. *Almanac for Computers for the Year 1978.* Washington, D.C.: Nautical Almanac Office.
3. Tricker, R. A. R. 1970. *Introduction to Meteorological Optics.* New York: American Elsevier.
4. Humphreys, W. J. 1940. *Physics of the Air.* New York: McGraw-Hill.
5. Abell, G. O. 1975. *Exploration of the Universe.* New York: Holt, Rinehart and Winston.
6. *The Handbook of the British Astronomical Association.* England: Sumfield and Day, Ltd. Published yearly.
7. *The Astronomical Almanac.* Washington, D.C.: Government Printing Office. Issued annually.
8. Reid, F., and Honeycutt, R. K. 1976. *Sky and Tel.* **52**, 59.
9. Prager, R. 1932. *Klein. Veroff. Univ. Sternw. Berlin-Babelsberg,* no. 12.
10. Landolt, A. U., and Blondeau, K. L. 1972. *Pub. A. S. P.* **84**, 784.
11. Bateson, F. M. 1963. In *Photoelectric Astronomy for Amateurs.* Edited by F. B. Wood. New York: Macmillan, p. 97.
12. Binnendijk, K. L. 1960. *Properties of Double Stars.* Philadelphia: Univ of Pennsylvania Press, pp. 228–232.
13. Smart, W. M. 1962. *Text-Book on Spherical Astronomy.* Cambridge: Cambridge Univ. Press.
14. S. M. Selby, ed. *CRC Standard Mathematical Tables.* Cleveland: The Chemical Rubber Co. Published yearly.

CHAPTER 6
CONSTRUCTING THE PHOTOMETER
HEAD

Careful design and construction of the photometer head is very important and it requires substantial comment. The goal of this chapter is to supply you with enough background information to allow you to design and construct a photometer head intelligently. We have not included detailed construction plans because the requirements of individual observatories and researchers varies greatly. Amateur and professional astronomers approach the construction of photometers somewhat differently. The professional intends to mount the completed photometer head on a rather large telescope. Hence the components can be made from heavy metal stock and the tube can be totally enclosed in a cold box. The total weight of the finished photometer can be as much as 45 kilograms (100 pounds), which exceeds the weight of many an amateur's telescope! Obviously, the amateur must keep weight and size as primary restrictions on the design. Our emphasis in this chapter is on the needs of this small telescope user. We first make some comments on design and construction. We then describe a simple, lightweight design in Section 6.5.

We discuss briefly designs utilizing a photodiode as a detector because such designs are difficult to find in the literature. We refer interested readers to papers by Persha[1] and De Lara et al.[2] Finally, a photodiode photometer is available commercially from Optec, Inc.[3]

6.1 THE OPTICAL LAYOUT

The first step in designing a photometer head is to position the optical elements on a drawing showing the correct relative sizes and spacing.

This layout depends on the F-ratio of the telescope to be used, because this determines the rate at which the light cone formed by the telescope's objective diverges from the focal point. For instance, if you are using an F/8 telescope, the light cone will have a 1-centimeter diameter at a distance of 8 centimeters from the focus, a 2-centimeter diameter at a distance of 16 centimeters, and so forth. A small F-ratio telescope causes special problems because the cone diverges very rapidly, forcing the photometer components to be placed within an uncomfortably small distance from the focal point. If you plan to use a small F-ratio telescope, say F/5 or less, consider the design described by Burke and Pippin.[4]

The optical layout procedure is best accomplished by using a large sheet of graph paper so that the drawing can be made full size. Pick a spot near the left side of the paper to be the focal point. Draw a horizontal line through the focal point across the page to represent the optical axis of the photometer. Now draw the expanding light cone from the focal point according to your F-ratio as described above. The diaphragm is of course located at the focal point. The filters are positioned at a distance from the focal point where the light cone has a diameter of 5 to 10 millimeters. This is a compromise between the desire to use small filters and the need to illuminate an area of the filter large enough so that dust or small defects in the filter do not affect the light cone significantly. The amount of available space between the filter and diaphragm is now fixed. For an F/8 light cone, this distance is 80 millimeters for a 10-millimeter spot size on the filter. Within this space, the photometer builder must find room for the filter assembly and the flip mirror with its associated lenses. In Figure 6.1, we have positioned the diaphragm and filter. Consult this figure as you read the remainder of this section.

The next element to be positioned is the Fabry or field lens. This lens has a very important function. It focuses an image of the telescope's objective, illuminated by the light of the star on the photocathode. This spot of light remains at the same place on the photocathode no matter where the star drifts within the diaphragm. This is important because no photocathode can be made with uniform sensitivity. Without the Fabry lens, the photomultiplier output could change considerably depending on the position of the star in the diaphragm. The desired spot size depends on the size of the photocathode of the photomultiplier. If the spot is too large, light will be thrown away because some of it will

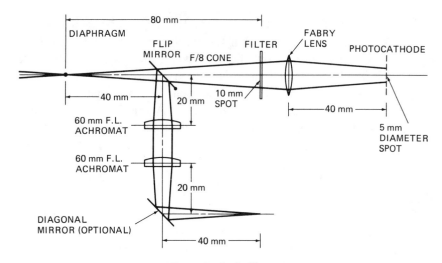

Figure 6.1 Optical layout.

miss the photocathode. If the spot is too small, local defects in the photocathode may have a degrading effect on the tube's output. For the 1P21 photomultiplier, a spot size of about 5 millimeters is about right. To calculate the Fabry lens's focal length, recall from elementary optics that for a thin lens the ratio of the object size to the object distance equals the ratio of the image size to the image distance. The object size is the diameter of the telescope's objective, D, and the object distance is essentially the telescope's focal length, f_t, so the relation becomes

$$\frac{D}{f_t} = \frac{a}{\text{image distance}}$$

where a is the image size. Because the focal length of the telescope is very large compared to that of the Fabry lens, the image distance is very nearly equal to the focal length, f, of the Fabry lens. That is,

$$\frac{D}{f_t} = \frac{a}{f}$$

or

$$f = a \cdot F, \qquad (6.1)$$

where F is the focal ratio of the telescope, f, divided by D. For the F/8 telescope used in our example, the Fabry lens must have a focal length of 40 millimeters for a 5-millimeter spot size. The spot size can be adjusted slightly to give a focal length of a common lens that can be found easily in optics catalogs. The spacing between the Fabry lens and the photocathode is now fixed as the focal length of the Fabry lens. The diameter of the lens depends upon its distance from the diaphragm. This distance is not critical. We have arbitrarily placed it 12 millimeters behind the filter in Figure 6.1. Once the lens is positioned on your drawing, the size of the light cone at this point gives the size of the lens. The lens should actually be made a little larger to allow for small misalignment after construction and the fact that the lens mount covers the edges. The lens itself is just a simple double convex lens. For proper ultraviolet transmission, this lens should be made of crown glass or, preferably, quartz.

The flip mirror can now be added to the drawing. It is placed between the diaphragm and the filter at a 45° angle to the optical axis. This mirror directs light into the first lens of the diaphragm-viewing optics. This lens is an achromat of sufficient diameter to accept the total light cone. It is positioned at a distance from the telescope's focal point equal to its own focal length. This results in a collimated beam of light after passing through the lens. If you cannot afford the luxury of custom-made optics, it is best to consult an optics catalog to find which focal lengths are available before positioning this lens in your drawing. A 60-millimeter focal length lens is available from Edmund Scientific[5] or A. Jaegers.[6] We have positioned this lens at a distance of 60 millimeters from the diaphragm. The next lens is an identical achromat that can be positioned at any comfortable distance from the first lens. The second lens reconverges this light for the viewing eyepiece. This optical arrangement gives a focused image of both the diaphragm and the star within it. Figure 6.1 shows the optical elements with the dimensions indicated.

A look at Figure 1.8 should convince you that the head for a photodiode photometer is somewhat simpler. Because the detector is at the telescope's focus, the flip mirror can direct the light cone directly to a viewing eyepiece without the need of the two lenses discussed above. There is also no Fabry lens or diaphragm. The size of the active area of the photodiode defines the "diaphragm size." Unfortunately, this can not be adjusted. Without a diaphragm, it is necessary to have illuminated cross hairs in the viewing eyepiece. They are aligned such that if a star is centered, when the flip mirror is removed the star's light will fall directly on the photodiode. The mechanical design of the head must allow for the components to be adjusted to achieve this alignment. It is also necessary for the eyepiece focus to be adjusted and locked so that when a star appears focused in the eyepiece, the photodiode will be at the telescope's focus. These design problems are no more difficult to solve than those encountered in a photomultiplier-type photometer.

There is quite a large jump between laying out the optical components and performing the actual mechanical construction. We now offer some specific comments to make that jump seem a little smaller.

6.2 THE PHOTOMULTIPLIER TUBE AND ITS HOUSING

There are many manufacturers of photomultiplier tubes, each offering a wide array of devices. Suppliers of tubes frequently used by astronomers are EMI Gencom,[7] ITT,[8] and RCA.[9] The tube you select depends upon the spectral response required by your research. For example, Figure 1.5 shows that you should not try to use a tube with an S-4 response to measure stars at 8000 Å. An S-20 or S-1 tube response should be used instead. If you wish to obtain measurements on the *UBV* system, the choice of tube response is very crucial. As discussed in Chapter 2, the *UBV* system is defined by both the tube response and the filter transmission. For example, the *U* filter, and to a lesser extent the *B* and *V* filters, transmit light beyond 7000 Å. This means that these filters do not isolate the single spectral region they were meant to measure. However, the 1P21 has very little sensitivity beyond 7000 Å and the filter's red leaks, except for a small amount from the *U* filter, can be ignored. If the 1P21 is replaced with a tube with an S-1 or S-20 response, the filter set must be changed to "plug" the red leaks. Fernie[10] has used a single red-extended S-20, EMI 9658R tube to make *UBVRI* measurements. However, the *UBV* filters had to be altered from the type usually used with the 1P21. The point to be made here is that care must be taken to match detectors and filters to insure proper transformation to the standard system.

There are many tubes newer than the 1P21 that have been successfully used to make *UBV* measurements. The EMI 6256 has an S-11 response that is only slightly more red-sensitive than an S-4 response. This tube has a peak quantum efficiency of 21 percent compared to 13 percent for the 1P21. Tubes such as the ITT FW-118 (S-1), and FW-130 (S-20) and the RCA 7102 (S-1) have also been used successfully for *UBVRI* observations, with the appropriate filter modifications. Another tube of interest is the EMI 9789, which has a bialkali (cesium-potassium antimonide) surface with a spectral response very similar to S-4. However, it has a peak quantum efficiency of 20 percent and a smaller photocathode than the 1P21. A smaller photocathode has less area for thermionic emission, in this case resulting in about one-fifth of the dark current of the 1P21 at room temperature. The tube appears to transform well to the *UBV* system with the standard filters.

There are many different kinds of photomultipliers in successful use today. Despite all the advances in photomultiplier tube technology since the introduction of the 1P21, there are some good reasons to use this tube for UBV observations. The first is the fact that this tube was used to define the *UBV* system and requires little experimentation with filters. While many astronomers have used other tube and filter combinations successfully to make *UBV* observations, it may not always be apparent to the novice when there is a problem with the transformation. Another important reason for using the 1P21 is cost. The EMI 9789 and 6256 cost over $300 and $600, respectively. The 1P21 costs less than $100. The 1P21 has a companion tube called the RCA 931A, identical in all respects except that the 931A has a lower sensitivity and lower cost. This tube sells for less than $20 and is ideal for testing a new photometer and learning observational techniques. If the tube is somehow damaged, it will not cost hundreds of dollars to replace. Once confidence has been gained in both the photometer and the observer's abilities, the 931A can be replaced with a 1P21 without any modifications to the photometer. The 931A represents a good investment for the newcomer to astronomical photometry. If you are constructing a photometer of small size, the Hamamatsu Corporation[11] has introduced a line of miniature photomultipliers. Their R869 tube is equivalent to the RCA 1P21 but at one-half the size and about the same cost. In the following discussion of photometer construction, we assume that the detector is a 1P21 or a 931A. Modifications for other tubes can be made by the reader, based on the manufacturer's specification sheets.

Figure 6.2 shows a photograph of the 1P21. The photocathode is just behind the grid of wires seen near the front of the tube. Below the glass envelope is a base with 11 electrical pin contacts and a center post for positioning the tube in the socket. This center post has a key that must

Figure 6.2 A 1P21 photomultiplier tube.

face the incident light for proper tube orientation. Figure 6.3 shows the physical dimensions of the tube taken from the RCA specification sheets. The photocathode is about 5 millimeters in front of the central axis of the tube. You should account for this displacement when you position the Fabry lens.

The 1P21 has nine dynodes, a photocathode, and an anode. The photocathode is operated at a potential of about −1000 V with respect to ground. The first dynode is at a potential of about −900 V, or about 100 V more positive than the photocathode. This potential difference provides for the acceleration of the electrons released at the photocathode to the first dynode. Each succeeding dynode is 100 V less negative than its predecessor. Finally, the last dynode is −100 V with respect to

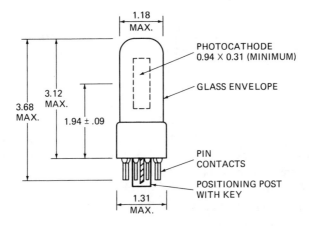

Figure 6.3 Physical dimensions of the 1P21 (all dimensions are in inches).

the anode that collects the cascade of secondary electrons. The pins on the tube base are provided so that the proper voltage can be applied to these tube elements. The voltage differences between dynodes are achieved by a simple voltage divider circuit that is wired directly to the tube socket. The tube socket is an Amphenol 78511T or equivalent. Figure 6.4 shows the tube socket with its voltage divider resistor string as viewed from the bottom. If you are pulse counting, it may be necessary to put a capacitor (0.01 mf, 1000 V, ceramic) between each pin (1 through 9) and ground. This reduces the instrumental sensitivity to external noise pulses.

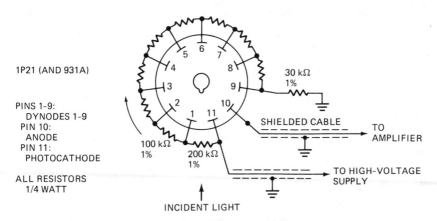

Figure 6.4 Wiring of tube socket (bottom view).

Note that the high voltage is applied to the photocathode on pin 11, which is next to pin 10, the anode pin from which the signal is collected. In order to prevent high voltage from leaking across to pin 10 and entering your amplifier, the socket must be made from a very high-resistance material such as mica or Teflon. Under no circumstances should a plastic socket be used.

After assembly, the socket should be cleaned with isopropyl alcohol to remove any fingerprints that may lead to leakage current. Because moisture at the tube socket can lead to leakage current, many astronomers seal the entire voltage divider string with silicon rubber. Prewired, sealed-tube sockets can be purchased from EMI and Hamamatsu. A hand-wired tube socket that is kept clean and dry is very adequate for a simple photometer.

The photomultiplier is a delicate device that should be handled with care. To avoid leakage-current problems, do not touch the tube at the base of the connector pins or the glass envelope. The photocathode is extremely sensitive and can be permanently damaged by exposure to bright light. The rule of thumb is never to allow light brighter than starlight to strike the tube when the high voltage is on. However, bright stars, especially on larger telescopes, can temporarily damage the tube, causing a condition known as *fatigue*. When a tube reaches the fatigue level, the tube seems to lose sensitivity and the output current drops. For the 1P21, fatigue occurs at an output current of about 1 μA. The sensitivity returns after the tube has been allowed to "rest" in total darkness. Fatigue can be avoided by lowering the high voltage applied to the tube, allowing brighter stars to be measured. Experience has shown that for most 1P21 tubes the transformation coefficients are not affected by a voltage change. There is no guarantee that this is true for all 1P21 tubes and it is certainly not true for many other tube designs. Even exposure to room light with the high voltage off can temporarily increase the dark current. Therefore, it is a good idea to handle the tube in subdued light during its installation in the tube housing. From then on, the dark slide should be kept closed except while observing. Another important precaution is to make sure that your high-voltage supply is connected properly so that negative high voltage is applied to the tube. The tube cannot be damaged by cold, but exposure to high temperatures for prolonged periods of time can lead to degraded performance. The best storage conditions for a photomultiplier tube are cool, dry, and dark.

The photomultiplier tube housing can be as simple as a pair of brass cylinders or as complex as a hermetically sealed thermoelectrically cooled chamber. The choice of housing depends on your commitment to serious observing and your budget. For the user of a small telescope who plans to observe brighter objects, we strongly recommend the simple approach. The function of the housing is to keep the tube in a dry, light-tight environment with the photocathode aligned to the optical axis of the photometer. The housing contains a dark slide which can be opened to allow the starlight to reach the photocathode or closed to keep the tube in total darkness when it is not being used. In a simple housing, one brass cylinder holds the tube socket, voltage divider resistors, and the cable connectors. This cylinder then snugly slides over the other cylinder, making a light-tight housing except for the small hole that allows light to reach the photocathode. The dark slide mechanism is mounted in front of this hole. A simple housing of this type will be shown in Section 6.5. The next step in complexity is to add a magnetic shield. This is a cylinder of mu-metal that fits into the housing and surrounds the photomultiplier. It shields the tube from external magnetic fields that might interfere with electrostatic focusing of the secondary electrons emitted from each dynode. External fields that would affect the tube significantly are rarely encountered. However, such a shield is a rather inexpensive precaution. Magnetic shields for the 1P21 can be supplied by the Hamamatsu Corporation[11] or Perfection Mica Company.[12]

The ultimate in photomultiplier tube housings incorporates a cooling system. Cooling the photomultiplier to dry-ice temperature can eliminate most of the tube's dark current. This has significant advantages for measuring faint stars that may produce a tube current comparable only to the dark current. Among professional astronomers, cooled tubes are the rule, not the exception. Cooling the 1P21 reduces the dark current from about 200 counts per second, for pulse counting, to less than one count per second. Essentially any output from the tube then results from starlight. A cooled tube has less sensitivity to red light, reducing the amount of the red leak through the U filter. This also means that the transformation coefficients of a tube change when it is cooled. If you determine these coefficients when the tube is uncooled, they will not be valid for observations made when the tube is cooled.

The usual means of cooling the tube is to replace the simple housing discussed previously with a cold box. The layout of a cold box is nicely illustrated in an article by Johnson.[13] A cold box consists of three boxes. The photomultiplier tube is sealed in an airtight container that has a small window allowing light to reach the photocathode. This inner container is surrounded by a larger box which holds one-half to one kilogram of dry ice. This box is, in turn, surrounded by the outermost box that holds styrofoam or polyurethane foam to insulate the dry-ice container. The light entrance to the cold box is a window and/or the Fabry lens. It is sometimes necessary to mount a small heating element near these glass components to prevent them from developing a coating of frost. Cold boxes can add considerable weight to the photometer. For this reason, special lightweight designs are required for telescopes less than 40 centimeters (16 inches) in aperture. Recently, thermoelectric cooling systems have begun to be used in astronomy. They can reduce the tube temperature typically by 20 to 40 Celsius degrees below the outdoor temperature. These cooling systems are large, heavy, and expensive. They probably work as well as a dry-ice cold box but may require a water supply or a fluid-circulation system. It is possible to purchase simple uncooled housings and dry-ice cold boxes. Suppliers are EMI Gencom,[7] Hamamatsu,[11] Pacific Precision Instruments,[14] EG & G Princeton Applied Research,[15] and Products for Research.[16] There is a word of caution to note before you place an order for a cooled photomultiplier tube housing. Most of the housings built by these companies are intended for laboratory use. Consequently, not every model can support its own weight properly if it is held to the photometer by a simple mounting flange around the light input port. Before placing an order, it is advisable to call the company and make certain that the model of your choice can be mounted to a telescope, that it can work in any position, and that it can function in the sometimes hostile environment of your observatory.

6.3 FILTERS

Most of the wide-band filters used in optical astronomy are made by Corning Glass Works[17] or Schott Optical Glass.[18] Table 6.1 lists a recommended filter set for *UBV* photometry using the 1P21. Note that it is important to order the specified thickness. Filters of different thicknesses have slightly different transmission curves. The *B* filter is actually a sandwich of two filters. The GG13 filter looks like clear glass

TABLE 6.1.   Recommended *UBV* Filters

Bandpass	Filter and Thickness (Schott Filters)
U	UG2[a] (2 mm)
B	GG13 (2 mm) + BG12 (1 mm)
V	GG14 (2 mm)
Red leak	UG2[a] (2 mm) + GG14 (2 mm)

[a]These two filters are from the same melt.

but it is designed to prevent transmission of light shortward of the Balmar discontinuity. Some observers have reported difficulty in making the *U* filter transformations unless the filter matches the one used to define the *UBV* system. This filter is a Corning 7-54 made from Corning 9863 glass. Unfortunately, this filter has a larger red leak than the Schott UG2. The red-leak filter listed in Table 6.1 is just a sandwich made from a second *U* filter and a *V* filter. The *V* filter does not transmit ultraviolet light normally passed by the *U* filter. However, it does transmit any red light which the *U* filter transmits. The combination of the two filters transmits only the red light "leaked" by the *U* filter. After a star has been measured with the ordinary *U* filter, it is measured again with the red-leak filter. The red-leak measurement can then be subtracted from the *U* measurement to obtain a corrected *U* measurement. When ordering these *U* filters, you should request that they both come from the same melt or order a single piece from which you can cut two filters. This helps to insure that the red-leak properties of the two filters are as nearly identical as possible.

If you are using a photometer that places the filters inside the telescope's focal point, be sure to add a Schott cover glass to make all filters the same total thickness. The passage of the telescope's light cone through glass alters the focal point slightly. If the filters are of different thicknesses, they will each cause the light to focus at a different point. This is not of concern for any photometer design discussed in this book, with the exception of the photodiode photometer.

Because of its different spectral response, a photodiode must use a different set of filters to match the *UBV* system. De Lara et al.[2] used an EG & G Electro-Optics Division[19] SGD-040L PIN photodiode with the filters listed in Table 6.2. The thicknesses of the Corning filters are not specified because they are adjusted by the manufacturer to achieve the

TABLE 6.2.   Filters Used with a Photodiode by De Lara et al.

Bandpass	Filters
B	Corning 5030 + Corning 9782 + Schott GG13 (2 mm)
V	Corning 9780 + Corning 3384
R	Corning 3480 + Corning 4600
I	Corning 2600 + Corning 3850

required bandpasses. It should be noted that De Lara et al. were not satisfied with this filter set. It is presented here as a starting point for those who wish to experiment with photodiode and filter combinations.

The *UBV* filters can be ordered in a 2.5 × 2.5 centimeter (1 × 1 inch) size at a cost of a few dollars per filter. They should be handled with care because they are very thin and made from soft glass that can be scratched easily. The surface of the *U* filter may appear to develop a water-spotlike pattern on its surface with age. This can be removed by polishing the surface with rouge or barnesite.

Normally, filters are mounted in a photometer in one of two ways. One technique uses a filter slide. The filters are held side by side in a long rectangular holder. The holder slides lengthwise so that the filters can be positioned one at a time in the light beam. This design presents a minor problem for a small photometer. The slide must be long enough to accommodate each filter and the width of the slide walls. For a four-filter photometer, the slide is at least 11.4 centimeters (4.5 inches) long for 2.5 centimeter (1 inch) wide filters. With either end filter in the light path, the slide sticks out about 10 centimeters (4 inches) to either side of the optical axis. That requires a total linear span of more than 19 centimeters (7.5 inches). This makes it very difficult to contain the filter slide within the main chassis of a small photometer head, which would simplify the design and make it easier to keep light-tight. One is forced to adopt a design that is frequently used by professional astronomers. Figure 6.5 illustrates the idea schematically. The filter slide fits within a rectangular housing which is light-tight except for holes on the top and bottom plates that allow the telescope's light cone to enter, pass through the filter, and exit. The outer housing is inserted into the photometer chassis and allows the slide to move its entire length, while eliminating the need to enlarge the photometer chassis. It is important to incorporate some sort of detent device so that each filter "clicks" into

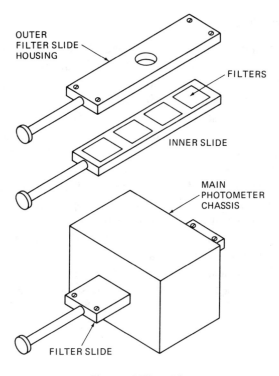

OUTER
FILTER SLIDE
HOUSING

FILTERS

INNER SLIDE

MAIN
PHOTOMETER
CHASSIS

FILTER SLIDE

Figure 6.5 Filter slide.

place and is held in the light path during a measurement. This is usually accomplished by notching the positioning rod and mounting a spring-loaded ball bearing in the rod's bearing at the end of the outer housing.

The second approach to filter mounting is the filter wheel. A flat circular disk has filters mounted around its periphery. There is a small hole under each filter to allow light to pass through the disk. The filter wheel is aligned perpendicular to the optical axis of the photometer with its rotation axis offset from the optical axis so that each filter passes into the light beam as the wheel rotates. Looking ahead to Figure 6.16, you find a sketch of a filter wheel. Once again, a detent mechanism is necessary to insure proper positioning of the filters. Of course, there are other methods of mounting filters. In a design by Dick et al.[20] the filters are mounted on a four-sided carousel that rotates around the photomultiplier. This very simple design has the advantages of compactness and ease of construction.

6.4 DIAPHRAGMS

Photometer diaphragms are usually made by drilling small holes in a metal plate. The first step is to decide on the desired sizes. We speak commonly of the size of a diaphragm in terms of the angular size of the field of view it permits us to see in the telescope's focal plane. That is, a diaphragm which is said to be 20 arc seconds exposes a portion of the sky 20 arc seconds in diameter to our detector. To translate an angular size to the physical diameter of the hole we need to drill requires a knowledge of the plate scale of the telescope. If we took a photographic exposure of the full moon (0.5° across) at the focus of our telescope and it appeared 1 centimeter wide on the developed film, the plate scale would be 0.5° per centimeter. In other words, this is simply a statement of how angular sizes in the sky project to the telescope's focal plane. The plate scale depends upon focal length. Short focal length telescopes have large plate scales; that is, they are wide field instruments. Long focal length telescopes have very small plate scales, hence narrow fields and high magnification. The plate scale can be computed in units of arc seconds per millimeter by

$$\text{plate scale} = \frac{K}{f_t}$$

where K is 20626 (8120) if the focal length of the telescope is expressed in centimeters (inches).

Let us suppose that the F/8 telescope discussed in Section 6.1 has a 20.3-centimeter (8-inch) diameter. Its focal length is then 162.4 centimeters (64 inches) and by the above equation it has a plate scale of 127 arc seconds per millimeter. Table 6.3 contains a list of twist drill numbers in the U.S. system and their corresponding diameters. We can use this table together with the plate scale to predict the angular size of a diaphragm made with any of these drills. For instance, a number 75 drill has a diameter of 0.533 millimeters, which gives a diaphragm of 0.533 × 127 or 67.7 arc seconds for this telescope. It is desirable to make the diaphragms rather small to minimize the amount of sky background light seen. Typically, professional astronomers use a diaphragm which is 20 arc seconds or less. This is practically impossible with small telescopes because their focal lengths are shorter, making the necessary drill sizes impossibly small. Even with a number 80 drill, which is only

TABLE 6.3. Twist Drill Diameters

Drill No.	Inches	Millimeters	Drill No.	Inches	Millimeters
40	0.0980	2.489	60	0.0400	1.016
41	0.0960	2.438	61	0.0390	0.991
42	0.0935	2.375	62	0.0380	0.965
43	0.0890	2.261	63	0.0370	0.940
44	0.0860	2.184	64	0.0360	0.914
45	0.0820	2.083	65	0.0350	0.889
46	0.0810	2.057	66	0.0330	0.838
47	0.0785	1.994	67	0.0320	0.813
48	0.0760	1.930	68	0.0310	0.787
49	0.0730	1.854	69	0.0293	0.743
50	0.0700	1.778	70	0.0280	0.711
51	0.0670	1.702	71	0.0260	0.660
52	0.0635	1.613	72	0.0250	0.635
53	0.0595	1.511	73	0.0240	0.610
54	0.0550	1.397	74	0.0225	0.572
55	0.0520	1.321	75	0.0210	0.533
56	0.0465	1.181	76	0.0200	0.508
57	0.0430	1.092	77	0.0180	0.457
58	0.0420	1.067	78	0.0160	0.406
59	0.0410	1.041	79	0.0145	0.368
			80	0.0135	0.343

a few times the width of a human hair, the diaphragm is 44 arc seconds for our 20.3-centimeter (8-inch) telescope. The same diaphragm used with a 76.2-centimeter (30-inch) diameter F/8 telescope is 12 arc seconds. This points out a basic disadvantage that the small telescope user must face. The larger plate scale of the small telescope means that photometry must be done with diaphragms that admit a fairly large amount of sky background light. This leads to a poorer signal-to-noise ratio, with the result that faint stars cannot be measured as well.

Even a simple photometer should contain at least three different diaphragm sizes, one of which is fairly large. This allows the observer to use a larger diaphragm on nights of poor seeing conditions, or a small one when the moon is bright. An intermediate size probably is used the most and should be of such a size that your clock drive can keep a star within this diaphragm for at least 5 to 10 minutes. Additional observational considerations for diaphragm selection are discussed in Section 9.4.

Section 6.5 contains a description of a photometer designed for a 20.3-centimeter (8-inch) F/8 telescope discussed in this section. The diaphragm selection in this design is based on the above considerations and on the availability of small drills. The largest diaphragm was made with a number 47 drill, which for a plate scale of 127 arc seconds per millimeter yields 253 arc seconds, or 4.2 arc minutes. The remaining two diaphragms were made with number 61 and 76 drills, yielding sizes of 126 and 64.5 arc seconds, respectively.

The diaphragm holes can be drilled in a brass or steel plate. A drill press must be used to insure that the holes are drilled straight and to minimize drill breakage. This latter point becomes important because these drills are very thin and break easily. Drills of this size usually must be purchased at large hardware stores or dealers in machinists' supplies. Purchase at least two of the smaller drills as you are bound to break at least one. The chucks on many drill presses do not close down far enough to hold drills this small. It may be necessary to find a local machinist who can drill these holes for you. It is important to counterbore the holes to avoid a tunneling effect when looking through the diaphragm viewing eyepiece. The drill for the counterbore should be several times the size of the diaphragm drill. The counterbore should be made as deep as possible without enlarging the diaphragm hole. It is possible to make holes about half the size of a number 80 drill by pricking aluminum foil with a sharp needle. The foil is placed on a flat metal surface, and the hole is made by turning the needle between your fingers. Make several holes and inspect them with a magnifying glass. The one which appears most round can be used as a diaphragm by gluing the foil to a piece of metal that has a larger hole in it.

Like filters, the diaphragm position usually is selected by a diaphragm slide or wheel. A diaphragm slide is usually used because, unlike the case of filters, it can be very short and completely contained within the main photometer chassis. The diaphragm holes are drilled in a flat rectangular piece of metal. It is also necessary to provide some sort of detent system so each diaphragm "clicks" into position on the optical axis. A diaphragm slide assembly is described in Section 6.5.

There are two final points to be made. First, when you view a star in the diaphragm through the viewing eyepiece it may be very difficult to tell if it is centered. This is because the sky background light does not outline the diaphragm sufficiently. As a result, everything except the star looks black. An exception to this occurs if you are observing near an urban area. In this case, the sky background is such that the diaphragm appears as a gray circle in the eyepiece. This is about the only benefit that light pollution provides for astronomy! Hopefully, you will have the opportunity to observe from a site that requires an internal source of diaphragm illumination. The simplest method is to mount a very tiny light bulb or a light-emitting diode (LED) just above the diaphragm slide. The electric current to this lamp is controlled by a contact switch attached to the flip mirror. When the flip mirror is moved out of the light path, the lamp is automatically shut off. It is a good idea to have a potentiometer in the circuit in order to adjust the lamp brightness.

Second, make sure that the focus of the diaphragm viewing eyepiece is at least initially adjustable. A quick look at Figure 6.1 should convince you that the spacing and size of the optical components depends on the assumption that the diaphragm is placed at the telescope's focal plane. This is a condition that must be established at the beginning of each observing session. This is accomplished first by focusing the diaphragm eyepiece until the diaphragm appears with sharp definition. Then center a star in the diaphragm. If this star appears out of focus, the diaphragm plane and focal plane do not coincide. This is remedied by adjusting the *telescope's* focus until the star's image appears sharp. Many photometers are designed so that the eyepiece focus is adjusted once during construction and locked in place. When observing, it is then only necessary to adjust the telescope's focus to make the stellar image clear. The disadvantage of this procedure is that eyeglass wearers must use their glasses when looking through the eyepiece. If they focus the star without their glasses on, the diaphragm will not appear focused because this was adjusted in the workshop by someone who, presumably, had normal vision. For the eyeglass wearer who does not use his or her glasses at the eyepiece, it is best to leave the eyepiece focus adjustable.

6.5 A SIMPLE PHOTOMETER HEAD DESIGN

In this section, we describe a simple photometer head design suitable for use by amateur astronomers or any user of a small telescope. Detailed construction plans are not presented. Instead, the sketches and discussion presented are intended as a guide and a source of ideas for the photometer builder. We recommend that this person look at the designs of the AAVSO photometry manual,[21] Allen,[22] Burke and Pippin,[4] Code,[23] Dick et al.[20], Grauer et al.[24] and Nye.[45]

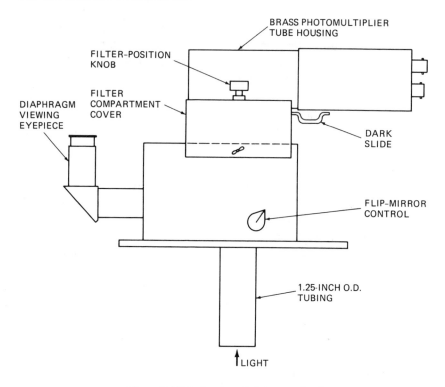

Figure 6.6 Exterior view of photometer head.

The design presented below was built originally for a 20.3-centimeter (8-inch) F/8 Newtonian telescope. Because it is difficult to counterbalance objects placed at a Newtonian focus, this photometer head was made as lightweight as possible, 1.4 kilograms (3.1 pounds). It has been used successfully for years and has produced a lot of observational data with the 20.3-centimeter (8-inch) and larger telescopes. The basic design is patterned after one by D. Engelkmeir.[21] Figure 6.6 shows a sketch of the exterior of the photometer head. The central box is made from a standard 12.7 × 10.2 × 7.6-centimeter (5 × 4 × 3-inch) aluminum electrical chassis. This choice was made to avoid machining and to provide a lightweight box at a cost of a few dollars. The interior was spray painted with flat black paint to reduce scattered light. The bottom of the box is mounted on a 19.0 × 19.0-centimeter (7.5 × 7.5-inch) base that is oversized to help mount the photometer head to the telescope securely. This is illustrated later. The starlight enters a 8.18-centimeter (1.25-inch) O.D. brass tube that fits the standard focusing drawtube of U.S.-made amateur telescopes. The diaphragm viewing eyepiece is attached to a diagonal mirror for ease of viewing. This is especially helpful when using Newtonian telescopes. The filters are contained in a separate compartment above the main box for easy access. The photomultiplier tube, a 1P21, is mounted in a simple, uncooled housing made from brass tubing. There are four external controls: the dark slide, the filter position, the diaphragm slide, and the flip mirror. Figure 6.7 shows a photograph of this head, seen in a perspective slightly different from Figure 6.6. Obviously, a photometer head should be made light-tight except for incident starlight.

Figure 6.8 shows a cut-away view of the interior of the photometer head. Wherever possible, plastic and aluminum have been used to reduce weight. The flip mirror is a quarter-wave optical flat. This mirror is mounted to a flat metal plate with double-sided adhesive tape. The metal plate is soldered to a rod that attaches to a knob on the outside of the box. The mirror directs light to the collimating and imaging lenses used for viewing the diaphragm. These lenses are identical achromats mounted in a single tube that helps to insure their mutual align-

Figure 6.7 The photomultiplier head.

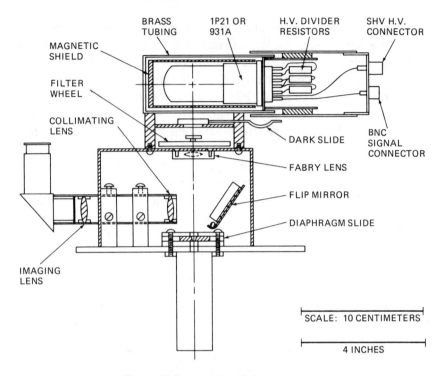

Figure 6.8 Cutaway view of photometer head.

ment. This tube is held in place by two plastic blocks. The tube passes through a hole in each block and is held in place by three adjustment screws similar to the way finder telescopes are mounted. In the workshop, the screws can be adjusted until the image of the diaphragm appears centered in the eyepiece. The ability to make this adjustment is valuable especially if you are unable to build components to machine-shop precision.

The top plate of the box is removable. On its interior side, the Fabry lens is held by a small plastic block. The exterior side holds a filter compartment and the tube housing. The left half of the housing, as shown in Figure 6.8, contains a magnetic shield and the photomultiplier tube. The right half of the housing is made from slightly larger tubing so that it slides over the left half. It holds the tube socket, voltage divider resistors, and cable connectors. The tube socket is held in place by a short length of tubing, which in turn is held snugly in place by a spacer between it and the interior housing wall. It is important to establish an electrical connection between the walls of the tube housing and electrical ground. This is necessary to provide good electrical shielding for the tube. The recommended BNC and SHV connectors should be installed so that the outside of the connector makes electrical contact with both the housing walls and the cable shield.

Just below the housing is the dark slide. This is simply a narrow compartment in which a small metal plate can be moved by a rod over the light opening. The floor of this compartment is lined with felt to make the slide move smoothly and to enhance the light seal.

Below the dark slide is the filter compartment. In this design, the filters were placed behind the Fabry lens rather than in front. This was purely a matter of convenience. It is preferable to place filters in a light beam that is nearly parallel so they do not deviate the beam. Both the telescope and Fabry lens have about the same F ratio, so it makes little difference where the filters are placed. Figure 6.9 shows some details of the filter assembly. The filters are mounted on a circular disk 6 centimeters (2.4 inches) in diameter. Because of this small size, the filters had to be cut smaller than their normal one-inch size. Access to the filter wheel is gained by removing a cover plate that is held in place by a single wing nut. The filter wheel is turned by two identical gears. One is mounted on the central shaft of the filter wheel, high enough to clear the filters. The second gear is mounted on a shaft that comes down from the top of the filter cover. This gear system was necessary since the filter wheel shaft is covered partially by the tube housing, leaving no room for a positioning knob. The two gears move this knob about 1.5 centimeters (0.6 inch) to the right in Figure 6.9. The detent positioning is accomplished by a scheme suggested by Burke and Pippin[4] and Stokes[25]. The shaft that holds the gear on the filter cover is actually the shaft from an electronic rotary switch. Such switches are inexpensive and contain an accurate detent system. All that is necessary is to remove the wafers containing the switch contacts. Usually these switches have a stop that prevents 360° rotation. This stop is often just a metal tab that can be bent out of the way. The switch positions should be spaced evenly around the knob. The number of switch positions should be a whole number times the number of filters. In this case, a 12-position switch was used with four filters.

Figure 6.9 also shows the diaphragm assembly. This slide consists of five pieces made from flat steel stock. The top and bottom plates are both 6.4 × 5.1 × 0.3 centimeters (2.5 × 2.0 × ⅛ inches) with a 0.64-

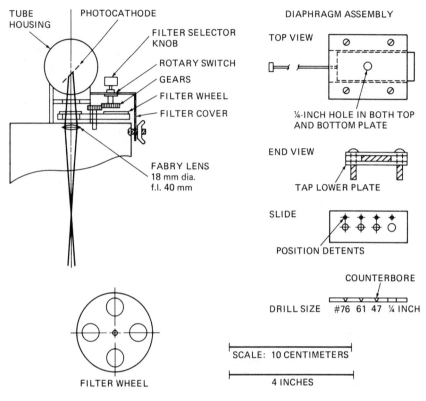

TUBE HOUSING

PHOTOCATHODE

FILTER SELECTOR KNOB

ROTARY SWITCH

GEARS

FILTER WHEEL

FILTER COVER

FABRY LENS
18 mm dia.
f.l. 40 mm

DIAPHRAGM ASSEMBLY

TOP VIEW

¼-INCH HOLE IN BOTH TOP AND BOTTOM PLATE

END VIEW

TAP LOWER PLATE

SLIDE

POSITION DETENTS

COUNTERBORE

DRILL SIZE   #76 61 47 ¼ INCH

SCALE: 10 CENTIMETERS

4 INCHES

FILTER WHEEL

Figure 6.9 Detail of filter assembly and diaphragm slide.

centimeter (0.25-inch) central hole. There are two 6.4 × 1.3 × 0.3-centimeter (2.5 × 0.5 × ⅛-inch) metal strips separating the top and bottom plates and forming the 2.54-centimeter (1-inch) cavity for the diaphragm slide. The fifth piece is 6.4 × 2.5 × 0.3 centimeters (2.5 × 1.0 × ⅛ inches) and contains the diaphragm holes. There are three diaphragms, as discussed in Section 6.4 and a 0.6-centimeter (0.25-inch) hole for a wide field of view. Detent positioning is accomplished by a spring-loaded ball bearing mounted in the bottom plate. This ball pushes against the bottom of the slide. As seen in Figure 6.9, there is a series of holes drilled just above each diaphragm position. When a diaphragm is on the optical axis, the spring pushes the ball into the detent hole and the slide locks into position. Because the detent holes are smaller than the ball bearing, pressure on the diaphragm rod pushes the ball bearing down and the slide moves until the next detent hole is aligned.

While the photometer described here has worked well for many years, we recommend two design changes. First, the filter wheel and filter compartment should be made larger in order to accept standard 1-inch filters. The second change concerns the flip mirror. A look at Figure 6.8 reveals the problem. When the mirror is swung back to make a measurement, it reflects any room light entering the eyepiece into the Fabry lens. It has been found necessary to place a cap over the eyepiece when a measurement is being made. The solution is to hinge the mirror about a point in the upper left of Figure 6.8 so that when the mirror is swung out of the light cone it covers the front of the collimating lens. A foam-rubber ring placed around the front of the lens housing would cushion the mirror.

It is very important to mount the photometer head solidly to the telescope. Any flexure can cause misalignment and move the star out of the diaphragm. Supporting the photometer head solely with the drawtube of the typical small telescope is insufficient unless the telescope's focuser has been redesigned. Figure 6.10 shows the photometer head just described mounted at the Cassegrain focus of a 30.5-centimeter (12-inch) telescope. The large base plate of the head is attached to a mounting rail on the telescope. A similar mounting rail could be used with Newtonian telescopes. The Cassegrain telescopes used by professional astronomers usually focus by moving the secondary mirror rather than the rack-and-pinion devices used by amateurs. This allows the photometer to be bolted firmly to the tail piece of the telescope, eliminating most flexure. This focusing arrangement should be considered more seriously by amateur astronomers.

6.6 ELECTRONIC CONSTRUCTION

In this and succeeding chapters, we present designs for electronic circuitry. These designs represent in most cases prototype units that have been constructed and tested. However, we would like to make three points:

1. You should not attempt to construct these circuits unless you are familar with high-frequency, high-voltage, and high-gain construction techniques. Otherwise, we recommend purchasing commercial units.
2. While the prototype units work as reported, different layouts and components may require minor modifications to perform properly.

Figure 6.10 The photometer head mounted on a telescope.

3. Because you are building high-performance circuits, you should use the best quality components that you can afford.

Finding sources of components can be complicated. Other than Radio Shack, you can generally find components at large electronic distributors. These companies usually have a $25 minimum order. Other excellent sources are hamfests, especially the larger ones in Dayton and Atlanta. These are advertised in *QST* and other amateur radio magazines. For most of us, the primary and cheapest source of electronic components is the mail-order house. *The Radio Amateur's Handbook*[26] lists many sources of parts in the chapter on construction techniques. We suggest reading this chapter as it contains much information that the amateur astronomer can use.

6.7 HIGH-VOLTAGE POWER SUPPLY

The high-voltage power supply for the photomultiplier tube is one of the most important components of the photometer. It should be adjustable, in order that the correct operating point for each tube can be found, and it should be well regulated. A 1 percent change in the output voltage can make a much larger change in the photomultiplier tube output because the gain of each stage is multiplicative. This kind of systematic error should be kept to a value smaller than anticipated from observational error (photon statistics); that is, the power supply should be regulated to better than 0.1 percent. Most variations are caused by voltage fluctuations from the power line, and may occur on a very short time scale.

The requirements listed above would be relatively simple with modern technology if not for the magnitude of the voltage required. A 1P21 tube uses approximately 1000 V (1 kV) and some other tubes, such as the FW-118, may require 2 kV. No integrated circuit (IC) voltage regulator and few transistors can handle these voltages.

Of course, one can always purchase a commercial, adjustable high-voltage supply. Appropriate used units can be obtained from many firms that deal in reconditioned test equipment, such as the Ted Dames Co.[27] New units are available from companies such as EMI,[7] Kepco,[28] Lambda,[29] Ortec,[30] or Princeton Applied Research.[15] Be advised, however, that some of these new units cost $200 to $1000.

You can construct your own power supply. There is a dearth of up-to-date circuits and we try to present those that we could find or derive. However, these circuits handle *lethal* voltages, so be extremely careful in working with them.

There are three general approaches used in building adjustable high-voltage supplies. The simplest is to use a bank of high-voltage batteries. The easiest electronically regulated supply is to obtain approximately 2 kV from a filtered supply and then use a voltage divider to pick off the appropriate voltage. The third method is also the most elegant: amplitude-modulate an RF oscillator and rectify the output voltage. Each of these approaches is discussed in more detail.

6.7a Batteries

The use of a battery bank has the advantage of excellent regulation and noise immunity. In addition, the bank is portable and the current drain

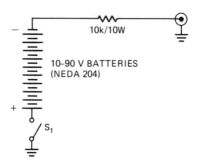

Figure 6.11 Battery supply.

is low enough that the batteries last their normal shelf life. The two disadvantages are that batteries are temperature-sensitive (keep them warm!) and expensive. Expect to pay about $1 per 10 V. Typical available batteries are the PX18 (45 V) and the NEDA 204 (90 V). Some high-voltage batteries used by the military can be obtained from surplus supply houses at a much lower cost; check electronics magazines for names and addresses. The U200 batteries (300 V) were available formerly and may still be found in local stores.

A typical battery-operated system is shown in Figure 6.11. The 10 K series resistor acts as a current limiter when an external short occurs. The case for this system should have insulation to prevent leakage paths to ground, moisture proofing to prevent leakage paths and damage to the batteries, and shielding on the outside for safety and noise immunity.

6.7b Filtered Supply

A schematic for a typical voltage divider supply is shown in Figure 6.12. This involves an AC transformer with a voltage doubler consisting of diodes D1 through D4. Each diode is bypassed with an RC combination to equalize voltage drops across the diodes and to guard against transients. Current-limiting resistors R1 and R4 protect the diodes against the initial turn-on surge and to allow some current to flow through the zener chain at all times. The output is filtered by capacitors C7 through C10, with equalizing resistors R7 through R10 doubling as bleeder resistors when the supply is shut off. The filtered output is fed to the zener bank. These diodes regulate the voltage and by switch or jumper

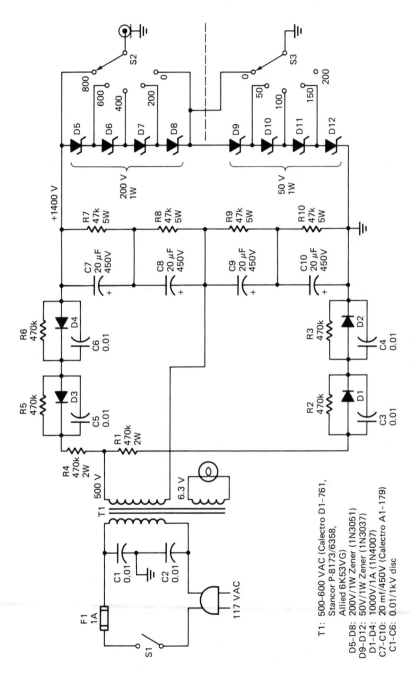

Figure 6.12 Zener voltage supply.

T1: 500-600 VAC (Calectro D1-761, Stancor P-8173/6358, Allied 6K53VG)
D5-D8: 200V/1W Zener (1N3051)
D9-D12: 50V/1W Zener (1N3037)
D1-D4: 1000V/1A (1N4007)
C7-C10: 20 mf/450V (Calectro A1-179)
C1-C6: 0.01/1kV disc

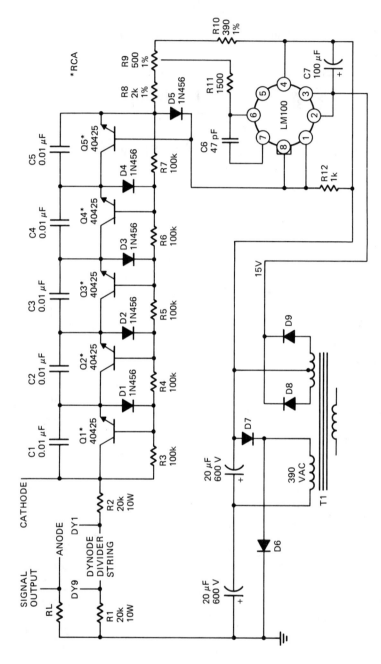

Figure 6.13 Current-regulated supply. (Copyright 1981 National Semiconductor Corporation)

selection can allow some voltage adjustment. A simplified chain of five 200 V zeners could be used if adjustment is not desired.

The regulation from this supply is not as good as might be expected. Because the zener knee is not infinitely sharp, there is some voltage change with current. In addition, zeners are very temperature-sensitive. The amount of regulation can be determined by comparing the current-limiting resistor to the dynamic resistance of the zeners, as this circuit is basically a voltage divider. If there is 20 percent ripple on the unregulated supply and the resistance ratio is 100 (typical values), then the regulation is approximately 0.2 percent. The advantage of this supply is that it is the least expensive to build of the electronically regulated supplies. If you do build it, try to thermostat the supply.

A novel variation of the filtered high-voltage supply was designed by Elkstrand[31] and is shown in Figure 6.13. Instead of trying to regulate the voltage, this circuit uses an LM100 IC regulator and regulates the current passing through the photomultiplier tube. A full-wave rectifier operating off one winding of the power transformer T1 provides a 15-V bias voltage for the LM100. The other winding is used in a voltage doubler as in Figure 6.12 with the output passing through the photomultiplier tube divider chain that develops the operating voltages for the cathode and dynodes. Five cascaded transistors, Q1 through Q5, are used as the pass transistors, each therefore passing one-fifth of the total voltage. This is the most economical solution to the problem of handling the required voltage levels. Base drive is provided for the cascade string by R3 through R7 in a manner that does not affect regulation. Capacitors C1 through C5 suppress and equalize transients across the pass transistors, and clamp diodes across the sensitive emitter-base junctions of the transistors prevent damage from voltage transients.

6.7c RF Oscillator

This approach was used by Code.[23] A schematic of this circuit is reproduced in Figure 6.14. Because of the high voltages involved, the only convenient oscillator involves vacuum tubes, and therefore the design is cumbersome. Basically, part of the rectified output voltage from an RF oscillator running at 100 kHz is used in a feedback loop to control the amplitude of the oscillator. By changing the amount of feedback voltage, the output voltage is adjustable. Because the current drain from a photomultiplier tube is negligible (less than 1 μA), the RF oscillator does not need much power capability.

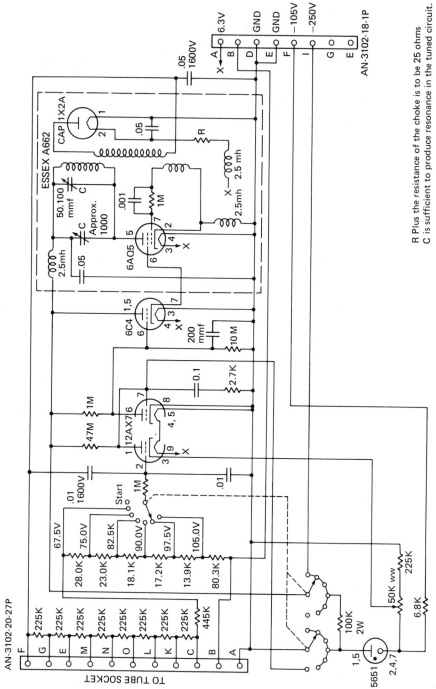

Figure 6.14 RF oscillator supply. (Reproduced from *Photoelectric Astronomy for Amateurs*, ed. F. B. Wood, Macmillan)

R Plus the resistance of the choke is to be 25 ohms
C is sufficient to produce resonance in the tuned circuit.

While obtaining the proper photomultiplier tube voltage in one step is impossible with transistors, there is another approach. Electronic flash units use an oscillator type of DC-DC supply that takes 4 to 6 V and transforms it to voltages in the 300 V range. These DC-DC supplies are available on the surplus market, and can be tied together in a series fashion to obtain the 1 kV voltage necessary for photomultiplier tubes. Regulation is then provided in the input voltages to the supplies, which can be obtained from standard IC regulators.

Commercial DC-DC supplies are available from companies such as RCA,[9] Venus,[32] Ortec,[30] EMI,[7] and Hamamatsu.[11] These supplies range from $100 to $500, and offer a small, convenient method of generating the high voltage for the photomultiplier tube. The input voltage is generally between 6 and 20 V to provide 900 to 1500 V output, with output regulation again controlled by the input voltage regulation. A DC-DC supply is an alternative to batteries for a small, portable supply.

6.7d Setup and Operation

To connect a high-voltage supply to the photomultiplier tube, coaxial cable such as RG58 can be used. For voltages above 1 kV, special high-voltage connectors of the SHV or MHV type should be used to gain immunity from possible dielectric breakdown. Always remember these precautions:

1. Never work on the high-voltage power supply with the power turned on.
2. Never disconnect the photomultiplier tube or the high-voltage cable to the photomultiplier tube with the high voltage turned on.
3. Bring the high voltage up and down slowly to avoid rapid changes.
4. Observe the correct polarity of the high-voltage power supply.

6.8 REFERENCE LIGHT SOURCES

As we mention in this and subsequent chapters, electronic equipment is generally temperature-sensitive. This means that if you use a set of A0 stars at the beginning of a night to determine the zero-point coefficients in the transformation equations, and then use these coefficients to reduce data taken many hours later, the results can be in error. There are other factors, such as telescope position dependence as a result of equipment flexure or magnetic fields, that also contribute errors to your results. To calibrate these irregularities out of the observations, astronomers use *standard light souces*. These come in three varieties: ground-mounted standard lamps, small radioactive sources, and stars.

Standard lamps are usually filament-operated devices with operating parameters kept constant. They cannot be mounted on the telescope because irregularities in the light output are common because of filament sag. In addition, they are difficult to use for astronomical purposes because of their relatively large output energy. To image the light source through the telescope requires that the energy collected by the telescope from the source must be equivalent in intensity to an average star. In general, such a lamp must be placed more than 100 meters away from the telescope. In addition, the filaments operate at a cool temperature in comparison to most stars and therefore temperature-sensitive errors tend to propagate in opposite directions.

Radioactive sources are usually weak beta emitters that are placed in contact with a phosphor. The fast electrons enter the phosphor crystals and produce light in one or more bands whose width is usually on the order of a hundred Angstroms. These sources can be made very small and are usually placed in the filter side or near the photomultiplier. This allows the observer to test the photometer for positional variations in addition to temperature and aging effects. The light output of these sources is usually blue-green, making calibrations a little easier than for the standard lamps. The phosphor in radioactive sources suffers from temperature effects equal to or greater than those of the photometer, and cannot be used for calibration unless thermostatted. In addition, the phosphor is highly light-sensitive, and there are long-term brightness variations that preclude calibrations over periods longer than a few months.

For the reasons listed above, few astronomers regularly use standard lamps or radioactive sources. They are used in initial calibration of the telescope and photometer and in cases where long-term accuracy (months for radioactive sources, longer for other types) is needed. An alternative to the ground-based calibration techniques is to use standard stars to monitor any equipment changes. This method has the advantage that it also measures atmospheric transparency changes. However, it suffers from increased complexity (extinction must be taken into account and often several stars are used), the problem of finding standard stars over the entire sky to measure flexure errors, and that calibrations take up observing time.

In general, we recommend using differential techniques in photometry. This eliminates almost all instrumental variations as they occur equally to both the comparison and the program star. If you intend to measure stars over the entire sky, to standardize your comparison stars for example, then use the North Polar Sequence stars to check transparency and temperature effects as their air mass (and therefore extinction) changes very little in the course of a night. In all cases, including extinction determinations, observe standards throughout the night, not just at the beginning or end.

6.9 SPECIALIZED PHOTOMETER DESIGNS

Earlier in this chapter we detailed the construction of a simple photometer that is certainly adequate for amateur and small telescopes. It is light, compact, and requires few specialized tools to construct. This section discusses other, more complicated designs that observatories have constructed. While the treatment is brief, it should be sufficient to inform you of other ideas and direct you to references where more detail can be found.

6.9a A Professional Single-beam Photometer

The photometer used at the Morgan Monroe Station of Goethe Link Observatory is a prime example of a professional instrument. Based on a design pioneered by William Hiltner, the photometer is shown in Figure 6.15. All external framework components are made of 0.635-centimeter (¼-inch) aluminum stock, milled with rabbet joints to form light-tight boxes. The assembled unit including the photomultiplier's cold box, weighs about 32 kilograms (70 pounds).

As seen from the top, where light enters the photometer from the telescope, we can identify the three major subdivisions of the instrument: *guide box, filter and diaphragm assembly,* and the *cold box.* The guide box has a military surplus eyepiece mounted on a movable X-Y platform for offset guiding and accurate star centering. This eyepiece and its associated mirror are placed in front of the diaphragm slide. The eyepiece has an illuminated reticle, with 30 arc second arms on the cross pattern. Once having centered the star in the diaphragm and adjusted the eyepiece position, the observer can repeatedly center stars in a 10 arc second diaphragm using the cross hairs without checking the diaphragm viewing eyepiece. Once a star is centered on the reticle the

Figure 6.15 The Goethe Link Observatory photometer.

viewing mirror is slid, parallel to its surface, until a hole in the mirror aligns with the optical axis and the starlight can enter the photometer. The eyepiece can be moved using its X-Y motion to find a guide star because the rest of the field is still available for viewing. The Erfle viewing eyepiece was chosen to provide sufficient eye relief so that an observer with eyeglasses can use the photometer easily.

The filter and diaphragm assembly begins with a detented filter slide that under normal circumstances contains an open hole and two neutral density filters, allowing the observer to perform photometry on stars as bright as zero magnitude. This slide can also be used to hold polarizing filters. The light beam then encounters a detented diaphragm slide with holes ranging from 10 to 120 arc seconds. Next the beam passes to a rotating filter wheel. Electronics control the motion of this wheel to move from one filter to another under programmed control. Manual motion is available with an externally mounted pushbutton, and the filter position number is shown on a seven-segment LED readout. The filter assembly is carefully machined and is removable with one screw, allowing convenient filter wheel and/or mechanism replacement.

The cold box has a self-contained dark slide and Fabry lens, allowing the observer to change photomultipliers during the night by switching cold-box assemblies. Through careful design, the Fabry lens does not require heating to remain frost-free. A single dry ice charge, about 1 kilogram (2.2 pounds), usually lasts an entire night. The pulse preamp and discriminator is mounted on the cold box, making good ground contact and matching the cold-box tube assembly with a preamp tailored to the photomultiplier tube's best operating conditions.

6.9b Chopping Photometers

The next level of complexity is to provide two light paths and to switch the detector back and forth between them. For instance, you could use two diaphragms in the focal plane and pick out the program star and a nearby comparison star. By directing the program or comparison star's light to the photomultiplier by the use of a mirror, you can "move" from one star to the other in a fraction of a second, nullifying any atmospheric changes. This setup allows differential photometry in one color during very poor sky conditions, such as uniform cirrus or broken cloud cover. An example of the dual-diaphragm arrangement is the photometer designed by Taylor[33] and shown in Figure 6.16. Here the photometer only chops between star and sky, which makes the mechanism simpler because the only moving element is the optical detent system; the filter and photometer assemblies remain the same. Because you are chopping between star and sky, you can only obtain accurate color indices. You must "intercompare" two stars to obtain differential magnitudes.

A similar system is used at Skibotn Valley in the Arctic Circle.[34] In this photometer the secondary mirror of the telescope is moved to pass the light of two separate stars, or the star and sky through a single diaphragm. This arrangement allowed the photometry of an eclipsing

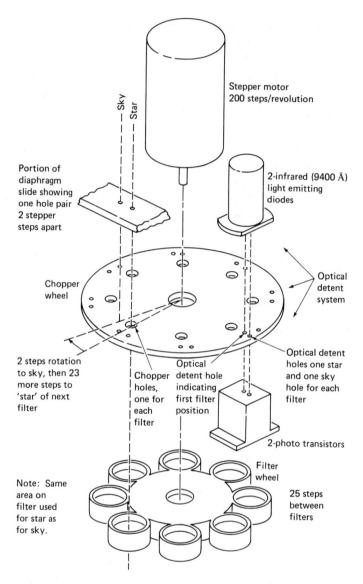

Stepper motor
200 steps/revolution

Sky
Star

Portion of
diaphragm
slide showing
one hole pair
2 stepper
steps apart

2-infrared (9400 Å)
light emitting
diodes

Chopper
wheel

Optical
detent
system

2 steps rotation
to sky, then 23
more steps to
'star' of next
filter

Chopper
holes,
one for
each
filter

Optical
detent hole
indicating
first filter
position

Optical detent
holes one star
and one sky
hole for each
filter

2-photo transistors

Filter
wheel

Note: Same
area on
filter used
for star as
for sky.

25 steps
between
filters

Figure 6.16 The Taylor dual-diaphragm photometer. (Courtesy of the *Publications* of the Astronomical Society of the Pacific)

binary star during an aurora that was as bright as a sixth-magnitude star and that varied by five magnitudes in 1 minute!

Chopping photometers work because clouds are relatively neutral in extinction; Serkowski[35] and Honeycutt[36] have shown that the effect of one magnitude of cloud extinction is only about 0.01 magnitude on the *UBV* colors. The biggest error is the variable transparency, easily accounted for by chopped photometers. Because only one detector is used, half of the time is usually spent observing the sky, decreasing the collecting efficiency.

An interesting variation of the chopping photometer was designed at Indiana University by De Veny.[37] This photometer uses two diaphragms of different sizes on the same star. By switching between the two diaphragms, you obtain a star and sky reading, and then a star and sky reading with a known additional amount of sky. You can then determine the sky background around the star mathematically and subtract it. The advantage of this system is that you are always measuring sky surrounding the star, while continuously observing the star, effectively multiplexing in the sky observations.

6.9c Dual-beam Photometers

A dual-beam photometer in this context means any system where two separate detectors are used. It can be built in one of two ways: either dividing the light from a single star into two components, or using the light from two stars separately.

The single-star photometer usually uses a dichroic beam-splitter to divide the beam into a blue and a red component. The response curve for such a beam splitter was calculated by Morbey and Fletcher[38] and is shown in Figure 6.17. Note that the division is not pure and sharp. This means that it is difficult to use a filter with the beam-splitter output and match the *UBV* colors exactly. Also, two separate detectors are used and their transformation coefficients must be known very accurately to obtain color indices. Half-aluminized mirrors could be used for the beam splitter, but then only half of the light in a given wavelength would be available, offering little gain over a chopping photometer. By using a dichroic splitter, you double throughput and prevent atmospheric variations from affecting the derived color index. An example of a single-star photometer as designed by Wood and Lockwood[39] is shown in Figure 6.18.

Basically, the dual-star photometer is two separate photometers mounted at the focal plane of the telescope. Usually one photometer is fixed on the optical axis and the other is movable in angle and radius to measure sky or a nearby comparison star. Because there is no beam splitter, no light is lost and no filter response change is involved. Usually

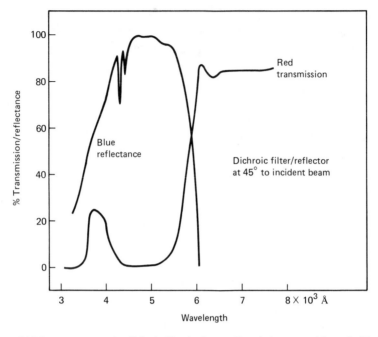

Figure 6.17 Response curves for dichroic filter/reflector. (Permission granted from the National Research Council of Canada.)

for accurate measurements, the role of the two photometers is interchanged to eliminate the instrumental response differences. An example of such a photometer as designed by Geyer and Hoffmann[40] is shown in Figure 6.19.

A novel approach to the dual-star photometer is the twin photometric reflector at Edinburgh.[41] Here two telescopes are contained on the same mount, with one continuously adjustable with respect to the other by several degrees. By pointing at one standard star with one telescope, the other telescope can determine a photoelectric sequence in a cluster in short order, or both telescopes can be used on a star for simultaneous two-color photometry.

PIN photodiodes would make an excellent dual-beam photometer. Small and lightweight, such a photometer would be feasible for moderate-sized amateur telescopes. This photometer would work well in areas with few photometric nights, such as the eastern U.S. The authors would like to hear about the design of this type of photometer for possible inclusion in future editions of this text.

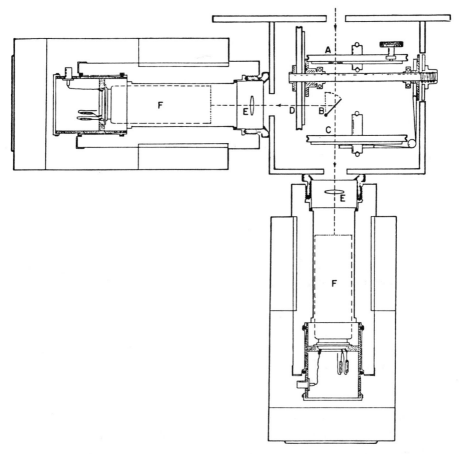

Figure 6.18 Single star photometer by Wood and Lockwood. (By permission of the Leander McCormick Observatory)

6.9d Multifilter Photometers

A multifilter photometer can also be classified as a coarse spectrometer. Light from a single star is broken into several beams that are measured individually. Dichroic beam splitters are not used because of their response curves; adequate separation of three or more colors is extremely difficult. Roberts[42] used aluminum beam splitters to obtain a three-channel photometer. Since aluminum is essentially neutral, three equal beams can be obtained with each passing through an appropriate

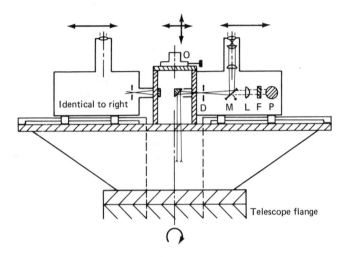

Figure 6.19 Schematic drawing of the Greyer photometer. *O* is the wide angle offset eyepiece, *D* the diaphragm wheel, *M* the periscope flip-flop mirror, *L* the Fabry lens, *F* the color filter wheel, and *P* the photomultiplier tube. (Courtesy of *Astronomy And Astrophysics*)

filter. However, each beam then contains only one-third of the light at any given wavelength so that the net result is the same as if you switched from one filter to another, in terms of throughput or net counts. However, the measurements are simultaneous.

A much more practical multifilter arrangement is the Walraven photometer.[43] Here a quartz prism is used to disperse the light, as in a spectrograph, and the resultant spectrum is sampled by five filter and detector combinations. It is impossible with such a combination to match the *UBV* system, as its wide-band response curves overlap each other. Medium- and narrow-band systems such as the Strömgren four-color and the Walraven five-color systems are ideally suited to multifilter photometers. The Mira group in California[44] have a 512-channel "photometer" covering the visible spectrum that they intend to use to acquire rapid spectrophotometry of the 125,000 stars of the Henry Draper Catalog visible in the Northern Hemisphere. As you can see, as the photometric instrumentation becomes more complicated, the dividing lines between types of instruments become very nebulous.

REFERENCES

1. Persha, G. 1980. *IAPPP Com.* **2**, 11.
2. De Lara, E., Chavarria K., Johnson, H. L., and Moreno, R., 1977. *Revista Mexicana de Astron. y Astrof.* **2**, 65.

3. Optec, Inc., 199 Smith, Lowell, MI 49331.
4. Burke, E. W. Jr., and Pippin, D. M. 1976. *Pub. A. S. P.* **88**, 561.
5. Edmund Scientific, 101 E. Gloucester Pike, Barrington, NJ 08007.
6. Jaegers, A., 691S Merrick Rd., Lynbrook, NY 11563.
7. EMI Gencom Inc., 80 Express St., Plainview, NY 11803.
8. ITT, Electro-Optical Products Division, 3700 E. Pontiac St., Fort Wayne, IN 46803.
9. RCA, Electro Optics and Devices, Lancaster PA 17604. RCA photomultipliers are available from electronics suppliers.
10. Fernie, J. D. 1974. *Pub. A. S. P.* **86**, 837.
11. Hamamatsu Corp., 420 South Ave., Middlesex, NJ 08846.
12 Perfection Mica Co., Magnetic Shield Division, 740 N. Thomas Drive, Bensenville, IL 60106.
13. Johnson, H. L. 1962. In *Astronomical Techniques,* Edited by W. Hiltner. Chicago: Univ. of Chicago Press, p. 157.
14. Pacific Precision Instruments, 1040 Shary Court, Concord, CA 94518.
15. EG & G Princeton Applied Research, P.O. Box 2565, Princeton, NJ 08540.
16. Products for Research, Inc., 88 Holten St., Danvers, MA 01923.
17. Corning Glass Works, Houghton Park, Corning, NY 14830. Corning filters may be ordered from Swift Glass Co., 104 Glass St., Elmira, NY 14902.
18. Schott Optical Glass Inc., 400 York Ave., Duryea, PA 18642.
19. EG & G Electro-Optics Division, 35 Congress St., Salem, MA 01970.
20. Dick, R., Fraser, A., Lossing, F., and Welch, D. 1978. *J. R. A. S. Canada* **72**, 40.
21. Photometry Committee. 1962. *Manual for Astronomical Photoelectric Photometry,* AAVSO, 187 Concord Ave., Cambridge, MA 02138.
22. Allen, W. H. 1980. *IAPPP Com.* **2**, 7.
23. Code, A. D. 1963. In *Photoelectric Astronomy for Amateurs.* Edited by F. B. Wood. New York: Macmillan.
24. Grauer, A. D., Pittman, C. E., and Russwurm, G. 1976. *Sky and Tel.* **52**, 86.
25. Stokes, A., 1980. In paper presented at IAPPP. Symposium, Dayton, OH.
26. *The Radio Amateur's Handbook.* Newington: The American Radio Relay League. Published yearly.
27. The Ted Dames Co., 308 Hickory St., Arlington, NJ 07032.
28. Kepco Inc., 131–38 Stanford Ave., Flushing, NY 11352.
29. Lambda Electronics Corp., 515 Broad Hollow Rd., Melville, NY 11747.
30. EG & G Ortec Inc., 100 Midland Rd., Oak Ridge, TN 37830.
31. Elkstrand, J. P. 1973. In *Linear Applications Handbook,* volume 1. National Semiconductor Corp. (A.N. 8).
32. Venus Scientific Inc., 399 Smith St., Farmingdale, NY 11735.
33. Taylor, D. J. 1980. *Pub. A. S. P.* **92**, 108.
34. Myrabø, H. K. 1978. *Observatory* **98**, 234.
35. Serkowski, K. 1970. *Pub. A. S. P.* **82**, 908.
36. Honeycutt, R. K. 1971. *Pub. A. S. P.* **83**, 502.
37. De Veny, J. B. 1967. *An Improved Technique for Photoelectric Measurement of Faint Stars.* Masters thesis, Indiana University.
38. Morbey, C. L., and Fletcher, J. M. 1974. *Pub. Dom. Ap. Obs.* **14**, 11.
39. Wood, H. J., and Lockwood, G. W. 1967. *Pub. Leander McCormick Obs.* XV, 25.

40. Geyer, H., and Hoffmann, M. 1975. *Ast. and Ap.* **38**, 359.
41. Reddish, V. C. 1966. *Sky and Tel.* **32**, 124.
42. Roberts, G. L. 1967. *Appl. Opt.* **6**, 907.
43. Walraven, T. and Walraven, J. H. 1960. *Bul. Ast. Inst. Neth.* **15**, 67.
44. Overbye, D. 1979. *Sky and Tel.* **57**, 223.
45. Nye, R. A. 1981. *Sky and Tel.* **62**, 496.

CHAPTER 7
PULSE-COUNTING ELECTRONICS

Pulse-counting systems are rapidly becoming comparable in expense to any other method of photoelectric photometry. A typical but very general layout of such a system is shown in Figure 7.1. The output from the photomultiplier is fed to the preamp, which amplifies the pulse, shapes it, and rejects noise pulses. This conditioned pulse is the input to the pulse counter, also known as a *frequency counter*. The pulse counter consists of three major parts: a counting circuit that counts every input pulse, a gate that allows pulses to reach the counter only for a specified time interval, and the timing circuit controlling gate.

The counts can be read directly from the counter or sent to a small computer through an interface. There the counts may be transformed to a crude magnitude scale. The data can be printed out on a teletype or displayed visually. It may be transferred to magnetic tape or disk to await further data reduction or for permanent storage.

Preamps and pulse counters are described in this chapter, along with some representative circuits. Some interfacing and testing procedures follow.

It should be emphasized that pulse counting cannot be performed with PIN diode photometers. Pulse counting requires hundreds of thousands of electrons for each incident photon. An incident photon produces only one electron-hole pair in a photodiode. Thus, with present photodiode technology, you must use DC methods.

7.1 PULSE AMPLIFIERS AND DISCRIMINATORS

The pulse amplifier increases the size and shapes the feeble pulse from the photomultiplier tube. The discriminator rejects pulses that are

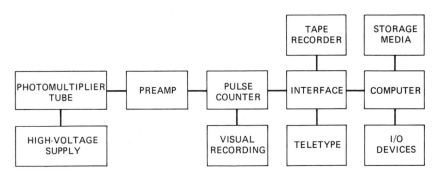

Figure 7.1. Block diagram of pulse counting system.

inherent to the photomultiplier tube itself and not from the source. The electronics that accomplish these two purposes is often in a single package, commonly called a *preamp.*

The amplification is necessary because each pulse contains on the order of a million (10^6) electrons, a current of only 10^{-12} A if averaged over 1 second. Most frequency counters require inputs of 100 mV (0.1 V) to count correctly. Therefore, using Ohm's law, we would have to use a series resistor of 10^{11} ohms to yield adequate counting voltage. This is a very difficult value to obtain.

If you look at the output of a typical photomultiplier tube at high time resolution, you would see something similar to Figure 7.2. Each pulse represents the output from a photon event, and the signal between pulses is the background or dark current of the tube. If you counted all of the pulses of a certain size occurring in a fixed time interval and

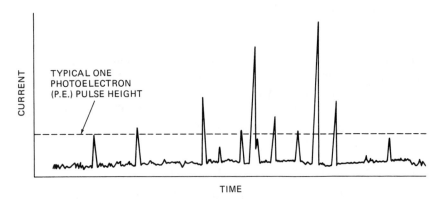

Figure 7.2. Typical photomultiplier output.

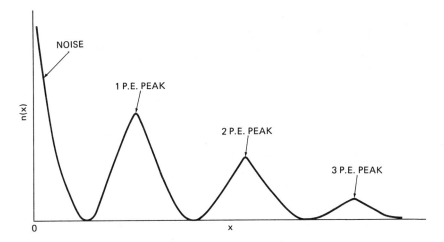

Figure 7.3. Pulse height distribution.

plotted your results, you would obtain a pulse height distribution. A theoretical pulse height distribution is shown in Figure 7.3. This shows that the number of background noise pulses decrease rapidly with the energy of the pulse. There are several peaks in the distribution, corresponding to the ejection of one or more electrons from the photocathode by the photon. Most events ejecting more than one electron are caused by cosmic rays and are few in number.

We do not want to amplify the noise pulses and count them along with photon events. Instead, we want to discriminate against them. This is usually achieved by setting a minimum threshold level below which no output pulse results. You can never eliminate all of the noise pulses because some arise on the photocathode itself and look like photon events, but by setting the threshold near the minimum between the noise and the one-photoelectron distribution, you will reject the maximum noise and accept the maximum signal. To be highly accurate, you would also reject the two and higher photoelectron pulses, because they are caused primarily by cosmic rays, and create a window discriminator. However, this trade-off is unnecessary because only a few pulses would be rejected with a large increase in circuit complexity.

A good pulse amplifier and discriminator should:

1. Have an output pulse no more than 50 nanoseconds wide, thereby providing a counting rate of about 20 MHz.

2. Have minimal temperature sensitivity.
3. Have stability and high noise immunity.
4. Be small, simple, and require only one operating voltage.
5. Be able to amplify a 0.5-mV pulse and provide a TTL-compatible output.

There are readily available commercial preamps. These include models from Princeton Applied Research,[1] Hamamatsu,[2] and Products for Research.[3] However, be prepared to spend several hundred dollars for one of these commercial devices. Amptek[4] has recently introduced hybrid charge-sensitive preamps that are the size of a dime. These could be mounted on the tube base and provide a very compact package. However, the current models are not sensitive enough for most astronomical applications. DuPuy[5] has recently published a circuit based on the MVL 100 single-chip amplifier. One limitation of this chip is that it may not have enough gain for some photomultiplier tubes.

7.2 A PRACTICAL PULSE AMPLIFIER AND DISCRIMINATOR

A preamp circuit that has been used by many observatories was described in 1973 by Taylor,[6] who recently revised the original circuit.[7] This enhanced preamp is presented in this section. The Taylor preamp was designed with simplicity and low cost in mind. The circuit is shown in Figure 7.4. It consists of nine 2N4124 transistors ($0.30 each) and a 1N3717 tunnel diode (about $10).

The first six transistors comprise the amplifier section and are connected as shunt-series feedback pairs, cascaded for an overall gain of about 1000. The tunnel diode monostable oscillator acts as the discriminator. When triggered, it generates a standard −0.5V pulse, which is buffered by an emitter follower, amplified and inverted, and fed to a second emitter follower to drive a 50-ohm cable to + 5V. The shape of the output pulse is similar to the positive half of a sine wave with a base width of 20 nanoseconds. The discriminator level is adjusted by means of a current bias potentiometer. An IC regulator is included in the circuit to improve stability and eliminate the need for a separate zener regulator for the tunnel diode.

The circuit should be constructed on a single board. Point-to-point wiring is recommended, using a double-sided printed-circuit board as the chassis. Layout of the parts is not critical and no shielding between

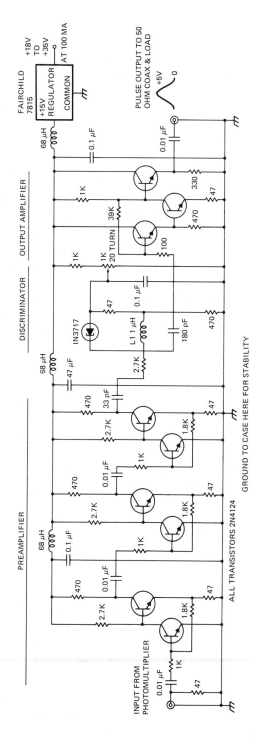

Figure 7.4. Schematic diagram of the improved pulse and amplifier circuit. All transistors are 2N4124's, L_1 is 1 μH (30 turns on a 1 Meg ½ watt resistor as a coil form). (Courtesy of the *Publications* of the Astronomical Society of the Pacific.)

stages is necessary, but a layout resembling the circuit diagram is suggested. After construction, the board should be mounted in a metal box for shielding. This can be a commercial box such as Pomona Electronics[8] model 3302 or constructed out of double-sided printed-circuit board material. The board should be grounded to the case in several places to prevent pulse doubling. BNC-type connectors should be used for the input and output.

The Taylor preamp is somewhat temperature-sensitive, losing sensitivity as the temperature decreases. The 1973 version had up to a 20 percent variation in the count rate with a 40 Celsius degree change. For this reason, obtaining accurate measurements requires thermostatting the circuit. Problems with temperature sensitivity can be minimized by using differential photometry and/or never observing near sunset when temperature variations are at their maximum.

With the pulse resolution of this preamp, dead-time corrections start to become important at around 100,000 counts per second. Use the methods discussed in Chapter 4 to correct for this error.

7.3 PULSE COUNTERS

A frequency or pulse counter for astronomical purposes has certain requirements:

1. Counting ability to 100 MHz or higher.
2. Selectable time base, with at least 1- and 10-second gating times for manual use, and 0.001- and 0.01-second gating for occultation observations.
3. Capability of external gate triggering and counter reset.
4. BCD or binary output for computer interfacing.

The last two items may not be necessary immediately when the counter purchase is contemplated, but should be considered for future applications. A rule of thumb is to be able to count 30 times faster than the most rapid anticipated nonuniform rate; 100 MHz gives a large margin of error in most cases. For astronomical purposes, a counting accuracy of 0.1 percent is entirely adequate. This is a condition met by all commercial frequency counters.

Examples of adequate commercial frequency counters are the Optoelectronics[9] 7010, Heathkit[10] SM-2420, and Hal-Tronix[11] HAL-600A;

all are 600-MHz counters using the newly released ICM 7216 frequency counter IC. Introduced by Intersil,[12] the 7216 has enormous potential for astronomical use because of its simplicity and low cost (under $25). The only additional major parts required for a 100-MHz counter with a selectable timebase are a 10-MHz crystal, a divide-by-ten prescaler (11C90 or 95H90), and a LED display of up to eight digits. Its only disadvantage is the very complicated interface for computer applications. Still, the ICM 7216 has allowed manufacturers to supply adequate frequency counters for manual use in the $100 to $200 price range.

If you want to build your own counter from scratch, consider the ICM 7216 and consult the data sheets supplied by Intersil. Other ICs are available to perform the major functions, such as a six-decade counter. The use of discrete ICs in building a counter makes for a cumbersome design, but has the advantage of easy computer interfacing as all signals are present continuously.

Normal quoted accuracies of the time bases for frequency counters are around 10 ppm/C°. This means that a change of 10 Celsius degrees causes a 0.01 percent change in the gating time, which is insignificant for overnight use. This error could become important if a less accurate time base were used. In addition, most commercial grade ICs quit working at 0°C (32°F), and the frequency response of both the pulse shaping input and the counter degrade as the temperature approaches zero. In other words, for best results the counter should be thermostatted to a constant temperature in summer and winter, just like the preamp. If you must operate without thermostatting, use the military (5400 series) instead of the commercial grade (7400 series) ICs.

7.4 A GENERAL-PURPOSE PULSE COUNTER

In this section, we describe a general-purpose frequency counter constructed from discrete integrated circuits. It contains 19 ICs and would cost around $100 to construct. Though more complicated than a counter using the ICM 7216 frequency counter IC, its main advantage is ease of computer control. All outputs are latched and can be brought out to a connector for computer input, and time base select and reset functions are simple to interface for computer control.

The counter is shown in Figures 7.5 through 7.7. The maximum count rate is 100 MHz, controlled by the 74S00 gate and the 74S196

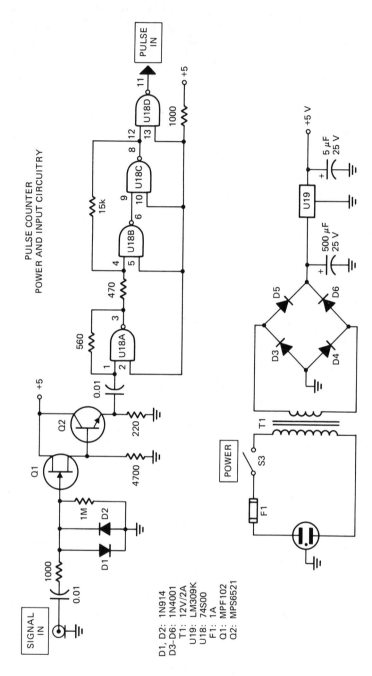

·Figure 7.5. Power and input circuitry.

174

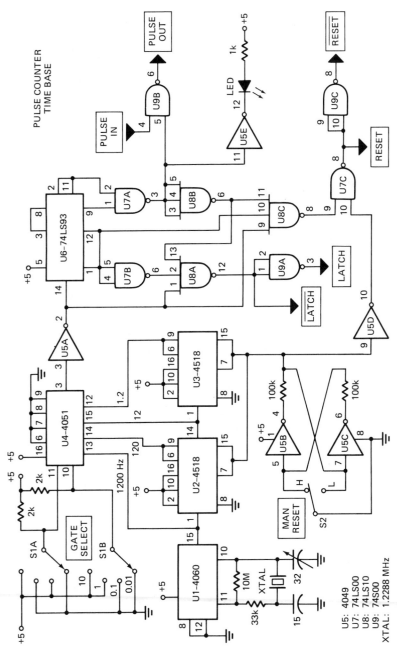

Figure 7.6. Time base.

175

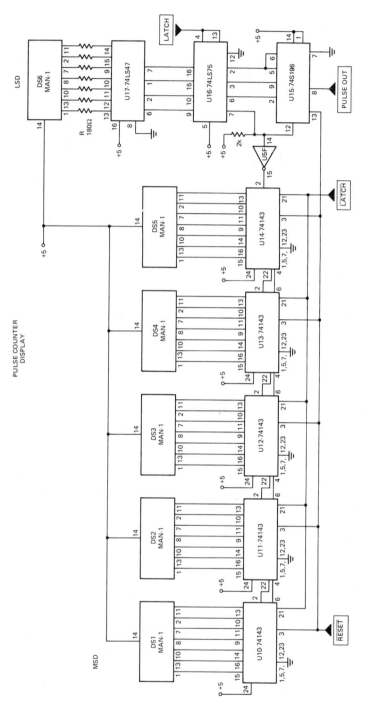

Figure 7.7. Display.

decade counter. If lower count rates are acceptable, the 74S196 can be replaced by a 74196 or another decade chip with some minor rewiring.

The input section amplifies the signal using a field-effect transistor (FET) and then conditions it into a square wave using device U18. This section can be eliminated if the counter's only use is for photometry, where there is a separate preamp in which the output pulse drives the gating circuitry directly. The pulse is routed through a timing gate and on to a series of decade counters. The 74143 is a combination counter, latch, and decoder-driver and would be used for all stages except that it has a low counting rate, 18 MHz. The 74S196 is negative-edge triggered, and its output must be inverted to drive the positive-edge triggered 74143. All LED displays are common-anode MAN-1 equivalents.

A CMOS 4060 IC is used as the oscillator. It divides the 1.2288-MHz crystal frequency by 2^{10} (1024) to provide a 1200-Hz square-wave output. This is further divided by the dual-decade 4518 counters, and four frequencies (1200, 120, 12, and 1.2 Hz) are fed to a 4051 demultiplexer. The desired frequency is selected by a DP4T rotary switch and routed to a divide-by-12 circuit. This opens the gate for 10 pulses, latches for one, and resets for one. Therefore, the final output gating times are 0.01, 0.1, 1, and 10 seconds, with 0.002, 0.02, 0.2, and 2 seconds, respectively, of dead-time between subsequent gatings. Note that the 4051 can accept up to 8 inputs, so that the second output stage of U3 (100 seconds) and the 2^7 output of the 4060 (1.2 milliseconds) could also be included in the gating selection with a larger switch.

The power supply is conventional with a full-wave bridge and an IC regulator. The bridge could be replaced by a single unit instead of four individual diodes. Be sure that the +5 V line on each board is bypassed by a 10-μF tantalum capacitor and that each counter IC is bypassed individually by 0.01-μF disc capacitors for noise immunity.

Our version of the counter was constructed on four boards: preamp, time base (and 74S196/74LS75), display, and power supply. Wire-wrap techniques were used and the final product was placed in a Radio Shack 270-270 cabinet.

To interface this counter to a computer, bring the 24 latched BCD lines to a back 25-pin connector along with a ground lead. The latch signal should also be available to the computer as you should not read the data while latching occurs. The computer should control the time base selection (add a DPDT toggle switch to change from manual to automatic time base select) and a reset signal to start counting (use one of the unused NAND gates in a similar manner to U7C).

7.5 A MICROPROCESSOR PULSE COUNTER

A high-speed pulse-counting board has been designed and built by Kephart.[13] This versatile board for the S-100 microcomputer bus satisfies the need for high time resolution (1 millisecond) for lunar occultation work and for moderate time resolution (0.1 second to several minutes) for multichannel applications.

Because of the complexity of the board and the fact that it is designed around a specific computer system (an 8080 with the S-100 bus), we do not give a complete schematic. Rather, Figure 7.8 shows a block diagram of the basic circuit in sufficient detail so that its logic can be implemented in other designs.

Two 21-bit counters are used as data counters. They each use one-half of a high-speed 74S112 J-K flip-flop for the least significant bit (LSB), with the pulse input routed to the J input and a control select signal to the K input. The remaining 20 bits are obtained from a 74197 and two 74393 binary counters. A third 16-bit counter using two 74393 ICs is used for interval timing.

For the millisecond time resolution application, the two data counters are used in a double-buffer mode to reduce the dead-time to a few nanoseconds of gate propagation time. One counter is disabled, read, and cleared while the other counter is acquiring data; at the end of the counting period the roles of the two counters are reversed. Dual-channel counting is performed by disabling, reading, and clearing both counters simultaneously, resulting in a dead-time of a few tens of microseconds per readout.

Communication with the microcomputer is through two parallel I/O ports (implemented on the pulse-counting board with Intel 8212 chips) and an interrupt instruction latch. One of the output ports from the microprocessor is used as a counting control latch. The other output port is used to set a comparison latch (with 7485 comparators) for the third onboard interval timer counter. An input port to the microcomputer is used to transfer any selected eight-bit byte from either 21-bit data counter to the CPU. The multiplexing is accomplished with 8T97 tri-state buffers. The CPU can be interrupted by the board, indicating to the CPU that service to the board is required.

The counting control latch byte from the CPU to the board is used to select functions of the pulse-counting board. From information written into the counting control latch, either interrupts or pulse counters

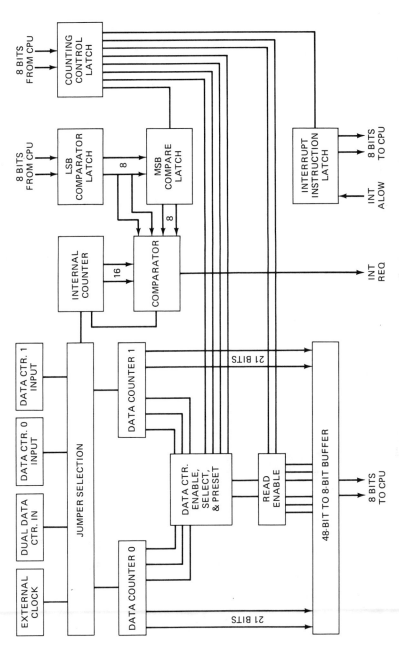

Figure 7.8. Block diagram of photon counting board. Published in the Proceedings of The Society of Photo-Optical Instrumentation Engineers, Volume 172, *Instrumentation in Astronomy III*, Bellingham, Washington.

or both can be disabled, counter selection (determining which counter is in the read mode) can be made, complete board reset or individual counter resets can be performed, byte selection between the MSB and LSB of the interval comparison latch, and byte selection for reading the 21-bit counters can be made.

The interval counter can be used to count either an external clock pulse or a signal from the S-100 bus. By setting the desired interval through software into the interval counter comparison latch, time resolution can be controlled by the user. The board creates an interrupt when the interval counter reaches the number held in the interval counter latch. This counter has 16-bit resolution allowing up to 65,535 clock pulses to be counted per interval. If a millisecond clock is used, then intervals from 0.001 to 65.535 seconds can be selected. This design allows the user to select the desired time resolution using interrupt control. The CPU can be used to display real-time data, reduce a previous observation, or perform any other desired task until an interrupt is issued from the pulse counting board, at which time the board is serviced and the CPU then returns to its previous task.

Figure 7.9. Microprocessor pulse counter.

Construction is straightforward, using wire-wrap techniques on a Vector prototype design board. As constructed, the board would cost about $125. Figure 7.9 shows the finished pulse counter. A second-generation counter would use the Intel 8255 triple-port I/0 chips to decrease chip density and power consumption. Such a microprocessor-controlled pulse-counting board demonstrates the versatility that can be achieved with a computer–pulse counting marriage.

7.6 PULSE GENERATORS

A useful piece of test equipment for the photometrist is the pulse generator. It produces pulses of known frequency, height, and duration that can be used to test frequency counters and preamps.

An example of a commercial pulse generator is the Continental Specialties Corporation[14] model 4001 (under $200). It has a frequency range of 0.5 Hz to 5 MHz, with pulses 100 mV to 10 V high and 100 nanoseconds to 1 second wide. Other generators are available from large manufacturers like Hewlett-Packard with tighter specifications and more ranges.

However, for testing photomultiplier preamps, pulses of −5.0 mV are desirable. A simple pulser satisfying this need is shown in Figure 7.10. Constructed at the Indiana University electronic shop, this pulser puts out a 5.0-mV, 500-nanosecond negative pulse to a 50-ohm load. This is a simple, inexpensive way to test a photomultiplier preamp. The

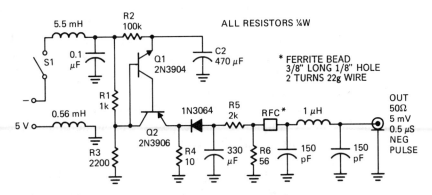

Figure 7.10. Simple pulse generator.

transistors Q1 and Q2 generate a ramp, with R2 and C2 controlling the ramp frequency. The R4/C2 pair provide the decay time of the ramp and D1 shapes the pulse. A voltage divider is formed by R5/R6, providing the 0.5-mV output pulse.

7.7 SETUP AND OPERATION

Pulse-counting systems are very sensitive to stray capacitances and noise. Stray impulses caused by heaters, motors, and relays turning on and off, along with other sources, are counted by the pulse counter and preamp just as if they came from the photomultiplier tube itself. To prevent this interference, connect the preamp solidly to the photomultiplier tube assembly. This keeps the interconnecting cable as short as possible and creates a common ground plane. Bypass all power leads with LC circuits to route all high-frequency interference to ground.

RG58 coaxial cable should be connected between the tube and the preamp, and again between the preamp and the pulse counter. RG58 coax matches the input and output impedances of the preamp properly, and if connected to the 50-ohm input of a pulse counter will present proper termination to the preamp. If the coax is not terminated with 50 ohms, there will be a mismatch, and the fast pulses will be reflected back and forth giving rise to "ringing," where the pulse counter will count several pulses for each actual pulse from the preamp.

The discriminator level adjustment is one of trial and error. For an uncooled 1P21 tube, the final count rate for dark current should be about 200 counts per second. For a dry ice cooled tube, adjust the discriminator to allow about one or two counts per second. Taylor suggests that his preamp can be adjusted by attaching the preamp to a counter (but with no photomultiplier attached) and increasing the discriminator bias by the potentiometer until the discriminator oscillates. Then back off on the bias until first the oscillation and then the stray counts from amplifier-noise peaks cease. You still have to make final adjustments at the telescope to get optimum noise discrimination.

Setting the high voltage for an optimum signal-to-noise ratio is easier than in the case of DC amplifiers. First expose the photomultiplier tube to a constant light source (starlight for example) and then increase the voltage in steps of about 100 V. The observed count rate increases rapidly until a plateau is reached at which the count rate from the source increases only slightly with increased voltage. Further increases in voltage serve no useful purpose; generally the dark current rises with no significant corresponding increases in signal count. For the 1P21 photometers in use at Indiana University, we have found that a high voltage around −900 to −950 V is optimum. To avoid dead-time effects during the voltage increase, pick a source that should eventually yield about 100,000 counts per second.

REFERENCES

1. EG & G Princeton Applied Research, P. O. Box 2565, Princeton, NJ 08540.
2. Hamamatsu Corp. 420 South Ave., Middlesex, NJ 08846.
3. Products for Research, Inc., 88 Holten St., Danvers, MA 01923.
4. Amptek, Inc., 6 De Angelo Dr., Bedford, MA 01730.
5. DuPuy, D. L. 1981. *Pub A.S.P.,* **93**, 144.
6. Taylor, D. J. 1972. *Pub. A. S. P.* **84**, 379.
7. Taylor, D. J. 1980. *Pub. A. S. P.* **92**, 108.
8. ITT Pomona Electronics, 1500 E. Ninth St., Pomona, CA 91766.
9. Optoelectronics Inc., 5821 N.E. 14th Ave. Ft. Lauderdale, FL 33334.
10. Heath Co., Benton Harbor, MI 49022.
11. Hal-Tronix, P. O. Box 1101, Southgate, MI 48195.
12. Intersil Inc., 10710 N. Tantau Ave., Cupertino, CA 95014.
13. Honeycutt, R. K., Kephart, J. E., and Henden, A. A., 1979. In *Instrumentation in Astronomy III.* Edited by D. L. Crawford. Society of Photo-Optical Instrumentation Engineers Proceedings, **172**, 408.
14. Continental Specialties Corporation, P. O. Box 1942, New Haven, CT 06509.

CHAPTER 8
DC ELECTRONICS

The photomultiplier tube is a high-gain current amplifier. For each electron released at the photocathode by a detected photon, about one million electrons are collected at the anode. A stream of incident photons generates a series of closely spaced bursts of current at the anode. In the pulse-counting mode, the goal is to count these bursts over a selected time interval. In the DC technique, the current is not resolved into bursts of current, but instead is averaged to give a continuous current. Despite the large amplification of the tube, the output current is extremely small and requires further amplification so that it can be measured easily. This current amplifier must be extremely linear because the photomultiplier's output current is directly proportional to the incident light flux. The 1P21 photomultiplier has a typical dark current of 10^{-9} A at room temperature. The amplifier should be capable of raising this to an easily measurable value, of about 1 mA (10^{-3} A). Thus, the amplifier should have a current gain of 10^6. This is easily achieved with some very simple electronics. On the other hand, the photodiode has an internal gain of unity and therefore requires an amplifier of much higher gain. This presents some special amplifier design problems, as discussed by Persha.[1] To date, very little has been published about amplifier designs for photodiodes used as astronomical detectors. For this reason, we restrict this chapter to an amplifier designed for use with a photomultiplier tube.

At this point, a very brief review of operational amplifiers (op amps) is needed. A more complete and lucid discussion of this topic can be found in the book by Melen and Garland.[2] The following discussion assumes a background in elementary electronics.

8.1 OPERATIONAL AMPLIFIERS

A few years ago, an *operational amplifier* was large, costly, fragile, and had a rather large power consumption. A modern op amp can be fabricated on a tiny silicon chip at a cost of a few dollars. Each chip may contain the equivalent of dozens of transistors, resistors, and capacitors. The details of the internal operation are not necessary for the present discussion. Figure 8.1 shows the symbol for an op amp. The op amp is a high-gain voltage amplifier. The "−" terminal is called the *inverting input* and the "+" terminal is called the *noninverting input*. An increasing voltage applied to the inverting input results in a decreasing voltage at the output (E_{out}). The same voltage applied to the noninverting input results in an increasing voltage at the output. If the same signal voltage was applied simultaneously to both inputs, the two amplified signals would be 180° out of phase and would cancel each other completely. The output is the amplified voltage difference between the two inputs. The output is unaffected by voltage changes that occur at both inputs; only the difference is amplified. It is sufficient for most of this discussion to consider the op amp to have "ideal" characteristics, namely infinite input impedance, infinite voltage gain, and zero output impedance. Figure 8.2 shows the op amp used as an inverting *voltage* amplifier. The *open-loop gain, A,* is defined as

$$A = \frac{E_{out}}{E_{in}}$$

where E_{in} and E_{out} are the input and output voltages, respectively. For an ideal op amp, A is infinite. For a practical op amp, A is 10^4 to 10^6. Real input impedances are typically 100 kΩ but the input impedance of op amps utilizing FETs can reach 10^{12} ohms or more. A typical output impedance is 50 ohms.

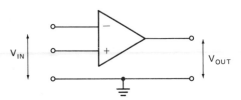

Figure 8.1. Op amp symbol.

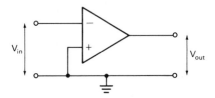

Figure 8.2. Voltage amplifier.

With the background developed above, it is now possible to discuss how the op amp is used as a *current* amplifier for DC photometry. Figure 8.3 shows a simplified current amplifier circuit. This particular type of circuit is *not* recommended. It is illustrated here as an example of a circuit design to be avoided. This type of circuit has been used in astronomical photometry in the past without a general appreciation of its inherent inaccuracy. An example of this type of circuit can be found in Wood.[3] We do not discuss the operation of this circuit except to point out the source of the problem. An input current from the photomultiplier tube, I_i, flows through R_L to ground instead of entering the higher-impedance amplifier. This elevates the potential at point B to $I_i R_L$. This means that the potential difference between the anode of the photomultiplier and ground has been changed slightly. The amount of change depends on I_i, which in turn depends on the brightness of the star. Young[4] has shown that this can result in a nonlinear tube response of a few tenths of a percent. This is a small error, but it need not be tolerated because there is a very simple solution. Circuits that use an anode load resistor should be avoided. The anode should always see ground potential directly.

Figure 8.4 illustrates the necessary circuit. In this type of circuit point a, the input seen by the anode, is always very nearly at ground potential. To see this, suppose a small positive external voltage, E_i, is applied at

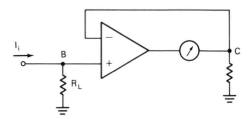

Figure 8.3. Current amplifier (not recommended).

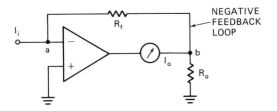

Figure 8.4. Current amplifier utilizing virtual ground.

the inverting input. This results in a negative output voltage, E_o. The output is connected, via the feedback loop, to the inverting input. The total input voltage at point a, E_a, is then

$$E_a = E_i + E_o. \tag{8.1}$$

The output voltage, E_o, is related to the input, E_a, and the voltage gain, A, by

$$E_o = -AE_a.$$

The minus sign results from the use of the inverting input. Combining the above two equations yields

$$E_i = E_a(1 + A).$$

By Equation 8.1,

$$E_o = E_a - E_i$$
$$= E_a - E_a(1 + A).$$

Thus the input and output voltage are related by

$$\frac{E_o}{E_i} = \frac{E_a - E_a(1 + A)}{E_a(1 + A)} = \frac{-A}{1 + A}.$$

As long as A is a large number, then

$$E_o \simeq -E_i. \tag{8.2}$$

Combining Equations 8.1 and 8.2, we obtain

$$E_a \simeq 0.$$

Point a is said to be at *virtual ground* because it is essentially at ground potential, but current does not flow to ground at this point. The anode of the photomultiplier always sees ground potential when connected to this circuit and the tube linearity is not affected.

Now consider specifically how this circuit is used as a current amplifier. An input current from the photomultiplier flows through resistors R_f and R_o to ground. Only a negligible amount of current enters the amplifier because of its very high input impedance. Because R_o is always made very small compared to R_f, point a would seem to be at a potential of $I_i R_f$ with respect to ground. This cannot happen, by our discussion above. By Equation 8.2, the voltage at point b must be $-I_i R_f$. This potential results in current flowing between the amplifier output, resistor R_o, and ground. This output current, I_o, must be related to the input current by

$$I_i R_f = -I_o R_o$$

or

$$I_o = -I_i \frac{R_f}{R_o}. \tag{8.3}$$

There is a linear amplification value that depends on the ratio of these two resistors and not on the characteristics of the op amp itself. While this is strictly true only for an ideal amplifier, it does show that a circuit that is very insensitive to changes within the op amp can be built. It would be very difficult to find an op amp with amplification stable enough for photometry, especially with the large temperature changes found in an observatory, if the feedback loop were not utilized. Even so, it is advisable to purchase a high-quality op amp to insure stability.

8.2 AN OP-AMP DC AMPLIFIER

Figure 8.5 shows a practical DC amplifier circuit. The op amp used is a Sylvania ECG 940 which has an FET input with an impedance of

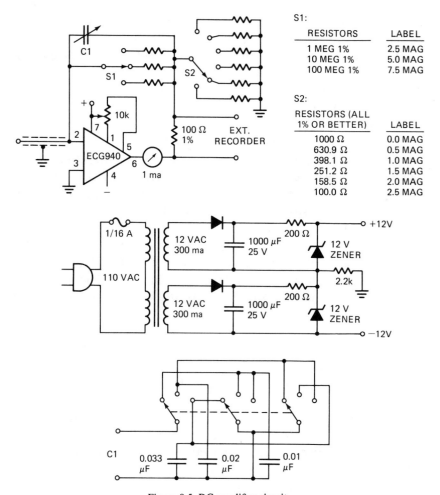

S1:

RESISTORS	LABEL
1 MEG 1%	2.5 MAG
10 MEG 1%	5.0 MAG
100 MEG 1%	7.5 MAG

S2:

RESISTORS (ALL 1% OR BETTER)	LABEL
1000 Ω	0.0 MAG
630.9 Ω	0.5 MAG
398.1 Ω	1.0 MAG
251.2 Ω	1.5 MAG
158.5 Ω	2.0 MAG
100.0 Ω	2.5 MAG

Figure 8.5. DC amplifier circuit.

about 10^{12} ohms and an open-loop gain of 10^6. This amplifier has a specified operating range from 0° to 70°C (32° to 158°F), which means that the amplifier must be kept warm in the winter. This is not a big disadvantage because it is always a good idea to operate the electronics at a constant temperature to avoid drift. Other op amps with a wider temperature range, such as the Analog Devices AD523K can be used. This latter device has a range from −55° to +125°C, but costs twice as much.

The resistors R_f and R_o have been replaced by switches that allow various combinations of resistors, and hence, various combinations of current gain to be selected. To make the gain large, the resistors on switch S1 (R_f) must be made large and those on switch S2 (R_o) rather small. The 1-megohm resistor of switch S1 is used for the brightest stars and the 100-megohm resistor is used for the faintest stars. As discussed in Section 6.2, the 1P21 shows fatigue effects if the tube current exceeds 10^{-6} A. Because our amplifier does not give a direct readout of the tube current, it would be advantageous to have some safety mechanism to let us know when this level is reached. The simplest approach is to design the amplifier so that a tube current of 10^{-6} A yields a full-scale deflection on the amplifier meter when the lowest gain setting is used. Because a full-scale reading on the meter is 10^{-3} A, the lowest current gain should be 10^3. This sets the value of the largest R_o resistor at 1000 ohms by Equation 8.3, since the lowest R_f is 10^6. The remaining resistors in switch S2 decrease in 0.5 magnitude steps; that is each is smaller than its predecessor by a factor of 0.6310. The resistors in switch S1 change by a factor of 10, yielding 2.5 magnitude steps. With the highest current gain ($R_f = 10^8$, $R_o = 10^2$), an input current of 10^{-9} A, which is the dark current of the 1P21 at room temperature, gives a full-scale deflection.

If you intend to use this amplifier with a cooled photomultiplier tube, one or two more resistors should be added to switch S1 with values of 1000 and 10,000 megohms, respectively. These resistors are required to take advantage of the reduction (by a factor of 100) in dark current, which allows much fainter stars, and hence, much lower currents to be measured. Unlike the idealized case, an actual op amp draws a small amount of input current during operation. This is referred to as the *input bias current*. This current itself can be a noise source just like the dark current from the photomultiplier. The op amp used in this circuit has an input bias current of 10^{-10} A, which is 10 times less than the dark current from an uncooled 1P21 and is therefore negligible. If you use a cooled tube, however, the bias current will become the dominant noise source when measuring faint stars. If you plan to use a cooled tube, the op amp in Figure 8.5 should be replaced by one with an input bias current of 10^{-12} A or less. Such op amps are available but are more expensive.

The feedback resistors have large values to achieve high amplifier gain and to minimize noise. Thermal (or Johnson) noise in these resistors varies with the square root of the resistance. Large values of R_f make this noise small compared to the current to be measured. The feedback resistors, R_f, should be accurate to 1 percent or better. Victoreen Instrument Company[5] can supply high-megohm resistors in glass encapsulation for the required accuracy. The R_o resistors have much lower values of resistance, which makes them inherently more stable, and they need not be glass-encapsulated. However, they should be accurate to 1 percent or better, because precision resistors are more stable than ordinary carbon resistors. It is impossible to find 1 percent resistors that equal the listed values exactly, so the values should be matched within 10 percent. A perfect match is not necessary because the amplifier is calibrated after construction.

The 10 kΩ potentiometer in Figure 8.5 is used to balance the circuit so that a zero input current produces a zero output current. An ordinary one-turn pot can be used but a five-turn pot makes circuit balancing much easier, especially at the high-gain settings. The purpose of selector switch C1 is to add a time constant that helps to smooth variations resulting from atmospheric scintillation and tube noise. A disadvantage of this circuit is that the time constant varies with the S1 switch position. The time constant, which is the product of R_f and C1, is negligible at the lowest gain setting and becomes significant only on the highest setting. Table 8.1 lists the time constant for each combination of R_f and C1. The capacitor values in this circuit can be changed to obtain other time constants. The variation in time constant with R_f is not a serious problem because larger time constants are preferred when higher gain settings are in use. It would be more convenient to be able to use the same time constant for all gain settings. The circuit designed by Oliver[6] avoids this problem by using a second op amp, of unity gain, connected to the output of the first op amp. This second amplifier drives the meter and any external recorder. It also has its own adjustable RC time constant in its feedback loop, which is independent of R_f in the first amplifier.

Selector switch C1 is wired so that each capacitor is shorted when

TABLE 8.1. Amplifier Time
Constants

R_f\C1	0.01 µF	0.02 µF	0.03 µF
1 Meg	0.01 sec	0.02 sec	0.03 sec
10 Meg	0.1	0.2	0.3
100 Meg	1.0	2.0	3.0

Figure 8.6. The DC amplifier, front view (top), and rear view (bottom).

not in use. This prevents some unwanted voltage spike from appearing at the amplifier input when a new capacitor is switched into the circuit. The 100-ohm resistor in the output circuit produces a voltage drop for an external chart recorder. An output of 1 mA produces a 100-mV drop, which produces a full-scale reading on a 100-mV chart recorder. The value of this resistor may be changed for recorders with different full-scale sensitivity.

The power supply circuit is taken from Stokes.[7] He found this simple zener-regulated design adequate for an earlier DC amplifier design. Both the amplifier and power supply can be built into one small chassis. Figure 8.6 shows a photograph of the completed unit, which is small enough to be mounted directly on the telescope if so desired.

There are two important comments to be made about the operation of this amplifier. First, FET devices, such as the op amp in this circuit, are damaged easily by an electrostatic charge at the input. As a precaution, always turn the amplifier on before connecting the signal cable. This prevents damage from any charge accumulated by the cable. Also, be careful when handling the op amp in a dry-air environment. Always "discharge" yourself by touching a ground, such as a water pipe, before handling the op amp. The second comment concerns zero-point drift. During the first 20 minutes of operation, there is substantial drift on the high-gain settings. It is therefore a good idea to turn on the electronics at least one-half hour before observing.

The circuit presented here is inexpensive and very simple to build. A more advanced circuit has been designed by Oliver.[6] As already mentioned, this circuit handles the time constant problem nicely. It has some other valuable features such as an internal constant current source for calibration and sky background cancellation. Although these extra features increase the cost, this circuit should be seriously considered by the advanced observer.

8.3 CHART RECORDERS AND METERS

Once your amplifier, high-voltage supply, and photometer head are built, you are ready to begin making some measurements. The question then arises as to the method of recording the data. The simplest technique is to read the amplifier meter and record the measurement with pencil and paper. To achieve good photometric accuracy, you must be able to read the meter to an accuracy of at least 1 percent. This is obviously not possible with the tiny edge meter seen in Figure 8.6. This meter was intended to be used only to monitor the functioning of the amplifier. If you plan to "meter read," you must invest in a larger meter of good quality. The minimum size should be 7.5 centimeters (3 inches) or preferably larger. The meter should have a quoted accuracy of 1 percent or better at full scale. Meters with a mirrored scale are preferred because they minimize parallax. The meter can be mounted in the amplifier chassis or in its own separate chassis connected to the amplifier with a cable. The later arrangement is convenient if you plan to mount the amplifier on the telescope. If you plan to take measurements with a meter, invest in a good one.

The disadvantages to meter reading are obvious. Atmospheric scintillation causes the needle position to jitter, making estimates difficult. The problem is complicated by observer fatigue, especially after 3 a.m.! Above all, there is no permanent record of the actual meter output. If the meter reading is written incorrectly, the observation is lost forever. Any DC observer who can afford it quickly invests in a *strip-chart recorder*. A strip-chart recorder consists of a device that drives a long roll of chart paper under a pen whose transverse displacement across the width of the paper is proportional to the input voltage. This device reduces the amount of effort required at the telescope. The observer needs only to write comments on the paper occasionally such as the amplifier gain or the time. Because the chart paper advances at a constant rate, the time of any observation can be found by interpolation. The chart record can be studied by an alert observer the following day. A permanent record exists that can be checked if an observation fails to reduce properly. Figure 9.9 illustrates the appearance of a chart recording for a series of observations.

There are a number of characteristics you should look for in a chart recorder to be used for photometry. There are a number of small and inexpensive models on the market. Unfortunately, these units must use narrow paper. This limits the accuracy to which the pen tracing can be read. It is best to buy a recorder that uses chart paper at least 25 centimeters (10 inches) wide. The recorder should be a DC voltmeter type with a range from zero to a few hundred millivolts. The latter value is not critical because the resistor in the output circuit of Figure 8.5 can be changed. A 100-mV input is used commonly by chart recorder manufacturers. The accuracy of the recorder at full scale should be at least one percent. Recorders with 0.5 percent accuracy are readily available. Finally, the chart speed must be considered. Most recorders have an adjustable speed. Experience has shown that a speed of 1 to 5 centimeters per minute is a good choice for most kinds of photometry. Be sure that the recorder you consider has a speed in this range.

There are many companies that manufacture chart recorders to meet the above criteria. Examples are the Markson Science Incorporated[8] model 5740, the Cole-Parmer Instrument[9] models C-8386-32 and C-8373-00, the Hewlett-Packard[10] model 7131A, and the Heath[11] model

IR-18M. This is just a very short list and the inclusion or omission of a company's name does not constitute an endorsement or criticism of their products. This list is merely a starting place for the would-be chart recorder owner. Unfortunately, all of these recorders, with the exception of the Heath IR-18M, cost over $700. This price is certainly beyond a limited budget. Consequently, most amateur astronomers have turned to the less expensive $230 Heath recorder. This recorder is not so strong mechanically as the other recorders but it does meet all of the selection criteria listed above. Experience has shown that this recorder, as most others, does not function well in the cold, winterlike environment of an observatory. A small heated enclosure solves the problem nicely. If you plan to do a lot of DC photometry, a strip-chart recorder is a very worthwhile investment.

8.4 VOLTAGE-TO-FREQUENCY CONVERTERS

One of the advantages of pulse counting over DC is the digital output, which frees the observer from making amplifier gain adjustments and calibrations. There is another approach to DC photometry that has these same attributes. The traditional DC amplifier is replaced by a voltage-to-frequency converter (VFC) circuit. The basic idea is to convert the current output of the photomultiplier to voltage which can serve as the input of a voltage-controlled oscillator. This oscillator has a frequency that varies linearly with the input voltage. The output of this oscillator is fed to a frequency counter in exactly the same way the output of a pulse amplifier is when pulse counting (see Sections 7.3 and 7.4).

The VFC design of Dunham and Elliot[12] is shown in Figure 8.7. The current from the photomultiplier tube is converted to a voltage by the first op amp. If the signal is weak, a second op amp is switched into the circuit for additional amplification. This voltage is applied to the input of a voltage-controlled oscillator. This single-chip device produces an output frequency of 10^5 Hz per volt at the input. The frequency counter is not shown in Figure 8.7. Before constructing this circuit, you should consult Dunham and Elliot for valuable commentary. The purpose for showing this circuit is to emphasize its simplicity. It is also possible to use a voltage-controlled oscillator and frequency counter with a conventional DC amplifier. This is certainly better than meter reading and may be less expensive than a chart recorder.

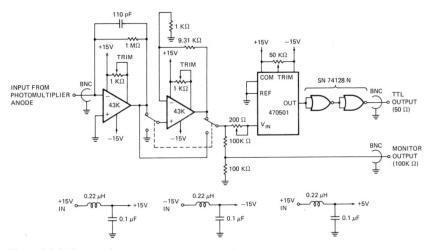

Figure 8.7. Voltage to frequency converter circuit diagram. The current to voltage converter is at left followed by the optional gain of 10.3 amplifier. The 470501 is the voltage controlled oscillator and the NOR gates on the right are line drivers. The filters at the bottom are lowpass power supply filters. Courtesy of the *Publications* of the Astronomical Society of the Pacific.

The VFC approach has some definite advantages over the conventional DC amplifier. There are fewer gain switches to adjust, which is especially valuable when light levels change very rapidly as occurs during occultation photometry. This also does away with the need for frequent amplifier gain calibration. Unlike pulse counting, there are no dead-time corrections to be made, and the digital output does away with the tedium of reading chart recorder tracings. However, unless you have some recording device such as a minicomputer with a disk drive and/or a printer, there is no permanent record of an observation. One approach that has been used by McGraw et al.[13] is to record the output frequency on magnetic tape as an audio signal. Then, as with a chart recorder, observations can be reviewed the following day. Finally, it must be kept in mind that just because you get a digital output from a VFC, this does not mean that you are photon counting. This is still DC photometry and the conclusion of Section K.5b still applies; the signal-to-noise ratio of DC photometry is inferior to pulse counting.

8.5 CONSTANT CURRENT SOURCES

The most common method of calibration of a DC amplifier requires a constant input current. In principle, the photomultiplier tube could be

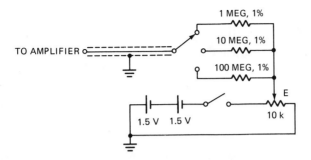

Figure 8.8. Constant current source.

used by exposing it to a constant light source, but in practice such a source is difficult to find. For instance, the brightness of an ordinary light bulb is very sensitive to changes in line voltage. Furthermore, an uncooled tube introduces noise that limits the accuracy of the calibration. A much better approach is to build a constant current source. Figure 8.8 shows such a circuit, which is extremely simple to build. The rotary switch and the potentiometer are used to adjust the current. The resistors used on this switch are the same value as those used on switch S1 of Figure 8.5. The rotary switch steps the current by factors of 10 just as switch S1 steps the amplifier gain by factors of 10. The 10 kΩ potentiometer is for fine adjustment of the current. Because the amplifier input is a virtual ground, the calibration current is given by E/R, where E is the voltage at the potentiometer wiper, 0 to 3 V, and R is the value of the rotary switch resistor. This circuit draws very little current, so two ordinary 1.5-V batteries comprise a sufficient power supply. We now describe how this circuit is used to calibrate the amplifier.

8.6 CALIBRATION AND OPERATION

The current gain of a DC amplifier is established by the resistors associated with its gain switches. The accuracy of your photometry depends, in part, on an accurate knowledge of the gain differences between switch positions. The actual sizes of these gain steps must be measured for two other reasons. First, it is very difficult to find resistors that exactly match the required values for 0.5 magnitude steps. Second, resistors tend to change value with time. This is especially true for the feedback resistors with values exceeding 10^8 ohms. This means that the calibration of the amplifier must be checked regularly. The frequency of these calibrations depends upon the quality of the resistors and their storage environment. Initially, you should plan to do a calibration every few months. You may find this is too frequent if the calibration appears to change little. On the other hand, you may find this is not frequent enough if significant calibration changes are seen. If calibration drifts seem to be associated with just one switch position, you may wish to replace that resistor with a more stable one.

There are usually two approaches to the amplifier calibration. The first measures the resistances of the amplifier resistors with a laboratory Wheatstone bridge. It is best to make these measurements with the resistors actually in place in the circuit. The process of cutting the resistor leads and soldering them to the switch may alter their values slightly. As a rule, most commonly found Wheatstone bridges cannot measure the large megohm resistors found in the feedback loop. Unfortunately, it is these large resistors that tend to be the most unstable. The second approach uses a constant current source. This has the advantage that you actually measure the amplifier gain directly and both gain switches can be calibrated by this process. We now describe the calibration using a constant current source in detail.

The actual calibration procedure is quite simple. Turn the amplifier on at least 30 minutes early to minimize drift while measurements are being taken. The fine gain steps are calibrated first. Place the coarse gain switch to its lowest position (2.5) and connect the constant current source to the amplifier input. Turn the fine gain switch to its lowest position (0.0) and adjust the rotary switch of the current source to its highest position, that is, the 1-megohm position. Turn the current source on and adjust its potentiometer to obtain an amplifier meter deflection of about one-half of full scale. Record the reading, turn the current source off, and record the zero-point level. Turn the current source on and repeat the process. Once a half dozen measurement pairs have been taken, increase the fine gain setting by one step (0.5 magnitude) and repeat the entire process. The ratio of the net deflections at these two switch positions yields the actual magnitude difference.

With the fine gain set at 0.5 magnitude, adjust the current source to reduce the meter reading to about half scale and take another series of readings at 0.5 and 1.0 magnitude. The entire process is repeated until measurements have been made at every fine gain switch position. In Table 8.2, we have listed a set of calibration readings. To save space, only one measurement per switch position is shown.

The next step is to subtract the zero-point readings to obtain the net

TABLE 8.2.   Data for Fine Calibration

Gain Position	Deflection	Zero Point	Net	Magnitude Difference
0.0	48.6	7.1	41.5	
0.5	74.8	6.3	68.5	0.544
0.5	57.3	6.3	51.2	
1.0	86.9	5.3	81.6	0.506
1.0	53.8	5.2	48.6	
1.5	82.4	4.3	78.1	0.515
1.5	58.9	4.3	54.6	
2.0	90.4	3.8	86.6	0.501
2.0	58.1	3.8	54.3	
2.5	90.5	3.8	86.7	0.508

deflection for each measurement. Finally, the magnitude difference between each switch position is calculated by

$$\Delta m = 2.5 \log (d_H / d_L),$$

where d_H and d_L are the net deflection at the high and low gains, respectively. These values are listed in the last column in Table 8.2. You have about a half dozen such values for each switch position pair. If you determine an average and compute the standard deviation of the mean, you will have the best estimate of the gain difference and its error. You should strive to obtain a standard deviation of less than 0.005 magnitude. With the amplifier in Figure 8.5 and the current source of Figure 8.6, a standard deviation of 0.002 magnitude was easily obtained in laboratory tests.

The next step is to use these magnitude differences to construct a gain table. This table is used during data reduction. It allows the researcher to find the gain difference between any two switch positions at a glance. Table 8.3 shows a gain table constructed from the magnitude differences listed in Table 8.2. The horizontal and vertical axes are the gain positions. For example, to find the gain difference between the 1.5 and the 0.5 positions we simply look to where the "1.5 row" intersects the "0.5 column" and read 1.021 magnitudes. The entries in this table were determined by simply summing the magnitude differences of Table 8.2 between each combination of switch positions.

TABLE 8.3. Gain Table for Fine
Adjustment Switch

	0.0	0.5	1.0	1.5	2.0
2.5	2.574	2.030	1.524	1.009	0.508
2.0	2.066	1.522	1.016	0.501	
1.5	1.565	1.021	0.515		
1.0	1.050	0.506			
0.5	0.544				

Once the fine gain switch positions have been calibrated, the coarse positions can be calibrated with respect to them. The rotary switch of the constant current source is placed in the next position (10-megohm resistor) with both the coarse and fine gain set to 2.5. Again the series of measurements are made. The fine gain is then reduced to 0.0 and the coarse gain increased to 5.0. Another set of measurements is then made. In Table 8.4, we list a sample measurement. If the amplifier had a perfect set of resistors, these two sets of measurements would be identical because the total gain of the two switches is the same (5.0). The rotary switch of the current source is moved to the last position (100-megohm resistor) and the procedure is repeated. The first set of measurements is taken with the coarse gain at 5.0 and the fine gain at 2.5. For the second set, the coarse and fine gains are set to 7.5 and 0.0, respectively.

Once the net deflections have been calculated, the first step is to correct for the fact that the fine gain difference is not exactly 2.5 magnitudes. According to Table 8.3, the gain difference between the 0.0 and 2.5 position is actually 2.574. Because this gain is larger than it should be, the deflections taken when the fine gain was set to 2.5 need to be corrected downward. If D_H is the net deflection, then the corrected deflection, D_H^*, is given by

$$D_H^* = D_H \, 10^{-0.4(\Delta f - 2.5)},$$

where Δf is the actual magnitude difference of the fine gain control (2.574). The results appear in column 6 of Table 8.4. Finally, the true coarse gain differences, Δm, can be calculated by

$$\Delta m = 2.500 - 2.5 \log (D_H^*/D_L)$$

TABLE 8.4. Data for Coarse Gain Calibration

Gain Coarse	Fine	Deflection	Zero Point	Net	D_H^*	Δm
2.5	2.5	72.2	14.8	57.4	53.6	
5.0	0.0	75.4	21.2	54.2		2.512
5.0	2.5	83.4	15.2	68.2	63.7	
7.5	0.0	83.2	21.4	61.8		2.467

where D_L is the net deflection obtained when the fine gain is set to 0.0. The coarse gain differences appear in the last column of Table 8.4.

The operation of the amplifier is straightforward, requiring only a little care and common sense. This is a sensitive device that should be used only to measure the output of the photomultiplier tube or the constant current source. As mentioned earlier, the amplifier should be turned on before connecting the signal cable as a precaution against damaging the FET input of the op amp. Finally, when measuring an unknown star for the first time, begin at the lowest gain setting. Gradually increase the gain until the desired deflection is reached. This procedure avoids possible damage to your meter or chart recorder if a bright star is measured with a gain setting that is too high.

REFERENCES

1. Persha, G., 1980. *IAPPP Com.* **2**, 11.
2. Melen, R. and Garland, H. 1971. *Understanding IC Operational Amplifiers.* Indianapolis: Howard W. Sams and Co.
3. Wood, F. B. 1963. *Photoelectric Astronomy for Amateurs.* New York: Macmillan, p. 70.
4. Young, A. T. 1974. In *Methods of Experimental Physics: Astrophysics.* vol. **12A**. Edited by N. Carleton. New York: Academic Press, p. 52.
5. The Victoreen Instrument Company, 10101 Woodland Ave., Cleveland, OH 44104.
6. Oliver, J. P., 1975. *Pub. A. S. P.* **87**, 217.
7. Stokes, A. J., 1972. *J. AAVSO* **1**, 60.
8. Markson Science Inc., 565 Oak St., Box 767, Del Mar, CA 92014.
9. Cole-Parmer Instrument Co., 7425 N. Oak Park Ave., Chicago IL 60648.
10. Hewlett-Packard Co., 5201 Tollview Dr., Rolling Meadows, IL 60008.
11. Heath Co., Benton Harbor, MI 49022.
12. Dunham, E., and Elliot, J. L. 1978. *Pub. A. S. P.* **90**, 119.
13. McGraw, J. T., Wells, D. C., and Wiant, J. R. 1973. *Rev. Sci. Inst.* **44**, 748.

CHAPTER 9
PRACTICAL OBSERVING TECHNIQUES

Chapters 1 through 5 present the foundation for understanding photometry and starlight in general, along with the rudiments of data reduction. Chapters 6 through 8 show how to construct or buy the necessary equipment, set it up, and perform the necessary calibrations. We are now ready to discuss using your photometer. This chapter explains in more detail how to perform photometric measurements, from selecting comparison stars and making a finding chart, through the actual acquisition of data. It ends with some comments about sources of error external to your equipment with which you must contend.

No book can replace actual experience with the equipment at hand. We can give you some practical advice and try to guide you past some of the pitfalls that we found, but you must learn much of photometry by trial and error. One suggestion we would like to make is to pick one variable that is bright, short period, and very well observed as your first trial. In this manner, you can be sure that your data compares favorably with previous results.

9.1 FINDING CHARTS

Sirius, Polaris, and other bright stars are easy to find in the sky. Fainter stars become increasingly difficult to find, not only because they are harder to see but also because there are more of them. With care, stars fainter than those visible by eye through a telescope can be measured by photoelectric photometry. Fainter stars, being more difficult to locate, require the use of a good finding chart.

The usual method of identifying program stars is through the preparation of a finding chart: a sketch or photograph of the region of the sky containing the object. You can prepare a finding chart from various atlases, from your own photographs of the area, or by obtaining previously prepared charts from published sources. Each of these methods is described below.

9.1a Available Positional Atlases

Positional atlases are drawn from catalogs of star positions. In many cases, stars are omitted for lack of data or were positioned incorrectly. Still, they can contain more information about the stars than a photograph. Several atlases include stars brighter than eighth magnitude. Most of these atlases have been reviewed by Larson[1] and are readily available. For objects brighter than ninth or tenth magnitude, three atlases are commonly available. They are:

1. *Bonner Durchmusterung (BD) and Córdoba Durchmusterung (CD) Atlases.*[2,3] The BD was produced by Argelander and Schönfeld in the period 1859–1886, covering the northern sky, and the CD was published between 1892 and 1932, covering the southern sky. Together, they contain approximately 580,000 stars to a limiting visual magnitude of 10 and have been the mainstay for almost a century. These catalogs are available at existing libraries and observatories. New copies are available in magnetic tape form only. Epoch 1855 coordinates are used and must be precessed.

2. *The Smithsonian Astrophysical Observatory (SAO) Atlas.*[4] These charts contain approximately the same stars as the BD and CD atlases, but the charts are smaller and stars are plotted closer together on a smaller scale. Most variables brighter than ninth magnitude are marked. All stars are identified in the accompanying catalog, available from the U. S. Government Printing Office. Transparent overlays allow the location of stars with arc minute accuracy. The coordinates are for epoch 1950.

3. *Atlas Borealis, Eclipticalis, and Australis.*[5] These charts by Becvar cover the sky to approximately tenth magnitude and identify variables by their variable star designations. One of the nice features of these charts is the color coding of spectral type. Epoch 1950 coordinates are used with transparent overlays. This atlas set is widely used by amateur astronomers and is relatively inexpensive.

9.1b Available Photographic Atlases

For stars fainter than ninth magnitude, photographic atlases must be used because of the large number of stars involved. These atlases consist of either photo-offset charts from original plates or actual photographic prints. Ingrao and Kasperian[6] review early photographic atlases. The major photographic atlases are listed below.

1. *Photographic Star Atlas (Falkau Atlas).*[7] This atlas used plates that were blue-sensitive and covers the entire sky in two volumes. The limiting magnitude is 13, the scale is 1 millimeter = 4 arc minutes, and each chart is about 10° on a side.
2. *Atlas Stellarum 1950.0.*[8] This atlas covers the entire sky in three volumes using blue-sensitive plates. The limiting magnitude is 14.5, the scale is 1 millimeter = 2 arc minutes, and a complete set of extremely useful transparent overlay grids is included. This atlas costs $225 in 1980.
3. *True Visual Magnitude Photographic Star Atlas.*[9] This atlas is very similar to Atlas Stellarum in that it covers the entire sky in three volumes with the same scale. The limiting magnitude is 13.5, and a green-sensitive emulsion has been used. For finding charts, green sensitivity is a great advantage as it closely matches the response of the eye.
4. *Lick Observatory Sky Atlas (North)*[10] *and Canterbury Sky Atlas (South).*[11] Rather than using the photo-offset methods of the previously listed photographic atlases, these two atlases are actual prints of blue plates. The scale is 1 millimeter = 3.88 arc minutes, the limiting magnitude is 15, and each print covers about 18° on a side. No overlays exist and copies are no longer available except at existing libraries and observatories.
5. *National Geographic–Palomar Observatory Sky Survey (POSS).*[12] This survey with the Palomar 48-inch Schmidt is the Rolls Royce of the astronomical atlases. Both red and blue plates were used, with the atlas consisting of positive prints with a scale of 1 millimeter = 1.1 arc minutes and a limiting magnitude of 20 (red) or 21 (blue). Each print is 6.6° on a side and a sequence of overlays exists, though less useful than most as no fiducial marks are found on the prints. The POSS is complete to −24° declina-

tion, with a red-plate extension to −45°. The plates were taken in the early 1950s, and Palomar intends to redo the survey starting sometime in 1985. A complete set of prints costs several thousand dollars.

6. *The European Southern Observatory (ESO)/Science Research Council (SRC) Atlas of the Southern Sky.*[13] In a similar manner to that of the POSS, the southern sky is presently being photographed by the two large Schmidt telescopes in the Southern Hemisphere.[14] The ESO 1 meter at La Silla is taking red plates and the SRC 1.2 meter at Siding Spring is taking the blue survey plates, both with a scale of 1 millimeter = 1.1 arc minutes and a limiting magnitude of 22. The atlas covers the sky from −90° to −17° declination with plate centers at 5° spacing. This atlas is being released in limited quantities (150 copies) only on 36-centimeter (14-inch) Aerographic Duplicating Film.

9.1c Preparation of Finding Charts

The goal of a finding chart is to allow easy identification of the program object at the telescope. Generally, two charts are prepared. A small-scale chart matching the field of view of the main telescope, typically 15 arc minutes square, should be prepared carefully, including stars two to three magnitudes fainter than the variable. Mark the program object, any nearby comparison stars, and an area with no stars to be used for sky background measurements. Many observers prefer these charts to match exactly the view of the telescope, that is, reversed and/or inverted. Cardinal directions should be indicated as well as the chart scale, perhaps by an angular measurement grid. A large field chart roughly matching the finder can provide pointing information for the main telescope, and at the same time identify photoelectric comparison stars and readily identifiable patterns to help locate the field.

The best charts are Polaroid copies of photographic atlases, negative copies of atlas prints, which can then be enlarged, or prints made from your original negatives of the sky. Direct tracings of atlases or xeroxes may be acceptable provided that the limiting magnitude near the program object, comparison stars, and sky measurement position is sufficiently faint.

9.1d Published Finding Charts

In most cases, earlier observers have published finding charts for your object of interest. These charts may lie in obscure journals or suffer from poor quality. However, it is highly recommended to search for published finding charts of variables fainter than ninth magnitude before preparing your own.

The major source for finding charts is the General Catalog of Variable Stars (GCVS).[15] Its extensive reference list contains chart references for the vast majority of identified variable stars. However, many of these finding charts are published in Russian journals, which are identified only in the Cyrillic alphabet rather than the English transliterated names under which they are cataloged in most major libraries.

There are several collections of finding charts available if the GCVS itself or its referenced charts are not available. These are listed below.

1. *AAVSO Variable Star Atlas.*[16] There are 178 charts in this atlas, measuring 11 × 14 inches with a scale of 15 millimeters per degree. These charts contain all of the American Association of Variable Star Observers' program stars and all variables that reach 10.5 visual magnitudes or brighter at maximum. The charts are very similar to the SAO Atlas.

2. *The Sonneberg charts.*[17] Several thousand variables were discovered at Sonneberg during the early part of the twentieth century. The charts contained in reference 17 cover 3600 of the Sonneberg variables.

3. *The Odessa charts.*[18] This reference contains light curves and finding charts for 266 stars.

4. *Atlas Stellarum Variabilium.*[19] These charts cover all variables brighter than tenth magnitude at minimum that were known by 1930. The entire sky was covered, with each chart measuring 20° on a side and plotting stars to a limiting magnitude of 14.

5. *Charts for Southern Variables.*[20] The 400 charts in this collection were sponsored by the International Astronomical Union and cover all long-period variables brighter than thirteenth magnitude at maximum and south of −30° declination. Later volumes in the series have photoelectric sequences for nearby stars.

6. *Atlas of Finding Charts of Variable Stars.*[21] This work is hard to find in Western libraries.

Goddard Space Flight Center (GSFC) in Greenbelt, Maryland is the distributor for the magnetic tape version of the GCVS. The tape also includes a cross-reference list for the Sonneberg variables, which is extremely helpful. In addition, GSFC can generate POSS Atlas overlays to identify faint variable stars. Write to Code 680 of GSFC for more details.[22]

9.2 COMPARISON STARS

Now that you have located your program star, you need to decide whether or not to use a comparison star in your measurements. These are stars that are near to your variable and are observed immediately before and/or after your program star. Usually, measurements are reported as differential observations, star A minus star B. This difference in the magnitudes is less likely to vary, as conditions that affect one star usually affect the other. Use of comparison stars has several advantages as noted below.

1. Slow atmospheric variations are eliminated, as the variation affects both stars equally.
2. First-order extinction corrections are nearly equal for both stars and becomes unimportant for differential measurements. Extinction measures are not necessary except to place the comparison star on the standard system.
3. Zero-point differences between you and other observers are removed if common comparison stars are used.
4. If a comparison star of similar color is used, errors in the transformation equations will have less effect.
5. If a comparison star of a similar magnitude is used, differential dead-time corrections become unimportant in pulse counting, and gain correction errors are removed if the same gain setting is used for both stars in DC photometry.
6. The comparison star can serve a double purpose as an extinction star if several measurements over wide air mass differences are made. In addition, if advantage 4 holds, second-order extinction is automatically taken into account.
7. For high accuracy and long-term reproducibility, errors in differential measurements with respect to a comparison star can approach the equipment short-term accuracy, less than $0^m.01$,

instead of the night-to-night transformation variation of $0^m.02$ or more. This is very important for small amplitude variables.

You can observe variable stars without using comparison stars. Many extensive surveys of variables have been carried out in the past without these aids, especially in the southwestern United States where photometric skies are common. However, for accurate low-amplitude photometry they are almost a necessity.

9.2a Selection of Comparison Stars

Make every effort to use the same comparison star as previous observers of the variable star. This should be done to minimize systematic differences between data sets of various observers. However, if this cannot be done (because no one has observed this star before or previous observers did not specify their comparison star), you will need to select your own.

Comparison stars should meet five criteria: (1) less than 1° from the program star, (2) of similar color, (3) equal in magnitude, (4) nonvarying, and (5) not red in color. Red stars are almost always variable, and are quite likely flare stars. Rules 2 and 3 are not rigid, as few stars will be near the variable and be the same brightness and color. But make every effort to enforce rules 1 and 4! Pick a brighter comparison star rather than one which is fainter than the variable, as better statistics can be obtained in a shorter time.

Selection of similarly colored stars can be difficult. For stars brighter than tenth magnitude, the Becvar atlases[5] indicate spectral class by the color of the dot representing the star. A more exact method is to use the Henry Draper (HD) Catalog,[23] which lists accurate spectral types for over 200,000 stars. This catalog is available at most colleges. A microfiche version is available from the University of North Carolina at Greensboro,[24] and a magnetic tape version from GSFC. Modern spectral classification yielding more accurate spectral types for the HD stars is being carried out by the University of Michigan[25] and by the Mira group in California.[26]

Nearby comparison stars of similar brightness can be found by examining the prepared finding charts for the variables. If you have a choice, pick a star listed in one of the major catalogs: BD, CD, HD, or SAO. This allows easy publication of your results without the necessity of including a finding chart for your comparisons.

If all else fails, a few minutes of observation in the field surrounding your variable will usually find a nearby comparison star candidate of the same magnitude. These observations can be performed quickly, as you are looking for a star with similar deflections or count rate to those of your variable and can easily eliminate stars that differ widely.

9.2b Use of Comparison Stars

Two comparison stars for each variable are usually chosen. One is considered to be the actual comparison star. The other is called a *check star*, and is used to test the stability of the comparison star. Differential measurements between the comparison and check stars should remain constant to within the nightly errors, usually $0^m.02$ or less with good skies. If variations larger than this consistently occur, either the comparison or the check star is variable, a fairly frequent occurrence! Which one is the culprit can be decided by comparing the nightly standardization of the comparisons or by deciding which star gives a light curve for the variable that has the smallest scatter. The check star is observed once or twice a night; the remaining measurements use only the comparison star.

The recommended observing sequence for each variable star observation is:

1. Sky
2. Comparison
3. Variable
4. Comparison
5. Variable
6. Comparison
7. Sky
8. Check (optional)

Each step in turn is comprised by the U, B, V, red leak, and perhaps dark-current measurements as discussed in Section 9.3. If the variable is faint, so that steps 3 and 5 would take several minutes each to reach 1 percent accuracy, it is much better to perform several sequences with less accuracy and average them than to risk sky transparency changes during the variable and comparison star observations.

If the comparison star is to be placed on the standard UBV system, it should be done on several occasions: at the beginning of the program, in the middle, and at the end. This can be done through differential measurements of nearby standard stars, or by using the transformation equations and nightly determination of the extinction.

9.3 INDIVIDUAL MEASUREMENTS OF A SINGLE STAR

An individual star observation really consists of four separate determinations in UBV photometry: U, B, V, and red leak. If you are doing only BV photometry, the U and red-leak measurements are removed. Red leak is unimportant in blue stars because little of their energy falls in the red. Sometimes observers also measure the dark current. This is usually negligible for bright stars or a dry-ice photomultiplier tube, and is subtracted automatically during sky background subtraction.

For pulse counting, the usual measurement sequence is V, B, U, red leak, and dark current. This is because V is the most commonly listed magnitude and gives a check for proper star selection and equipment operation. If you are using a filter wheel, you will end on the dark filter position, allowing movement to the next star, and then will be ready to perform the V observation with the next rotation of the wheel. The time of the observation is the average of the starting and stopping times of the sequence.

For DC photometry, the usual sequence is V, B, U, red leak, U, B, and V. This sequence allows checking for instrumental drift effects during the sequence.

Achieving one percent accuracy in a star measurement always requires a signal-to-noise ratio (S/N) of 100. How this is determined is different for pulse counting and DC photometry.

9.3a Pulse-Counting Measurements

Remember from Chapter 3 that 10,000 total source counts are necessary from a star to approach one percent or $0^m.01$ accuracy. Figure 9.1 shows the typical count rate for telescopes of 20-, 40-, and 75-centimeter diameters. For example, an $11^m.7$ star produces roughly the count rates shown in Table 9.1. For faint stars, measuring the U magnitude is always a problem. For example, the count rate for cepheids in U is ten times less than in V. You must decide in these cases if having the $(U - B)$ color index is essential to your program and make allowances for the increased time if it is.

TABLE 9.1. Pulse-Counting Rates

Telescope Size (centimeters)	Rate (counts/second)	Integration Time to Achieve 1% Accuracy (seconds)
20	100	100
40	380	26
75	1400	7

The times quoted in Table 9.1 are only for measuring the star in a single color. However, the sky must also be measured accurately to subtract its contribution from the star measurement. The ideal ratio of time spent measuring the sky background to time spent on star and sky is

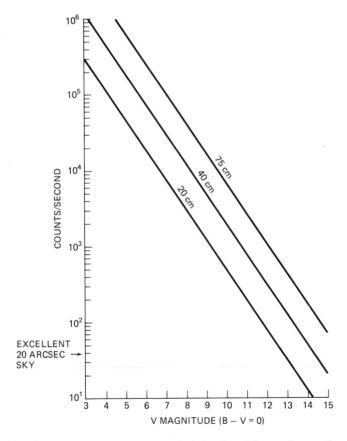

Figure 9.1. Count rate versus apparent magnitude for three different telescope diameters.

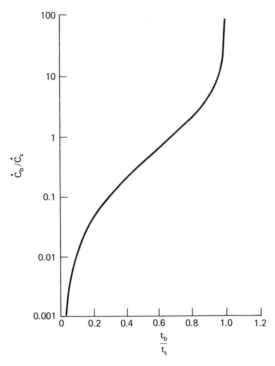

Figure 9.2. The optimum fraction of observing time to be spent on sky background.

found by taking the derivative of Equation K.41 with respect to the source time. The result is

$$\frac{t_b}{t_s} = \sqrt{\frac{\dot{C}_b/\dot{C}_s}{\dot{C}_b/\dot{C}_s + 1}} \qquad (9.1)$$

where the subscript s refers to source measurements and the subscript b refers to background measurements, $\dot{C}$ is the count rate, and t is the time per measurement. This ratio is plotted in Figure 9.2. From a known count rate ratio the corresponding time ratio can be read directly from this figure.

Example: $11^m.7$ star produces roughly 100 counts per second in the 20-centimeter telescope. Assume the sky background gives roughly 50 counts per second in the chosen diaphragm. How long do we have to observe the star and the background?

$$\frac{t_b}{t_s} = \sqrt{\frac{50/100}{(50/100) + 1}} = 0.577$$

Or, $\dot{C}_b/\dot{C}_s = 50/100 = 0.5$, and reading from Figure 9.2, the corresponding time ratio of 0.56. Because we need to observe the star for 100 seconds for 1 percent accuracy, we need to observe sky alone for at least 56 to 58 seconds.

9.3b DC Photometry

When pulse counting, there is a fairly simple rule to follow to achieve an accuracy of 1 percent. This requires an S/N of 100, which means that a total of 10,000 counts must be accumulated. If a star produces only 1000 counts in one second, you simply observe it for at least 10 seconds. The guidelines are not so simple in DC photometry. If you were to watch the output of a DC amplifier on a chart recorder as starlight strikes the detector, you would see the pen rise and then jitter about some mean level.

Figure 9.3 shows the chart recorder tracing for the first observation of UZ Leonis in Table 4.1. The mean level of the pen represents the signal from the star and the jitter is the noise. It is noise that prevents us from determining the stellar signal with perfect accuracy. Unlike

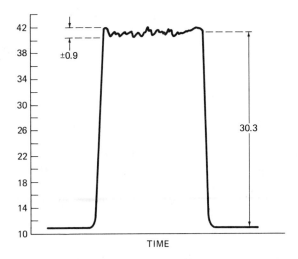

Figure 9.3. Chart recorder tracing.

pulse counting, the S/N does not improve when we observe the star longer, the chart tracing just gets longer and continues to look much the same. The same is true if we watch the amplifier meter. Increasing the observing time improves the photometric accuracy to some extent because the longer chart tracing makes it easier to estimate the mean level using a straightedge. However, once the tracing is several centimeters long, continuing the deflection brings diminishing returns (unlike pulse counting). The problem is that in DC photometry the integration time is set by the RC time constant at the amplifier input. The obvious way to improve the S/N is to increase this time constant. Indeed, the tracing does become smoother when the time constant is increased. However, there is a trade-off when using a capacitor to smooth the signal. When the detector is exposed to light, the current entering the amplifier must charge the capacitor. The rate at which the capacitor charges depends on the RC time constant. As the capacitor charges, the pen makes an exponential rise to its final value. For the pen to reach 99 percent of its final value requires a period of 4.6 time constants. If a large time constant is used, a significant amount of observing time is spent waiting for the pen to reach its final level. For this reason, DC amplifiers seldom use time constants that exceed a few seconds. The DC amplifier in Chapter 8 has an adjustable time constant. For bright stars that have a large S/N, a small time constant is used to save observing time, while for fainter stars a longer time constant is used to improve the S/N.

For many stars, a time constant of less than a second is not enough to achieve a S/N of 100. Figure 9.3 shows a case with a 0.5 second time constant. We can estimate the S/N by the amount of jitter about the mean. The mean signal level is 30.3 units on the chart paper. The noise causes variations of 0.9 unit to either side of the mean. If the sky background is large, it would be necessary to subtract this from the star to obtain the net signal. In this particular example, the sky background is low so that the S/N is very nearly $30.3/0.9 = 34$. By Equation K.25, we see that the S/N increases with the square root of the total integration time, t. Therefore, we would need to increase the amplifier time constant by a factor of nine to achieve an S/N of 100. A time constant of this length is not available for this amplifier. Then the procedure is to take several deflections (each many time constants in duration) and form an average to make a single observation. A rough estimate of the necessary number, n, of such observations is given by

$$n = \left(\frac{100}{S/N} \right)^2 \qquad (9.2)$$

The time between each of these deflections can be spent recentering the star in the diaphragm (if necessary) or making a deflection in another filter. For the chart tracing in Figure 9.3, the S/N implies that a single measurement would have an error of 0.03 magnitude. The formula above implies that nine observations should be averaged for a 0.01 magnitude error. In fact, the actual standard deviation from the mean of nine observations that night was 0.012 magnitude.

This example points out a disadvantage of DC compared to pulse counting. The nine observations required would take several minutes of observing time. With a pulse-counting system, if we obtained a S/N of 34 in 0.5 second (the time constant used that night), we would need only to integrate nine times longer (because $S/N \propto t^{1/2}$) or 4.5 seconds for a S/N of 100. For many observing projects, this difference in observing time is unimportant. But there are rapid variable stars and short-period binaries that have measurable changes of brightness in just a few minutes. We must observe the light curve on more nights to obtain the same quality of data as that obtained with a pulse-counting system. Alternatively, you can retain the time resolution by not averaging as many deflections but you obtain a noisier light curve.

Note that this disadvantage of DC photometry disappears if the chart recorder is replaced by a voltage-to-frequency converter and a counter. A very small amplifier time constant can then be used to integrate on the star until the desired S/N is reached. However, the S/N analysis has a further complication. Unlike pulse counting, the number that appears on your counter is not equal to the number of detected photons. Instead, it corresponds to some level of current flowing in the feedback loop of the amplifier. This in turn depends on both the brightness of the star and the amplifier gain. In this case, an empirical method is the simplest way to determine S/N. Take a series of short test integrations and calculate the standard deviation from the mean. If $\bar{c}$ is the mean counts and s.d. is the standard deviation, then

$$S/N = \frac{\bar{c}}{s.d.} \qquad (9.3)$$

To obtain an S/N of 100, the required integration time, T, is

$$T = \left(\frac{100}{S/N}\right)^2 t. \tag{9.4}$$

where t is the total time of all the test integrations.

The amount of observing time spent on sky measurements can be estimated by Equation 9.1 just as it is for pulse counting. The count rates in that equation are simply replaced by net pen deflections. In the example above, the sky background was ⅕₅ of the stellar signal. Equation 9.1 then tells us that 20 percent of our observing time should be spent on sky background.

There are also some differences in the observing procedure between pulse counting and DC photometry. These are discussed in Section 9.7.

In Sections 9.3a and 9.3b, much emphasis has been placed on the S/N as an indicator of the quality of an observation. However, a high S/N is a necessary but not a sufficient condition for an accurate observation. There are many other factors that can come into play. For instance, electronic drift or the slow passage of cirrus clouds are not obvious in the noise level in a single measurement. However, they become apparent when measurements of the same object, such as the comparison star, fail to repeat. Discrepancies that exceed the noise levels are indicators of a problem. Even if a single measurement has a very high S/N, never assume that it will be reproducible; always take at least two. There is no substitute for an alert, experienced observer who can tell when "things are not quite right."

9.3c Differential Photometry

Differential photometry is the simplest and potentially the most accurate of photometric techniques. The basic idea is to compare the brightness of the variable star to that of a nearby and constant comparison star. However, simple as it sounds, certain observing procedures must be followed strictly if differential photometry is to be done properly.

The golden rule of differential photometry is: *interpolate, never extrapolate.* To illustrate the meaning of this rule, consider what happens as we observe our two stars during the night. Suppose that early in the evening the variable and comparison star are near the eastern horizon. We measure the comparison star and then, for some reason, delay measuring the variable for 20 minutes. During those 20 minutes, the stars have risen higher and the extinction is considerably less than it was when the comparison star was measured. The result is that the variable looks too bright with respect to the comparison star measurement. This is an example of extrapolation; we took a comparison star measurement and assumed it was valid 20 minutes later. Obviously, a better procedure is to measure the comparison, variable, and then the comparison star again. We can then interpolate to estimate the apparent brightness of the comparison star at the time of the variable star measurement. Our golden rule can be restated: *always sandwich the variable star measurements between comparison star measurements.*

If the variable star is faint or varies slowly in brightness, the observing sequence in Section 9.2b is recommended. However, if you are observing a star that varies rapidly, such as an eclipsing binary with a half-day orbital period, a slightly different observing pattern is preferred. If we let C and V represent an observation through each filter of the comparison and variable star respectively, then the observing sequence might look like the following.

$$CVV \ldots VVCVV \ldots VVCVV \ldots VVCVV \ldots$$

The brackets mark a data group that we refer to as a *block*. Each block begins and ends with a comparison star measurement. The number of variable star measurements in a block depends on three factors. First, the required number of measurements needed so that when combined, a single observation with a S/N of at least 100 is produced. (This was discussed in Sections 9.3a and 9.3b.) Second is the speed with which the variable changes. Obviously, if the star only varies by 0.1^m during the entire night, you need not look at it as often as one that changes by the same amount in 30 minutes. In the latter case, it would be desirable to obtain several observations per block (i.e., spend a higher percentage of the observing time on the variable). The third factor is zenith distance. When the air mass is large, variations in extinction can have a large impact. Therefore, the comparison star must be observed more frequently. There is no simple rule on how long to make a block, but of course, there is no substitute for experience. However, it is certainly advisable to observe the comparison star as frequently as possible. Experience with short-period eclipsing binaries observed through the somewhat variable skies of the midwestern United States suggests that the comparison star should be observed at intervals of 20 minutes or less. If the observing sequence must be interrupted at any point, it is important to end with a comparison star measurement. If observing resumes later, you should begin with a comparison star measurement.

The block structure outlined above does not indicate sky background measurements. The reason is that the amount of time spent measuring the sky depends on the relative brightness of the star and the sky background. The method of Section 9.3a can be used to estimate the percentage of observing time spent monitoring the sky background. If, for instance, it turns out that 25 percent of your time should be spent on the sky, then every fourth measurement in the block should be of the sky. If you suspect the sky background is changing rapidly (for example, if the moon is rising), then you should measure the sky more frequently.

Note that our block structure does not contain separate measurements of the dark current. Some authors recommend measuring the dark current frequently. However, our experience has been that with well-designed amplifiers and fairly stable photomultiplier tube temperatures, the dark current is very constant. Every time the sky background is observed, we actually measure sky plus dark current (plus any zero-point shift if a DC system is used). When this is subtracted from the stellar measurement, the dark current (plus any zero-point shift) is subtracted automatically. There is no need to measure and subtract the dark current specifically from all the measurements. Therefore, the dark current need be measured only occasionally as a check on the stability of the photometer.

9.3d Faint Sources

Photometry of faint sources can be a time-consuming and exasperating project that should only be undertaken by the experienced observer. By faint sources we mean objects that are comparable to the sky background in brightness, or objects near the visual limit of the telescope. There are several points to consider when observing faint sources.

First, pulse counting with a cooled photomultiplier tube is the most practical method of observing faint sources. DC methods yield chart recorder deflections that are not significantly greater than the random fluctuations in the sky background. A smoother trace can be obtained by increasing the time constant, thereby integrating over a longer period. However, the time required to reach a constant level is also increased. Eye measurement of a star plus sky trace that is only a few percent greater than the sky trace alone is very difficult. Long integrations with pulse counting are very easy, requiring only the selection of a longer gating time on the pulse counter.

Second, time is limited by the accuracy of your telescope drive and by sky conditions. Generally, never integrate on one star for more than 5 minutes, including time to measure *all* colors. If you have insufficient counts with the 5-minute limitation, move to the comparison star or background and then return to the program object for another 5-minute observation.

Third, never observe except under optimum conditions. This includes using only moonless nights, observing near the zenith, and with the best possible seeing conditions. Under these conditions, you can use the smallest diaphragm to reduce the sky background and increase the contrast between the star and the sky.

For stars that approach the sky background in intensity, the time spent on observing the star and observing the sky should be about equal (see Figure 9.2). This means that you should alternate 5-minute integrations between star and sky. Always cycle through all filters on one object before moving the telescope to look at sky or a comparison source.

If you are observing one source for a significant amount of time, say 30 minutes or more, plot the sky values versus time. You may find a significant trend because of a brighter sky near the horizon or slowly varying sky brightness that allows you to interpolate between adjacent sky readings to give a better sky value at the time of observation of your program star.

Stars near the visual limit or fainter can be measured photoelectrically, but are very difficult to place in the diaphragm. The usual procedure is to have the guiding or finding eyepiece on a stage with X and Y movements and offset to a brighter star in the same field. This requires the ability to measure the amount of offset in both axes and the knowledge of the plate scale of the telescope. For simple systems, the first requirement can be met by counting screw turns between two stars in the field with known positions. To perform offset photometry, first position the cross hairs on the center of the diaphragm, and then move the eyepiece in X and Y the distance between the object to be measured and the nearby bright star. The positioning of the bright star on the cross hairs places the source to be measured in the diaphragm.

You must find a region near the star where no stars within five magnitudes of the program star's brightness exist. For example, a ninth magnitude variable must have a sky reading with no stars brighter than fourteenth magnitude in the diaphragm. Otherwise, the sky background reading gives a sky value significantly higher than the sky reading at the star itself, and the measurement for the star becomes fainter than it actually is when you subtract the incorrect brighter sky value from it. This becomes troublesome particularly around tenth magnitude for the program object, as there are many fifteenth magnitude stars within an average 30 arc second area. It is difficult to find a clear region for the sky reading. Also, there is a large chance of including a faint companion near the star itself. A secondary problem is finding charts that go faint enough; even using Atlas Stellarum with its fourteenth magnitude limit, you cannot observe any stars fainter than ninth magnitude without the chance of significant sky background subtraction errors.

9.4 DIAPHRAGM SELECTION

Chapter 6 presented the practical details of constructing the photometer head and the diaphragms. However, there are some basic considerations to be made when using these diaphragms in your observing program.

The most obvious reason for having more than one diaphragm is to prevent unwanted stars from contributing to the light entering the diaphragm. In addition, a smaller diaphragm allows less sky background radiation to pass through, while permitting most of the program star's light to pass through unhindered.

It is tempting when using a photometer with several diaphragms to use a small one on one star, then to use a larger one on another star, because it is brighter or has no companions. There are several reasons for *not* doing this, and these are presented in this section.

*9.4a The Optical System

The image of a point source created by a telescope is not a point source but rather a very complicated distribution. Because the telescope is not infinite in size, only a portion of the total wave front of light from the star is intercepted by the telescopic mirror or lens. The mirror is then called the *entrance aperture* of the optical system.

As the light is focused by this aperture, the path length of light rays from a given wave front is different for different parts of the image. Some of these rays add together in phase, resulting in *constructive interference;* others add together 180° out of phase, resulting in *destructive interference.* The resultant image of a point source by a circular aperture looks like a bright central disk, the *Airy disk,* surrounded by fainter concentric rings of light. This image can be seen with good optics on a good night and high magnification, and actually can be used to collimate the optical system. The important point to remember is that the image is *not* concentrated at a point even if the source appears pointlike. The size of the central disk and the brightness of the secondary rings are inversely proportional to the diameter of the telescope.

An additional problem arises when a secondary mirror is used, because part of the circular aperture is obscured and an annular entrance aperture results. A theoretical description of the resultant image of a point source is discussed by Young.[27] The major change from a strictly uniform, circular aperture is an increase in the amount of light in the secondary rings.

If a diaphragm is placed in the focal plane of the telescope, a certain amount of the energy from the star will be removed, the amount depending on how many of the secondary rings are larger than the diaphragm. A good approximation to the excluded energy is

$$X(d) = \left[\frac{82,500\lambda}{d\,D(1 - t)} \right] \qquad (9.5)$$

where $X(d)$ is the fractional excluded energy as a function of diaphragm diameter, λ is the wavelength of light, D is the diameter of the lens or mirror, d is the diameter of the diaphragm in arc seconds, and t is the fractional obscuration of the primary mirror by the secondary mirror. The variables D and λ must be in the same units. The total energy included by a diaphragm is then given by

$$I(d) = 1 - X(d) \qquad (9.6)$$

For a 40-centimeter (16-inch) telescope with a 40 percent central obscuration and a wavelength of 5000 Å (5 × 10⁻⁵ centimeters),

$$I(d) = 1 - \frac{82{,}500(5 \times 10^{-5})}{40d(1 - 0.4)}$$

$$I(d) = 1 - \frac{0.1718}{d} \tag{9.7}$$

Figure 9.4 shows the result of Equation 9.7. The approximation breaks down for small diaphragms, which is why the included energy from the figure does not approach zero for small diaphragms. The point to note, however, is that for a 40-centimeter telescope, changing from a 10 arc second diaphragm (2 percent excluded energy) on one star to a 20 arc second diaphragm (1 percent excluded) on another star causes at least a 1 percent error. However, the difference between a 20 arc second and a 30 arc second diaphragm is small enough to neglect unless

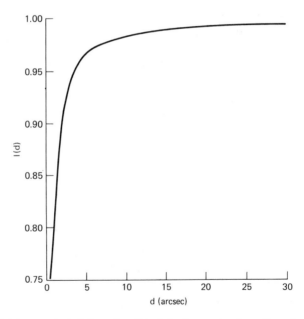

Figure 9.4. Total energy included as a function of diaphragm size, for a 40-centimeter aperture telescope.

precision greater than $\pm$ 0.01 magnitude is desired. But reducing the size of the telescope to 20 centimeters would then make the 20 to 30 arc second change as large as the 10 to 20 arc second change with the larger telescope. Therefore, use as large a telescope as possible to eliminate this error; many observers even do not use diaphragms smaller than 20 arc seconds with telescopes smaller than about 20 centimeters in diameter.

We have not included other effects that result from diffraction spikes from the secondary supports or the optical aberrations caused by the mirror itself, all of which increase the amount of energy outside of the central disk. In other words, consider the above estimates to be lower limits on the errors involved from the optical system itself.

9.4b Stellar Profiles

Just as the light from the sun scatters, making the sky blue, the light from any star scatters over the entire sky. The profile of a stellar image on the sky is therefore not strictly pointlike, but rather spread out by refraction, diffraction, and scattering in the atmosphere and diffraction and scattering within the telescope. The profile concentrates heavily towards the center, producing a "seeing disk" typically 2 arc seconds across and then decreases rapidly outside that diameter. The seeing disk or stellar profile is *not* constant for a given instrument. A hazy night can broaden the image greatly.

Figure 9.5 shows a typical stellar profile for a $m_v = 0$ star based on the results by King[28] and Picarillo.[29] Note that, although the intensity falls off rapidly to a 10 arc second radius, the decreasing intensity soon approaches an inverse square law drop. You might think because at a 10 arc second radius, equivalent to a 20 arc second diaphragm, the starlight is ten magnitudes fainter than near the profile center that the remaining radiation could be neglected. However, the total light entering the diaphragm is the product of the intensity per unit area and the total area of the diaphragm, which increases as the square of the radius. The resultant total light pattern is shown in Figure 9.6. Here you can see that a 30 arc second radius circle, 60 arc second diaphragm, includes most of the light of a star, but that using a 20 arc second diaphragm on one star and a 10 arc second diaphragm on another can cause significant error.

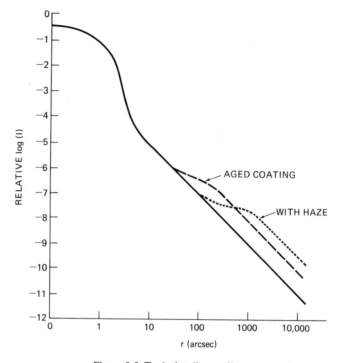

Figure 9.5. Typical stellar profile.

9.4c Practical Considerations

The fact that a stellar image is not concentrated at one point has several direct consequences to photometry:

1. Changing diaphragms between a comparison and the variable star causes different fractions of each star's total light to reach the photometer.
2. On hazy nights, even observations with the same diaphragm size can be in error as the haze scatters a changing percentage of the starlight out of the diaphragm, depending on observation time or altitude.
3. A miscentered image increases the chance for observational error greatly, because a significant fraction of one star's light may be misplaced out of the diaphragm.
4. A misfocused image enlarges the seeing disk and allows less light to reach the photomultiplier tube and increases the chance of mis-

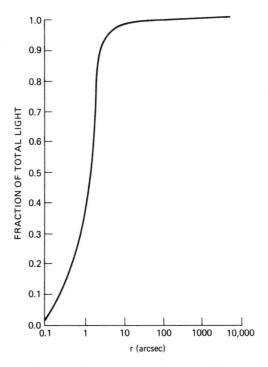

Figure 9.6. Integral of starlight versus radius.

centering errors. This error is common when comparing early and late evening observations if the telescope has not been refocused for temperature changes.

5. Never change diaphragms between star and sky measurements. Whereas the stellar contributions through a 20 or a 60 arc second aperture is the same to within 1 percent, the 60 arc second aperture allows nine times more skylight to pass through. At times it is difficult to find a clear patch of sky for the background measurement. It is then the observer's discretion whether to make the sky measurement further from the program star, or to use a smaller diaphragm for all measurements.

6. There is a limit on the smallness of the diaphragm because of the stellar profile size. If apertures much less than 10 arc seconds are used, a significant fraction of the star's light is rejected. One reason the 2.1-meter Space Telescope (to be launched from the space shuttle by NASA in 1990) is expected to outperform the largest earth-based telescopes is that with no atmospheric seeing, a dif-

fraction-limited star profile is obtained, where 70 percent of the light is concentrated within a 0.1 arc second circle. Then diaphragms of 0.4 and 1 arc second are easily used, removing much more of the sky background from the measurement than is possible from the ground.

7. The diameter of the seeing disk varies with altitude above the horizon because of the differing air mass. Near the zenith the disk may be 1 or 2 arc seconds in diameter, but near the horizon it has expanded to perhaps 10 arc seconds. Therefore, even using the same diaphragm on stars at differing altitude, differing amounts of the total starlight are admitted. Young[27] gives a good review of this and other seeing and scintillation effects.

At all costs, try to use one diaphragm size for all observations that are to be compared on a given night. You do not have to measure 100 percent of the light from a star, or even 95 percent, to get accurate results. What you must try to do is measure the same *fraction* of light from every star you want to compare.

9.4d Background Removal

Because the sky background acts like an extended source, a larger diaphragm will admit more background radiation since a larger area of the sky is seen by the photometer. However, few more star photons are acquired as they come from a nearly pointlike image amply covered by the diaphragm. The light from the sky passing through the diaphragm cannot be distinguished from the light of some faint star as the photometer knows only that a certain *number* of photons have reached it, not the *origin* of those photons in the area covered by the diaphragm. Therefore, we can compute the magnitude of an equivalent star that produces the same number of photons as produced by the sky. This is shown in Figure 9.7 for a typical site where the sky brightness is $22^m.6$ per square arc second at the zenith. You can see that if a 30 arc second diaphragm is used, as much light reaches the photometer from the sky as if a $15^m.5$ star were in the aperture. As Equation 9.1 indicates, the larger the sky-to-star ratio becomes, the longer is the time required to complete an observation. Therefore, you should use the smallest diaphragm feasible when measuring faint sources. A size of 15 to 20 arc seconds is usually considered the minimum size for amateur telescopes,

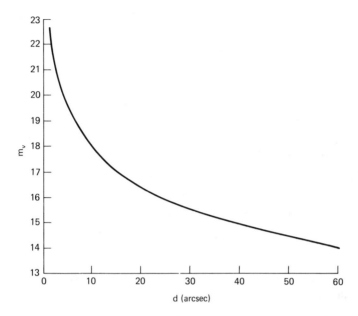

Figure 9.7. Sky brightness as seen through different diaphragms assuming a surface brightness of $22^{m}.6$ per square arcsec.

though diaphragms of 4 to 7 arc seconds have been used on the Hale 5-meter (200-inch) telescope with good seeing and the advantage of its superior drive.

The full moon can easily increase the brightness indicated in Figure 9.7 by three or more magnitudes. Also, because of the increased scattering near the horizon, the sky is two to three times brighter there than near the zenith. Faint star observations are therefore usually only performed under moonless conditions near the zenith and with good seeing.

9.4e Aperture Calibration

There are two main reasons why an accurate calibration of the aperture size might be necessary. When photometry of extended objects such as galaxies or comets is intended, the measurements must be reduced to magnitudes per square arc second. When you want to compare measurements taken with different apertures, both measurements must be reduced to a common aperture size.

Because of the small size involved, not many methods are available to measure the diameter or area. A direct measurement of a 0.01 inch hole to 0.1 percent accuracy requires a precision of $\pm$ 10 microns, not available from your typical ruler! Usually this is performed with a large instrument called a *measuring engine,* and must be done at an astronomy department possessing such an instrument. An indirect measurement of the area can be obtained (and the diameter from $A = \pi D^2/4$) by measuring a uniform object like a white card on a dome through each diaphragm and noting the intensity ratios. After the relative aperture sizes have been obtained, the size of one aperture can be obtained by measuring an object with known surface brightness, such as a constant light source, or by direct measurement of the largest diaphragm.

9.5 EXTINCTION NOTES

Chapter 4 gave the types of stars to be used for extinction measurements. Listed below are some of the methods for obtaining these observations during a program of all-sky photometry (i.e., not differential photometry).

1. Use more than one star to determine extinction. This reduces errors due to the non-uniform sky.
2. Use stars near the celestial equator so that they move through air mass values (X) quickly. Also, measure them several times while they are near the horizon, as X varies quickly there and you want to fill in the plot with more than one point at large X. Do not get too close to the horizon. Refraction and particulate problems are much more severe at low altitudes. A practical limit is $X < 5$.
3. If you are in a dry climate or are under an extended high-pressure system, you can average values from several consecutive nights to obtain mean extinction coefficients.
4. Observe in the following sequence: extinction stars, program stars, extinction stars, etc., spending about 80 percent of time on your program stars but obtaining extinction measurements throughout the night.
5. To check on the temporal, that is, variation with time, consistency of the sky, look at some of the North Polar Sequence stars from Appendix E throughout the night, as the zenith distance of these stars (and therefore X) changes very little. Temporal variations occur most frequently near sunrise, sunset, and when there is an approaching atmospheric frontal zone.

6. Always interpolate, never extrapolate. In other words, make sure that you have extinction measurements at air masses larger and smaller than those for your program stars.

9.6 LIGHT OF THE NIGHT SKY

Even when the sun disappears beneath the horizon, our world is filled with light. It may be fainter than daylight or present in the infrared and therefore undetectable by the eye, but is a major contributor to the errors of photometric observations. Roach and Gordon[30] give a good review of the light of the night sky, which should be studied if more details are needed. In this section we will consider only the natural sources of night sky light, neglecting man-made light pollution.

There are six general contributors to the night sky brightness: (1) integrated light from distant galaxies; (2) integrated starlight from within our galaxy; (3) zodiacal light; (4) night airglow; (5) aurora; and (6) twilight emission lines. Night airglow, aurora, and twilight emission lines are results of a planet with an atmosphere and magnetic field. Zodiacal light is a result of being within a solar system. The remaining two contributors would be present anywhere within our galaxy. We discuss only the spectral region covered by the *UBV* system with some digression into the near-infrared.

Background light from faint stars and galaxies is probably the limiting factor in photometry of faint sources. Miller[31] notes that the sky background can vary over distances of a few arc minutes. This means that if you observe a star and then offset to another location to measure only the sky, the two sky values may not agree. However, in most cases the light from these background stars and galaxies will not be important unless the program object is very faint and difficult to observe even if you are using a very large telescope. In addition, these contributors are static; if you always offset to the same location to measure sky, the contribution from these faint sources will always be the same.

Zodiacal light is caused by sunlight reflecting off dust in the plane of the solar system. It increases in brightness as the observer looks closer to the sun, and is always confined to the ecliptic plane. Zodiacal light may or may not be important as a background source in your observations depending on the location of your source with respect to the sun and the ecliptic. For instance, within 50° of the sun the zodiacal light in the ecliptic is brighter than the brightest part of the Milky Way, and it is brighter than integrated starlight over most of the sky. The zodiacal light is relatively uniform in the range of arc minutes, follows the solar spectrum, and is highly polarized like the blue sky.

Twilight emission lines are only important for a very short time after sunset and seldom interfere with astronomical observations. A layer in the upper atmosphere containing sodium atoms is illuminated by the sun after sunset as seen from the earth's surface. This illumination excites the atoms, causing them to emit the sodium D lines (5892 Å). However, only at a *solar depression angle* (the distance at which sun is found below the horizon) of 7° to 10° is this emission observable. If the sun is closer to the horizon, scattering overpowers the emission; below 10°, the layer is no longer illuminated. A similar case is noted for the red lines of oxygen atoms (6300, 6364 Å). Both of these effects contribute to errors in the V magnitude, but are important for less than an hour. Note, though, that observing in twilight carries its disadvantages.

All of the effects discussed in detail so far are minor contributors that cause errors only for short intervals or when very faint stars, those whose brightness is comparable to the sky brightness, are to be observed.

The final two terrestrial contributors can cause larger errors, both spatial and temporal. *Night airglow* is the fluorescence of the atoms and molecules in the air from photochemical excitation. It occurs primarily in a layer about 100 kilometers above the earth and is variable, depending on sky conditions, local time, latitude, season, and solar activity. There is a component that is present at most wavelengths, called the continuum, primarily caused by nitrous oxide and other molecules, but the major component is caused by distinct emission lines. Both components are always present, tend to increase in brightness near the horizon, and are not strongly affected by geomagnetic activity. The primary lines in the airglow are atomic oxygen (5577 Å), sodium (5892 Å), molecular oxygen (7619, 8645 Å), and hydroxyl, OH^- (mostly in the near-infrared). All of these emissions can be fairly strong, with some observers seeing the 5577 Å structure with the unaided eye at dark locations. Peterson and Kieffaber[32] present photographs of the hydroxyl near-infrared emission showing the mottled structure of the emission. As observed with infrared sensors, the night airglow can look like bands of cirrus clouds and move across the sky. Therefore, at least in the V filter and certainly in any filter redward of this, the airglow is a variable that always reduces the consistency of the measurements during any given night.

The *aurora* again occurs with the same mechanisms and altitudes as airglow, but varies with the solar cycle. The primary excitation mechanism is incoming charged particles from the sun. These particles become trapped in the geomagnetic field and spiral towards the poles, where they excite the atoms and molecules in the air. These polar auroras differ from airglow primarily in their strength, being up to several hundred times brighter, and their higher degree of excitation. The main auroral lines are atomic oxygen (5577, 6300, 6364 Å), hydrogen (6563 Å), and the red molecular nitrogen bands. These lines vary according to three factors: (1) solar activity, during which aurora occur more often near sunspot maxima when flares are more common; (2) latitude, because the particles concentrate near the poles, most of the radiation occurs there; and (3) time of year, peaking in March and October. Our suggestion is not to observe if an aurora is visible at your site. Though photometry can be accomplished, auroras vary rapidly in intensity and direction. Special techniques are necessary to achieve accurate results. This is one of the reasons few observatories are located above the Arctic Circle or in auroral zones. Myrabø[33] gives an example of the possible results when a chopping technique is used to remove the effects of a bright aurora that can vary five magnitudes within 1 minute.

The conclusions of this section are threefold. First, the light of the night sky is not constant in time or space, and therefore will always limit the accuracy of your measurements. Do not expect $\pm\ 0^{m}.001$ results! Second, do not observe during an aurora, near the horizon, or at twilight. And last, measurements redward of the V filter are strongly affected by the varying night sky and should be avoided until experience is gained with the UBV system. Except for auroras or while observing very faint stars, the night sky variations will probably never be noticeable in your photometry, but knowledge of the possibility of these errors should be filed in your mind for later reference.

9.7 YOUR FIRST NIGHT AT THE TELESCOPE

For the newcomer to photometry, the previous sections may seem helpful but somehow cloud the answer to the question "What do I do at the telescope?" In this section, we attempt to pull together the concepts of earlier chapters to outline some procedures to follow at the telescope.

It is important to be prepared before going to the telescope. Unless you plan to observe some very bright objects, you should prepare a set of finding charts in order to identify your "targets" for the night. It is important to mark the charts to indicate the orientation and the size of the field of view of your guide telescope or wide-field eyepiece of the photometer. This can save hours of frustration when you try to identify the star fields at the telescope. If you are doing differential photometry, be sure the comparison and check stars are marked on the chart in addition to the variable star. If you are using a pulse-counting system, you should determine the dead-time coefficient as outlined in Section 4.2. For a DC photometer, you should calibrate the gain settings as described in Section 8.6.

It is a good idea to arrive at the telescope early to uncap the tube and let the optics adjust to the outdoor temperature. All the electronics should be turned on at least 60 minutes prior to observing. This is necessary to allow the electronics time to stabilize. DC amplifiers, for example, tend to drift rapidly for the first few minutes after they are turned on. The high voltage should also be applied to the photomultiplier tube (with the dark slide closed) because the tube tends to be noisier than normal during the first few minutes of operation. If your photometer uses a cooled detector, this is the time to turn on the cooling system or to add dry ice to the cold box.

If you are using a photomultiplier tube, the next step is very important. In order for the photometer's optical elements to be in the proper location within the telescope's light cone, it is important that the diaphragm be positioned in the focal plane of the telescope. To do this, first aim the telescope at some bright background (such as the observatory wall, or the twilight sky) so that the outline of the diaphragm can be seen clearly in the diaphragm eyepiece. This can also be accomplished with a diaphragm light. This eyepiece is then focused to make the diaphragm as clear as possible. *Do not adjust this eyepiece focus again the rest of the night.* Next, a bright star is centered in the diaphragm and focused sharply using the *telescope focus.* Now both the star and the diaphragm appear sharp when viewed in the diaphragm eyepiece. The diaphragm is now in the focal plane of the telescope.

This procedure is unnecessary for a photodiode photometer. In this case, the photometer head does not have a diaphragm. The head is constructed so that when the stellar image appears focused in the eyepiece, it is also focused on the photodiode when the flip mirror is removed from the light path. The set-up procedure is concluded by choosing the diaphragm to be used (see Section 9.4), setting the telescope coordinates, and setting the observatory clock.

There are some important comments to be made about the art of data taking at the telescope. Making a stellar measurement with a pulse-counting system is the simplest. The star is centered in the diaphragm, the dark slide is opened, and the counts are recorded. For this system, use the advice of Section 9.3a to estimate the total observing time through each filter. Measurements through the red-leak filter should have the same duration as the U filter. If you are using a DC system, some additional advice is in order. The DC amplifier zero point may drift slightly during the night. This drift may be either positive or negative. Most chart recorders and meters do not follow a negative drift off the bottom of the scale. For this reason, it is a good idea to put the zero point at about 10 percent of full scale. To do this, simply close the dark slide (with the high voltage on) and adjust the "zero adjustment" knob on the DC amplifier. Chart recorders and meters are most accurate at their maximum (full-scale) reading. Therefore, whenever possible, adjust the amplifier gain so that a stellar measurement gives a nearly full-scale reading.

There are three additional rules to follow when doing DC photometry. When you measure a star for the first time, be sure the amplifier gain is at its lowest setting. You then increase the gain to achieve the desired meter deflection. This procedure is designed to protect the meter and/or chart recorder from damage if too high a gain setting is used. If this happens, the pen or meter needle will slam beyond full scale. With a little practice, you can estimate a safe gain setting simply by observing the apparent brightness of the star in the eyepiece. The second rule is to use the same gain settings for the sky measurements as was used for the stellar measurements. A much higher gain may be used for the U measurements than is used for B or V. The U sky background measurement also must be made at this higher gain setting. This is obviously necessary if we are to subtract the sky measurement from the stellar measurement directly. However, this is also necessary because it is possible for the amplifier zero point to change slightly with different gain settings. The third rule is to record the coarse and fine gain settings separately and not their total. The reason is that each gain position requires a calibration correction as discussed in Section 8.6. More than one combination of switch positions can yield the same total. If your records only contain the total gain, you will not be able to determine the proper gain correction without ambiguity.

The observing pattern used at the telescope depends strongly on the

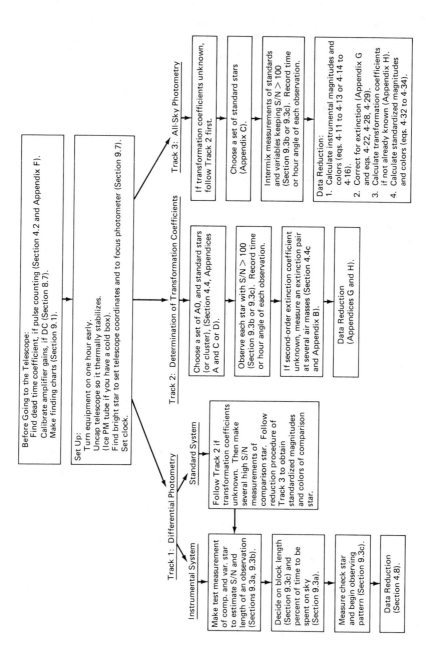

Before Going to the Telescope:
Find dead time coefficient, if pulse counting (Section 4.2 and Appendix F).
Calibrate amplifier gains, if DC (Section 8.7).
Make finding charts (Section 9.1).

Set Up:
Turn equipment on one hour early.
Uncap telescope so it thermally stabilizes.
(Ice PM tube if you have a cold box).
Find bright star to set telescope coordinates and to focus photometer (Section 9.7).
Set clock.

Track 1: Differential Photometry

Instrumental System

Make test measurement of comp. and var. star to estimate S/N and length of an observation (Sections 9.3a, 9.3b).

Decide on block length (Section 9.3c) and percent of time to be spent on sky (Section 9.3a).

Measure check star and begin observing pattern (Section 9.3c).

Data Reduction (Section 4.8).

Standard System

Follow Track 2 if transformation coefficients unknown. Then make several high S/N measurements of comparison star. Follow reduction procedure of Track 3 to obtain standardized magnitudes and colors of comparison star.

Track 2: Determination of Transformation Coefficients

Choose a set of A0, and standard stars (or cluster), (Section 4.4, Appendices A and C or D).

Observe each star with S/N > 100 (Section 9.3b or 9.3c). Record time or hour angle of each observation.

If second-order extinction coefficient unknown, measure an extinction pair at several air masses (Section 4.4c and Appendix B).

Data Reduction (Appendices G and H).

Track 3: All-Sky Photometry

If transformation coefficients unknown, follow Track 2 first.

Choose a set of standard stars (Appendix C).

Intermix measurements of standards and variables keeping S/N > 100 (Section 9.3b or 9.3c). Record time or hour angle of each observation.

Data Reduction:
1. Calculate instrumental magnitudes and colors (eqs. 4-11 to 4-13 or 4-14 to 4-16).
2. Correct for extinction (Appendix G and eqs. 4-22, 4-28, 4-29).
3. Calculate transformation coefficients if not already known (Appendix H).
4. Calculate standardized magnitudes and colors (eqs. 4-32 to 4-34).

Figure 9.8. Observing flowchart.

234

research program and the habits of the observer. For example, one might begin the night with simple differential photometry of a rapid variable but after an hour or two start a program of observing cepheid variables on the *UBV* system scattered all over the sky. Clearly, this calls for a combination of observing techniques. However, on any given night, the observing pattern can be broken into three categories. The first category is differential photometry either on the standard or the instrumental photometric system. The second is a sequence of observations designed to yield the transformation coefficients to the standard system. The third category is what we call "all-sky" photometry in which many objects are observed throughout the night, located at various positions in the sky. The cepheid observations mentioned above fall into this category. We must stress that there are several other forms of photometry, such as occultation or galaxy surface photometry, that do not fit these categories directly. These categories are merely the most common types and they are defined to help the novice to see how things are done. Figure 9.8 illustrates possible observing patterns with the three categories labeled as tracks 1, 2, and 3. This figure is a flowchart that can be followed from observing preparations to data reductions. For your reference, we have labeled the appropriate sections where a discussion or a worked example can be found.

A final comment about data recording is in order for those using DC photometers. If you are using the amplifier meter to make your measurements, it is a good idea to follow a simple pattern. As you watch the needle, it appears to jitter above and below some mean value. Rather than watching the meter for a long stretch of time, it is better to watch the meter for, say, 10 seconds and then estimate and record the mean value. This procedure should be repeated several times and averaged to make a single measurement. When using a chart recorder, the jitter of the needle is transformed to the jitter of a pen recording on strip-chart paper. The main advantage of the chart recorder is that you have a permanent record of the actual observations and you can transform the pen tracings to numbers the next day. Figure 9.9 shows a sample chart tracing to illustrate the technique of extracting the data. Each measurement is estimated by drawing a straight line through the middle of the jitter. The two sets of sky measurements illustrate that our golden rule of differential photometry really applies to all photometry. By drawing a line connecting the sky measurements, we can interpolate the sky background to the time of each stellar measurement. In this exam-

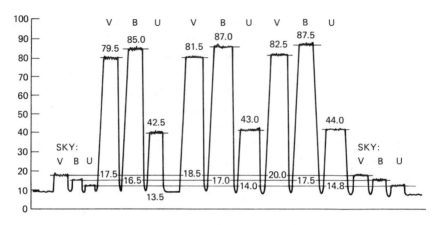

Figure 9.9. Typical chart tracing.

ple, the sky background was increasing because of a rising moon. Note that if we had made only the first sky measurement, it would have appeared that the star was brightening steadily. With the two sets of sky measurements and the graphical interpolation, you can see that the star was essentially constant once the sky background is subtracted.

We wish you good luck on your first night of photometry.

REFERENCES

1. Larson, W. J. 1978. *Sky and Tel.* **56**, 507.
2. Argelander, F. W. A. and Schönfeld, E. 1859–1886. *Astronomiche Beobachten Sternwarte Konigl.* **3, 4, 5, 8.**
3. Thome, J. M. and Perrine, C. D., 1892–1932. *Resultados Observatorios Nacional Argentino* **16, 17, 18, 21.**
4. Staff, 1969. *The Smithsonian Astrophysical Observatory Star Atlas.* Cambridge: MIT Press.
5. Becvar, A., 1964. *Atlas Borealis, Eclipticalis, and Australis.* Cambridge: Sky Publishing Co.
6. Ingrao, H. C. and Kasperian, E. 1967. *Sky and Tel.* **34**, 284.
7. Vehrenberg, H. 1963. *Photographic Star Atlas.* Düsseldorf: Treugesell-Verlag KG.
8. Vehrenberg, H., 1970. *Atlas Stellarum 1950.0.* Düsseldorf: Treugesell-Verlag KG.
9. Papadopoulos, C. 1979. *True Visual Magnitude Photographic Star Atlas.* Elmsford, NY: Pergamon.
10. Lick Observatory 1965. *Lick Observatory Sky Atlas.* Mt. Hamilton, California.
11. Doughty, N. A., Shane, C. O., and Wood, F. B. 1972. *Canterbury Sky Atlas (Australis).* New Zealand: Mount John University Observatory.

12. Palomar Observatory, 1954. *National Geographic–Palomar Observatory Sky Survey.* Pasadena: California Institute of Technology.
13. ESO/SRC. *Atlas of the Southern Sky.* In preparation.
14. Overbye, D. 1979. *Sky and Tel.* **58**, 30.
15. Kukarkin, B. V., Kholopov, P. N., Efremov, Yu. N., Kukarakina, N. P., Kurochkin, N. E., Medvedera, G. I., Peruva, N. B., Fedorovich, V. P., and Frolov, M. S. 1969–1974. *General Catalog of Variable Stars.* Moscow: Academy of Sciences of the U.S.S.R.
16. Scovil, C. E. 1980. *AAVSO Variable Star Atlas.* Cambridge: Sky Publishing Co.
17. Hoffmeister, C. *Mitteilungen der Sternwarte zu Sonneberg,* No. 12–22 (1928–1933), No. 245–330 (1957).
18. Anon., 1954. *Communications of the Observatory of the University at Odessa* **4**, 1–3.
19. Hagen, J. G. 1934. *Atlas Stellarum Variabilium.* Vatican.
20. Bateson, F. M., Jones, A. F., et al. 1958–1977. *Charts for Southern Variables.* Wellington.
21. *Odessa Universitet Observatoriia Izvestiia,* 1953, 1954, 1955, vol. IV, parts I, II, III.
22. Code 680, Goddard Space Flight Center, Greenbelt, MD 20771
23. Cannon, A. J., and Pickering, E. C. 1918–1924. *Henry Draper Catalog and Extensions,* Harvard Annals 91–100.
24. Danford, S., and Muir, R., 1978. *Bul. Amer. Astr. Soc.* **10**, 461.
25. Houk, N. and Cowley, A. P. 1975. *University of Michigan Catalogue of Two Dimensional Spectral Types for the HD Stars.* Ann Arbor: Univ. of Michigan Press, vol. 1.
26. Overbye, D. 1979. *Sky and Tel.* **57**, 223.
27. Young, A. T. 1974. In *Methods of Experimental Physics: Astrophysics.* vol. **12A**. Edited by N. Carleton. New York: Academic Press.
28. King, I. R. 1971. *Pub. A. S. P.* **83**, 199.
29. Picarillo, J. 1973. *Pub. A. S. P.* **85**, 278.
30. Roach, F. E., and Gordon, J. L. 1973. *The Light of the Night Sky.* Boston: D. Reidel.
31. Miller, R. H. 1963. *Ap. J.* **137**, 1049.
32. Peterson, A. W. and Kieffaber, L., 1973. *Sky and Tel.* **46**, 338.
33. Myrabø, H. K. 1978. *Observatory* **98**, 234.

CHAPTER 10
APPLICATIONS OF PHOTOELECTRIC
PHOTOMETRY

By now, you probably have built or purchased a photoelectric photometer and have measured the magnitudes of a few bright stars. You may rightfully wonder what to do next! Happily, this is the least of your worries, as there are thousands of interesting stars and projects within the range of most amateur and small college telescopes.

In this chapter, we present a few of these projects. By no means is this an exhaustive compendium and we invite you to branch out and pursue other topics. However, the ideas mentioned here should give you a feeling of the breadth and diversity of the field of photometry. Not only can it be as fun and interesting as photography or visual observing, but you can help in the advancement of scientific knowledge.

10.1 PHOTOMETRIC SEQUENCES

Are you unselfish and like to share your work? Then determining photometric sequences should be right up your alley! The object is to determine the magnitudes of several standard stars in a field surrounding or near some interesting source. These sequences have to be determined carefully, as many observers following in your footsteps will be using your data as the foundation for their own research. For the purposes of this section, we identify three types of comparison star sequences: for visual observers, for photoelectric observers, and for calibrating photographic plates.

Visual variable star observers have two primary advantages over photoelectric observers: they are less influenced by light cloud cover because the comparison is made almost instantaneously, and they can work faster because the object's light does not have to be centered in a diaphragm. For these reasons, among others, visual photometry still flourishes in the ranks of amateur astronomers. However, the comparison star sequences around visual variables are generally not very accurate. The stars should cluster uniformly in space and brightness around the variable, appear similar in color, and have their magnitudes measured in a filter bandpass approximating the response of the unaided eye. This latter requirement has been difficult to achieve. Landis[1] mentions that the V filter does not match the eye's response, as blue stars look fainter and red stars brighter in V than with the eye. Stanton[2] experimented with filter responses and found that a Schott GG4 filter along with an EMI 9789B (S-11 cathode) matched the eye's response best. Each visual observer's eye has a slightly different response because of inherent and dark adaptation variations. We suggest that you cooperate with the American Association of Variable Star Observers (AAVSO)[3] and help them in determining photoelectric sequences in poorly defined fields and in finding good filter-photometer combinations for visual magnitude sequences.

Photoelectric observers need fewer comparison stars per variable than do visual observers, but the selection of suitable comparisons can be very tedious. The color (especially) and magnitude should match as closely as possible, and the star should be within 1° of the variable. Unlike visual observers, where 0.1 magnitude accuracy is acceptable, photoelectric observers need to determine their variables to 0.01 magnitude or better. This means the comparison stars must be at least this stable. Two stars should be located and measured on several occasions to ascertain whether they are truly constant in magnitude. It is difficult to obtain comparison stars for red variables because a large fraction of cool stars are variable, often with long periods, so that they may be constant during a few night's observations. Try to determine comparison stars for a group of variables, such as bright flare stars, cepheids with 5-day periods, etc. Another project is to reobserve comparison stars used in the literature to see if they remain constant or are long-period variables. Check with a local professional astronomer or the AAVSO for additional or more specific ideas.

Photographic photometry is still valuable today because of its great multiplexing advantages. By calibrating a cluster plate accurately, for example, you can measure the brightness of many hundreds of stars in a few hours. In crowded fields, photographic photometry may be the only practical method of determining magnitudes. It is also much faster in measuring faint stars than photoelectric methods. Calibrating photographic plates is impossible unless a good photoelectric sequence appears in the plate field. This sequence should cover as wide a magnitude range as possible, and be obtained in the filter bandpass of the plate, which is usually blue. The plate calibration of the large surveys such as the National Geographic–Palomar Sky Survey is particularly important, as the Space Telescope will require accurate magnitudes over the entire sky, obtainable only from such surveys. Argue et al.[4] have gathered the known photoelectric sequences, which are usually around galactic and globular clusters. Complete coverage of the sky is lacking, though, and amateur observations are particularly needed here to take some of the burden from the professional observatories. There are over 1000 fields in the National Geographic–Palomar Sky Survey alone, each requiring 10 to 20 sequence stars to fifteenth visual magnitude for the fine guidance system of the Space Telescope. You can see that there is plenty of opportunity here for your photometer to feel needed!

10.2 MONITORING FLARE STARS

In 1924, the astronomer E. Hertzsprung[5] was photographing an area of sky in the constellation of Carina. He discovered that on one photograph a star was two magnitudes brighter than it had been on previous photographs. The rate at which the star brightened was much too fast to be either a nova or any kind of intrinsic variable then known. Hertzsprung tried to explain the event as the result of an asteroid falling into a star. This is the first known observation of what we now call a *flare star*. Later, this same star was seen to flare many more times and was given the variable star designation DH Car. In the years that followed, other M-type dwarfs were seen to flare but they did not receive recognition as a new class of variable stars until 20 years after Hertzsprung's initial observation.

In 1947 the American astronomer Carpenter (Luyten[6]) was photographing a red dwarf. This star was known to have a large proper motion, which implied that it was nearby. Carpenter was attempting to measure its parallax. On a single plate, he took a series of five 4-minute exposures, moving the telescope slightly after each one. When the plate was developed, he expected to see five equally bright images. But the second image was much brighter than the first. The star faded in the later images, returning to its normal brightness. The star had become 12 times brighter in about 3 minutes. This rate of increase is even faster than a supernova, though the total luminosity is much less. This star is now called UV Ceti and flare stars are now commonly referred to as *UV Ceti variables.*

The first photoelectric recording of a flare was obtained by Gordon and Kron[7] in 1949. They were observing a late-type eclipsing binary with the 0.9-meter (36-inch) refractor at Lick Observatory. They were measuring the comparison star when the needle on the DC amplifier went off the top of the scale. After several frantic minutes of experimentation, they realized their equipment was not malfunctioning and the comparison star had flared. They were able to observe the star slowly return to its normal brightness. This star is known today as AD Leo. This story simultaneously points out the sudden nature of flare star eruptions and one of the dangers of using a red comparison star!

Flare stars are usually M-type dwarfs that have emission lines in their spectra. K-type stars occasionally have been seen to flare but they do so much less frequently. Flare stars are typically one-twentieth to one-half the mass of the sun and only 10^{-5} times as luminous. They are so intrinsically faint that they must be nearby to be seen at all. Their sudden increases in luminosity have been likened to solar flares, only thousands of times stronger. These are very remarkable events for such small stars. Flare amplitudes can range from a few tenths of a magnitude or less to several magnitudes. There are two general types of flares. A spike flare increases suddenly with a rise time of only a few seconds and then fades in a few minutes. A slow flare brightens gradually over an interval of minutes to tens of minutes and then fades at about the same rate.

However, these classifications should not be taken too literally. Many flares are a combination of both types and there is great variability from flare to flare even in the same star. A more complete description of these interesting objects is beyond the scope of this section. The interested reader is referred to the work of Moffett,[8] Lovell,[9] Gershberg,[10] and Gurzadyan.[11]

The monitoring of flare stars can only be recommended to the beginner with some reluctance. Catching a flare photoelectrically can be every bit as exciting today as it was for Gordon and Kron in 1949. However, the observer must be prepared for possibly spending many tens of hours at the telescope and recording nothing but a constant star. Flares cannot be predicted, and catching one is a matter of looking in the right place at the right time. For those who cannot resist the chance of actually seeing a flare, we supply a list of flare stars, brighter than twelfth visual magnitude, in Table 10.1. Finder charts for some of these stars are available from the AAVSO at a modest cost.

Besides the requirement of patience, there are certain requirements of your equipment. Unlike normal photometry, in flare star monitoring you measure the same star for hours at a time, interrupted occasionally by a measurement of the sky background. It is therefore important that your telescope can track well and keep the star centered in the diaphragm as long as possible. Because the flare may occur very rapidly and at some unknown time, the observations are usually made in a single filter. Flares are brightest in the ultraviolet, so an ultraviolet or blue filter is preferred. Pulse-counting photometers cannot be used unless a large digital memory that can store hundreds or thousands of measurements is available. Such a system has been described by Warner and Nather[12] and Nather.[13] This instrumentation is fairly elaborate and a much simpler system for the beginner is a DC amplifier and a strip-chart recorder. If the telescope tracks well, the equipment can be left unattended for small intervals of time and the chart recorder will preserve a record of any flare activity. It is important to use the shortest possible amplifier time constant. This is necessary so the amplifier can follow any rapid flickering during the flare event. Unlike the normal procedure, it is a good idea to adjust the amplifier gain so that the star does *not* read nearly full scale. After all, if the star flares it would be helpful if the amplifier and chart recorder do not go off the top of the scale.

As mentioned above, catching a flare involves a lot of luck. One of the authors (RHK) recalls accumulating over 23 hours of monitoring of a flare star only to collect what seemed like miles of chart paper with a constant ink line. In utter frustration, the telescope was moved to the flare star EV Lac. Within the first hour of monitoring the spike flare shown in Figure 10.1 was recorded. Note that this flare lasted only 82 seconds. It would have been very unfortunate if during those 82 seconds the sky background was measured instead!

TABLE 10.1. Flare Stars

Star	(1950.0) RA	Dec.	(1985.0) RA	Dec.	Vis. Mag.	Comments
BD +43°44	00h15.5m	43°44.4	00h17.3m	43°56.0	8.1	Visual double
CQ And	00 15.5	43 44.4	00 17.3	43 56.0	11.0	
BD +66°34	00 29.3	66 57.8	00 31.3	67 09.3	10.5	
Butler's Star	00 58.1	−73 13.4	00 59.2	−73 02.0	10.6	
LPM 63	01 09.9	−17 16.0	01 11.6	−17 04.9	11.6	
CC Eri	02 32.5	−44 00.6	02 33.8	−43 51.4	8.7	
40 Eri C	03 13.1	−07 44.1	03 14.8	−07 36.3	11.2	
Ross 42	05 29.5	09 47.3	05 31.4	09 48.8	11.5	
V371 Ori	05 31.2	01 54.8	05 33.0	01 56.2	11.7	
BD −21°1377	06 08.5	−21 50.6	06 10.0	−21 51.0	8.1	
Ross 614	06 26.8	−02 46.2	06 28.5	−02 47.6	11.1	
PZ Mon	06 45.8	01 16.6	06 47.6	01 14.2	10.8	
AC +38°23616	07 06.7	38 37.5	07 09.1	38 34.1	11.5	
YY Gem	07 31.6	31 58.8	07 33.6	31 54.2	9.1	
YZ CMi	07 42.1	03 40.8	07 43.9	03 35.7	11.2	
BD +33°1646B	08 05.7	32 56.0	08 07.9	32 49.8	11.0	
AD Leo	10 16.9	20 07.3	10 18.8	19 56.7	9.4	
SZ UMa	11 17.5	66 07.0	11 19.6	65 55.5	9.3	
Ross 128	11 45.2	01 01.0	11 47.0	00 49.3	11.1	
DT Vir	12 58.3	12 38.7	13 00.0	12 27.4	9.8	
EQ Her	13 32.1	−08 05.1	13 33.9	−08 15.8	9.3	
V645 Cen	14 26.3	−62 28.1	14 29.0	−62 37.4	11.1	
DM +16°2708	14 52.1	16 18.3	14 53.7	16 09.8	10.2	
DM +55°1823	16 16.0	55 23.8	16 16.8	55 18.7	10.0	
V1054 Oph	16 52.8	−08 14.7	16 54.7	−08 18.0	9.8	Visual Companion, Ross 867, also flare star (12.9 mag.)
Ross 868	17 17.9	26 32.8	17 19.3	26 30.7	11.4	
BY Dra	18 32.7	51 41.0	18 33.5	51 42.7	8.6	
V1216 Sgr	18 46.8	−23 53.5	18 48.9	−23 51.1	10.6	

TABLE 10.1.. Flare Stars (continued)

Star	(1950.0) RA	Dec.	(1985.0) RA	Dec.	Vis. Mag.	Comments
V1285 Aql	18 53.0	08 20.3	18 54.7	08 26.0	10.1	
WOLF 1130	19 20.1	54 18.2	19 20.9	54 22.2	11.9	
AT Mic	20 38.7	−32 36.6	20 40.9	−32 29.1	10.8	
AU Mic	20 42.1	−31 31.1	20 44.2	−31 23.5	8.6	
AC +39° 57322	20 58.1	39 52.7	20 59.4	40 00.9	10.3	⎫ Visual Companion, DO Cep,
BD +56° 2783	22 26.2	57 26.8	22 27.5	57 37.5	9.9	⎬ also flare star (13.3 mag.)
L717-22	22 36.0	−20 52.8	22 37.9	−20 41.9	11.5	⎭
EV Lac	22 44.7	44 04.6	22 46.2	44 15.5	10.2	
DM +19° 5116	23 29.5	19 39.7	23 31.2	19 51.3	10.4	
BD +1° 4774	23 46.6	02 08.2	23 48.4	02 19.9	9.0	

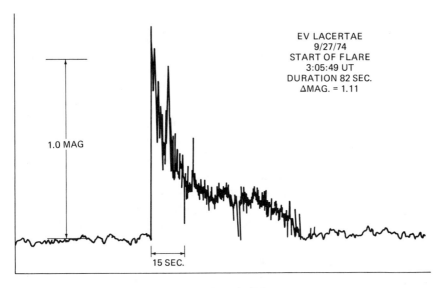

Figure 10.1. Flare of EV Lacertae.

10.3 OCCULTATION PHOTOMETRY

Occultations are among the oldest astronomical observations. With the advent of modern photoelectric photometers, chart recorders, and accurate timekeeping via WWV, amateur astronomers now have the means to make high-quality observations of occultation events. As more and more observers couple microcomputers to their equipment, the limit to complex occultation projects will depend only on the ingenuity of the astronomer. Space does not permit a thorough coverage of the methods of observing occultations. Instead, the reader is urged strongly to study the appropriate references in this section for a more in-depth treatment.

   This section describes several types of occultation observations. Occultation observers routinely seek information on the figure of the lunar limb, the separation of otherwise unresolvable binary stars, the diameter of an asteroid, or the angular size of a star. No matter what sort of occultation project is undertaken, one theme underlies each of these observations: occultations yield very high angular resolution. Observers can resolve angles as small as a few arc milliseconds. Measuring, say, 5 arc milliseconds is like determining the angular size of an orange at a distance of 3200 kilometers (1920 miles). The reason for this greatly enhanced resolution over the Dawes limit is that you no longer use the telescope's optics to do the resolving. Instead, you take advantage of the geometry of the occultation by using the separation between your earth-bound location and the occulting body as a sort of "interplanetary optical bench" in probing the object of interest.

Requirements for observing occultations vary with the complexity of the project. For many observations, only a strip-chart recorder and an accurate timepiece are needed. In order to obtain the high resolution afforded by occultations, observations must be made at high time resolution. Instrumentation such as that described by McGraw et al.[14] provides a great deal of versatility and high time resolution. Integrations must be less than 1 second and should be somewhat less for some of the projects described. This may be accomplished by running the chart recorder at high speed or for those with microcomputers, reading photometer counts into a "circulating" memory at a rate controlled by the computer. By use of microcomputers, a time resolution of 0.001 second is not difficult to obtain. This high time resolution is necessary for angular diameter studies of stars.

Grazing lunar occultations have long been of interest to amateur astronomers. Amateurs have banded themselves into groups that pack up their portable equipment, travel to "graze lines," and through cooperative efforts obtain lunar limb profiles. Many graze observers obtain very good results with little more than a stopwatch and telescope. Use of photometry for the quick disappearances and reappearances characteristic of grazes yields an unbiased, more accurate recording of grazes. Harold Povenmire[15] has devoted considerable effort to the observation of grazing occultations.

From time to time, the planets occult stars. During such events, observers are afforded the chance to obtain accurate diameters of these objects or information on their upper atmospheres. Rather startling discoveries have recently come from occultations of stars by planets. The discovery of the Uranian rings in 1977 by Elliot et al.[16] was made by occultation. Almost all information on those rings continues to be from occultation observations. In April 1980, Pluto nearly occulted a star. Such an observation would be extremely valuable as a measure of Pluto's diameter; no such occultation has yet been reported. During that 1980 appulse, Pluto's moon Chiron did occult the star as seen by one observer, A. R. Walker[17] in South Africa. An upper limit of 1200 kilometers for the diameter was deduced from the observation. Occultations of stars by planets is still fertile ground for new discoveries.

In the past few years, astrometric techniques have been pushed toward the goal of providing better predictions of occultations by asteroids. Accurate predictions are important because the path of observability is equal to the diameter of the occulting body, and asteroids are generally less than a few hundred kilometers across. Results from these measurements are impressive. Often, diameter determinations are accurate to within 1 percent.

The observations just described do not require microcomputer control of the occultation event. However, as more observers couple computers to their telescopes, it is probably only a matter of time before an intrepid amateur attempts to determine a stellar angular diameter. During a lunar occultation, the light from a star is diffracted by the lunar limb. What the photometer "sees" during the occultation is the passage of the fresnel diffraction fringes: an oscillation of the stellar flux just prior to occultation. By analysis of the diffraction fringe spacing and height, the angular size of the occulted star may be determined. References concerning aspects of lunar occultations may be found in a two-article sequence by Evans.[18,19] A more rigorous development of the topic may be found in Nather and Evans,[20] Nather,[21] Evans,[22] and Nather and McCants.[23] The fresnel diffraction pattern is only seen at high time resolution, that is, integrations of around 1 millisecond.

Related to occultations are mutual phenomena of planetary satellites, that is the mutual occultations, eclipses, and transits of satellites during the time the nodes of their orbital planes align with the earth. Accurate timing of these events can give accurate shapes and sizes of these satellites.

Predictions of the described occultations may be found from several sources such as *Sky and Telescope,* the *Astronomical Almanac,*[24] or the *Observer's Handbook,*[25] to name a few. Ambitious astronomers may wish to try their hand at predicting occultations for their particular location. These readers are referred to Smart's *Spherical Astronomy,*[26] where an excellent treatment may be found. Amateurs interested in any part of occultation observing are urged to join the International Occultation Timing Association.[27] IOTA provides excellent predictions, information, and hints on observing all types of occultations. Furthermore, this organization serves as a clearing house for observations of almost all types of occultations.

[Note: Section 10.3 was contributed by T. L. Mullikin, Space Operations and Satellite Systems Development, Rockwell International.]

10.4 INTRINSIC VARIABLES

Intrinsic variables are those stars that vary in brightness because of internal changes. Normally, this is evidenced by pulsational behavior: the star periodically shrinks and expands. Sometimes the light variations are highly regular, as in the case of cepheids and RR Lyrae variables; sometimes it is quite erratic, as for Mira and RV Tauri variables.

A thorough description of the characteristics and pulsational mechanisms for these stars would occupy more space than this text. Therefore, we refer the interested reader to Glasby,[28] Strohmeier,[29] and Kukarkin[30] for more detail. The major point of interest in this section is the fact that there are thousands of intrinsic variables, each one unique though they are placed in general categories. Astronomers have neither the manpower nor the telescope time to investigate even a majority of these stars with the thoroughness they deserve. The energies of the amateur variable star observer should be channeled in the following directions:

1. Determining standard comparison stars and preparing finding charts for those variables where no charts exist.
2. Obtaining light curves for stars with missing or incomplete curves.
3. Observing a variable star at an epoch several years removed from previous measurements, in order to detect temporal variations.
4. Investigating stars mentioned in the *Catalog of Suspected Variables*[31] or other publications to determine their nature and period.

Two rules should be followed for accurate data: use comparison stars for all measures, and obtain as many observations as possible, covering the entire light curve.

In this section, several tables of stars are presented. In each case, the 1950 coordinates are as accurate as could be found. Those variables for which coordinates are less accurate can be identified by their 1950 declination, where the arc seconds are multiples of six. The magnitudes are a general range, with the particular color indicated with a letter: *P* for photographic, *B* for the *B* filter of the *UBV* system, and *V* for the visual. Each list contains approximately 30 bright variables in each period range, as culled from the magnetic tape version of the *General Catalog of Variable Stars*. For those of you with access to large computer facilities, we highly recommend acquiring a copy of this magnetic tape through Goddard Space Flight Center in Greenbelt, Maryland.[32] Another good source of bright variables is the *Atlas of the Heavens Catalog*,[33] which has 13 pages of variables with 1950 coordinates.

Note that as the periods of the stars mentioned in this section increase, the accuracy with which they are determined decreases. This is because photoelectric data are missing on most of the long-period variables. They have not been observed for nearly as many periods as those variables with short cycles. The use of the terms *epoch* and *period* is explained in Section 10.5.

10.4a Short-Period Variables

As with the other classifications, as soon as researchers find more than one star with similar characteristics, they invent a new group of variables. The short-period intrinsic variables have therefore been divided into four major groups:

1. *δ Scuti stars*. These have low amplitude, sinusoidal light curves. Periods are less than 0.3 day.
2. *Dwarf cepheids*. These have larger amplitudes (though less than one magnitude), varied light curve shapes (either sinusoidal or asymmetric with a faster rise to maximum brightness than the ensuing decline), and periods also less than 0.3 day.
3. *RR Lyrae variables*. Named after their prototype, these are similar to dwarf cepheids but with periods ranging between 0.3 and 1.0 day. They are commonly called *cluster variables* because of their affinity to globular clusters.
4. *Cepheids*. Again similar to dwarf cepheids, these variables have periods ranging between 1 and approximately 50 days.

Eggen[34] and Tsesevich[35] give more information on these stars. For the amateur, δ Scuti stars are very difficult to observe as the amplitude is seldom greater than 0.10 magnitude in the visual. Therefore, we concentrate on the latter three groups.

Dwarf cepheids brighter than twelfth visual magnitude and with a ΔV of 0.5 or less have been listed by Percy et al.[11] The coordinates that they give are for 1900.0 and will have to be precessed to be usable. Fourteen stars are included on their list. A complete list (but without coordinates) is given by Eggen,[34] including all δ Scuti and dwarf cepheids known to date that are brighter than visual magnitude 11.5 at maximum. Coordinates can be found in Eggen's references or by using the BD or HD catalogs.

No exclusive catalog exists for RR Lyrae variables. Tsesevich[35] presents older visual observations for several hundred RR Lyrae stars and this work should be reviewed by the interested reader. A complete catalog of the several thousand Magellanic Cloud RR Lyrae variables has been published by the Gaposchkins,[37,38] but these stars are too faint and in overcrowded fields for photoelectric work by all but the large professional telescopes. Sturch[39] lists photoelectric observations on 100 field RR Lyrae stars.

Table 10.2 lists the magnitudes and coordinates for selected very short-period (less than 1 day) variables. Table 10.2 is by no means complete, but can be used as a stepping stone to more difficult objects.

Because of their relative rarity and larger luminosity, cepheid variables have been cataloged more carefully than the other variables. Schaltenbrand and Tammann[40] give a complete list of those cepheids with photoelectric data. Henden[41,42] gives an extensive list of short-period (less than 5 days) cepheids that are visible from the Northern Hemisphere. Table 10.3 lists a representative sample of cepheid variables with periods less than 10 days.

10.4b Medium-period Variables

These stars are classified primarily as *RV Tauri stars* or *long-period cepheids*. Eggen[43] gives a review of these stars whose periods range from 30 to 100 days or so. Most of the long-period cepheids are found in the Small Magellanic or Large Magellanic Cloud. Very little data exist on these variables because of their rarity and long periods. These and the longer period Miras are prime candidates for dedicated amateurs as their periods are too long for good coverage from national observatories. RV Tauri light curves are unstable and show irregularities in both shape and period. Like RR Lyrae stars, they belong to the old galactic halo star population type. The long-period cepheids have not been studied extensively, and in some cases, such as RU Cam, they have quit pulsating for extended periods of time. Representative members of both of these classes with periods between 10 to 100 days are shown in Table 10.4.

TABLE 10.2. Intrinsic Variables, 0.1 ≤ P < 1.0 Days

NAME	R.A. (1950.0)	DEC. (1950.0)	R.A. (1985.0)	DEC. (1985.0)	TYPE	MAG.	EPOCH	PERIOD
BS AQR	23 46 11.6	− 8 25 24.5	23 47 59	− 8 13 44	RRS	9.4−10.0B	28095.330	0.19782278
DN AQR	23 16 28.5	−24 33 28.7	23 18 19	−24 21 59	RRAB	10.0−10.5P	28425.284	0.63464
X ARI	3 8 48.0	10 15 23.8	3 7 41	10 23 25	RRAB	9.2−10.5B	37583.568	0.651139
VZ CNC	8 38 9.5	10 0 10.4	8 40 3	9 38 41	RRS	7.5− 8.2P	37631.8461	0.17836376
AD CMI	7 50 11.7	1 43 39.1	7 52 0	1 38 12	RRS	9.1− 9.4B	36601.8228	0.122974
V743 CEN	13 25 17.7	−51 1 58.5	13 27 26	−51 12 50	RR	8.3− 8.5P	−	0.104
RZ CEP	22 37 27.9	64 35 42.6	22 38 40	64 46 39	RRAB	9.5−10.3B	38207.938	0.308645
RR CET	1 29 34.0	5 18 12.0	1 31 21	5 15 59	RR	9.3−10.3P	17501.4421	0.5530253
XZ CET	1 57 52.6	−16 35 15.2	1 59 33	−16 25 25	RRAB	8.5− 9.2P	−	0.451
XZ CYG	19 31 27.4	56 16 47.2	19 32 10	56 21 20	RRAB	9.1−10.5B	36933.981	0.466579
DX DEL	20 45 5.0	−12 16 42.0	20 46 44	−12 24 26	RRAB	9.5−10.3V	30950.506	0.47261673
SU DRA	11 35 6.8	67 36 27.0	11 37 37	67 24 49	RRAB	9.2−10.2V	20605.7569	0.66041926
XZ DRA	19 30 24.4	64 46 33.1	19 31 9	64 50 2	RRAB	9.6−10.6V	27985.648	0.4764944
RX ERI	4 47 28.5	−15 49 35.3	4 49 3	−15 45 59	RRAB	9.2−10.1V	21692.479	0.58724622
SV ERI	3 9 27.9	−11 32 36.0	3 11 7	−11 24 42	RRC	9.6−10.2V	28398.200	0.7137590
CS ERI	2 35 10.0	−43 10 47.3	2 36 30	−43 1 41	RRC	8.7− 9.2V	−	0.311331
SS FOR	2 5 36.1	−27 6 5.9	2 7 11	−26 56 8	RRAB	9.5−10.6V	38668.951	0.495432
RS GRU	21 39 48.2	−48 25 6.5	21 42 5	−48 15 30	RRS	7.9− 8.5V	34325.2931	0.14701147
TT IND	21 11 11.0	−45 16 42.0	21 12 30	−45 8 6	RRAB	9.1−10.5V	36651.358	0.479591
RR LYR	19 23 52.1	42 41 11.9	19 24 59	42 45 47	RRAB	9.5−10.2V	38241.460	0.5974379
TY MEN	5 40 38.1	−81 38 19.1	5 37 27	−81 37 24	RRAB	7.2− 8.6B	38314.493	0.5668054
V429 ORI	4 53 43.0	1 36 30.0	4 55 27	1 33 14	RRS	7.7− 7.9P	28876.413	0.18747
DH PEG	22 12 55.0	6 34 6.0	22 14 40	6 44 39	RRC	9.3− 9.8V	38251.872	0.255510
RU PSC	1 11 42.0	24 9 6.0	1 13 36	24 20 12	RRC	10.0−10.4V	24057.945	0.3903174
V440 SGR	19 29 20.0	−23 57 36.0	19 31 26	−23 53 6	RRAB	9.8−11.3B	37526.324	0.477474
V703 SCO	17 39 20.0	−32 30 0.0	17 41 17	−32 31 0	RRC	7.8− 8.5B	37186.365	0.11521789
MT TEL	18 58 30.8	−46 43 27.3	19 1 6	−46 40 26	RRC	8.7− 9.3V	38479.332	0.316899
TU UMA	11 27 9.7	30 20 37.7	11 29 35	30 9 2	RRAB	9.3−10.2V	38510.756	0.557659
AI VEL	8 12 26.2	−44 25 21.8	8 13 35	−44 31 46	RRS	6.4− 7.1V	−	0.11157396

TABLE 10.3. Intrinsic Variables, 1.0 < P < 10.0 Days

NAME	R.A. (1950.0)	DEC. (1950.0)	R.A. (1985.0)	DEC. (1985.0)	TYPE	MAG.	EPOCH	PERIOD
FF AQL	18 56 1.2	17 17 32.4	18 57 34	17 20 24	CDEL	5.8- 6.4B	41576.428	4.470916
V1162 AQL	19 49 35.2	-11 29 46.2	19 51 31	-11 24 20	CEP	8.6- 9.3P	25803.400	5.3761
ETA AQL	19 49 55.5	0 52 33.2	19 51 42	0 57 59	CDEL	4.1- 5.4B	32926.749	7.176641
V CAR	8 27 42.5	-59 57 17.9	8 28 25	-60 4 20	CDEL	7.8- 8.8B	35621.16	6.69638
GI CAR	11 11 48.0	-57 38 18.1	11 13 20	-57 49 44	CEP	8.8- 9.2B	34521.40	4.43061
TU CAS	0 23 36.7	51 0 13.5	0 25 30	51 11 51	CW	7.4- 8.9B	36792.94	2.139292
V381 CEN	13 47 22.5	-57 19 58.4	13 49 43	-57 30 22	CW	7.9- 9.0B	34932.29	5.07878
V419 CEN	11 28 34.2	-56 37 22.1	11 30 12	-56 48 20	CEP	8.6- 9.2B	34906.43	5.50746
V553 CEN	14 43 32.2	-31 57 42.0	14 45 38	-32 6 30	CEP	8.7- 9.3P	34235.65	2.06119
V659 CEN	13 28 12.8	-61 19 29.7	13 30 32	-61 30 18	CEP	7.1- 7.4P	30049.637	5.621605
DELTA CEP	22 27 18.5	58 9 31.8	22 28 36	58 20 17	CDEL	3.9- 5.2B	42756.458	5.366270
AX CIR	14 48 29.4	-63 36 17.8	14 51 21	-63 44 55	CEP	5.6- 6.1V	38199.325	5.2734
V1334 CYG	21 17 22.4	38 1 31.8	21 18 46	38 10 25	CW	5.8- 6.0V	41760.900	3.333020
TX DEL	20 47 42.0	3 27 54.8	20 49 27	3 35 45	CDEL	8.8- 9.5V	42947.033	6.165907
BETA DOR	5 32 11.3	-62 15 20.2	5 33 5	-62 29 58	CDEL	4.0- 5.1B	40905.26	9.84206
W GEM	6 32 5.6	15 22 16.4	6 34 31	15 20 35	CEP	7.3- 8.5B	42755.172	7.913779
GH LUP	15 20 56.5	-52 40 38.9	15 23 31	-52 48 4	CEP	7.8- 8.2P	38202.145	9.285
V526 MON	6 59 21.1	-1 3 29.9	7 1 7	-1 1 32	CEP	9.0- 9.4P	40286.290	2.674985
AU PEG	21 21 40.4	18 1 49.4	21 23 39	18 12 51	CW	9.2- 9.4V	41739.439	2.40525
16 PSA	23 0 44.1	-35 1 12.7	23 2 2	-34 49 53	CEP	5.2- 5.5P	38260.250	7.975
AP PUP	7 56 1.0	-39 59 14.8	7 57 14	-40 4 56	CDEL	7.1- 7.8V	40689.21	5.0843102
S SGE	19 53 44.9	16 30 4.0	19 55 20	16 35 40	CDEL	5.9- 7.0B	42678.783	8.382086
V636 SCO	17 19 5.4	-45 34 1.1	17 21 19	-45 36 15	CEP	7.2- 8.0B	34906.47	6.79663
ST TAU	5 42 13.3	13 33 23.8	5 44 12	13 34 48	CW	8.5- 9.6B	41761.963	4.034229
SZ TAU	4 34 20.2	18 26 35.2	4 36 22	18 30 15	CDEL	7.1- 7.8B	41659.194	3.148380
U TRA	16 2 51.2	-62 46 36.6	16 5 58	-62 52 48	CEP	7.7- 9.1B	19722.284	2.568438
ALFA UMI	1 48 48.8	89 1 43.7	2 16 16	89 11 56	CW	1.9- 2.1V	39253.23	3.96978
AH VEL	8 10 25.6	-46 29 36.8	8 11 31	-46 35 35	CEP	5.5- 5.9V	40742.14	4.22713
BG VEL	9 6 39.1	-51 14 0.0	9 7 46	-51 22 22	CDEL	7.4- 7.9V	41053.30	6.92357
T VUL	20 49 26.8	28 13 43.7	20 50 49	28 11 31	CDEL	5.4- 6.1V	41705.121	4.435462
U VUL	19 34 26.5	20 13 12.3	19 35 58	20 17 55	CDEL	6.8- 7.5V	42526.328	7.990629

TABLE 10.4. Intrinsic Variables with 10 < P < 100 Days

NAME	R.A. (1950.0)	DEC. (1950.0)	R.A. (1985.0)	DEC. (1985.0)	TYPE	MAG.	EPOCH	PERIOD
DS AQR	22 50 36.0	-18 51 30.0	22 52 28	-18 40 19	RV	10.3-11.6P	30972.6	78.30
V341 ARA	16 53 2.0	-63 7 54.0	16 56 18	-63 11 11	CEP	10.9-11.3V	34237.6	11.95
RU CAM	7 16 20.4	69 45 53.4	7 20 7	69 41 58	CW	9.3-10.4B	37356.9	22.055
TW CAM	4 16 39.0	57 19 18.0	4 19 32	57 24 19	RVA	10.4-11.5P	28647.	85.6
TW CAP	20 11 40.0	-13 59 30.0	20 13 37	-13 53 6	CW	10.3-12.0B	35664.8	28.5578
U CAR	10 55 45.6	-59 27 50.8	10 57 11	-59 39 5	CDEL	6.7-8.5B	41118.2	38.7681
IW CAR	9 25 42.9	-63 24 43.3	9 26 32	-63 33 52	RVB	7.9-9.6P	29401.	67.5
L CAR	9 43 52.4	-62 16 36.4	9 44 50	-62 26 18	CDEL	4.3-5.5B	40736.44	35.5330
V420 CEN	11 37 24.0	-47 41 6.0	11 39 39	-47 52 44	CW	9.9-11.6B	25350.67	24.7678
RS COL	5 13 33.0	-28 48 24.0	5 14 55	-28 46 44	CEP	9.0-9.4P	27809.	14.66
X CYG	20 41 26.6	35 24 23.9	20 42 48	35 31 59	CDEL	6.6-8.4B	25739.90	16.3866
SS GEM	6 5 33.5	22 37 32.8	6 7 3	22 37 12	RV	9.3-10.7P	34365.	89.31
ZETA GEM	7 1 8.6	20 38 43.4	7 3 13	20 35 35	CDEL	3.7-4.2V	34416.78	10.15082
AC HER	18 28 13.0	21 40 53.1	18 29 37	21 21 21	RVA	7.4-9.7B	35052.	75.4619
AP HER	18 48 13.0	15 52 42.0	18 49 47	15 55 10	CW	10.4-11.2V	–	10.408
FW LUP	15 19 7.2	-40 44 53.3	15 21 25	-40 52 23	CEP	9.2-9.6P	38197.3	16.73
T MON	6 22 33.2	7 6 51.0	6 24 26	7 5 39	CDEL	5.6-6.0V	40838.59	27.0205
U MON	7 28 24.3	-9 40 15.4	7 30 4	-9 44 41	RVB	6.1-8.1P	30347.	92.26
Y OPH	17 49 57.8	-6 7 59.0	17 51 50	-6 8 26	CEP	7.1-7.9B	34921.49	17.12326
EI PEG	23 19 15.0	-12 19 18.0	23 21 0	-12 30 48	SRA	10.0-11.5P	30961.0	61.15
RS PUP	8 11 9.0	-34 25 35.6	8 12 29	-34 31 57	CDEL	6.5-7.6V	35734.426	41.3876
ST PUP	6 47 12.0	-37 11 8.0	6 48 24	-37 15 31	CW	9.7-11.5B	35617.45	18.8864
AR PUP	8 1 10.0	-36 27 18.0	8 2 27	-36 33 13	RVB	8.7-10.9P		75.
LS PUP	7 56 58.0	-29 10 18.0	7 58 22	-29 16 2	CEP	9.8-10.8P	38376.500	14.1464
LX PUP	8 6 6.7	-16 18 48.0	8 7 41	-16 24 56	CEP	9.5-10.0P	37314.25	13.88
R SGE	20 11 46.7	-16 34 26.2	20 13 22	-16 40 49	RVB	9.5-11.5B	23627.0	70.594
AL VIR	14 8 26.8	-13 4 32.9	14 10 20	-13 14 25	CW	9.1-9.9V	37462.5	10.3040
W VIR	13 23 26.9	-3 7 8.8	13 25 15	-3 18 3	CW	9.5-10.7V	32697.783	17.2736
V VUL	20 34 24.0	26 25 48.0	20 35 53	26 33 7	RVA	8.1-9.3V	14871.1	75.72
SV VUL	19 49 27.8	27 19 52.8	19 50 53	27 25 17	CDEL	6.7-7.8V	38268.9	45.035

10.4c Long-period Variables

The *Mira* type of variable has regular periods of 150 to 450 days. They differ from the *semiregular* (SR) variables primarily in their amplitude of pulsation. Miras vary by more than 2.5 magnitudes in the visual, whereas SR variables are defined to have smaller amplitudes than this. Miras are red giants, and are named after their prototype Mira Ceti, the first intrinsic variable star ever discovered. Most long-period variables show bright hydrogen emission lines and titanium oxide bands in their spectra. Table 10.5 lists the red long-period variables whose periods range from 100 to 1000 days.

Landolt has one of the longest series of *UBV* observations on long-period variables. The papers in his series are listed below.

I: 1966, *Pub. A.S.P.* **78**, 531.
II: 1967, *Pub. A.S.P.* **79**, 336.
III: 1968, *Pub. A.S.P.* **80**, 228.
IV: 1968, *Pub. A.S.P.* **80**, 450.
V: 1968, *Pub. A.S.P.* **80**, 680.
VI: 1969, *Pub. A.S.P.* **81**, 134.
VII: 1969, *Pub. A.S.P.* **81**, 381.
VIII: 1973, *Pub. A.S.P.* **85**, 625.

From these papers, it is immediately obvious that one of the problems of observing this class of variables is: they are very red, with typical $(B - V)$ indices of 1.5 to 4.0 magnitudes. Therefore, when a long period variable is near minimum at V equals 10, it may be fourteenth magnitude at B!

10.4d The Eggen Paper Series

Eggen was one of the pioneers in observing variable stars photoelectrically, and has been classifying variables systematically for many years. His series of papers should be consulted for information concerning any variable class, and contain many observations that are useful in setting up your own program. The papers are somewhat technical and may be difficult for the amateur to read, but are listed below.

I: "The Red Variables of Type N," 1972. *Ap. J.* **174**, 45.
II: "The Red Variables of S and Related Types," 1972. *Ap. J.* **177**, 489.

TABLE 10.5. Intrinsic Variables, 100 < P < 1000 Days

NAME	(1950.0) R.A.	(1950.0) DEC.	(1985.0) R.A.	(1985.0) DEC.	TYPE	MAG.	EPOCH	PERIOD
VX AND	0 17 15.0	44 26 0.9	0 19 6	44 37	SRA	7.8– 9.3V	25558.	369.
THET APS	14 0 23.3	-76 33 24.7	14 3 50	-76 43	SRB	6.4– 8.6P	28625.	119.
V AQR	20 44 17.7	-2 15 11.9	20 46 3	-2 22	SRB	7.6– 9.4V	34275.	244.
RV BOO	14 37 9.3	32 45 15.2	14 38 37	32 36	SRB	7.9– 9.6P	—	137.
RW BOO	14 39 6.2	31 47 6.6	14 40 35	31 31	SRB	8.0– 9.5P	28861.	209.
RV CAM	4 26 31.9	57 18 12.7	4 29 26	57 22	SRB	8.2– 9.0P	34930.	101.
V CVN	13 17 17.1	45 47 22.4	13 18 48	45 36	SRA	8.2– 8.8V	—	191.88
RU CEP	1 14 23.7	84 52 10.1	1 19 5	85 3	SRD	8.2– 9.4V	—	109.
T CET	0 19 14.5	-20 20 6.2	0 21 0	-20 8	SRB	6.6– 7.7P	36460.	159.
OMI CET	2 16 49.0	-3 12 13.4	2 18 35	-3 2	M	2.0–10.1V	38457.	331.65
W CYG	21 34 8.2	45 9 0.4	21 35 27	45 18	SRB	6.8– 8.9P	30684.	130.85
RS CYG	20 11 34.5	38 34 36.4	20 12 50	38 40	SRA	6.5– 9.3V	37930.	418.0
R DOR	4 36 0	-62 10 31.8	4 36 35	-62 6	SRB	5.9– 6.9V	—	338.
UX DRA	19 23 22.4	76 27 41.7	19 22 7	76 31	SRA	5.9– 6.5V	—	168.
AH DRA	16 47 24.0	57 53 59.2	16 48 0	57 50	SRB	8.5– 9.3P	30520.	158.
TV GEM	6 8 50.9	21 52 51.6	6 10 57	21 52	SRC	8.7– 9.5P	—	182.
UW HER	17 12 39.0	36 25 26.7	17 13 52	36 23	SRB	8.6– 9.5P	—	100.
AK HYA	8 37 35.7	-17 7 23.4	8 39 12	-17 14	SRB	7.8– 8.2P	—	112.
T IND	21 16 52.2	-45 14 3.6	21 19 10	-45 5	SRB	7.7– 9.4P	30100.	320.
T MIC	20 24 52.5	-28 25 39.2	20 27 0	-28 18	SRB	7.7– 9.6P	23743.	347.
RY MON	7 4 31.0	-1 28 48.0	7 6 12	-1 32	SRA	7.7– 9.2V	38475.	466.
X OPH	18 35 57.6	8 47 19.7	18 37 37	8 49	M	5.9– 9.2V	30370.	334.22
TW PEG	22 1 43.2	22 6 20.4	22 3 21	22 16	SR	7.0– 9.2V	36946.	956.4
L2 PUP	7 12 0.7	-44 33 26.4	7 13 4	-44 37	SRB	2.6– 6.0V	—	140.83
U PYX	8 27 49.1	-30 9 25.9	8 29 14	-30 16	SR	8.6– 9.4P	—	345.
BM SCO	17 37 42.8	-32 11 21.1	17 39 59	-32 12	SRD	6.8– 8.7P	—	850.
CE TAU	5 29 16.8	18 33 32.0	5 31 19	18 35	SRC	6.1– 6.5P	34670.	165.
RY UMA	12 18 4.0	61 35 13.3	12 19 44	61 23	SRA	6.1– 9.3P	—	311.2
VW UMA	10 55 38.0	70 15 25.5	10 58 27	70 4	SR	8.4– 9.1P	38890.	125.
SS VIR	12 22 40.0	1 2 48.0	12 24 27	0 51	M	6.0– 9.6V	—	354.66
SW VIR	13 11 29.7	-2 32 32.6	13 13 17	-2 43	SRB	8.2– 9.4P	—	150.

III: "Calibration of the Luminosities of Small-Amplitude Red Variables of the Old Disk Population," 1973. *Ap. J.* **180**, 857.
IV: "Very-Small-Amplitude, Very Short-Period Red Variables," 1973. *Ap. J.* **184**, 793.
V: "The Large-Amplitude Red Variables," 1975. *Ap. J.* **195**, 661.
VI: "The Long-Period Cepheids," 1977. *Ap. J. Supl. Ser.* **34**, 1.
VII: "The Medium-Amplitude Red Variables," 1977. *Ap. J.* **213**, 767.
VIII: "Ultrashort-Period Cepheids," 1979. *Ap. J. Supl. Ser.* **41**, 413.
IX: "The Very Short-Period Cepheids," *Ap. J.* In press.

10.5 ECLIPSING BINARIES

At least 50 percent of all stars are members of systems in which two or more stars orbit around their common center of mass. Many of the stars that appear single are in fact unresolved binaries. Some of these systems have orbital planes that lie nearly along our line of sight. As a result, the two stars take turns blocking each other from our sight during each orbital period. The apparent single point of light seen on earth fades and recovers as a star goes through eclipse. There are two eclipses each orbital period. The amount of light lost depends on the temperature of the two stars. The greatest light loss, called *primary eclipse,* occurs when the hotter star is blocked from view. The shallower, *secondary eclipse* occurs when the cooler star is blocked from view. These stellar systems are referred to as eclipsing binary systems. Their light curves contain valuable information about the stellar sizes, shapes, limb darkening, mass exchange, and surface spots, to name but a few items. As a result, the study of these systems forms an important part of stellar research.

It has been traditional to classify an eclipsing binary system as one of three types based on the shape of its light curve. When binaries are classified in this way, many systems of diverse physical structure and evolutionary state are grouped together. Furthermore, there are systems for which light curves defy classification in this scheme. It has become clear in recent years that this classification system is now obsolete. However, there is no new classification scheme that is universally accepted. For this and historical reasons, we describe the three traditional classification types.

Algol or β Persei is a naked-eye star that was discovered to be a variable star by ancient Arab astronomers. This was the first known variable star. It is now the prototype of the *Algol class* of eclipsing binaries, which now numbers several hundred. Typically, these systems contain an early-type (B to A) star that is brighter and more massive than its late-type (G to K) companion. The primary eclipse is deep because of the loss of light from the hot early-type star. On the other hand, the secondary eclipse, because of the light loss of the cooler star, is very shallow and difficult to detect. The orbital periods of Algol systems range from about 1 day to more than a month. The light curve in Figure 10.2a is from a typical Algol system. Table 10.6 lists a few of the brighter systems.

The light curve of Figure 10.2b is that of a typical β Lyrae type eclipsing binary. In these systems, the apparent magnitude changes con-

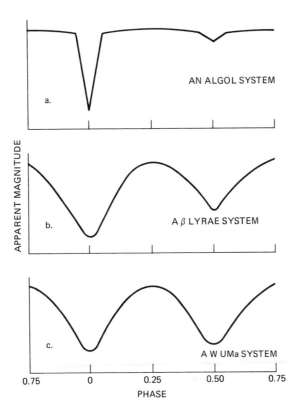

Figure 10.2. Light curves of eclipsing binaries.

TABLE 10.6. Algol-Type Binary Systems

Name	(1950.0) RA	(1950.0) Dec.	(1985.0) RA	(1985.0) Dec.	Mag.	Epoch	Period (Days)
XZ And	01h53m49s	41° 51′26″	01h55m57s	42° 01′41″	10.02–12.99 p	2441954.340	1.357293
V889 Aql	19 16 34	16 09 30	19 18 09	16 13 22	8.7–9.3 p	27210.596	11.12071
RZ Cas	02 44 23	69 25 36	02 47 33	69 34 21	6.38–7.89 p	39025.3025	1.1952499
TV Cas	00 16 36	58 51 40	00 18 30	59 03 19	7.3–8.39 p	36483.8091	1.8126130
V636 Cen	14 13 40	−49 42 48	14 15 58	−49 52 32	8.7–9.2 v	34540.340	4.28398
U Cep	00 57 46	81 36 25	01 00 56	81 47 43	6.80–9.10 V	42327.7697	2.493083
U CrB	15 16 09	31 49 42	15 17 35	31 42 04	7.04–8.35 p	16747.964	3.45220416
SW Cyg	20 05 24	46 09 21	20 06 30	46 15 27	9.24–11.83 V	38602.6009	4.573116
AI Dra	16 55 09	52 46 30	16 55 57	52 43 15	7.05–8.09 V	37544.5095	1.19881520
TW Dra	15 33 07	64 04 23	15 33 38	63 57 24	8.2–10.5 p	38539.4457	2.8068352
S Equ	20 54 44	04 53 10	20 56 29	05 01 16	8.0–10.08 V	37968.345	3.436072
CD Eri	03 45 21	−08 46 04	03 47 03	−08 39 37	9.5–10.2 p	29910.567	2.876766
TT Hya	11 10 46	−26 11 36	11 12 29	−26 23 02	7.5–9.5 p	24615.388	6.9534124
AU Mon	06 52 22	−01 18 42	06 54 09	−01 21 24	8.2–9.5 v	32888.554	11.11306
β Per (Algol)	03 04 55	40 45 50	03 07 12	40 53 53	2.12–3.40 V	40953.4657	2.8673075
IZ Per	01 28 56	53 45 42	01 31 08	53 56 30	7.8–9.0 p	25571.360	3.687661
RW Per	04 16 48	42 11 41	04 19 14	42 16 43	9.7–11.45 V	39063.684	13.19891
Y Psc	23 31 53	07 38 52	23 33 40	07 50 28	9.0–12.0 v	41225.473	3.765859
BH Pup	08 06 34	−41 52 55	08 07 46	−41 59 05	8.4–9.1 p	26100.891	1.915854
U Sge	19 16 37	19 31 06	19 18 09	19 34 58	6.58–9.18 V	40774.4638	3.3806260
λ Tau	03 57 54	12 21 04	03 59 50	12 26 58	3.3–3.80 p	35089.204	3.952955
RW Tau	04 00 49	27 59 24	04 02 58	28 05 10	8.02–11.59 V	40160.3771	2.7688425
X Tri	01 57 43	27 38 48	01 59 43	27 48 57	8.9–11.5 p	40299.296	0.9715330
AC UMa	08 51 36	65 09 45	08 54 37	65 01 44	9.2–10.2 p	42521.58	6.85493
TX UMa	10 42 24	45 49 47	10 44 27	45 38 44	7.06–8.76 V	39193.310	3.063243

tinuously even outside of eclipse because of the distorted shapes of the stars. The stars in these systems are nearly touching, and their mutual gravitational attraction has distorted them into elongated, egg-like shapes whose long dimensions always point toward each other. As the stars move in their orbits, their projected surface area as seen by the observer varies. The light curve then peaks when both stars are seen "broadside" and then fade as they turn. These systems usually contain early-type stars and often show complications in their spectra indicating gas streams and shells. Their orbital periods usually exceed 1 day. Table 10.7 is a list of some bright β Lyrae-type systems.

The curve in Figure 10.2c belongs to a typical member of the W *Ursae Majoris (W UMa) class*. These systems too are highly distorted by gravitational fields. The two component stars have nearly identical surface temperatures, which results in near equality in the depths of the two eclipses. The similarity in temperature is believed to be the result of a common atmosphere that surrounds both stars. These stars really are touching! Unlike the β Lyrae systems, these stars belong to spectral classes F, G, and K. The orbital periods are less than 1 day. Table 10.8 is a list of some brighter W UMa-type systems.

There is a newly recognized type of eclipsing binary, *RS Canun Venaticorum (RS CVn) systems*, which shows one of the shortcomings of the old classification system. In the past, members of this group had been classified with the Algols, yet they clearly contain stars that are very different from those found in Algol systems. The hotter star is type F or G and the cooler is late G to early K. They have orbital periods of a few days. The curious feature of their light curve is a broad depression of about $0^m.1$ which slowly migrates in phase. Several of these systems are now known to flare in the radio and x-ray regions of the spectrum. The depression in the light curve is believed to be the result of large starspots that migrate slowly in longitude on the surface of the cooler star. These spots are like sunspots, only they cover a much higher percentage (about 10 percent) of the stellar surface. The x-ray and radio emissions are believed to be related to strong coronal activity around the spotted star. A more complete review can be found in an article by Zeilik et al.[44] Table 10.9 contains a partial list of some RS CVn-type systems. Anyone seriously considering observing these systems would do well to contact Douglas Hall,[45] who is coordinating the photometric work of amateur and professional observers. When monitoring these systems, it is important to follow the light curve distortions and to cor-

TABLE 10.7. β Lyrae-Type Binary Systems

Name	RA (1950.0)	Dec. (1950.0)	RA (1985.0)	Dec. (1985.0)	Mag.	Epoch	Period (Days)
AN And	23h16m01s	41°29'59"	23h17m41s	41°41'28"	6.0–6.16 p	2421060.326	3.219565
σ Agl	19 36 43	05 16 58	19 38 27	05 21 48	5.18–5.36 B	22486.797	1.95026
LR Ara	16 49 07	−61 30 08	16 52 17	−61 33 37	10.0–10.6 p	28004.430	1.519304
TT Aur	05 06 15	39 31 24	05 08 40	39 34 03	8.3–9.2 p	21242.2564	1.33273365
SZ Cam	04 03 24	62 11 59	04 06 29	62 17 37	7.0–7.29 B	27533.5191	2.6984378
CX CMa	07 19 57	−25 46 44	07 21 23	−25 50 46	9.9–10.6 p	28095.601	0.954608
X Car	08 30 11	−59 03 27	08 30 57	−59 10 35	8.0–8.7 p	15021.114	1.0826310
AO Cas	00 15 04	51 09 22	00 16 56	51 21 02	8.0–8.7 p	24002.579	3.523487
LW Cen	11 35 12	−63 04 18	11 36 50	−63 15 56	5.96–6.11 B	24824.462	1.0025674
LZ Cen	11 48 05	−60 30 59	11 49 49	−60 42 40	8.0–8.6 p	26096.384	2.757717
AH Cep	22 46 04	64 47 49	22 47 20	64 58 55	6.9–7.12 p	34989.3702	1.7747274
V366 Cyg	20 43 06	53 55 10	20 44 05	54 02 49	10.0–10.46 p	34489.593	1.0960183
V548 Cyg	19 55 47	54 39 51	19 56 37	54 45 32	8.9–9.72 p	38972.1706	1.805244
V836 Cyg	21 19 21	35 31 25	21 20 47	35 40 22	8.59–9.30 B	26547.5224	0.65341090
u Her	17 15 29	33 09 13	17 16 47	33 06 59	4.6–5.28 p	27640.654	2.0510272
β Lyr	18 48 14	33 18 13	18 49 32	33 20 41	3.34–4.34 V	36379.532	12.93016
η Ori A	05 21 58	−02 26 27	05 23 44	−02 24 34	3.14–3.35 B	33420.215	7.98926
VV Ori	05 30 59	−01 11 24	05 32 46	−01 09 58	5.14–5.51 p	40545.899	1.48537769
AU Pup	08 15 56	−41 33 05	08 17 09	−41 39 39	8.50–9.40 V	39237.985	1.126411
V Pup	07 56 48	−49 06 30	07 57 48	−49 12 14	4.74–5.25 p	28648.3048	1.4544867
V525 Sgr	19 04 02	−30 14 24	19 06 16	−30 11 07	7.9–8.8 p	29662.4593	0.70512200
V453 Sco	17 53 00	−32 28 08	17 55 17	−32 28 26	6.36–6.73 V	41762.58	12.0061
V499 Sco	17 25 45	−32 57 54	17 28 03	−32 59 35	8.8–9.36 p	28340.405	2.3332977
AC Vel	10 44 18	−56 33 59	10 45 43	−56 45 03	8.5–9.0 p	23936.285	4.5622426
AY Vel	08 18 37	−43 43 27	08 19 48	−43 50 07	9.1–9.8 p	26308.903	1.617653

TABLE 10.8. W UMa- Type Binary System

Name	RA (1950.0)	Dec.	RA (1985.0)	Dec.	Mag.	Epoch	Period (Days)
AB And	23h09m08s	36° 37'22"	23h10m48s	36° 48'47"	10.4–11.27 p	2440128.7945	0.33189305
BX And	02 05 58	40 33 30	02 08 07	40 43 26	8.9–9.57 v	43809.8873	0.61011508
S Ant	09 30 07	−28 24 25	09 31 39	−28 33 43	6.7–7.22 B	35139.929	0.648345
OO Aql	19 45 47	09 11 03	19 47 28	09 16 18	9.2–10.0 v	40522.294	0.5067887
i Boo	15 02 08	47 50 51	15 03 19	47 42 41	6.5–7.10 v	39370.4222	0.2678160
XY Boo	13 46 48	20 26 02	13 48 28	20 15 37	10.0–10.36 p	39953.9621	0.37054663
TX Cnc	08 37 11	19 10 37	08 39 11	19 03 10	10.45–10.78 p	38011.3909	0.382881537
RR Cen	14 13 25	−57 37 19	14 15 54	−57 47 03	7.46–8.1 B	29036.0321	0.60569121
VW Cep	20 38 03	75 24 57	20 37 31	75 32 23	7.8–8.21 p	41880.8027	0.2783161
RZ Com	12 32 35	23 36 51	12 34 20	23 25 17	10.96–11.66 B	34837.4198	0.33850604
ε CrA	18 55 21	−37 10 25	18 57 43	−37 07 34	4.96–5.22 p	39707.6619	0.5914264
YY Eri	04 09 46	−10 35 41	04 11 26	−10 30 19	8.8–9.50 B	33617.5198	0.321496212
AK Her	17 11 43	16 24 32	17 13 17	16 22 08	8.83–9.32 B	38176.5092	0.42152368
SW Lac	22 51 22	37 40 20	22 52 59	37 51 31	10.2–11.23 p	43459.7476	0.3207216
AM Leo	11 59 35	10 09 59	11 01 25	09 58 42	8.2–8.65 v	39936.8337	0.36579720
UZ Leo	10 37 53	13 49 42	10 39 45	13 38 44	9.58–10.15 V	40673.6666	0.6180429
XY Leo	09 58 55	17 39 07	10 00 50	17 29 00	10.43–10.93 B	41005.5351	0.28411
V502 Oph	16 38 48	00 36 07	16 40 35	00 32 06	8.34–8.84 V	41174.2288	0.45339345
V566 Oph	17 54 26	04 59 29	17 56 09	04 59 15	7.60–8.09 p	41835.8618	0.40964399
V839 Oph	18 06 59	09 08 26	18 08 39	09 08 50	9.4–9.99 p	36361.7317	0.4089946
U Peg	23 55 25	15 40 30	23 57 12	15 52 11	9.23–9.80 V	36511.6688	0.3747819
AW UMa	11 27 26	30 14 35	11 29 17	30 03 00	6.84–7.10 V	38044.7815	0.4387318
W UMa	09 40 16	56 01 52	09 42 43	56 01 15	7.9–8.63 V	41004.3977	0.33363696
AG Vir	11 58 29	13 17 12	12 00 17	13 05 31	8.4–8.98 V	39946.7472	0.64264787
AH Vir	12 11 48	12 06 00	12 13 35	11 54 20	9.6–10.31 p	35245.6522	0.40752189

TABLE 10.9. Eclipsing Binaries of the RS CVn Type

Name	RA (1950.0)	Dec. (1950.0)	RA (1985.0)	Dec. (1985.0)	Mag.	Epoch	Period (Days)
CQ Aur	06ʰ00ᵐ39ˢ	31°19′52″	06ʰ02ᵐ55ˢ	31°19′37″	9.6–10.6 p	2429558.78	10.62148
SS Boo	15 11 39	38 45 15	15 12 59	38 37 26	10.2–11.2 p	20707.375	7.606215
SS Cam	07 10 19	73 25 16	07 14 36	73 21 38	10.1–10.7 v	35223.28	4.8241
RU Cnc	08 34 34	23 44 15	08 36 38	23 36 55	9.9–11.5 v	22650.720	10.172988
RS CVn	13 08 18	36 12 00	13 09 55	36 00 50	8.4–9.92 p	38889.3300	4.797855
AD Cap	21 37 03	−16 14 00	21 38 58	−16 04 29	9.3–9.9 p	30603.55	6.11826
UX Com	12 59 07	28 53 50	13 00 48	28 42 32	10.91–11.8 B	25798.370	3.642386
RT CrB	15 35 59	29 39 01	15 37 25	29 32 10	10.2–10.7 v	28273.280	5.11712
WW Dra	16 38 21	60 47 45	16 38 50	60 43 41	8.29–9.49 V	28020.3693	4.629583
Z Her	17 55 52	15 08 31	17 57 27	15 08 21	7.3–8.1 p	13086.348	3.9928012
AW Her	18 23 27	18 15 50	18 24 59	18 17 04	9.5–10.9 v	27717.2151	8.80086
MM Her	17 56 32	22 08 58	17 58 01	22 08 50	9.8–10.8 p	31302.451	7.96037
PW Her	18 08 35	33 22 34	18 09 52	33 23 02	10.7–11.8 p	28248.564	2.8810016
GK Hya	08 28 13	02 26 55	08 30 02	02 19 50	9.1–9.8 p	26411.460	3.587035
RT Lac	21 59 29	43 38 55	22 00 54	43 49 03	8.84–9.89 V	39073.8020	5.074012
AR Lac	22 06 39	45 29 46	22 08 04	45 40 04	6.11–6.77 V	39376.4955	1.9831987
RV Lib	14 33 02	−17 49 05	14 34 59	−17 58 14	9.8–10.4 p	30887.236	10.722164
VV Mon	07 00 51	−05 39 42	07 02 34	−05 42 49	9.6–10.4 v	26037.529	6.05079
LX Per	03 09 52	47 55 05	03 12 18	48 02 56	8.4–9.4 p	27033.120	8.038044
SZ Psc	23 10 50	02 24 06	23 12 37	02 35 32	8.02–8.69 B	36114.565	3.96637
TY Pyx	8 57 36	−27 37 14	08 59 06	−27 45 26	6.87–7.47 V	27154.325	1.599292
RW UMa	11 38 05	52 16 29	11 39 58	52 04 50	10.3–11.9 p	33006.308	7.328251

relate any optical changes that occur simultaneously with radio and x-ray outbursts.

Finally, there is a group of binary systems that display dramatically the results of stellar evolution. The *cataclysmic systems* contain a faint red dwarf star and a white dwarf companion. The red dwarf star is slowly expanding, as stars are known to do when their evolution carries them from the main sequence to the red giant stage. In this case, however, as the star expands, its atmosphere is drawn by the gravitational attraction of the white dwarf. This transferred matter forms a disk around the white dwarf as it spirals into the star. This process of mass transfer occurs in many binary systems, including Algols, but nowhere are the effects as visibly dramatic as in cataclysmic systems. For these systems, the mass transfer is so rapid that a thick, extensive accretion disk forms. The continuous emission from the disk becomes so bright that it can outshine the stars. Matter streams in, striking the disk and producing a flickering hot spot. High-speed photometry (with time resolution of a fraction of a second) shows this flickering clearly. It disappears when the spot is eclipsed. There are several subclasses within the cataclysmic group, one of which is *novae*. It is believed that the explosive events in these systems are a direct result of the mass accretion process. A very interesting review of cataclysmic systems has been given by Trimble.[46] A review of high-speed photometry of these systems has been published by Warner and Nather.[12] Unfortunately, nearly all these systems are faint and beyond the grasp of small telescopes. For this reason, we have not included a list of these objects. However, one can be found in a well-written review article by Robinson.[47]

In general, a photometric study of an eclipsing system can have one or both of the following goals. The first is a set of observations to determine the time of mideclipse, which is often called the *time of minimum light*. This is done in order to determine the orbital period. In many eclipsing systems, the orbital periods are not constant. Mass transfer or mass ejected from the system may cause a slight shift in the position of the center of mass of the system. As a result, there is a small change in the orbital period. With observations of the time of minimum light, we can check to see if the eclipses are occurring "on time." Eclipses that occur earlier or later than predicted indicate a period change. Variations in the orbital period give us indirect information about the mass transfer or mass loss processes. A second reason for observing the times of minimum light is so that spectroscopists can determine accurately the orbital phases at which their spectrograms are taken. This is essential for the proper interpretation of the spectroscopic data.

The second observational goal mentioned above is the observation of the entire light curve. For short-period systems like the W UMa binaries, it is possible to observe a sizable portion of the light curve in one night. The data from several nights, covering portions of different orbital periods, can be combined into a composite light curve similar to Figure 1.1. Then you can calculate the orbital phase of each observation. This is explained below.

The analysis of a light curve can yield many physical parameters of the stars. However, analysis is a rather advanced topic and the reader is referred to Irwin,[48] Binnendijk,[49] and Tsesevich[50] for an introduction. A review of the most modern synthetic light curve analysis can be found in Binnendijk.[51] By no means should an observer be discouraged from obtaining a complete light curve even if the analysis appears too difficult. There are many professional astronomers who specialize in these studies and would welcome the data. Many binary systems show distorted light curves whose shapes can change because of circumstellar matter or starspots. Such systems should have their entire light curves monitored frequently. A comparison of light curves over many years can often provide clues as to the location and nature of the matter responsible for the distortions. See Bookmyer and Kaitchuck,[52] for example.

The determination of the time of minimum light is a good program for the newcomer to photometry. This involves simple differential photometry without the need to transform to the standard system. It provides valuable practice in observing techniques and data reduction. In addition, it provides valuable information. After the binary has been chosen and a comparison star has been found, the next step is to calculate the predicted time of minimum light. Tables 10.2 through 10.5 contain two numbers for each binary labeled *epoch* and *period*. These numbers are referred to as the *light elements*. They allow for calculation of binary orbital phase for any given date and time. The epoch is a heliocentric Julian date of a primary eclipse. The second number is the orbital period in days. You may be surprised by the accuracy to which the orbital periods are quoted. Although the time of minimum light can be determined only to an accuracy of a minute or so, we can measure the orbital period to an accuracy of a few seconds or even less. This is because for short-period systems a small error in the orbital period can accumulate in a few years to a large discrepancy between the predicted and observed times of eclipse.

Orbital phase is defined to be zero at mideclipse and 0.50 at one-half an orbit later, etc., as seen in Figures 1.1 and 10.2. The first step in predicting the time of minimum light is to compute the heliocentric Julian date (HJD) at 0 hour UT, as explained in Sections 5.3d and 5.3e for the day and time in question. We then compute a quantity called H, by

$$H = \text{fractional part of} \left(\frac{\text{HJD} - \text{epoch}}{\text{period}} \right)$$

if HJD is greater than the epoch, or

$$H = 1 - \text{fractional part of} \left(\frac{\text{HJD} - \text{epoch}}{\text{period}} \right)$$

if HJD is less than the epoch.

The heliocentric phase is then given by

$$\text{Phase (Hel.)} = H + \frac{\text{UT(in hours)}/24 \text{ hours}}{\text{period}}.$$

To predict the time of minimum light, we need only to find a day and time for which phase 0.0 or equivalently 1.0, occurs after dark and with our star above the horizon. Because the orbital periods change, the light elements in Tables 10.2 through 10.5 give only an approximate time of minimum light. This is especially true for light elements with small epoch values where the error could be as much as an hour. You should begin observing early to avoid the possibility of missing part of the eclipse. The most recent references to published light elements can be obtained from the astronomy department at the University of Florida.[53] They maintain a file of index cards containing literature references to research papers, times of minimum light, and the most recent light elements for hundreds of eclipsing-binary systems. A xerox of these cards can be obtained by writing to them and specifying which binary systems you are studying.

The actual observing procedure to follow is outlined in Section 9.3c and the data reduction is explained in Section 4.8. For short-period systems, you can observe most or all of the eclipse in a few hours. For long-period systems, the eclipse can last days and you have to spread your observing over several nights. It is important to observe as much of the descending and ascending branches of the curve as possible. This improves the accuracy of your determination of the time of minimum light greatly. Because of observational error, the time of minimum light does not simply refer to the time of your lowest measurement. There are several methods for determining the time of minimum light from the observations.

The *bisection of chords technique* can be applied if the eclipse curve is symmetric about mideclipse. First, a plot is made of Δm versus HJD. A smooth freehand curve is drawn through the data points and several horizontal lines are drawn connecting points of equal brightness on the ascending and descending sides of the curve. The midpoint of each line is measured and the average is taken to give an estimate of the time of mideclipse. The standard deviation from the mean gives an error estimate.

The *tracing-paper method* is still simpler. On the data plot, a vertical line is drawn to indicate your best estimate of the time of minimum light. The data points, the vertical line, and the horizontal axis are then transferred to a piece of tracing paper. The tracing paper is then turned over, so the time axis is reversed, and laid back on the original plot. The tracing paper is then moved horizontally so that data points and their tracing-paper counterparts give the best fit with a minimum of scatter. In general, the vertical lines on the plot and tracing paper do not align. The time of minimum light is midway between these two lines and can be read directly from the horizontal axis. Shifting the tracing paper to the right and left until the fit obviously worsens gives an error estimate.

A more analytical technique has been devised by Hertzsprung.[54] Because this reference is difficult to find in many libraries, we illustrate it in detail. This method is more time-consuming but has the advantage of eliminating most individual bias. It can also be implemented easily on a computer or programmable calculator. A plot of the observations, Δm versus HJD, is made on a large sheet of graph paper, say 50×100 centimeters. The plotting scales should be chosen so that the eclipse curve has a slope of about $45°$. Each data point is then connected by straight line segments. Figure 10.3 shows this plot (greatly reduced in size) for an eclipse of V566 Oph observed by Bookmyer.[55] First, esti-

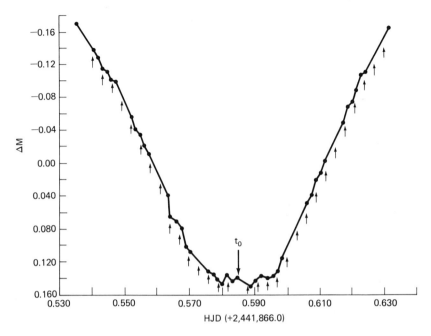

Figure 10.3. Eclipse observations.

mate the time of minimum light, called t_0, by simply looking at the plot. In this case, t_0 was estimated to be 0.5850, the Julian decimal. Place an arrow on the plot at 10 or more time intervals Δt to either side of t_0. In this case, Δt was chosen as 0.003 day. Read Δm from the plot at each arrow, using the straight line segments. These values are recorded in pairs that correspond to the same time interval on either side of t_0. The absolute value of the differences between the numbers in each pair is then found. The middle three columns of Table 10.10 shows these measurements and their differences. Ideally, if we had guessed t_0 exactly right, and the light was symmetric with no observational error, the column of differences would only contain zeros.

This process is then repeated, taking the first arrow on the right to be a new estimate of t_0 (the rightmost three columns of Table 10.10). This really does not involve much work; it requires moving some numbers in the table to different rows. The process is repeated a third time using the first arrow on the left as the new t_0 (the leftmost three columns in Table 10.10). We now let Y^-, Y^0, and Y^+ be the sum of the squares

TABLE 10.10.   Time of Minimum Light Data

$t_0 - \Delta t = 0.5820$			$t_0 = 0.5850$			$t_0 + \Delta t = 0.5880$		
Δm			Δm			Δm		
Decending	Ascending	|Diff.|	Descending	Ascending	|Diff.|	Decending	Ascending	|Diff.|
−0.141	−0.108	0.033	−0.117	−0.130	0.013	−0.101	−0.152	0.051
−0.117	−0.083	0.034	−0.101	−0.108	0.007	−0.083	−0.130	0.047
−0.101	−0.057	0.044	−0.083	−0.083	0.000	−0.058	−0.108	0.050
−0.083	−0.028	0.055	−0.058	−0.057	0.001	−0.033	−0.083	0.050
−0.058	−0.004	0.054	−0.033	−0.028	0.005	−0.007	−0.057	0.050
−0.033	+0.022	0.055	−0.007	−0.004	0.003	+0.018	−0.028	0.046
−0.007	+0.053	0.060	+0.018	+0.022	0.004	+0.048	−0.004	0.052
+0.018	+0.078	0.060	+0.048	+0.053	0.005	+0.076	+0.022	0.054
+0.048	+0.104	0.056	+0.076	+0.078	0.002	+0.107	+0.053	0.054
+0.076	+0.132	0.056	+0.107	+0.104	0.003	+0.119	+0.078	0.041
+0.107	+0.139	0.032	+0.119	+0.132	0.013	+0.132	+0.104	0.028
+0.119	+0.140	0.021	+0.132	+0.139	0.007	+0.142	+0.132	0.010
+0.132	+0.148	0.016	+0.142	+0.140	0.002	+0.137	+0.139	0.002
+0.142	+0.137	0.005	+0.137	+0.148	0.011	+0.148	+0.140	0.008
	$Y^- = \Sigma\|\text{Diff.}\|^2$			$Y^0 = \Sigma\|\text{Diff.}\|^2$			$Y^+ = \Sigma\|\text{Diff.}\|^2$	
	$= 0.02836$			$= 0.00065$			$= 0.02560$	

of the values in columns 3, 6, and 9, respectively. The time of minimum light, t_{min}, is then computed by

$$t_{min} = t_0 + \tfrac{1}{2}\left(\frac{Y^- - Y^+}{Y^- - 2Y^0 + Y^+}\right)\Delta t.$$

In this particular example,

$$t_{min} = 0.5850 + \tfrac{1}{2}\left(\frac{0.02836 - 0.02560}{0.02836 - 2(0.000650) + 0.02560}\right)0.003$$
$$= 0.5851$$

For even higher accuracy, the entire procedure can be iterated using the above value as a new estimate of t_0. However, this is probably not justified unless the observational data is of very high quality. An estimate of the error in the time of minimum light can be obtained by changing Δt and recomputing t_{min}.

When reporting a time of minimum light, it is customary to also include a second number called the *(O − C) value*. This is the difference in decimal day between the *observed* and *computed* time of minimum light. Because this computed time of minimum light depends on the set of light elements used, they should also be reported. The computed time of minimum light can be calculated by

$$T_{min} = T_0 + P \cdot E,$$

where T_0 and P are the initial epoch and period, respectively, and E is an integer. With a little trial and error, a value of E can be found, which gives a value of T_{min} as close as possible to the observed time of minimum light. In our example above, the observed time of minimum light is calculated from a set of light elements published by Bookmyer[56] many years before, namely

$$T_{min} = 2,436,744.4200 + 0.40964091E.$$

If E is chosen as 12,504, then the calculated time of minimum light is 2,441,866.5699. The *observed* time of minimum, t_{min}, minus the *computed* time of minimum light, T_{min}, is

$$(O - C) = 0.5851 - 0.5699$$
$$= 0.0152 \text{ day}$$

or about 22 minutes. This large difference is certainly easy to measure.

When $(O - C)$ values over intervals of a few years are collected and plotted versus Julian date, the story of period variations is told. For instance, if the $(O - C)$ values scatter about zero, resulting in a horizontal line on the plot, the period is constant. If the $(O - C)$ points trace out a curved path on the plot, this indicates that the period is continuously changing. The $(O - C)$ plot for V566 Oph shows a long interval of a constant period and then abruptly at about Julian date 2,440,000, or the year 1968, the $(O - C)$ values begin to rise following a straight line.[57] Such a straight, sloping line on an $(O - C)$ plot indicates that a single abrupt period change occurred. From this date (2,440,000) until the time of minimum light measured in our example above, the binary system completed a number of orbits given by

$$\frac{2,441,866.6 - 2,440,000}{\text{period}}$$

or

$$\frac{1866.6}{0.409644} = 4556.$$

If it took 4556 orbits to accumulate an $(O - C)$ value as large as 23 minutes, then the change in orbital period must have been

$$\frac{23 \text{ minutes}}{4556} = 0.005 \text{ minute}$$

or 0.3 second! This example demonstrates that times of minimum light determined to an accuracy of only a few minutes can often detect period changes of just a few tenths of a second.

10.6 SOLAR SYSTEM OBJECTS

In the past, less photoelectric photometry has been done on solar system objects than on stellar or galactic objects. There are many reasons for this, among them being, that there are fewer objects to study and an incorrect impression that little new information could be learned. There are three areas that amateurs can contribute most readily: comets, asteroids, and satellites.

Very little comet photometry has been performed. Most astronomers concentrate on spectra when comets appear, trying to decipher the composition of comets. However, recent research at GSFC by Niedner[58] has shown that magnetic sector boundaries emanating from the sun cause tail disconnections and brightness flareups. This latter phenomenon may be related to the brightness variations shown by periodic comets such as Schwassmann-Wachmann and therefore observing these comets photoelectrically may help in our understanding of the interplanetary magnetic field. Observing comets as they approach from beyond Jupiter can provide a probe at great distances from the sun. One problem with comets is that most of the light from the coma/nucleus region is from emission lines, making interpretation of wide-band colors as used in the *UBV* system difficult. We have the following suggestions for comet observations:

1. Use *UBV* photometry on new comets as soon as they are bright enough to be detected by your telescope. Be careful in measuring

a comet with a tail and coma, as your diaphragm will not contain the entire comet. Center on the nucleus and keep accurate records of what diaphragms you use. Sky determinations are also difficult because of contamination by the comet.

2. On large, bright comets, you can obtain intensity *isophotes* (contours of equal intensity) by centering on the comet nucleus and measuring its brightness in diaphragms from as small to as large as possible.

3. On bright comets, use narrow-band or interference filters to isolate particular emission features. Borra and Wehlau[59] used 75 Å wide bandpasses centered at 3878 Å (CN bands), 4870 Å (reflected sunlight continuum), and 5117 Å (Swan C_2 bands) for their photographic photometry.

There are several hundred asteroids brighter than eleventh magnitude. All are within range of amateur telescopes but only a few have been observed photoelectrically. Not only can photoelectric measurements provide information about their albedo and size, but most asteroids are nonspherical and show brightness variations during their rotations. Obtaining light curves can give clues as to their shape and the orientation of their spin axis. A study of 43 Ariadne by Burchi and Milano[60] gives examples of parameters obtainable from asteroid photometry. The current hypothesis that many asteroids have satellites also means that eclipsing asteroids should be visible, but have not yet been detected. Because asteroids are constantly moving with respect to stars, you need to obtain ephemerides from the Almanac[24] or another similar source. Comparison stars are difficult to obtain because of the asteroids' movement. Stars from the *UBV* catalog[61] should probably be used.

Planetary satellites are very difficult to measure. They are always much fainter than their parent body and lie very close in angular distance. You must be very careful to avoid contamination from the brighter planet. Eclipses behind the shadow of the planet can yield three main pieces of information: the diameter of the satellite, its orbit, and the structure of the planetary upper atmosphere. The Galilean satellites also have intervals of mutual eclipses twice per Jovian year. These eclipses of one satellite by another can give better information about their diameter and orbits, and can occur at a greater angular separation from the planet. In all eclipse observations, record the eclipse time to the nearest tenth of a second, preferably from inspection of the strip chart or microcomputer time series. Williamon[62] gives examples of the photometric appearance of this eclipse.

Observations of the planets have been carried out at major observatories. Uranus and Neptune have been observed for many years at Lowell Observatory to check the constancy of their solar luminosity. These two planets are faint enough that nearby comparison stars can be found. The rotation period of Pluto may be best detected photoelectrically[63] because of the low amplitude of its light variations, about 0.2 magnitude in V. The variation may be partially a result of the newly discovered satellite. You too can participate in such determinations if you have access to a meter-sized telescope.

10.7 EXTRAGALACTIC PHOTOMETRY

Extragalactic photometry is a very active area of research for many professional astronomers. This type of photometry can take many different forms. For example, drift scan photometry is a way of obtaining brightness and color profiles by drifting the photometer aperture across the face of a galaxy. Such data yield information about the distribution of dust and stellar populations within the galaxy. Aperture photometry is another technique that yields much the same information. Measurements of a galaxy are made through photometer diaphragms of various sizes centered on the galactic nucleus. Quasars, BL Lac objects, compact galaxies, and many radio galaxies appear starlike in a telescope. Photometry of these objects is done much as it is for ordinary stars.

The problem with all these projects is that we are dealing with very distant objects that appear very faint. Because much of this book has been aimed at small telescope users, it would be out of place to discuss in detail projects that exceed the capabilities of their equipment. We instead mention one particular project which is within the reach of a 30- to 40-centimeter (12- to 16-inch) telescope and is of great scientific value. Many quasars, BL Lac objects, and radio galaxies are variable in the optical region of the spectrum. For many such objects, there is a serious shortage of observations over the long term, necessary for an understanding of the nature of these variations. The reason for the shortage of data is simply that these objects greatly outnumber the number of astronomers working in this field.

There are very few quasars brighter than thirteenth visual magnitude. The quasar 3C273 is about visual magnitude 12.5 and its variations have been well documented. The AAVSO[3] can supply a finder chart for this object at a modest cost. There are several radio galaxies and BL Lac objects brighter than thirteenth visual magnitude which could be monitored profitably. Burbidge and Crowne[64] have compiled an optical catalog of radio galaxies. A similar catalog for quasistellar objects has been published by Hewitt and Burbidge.[65] Both references represent a good starting place for finding potential objects to study and for further references to published papers and finding charts. It should be emphasized that these objects are faint and are difficult to measure accurately with a small telescope. However, even observations with an error of 0.1 magnitude are valuable, particularly if they are made on a routine basis.

10.8 PUBLICATION OF DATA

The acquisition of photoelectric data is enjoyable in itself. As you gain experience and observational data, you may reach the conclusion that you would like to publish your data. Publication serves three purposes: it provides a means of rapid dissemination of important data or results, it gives permanence to results so that they may be used decades in the future, and it gets your name in print.

There are several methods to publish your data. These are listed below.

1. The American Association of Variable Star Observers (AAVSO) publishes newsletters and its own journal. They are the central depository for all visual observations and also most amateur photoelectric data. Check with them at their headquarters.[3] They are often consulted by professional observatories for information on long-period variables.
2. The International Astronomical Union (IAU) has a depository of photoelectric data.[66] This is a good alternative if you do not wish to publish your results in meeting abstracts or a journal. It is used heavily for extensive sets of data on a particular star such as RW Tau or SS 433.
3. Societies such as the American Astronomical Society, the Astronomical Society of the Pacific, and the International Astronomical

Union sponsor meetings and publish the proceedings. Generally, only the abstract of your paper or talk is published, but interested parties then know who to contact for further details.

4. Among the small journals are the *Information Bulletin of Variable Stars,* the *Journal of the AAVSO,* the *Journal of the Royal Astronomical Society of Canada,* and the *Monthly Notices of the Astronomical Society of South Africa.* In many cases, these journals do not have page charges and may not have your paper refereed formally.

5. Major astronomical journals include the *Publications of the Astronomical Society of the Pacific, Astronomy and Astrophysics,* the *Astronomical Journal,* the *Astrophysical Journal,* and the *Monthly Notices of the Royal Astronomical Society.* These journals send submitted papers to independent referees who assess the quality of the paper and who can ask for changes in addition to recommending acceptance or rejection. In addition, most major journals have page charges because of the technical nature of the papers, the cost of typesetting, and the large volume of papers. The cost may range from around $40 to $100 per page or more.

The large number of astronomers and the use of modern techniques yield more data than in the past, and the emphasis on professional publication forces more papers to be written, contributing to the necessity of these page charges. At the same time, avenues have been opened to amateur observers, as few professionals can devote time to long-term projects or projects that contain classical astronomy that do not yield immediate results.

When you decide that you would like to publish results, we suggest that you find a professional astronomer with whom to collaborate. The astronomer probably knows more about photometry theory and publishing procedures than you do, and in addition may be able to give you guidance and access to a library or computer center. Other reasons for collaboration are that the astronomer may have an ongoing project to which you can contribute, the astronomer may be a good reference if you are contemplating a career in astronomy, and the astronomer's institution may be able to pay page charges on a joint publication. Check with local universities or read journals to find someone who appears to be interested in the same field that you are.

There is not enough room in this text to give complete details of the techniques of technical writing. The IAU Style Book[67] and the AIP Style Manual[68] give the grammatical aspects for astronomical papers. There are several texts on scientific writing, and each journal mentions the format that they wish submitted papers to obey. The best method is to read the journals and see how others write and learn by example.

REFERENCES

1. Landis, H. J. 1977. *J. AAVSO* **6**, 4.
2. Stanton, R. H. 1978. *J. AAVSO* **7**, 14.
3. American Association of Variable Star Observers, 187 Concord Avenue, Cambridge, MA 02138.
4. Argue, A. N., Bok, B. J., and Miller, P. W. 1973. *A Catalog of Photometric Sequences.* Tucson: Univ. of Arizona Press.
5. Hertzsprung, E. 1924, *Bul. Ast. Inst. Neth.* **2**, 87.
6. Luyton, W. J. 1949. *Ap. J.* **109**, 532.
7. Gordon, K., and Kron, G. 1949. *Pub. A. S. P.* **61**, 210.
8. Moffett, T. J., 1974. *Sky and Tel.* **48**, 94.
9. Lovell, Sir Bernard 1971. *Quart. J.R.A.S.* **12**, 98.
10. Gershberg, R. E. 1971. *Flares and Red Dwarf Stars.* D. J. Mullan, trans. Armagh, Ireland: Armagh Observatory.
11. Gurzadyan, G. A. 1980. *Flare Stars.* Elmsford, NY: Pergamon.
12. Warner, B., and Nather, R. E. 1972. *Sky and Tel.* **43**, 82.
13. Nather, R. E. 1973. *Vistas in Astr.* **15**, 91.
14. McGraw, J. T., Wells, D. C., and Wiant, J. R. 1973. *Rev. Sci. Inst.* **44**, 748.
15. Povenmire, H. R. 1979. *Graze Observer's Handbook.* Indian Harbor Beach, Florida: JSB Enterprises.
16. Elliot, J. L. 1978. *A.J.* **83**, 90.
17. Walker, A. R. 1980. *I.A.U. Cir.* 3466.
18. Evans, D. S. 1977. *Sky and Tel.* **56**, 164.
19. Evans, D. S. 1977. *Sky and Tel.* **56**, 289.
20. Nather, R. E., and Evans, D. S. 1970. *A.J.* **75**, 575.
21. Nather, R. E. 1970. *A.J.* **75**, 583.
22. Evans, D. S. 1970. *A.J.* **75**, 589.
23. Nather, R. E., and McCants, M. M. 1970. *A.J.* **57**, 963.
24. *The Astronomical Almanac.* Washington, D.C.: Government Printing Office. Issued annually.
25. J. R. Percy, ed. *The Observer's Handbook.* Royal Astronomical Society of Canada. Toronto: Univ. of Toronto Press. Issued annually.
26. Smart, W. M. 1971. *Text-Book on Spherical Astronomy.* New York: Cambridge Univ. Press.
27. International Occultation Timing Association, P.O. Box 596, Tinley Park, IL 60477.
28. Glasby, J. S. 1969. *Variable Stars.* Cambridge: Harvard Univ. Press.

29. Strohmeier, W. 1972. *Variable Stars.* Edited by A. J. Meadows. Elmsford, New York: Pergamon.
30. Kukarkin, B. V. 1975. *Pulsating Stars.* New York: Halsted (translation).
31. Kukarkin, B. V., Kholopur, P. N., Efremuv, Yu. N., and Kurochkin, N. E. 1965. *The Second Catalogue of Suspected Variable Stars.* Moscow: U.S.S.R. Academy of Sciences.
32. Code 680, Goddard Space Flight Center, Greenbelt, MD 20771.
33. Becvar, A. 1964. *Atlas of the Heavens—II Catalogue.* Cambridge: Sky Publishing Co.
34. Eggen, O. J. 1979. *Ap. J. Supl. Ser.* **41**, 413.
35. Tsesevich, V. P. 1969. *RR Lyrae Stars.* Springfield, Virginia: National Technical Information Service, U.S. Department of Commerce.
36. Percy, J. R., Dick, R., Meier, R., and Welch, D. 1978. *J. AAVSO* **7**, 19.
37. Payne-Gaposchkin, C. H. 1971. *Smithsonian Contributions to Astrophysics.* No. 13 (LMC).
38. Payne-Gaposchkin, C. H., and Gaposchkin, S. 1966. *Smithsonian Contributions to Astrophysics.* No. 9 (SMC).
39. Sturch, C. 1966. *Ap. J.* **143**, 774.
40. Schaltenbrand, R., and Tammann, G. A. 1971. *Ast. and Ap. Supl.* **4**, 265.
41. Henden, A. A. 1979. *MNRAS* **189**, 149.
42. Henden, A. A. 1980. *MNRAS* **192**, 621.
43. Eggen, O. J. 1977. *Ap. J. Supl. Ser.* **34**, 1.
44. Zeilik, M., Hall, D. S., Feldman, P. A., and Walter, F. 1979. *Sky and Tel.* **57**, 132.
45. Dr. Douglas S. Hall, Dyer Observatory, Vanderbilt University, Nashville, TN 37235.
46. Trimble, V. 1980. *Mercury* **9**, 8.
47. Robinson, E. L. 1976. *Ann. Rev. Astr. and Ap.* **14**, 119.
48. Irwin, J. B. 1962. *Astronomical Techniques.* Edited by W. A. Hiltner. Chicago: Univ. of Chicago Press, p. 584.
49. Binnendijk, L. 1960. *Properties of Double Stars.* Philadelphia: Univ. of Pennsylvania Press, p. 258.
50. Tsesevich, V. P., ed. *Eclipsing Variable Stars.* New York: Halsted Press.
51. Binnendijk, L. 1977. *Vistas in Astr.* **21**, 359.
52. Bookmyer, B. B., and Kaitchuck, R. H. 1979. *Pub. A. S. P.* **91**, 234.
53. Curator, Card Catalog of Eclipsing Variables, Department of Physics and Astronomy, University of Florida, Gainesville, FL 32611.
54. Hertzsprung, E. 1928. *Bul. Astr. Inst. Neth.* **4**, 179.
55. Bookmyer, B. B. 1976. *Pub. A. S. P.* **88**, 473.
56. Bookmyer, B. B. 1969. *A. J.* **74**, 1197.
57. Kaitchuck, R. H. 1974. *J. AAVSO* **3**, 1.
58. Niedner, M. B. 1980. *Ap. J.* **241**, 820.
59. Borra, E. F., and Wehlau, W. H. 1971. *Pub. A. S. P.* **83**, 184.
60. Burchi, R., and Milano, L. 1974. *Ast. and Ap. Supl.* **15**, 173.
61. Blanco, V. M., Demers, S., Douglass, G. G., and Fitzgerald, M. P. 1968. *Photoelectric Catalog.* Washington, D.C.: U.S. Naval Observatory. **XXI**, second series.

62. Williamon, R. M., 1976. *Pub. A. S. P.* **88**, 73.
63. Neff, J. S., Lane, W. A., and Fix, J. D. 1974. *Pub. A. S. P.* **86**, 225.
64. Burbidge, G., and Crowne, A. H. 1979. *Ap. J. Supl. Ser.* **40**, 583.
65. Hewitt, A., and Burbidge, G. 1980. *Ap. J. Supl. Ser.* **43**, 57.
66. Breger, M. 1979. *Information Bulletin on Variable Stars,* No. 1659.
67. Anon., 1971. *International Astronomical Union Style Book.* Transactions IAU, **XIVB**, 261.
68. Hathwell, D., and Metzner, A. W. K., for the AIP Publications Board, *American Institute of Physics Style Manual.* New York: AIP. Revised periodically.

APPENDIX A
FIRST-ORDER EXTINCTION STARS

This appendix lists those stars that are particularly useful in determining the first-order extinction coefficients. Several sources were consulted with the following criteria used for star selection:

1. The star must be fainter than $4^m.0$ (V).
2. $-0.15 \leq B - V \leq +0.15$.
3. $-0.15 \leq U - B \leq +0.15$.
4. No star is a common close visual or spectroscopic binary.
5. There are no peculiar spectral types.
6. No star is a known variable.

The following tables indicate the SAO 1950.0 coordinates along with precessed 1985 coordinates (with no proper motion corrections). Those stars with no HR number or Flamsteed number are designated by their HD or BD number in an obvious manner.

Table A.1 lists the northern declination stars, while Table A.2 lists the southern declination stars. The observer is indicated in the rightmost column of each table.

AZ-TNT. = Iriarte et al.[1]
COUSINS = Cousins[2]
JOHNSON = Johnson[3]

For those who need fainter standards, the list of equatorial standards ($10 - 13^m$) by Landolt[4] is extremely useful.

REFERENCES

1. Iriarte, B., Johnson, H. L., Mitchell, R. I., and Wisniewski, W. K. 1965. *Sky and Tel.* **30**, 25.
2. Cousins, A. W. J. 1971. *Roy. Obs. Annals,* No. 7.
3. Johnson, H. L. 1963. In *Basic Astronomical Data.* Edited by K. AA Strand. Chicago: Univ. of Chicago Press, p. 208.
4. Landolt, A. U. 1973. *A. J.* **78**, 959.

TABLE A.1. Northern First-Order Extinction Stars

HR	R.A. (1950.0)	DEC. (1950.0)	R.A. (1985.0)	DEC. (1985.0)	V	B-V	U-B	SPEC.	NAME	OBS.
0063	0 14 28.3	+38 24 14.9	0 16 18	38 35 54	4.61	0.06	0.07	A2V	THE AND	JOHNSON
0068	0 15 42.5	+36 30 29.7	0 17 32	36 42 9	4.50	0.06	0.07	A2V	SIG AND	AZ-TNT.
0343	1 08 2.6	+54 53 4.3	1 10 1	55 3 14	4.36	0.05	0.13	A7V	THE CAS	JOHNSON
0378	1 15 13.0	+3 21 6.2	1 17 3	3 32 9	5.15	0.07	0.10	A3V	89 PSC	COUSINS
0383	1 16 42.7	+27 0 6.8	1 18 38	27 11 8	4.76	0.03	0.10	A3V	UPS PSC	AZ-TNT.
0580	1 59 27.2	+72 50 0.8	2 07 34	72 20 57	3.98	0.01	0.03	A1V	50 CAS	AZ-TNT.
0620	2 05 27.7	+37 37 22.8	2 16 24	37 47 20	4.83	0.12	0.14	A4V	58 AND	AZ-TNT.
0664	2 14 20.0	+33 37 1.5	2 27 21	33 46 44	4.01	0.03	0.01	A0V	GAM TRI	AZ-TNT.
0718	2 25 29.8	+8 14 13.1	2 57 47	8 23 36	4.28	-0.06	-0.13	B9III	CHI2 CET	JOHNSON
0879	2 55 33.3	+39 27 50.7	3 07 16	39 36 13	4.70	0.06	0.12	A2V	PI PER	AZ-TNT.
0932	3 06 27.7	+74 22 22.1	3 14 2	74 20 19	4.87	0.06	0.01	A0V		AZ-TNT.
0972	3 12 1.3	+20 51 37.9	3 20 26	20 59 25	4.89	-0.02	0.01	A0IV	ZET ARI	AZ-TNT.
1002	3 18 5.0	+43 9 2.0	3 48 45	43 16 34	4.94	0.06	0.05	A3V	32 PER	AZ-TNT.
1148	3 45 2.9	+71 10 51.6	4 17 6	71 17 16	4.66	0.03	0.05	A3IV	GAM CAM	AZ-TNT.
1261	4 02 50.9	+50 13 3.3	4 24 28	50 18 43	4.02	-0.02	-0.04	B9V	LAM PER	AZ-TNT.
1324	4 14 28.4	+50 10 28.9	4 24 36	50 15 37	4.65	0.05	0.05	A2	B PER	AZ-TNT.
1387	4 22 23.1	+22 10 51.9	4 33 20	22 15 38	4.23	0.12	0.15	A7V	KAP TAU	AZ-TNT.
1389	4 22 35.6	+17 48 55.2	4 49 47	17 53 41	4.29	0.04	0.08	A3V	68 TAU	AZ-TNT.
1448	4 31 28.5	+2 27 54.9	4 54 3	8 52 16	5.68	0.05	0.10	A3		COUSINS
1544	4 47 53.0	+8 48 57.6	4 54 54	10 52 31	4.35	0.01	0.03	A0V	PI2 ORI	AZ-TNT.
1570	4 52 8.4	+10 4 22.5	5 25 50	1 55 44	4.66	0.08	0.08	A0V	PI1 ORI	AZ-TNT.
1724	5 14 5.2	+1 53 36.6	5 33 29	6 51 53	6.42	-0.02	0.02	B8V		COUSINS
1807	5 23 57.1	+6 1 38.7	5 52 22	3 45 25	6.42	-0.02	-0.05	B9		COUSINS
1872	5 31 38.8	+3 44 3.5	5 58 3	27 36 35	5.35	0.04	0.06	A2	38 ORI	COUSINS
2034	5 50 11.0	+27 36 8.5	6 10 8	27 36 8	4.61	-0.02	0.01	B9.5V	136 TAU	AZ-TNT.
2103	5 56 15.2	+2 32 59.7	6 11 17	2 33 8	5.21	0.06	0.01	A1	60 ORI	COUSINS
2174	6 13 20.4	+2 30 32.8	6 18 17	2 30 10	5.73	0.06	0.04	A0.5I	22 CAM	COUSINS
2209	6 15 21.2	+69 1 27.1	6 33 57	69 19 40	4.79	0.03	0.01	A0V	2 LYN	COUSINS
2238	6 32 12.7	+59 1 54.2	6 52 52	59 19 2	4.47	0.01	0.03	A2V	14 MON	AZ-TNT.
2404	6 49 2.1	+7 36 46.8	6 50 45	7 35 6	6.44	-0.01	0.03	A0	16 LYN	AZ-TNT.
2543	6 52 51.4	+3 6 10.6	6 54 45	3 38 38	6.38	0.09	0.09	A0		COUSINS
2584	6 53 58.3	+8 23 23.1	6 56 31	8 20 39	6.28	0.04	0.06	A0		COUSINS
2535	6 56 2.2	+45 9 40.7	7 3 33	45 6 53	4.90	0.04	0.03	A2V		COUSINS
2629	7 09 44.8	+1 33 26.2	7 33 53	4 50 24	6.63	0.06	0.09	A0		AZ-TNT.
2654	7 11.3	+1 33 50.6	7 33 33	1 50 41	6.56	0.01	0.07	B9		COUSINS
2710	7 11 3	+5 44 20.7	7 11 23	5 40 49	6.08	-0.02	-0.05	A0		COUSINS
2751	7 14 44.3	+49 33 22.1	7 17 23	49 29 33	5.04	0.08	0.09	A3III		AZ-TNT.

281

NORTHERN FIRST ORDER EXTINCTION STARS

HR	R.A. (1950.0)	Dec. (1950.0)	R.A. (1985.0)	Dec. (1985.0)	V	B-V	U-B	Spec.	Name	Obs.
2818	7 22 56.8	+49 18 46.7	7 25 35	49 14 34	4.63	-0.02	-0.02	A1IV	21 LYN	AZ-TNT.
2946	7 38 47.2	+58 49 47.0	7 41 44	58 44 49	4.99	0.08	0.09	A3III	24 LYN	AZ-TNT.
3067	7 50 26.4	+26 53 48.7	7 52 34	26 48 20	4.99	0.09	0.12	A4V	PHI GEM	AZ-TNT.
3136	7 58 35.2	+5 1 7.3	8 0 26	4 55 17	5.64	0.00	0.01	A0		COUSINS
3173	8 4 42.3	+51 39 9.9	8 7 20	51 33 3	4.84	0.05	0.00	A2V	27 LYN	AZ-TNT.
3410	8 35 0.6	+5 52 45.6	8 36 51	5 45 24	4.17	0.00	0.02	A0V	DEL HYA	AZ-TNT.
3412	8 35 22.7	+9 45 2.4	8 37 16	9 37 40	6.52	-0.02	-0.04	A0	37 CNC	COUSINS
3449	8 40 23.7	+21 38 58.8	8 42 25	21 31 24	4.66	0.02	0.01	A1V	GAM CNC	COUSINS
3492	8 45 47.1	+6 1 25.1	8 47 38	5 53 38	4.37	-0.05	-0.05	A0V	RHO HYA	AZ-TNT.
3573	8 55 33.2	+1 44 8.5	8 57 21	1 36 0	6.59	0.06	0.08	A0		COUSINS
3651	9 9 36.2	+4 4 23.2	9 11 25	3 55 44	6.14	0.00	0.00	A0		COUSINS
3799	9 31 24.6	+52 16 30.2	9 33 48	52 7 8	4.50	0.00	0.04	A2V	26 UMA	AZ-TNT.
3906	9 49 37.4	+2 41 17.3	9 51 26	2 31 24	6.02	-0.04	-0.08	A1V	7 SEX	COUSINS
3974	10 4 29.2	+35 29 21.4	10 6 32	35 19 5	4.49	0.19	0.07	A7V	21 LMI	JOHNSON
4248	10 51 6.5	+43 27 24.0	10 53 6	43 16 12	4.71	-0.05	-0.06	A1V	OMI UMA	AZ-TNT.
4300	10 59 39.8	+20 26 54.2	11 1 31	20 15 36	4.41	0.04	0.04	A1V	60 LEO	AZ-TNT.
4356	11 11 11.9	+6 18 13.1	11 13 1	6 6 43	5.42	-0.02	-0.05	A0	69 LEO	COUSINS
4386	11 18 33.5	+38 27 36.4	11 20 21	38 16 6	4.06	-0.07	-0.12	B9V	SIG LEO	AZ-TNT.
4380	11 16 24.7	+8 20 25.3	11 18 19	8 19 44	4.79	0.12	0.03	A2V	55 UMA	AZ-TNT.
4528	11 45 20.8	+3 56 1.0	11 47 8	3 44 19	5.31	0.02	0.04	A1	4 VIR	COUSINS
4585	11 57 23.2	+6 53 35.1	11 59 10	6 41 53	5.36	0.00	0.00	A0	7 VIR	COUSINS
4589	11 58 18.6	+22 54 15.4	12 0 6	22 42 41	4.67	0.13	0.10	A4V	PI VIR	AZ-TNT.
4789	12 32 21.6	+10 33 26.5	12 34 6	10 21 53	4.81	0.00	-0.01	A3III	23 COM	AZ-TNT.
4805	12 35 31.4	+3 30 39.2	12 37 18	3 19 8	6.32	0.01	0.01	A0		COUSINS
4828	12 39 21.2	+2 9 1.6	12 41 7	1 58 5	4.88	0.06	0.02	A1V	RHO VIR	AZ-TNT.
5021	13 16 19.0	+55 14 53.0	13 18 5	55 3 9	6.62	0.06	0.02	A1IV		COUSINS
5037	13 19 9.0	+49 16 15.5	13 20 55	49 9 2	5.70	0.05	0.09	A0	80 UMA	COUSINS
5062	13 23 16.5	+55 14 53.0	13 24 39	55 3 57	4.03	0.15	0.11	A5V	24 CVN	COUSINS
5112	13 32 24.1	+49 16 15.5	13 33 50	49 5 31	4.70	0.12	0.14	A4V	TAU VIR	AZ-TNT.
5264	13 59 5.9	+1 47 5.0	14 0 52	1 37 37	4.27	0.09	0.03	A3III		JOHNSON
5859	15 42 55.0	+22 56 8.4	15 44 38	22 50 29	5.58	0.04	0.05	A0V	PI SER	AZ-TNT.
5972	16 8 8.4	+68 52 4.2	16 10 38	68 48 42	4.83	0.07	0.10	A3V	15 DRA	AZ-TNT.
6161	16 28 4.2	+42 29 29.3	16 30 37	42 28 0	5.01	-0.06	-0.10	B9IV	SIG HER	AZ-TNT.
6168	16 32 29.3	+12 48 3.4	16 34 28	12 45 1	4.20	-0.02	-0.10	B9V	60 HER	AZ-TNT.
6355	17 3 3.4	+37 20 56.7	17 4 40	37 18 38	4.91	0.12	0.06	A3IV	69 HER	AZ-TNT.
6436	17 15 56.7	+20 48 34.1	17 17 9	20 37 21	4.66	0.05	-0.03	A2V		AZ-TNT.

HR	RA (1950)	Dec (1950)	RA (2000)	Dec (2000)	V	C1	C2	Sp	Name	Source
6723	17 59 12.9	+1 18 17.3	18 0 59	+1 18 17	4.42	0.02	0.04	A1V	68 OPH	AZ-TNT.
6789	17 48 18.3	+86 35 34.8	17 37 0	+86 35 41	4.35	0.04	0.01	A1V	DEL UMI	AZ-TNT.
6923	18 23 10.7	+58 47 16.5	18 23 41	+58 47 28	4.98	0.05	0.08	A1V	39 DRA	AZ-TNT.
7069	18 44 48.7	+18 9 28.8	18 46 21	+18 9 46	4.36	0.07	0.13	A3V	111 HER	AZ-TNT.
7085	18 47 4.2	0 49 40.6	18 48 51	0 49 6	6.24	0.01	0.03	A0		COUSINS
7313	19 15 16.6	+2 0 26.7	19 17 2	+2 0 15	6.18	0.01	0.01	A0		COUSINS
7371	19 20 24.9	+65 6 5.2	19 20 35	+65 6 6	4.59	0.06	0.02	A2IV	PI DRA	AZ-TNT.
7546	19 46 45.4	+19 2 55.5	19 48 18	+19 2 12	5.00	0.10	0.10	A3V	ZET SGE	AZ-TNT.
7592	19 51 20.1	+24 2 52.8	19 52 49	+24 2 22	4.58	−0.13	0.06	B9.5I	13 VUL	AZ-TNT.
7724	20 11 57.7	+15 9 38.4	20 13 34	+15 9 2	4.95	0.01	0.09	A2V	RHO AQL	AZ-TNT.
7730	20 12 43.6	+46 46 48.9	20 12 49	+46 46 11	4.82	0.14	0.10	A3III	30 CYG	AZ-TNT.
7736	20 12 39.6	+36 45 7.8	20 13 58	+36 45 33	4.99	0.08	0.12	A2III	29 CYG	AZ-TNT.
7740	20 12 14.1	+56 31 50.9	20 13 2	+56 31 14	4.30	0.08	0.11	A3IV	33 CYG	AZ-TNT.
7857	20 31 29.1	+10 0 15.0	20 33 10	+10 0 27	6.56	0.05	0.08	A0		COUSINS
7871	20 32 58.2	+14 37 2.2	20 34 36	+14 37 18	4.69	0.11	0.11	A3V	ZET DEL	AZ-TNT.
7891	20 36 17.2	+21 8 58.7	20 37 50	+21 8 52	4.82	0.07	0.02	B9.5V	29 VUL	AZ-TNT.
8098	21 8 5.4	+9 59 38.4	21 9 47	+9 59 13	6.07	0.04	0.02	A2V	6 EQU	COUSINS
8265	21 35 14.1	+6 33 33.9	21 36 58	+6 33 1	6.20	0.01	0.02	A1V	3 PEG	COUSINS
8328	21 44 41.8	+8 28 14.6	21 46 28	+8 28 58	6.20	0.04	0.02	A0	11 PEG	COUSINS
8491	22 13 30.3	+29 13	22 15 14	+29 13 45				A0		COUSINS
8641	22 39 24.3	+13 44 46.1	22 41 28	+13 44 8	4.79	0.00	0.01	A1V	OM PEG	AZ-TNT.
8717	22 52 42.5	+9 7 55.9	22 54 57	+9 7 36	4.91	0.01	0.00	A1V	RHO PEG	AZ-TNT.
8738	22 56 11.2	+7 15 21.7	22 57 18	+7 15 26	6.33	0.06	0.06	A0		COUSINS
9042	23 50 31.0	+2 0 45.3	23 52 18	+2 0 26	6.28	0.01	0.00	A2	25 PSC	COUSINS

TABLE A.2. Southern First-Order Extinction Stars

HR	R.A. (1950.0)	Dec. (1950.0)	R.A. (1985.0)	Dec. (1985.0)	V	B-V	U-B	SPEC.	NAME	OBS.
0125	0 29 6.6	-49 04 47.3	0 30 41	-48 53 11	4.77	0.01	0.04	A0V	LAM1PHE	COUSINS
0191	0 41 6.8	-57 44 13.2	0 42 40	-57 32 43	4.36	0.00	-0.03	A0V	ETA PHE	COUSINS
0444	1 30 33.9	-42 16 16.3	1 32 18	-42 05 29	6.59	-0.05	-0.10	A0		COUSINS
0558	1 52 17.6	-42 30 42.3	1 53 44	-42 25 22	5.11	-0.05	-0.14	B9	PHI PHE	COUSINS
0607	2 00 37.6	-9 41 52.7	2 02 25	-9 32 07	5.42	0.14	0.13	A5	60 CET	COUSINS
0653	2 13 9.4	-9 34 09.6	2 14 43	-9 24 50	6.54	-0.01	-0.07	A0		COUSINS
0634	2 17 9.4	-4 28 11.8	2 18 55	-4 24 32	6.50	0.07	0.08	A2		COUSINS
0705	2 20 51.2	-68 34 54.3	2 21 29	-68 43 39	4.08	0.03	0.05	A2V	DEL HYI	COUSINS
0708	2 23 32.0	-12 53 11.8	2 25 13	-12 51 27	4.89	-0.02	-0.04	B9V	RHO CET	AZ-TNT.
0789	2 37 53.6	-43 60 54.3	2 39 20	-42 57 19	4.74	0.06	0.06	A2V		COUSINS
0806	2 38 48.8	-68 28 19.7	2 45 18	-68 46 51	4.11	-0.06	-0.13	B9III	EPS HYI	COUSINS
0837	2 44 45.9	-67 49 50.9	2 47 40	-67 40 40	4.83	0.05	0.08	A2	ZET HYI	COUSINS
0875	2 54 6.9	-3 54 35.4	2 55 18	-3 46 03	5.16	0.08	0.06	A1V		JOHNSON
0892	2 56 10.7	-8 59 45.0	2 57 52	-2 50 02	5.23	0.00	0.04	A2		COUSINS
1272	4 3 31.1	-3 51 51.2	4 22 56	-8 53 44	6.26	0.06	0.08	A3V		COUSINS
1383	4 21 11.3	-3 02 34.8	4 22 55	-3 46 48	5.18	0.07	0.08	A1V	XSI ERI	COUSINS
1522	4 43 53.7	-2 17 35.1	4 45 38	-2 14 06	6.33	0.04	0.06	A2		COUSINS
1596	4 55 39.6	-20 17 18.2	4 57 25	-3 22 22	6.34	0.09	0.11	A0		AZ-TNT.
1621	4 59 15.3	-21 17 24.0	5 19 46	-20 48 14	4.91	-0.05	-0.15	B9		COUSINS
1762	5 18 18.7	-3 20 19.2	5 28 11	-21 15 07	4.70	-0.05	-0.11	A0V		COUSINS
1826	5 26 26.9	-7 14 47.5	5 38 9	-3 19 12	6.38	-0.01	-0.06	B9	49 ORI	AZ-TNT.
1937	5 36 27.8	-9 13 21.4	5 51 24	-7 13 23	5.95	0.14	0.09	A4IV		COUSINS
2039	5 49 44.5	-4 14 11.3	5 54 50	-9 47 59	6.28	0.10	0.06	A0		COUSINS
2071	5 53 7.3	-14 47 41.5	6 10 28	-4 55 00	4.67	0.05	0.08	A1V	THE LEP	AZ-TNT.
2155	6 3 53.5	-6 44 45.6	6 11 5	-14 45 00	6.14	0.01	0.03	A0		COUSINS
2195	6 8 35.4	-2 29 31.6	6 22 17	-6 45 43	6.62	0.04	0.08	A0		COUSINS
2210	6 20 54.4	-4 39 26.5	6 26 38	-2 30 06	6.66	0.06	0.00	B9		COUSINS
2295	6 24 19.8	-7 28 37.4	6 34 1	-1 57 08	6.26	0.03	-0.10	A0		COUSINS
2328	6 32 57.6	-22 55 49.6	7 9 25	-22 28 01	4.54	-0.04	-0.02	A0V	CHI2CMA	AZ-TNT.
2414	7 9 18.6	-5 24 26.1	7 59 11	-5 18 25	4.15	0.03	0.03	A0IV	DEL MON	AZ-TNT.
2714	7 57 37.5	-18 15 30.4	8 33 16	-18 2 59	4.61	0.07	0.08	A3V		COUSINS
3131	8 31 29.9	-1 58 39.2	8 37 6	-42 56 10	5.80	0.00	0.00	A0		COUSINS
3383	8 35 53.1	-42 48 46.8	8 40 17	-8 56 53	4.14	0.10	0.12	A9II		COUSINS
3426	8 36 36.1	-1 52 47.1	8 40 43	-47 15 47	6.62	-0.02	0.02	A0		COUSINS
3452	8 39 34.6	-47 8 16.2	8 54 52	-27 37 21	4.77	0.12	0.12	A5II		COUSINS
3556	8 53 22.8	-27 29 18.7	8 54 52	-27 37 21	4.88	0.12	0.15	A3V	DEL PYX	COUSINS

284

HR	Name	Catalog	Sp	(V-R)	(R-I)	V
3615	ALF VOL	COUSINS	A5V	Ø.14	Ø.15	4.ØØ
3787	TAU2HYA	AZ-TNT.	A3III	Ø.Ø9	Ø.11	4.56
3832	34 HYA	COUSINS	AØ	-Ø.Ø9	-Ø.Ø4	6.4Ø
3981	ALP SEX	AZ-TNT.	AØIII	-Ø.Ø7	Ø.Ø2	4.49
3989	17 SEX	COUSINS	AØ	-Ø.Ø6	Ø.Ø4	5.9Ø
4109		COUSINS	AØ	Ø.Ø5	Ø.Ø3	6.Ø4
4138		COUSINS	A2V	Ø.Ø7	Ø.11	4.73
4293		COUSINS	A2IV	Ø.13	Ø.Ø3	4.38
4343	BET CRT	AZ-TNT.	A2III	Ø.Ø7	Ø.Ø4	6.52
5163		COUSINS	AØ	Ø.Ø2	Ø.ØØ	6.14
5342		COUSINS	A3	Ø.Ø1	-Ø.Ø1	4.Ø4
5367	PSI CEN	COUSINS	AØIV	-Ø.Ø1	-Ø.Ø3	4.92
5489		COUSINS	A1	-Ø.11	Ø.Ø2	4.Ø6
5670	BET CIR	COUSINS	A3V	-Ø.Ø4	Ø.Ø9	4.6Ø
5724		COUSINS	AØIV	Ø.Ø8	Ø.ØØ	5.55
5959	5Ø LIB	COUSINS	A1	Ø.Ø7	Ø.Ø4	4.92
6031	PSI SCO	COUSINS	A2V	-Ø.Ø4	Ø.Ø9	4.77
6070	D SCO	AZ-TNT.	AØV	Ø.1Ø	Ø.Ø2	4.31
6446	NU SER	AZ-TNT.	A1V	-Ø.Ø1	Ø.Ø3	4.81
6519	51 OPH	COUSINS	A1	Ø.Ø3	Ø.ØØ	4.24
6581	OMI SER	AZ-TNT.	A2V	-Ø.Ø3	-Ø.Ø3	4.71
6930	GAM SCT	AZ-TNT.	A3V	Ø.1Ø	Ø.Ø8	6.36
6963		COUSINS	AØ	Ø.Ø4	Ø.Ø7	5.42
7029	14 AQL	COUSINS	AØ	-Ø.Ø7	Ø.Ø2	4.12
7254	ALF CRA	COUSINS	A2V	Ø.Ø7	Ø.ØØ	4.59
7440	52 SGR	AZ-TNT.	B9	-Ø.12	-Ø.Ø6	4.76
7773	NU CAP	AZ-TNT.	B9V	-Ø.11	-Ø.Ø4	4.Ø7
8075	THE CAP	AZ-TNT.	AØV	Ø.Ø1	-Ø.Ø1	4.5Ø
8431	MU PSA	AZ-TNT.	A2V	Ø.Ø5	Ø.Ø5	6.27
8451		COUSINS	AØ	-Ø.Ø7	Ø.ØØ	4.82
8573	THE AQR	AZ-TNT.	AØIV	-Ø.12	-Ø.Ø6	5.55
8840		COUSINS	A2	Ø.Ø5	Ø.Ø5	4.73
8959		COUSINS	A2V	Ø.Ø8	Ø.Ø8	4.51
8968	OM2 AQR	AZ-TNT.	B9.5V	-Ø.13	-Ø.Ø4	4.57
9016	DEL SCL	AZ-TNT.	AØV	Ø.ØØ	Ø.ØØ	4.56
9098	2 CET	AZ-TNT.	B9IV	-Ø.12	-Ø.Ø4	4.56

APPENDIX B
SECOND-ORDER EXTINCTION PAIRS

As mentioned in Section 4.4, second-order extinction can be determined by observing a close optical pair of widely differing colors as they pass through varying air mass. A list of bright pairs in the equatorial plane was published by Crawford, Golson, and Landolt.[1] Barnes and Moffett[2] extended this list to include R and I magnitudes and one additional star. Their paper is extremely useful as it gives finding charts for all 37 stars of their extinction network.

An examination of the Johnson, Tonantzintla, and Cousins lists of standard stars yielded 23 more stars useful in the extinction determination. Table B.1 lists all 60 stars.

Extinction examples using stars from this list are presented in Appendix G.

REFERENCES

1. Crawford, D. L., Golson, J. C., and Landolt, A. U. 1971. *Pub. A. S. P.* **83**, 652.
2. Barnes, T. G., III, and Moffett, T. J. 1979. *Pub. A. S. P.* **91**, 289.

TABLE B.1. Second-Order Extinction Pairs

Star	EPOCH 1950 RA h m s	EPOCH 1950 DEC d m s	EPOCH 1985 RA h m s	EPOCH 1985 DEC d m s	V	B-V	U-B	SPEC.	NAME	OBS.
HR0607	2 0 38	-0 6 42	2 2 26	0 3 23	5.42	0.14	0.13	A5	60 CET	COUSINS
HR0610	2 1 14	-0 34 45	2 3 1	-0 24 41	5.92	0.88	0.51	G5II	61 CET	COUSINS
HR0718	2 25 30	8 14 13	2 27 22	8 23 36	4.28	-0.06	-0.13	B9III	CH12 CET	JOHNSONS
HR0725	2 26 55	9 20 37	2 28 47	9 29 58	6.07	1.02	0.86	K2III		COUSINS
HD16581	2 37 0	1 9 14	2 38 48	1 18 16	8.19	-0.06	-0.27	B9		KITT PK.
HD16608	2 37 11	1 54 57	2 38 60	2 3 58	8.31	1.51	1.79	K4		KITT PK.
HR1373	4 20 3	17 25 37	4 22 4	17 30 31	3.76	0.99	0.83	K1III	DEL TAU	AZ-TNT.
HR1389	4 22 36	17 48 55	4 24 37	17 53 41	4.29	0.04	0.08	A3V	68 TAU	AZ-TNT.
HD30544	4 46 2	3 33 45	4 47 52	3 37 25	7.32	-0.06	-0.31	B9		KITT PK.
HD30545	4 46 7	3 30 7	4 47 57	3 33 47	6.01	1.21	1.15	K0		KITT PK.
HR1826	5 26 27	-3 20 47	5 28 12	-3 19 7	6.38	-0.01	-0.06	B9		COUSINS
HR1830	5 26 54	-3 29 5	5 28 39	-3 27 27	5.80	1.15	1.07	G8		COUSINS
HR2071	5 53 7	-4 47 41	5 54 51	-4 47 23	6.28	0.05	0.06	A0		COUSINS
HR2070	5 53 2	-4 37 24	5 54 46	-4 37 5	5.87	1.17	1.22	K2		COUSINS
HD40983	5 59 47	1 5 26	6 1 35	1 5 24	8.56	0.00	-0.04	B9		KITT PK.
HD41029	6 0 5	1 6 55	6 1 53	1 6 52	8.17	0.98	0.76	K0		KITT PK.
HD50279	6 50 1	1 9 5	6 51 49	1 6 30	8.17	-0.06	-0.28	B8		KITT PK.
HD50167	6 49 29	1 18 45	6 51 18	1 16 12	7.85	1.55	1.72	K5		KITT PK.

SECOND ORDER EXTINCTION PAIRS (CONT)

Star	EPOCH 1950 RA h m s	EPOCH 1950 DEC d m s	EPOCH 1985 RA h m s	EPOCH 1985 DEC d m s	V	B-V	U-B	SPEC.	NAME	OBS.
HR2710	7 9 11	5 44 21	7 11 3	5 40 50	6.08	-0.02	-0.05	A0		COUSINS
HR2713	7 9 28	5 33 33	7 11 20	5 30 1	6.15	1.15	0.97	K0		COUSINS
HD63390	7 46 10	-0 8 0	7 47 57	-0 13 16	8.74	0.05	0.05	B9		KITT PK.
HD63368	7 46 4	-0 37 7	7 47 51	-0 42 23	8.43	0.95	0.57	K0		KITT PK.
HD75012	8 45 1	0 15 44	8 46 49	0 7 59	7.83	0.08	0.09	B9		KITT PK.
HD75138	8 45 44	0 44 25	8 47 32	0 36 39	7.24	1.48	1.78	K2		KITT PK.
HD84971	9 46 12	-2 28 50	9 47 58	-2 38 35	8.65	-0.17	-0.76	B5		KITT PK.
HD84916	9 46 51	-4 10 25	9 47 37	-4 20 11	8.66	1.16	1.12	K5		KITT PK.
HR3989	10 7 38	-8 9 43	10 9 22	-8 20 3	5.90	0.02	-0.06	A0	17 SEX	COUSINS
HR3996	10 8 27	-8 10 16	10 10 11	-8 20 37	5.64	1.31	1.41	K2	18 SEX	COUSINS
HD97991	11 13 39	-3 11 57	11 15 26	-3 23 25	7.41	-0.24	-0.93	B3		KITT PK.
HD98007	11 13 44	-3 29 19	11 15 31	-3 40 47	8.94	0.71	0.32	K0		KITT PK.
HD111133	12 44 30	6 13 27	12 46 17	6 1 59	6.36	-0.06	-0.05	B9		KITT PK.
HD111165	12 44 43	7 16 51	12 46 29	7 5 23	8.46	1.16	1.21	K0		KITT PK.
HD118246	13 33 7	-5 54 4	13 34 57	-6 4 47	8.07	-0.16	-0.63	B8		KITT PK.
HD118129	13 32 27	-6 42 44	13 34 17	-6 53 28	8.18	1.07	0.95	K2		KITT PK.
HD129956	14 42 57	0 55 38	14 44 44	0 46 48	5.70	-0.03	-0.06	B9		KITT PK.
HD129975	14 43 4	-0 6 17	14 44 52	-0 15 7	8.37	1.50	1.86	K5		KITT PK.

SECOND ORDER EXTINCTION PARIS (CONT)

Star	EPOCH 1950 RA h m s	EPOCH 1950 DEC d m s	EPOCH 1985 RA h m s	EPOCH 1985 DEC d m s	V	B-V	U-B	SPEC.	NAME	OBS.
HD140873	15 43 30	-1 38 56	15 45 19	-1 45 27	5.40	-0.03	-0.42	B8		KITT PK.
HD140850	15 43 23	-1 17 26	15 45 11	-1 23 58	8.80	1.66	2.02	K5		KITT PK.
HD161261	17 41 49	5 44 7	17 43 32	5 43 14	8.31	0.05	-0.14	B9		KITT PK.
HD161242	17 41 45	5 16 17	17 43 28	5 15 24	7.80	1.28	1.10	K2		KITT PK.
HD171732	18 33 56	-3 7 13	18 35 46	-3 5 27	9.12	0.28	-0.10	B9		KITT PK.
HD171731	18 33 56	-2 31 36	18 35 46	-2 29 50	9.06	1.13	1.05	K2		KITT PK.
HR7313	19 15 17	1 56 27	19 17 3	2 0 16	6.18	0.01	0.01	A0	23 AQL	COUSINS
HR7319	19 16 0	0 59 34	19 17 47	1 3 25	5.09	1.15	1.01	K2II		COUSINS
HD184790	19 33 36	-2 55 07	19 35 26	-2 50 26	8.12	0.17	-0.32	B8		KITT PK.
HD184914	19 34 07	-4 24 44	19 35 58	-4 20 1	8.16	1.20	0.93	K5		KITT PK.
HD196426	20 34 45	-0-04 41	20 36 33	0 2 40	6.23	-0.09	-0.39	B8		KITT PK.
HD196395	20 34 33	-0-41 34	20 36 21	-0 34 14	8.72	1.66	2.04	K5		KITT PK.
HD205556	21 33 26	5 15 7	21 35 11	5 24 32	8.32	-0.06	-0.35	B9		KITT PK.
HD205584	21 33 44	5 54 46	21 35 29	6 4 11	7.72	1.26	1.32	K2		KITT PK.
HD209905	22 4 6	2 11 43	22 5 53	2 21 58	6.52	-0.06	-0.23	B9		KITT PK.
HD209796	22 3 29	1 0 48	22 5 16	1 11 2	8.94	1.21	1.17	K2		KITT PK.
HR8451	22 7 45	-4 8 24	22 9 34	-3 58 4	6.27	0.00	-0.07	A0		COUSINS
HR8453	22 7 57	-4 30 49	22 9 46	-4 20 28	6.00	0.98	0.84	K0		COUSINS
HR9042	23 50 31	1 48 45	23 52 18	2 0 26	6.28	0.00	-0.01			COUSINS
HR9033	23 49 24	2 39 09	23 51 11	2 50 50	5.55	1.53	1.86			COUSINS

APPENDIX C
UBV STANDARD FIELD STARS

Having a photometric system without standard stars is like measuring the distance from New York to Paris in meters without defining the length of the meter. The standard stars are an integral part of a photometric system. They are as important as the filter responses themselves.

After the definition of the *UBV* system by Johnson and Morgan,[1] Johnson and Harris[2] published a list of 108 stars intended for use as photometric standards for the system. There were 10 primary standards, stars that were measured every possible night, and 98 additional stars that were measured from two to 17 times, averaging 7.3 measurements each. Because of the few measurements of some of these stars, internal accuracy of the system is on the order of $0.^m03$ in *V*. That is, if you select a large subset of these stars and measure them, your mean probable error of a measurement should be about this size.

The Johnson standard list has no stars south of $-20°$ declination. Traditionally, this has made Southern Hemisphere transformations difficult. For this reason, Cousins[3] has proposed a second list of standards between $+10°$ and $-10°$ declination, and secondary standards in the E and F regions of the southern sky.[4] The equatorial standards are presented by Cousins with their HR numbers but without coordinates, making them difficult for the amateur to use. The E and F region stars have the coordinates listed, but the amateur may have difficulty finding the reference in the local library. For this reason, the E and F region stars are included in this appendix and the list is separated into stars north and south of the celestial equator. Table C.1 lists the northern standard field stars, while Table C.2 lists the southern standard field stars.

Another problem with the standard stars listed in references 2 through 4 is the preponderance of bright stars. Transformations using bright stars and large telescopes are very difficult because of dead-time corrections and photomultiplier tube fatigue. For instance, with the Goethe Link 40-centimeter (16-inch) telescope, you cannot easily look at stars brighter than $4.^m0$ in V, and seldom use stars brighter than $6.^m0$ as standards. Fainter stars that can be used as secondary standards can be found in the list by Landolt.[5] These equatorial stars range from seventh to fourteenth magnitude, with most about twelfth magnitude in V. Another list of brighter UBV secondary standards is readily available from Sky Publishing[6] and is recommended for purchase.

To use the stars from this appendix for transforming to the standard system, pick 20 or more from the list, distributed over the sky but greater than 30° above the horizon. This removes effects caused by a small number of standards and minimizes systematic regional errors.

REFERENCES

1. Johnson, H. L. and Morgan, W. W. 1953. *Ap. J.* **117**, 313.
2. Johnson, H. L. and Harris, D. L., III 1954. *Ap. J.* **120**, 196.
3. Cousins, A. W. J. 1971. *Roy. Obs. Annals.* No. 7.
4. Cousins, A. W. J. 1973. *Mem. Roy. Astr. Soc.* **77**, 223.
5. Landolt, A. U. 1973. *A. J.* **78**, 959.
6. Iriarte, B., Johnson, H. L., Mitchell, R. I., and Wisniewski, W. K. 1965. *Sky and Tel.* **30**, 25. (Available as a reprint.)

TABLE C.1. Northern *UBV* Standard Field Stars

HR	R.A. (1950.0)	DEC. (1950.0)	R.A. (1985.0)	DEC. (1985.0)	V	B-V	U-B	SPEC.	NAME	OBS.
0039	0 10 39.4	14 54 20.6	0 12 27	15 06 01	2.83	-0.23	-0.87	B2IV	GAM PEG	JOHNSON
0063	0 14 28.3	38 24 14.9	0 16 18	38 35 54	4.61	0.06	0.04	A2V	THE AND	JOHNSON
0226	0 47 2.8	40 58 25.2	0 48 58	40 59 51	4.53	-0.15	-0.58	B5V	NU AND	JOHNSON
0343	1 8 2.6	54 53 4.3	1 10 9	55 04 14	4.33	0.17	0.11	A7V	THE CAS	JOHNSON
0403	1 22 31.5	59 58 34.4	1 24 48	60 09 29	2.68	0.13	0.12	A5V	DEL CAS	JOHNSON
0437	1 28 46.6	15 58 19.4	1 30 40	16 12 07	3.62	0.97	0.76	G8III	ETA CAS	JOHNSON
0493	1 39 46.6	20 1 34.3	1 41 41	20 12 09	5.23	0.83	0.50	K1V	107 PSC	JOHNSON
0553	1 51 52.3	20 33 52.0	1 53 48	20 44 10	2.65	0.13	0.10	A5V	BET ARI	JOHNSON
0617	2 4 20.9	23 13 37.0	2 6 18	23 23 36	2.00	1.15	1.12	K2III	ALF ARI	PRIMARY
	2 5 3	2 57 54.4	2 6 54	3 07 52	10.03	1.44	1.08		2 348	JOHNSON
0718	2 25 29.8	8 14 13.1	2 27 21	8 23 36	4.28	-0.06	-0.13	B9III	CHI2 CET	JOHNSON
0753	2 33 20.1	6 38 57.8	2 35 11	6 48 08	5.82	0.97	0.79	K3V	A	JOHNSON
0753	2 33 20.1	6 38 57.8	2 35 11	6 48 08	11.65	1.61	1.12		B	JOHNSON
0996	3 16 44.1	8 51 15.2	3 18 33	9 03 18	4.82	0.89	0.18	G5V	KAP CET	JOHNSON
1030	3 22 7.1	8 50 8.8	3 24	8 58 53	3.59	0.05	0.62	G8III	OMI TAU	JOHNSON
1046	3 26 10.5	15 30 30.6	3 28 51	15 24 05	5.08	0.99	0.03	A1V	GAM TAU	JOHNSON
1346	4 16 56.7	25 36 8.4	4 18 55	15 35 32	3.65	0.98	0.82	K0III	DEL TAU	JOHNSON
1373	4 20 2.8	19 4 16.4	4 22	17 30 30	3.76	1.02	0.82	K0III	EPS TAU	JOHNSON
1409	4 25 41.6	52 32.3	4 27 44	19 8 54	3.54	1.02	0.88	K0III	PI3 ORI	JOHNSON
1543	4 47 7.4	31 16.3	4 49 0	6 56 48	3.19	0.45	-0.01	F8V	PI4 ORI	JOHNSON
1552	4 48 32.4	41 10 8.4	4 50 24	34 48	3.69	-0.17	-0.80	B2III	ETA AUR	JOHNSON
1641	5 3 2	18 1.7	5 5 27	41 12 57	3.17	-0.18	-0.67	B3V	GAM ORI	JOHNSON
1790	5 22 26.8	28 34 13.6	5 24 19	6 20 13	1.64	-0.23	-0.87	B2III	BET TAU	JOHNSON
1791	5 23 7.7	12 38 12.0	5 25 20	28 35 50	1.65	-0.13	-0.49	B7III	134 TAU	JOHNSON
2010	5 46 44.3	17 49 12.0	5 48 42	12 38 51	4.90	-0.07	-0.18	B9IV	17 1320	JOHNSON
2421	6 28 51.7	16 37 56.1	6 30 54	17 38 40	1.93	1.50	1.18	A0IV	GAM GEM	JOHNSON
2763	7 15 13.2	39 42.0	6 36 50	16 24 48	3.58	0.11	0.03	A3V	LAM GEM	JOHNSON
	7 19 35.0	31 53 8.3	7 17 14	16 34 06	9.63	1.56	0.10		5 1668	JOHNSON
2852	7 25 53.8	24 27.5	7 21 27	5 35 39	4.16	0.32	1.12	F0V	RHO GEM	JOHNSON
2985	7 41 25.9	20 27.7	7 28 8	31 48 48	3.57	0.93	-0.03	G8III	KAP GEM	JOHNSON
3249	8 13 48.3	34 45.7	7 43 32	24 26 07	3.52	1.48	0.68	K4III	BET CNC	PRIMARY
3454	8 40 36.7	14 21.8	8 15 42	3 27 11	4.30	-0.19	1.78	B3V	ETA HYA	PRIMARY
3569	8 55 47.6	31 34.6	8 42 26	48 6 12	3.15	0.18	-0.74	A7V	IOT UMA	PRIMARY
3665	9 11 45.8	21 14.7	8 58 12	2 22 51	3.88	-0.06	0.07	A0P	THE HYA	JQHNSON
3815	9 32 40.8	29 21.4	9 13 34	35 52 51	5.41	0.77	-0.13	G8IV-	11 LMI	JQHNSON
3974	10 4 29.2	29 21.4	9 34 47	35 19 5	4.48	0.18	0.45	A7V	21 LMI	JOHNSON

292

3982	1Ø	5	42.6	12	12	44.5	1Ø	7	34	12	2	26	1.36	-Ø.11	-Ø.36	B8V	ALF LEO	JOHNSON	
4Ø33	1Ø	14	5.4	43	9	53.5	1Ø	16	12	42	59	24	3.45	Ø.Ø3	Ø.Ø6	A2IV	LAM UMA	JOHNSON	
	1Ø	21	33.4	1	37	54.Ø	1Ø	23	21	1	27	15	9.63	1.52	1.19		1 2447	JOHNSON	
4133	1Ø	3Ø	1Ø.8	9	33	52.2	1Ø	32	1	9	23	2	3.85	-Ø.14	-Ø.95	B1IB	RHO LEO	JOHNSON	
4456	11	32	6.4	17	4	24.6	11	33	55	16	52	47	5.95	-Ø.16	-Ø.64	B3V	9ØAB LEO	JOHNSON	
4534	11	46	3Ø.6	14	51	5.8	11	48	18	14	39	25	2.14	Ø.Ø9	Ø.Ø7	A3V	BET LEO	JOHNSON	
454Ø	11	48	5.4	2	2	47.6	11	49	53	1	51	4	3.61	Ø.55	Ø.1Ø	F8V	BET VIR	JOHNSON	
455Ø	11	5Ø	6.2	38	4	39.2	11	51	55	37	52	58	6.45	Ø.75	Ø.17	G8VP		JOHNSON	
4554	11	51	12.6	53	58	22.Ø	11	53	2	53	46	4Ø	2.44	Ø.ØØ	Ø.Ø1	AØV	GAM UMA	JOHNSON	
466Ø	12	12	57.6	57	18	36.9	12	14	4Ø	57	6	56	3.31	Ø.Ø8	Ø.Ø7	A3V	DEL UMA	JOHNSON	
4931	12	53	35.4	56	38	7.8	13	Ø	4	56	26	49	4.93	Ø.36	Ø.Ø1	F2V	78 UMA	JOHNSON	
4983	13	9	32.4	28	7	52.Ø	13	11	12	27	56	43	4.28	Ø.57	Ø.Ø7	GØV	BET COM	JOHNSON	
5Ø62	13	21	55.8	55	1Ø	56.6	13	23	19	54	59	57	4.Ø1	Ø.16	Ø.Ø8	A5V	8Ø UMA	JOHNSON	
5Ø72	13	25	59.Ø	14	2	42.8	13	27	42	13	51	5Ø	4.98	Ø.71	Ø.26	G5V	7Ø VIR	JOHNSON	
5235	13	52	18.2	18	38	51.3	13	53	58	18	28	33	2.69	Ø.58	Ø.19	GØIV	ETA BOO	JOHNSON	
5511	14	43	43.1	2	6	9.Ø	14	45	29	1	57	2Ø	3.74	Ø.ØØ	-Ø.Ø3	AØV	1Ø9 VIR	JOHNSON	
5854	15	41	48.2	6	34	53.9	15	43	31	6	28	18	2.65	1.17	1.24	K2III	ALF SER	PRIMARY	
5867	15	43	52.7	15	34	37.4	15	45	29	15	28	6	3.67	Ø.Ø6	Ø.Ø7	A2IV	BET SER	JOHNSON	A
5868	15	44	Ø.8	7	3Ø	3Ø.7	15	45	43	7	24	Ø	4.43	Ø.6Ø	Ø.1Ø	GØV	LAM SER	JOHNSON	
5933	15	54	8.5	15	49	24.8	15	55	44	15	43	2Ø	3.85	Ø.48	-Ø.Ø3	F6V	GAM SER	JOHNSON	
5947	15	55	3Ø.9	27	1	17.4	15	56	58	26	55	16	4.15	1.23	1.28	K3III	EPS CRB	PRIMARY	
6Ø92	16	18	14.1	46	25	53.6	16	19	17	46	2Ø	53	3.89	-Ø.15	-Ø.56	B5IV	TAU HER	PRIMARY	
	17	23	15.9	2	1Ø	14.2	17	25	1	2	8	24	7.54	1.36	1.26	K7V	157881	JOHNSON	
6556	17	32	36.7	12	35	41.9	17	34	13	12	34	2Ø	2.Ø8	Ø.15	Ø.1Ø	A5III	ALF OPH	JOHNSON	
66Ø3	17	41	Ø.Ø	4	35	11.8	17	42	43	4	34	16	2.77	1.16	1.24	K2III	BET OPH	JOHNSON	
6629	17	45	23.Ø	2	43	28.3	17	47	8	2	42	46	3.75	Ø.Ø4	Ø.Ø4	AØV	GAM OPH	JOHNSON	
	17	5Ø	42.9	4	16	54.Ø	17	52	26	4	16	28	9.54	1.74	1.29	M5V	4 3561	JOHNSON	
7ØØ1	18	35	14.7	38	44	9.6	18	36	25	38	45	58	Ø.Ø4	Ø.ØØ	-Ø.Ø1	AØV	ALF LYR	JOHNSON	
7178	18	57	4.3	32	37	11.3	18	58	22	32	4Ø	6	3.25	-Ø.Ø5	-Ø.Ø9	B9III	GAM LYR	JOHNSON	
7235	19	3	6.6	13	47	15.9	19	4	43	13	5Ø	29	2.99	Ø.ØØ	-Ø.Ø1	AØV	ZET AQL	JOHNSON	
	19	9	51.8	4	57	54.Ø	19	11	35	5	1	27	9.13	1.49	1.16	M3.5V	4 4Ø48	JOHNSON	
	19	31	7.2	3	39	7.8	19	32	52	3	43	42	6.82	Ø.Ø2	-Ø.83	B5	184279	JOHNSON	
7557	19	48	2Ø.6	8	44	5.8	19	5Ø	1	8	49	27	Ø.77	Ø.22	Ø.Ø8	A7IV-	ALF AQL	JOHNSON	
76Ø2	19	52	51.4	6	16	49.8	19	54	34	6	22	23	3.71	Ø.86	Ø.48	G8IV	BET AQL	JOHNSON	
79Ø6	2Ø	37	18.9	18	44	4.3	2Ø	38	54	18	51	3Ø	3.77	-Ø.Ø6	-Ø.22	B9V	ALF DEL	JOHNSON	
8622	22	37	Ø.8	38	47	22.4	22	38	35	38	58	19	4.88	-Ø.2Ø	-1.Ø4	O9V	1Ø LAC	PRIMARY	
8781	23	2	16.1	14	56	9.2	23	4	Ø	15	7	29	2.49	-Ø.Ø5	-Ø.Ø6	B9V	ALF PEG	JOHNSON	
8832	23	1Ø	51.9	56	53	31.3	23	12	24	57	4	57	5.57	1.Ø1	Ø.89	K3V		PRIMARY	
8969	23	37	22.6	5	21	18.6	23	39	9	5	32	57	4.13	Ø.51	Ø.ØØ	F7V	IOT PSC	JOHNSON	
	23	46	35.6	2	8	11.7	23	48	23	2	19	52	8.98	1.48	1.Ø9	M2V	1 4774	JOHNSON	

TABLE C.2. Southern *UBV* Standard Field Stars

HR	R.A. (1950.0)	DEC. (1950.0)	R.A. (1985.0)	DEC. (1985.0)	V	B-V	U-B	SPEC.	NAME	OBS.
0331	1 5 31.0	-41 45 14.2	1 7 6	-41 34 1	5.21	0.16	0.08	A3	UPS PHE	COUSINS
0370	1 12 55.9	-45 47 53.1	1 14 28	-45 36 47	4.96	0.57	0.10	G0	NU PHE	COUSINS
	1 14 46.8	-42 47 43.9	1 16 20	-42 36 40	7.86	-0.08	-0.37	B9	HD7795	COUSINS
0411	1 22 31.7	-44 47 18.1	1 24 2	-44 36 22	6.27	1.14	1.08	K0	HD9733	COUSINS
	1 32 13.7	-45 56 52.2	1 33 42	-45 46 7	6.92	0.99	0.48	G5		COUSINS
0509	1 41 44.7	-16 12 0.5	1 43 16	-16 1 28	3.50	0.72	0.20	GBVP	TAU CET	JOHNSON
	1 58 0.2	-18 18 30.0	1 59 40	-18 8 20	10.18	1.53	1.16		-18 0359	JOHNSON
0875	2 54 6.9	-3 54 45.0	2 55 52	-3 46 18	5.17	0.08	0.05	A1V		PRIMARY
	3 25 47.0	-76 55 9.9	3 24 58	-76 47 51	6.80	0.20	0.10	A0	HD21940	COUSINS
1084	3 30 34.4	-9 37 34.8	3 32 15	-9 30 31	3.73	0.89	0.57	K2V	EPS ERI	JOHNSON
	3 36 47.6	-74 8 17.8	3 36 22	-74 1 26	7.61	1.14	1.01	K0	HD23128	COUSINS
	3 48 26.1	-45 32 8.6	3 49 33	-45 25 49	6.94	0.94	0.70	G5	HD24291	COUSINS
	3 49 3.4	-74 50 43.9	3 48 26	-74 44 23	7.12	0.39	-0.05	F2	HD24636	COUSINS
	4 0 40.2	-48 0 3.9	4 1 47	-44 42 16	8.20	0.13	0.15	A2	HD25653	COUSINS
1291	4 7 0.7	-45 59 46.3	4 8 5	-45 54 15	6.58	0.38	0.00	F0		COUSINS
1316	4 10 56.0	-44 29 42.2	4 12 2	-44 24 22	6.71	1.48	1.80	K0		COUSINS
	4 15 55.2	-75 55 50.9	4 17 55	-75 50 41	7.23	1.64	1.97	K0	HD27728	COUSINS
	4 16 27.9	-46 27 20.4	4 18 32	-46 41 15	7.54	0.64	0.17	G0	HD27471	COUSINS
	4 35 9.1	-73 18 39.5	4 34 31	-73 14 24	6.81	0.96	0.66	K0	HD29751	COUSINS
1666	5 5 23.4	-5 8 58.5	5 7 6	-5 6 15	2.80	0.13	0.10	A3III	BET ERI	JOHNSON
1781	5 21 8.8	-8 12 18.7	5 22 56	-8 10 23	5.70	-0.22	-0.87	B5V	35299	JOHNSON
	5 28 55.3	-3 41 4.1	5 30 39	-3 39 31	7.97	1.47	1.21	K2	36395	JOHNSON
1855	5 29 30.6	-7 20 12.9	5 31 12	-7 18 42	4.63	-0.26	-1.07	B0V	UPS ORI	JOHNSON
1861	5 30 9.5	-1 37 35.7	5 31 55	-1 36 7	5.35	-0.20	-0.94	B1V	36591	JOHNSON
1899	5 32 59.1	-5 56 28.1	5 34 41	-5 55 8	2.77	-0.25	-1.08	O9III	EPS ORI	JOHNSON
1903	5 33 40.5	-1 13 56.1	5 35 27	-1 12 38	1.70	-0.19	-1.04	B0IA	EPS ORI	JOHNSON
1998	5 44 41.3	-14 50 21.2	5 46 16	-14 49 36	3.55	0.10	0.05	A3V	ZET LEP	JOHNSON
2462	6 29 34.2	-43 40 51.4	6 30 37	-43 42 23	6.69	1.00	0.86	K0	HD46415	JOHNSON
	6 30 17.6	-48 10 28.8	6 31 13	-48 12 2	4.94	0.88	0.74	K0		COUSINS
2546	6 43 47.5	-47 10 8.9	6 44 45	-47 12 23	7.22	-0.16	-0.74	B3	HD49260	COUSINS
	6 46 47.2	-43 44 37.9	6 47 50	-43 47 1	7.42	-0.12	-0.74	A3	HD49850	COUSINS
	6 49 30.2	-45 23 24.0	6 49 31	-45 25 52	6.54	1.51	1.82	K0		COUSINS
3314	8 23 9.7	-3 44 31.5	8 24 54	-3 51 23	3.90	-0.02	-0.02	A0V		JOHNSON
3654	9 9 15.4	-44 39 45.2	9 10 31	-44 48 22	4.98	0.23	-0.57	B5		COUSINS
	9 17 1.1	-44 47 46.9	9 18 18	-44 56 39	7.20	1.11	0.94	K0	HD80527	COUSINS
3730	9 20 34.3	-45 50 0.5	9 21 51	-45 59 0	5.74	0.92	0.65	G5		COUSINS

294

Star catalogue data (photometry and positions).

Source	ID	SpType	Data
COUSINS	HD81347	B5	6.27 -0.14 -0.61 9 22 53 -48 13 20 21 39.1 -48 4 48 9 21 4519
JOHNSON	-12 2918	F5	10.06 1.53 1.15 9 25 56 -13 0 49 15.7 -12 51 24
COUSINS	HD82224	G0	6.60 0.48 0.06 9 28 47 -43 7 26 42.0 27.2 -42 1 47 9 27
COUSINS	HD101805	B8	6.47 0.52 0.05 11 41 34 -75 8 37 13.0 13.8 -74 1 47 11 40
COUSINS	HD103281	G5	5.29 -0.12 -0.55 11 44 59 -46 45 36 58.5 15.0 -46 15 43
COUSINS	HD104138	F8	7.22 1.04 0.83 11 52 50 -46 32 39 44.6 14.2 -46 1 51
COUSINS	—	K0	6.66 0.56 0.09 11 48 43 -74 7 32 50.2 1.9 -73 8.5 57
COUSINS	—	A2	6.45 0.22 0.98 12 57 7 -74 49 49 16.2 4.2 -44 18.1 2
COUSINS	HD106321	K0	5.75 0.24 0.15 12 8 7 -44 14 31 7.8 8.5 -44 6
JOHNSON	GAM CRV	BBIII	5.31 1.43 1.58 12 13 15 -45 38 25 49.5 18.1 -45 11 26
COUSINS	HD107145	F5	2.60 -0.11 -0.35 12 15 2 -17 27 32 45.3 25.3 -17 13 13
COUSINS	HD107547	A2	6.84 -0.01 -0.01 12 18 54 -76 43 14 52.0 51.4 -76 15 22
JOHNSON	—	B9	6.78 0.16 0.14 12 21 18 -73 25 15 35.6 21.8 -73 5 19
JOHNSON	0 2989	M0.5V	6.48 0.09 -0.23 12 38 21 -75 17 40 42.7 59.8 -75 0 35
JOHNSON	61 VIR	G6V	8.49 1.41 1.26 12 49 38 -18 13 13 26.3 9.7 -18 0 48
JOHNSON	ALF VIR	B1V	4.75 -0.71 0.25 13 17 57 -11 3 1.3 47.1 -10 22 15
COUSINS	—	A3	0.96 -0.23 -0.94 13 22 39 -24 11 58 3.4 33.3 -10 10 22
COUSINS	—	K2	5.82 0.31 0.14 14 24 24 -46 58 3.0 58.1 -45 23 34
JOHNSON	ALF1 LIB	G5	5.54 1.49 1.71 14 26 14 -15 19 50 41.6 1.9 -15 45 33
JOHNSON	ALF2 LIB	F5IV	6.30 1.08 0.88 14 35 19 -15 33 40 54.0 16.4 -15 44 47
COUSINS	OMI LUP	AM	5.16 0.41 -0.04 14 46 33 -43 15 6 24.9 55.0 -43 2 48
COUSINS	—	B5	2.75 -0.15 -0.08 14 47 51 -15 58 19 6.6 6.4 -15 6 48
PRIMARY	BET LIB	F8	4.32 -0.16 -0.62 14 50 27 -43 30 11.1 21.9 -43 17 56
JOHNSON	-7 4003	BBV	2.61 0.60 -0.28 14 58 16 -1 43 39.6 9.7 -1 44
JOHNSON	-12 4523	—	10.56 -0.11 0.37 15 16 11 -7 9 58.9 18.7 -7 11 42
JOHNSON	ZET OPH	O9.5V	10.13 1.61 1.20 15 13 13 -12 19 18.0 52.7 -12 11 16
JOHNSON	154363	K5V	2.56 1.60 -0.86 16 24 18 -10 32 6.0 13.9 -10 22 34
JOHNSON	-4 4226	M3.5V	7.73 0.02 1.18 16 36 20 -4 18 2.8 24.1 -4 27 57
COUSINS	—	G5	10.07 1.16 1.09 17 18 59 -44 36 44 58.4 27.0 -44 7
CQUSINS	HD157487	A0	5.07 1.43 0.56 17 23 36 -44 18 29 8.4 39.6 -44 15
COUSINS	HD159656	B8	6.64 0.88 0.05 17 24 19 -44 32 10 42.7 4.6 -44 20
COUSINS	-3 4233	K0	5.11 0.20 -0.40 17 36 23 -44 44 8 17.9 46.9 -44 22
JOHNSON	KAP AQL	G5	7.65 1.25 1.14 18 4 35 -44 46 8.1 35.3 -44 34
JOHNSON	—	K5	7.17 0.65 0.17 19 18 48 -42 44 3 8.4 18.3 -42 18
COUSINS	HD186502	B0.5I	9.38 1.52 1.21 19 2 18 -3 41 52.6 28.3 -3 2
JOHNSON	—	B0.51	4.96 -0.01 -0.87 19 34 4 -72 32 30 24.7 12.1 -72 7 34
JOHNSON	KAP AQL	A3	5.39 0.24 0.10 19 43 47 -72 30 49 24.4 41.3 -72 43 7446
COUSINS	HD186502	F8	7.30 0.46 0.02 19 49 30 -72 59 16.9 27.3 -72 45 7498

SOUTHERN UBV FIELD STANDARD STARS

HR	R.A. (1950.0)	DEC.	R.A. (1985.0)	DEC.	V	B-V	U-B	SPEC.	NAME	OBS.
7590	19 54 50.8	-73 2 43.8	19 58 51	-72 57 1	3.95	-0.03	-0.06	A0	EPS PAV	COUSINS
	19 58 39.6	-44 36 21.4	20 1 7	-44 30 30	7.91	-0.04	-0.25	A0	HD189502	COUSINS
	19 59 4.0	-45 20 10.2	20 1 32	-45 14 18	6.57	1.22	1.22	K0	HD189563	COUSINS
	20 7 48.0	-43 48 40.3	20 10 13	-43 42 25	6.54	0.88	0.57	G5	HD191349	COUSINS
	20 12 51.2	-73 8 3.7	20 16 46	-73 1 34	6.56	1.41	1.67	K2	HD191937	COUSINS
	20 12 56.8	-72 57 50.3	20 16 50	-72 51 20	6.93	1.03	1.87	K0	HD191973	COUSINS
	20 14 50.3	-43 0 55.0	20 17 13	-42 54 22	7.01	0.33	0.02	F0	HD192758	COUSINS
	20 15 14.2	-42 46 30.8	20 17 37	-42 39 57	7.45	0.59	0.16	G0	HD192826	COUSINS
7950	20 44 58.2	-9 40 48.2	20 46 51	-9 33 3	3.77	0.01	0.04	A1V	EPS AQR	JOHNSON
	22 27 18.1	-42 32 51.5	22 31 18	-42 22 5	6.92	-0.05	-0.08	A0	HD213155	COUSINS
	22 29 13.8	-43 31 14.2	22 31 18	-43 20 25	6.91	0.98	0.77	G5	HD213457	COUSINS
8657	22 42 44.1	-46 48 38.1	22 44 47	-46 37 34	5.51	1.32	1.43	K0	HD215657	COUSINS
8662	22 43 46.7	-47 12 12.3	22 45 50	-47 1 8	6.56	0.30	0.10	A5		COUSINS
	22 44 31.9	-45 13 44.8	22 46 34	-45 2 39	7.22	0.60	0.07	G0		COUSINS
	22 45 27.5	-15 0 42.0	22 47 18	-14 49 36	10.17	1.60	1.15		-15 6290	JOHNSON
8704	22 50 50.8	-11 52 58.3	22 52 41	-11 41 47	5.81	-0.08	-0.32	B9	74 AQR	JOHNSON

APPENDIX D
JOHNSON UBV STANDARD CLUSTERS

When Johnson and Morgan created the *UBV* system, they included a list of standard stars. This list covered the entire sky visible from the United States and is used by some observers as the primary method of calibrating their instrumental magnitudes. However, at the same time, Johnson observed stars in or near three open clusters. These standard clusters were also to be used in determining the transforming coefficients.

The advantages of using star clusters to obtain coefficients include:

1. First-order extinction corrections are very small because all stars are within 1° of each other.
2. It is easy to observe many stars quickly because they can be located on a single finding chart and only small movements are required to change from one star to another.

The disadvantages of using one of these standard clusters include:

1. Red stars are almost always fainter than blue ones, because most stars are on the main sequence and are at the same distance.
2. A clear spot for obtaining a sky reading can be hard to find.
3. The density of stars makes the use of a large diaphragm difficult because "companions" become included.
4. Transformation difficulties can exist because each cluster is in an isolated region in the sky and was placed on the standard system differently than the whole-sky standard list.

Still, for many observers the cluster method of calculating color coefficients is highly useful. We recommend that you use both the whole-sky and the cluster methods sometime during your observing season.

In observing these clusters, Johnson picked from one to three regional standard stars, and measured all cluster stars with respect to these standards. He then tied the regional standards to the *UBV* system by using the whole-sky standards. Therefore, the clusters are placed on the *UBV* system in a two-step process, though with exactly the same equipment which was used to define the *UBV* system.

Each cluster is discussed in a similar manner. There is a brief description of the cluster and of the pertinent references. This is followed by a list of 26 stars for each cluster. These stars were picked from the much larger lists by Johnson to include stars over a wide magnitude and spectral range, and with as many Johnson observations as possible.

Each star's coordinates are taken from the SAO catalog, or from the catalog reference if the star is fainter than tenth magnitude. The stars are named on the right by a letter of the alphabet and the zone BD number where available. The last item for each cluster is a finding chart with 26 stars identified.

D.1 THE PLEIADES

This famous naked-eye cluster is often called the Seven Sisters. It is a very young cluster, containing many bright blue stars and nebulosity. There are about 600 stars brighter than fourteenth magnitude in the central 1° field.

Because of the youth of the cluster, only three red stars were observed that are brighter than tenth magnitude. This places a large weight on their measurement, especially star D, and this should be recognized by the observer. Table D.1 lists the information for this cluster.

Approximately 250 stars were observed with the 53- and 103-centimeter (21- and 42-inch) Lowell reflectors. All stars in the region were observed differentially with respect to the regional standard stars E, I, and Alcyone.

Catalog:
Hertzsprung, E., 1947. *Ann. Leiden Obs.* **19**, 1A.
Photometry:
Johnson, H. L., and Morgan, W. W. 1953. *Ap. J.* **117**, 313.
Johnson, H. L., and Mitchell, R, I. 1958. *Ap. J.* **128**, 31.
Chart:
Red Palomar chart MLP 357 (E-641).

D. 2 THE PRAESEPE

The Praesepe, M44, or the Beehive, is one of the largest and nearest open clusters. It is visible to the naked eye, though not as easily as the Pleiades, and has several hundred members.

TABLE D.1. Pleiades Cluster Standards

HR	R.A. (1950.0)	DEC. (1950.0)	R.A. (1985.0)	DEC. (1985.0)	V	B-V	U-B	SPEC.	NAME	OBS.
1165	3 44 30.4	23 57 7.6	3 46 35	24 35 35	2.87	-0.09	-0.34	B7II	A	JOHNSON
1145	3 42 13.6	24 18 42.9	3 44 18	24 25 17	4.31	-0.11	-0.46	B6V	B	JOHNSON
1172	3 45 22.9	23 16 8.8	3 47 27	23 22 34	5.45	-0.07	-0.32	B8V	C	JOHNSON
	3 45 7.0	24 50 9.1	3 47 12	24 56 35	6.46	1.70	2.07	K5	D	JOHNSON
	3 44 0.3	24 22 0.4	3 46 5	24 28 30	6.82	0.03	-0.07	B9V	E	JOHNSON
	3 45 31.1	24 11 36.4	3 47 36	24 18 2	6.95	0.12	0.09	A0	F	JOHNSON
	3 44 28.8	24 20 42.1	3 49 34	24 27 2	7.42	0.13	0.12	A2	G	JOHNSON
	3 44 38.7	23 27 23.1	3 46 43	23 33 51	7.72	1.23	1.12	K0	H	JOHNSON
	3 43 36.2	23 28 12.2	3 45 40	23 34 42	8.11	0.35	0.29	A0	I	JOHNSON
	3 42 35.6	24 18 30.4	3 44 40	24 25 3	8.60	0.35	0.11	A2	K	JOHNSON
	3 44 44.2	23 23 26.6	3 46 48	23 29 54	8.79	1.15	0.81	K0	L	JOHNSON
	3 46 55.8	24 4 2.5	3 49 0	24 10 24	9.16	0.16	0.02	A0	M	JOHNSON
	3 44 11.1	24 7 26.0	3 46 16	24 13 55	9.46	0.47	0.15	F8	N	JOHNSON
	3 42 41.0	24 28 22.0	3 44 46	24 34 55	9.70	0.55	0.05	F8	O	JOHNSON
	3 45 27.5	23 53 48.0	3 47 32	24 0 13	10.02	0.56	0.09		P	JOHNSON
	3 43 55.7	23 25 50.0	3 46 0	23 32 19	10.52	0.64	0.16	F9	Q	JOHNSON
	3 46 25.5	23 41 19.0	3 48 30	23 47 42	11.35	0.78	0.38	G2	R	JOHNSON
	3 43 42.3	23 20 40.0	3 45 46	23 27 18	12.02	0.99	0.54	G8	S	JOHNSON
	3 43 8.3	24 42 47.0	3 45 13	24 49 54	12.05	1.01	0.84	G5	T	JOHNSON
	3 41 5.0	24 5 17.0	3 43 9	24 11 46	12.51	0.81	0.30	G1	U	JOHNSON
	3 44 19.0	24 14 18.0	3 46 24	24 20 22	12.61	1.18	1.00	G9V	V	JOHNSON
	3 43 7.7	25 0 51.0	3 45 13	25 7 21	14.36	1.01	0.47		X	JOHNSON
	3 46 26.1	23 49 58.0	3 48 30	23 56 21	15.72	1.15	0.98		Y	JOHNSON
	3 44 39.0	24 34 52.0	3 46 44	24 41 20	16.42	0.60	0.25		Z	JOHNSON

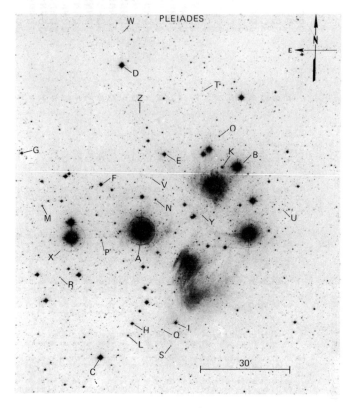

Figure D.1. The Pleiades cluster standards. Copyright by the National Geographic Society—Palomar Observatory Sky Survey. Reproduced by permission.

Johnson made observations of 150 stars in the region of the Praesepe cluster. The 26 stars listed in this table are therefore a small subset of the total. Two regional standards were used in this cluster, stars B and F. All stars in the cluster were then observed differentially with respect to these two standards. Table D.2 lists the information for this cluster.

Catalog:
Klein-Wassink, W. J. 1927. *Pub. of Kapetyn Astronomical Laboratory at Gröningen,* No. 41, 5.
Vanderlinden, H. L. 1933. *Étude de l'amas de Praesepe.* Gembloux: Joules Duculot.

Photometry:
Johnson, H. L. 1952. *Ap. J.* **116**, 640.

Chart:
Blue Palomar chart MLP 426 (O-1311).

TABLE D.2. Praesepe Cluster Standards

HR	EPOCH 1950 RA h	m	s	DEC d	m	s	EPOCH 1985 RA h	m	s	DEC d	m	s	V	B-V	U-B	SPEC.	NAME	OBS.
3429	8	36	59	19	43	7	8	38	59	19	35	41	6.590	0.960	0.720	K0II	A,2150	JOHNSON
3428	8	37	14	20	11	8	8	39	15	20	3	41	6.390	0.980	0.830	K0II	B,2158	JOHNSON
3428	8	37	30	19	50	53	8	39	31	19	43	26	6.440	1.020	0.900	K0II	C,2166	JOHNSON
	8	32	27	19	45	48	8	34	28	19	38	33	6.580	0.670	0.250	G0II	D,2118	JOHNSON
	8	37	35	19	43	23	8	39	35	19	35	55	6.300	0.170	0.160	A2	E,2171	JOHNSON
	8	37	19	20	8	57	8	39	20	20	1	30	6.610	0.010	0.020	A0	F,2159	JOHNSON
	8	38	4	19	45	32	8	40	4	19	38	3	6.780	0.170	0.140	A6V	G,2175	JOHNSON
	8	37	51	19	53	52	8	39	52	19	46	24	6.850	0.200	0.150	A9II	H,2172	JOHNSON
	8	38	58	20	3	13	8	40	59	19	55	42	6.900	0.960	0.740	K0II	J,2185	JOHNSON
	8	37	26	19	42	36	8	39	26	19	35	9	7.540	0.160	0.130	F0II	K,2163	JOHNSON
	8	36	17	19	46	10	8	38	18	19	38	45	8.500	0.250	0.070	A9V	L,2144	JOHNSON
	8	35	55	19	40	39	8	37	55	19	33	15	9.000	0.320	0.030	A5	M,2139	JOHNSON
	8	37	9	20	18	49	8	39	10	20	11	22	9.670	0.440	-0.020	F6V	N,2156	JOHNSON
	8	37	40	19	38	30	8	37	40	19	31	7	10.010	1.010	0.780	G5	P,2056	JOHNSON
	8	38	3	20	14	34	8	39	4	20	7	8	10.110	0.490	0.000		Q	JOHNSON
	8	38	34	20	7	22	8	40	35	19	59	52	10.720	0.600	0.100		R,2181	JOHNSON
	8	37	48	19	50	53	8	39	48	19	43	25	10.870	0.680	0.190		S	JOHNSON
	8	36	22	20	23	17	8	38	23	20	15	52	11.310	0.700	0.240		T	JOHNSON
	8	38	42	20	8	54	8	40	43	19	1	24	11.710	0.780	0.380		U	JOHNSON
	8	36	14	19	28	55	8	38	14	19	21	31	12.370	0.460	-0.050		V	JOHNSON
	8	36	37	19	57	51	8	38	38	19	50	26	12.640	1.000	0.760		W	JOHNSON
	8	38	24	19	55	37	8	40	25	19	48	7	13.700	0.810	0.400		X	JOHNSON
	8	37	13	19	56	12	8	39	14	19	48	45	14.610	0.950	0.690		Y	JOHNSON
	8	36	23	20	14	51	8	38	24	20	7	26	14.940	1.480	1.100		Z	JOHNSON

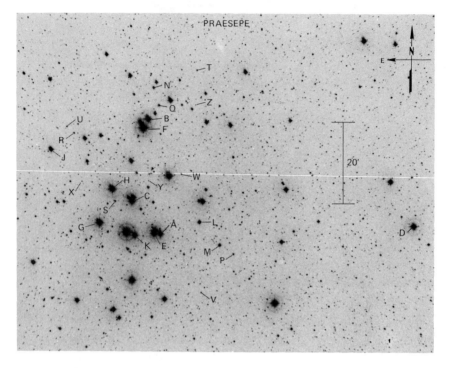

Figure D.2. The Praesepe cluster standards. Copyright by the National Geographic Society—Palomar Observatory Sky Survey. Reproduced by permission.

D.3 IC 4665

The standard region near the open cluster IC 4665 was observed by Johnson in 1954. The cluster itself contains a few blue stars, some of which were measured, but most of the standard stars in this region are field stars within 1° of the cluster center.

All stars in the region were measured differentially with respect to the regional standard, star A. Some of these stars were observed at McDonald and some at Mount Wilson observatories, but most were measured at Lowell observatory. Table D.3 lists the information for this cluster.

This region is interesting because several reasonably bright red stars are included, thereby reducing the error in the color transformation that can be troublesome on the other two standard regions.

Catalog:
Kopff. 1943. *Mitt. Hamburg Sternw.* **8**, 93.

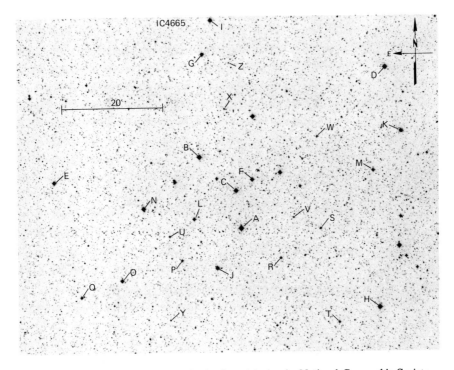

Figure D.3. The IC 4665 cluster standards. Copyright by the National Geographic Society—Palomar Observatory Sky Survey. Reproduced by permission.

Photometry:
Johnson, H. L. 1954. *Ap. J.* **119**, 181.

Chart:
Red Palomar chart MLP 569 (E-780).

TABLE D.3. IC 4665 Regional Standards

HR	R.A. (1950.0)	DEC.	R.A. (1985.0)	DEC.	V	B-V	U-B	SPEC.	NAME	OBS.
	17 43 40.1	5 32 54.5	17 45 23	5 32 7	6.85	0.01	-0.54	B4V	A,3483	JOHNSON
	17 44 14.0	5 47 31.0	17 45 56	5 46 45	7.12	0.02	-0.48	B8	B,3490	JOHNSON
	17 43 43.7	5 40 43.2	17 45 26	5 39 48	7.34	0.02	-0.46	B9	C,3484	JOHNSON
	17 41 36.9	6 4 51.4	17 43 19	6 3 57	7.43	0.33	-0.15	A2	D,3514	JOHNSON
	17 46 16.3	5 42 59.4	17 47 59	5 42 20	7.49	0.02	-0.41	B9	E,3504	JOHNSON
	17 43 29.9	5 42 46.4	17 45 12	5 41 58	7.59	0.00	-0.49	B6V	F,3432	JOHNSON
	17 44 9.8	6 8 18.1	17 45 52	6 7 32	7.74	-0.01	-0.55	B9	G,3525	JOHNSON
	17 41 45.4	5 16 16.6	17 43 28	5 15 23	7.83	1.28	1.10	K2	H,3469	JOHNSON
	17 44 2.1	6 15 14.2	17 45 44	6 14 27	7.89	1.03	0.77	KØ	I,3524	JOHNSON
	17 44 0.8	5 24 54.8	17 45 43	5 24 8	7.94	0.45	-0.01	FØ	J,3488	JOHNSON
	17 41 24.8	5 51 57.4	17 43 7	5 51 2	8.05	0.07	-0.17	AØ	K,3466	JOHNSON
	17 44 19.4	5 34 57.4	17 46 2	5 34 12	8.22	0.11	-0.30	B9	L,3491	JOHNSON
	17 41 48.6	5 44 6.7	17 43 31	5 43 13	8.31	0.06	-0.16	B9	M,3471	JOHNSON
	17 45 1.7	5 37 14.6	17 46 44	5 36 31	8.33	1.73	2.08	K5	N,3498	JOHNSON
	17 45 21.0	5 22 43.3	17 47 4	5 22 1	8.40	1.23	1.04	K2	O,3500	JOHNSON
	17 44 30.3	5 26 35.1	17 46 13	5 25 50	8.89	0.11	-0.27	B9V	P,3493	JOHNSON
	17 45 55.3	5 19 32.0	17 47 38	5 18 51	8.96	1.25	1.07		Q,3503	JOHNSON
	17 43 7.4	5 26 44.1	17 44 50	5 25 55	9.10	0.26	0.10		R,3479	JOHNSON
	17 42 33.6	5 32 33.6	17 44 16	5 31 42	9.39	0.31	-0.17	A2V	S,3473	JOHNSON
	17 42 19.0	5 13 14.0	17 44 1	5 12 22	9.68	1.27	1.04		T,3472	JOHNSON
	17 44 41.0	5 31 39.0	17 46 24	5 30 54	9.81	0.68	0.23		U,3496	JOHNSON
	17 42 55.0	5 35 1.0	17 44 37	5 34 11	10.10	0.12	0.01	AØ	V,3477	JOHNSON
	17 42 34.0	5 52 46.0	17 44 16	5 51 55	10.21	1.29	1.27		W,3474	JOHNSON
	17 43 52.0	5 57 21.0	17 45 34	5 56 34	10.61	0.45	0.15	A2	X,3485	JOHNSON
	17 44 41.0	5 13 15.0	17 46 24	5 12 30	10.75	0.37	0.22		Y,3495	JOHNSON
	17 43 45.0	6 6 44.0	17 45 27	6 5 56	11.33	0.53	-0.05		Z,3523	JOHNSON

APPENDIX E
NORTH POLAR SEQUENCE STARS

The North Polar Sequence (NPS) was developed at Harvard College Observatory in 1906 to provide stars with standard photographic magnitudes that could be used to derive magnitudes for other stars. The sequence began with 10 and rapidly expanded to 96 stars. Three separate sequences evolved: red (r), blue (no suffix), and supplementary (s, mostly yellow). Mount Wilson collaborated in the latter stages, and the sequences formed the basis of the International System of magnitudes adopted by the IAU in 1922. See Pickering,[1] Leavitt,[2] and Stebbins et al.[3] for more detail.

The NPS has only historical significance now because it has been superseded by sequences in clusters and in the equatorial plane, accessible by major telescopes in both hemispheres. In addition, only photographic magnitudes and colors have been derived for the majority of the stars, and even these are in error for the fainter members of the NPS.

One modern application for which the NPS is well suited is to determine temporal consistency of the atmosphere. This is because none of the stars lies more than 3° from the north celestial pole, and therefore remain at the same air mass with time. It is a good idea to observe one of these stars several times during the night to be sure that the atmosphere is remaining constant.

Table E.1 lists the sequence stars that are brighter than eleventh magnitude on photovisual plates. The V magnitudes of those stars in the table with no $(U - B)$ color indicated are photovisual magnitudes, and the color index is photographic-photovisual. The accompanying finding chart identifies the table stars.

For amateurs in the Southern Hemisphere, a short sequence near the south celestial pole has been set up by Soonthornthum and Tritton.[4] Their photoelectric sequence includes nine stars ranging from $V = 6.53$ to $V = 12.66$. They include a finding chart in their article.

NORTH POLAR SEQUENCE

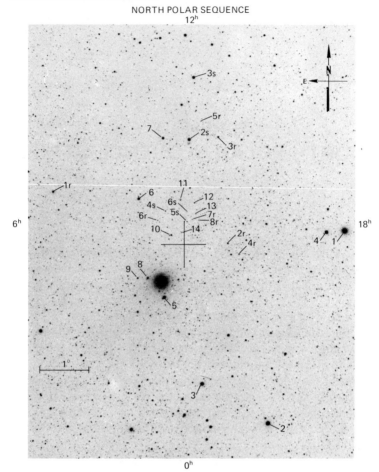

Figure E.1. The North Polar Region. Lick Observatory photograph.

REFERENCES

1. Pickering, E. C. 1912. *Harvard College Circular,* No. 170.
2. Leavitt, H. C. 1917. *Ann. Harvard College Obs.* **71**, 47.
3. Stebbins, J., Whitford, A. E., and Johnson, H. L. 1950. *Ap. J.* **112**, 469.
4. Soonthornthum, B., and Tritton, K. P. 1980. *Observatory* **100**, 4.

TABLE E.1. North Polar Sequence Stars

NP	R.A. (1950.Ø)	DEC. (1950.Ø)	R.A. (1985.Ø)	DEC. (1985.Ø)	V	B-V	U-B	SPEC.	NAME	OBS.
5	1 1Ø 57.3	88 45 18.9	1 25 44	88 56 2Ø	6.44	Ø.11	Ø.14	A2	BD88 4	JOHNSON
8	2 49 44.3	88 55 16.Ø	2 23 39	89 3 18	8.Ø8	Ø.41	-Ø.Ø6	FØ	BD88 9	JOHNSON
9	3 18 47.5	88 45 56.Ø	3 51 12	88 52 51	8.89	Ø.2Ø		A	BD88 13	NPS
1Ø	7 12 31.2	89 44 52.Ø	9 16 26	89 38 9	9.Ø5	Ø.12	Ø.ØØ	A5	BD89 3	NPS
1R	8 22 39.7	87 7 34.5	7 33 54	87 3 17	5.Ø4	1.57	Ø.ØØ	MØ	BD87 51	NPS
6R	8 45 53.6	89 21 3Ø.6	9 11 39	89 13 4Ø	9.24	1.23	Ø.ØØ	G8	BD89 9	NPS
6	9 49 27.5	88 46 14.8	9 12 37	88 38 Ø	7.Ø9	Ø.Ø6	Ø.ØØ	AØ	BD89 13	NPS
4S	9 13 59.6	89 19 44.9	1Ø 19 45	89 12 29	9.89	Ø.47	Ø.ØØ	GØ	BD89 12	NPS
7	11 23 15.7	87 54 43.3	11 19 36	87 43 14	7.55	-Ø.17	Ø.ØØ	B8	BD88 64	NPS
14	11 45 52.7	89 51 54.Ø	11 46 14	89 4Ø 15	1Ø.57	Ø.45	Ø.ØØ	F2	BD89 1	NPS
11	12 14 45.Ø	89 12 24.9	11 5Ø 16	89 Ø 44	9.61	Ø.22	Ø.ØØ	F2	BD89 18	NPS
2S	12 15 24.5	87 58 37.6	12 15 16	87 46 57	6.22	Ø.26	Ø.ØØ	FØ	BD88 71	NPS
3S	12 3Ø 4.4	86 42 49.3	12 16 17	86 31 9	6.33	Ø.33	Ø.ØØ	F2	BD87 1Ø7	NPS
6S	12 43 27.1	89 25 16.9	12 24 4	89 13 4Ø	1Ø.72	Ø.67	Ø.ØØ	G8	BD89 26	NPS
5R	12 58 22.1	88 37 45.6	12 39 44	88 26 15	8.63	1.53	1.51	KØ	BD89 22	NPS
3R	13 1 4Ø.6	87 55 5.7	12 55 7	87 43 45	7.47	1.42	Ø.ØØ	K2	BD88 76	JOHNSON
5S	13 15 1.8	89 38 11.9	12 41 4Ø	89 26 47	1Ø.Ø6	1.Ø8	Ø.ØØ	G5	BD89 37	NPS
12	13 46 56.8	89 33 28.9	13 1 42	89 2 17	9.78	Ø.35	Ø.ØØ	A3	BD89 25	NPS
7R	13 52 2Ø.5	89 25 26.3	13 16 6	89 22 38	9.87	1.12	Ø.ØØ	G8	BD89 35	NPS
13	14 47 18.5	89 29 1.4	13 26 12	89 14 23	1Ø.27	Ø.24	Ø.ØØ	A5	BD89 29	NPS
8R	17 48 18.3	89 29 12.7	14 4 12	89 19 45	1Ø.41	1.Ø2	Ø.ØØ	G8	BD89 31	NPS
1	17 49 12.2	86 36 34.8	17 37 Ø	86 35 41	4.35	Ø.Ø1	Ø.Ø4	A1V	BD86 269	JOHNSON
4	18 21 21.8	86 59 31.9	17 36 14	86 58 39	5.74	Ø.14	Ø.ØØ	A3	BD86 272	NPS
2R	18 53 29.5	89 3 3.5	17 36 2	89 2 59	6.34	1.56	Ø.ØØ	M3	BD88 112	NPS
4R	21 2 1.8	88 46 55.6	18 23 38	88 49 1	8.22	1.Ø2	Ø.ØØ	KØ	BD88 114	NPS
2	22 17 33.6	85 51 27.Ø	22 14 32	86 1 57	5.24	-Ø.Ø2	-Ø.22	AØ	BD85 383	JOHNSON
3	23 27 34.2	87 1 54.4	23 27 9	87 13 28	5.56	Ø.16	Ø.ØØ	FØ	BD86 344	NPS

APPENDIX F
DEAD-TIME EXAMPLE

This appendix gives an example of how to calculate the dead-time coefficient for a photomultiplier pulse-counting system. Section 4.2 presents the basis for this example and should be consulted for more detail.

The main requirement for determining the dead-time coefficient is a set of stars, some of which should have negligible correction and some with a large correction. For our system, this means stars with rates around 100,000 counts per second and 800,000 counts per second to bracket the changeover point. Our sample of eight stars should be considered the minimum necessary to determine the coefficient.

Several stars were measured with the neutral density filter used at Indiana University, which has the $v_1 - v_0$ relation:

$$v_1 - v_0 = -0.008(B - V) + 3.934 \qquad \text{(F.1)}$$

The data are listed in Table F.1. The steps required to obtain the coefficient follow.

1. Calculate $v_1 - v_0$ for each star from Equation F.1, using the known color index given in column 2.
2. Using Equation 4.7, calculate the intensity ratio $b \, (= I_0/I_1)$.
3. Using the observed count rate obtained with the filter in the light path (n_L) and the rate without the filter (n_H), calculate the true count rate without the filter using Equation 4.3a:

$$N_H = bn_L$$

TABLE F.1.   Dead-Time Coefficient Data

	Collected Data			Calculated Results			
Star	$B - V$	n_L	n_H	$v_1 - v_0$	b	N_H	A
HR8334	0.51	10,670	374,200	3.930	37.32	398,200	0.0622
HR8465	1.55	25,170	824,700	3.922	37.04	932,200	0.1225
HR8469	0.23	5190	190,100	3.932	37.40	194,100	0.0208
HR8494	0.27	11,720	407,300	3.932	37.39	438,200	0.0731
HR8498	1.46	12,400	427,400	3.922	37.06	459,600	0.0726
HR8585	0.01	17,190	582,700	3.934	37.46	643,900	0.0999
HR8622	−0.20	6170	224,200	3.936	37.52	231,500	0.0320
HR8694	1.05	21,430	708,100	3.926	37.17	796,600	0.1178

4. Calculate the quantity

$$A = \ln \left(\frac{N_H}{n_H} \right)$$

for each star (where ln is the natural logarithm).

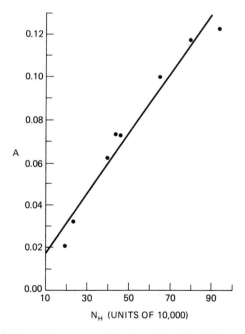

Figure F.1. A versus N_H, where $A = (N_H/n_H)$.

5. Now plot A versus N_H from Equation 4.4,

$$A = tN_H$$

The slope of the resultant line is t, the dead-time coefficient. The plot for this example is given in Figure F.1.

For our example using eight stars, the slope (using linear least squares) is t = 1.40×10^{-7} seconds. An example of the use of the dead-time coefficient can be seen in Appendix H.

APPENDIX G
EXTINCTION EXAMPLE

The approach used to determine the extinction coefficients depends, to some extent, on the type of observing program. In a program of differential photometry the atmospheric extinction corrections can usually be ignored. Occasionally, however, an extinction correction is advisable if the two stars are widely separated. In this case, the comparison star measurements themselves yield the extinction coefficients. When the observing program calls for measuring many different stars at various locations in the sky, it is necessary to follow another approach. In this case, a separate set of standard stars must be observed to determine the extinction coefficients. No matter which kind of observing program is conducted, another set of observations must be made to determine the second-order extinction coefficients.

We now take you through each of these procedures using actual photometric data.

G.1 EXTINCTION CORRECTION FOR DIFFERENTIAL PHOTOMETRY

Because the second-order extinction corrections applied to differential photometry are small enough to ignore, we concentrate on the principal extinction coefficients. As stated above, it is the comparison star measurements that allow us to find the principal extinction coefficients. The success of this method depends on the fact that the comparison star is usually observed through a large range of air mass. Second, the method assumes that the transmission of the atmosphere has remained constant and that the electronics remain free from gain drift throughout the night. These conditions are usually satisfied on a clear night and with well-designed electronics.

As the comparison star rises or sets, the amount of light detected changes as more or less light is absorbed by the earth's atmosphere. Using Equations 2.1 through 2.3 we can calculate the instrumental magnitude of the comparison star through each filter at each air mass. These magnitudes can be corrected for atmospheric absorption by using Equation 4.20 for each filter, that is

$$v_0 = v - k'_v X \tag{G.1}$$
$$b_0 = b - k'_b X \tag{G.2}$$
$$u_0 = u - k'_u X \tag{G.3}$$

where v, b, and u are the instrumental magnitudes, v_0, b_0, and u_0 are the instrumental magnitudes corrected for extinction and k'_v, k'_b, and k'_u are the principal extinction coefficients. These coefficients are, of course, unknown. However, a plot of v versus X yields a straight line slope k'_v. Similarly, plots of b versus X and u versus X yield the slopes k'_b and k'_u, respectively.

1. The comparison star used in this example has a right ascension of 2^h07^m and a declination of $40°23'$. The observatory has a latitude of $39°33'$ north. In Table G.1, column 1 contains the hour angle of each comparison star observation. Column 2 contains the air mass, X, calculated by Equations 4.17 and 4.18. Try calculating X to check a few entries in column 2. If you have difficulties, refer to the example in Section 4.4.
2. Columns 3, 4, and 5 of Table G.1 contain the counts per second recorded through each filter with the sky background subtracted. These have not been corrected for dead time because the count rates are rather low. If these observations had been made with a DC system, these three columns would contain the deflection (usually in percent of full scale) and the

TABLE G.1. Comparison Star Data

Star: $\alpha = 2^h07^m$, $\delta = 40°23'$ Observatory: $39°33'$ north latitude

		Counts per Second			Instrumental Magnitudes		
HA	X	v Filter	b Filter	u Filter	v	b	u
2:42E	1.165	5660	7550	1413	−9.382	−9.695	−7.876
1:53	1.076	5854	7948	1530	−9.419	−9.751	−7.962
1:14	1.032	5878	8110	1596	−9.423	−9.772	−8.008
0:30	1.005	5887	8143	1638	−9.425	−9.777	−8.036
0:09W	1.001	5897	8088	1611	−9.427	−9.770	−8.018
0:14	1.001	5883	8083	1617	−9.424	−9.769	−8.022
1:00	1.021	5838	8006	1588	−9.416	−9.759	−8.002
1:43	1.062	5655	7821	1528	−9.381	−9.733	−7.961
2:24	1.127	5568	7511	1424	−9.364	−9.689	−7.884
3:15	1.252	5415	7195	1297	−9.334	−9.643	−7.782
4:01	1.423	5187	6819	1188	−9.287	−9.584	−7.687
4:31	1.579	5042	6450	1033	−9.256	−9.524	−7.535

amplifier gain settings. Columns 6, 7, and 8 are the instrumental magnitudes calculated by Equations 2.1, 2.2, and 2.3. Check some of these
entries. If DC measurements had been made, we would substitute the
deflection for the count rate and add the amplifier gain (in magnitudes).
That is,

$$v = -2.5 \log (d_v) + G_v$$
$$b = -2.5 \log (d_b) + G_b$$
$$u = -2.5 \log (d_u) + G_u.$$

3. We now plot v versus X, b versus X, and u versus X. These are shown in
Figure G.1. A linear least-squares analysis yields

$$k_v' = 0.306$$
$$k_b' = 0.441$$
$$k_u' = 0.840.$$

(See Section 3.5 for an explanation of linear least-squares analysis.)
4. The magnitude difference between the variable and the comparison star
can now be corrected for extinction by using Equations 2.35 through 2.37
(or 2.38 through 2.40) and 2.43 through 2.45. The color indices are computed by Equations 2.41 and 2.42. These colors can be corrected for
extinction by noting that

$$k_{bv}' = k_b' - k_v'$$
$$k_{ub}' = k_u' - k_b'$$

and applying Equations 2.46 and 2.47. The third term on the right side
of Equation 2.46 can usually be dropped because k_{bv}'' is small. Furthermore, if the variable and comparison star are nearly the same color, $\Delta(b
- v)$ is nearly zero. However, if you wish, this term can be included by
finding k_{bv}'' as outlined in Section G.3.

G.2. EXTINCTION CORRECTION FOR "ALL-SKY" PHOTOMETRY

The procedure described in this section is applied to the situation in which stars
have been measured at various positions in the sky. Each star is observed
briefly through a limited range of air mass and hence the procedure of Section
G.1 cannot be used. There are two approaches that can be followed, depending
on whether or not the transformation coefficients to the standard system are
known.

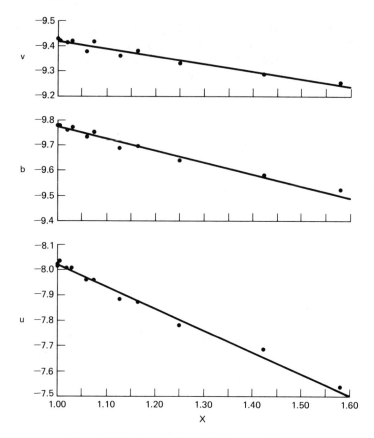

Figure G.1. Instrumental magnitudes versus air mass.

Unknown Transformation Coefficients

The observing procedure is quite simple. At various times during the night, one observes an early A-type standard star from the list in Appendix A or C. The reason for choosing this type of star becomes apparent in the following. If we substitute Equation 4.20 into 4.32, we obtain

$$V = v - k'_v X + \epsilon(B - V) + \zeta_v$$

or

$$V - v = -k'_v X + \epsilon(B - V) + \zeta_v. \tag{G.4}$$

For early A stars, $(B - V)$ is very small. Furthermore, ϵ is a small number, so their product is extremely small. Thus, to a good approximation the above equation becomes

$$V - v = \zeta_v - k'_v X \qquad (G.5)$$

A plot of $V - v$ versus X for the early A stars yields a straight line with slope k'_v. Substituting equation 4.29 into 4.33 yields

$$(B - V) = \mu(b - v) - \mu(b - v)k''_{b\,v}X - \mu k'_{bv}X + \zeta_{bv}. \qquad (G.6)$$

Because μ is usually very nearly equal to one for most photometers and k''_{bv} is very small, we can make the following approximation.

$$(B - V) - (b - v) \simeq -k'_{bv}X + \zeta_{bv} \qquad (G.7)$$

A plot of $(B - V) - (b - v)$ versus X yields a straight line with slope $-k'_{bv}$. A similar procedure with substitution of Equation 4.22 into 4.34 yields

$$(U - B) = \psi(u - b) - \psi k'_{ub}X + \zeta_{ub}. \qquad (G.8)$$

We again note that $\psi \simeq 1$ for most photometers. We thus obtain our final equation

$$(U - B) - (u - b) \simeq -k'_{ub}X + \zeta_{ub}. \qquad (G.9)$$

A plot of $(U - B) - (u - b)$ versus X yields a straight line with slope k'_{ub}.

1. Table G.2 contains the data for a number of extinction stars obtained during one night. Some stars appear more than once because they were observed later in the night at an appreciably different air mass. Most of the observing time was spent on program stars that do not appear in the table. Columns 2, 3, and 4 contain data taken from Appendices A and C. Column 5 contains the air mass calculated by Equations 4.17 and 4.18. Columns 6, 7, and 8 contain the count rates through each filter (after sky subtraction and a dead-time correction was made). Check some of the entries in column 9, using Equation 4.14 for v.

2. Check some of the entries in columns 10 and 11 using Equations 4.15 and 4.16.

3. Figure G.2 shows the plots of $(V - v)$ versus X, $(B - V) - (b - v)$ versus X and $(U - B) - (u - b)$ versus X. A linear regression analysis

TABLE G.2.   Extinction Star Measurements

Star	V	B − V	U − B	X	Counts per Second			V − v	(B − V) − (b − v)	(U − B) − (u − b)
					v	b	u			
80 UMa	4.03	0.15	0.09	1.042	399,726	799,296	140,792	18.014	0.912	−1.805
109 Vir	3.74	0.00	−0.03	1.269	524,038	1,152,529	201,823	18.038	0.856	−1.922
B Ser A	3.67	0.06	0.07	1.161	559,793	1,209,184	195,872	18.040	0.896	−1.906
τ Her	3.89	−0.15	−0.56	1.080	452,832	1,204,795	380,022	18.030	0.910	−1.813
γ Oph	3.75	0.04	0.04	1.868	454,939	887,150	122,538	17.895	0.765	−2.109
π Ser	4.83	0.07	0.05	1.097	194,252	407,561	71,059	18.051	0.875	−1.846
68 Oph	4.42	0.04	0.02	1.931	234,468	456,535	65,537	17.845	0.764	−2.088
68 Oph	4.42	0.04	0.02	1.340	260,411	559,110	94,773	17.959	0.870	−1.907
π Ser	4.83	0.07	0.05	1.082	192,633	402,426	71,980	18.042	0.870	−1.819
109 Vir	3.74	0.00	−0.03	1.673	458,829	974,150	148,048	17.894	0.817	−2.076
γ Oph	3.75	0.04	0.04	1.245	501,527	1,102,259	180,078	18.001	0.895	−1.927
57 Cyg	4.77	−0.14	−0.58	1.006	197,291	515,202	175,144	18.008	0.902	−1.752

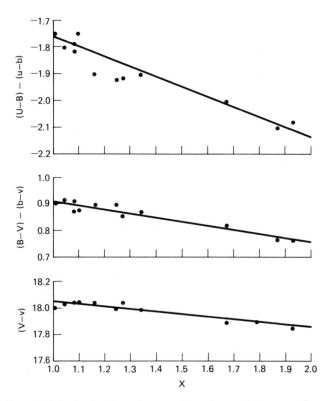

Figure G.2. Extinction plots when transformation coefficients are unknown.

yields

$$k'_v = 0.200$$
$$k'_{bv} = 0.153$$
$$k'_{ub} = 0.353.$$

Known Transformation Coefficients

When the transformation coefficients are known, the procedure of finding the extinction coefficients is simplified. Now all that is required are observations of five or more standard stars, of any color, at various air masses. These can be the same standards you would observe to determine your nightly zero-point constants (ζ_v, ζ_{bv}, ζ_{ub}). If Equation G.4 is rearranged, we obtain

$$V - v - \epsilon(B - V) = -k'_v X + \zeta_v. \qquad (G.10)$$

Because ϵ is known, we do not need to use A stars in order to approximate the $\epsilon(B - V)$ term as zero. A plot of $V - v - \epsilon(B - V)$ versus X yields a straight line with slope k'_v. Likewise, Equation G.6 becomes (assuming $k''_{bv} \sim 0$)

$$(B - V) - \mu(b - v) = -\mu k'_{bv} X + \zeta_{bv}. \qquad (G.11)$$

A plot of $(B - V) - \mu(b - v)$ versus X yields a slope $\mu k'_{bv}$. Rearranging Equation, G.8 becomes

$$(U - B) - \psi(u - b) = -\psi k'_{ub} X + \zeta_{ub}. \qquad (G.12)$$

Again, a plot of $(U - B) - \psi(u - b)$ versus X yields a slope $\psi k'_{ub}$.

1. Table G.3 contains data on 10 standard stars observed on one night. The first four columns contain values taken from Appendix C. Column 5 contains the air mass and columns 6, 7, and 8 contain the instrumental magnitudes and colors calculated by Equations 4.14, 4.15, and 4.16. The transformation coefficients were determined on a previous night to be

$$\epsilon = -0.084$$
$$\mu = 1.083$$
$$\psi = 1.006.$$

Compute the left-hand side of Equation G.10 for a few stars to check the entries in column 9. Likewise, compute the left-hand side of Equation G.11 and G.12 to check the entries in columns 10 and 11.

TABLE G.3. Observations of Standard Stars

Star	V	(B − V)	(U − B)	X	v	(b − v)	(u − b)	V − v − ε(B − V)	(B − V) − μ(b − v)	(U − B) − ψ(u − b)
i Psc	4.13	0.51	0.00	2.183	−13.721	−0.001	2.183	17.851	0.511	−2.196
HR8832	5.57	1.01	0.89	1.262	−12.502	0.334	2.741	18.157	0.648	−1.867
10 Lac	4.88	−0.20	−1.04	1.183	−13.206	−0.794	0.709	18.069	0.660	−1.753
ε Aqr	3.77	0.01	0.04	1.562	−14.199	−0.564	2.033	17.970	0.621	−2.005
α Del	3.77	−0.06	−0.22	1.103	−14.312	−0.694	1.612	18.077	0.692	−1.842
B Aql	3.71	0.86	0.48	1.191	−14.344	0.190	2.269	18.126	0.654	−1.803
γ Oph	3.75	0.04	0.04	1.514	−14.293	−0.514	2.002	18.046	0.597	−1.974
τ Her	3.89	−0.15	−0.56	1.361	−14.179	−0.721	1.288	18.056	0.631	−1.856
ε Crb	4.15	1.23	1.28	1.754	−13.862	0.618	3.342	18.115	0.561	−2.082
β SerA	3.67	0.06	0.07	2.340	−14.177	−0.352	2.286	17.852	0.441	−2.230

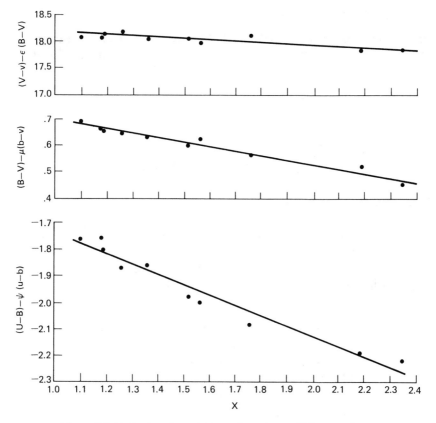

Figure G.3. Extinction plots when transformation coefficients are known.

2. Plots of $V - v - \epsilon(B - V)$ versus X, $(B - V) - \mu(b - v)$ versus X, and $(U - B) - \psi(u - b)$ versus X appears in Figure G.3. A linear regression analysis of each plot yields the following slopes.

$$k'_v = 0.212$$
$$k'_{bv} = 0.163$$
$$k'_{ub} = 0.373.$$

Note that this same linear regression analysis gives the intercepts that are the zero-point constants. These turn out to be

$$\zeta_v = 18.359$$
$$\zeta_{bv} = 0.875$$
$$\zeta_{ub} = -1.381.$$

G.3 SECOND-ORDER EXTINCTION COEFFICIENTS

Because k_v'' is very small and k_{ub}'' is defined as zero, we confine this example to k_{bv}''. Experience has shown that k_{bv}'' is both small and fairly stable. Therefore, k_{bv}'' need be determined only once or twice a year. The procedure is to observe a closely spaced pair of stars, of very different colors, at various air masses. If we let subscripts 1 and 2 refer to each star and use Equation 4.29 to form the differences in color indices, we obtain

$$(b - v)_{01} - (b - v)_{02} = (b - v)_1 - k_{bv}''X_1(b - v)_1$$
$$- k_{bv}'X_1 - (b - v)_2 + k_{bv}''X_2(b - v)_2 + k_{bv}'X_2.$$

Because $X_1 \simeq X_2$, this reduces to

$$\Delta(b - v)_0 = \Delta(b - v) - k_{bv}''X\Delta(b - v). \qquad (G.13)$$

Because $\Delta(b - v)_0$ is constant, a plot of $\Delta(b - v)$ versus $X\Delta(b - v)$ gives a straight line with slope k_{bv}''.

TABLE G.4.   Observations of HD30544 and HD30545

HD30544 $(b - v)$	HD30545 $(b - v)$	$\Delta(b - v)$	X	$\Delta(b - v)X$
−0.628	0.458	−1.086	2.079	−2.258
−0.676	0.396	−1.072	1.786	−1.915
−0.718	0.376	−1.094	1.551	−1.697
−0.756	0.344	−1.100	1.367	−1.504
−0.778	0.339	−1.117	1.279	−1.429
−0.783	0.335	−1.118	1.231	−1.376

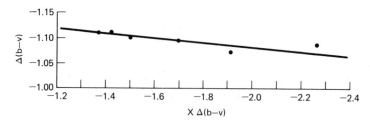

Figure G.4. Second order extinction plot.

1. The pair of stars used in this example is HD30544 and HD30545. These and other pairs can be found in Appendix B. Columns 1 and 2 of Table G.4 contain the color indices of each star calculated by Equation 4.15 and 4.16. Column 3 is just column 1 minus column 2. Column 4 is the mean air mass at the time of observation. Finally, column 5 is the product of columns 3 and 4.

2. Figure G.4 shows a plot of $\Delta(b - v)X$ versus $\Delta(b - v)$. A linear regression analysis yields a slope

$$k''_{bv} = -0.042.$$

APPENDIX H
TRANSFORMATION COEFFICIENTS
EXAMPLE

H.1 DC EXAMPLE

The transformation coefficients are often determined from standard stars within a cluster that is near the zenith. This procedure reduces the impact of the extinction corrections greatly. Appendix D contains finder charts and lists of standard stars for three clusters. In this particular example, however, a cluster was not used. Standard stars near the meridian were selected from the list in Appendix C. While this technique works, it usually gives inferior results under variable sky conditions to the cluster method. A 60-centimeter (24-inch) telescope was used. A completely different telescope and photometer were used for the pulse-counting example to follow.

1. The first step is to measure each star through each filter. The sky background should be measured in each filter using the same amplifier gain and diaphragm as used for each star. In fact, the same diaphragm should be used for all measurements. Record the gain setting of *each* gain switch, *not their total*. This is necessary because there is more than one combination of gain switch positions which gives the same apparent total gain. However, each combination has a different set of gain corrections as determined by the gain correction table.

Table H.1 lists the coordinates, magnitudes, and colors of the stars observed. For now, ignore the three columns on the right. While in this particular example, only nine stars were used, it is recommended that you observe as many as is practically possible. Table H.2 lists the actual observations.

2. The next step is to subtract the sky background to produce the net deflection shown in column 5 of Table H.2. The settings of the two gain switches are shown in column 6, separated by a slash. For the particular amplifier used in this example, the coarse switch requires no gain corrections. The corrections

TABLE H.1.   Standard Stars

Star	RA h m	Dec. ° ′	V	Standard B − V	U − B	Calculated V	B − V	U − B
11 LMi	9 34	35 56	5.41	0.77	0.45	5.43	0.78	0.38
21 LMi	10 06	35 22	4.48	0.18	0.08	4.52	0.18	0.13
λ UMa	10 16	43 03	3.45	0.03	0.06	3.47	0.05	0.11
α Leo	10 07	12 05	1.36	−0.11	−0.36	1.35	−0.13	−0.37
ε Leo	9 44	23 58	2.98	0.81	0.46	2.95	0.79	0.43
υ UMa	9 48	59 14	3.82	0.29	0.10	3.77	0.29	0.09
31 Leo	10 06	10 12	4.36	1.45	1.75	4.33	1.43	1.82
72 Leo	11 13	23 18	4.60	1.66	1.85	4.64	1.68	1.80
β Leo	11 48	14 43	2.14	0.09	0.07	2.13	0.09	0.05

TABLE H.2.   Stellar Measurements

Star	Filter	Deflection	Sky	Net	Gain	v	$b - v$	$u - b$
11 LMi	v	41.0	10.9	30.1	5/2	3.306	0.189	2.433
	b	36.2	10.9	25.3	5/2			
	u	37.8	10.9	26.9	7.5/2			
21 LMi	v	36.3	7.6	28.7	5/1	2.378	−0.462	2.199
	b	51.5	7.6	43.9	5/1			
	u	36.6	14.1	22.5	5/2.5			
λ UMa	v	35.5	5.8	29.7	5/0	1.318	−0.606	2.184
	b	57.7	5.8	51.9	5/0			
	u	36.6	8.7	27.9	5/1.5			
α Leo	v	37.5	6.4	31.1	2.5/0.5	−0.738	−0.739	1.847
	b	67.8	6.4	61.4	2.5/0.5			
	u	55.7	10.7	45.0	2.5/2			
ε Leo	v	52.3	6.0	46.3	5/0	0.836	0.212	2.487
	b	44.1	6.0	38.1	5/0			
	u	35.9	11.5	24.4	5/2			
υ UMa	v	40.6	6.7	33.9	5/0.5	1.668	−0.312	2.220
	b	51.9	6.7	45.2	5/0.5			
	u	35.5	12.0	23.5	5/2			
31 Leo	v	46.0	13.7	32.3	5/1	2.250	0.925	3.727
	b	34.6	13.0	21.6	5/1.5			
	u	27.5	10.2	17.3	7.5/2.5			
72 Leo	v	52.7	13.0	39.7	5/1.5	2.513	1.145	3.640
	b	44.6	10.3	34.3	5/2.5			
	u	45.0	14.1	30.9	10/1			
β Leo	v	53.3	13.8	39.5	2.5/1.5	0.019	−0.527	2.178
	b	78.0	13.8	64.2	2.5/1.5			
	u	69.2	14.1	55.1	5/1			

for the fine gain switch were determined by the procedure outlined in Section 8.6. The table below gives the actual fine gain values. The amplifier gain is then the total of the coarse switch position and the actual fine gain read from the table.

Fine Gain Switch Position	Actual Gain in Magnitudes
0	0
0.5	0.494
1.0	1.023
1.5	1.510
2.0	2.003
2.5	2.496

The atmospheric, instrumental magnitudes and colors can be computed by Equations 4.11, 4.12, and 4.13. Check some of the results in the last three columns of Table H.2.

3. The magnitudes and colors determined above must now be corrected for atmospheric extinction. It is necessary to determine the air mass, X, for each star. Because the three filter measurements were made within a few minutes of each other, a single value of X is used for each star. Column 2 of Table H.3 lists the hour angle at the time of observation of each star. In this case, the telescope had an hour angle read-out device. If your telescope is not so equipped, you need to calculate hour angle as described in Section 5.3c. The east-west notation in the table is really unnecessary because it makes no dif-

TABLE H.3. Extinction Correction and Transformation Coefficient Determination

Star	HA	X	v_0	$(b - v)_0$	$(u - b)_0$	$V - v_0$	$(B - V) - (b - v)_0$	$(U - B) - (u - b)_0$
11 LMi	1:23W	1.044	2.909	−0.124	1.898	2.501	0.895	−1.449
21 LMi	0:47W	1.014	1.993	−0.766	1.695	2.487	0.946	−1.615
λ UMa	0:33W	1.014	0.940	−0.917	1.665	2.510	0.948	−1.605
α Leo	1:24W	1.160	−1.179	−0.991	1.253	2.539	0.881	−1.613
ε Leo	1:18W	1.069	0.430	−0.109	1.940	2.550	0.919	−1.479
υ UMa	1:18W	1.118	1.243	−0.647	1.648	2.577	0.938	−1.547
31 Leo	1:06W	1.152	1.812	0.579	3.137	2.551	0.871	−1.387
72 Leo	0:11W	1.026	2.123	0.859	3.125	2.476	0.801	−1.275
β Leo	0.58E	1.102	−0.400	−0.858	1.614	2.540	0.948	−1.544

ference for the calculation of X. As an example, consider 21 LMi.

$$\begin{aligned}
\text{hour angle} = H &= 0{:}47 \\
&= \frac{47 \text{ minutes}}{60 \text{ minutes/hour}} \times (15°/\text{hour}) \\
&= 11.75° \\
\delta &= 35.37° \text{ (declination from Table H.1)} \qquad (4.18) \\
\phi &= 35.92° \text{ (latitude of observatory)} \\
X &= (\sin \delta \sin \phi + \cos \delta \cos \phi \cos H)^{-1} \\
X &= 1.014
\end{aligned}$$

The more precise method described in Section 4.4a (Equation 4.19) is not needed because measurements were made near the zenith.

The extinction coefficients were determined by the method outlined in Appendix G. They were found to be

$$\begin{aligned}
k'_v &= 0.380 \\
k'_{bv} &= 0.300 \\
k'_{ub} &= 0.512 \\
k''_{bv} &\simeq 0
\end{aligned}$$

The extinction corrections were then made by calculating for each star, assuming that $k''_{ub} = 0$:

$$\begin{aligned}
v_0 &= v - k'_v X \\
(b - v)_0 &= (b - v) - k'_{bv} X \\
(u - b)_0 &= (u - b) - k'_{ub} X.
\end{aligned}$$

The results of these calculations appear in columns 4 through 6 of Table H.3. These are the instrumental magnitudes and colors. Check some of these results.

4. To determine ϵ and ζ_v, a plot of $V - v_0$ versus $(B - V)$ is needed. The values of V and $(B - V)$ are found in Table H.1. The computed values of $V - v_0$ appear in Table H.3. The graph appears in Figure H.1. A linear least-squares fit yields a slope of -0.012 and an intercept of 2.532. From Equation 4.38,

$$\begin{aligned}
\epsilon &= -0.012 \\
\zeta_v &= 2.532.
\end{aligned}$$

5. To determine μ and ζ_{bv}, a plot of $[(B - V) - (b - v)_0]$ versus $(B - V)$ is required. Again, $(B - V)$ is found in Table H.1 and $[(B - V) - $

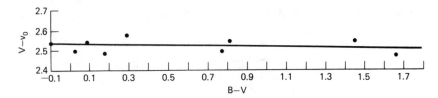

Figure H.1. Plot to determine ϵ and ζ_v.

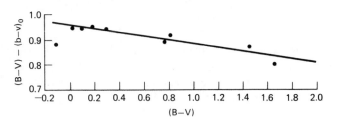

Figure H.2. Plot to determine μ and ζ_{bv}.

$(b - v)_0$] is calculated and shown in Table H.3. The graph appears in Figure H.2. A linear least-squares fit yields a slope of -0.059 and an intercept of 0.940. From Equation 4.40,

$$1 - \frac{1}{\mu} = -0.059$$

and
$$\mu = 0.944$$
$$\frac{\zeta_{bv}}{\mu} = 0.940$$
$$\zeta_{bv} = 0.887.$$

6. The procedure in step 5 is repeated for $[(U - B) - (u - b)_0]$ versus $(U - B)$. The graph appears in Figure H.3. A linear least-squares fit yields a slope of 0.139 and an intercept of -1.570. From Equation 4.41,

$$1 - \frac{1}{\psi} = 0.139$$
$$\psi = 1.161$$

and

$$\frac{\zeta_{ub}}{\psi} = -1.570$$
$$\zeta_{ub} = -1.823.$$

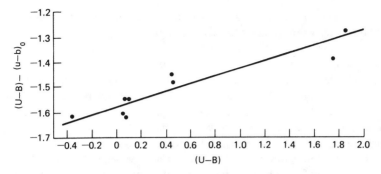

Figure H.3. Plot to determine ψ and ζ_{ub}.

Now the standardized magnitudes and colors of any star measured that same night can be found by the following expressions:

$$(B - V) = 0.944 \, (b - v)_0 + 0.887$$
$$V = v_0 - 0.012 \, (B - V) + 2.532$$
$$(U - B) = 1.161 \, (u - b)_0 - 1.823.$$

As a check on the quality of these transformation equations, the magnitudes and colors of the standard stars were computed and compared to the known values. The results appear in the rightmost three columns of Table H.1. Compare Figures H.1, H.2, and H.3 to Figures H.4, H.5, and H.6. This last set of figures, from the pulse-counting example, represents a very good set of observations and hence, a good set of transformation equations. The results of the DC example show that the observations are of marginal quality and the transformation equations are not very dependable. This is primarily because of poor sky conditions. The cluster method tends to work better when the sky conditions are less than excellent. Note that, because different telescopes and photometers were used, the color coefficients from the two examples are not the same.

As explained in Chapter 4, the coefficients ϵ, μ, and ψ are constant over fairly long time periods. However, ζ_v, ζ_{vb}, and ζ_{ub} *must be determined nightly.*

H.2 PULSE-COUNTING EXAMPLE

The transformation coefficients can be determined from standard stars within a cluster that is near the zenith. This procedure reduces the impact of the extinction corrections greatly. Appendix D contains finder charts and lists of standard stars for three clusters. In this case, the cluster IC 4665 was observed.

A 40-centimeter (16-inch) telescope was used. A completely different telescope and photometer were used for the DC example.

1. The first step is to measure each star through each filter. The sky background should be measured several times during this process. The same diaphragm should be used for all measurements. Table H.4 lists the coordinates, magnitudes, and colors of the stars observed. For now, ignore the three columns on the right. Table H.5 lists the actual observations. The third column contains the number of counts per second, which was found by averaging the counts obtained in several 10-second intervals and dividing by 10.

2. The next step is to correct the observations for dead time. The dead-time coefficient, t, was found by the technique outlined in Chapter 4 with a worked example in Appendix F. For the particular photomultiplier used in this example, $t = 1.54 \times 10^{-7}$ seconds per count. The observed count rate n is related to the true count rate N by

$$n = N e^{-Nt}.$$

A FORTRAN subroutine to solve this equation in an iterative fashion can be found in Section I.1. To illustrate the essential idea behind the solution, a numerical example is given using the first observation in Table H.5. The observed count rate is 28,925. As an initial guess, suppose that N is equal to this observed rate. Then

$$n = 28,925\ e^{-(28,925)1.54 \times 10^{-7}}$$
$$n = 28,796$$

TABLE H.4. The Standard Stars

Star	RA	Dec.	V	Standard B − V	U − B	V	Calculated B − V	U − B
A	17^{h} 45^{m}	5° 32′	6.85	0.011	−0.54	6.84	0.018	−0.554
F	17 45	5 42	7.59	0.002	−0.49	7.58	0.003	−0.491
G	17 45	6 08	7.74	−0.009	−0.55	7.76	−0.007	−0.544
I	17 45	6 15	7.89	1.028	0.77	7.88	1.034	0.735
J	17 45	5 24	7.94	0.449	−0.01	7.95	0.433	−0.019
N	17 46	5 37	8.33	1.728	2.08	8.34	1.711	2.098
O	17 47	5 22	8.40	1.232	1.04	8.40	1.243	0.992
P	17 46	5 26	8.89	0.106	−0.27	8.88	0.099	−0.264
S	17 44	5 32	9.39	0.314	0.17	9.39	0.306	0.221
U	17 46	5 31	9.81	0.676	0.23	9.80	0.701	0.201
V	17 44	5 34	10.10	0.122	0.01	10.11	0.111	0.036
W	17 44	5 51	10.21	1.292	1.27	10.21	1.296	1.301

TABLE H.5. Stellar Measurements

Star	Filter	Counts per Second	Dead-time Corrected	Net	v	b − v	u − b
A	v	28,925	29,055	29,001	−11.156		
	b	61,718	62,313	62,220		−0.829	
	u	18,575	18,628	18,599			1.311
F	v	14,819	14,853	14,799	−10.426		
	b	32,152	32,312	32,219		−0.845	
	u	9136	9149	9120			1.370
Sky	v	54.1					
	b	93.2					
	u	28.6					
G	v	12,539	12,563	12,510	−10.243		
	b	27,547	27,664	27,575		−0.858	
	u	8287	8298	8270			1.308
I	v	10,708	10,726	10,673	−10.071		
	b	10,139	10,155	10,066		0.064	
	u	911	911	883			2.642
Sky	v	51.8					
	b	84.6					
	u	28.2					
J	v	10,387	10,404	10,352	−10.038		
	b	15,994	16,033	15,949		−0.469	
	u	2917	2918	2891			1.854
N	v	6810	6817	6765	−9.576		
	b	3756	3758	3674		0.663	
	u	115	115	87			4.062
O	v	6613	6620	6568	−9.544		
	b	5310	5314	5230		0.247	
	u	387	387	360			2.906
P	v	4524	4527	4475	−9.127		
	b	9165	9178	9094		−0.770	
	u	2129	2129	2102			1.590
Sky	v	51.4					
	b	82.8					
	u	26.6					
S	v	2826	2827	2776	−8.609		
	b	4856	4860	4781		−0.590	
	u	723	723	698			2.090
U	v	1926	1926	1875	−8.183		
	b	2416	2416	2337		−0.239	
	u	373	373	347			2.070
V	v	1508	1508	1457	−7.909		
	b	3028	3029	2950		−0.766	
	u	542	542	516			1.893
W	v	1296	1296	1245	−7.738		
	b	1034	1034	955		0.288	
	u	76	76	50			3.211
Sky	v	50.2					
	b	75.8					
	u	25.2					

Because this value is lower than the actual observed rate, we *increase* the next guess of N by the difference between these two numbers, i.e.

$$N \text{ (second guess)} = 28{,}925 + (28{,}925 - 28{,}796)$$
$$= 29{,}054$$

We can now recompute n by

$$n = 29{,}054 \, e^{-(29{,}054)1.54 \times 10^{-7}}$$
$$= 28{,}924.$$

This differs from the observed rate by only 1. Thus as a third guess,

$$N \text{ (third guess)} = 29{,}054 + 1$$

and

$$n = 29{,}055 \, e^{-(29{,}055)1.54 \times 10^{-7}}$$
$$n = 28{,}925.$$

Because this value agrees with the observed rate, we know that the true count rate is 29,055. This number appears in column 4 of Table H.5 along with the other corrected count rates.

3. The sky background is now subtracted from each value in column 4. When the stellar measurement is sandwiched between two sky measurements, an average sky measurement is subtracted.

The atmospheric instrumental magnitudes and colors can be computed by Equations 4.14 through 4.16. The results appear in columns 6, 7, and 8 of Table H.5. Check some of the results with your calculator.

4. The magnitudes and colors determined in step 3 must be corrected for atmospheric extinction. It is necessary to determine the air mass, X, for each star. Because the three filter measurements were made within a few minutes of each other, a single value of X is used for each star. Column 2 in Table H.6 lists the hour angle at the time of observation of each star. In this case, the telescope had an hour angle read-out device. If your telescope is not so equipped, you need to calculate the hour angle as described in Section 5.3c. The east-west notation in the table is really unnecessary because it makes no difference for the calculation of X. As an example, consider star A.

$$\text{hour angle} = H = 1{:}54$$
$$H = \left(1 + \frac{54}{60}\right) \times (15°/\text{hour})$$

$$H = 28.50°$$
$$\delta = 5.53° \text{ (declination from Table H.4)}$$
$$\phi = 39.17° \text{ (latitude of observatory)}$$
$$X = (\sin \delta \sin \phi + \cos \delta \cos \phi \cos H)^{-1}$$
$$X = 1.353$$

The more precise method of finding X described in Section 4.4 (Equation 4.19) is not needed since the measurements were made near the zenith.

The extinction coefficients were determined by the method outlined in Appendix G. They were found to be

$$k'_v = 0.209$$
$$k'_{bv} = 0.162$$
$$k'_{ub} = 0.337$$
$$k''_{bv} = -0.088$$

The extinction corrections were then made by calculating, for each star, assuming $k''_{ub} = 0$,

$$v_0 = v - k'_v X$$
$$(b - v)_0 = (b - v)(1 - k''_{bv} X) - k'_{bv} X$$
$$(u - b)_0 = (u - b) - k'_{ub} X.$$

The results of these calculations appear in columns 4 through 6 of Table H.6. These are instrumental magnitudes and colors. Check some of these results.

TABLE H.6. Extinction Correction and Transformation Coefficient Determination

Star	HA	X	v_0	$(b - v)_0$	$(u - b)_0$	$V - v_0$	$(B - V) - (b - v)_0$	$(U - B) - (u - b)_0$
A	1:54E	1.353	−11.439	−1.146	0.855	18.289	1.157	−1.395
F	1:50E	1.339	−10.705	−1.161	0.919	18.295	1.163	−1.409
G	1:46E	1.320	−10.519	−1.171	0.863	18.259	1.162	−1.413
I	1:43E	1.311	−10.345	−0.141	2.200	18.235	1.169	−1.430
J	1:38E	1.313	−10.312	−0.736	1.412	18.252	1.185	−1.422
N	1:34E	1.300	−9.847	0.528	3.624	18.177	1.200	−1.544
O	1:31E	1.297	−9.815	0.065	2.468	18.215	1.167	−1.428
P	1:27E	1.288	−9.396	−1.066	1.156	18.286	1.172	−1.426
S	1:19E	1.270	−8.874	−0.862	1.662	18.264	1.176	−1.492
U	1:18E	1.269	−8.448	−0.471	1.642	18.258	1.147	−1.412
V	1:13E	1.259	−8.172	−1.054	1.469	18.272	1.176	−1.459
W	1:08E	1.247	−7.999	0.118	2.791	18.209	1.174	−1.521

5. To determine ϵ and ζ_v, a plot of $V - v_0$ versus $(B - V)$ is needed. The values of V and $(B - V)$ are found in Table H.4. The computed values of $V - v_0$ appear in Table H.6. The graph appears in Figure H.4. A linear least-squares fit yields a slope of -0.057 and an intercept of 18.284. From Equation 4.38,

$$\epsilon = -0.057$$
$$\zeta_v = 18.284.$$

6. To determine μ and ζ_{bv}, a plot of $[(B - V) - (b - v)_0]$ versus $(B - V)$ is required. Again $(B - V)$ is found in Table H.4 and $[(B - V) - (b - v)_0]$ was calculated and appears in Table H.6. The graph appears in Figure H.5. A linear least-squares fit yields a slope of 0.011 and an intercept of 1.164. From equation 4.40,

$$1 - \frac{1}{\mu} = 0.011$$
$$\mu = 1.011$$

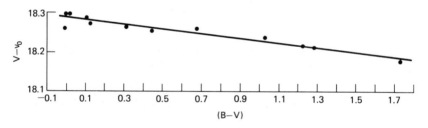

Figure H.4. Plot to determine ϵ and ζ_v.

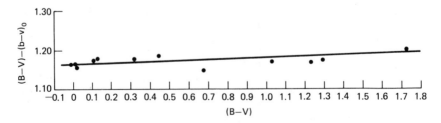

Figure H.5. Plot to determine μ and ζ_{bv}.

and

$$\frac{\zeta_{bv}}{\mu} = 1.164$$
$$\zeta_{bv} = 1.177$$

7. The procedure in step 6 is repeated for $[(U - B) - (u - b)_0]$ versus $(U - B)$. The graph appears in Figure H.6. A linear least-squares fit yields a slope of -0.045 and an intercept of -1.432. From Equation 4.41,

$$1 - \frac{1}{\psi} = -0.045$$
$$\psi = 0.957$$

and

$$\frac{\zeta_{ub}}{\psi} = -1.432$$
$$\zeta_{ub} = -1.370.$$

Now the standardized magnitudes and colors of any "unknown" star observed that same night can be found by the following expressions.

$$(B - V) = 1.011\,(b - v)_0 + 1.177$$
$$V = v_0 - 0.057\,(B - V) + 18.284$$
$$(U - B) = 0.957\,(u - b)_0 - 1.370$$

As a check on the quality of these transformation equations, the magnitudes and colors of the standard stars were computed and compared to the known values. The results appear in the rightmost three columns of Table H.4. This

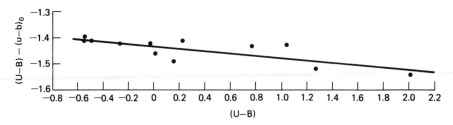

Figure H.6. Plot to determine ψ and ζ_{ub}.

comparison shows that the transformations are fairly good. Compare Figures H.4, H.5, and H.6 to H.1, H.2, and H.3. This last set of Figures, from the DC example, represents a rather poor set of observations and the resulting transformation equations are of questionable quality. Note that, because different telescopes and photometers were used, the color coefficients from the two examples are not the same.

As explained in Chapter 4, the coefficients ϵ, μ, and ψ are constant over fairly long time periods. However, ζ_v, ζ_{bv}, and ζ_{ub} *must be determined nightly.*

APPENDIX I
USEFUL FORTRAN SUBROUTINES

These routines were written by one of the authors (AAH) for the FORTRAN IV compiler of Control Data Corporation computers. The programming is functional but not elegant. Most of the routines are in constant use at Indiana University and have not been found in error.

Further information on programming and numerical analysis is available in many texts. Three books the authors have found most useful are:

- Bevington, A. R. 1969. *Data Reduction and Error Analysis for the Physical Sciences*. New York: McGraw-Hill.
- Carnahan, B., Luther, H. A., and Wilkes, J. O. 1969. *Applied Numerical Methods*. New York: Wiley and Sons.
- Murril, P. W., and Smith, C. L. 1969. *FORTRAN IV Programming for Engineers and Scientists*. Scranton: International Textbook Co.

I.1   DEAD-TIME CORRECTION FOR PULSE-COUNTING METHOD

```
       FUNCTION CNTCR (OBSD,TAU)
C
C      *** DEAD-TIME CORRECTION FOR PULSE COUNTING ***
C
C      INPUTS -
C              TAU     DEAD-TIME COEF IN SECONDS
C              OBSD    OBSERVED COUNT RATE IN INVERSE SECONDS
C      OUTPUTS -
C              CNTCR   CORRECTED COUNT RATE IN INVERSE SECONDS
C
C      *** COMMENTED VERSION BY ARNE A. HENDEN 1978 ***
C      *** FROM ORIGINAL FROM UBVLSQ AT I.U. ***
C
C      CALCULATE INITIAL COUNT VALUE FOR ITERATION
       A=OBSD*EXP(OBSD*TAU)
C      ITERATE FOR 2Ø TRIES.  IF NO CONVERGENCE,GET HELP
       DO 1Ø J=1,2Ø
C      CALCULATE NEXT GUESS FOR RATE
       B=OBSD*EXP(A*TAU)
C      IS THIS GUESS WITHIN Ø.ØØ1 COUNTS?
C      (ACTUALLY, PERCENTAGE ERROR WOULD BE BETTER)
       IF (ABS(A-B)-Ø.ØØ1) 2Ø,2Ø,5
C      NO...RESET OLD RATE VALUE TO NEW VALUE AND TRY AGAIN
5      A=B
1Ø     CONTINUE
       WRITE (6,9ØØ)
9ØØ    FORMAT( *NO CONVERGENCE AFTER 2Ø TRIES*)
2Ø     CNTCR=B
       RETURN
       END
```

I.2   CALCULATING JULIAN DATE FROM UT DATE

```
       SUBROUTINE JDAY (ID,IM,IY,UTHR,DATE)
C
C      *** CALCULATE JULIAN DATE FROM UT DATE ***
C
C      INPUTS -
C              ID      INTEGER UT DAY
C              IM      INTEGER UT MONTH
C              IY      INTEGER UT YEAR
C              UTHR    F.P. UT HOUR (24HR CLOCK)
C      OUTPUTS -
C              DATE    (JULIAN DATE - 24ØØØØØ)
C
C      *** PROGRAMMED BY ARNE A. HENDEN 1977 ***
C
C      MONTH IS NUMBER OF ELAPSED DAYS IN NORMAL YEAR
       DIMENSION MONTH(12)
       DATA MONTH/Ø,31,59,9Ø,12Ø,151,181,212,243,273,3Ø4,334/
C      LEAP IS NUMBER OF LEAP DAYS SINCE 19ØØ
       LEAP=IY/4
C      CHECK TO SEE IF THIS YEAR IS LEAP AND MONTH=JAN,FEB
       IF ((4*LEAP-IY).EQ.Ø.AND.IM.LT.3) LEAP=LEAP-1
C      CALCULATE INTEGRAL NUMBER OF JULIAN DAYS
       JDØ=15Ø2Ø+IY*365+LEAP+MONTH(IM)+ID
C      ADD IN UTHR AND SUBTRACT A HALF-DAY
       DATE=FLOAT(JDØ)+UTHR/24.-Ø.5
       RETURN
       END
```

I.3 GENERAL METHOD FOR COORDINATE PRECESSION

```
SUBROUTINE PRCS (R,DD,YRØ,YR,IH,IM,IS,ID,IDM,IDS)
C
C    *** RIGOROUS COORDINATE PRECESSION W/O P.M. CORRECTIONS ***
C
C
C    INPUTS-
C              R         R.A. IN DECIMAL HOURS
C              DD        DEC. IN DECIMAL DEGREES
C              YRØ       COORDINATE EPOCH
C              YR        YEAR TO BE PRECESSED TO
C    OUTPUTS-
C              IH,IM,IS    R.A. H,M,S IN INTEGER FORM
C              ID,IDM,IDS  PRECESSED DEC. IN INTEGER FORM
C
C    *** WRITTEN BY A. HENDEN 1978 ***
C
      DATA A,B,C,D,E/1.60017,5.25E-4,7.8E-5,1.60017,1.9E-3/
      DATA F,G,H,P/8.3E-5,1.39214,7.39E-4,1.8E-4/
      DATA PICON/0.0174532925/
C         CONVERT INPUTS TO RADIANS
      RA=R*PICON*15.
      DEC=DD*PICON
      TAU=(YR-YRØ)/250.
      ZET=TAU*(A+TAU*(B+TAU*C))*PICON
      Z=TAU*(D+TAU*(E+TAU*F))*PICON
      THET=TAU*(G-TAU*(H+TAU*P))*PICON
      AMU=ZET+Z
      BET=RA+ZET
      Q=SIN(THET)*(TAN(DEC)+COS(BET)*TAN(THET*0.5))
      GAM=0.5*ATAN(Q*SIN(BET)/(1.-Q*COS(BET)))
      DEE=2.*ATAN(TAN(THET*0.5)*COS(BET+GAM)/COS(GAM))
      DR=GAM+GAM+AMU
      RA=(RA+DR)/(PICON*15.)
      DEC=(DEC+DEE)/PICON
C         WE NOW HAVE DECIMAL FORMS...CONVERT TO INTEGER FORM
      IH=INT(RA)
      X=(RA-FLOAT(IH))*60.
      IM=INT(X)
      IS=INT((X-FLOAT(IM))*60.)
      ID=INT(DEC)
      RM=(DEC-FLOAT(ID))*60.
      IF (RM.LT.0.) RM=-RM
      IDM=INT(RM)
      IDS=INT((RM-FLOAT(IDM))*60.)
      RETURN
      END
```

I.4 LINEAR REGRESSION (LEAST-SQUARES) METHOD

```
Subroutine SMOOTH (X,Y,M,A,B)

c  *** Linear least squares routine from Nielson ***
c  Simple solution with no weighting factors
c
c  Inputs:
c               x,y    data arrays
c               m      number of points in arrays
c  Outputs:
c               a,b    where y=ax+b
c
c  *** written by A. Henden 1973 ***
c
       dimension x(m),y(m)
c  initialize summing parameters
       a2=0.
       a3=0.
       c1=0.
       c2=0.
       a1=m
c  loop to set up matrix coefficients
       do 10 i=1,m
       a2=a2+x(i)
       a3=a3+x(i)*x(i)
       c1=c1+y(i)
       c2=c2+y(i)*x(i)
10     continue
c  solve matrix - simple since only 2x2
       det=1./(a1*a3-a2*a2)
       b=-(a2*c2-c1*a3)*det
       a=(a1*c2-c1*a2)*det
       return
       end
```

I.5 LINEAR REGRESSION (LEAST-SQUARES) METHOD USING THE *UBV* TRANSFORMATION EQUATIONS

```
      SUBROUTINE SOLVE (N,X,SMAG,URMAG,SEXT,FEXT,COEF,ZERO)
C
C     LEAST SQUARES SOLUTION OF THE UBV TRANSFORMATION EQUATIONS
C  INPUT -
C     SMAG(N,3)  STANDARD MAGNITUDES AND COLORS IN THE FORM:
C                    SMAG(N,1) = V
C                    SMAG(N,2) = B-V
C                    SMAG(N,3) = U-B
C     URMAG(N,3) YOUR CORRESPONDING INSTRUMENTAL MAGNITUDES & COLORS
C     X(N)       AIR MASS VALUES
C     N          NUMBER OF OBSERVATIONS TO REDUCE
C     SEXT(3)    SECOND ORDER EXTINCTION
C  OUTPUT -
C     FEXT(3)    FIRST ORDER EXTINCTION
C     COEF(3)    TRANSFORMATION COLOR COEFFICIENTS
C     ZERO(3)    ZERO POINTS
C
C     TO HAVE FEXT, COEF AND ZERO TO ALL BE VALID, YOU
C     MUST USE STANDARDS WITH BOTH A WIDE RANGE OF COLORS
C     AND A WIDE RANGE OF AIRMASSES.  WITH A CLUSTER, YOU
C     WILL GET VALID COEF PARAMETERS, BUT FEXT AND ZERO MAY
C     BE INVALID...SO BEWARE!
C
C     WRITTEN BY A. HENDEN 1980
C
      DIMENSION X(N),SMAG(N,3),URMAG(N,3),SEXT(3)
      DIMENSION FEXT(3),COEF(3),ZERO(3)
C  LOOP OVER COLORS
      DO 20 K=1,3
C  ZERO MATRIX ELEMENTS
      A1=0 $ A2=0. $ A3=0. $ A4=0. $ A5=0. $ A6=0.
      A7=0. $ A8=0. $ A9=0. $ A10=0. $ A11=0. $ A12=0.
C  LOOP OVER NUMBER OF STANDARDS
      DO 10 I=1,N
C  CALCULATE MATRIX ELEMENT SUMS
      TEMP=URMAG(I,K)*(1.-SEXT(K)*X(I))
      STD=SMAG(I,K)
      IF (K.NE.1) GO TO 5
C  NOTE:  THE V EQUATION HAS SLIGHTLY DIFFERENT FORM
      TEMP=SMAG(I,2)
      STD=STD-URMAG(I,K)
    5 CONTINUE
C
C  THE MATRIX LOOKS LIKE:
C     ( A1    A2    A3   . A4   )
C     ( A5    A6    A7   . A8   )
C     ( A9    A10   A11  . A12  )
C  NOTE: A2=A5, A3=A9, AND A7=A10, BUT EXPLICIT HERE FOR CLARITY
C
      A1=A1+TEMP*TEMP
      A2=A2+TEMP*X(I)
      A3=A3+TEMP
      A4=A4+STD*TEMP
      A5=A5+TEMP*X(I)
      A6=A6+X(I)*X(I)
      A7=A7+X(I)
      A8=A8+STD*X(I)
      A9=A9+TEMP
      A10=A10+X(I)
      A11=A11+1
      A12=A12+STD
```

(Continued on p. 340)

I.5 LINEAR REGRESSION (LEAST-SQUARES) METHOD USING THE UBV TRANSFORMATION EQUATIONS (Continued)

```
10        CONTINUE
C       CALCULATE MINORS
          AA=A7*A10-A6*A11

          BB=A5*A11-A7*A9
          CC=A6*A9-A5*A10
          DD=A8*A11-A7*A12
          EE=A6*A12-A8*A10
          FF=A5*A12-A8*A9
C       CALCULATE DETERMINANT
          DET=A1*AA+A2*BB+A3*CC
C       SOLVE FOR WANTED VALUES
          COEF(K)=(A4*AA+A2*DD+A3*EE)/DET
          ZERO(K)=(A2*FF-A1*EE+A4*CC)/DET
          FEXT(K)=(A1*DD-A4*BB+A3*FF)/DET
          IF (K.NE.1) FEXT(K)=FEXT(K)/COEF(K)
20        CONTINUE
          RETURN
          END
```

I.6 CALCULATING SIDEREAL TIME

```
          SUBROUTINE STIME (DATE,UT,ALON,ST,IST)
C
C       *** CALCULATE SIDEREAL TIME ***
C
C       INPUTS -
C                 DATE      JULIAN DATE - 2400000.
C                 UT        UT IN DECIMAL HOURS
C                 ALON      OBSERVER LONGITUDE IN HOURS
C                           ( LONGITUDE IN DEG / 15)
C       OUTPUTS -
C                 ST        SIDEREAL TIME IN DECIMAL HOURS
C                 IST       S.T. IN FORMAT HHMM  (INTEGER)
C
C       *** PROGRAMMED BY ARNE A. HENDEN 1977 ***
C
C        STHR IS # SIDEREAL HRS SINCE JAN 1, 1900
         STHR=6.6460556+2400.0512617*(DATE-15020.)/36525.+
     S   UT*1.00273-ALON
C        GET S.T. FROM STHR - # WHOLE S.T. DAYS SINCE JAN 1,1900
         ST=STHR-INT(STHR/24.)*24.
C        NOW COMBINE TO GET IST
         IST=INT(ST)
         IST=IST*100+INT((ST-FLOAT(IST))*60.)
         RETURN
         END
```

I.7 CALCULATING CARTESIAN COORDINATES FOR 1950.0

```
      SUBROUTINE XYZ (DATE,X,Y,Z)
C
C     CALCULATE HELIOCENTRIC X,Y,Z COORDINATES FOR 1950.0
C
C     INPUTS-
C              DATE    JULIAN DAY - 2400000
C     OUTPUTS-
C              X,Y,Z   HELIOCENTRIC RECTANGULAR COORDINATES
C                      IN A.U.
C
C     EQUATIONS FROM ALMANAC FOR COMPUTERS, DOGGETT. ET. AL.
C        USNO 1978
C     *** PROGRAMMED BY ARNE A. HENDEN 1978 ***
C
      DATA PICON/0.01745329/
C     T IS A RELATIVE JULIAN CENTURY
      T=(DATE-15020.)/36525.
C     EL IS THE MEAN SOLAR LONGITUDE, PRECESSED BACK TO 1950.0
      EL=279.696678+36000.76892*T+0.000303*T*T-
     $  (1.396041+0.000308*(T+0.5))*(T-0.499998)
C     G IS THE MEAN SOLAR ANOMALY
      G=358.475833+35999.04975*T-0.00015*T*T
C     AJ IS THE MEAN JUPITER ANOMALY
      AJ=225.444651+2880.0*T+154.906654*T
C     CONVERT DEGREES TO RADIANS FOR TRIG FUNCTIONS
      EL=EL*PICON
      G=G*PICON
      AJ=AJ*PICON
C     CALCULATE X,Y,Z USING TRIGONOMETRIC SERIES
      X=0.99986*COS(EL)-0.025127*COS(G-EL)+0.008374*COS(G+EL)+
     $  0.000105*COS(G+G+EL)+0.000063*T*COS(G-EL)+
     $  0.000035*COS(G+G-EL)-0.000026*SIN(G-EL-AJ)-
     $  0.000021*T*COS(G+EL)
      Y=0.917308*SIN(EL)+0.023053*SIN(G-EL)+0.007683*SIN(G+EL)+
     $  0.000097*SIN(G+G+EL)-0.000057*T*SIN(G-EL)-
     $  0.000032*SIN(G+G-EL)-0.000024*COS(G-EL-AJ)-
     $  0.000019*T*SIN(G+EL)
      Z=0.397825*SIN(EL)+0.009998*SIN(G-EL)+0.003332*SIN(G+EL)+
     $  0.000042*SIN(G+G+EL)-0.000025*T*SIN(G-EL)-
     $  0.000014*SIN(G+G-EL)-0.000010*COS(G-EL-AJ)
      RETURN
      END
```

APPENDIX J
THE LIGHT RADIATION FROM STARS

J.1 INTENSITY, FLUX, AND LUMINOSITY

The concepts of intensity, flux, and luminosity are very important and yet they are often confused. These terms cannot be used interchangeably as they have very different meanings. The following discussion is based on treatments by Aller[1] and Gray.[2] Figure J.1 shows a small area ΔA on the surface of a star. What we wish to consider is the amount of energy emitted by this small area in the direction θ from the normal (a line perpendicular to the surface). Throughout this discussion, we assume symmetry about the normal. That is to say, the results are the same if θ is drawn to the left of the normal in Figure J.1 instead of to the right. In order to measure the energy, some detector must be used to collect the energy falling on its surface. In practice, you cannot measure energy at a "point" because a point has no area. In Figure J.1, $\Delta A'$ represents the energy-collecting area, and $\Delta\omega$ is the solid angle subtended by this area as seen from the star. Strictly speaking, the only point on the surface that can radiate energy into the cone, $\Delta\omega$, is the point at the vertex of this cone. For the moment, assume that ΔA is very small compared to this cone, so that ΔA looks almost like a point.

The amount of energy emitted each second into the cone depends on $\Delta\omega$. Obviously, if the cone is made larger, it will contain a larger fraction of the total energy emitted by ΔA. A second factor is the range of wavelength or frequency to be measured. No detector can be made to measure light in an infinitely narrow wavelength interval. Likewise, no single detector can measure every portion of the electromagnetic spectrum. It is for this reason we build x-ray, γ-ray, radio, and infrared as well as optical telescopes. A large bandpass contains more energy than a narrow one. Finally, the projected size of ΔA affects the energy in the cone $\Delta\omega$. To understand this, imagine you are viewing ΔA by looking down the axis of the cone. If θ equals zero, you are viewing ΔA perpendicular to its surface and it appears its actual size. As θ increases, the

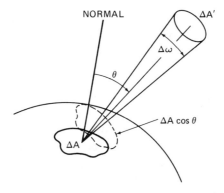

Figure J.1. Geometry used to define flux and intensity.

area appears smaller and smaller until at $\theta = 90°$ the apparent area is zero. Likewise, as θ increases, the apparent brightness decreases until at $\theta = 90°$ it reaches zero. The projected area is $\Delta A \cos \theta$.

Combining all of the above ideas, it can be said that the energy emitted (ΔE) in a time interval (Δt) into the cone is proportional to the size of the cone $(\Delta\omega)$, the wavelength interval $(\Delta\lambda)$, and the projected surface area $(\Delta A \cos \theta)$. Symbolically,

$$\frac{\Delta E}{\Delta t} \propto (\Delta A \cos \theta) \, \Delta\lambda\Delta\omega. \tag{J.1}$$

The "constant of proportionality" must contain the information that describes the radiation emerging from the star through its surface. Its value is set by the physical conditions in the star's atmosphere such as temperature, pressure, and gravity. This quantity, called the *specific intensity*, I_λ, is defined by rearranging Equation J.1 and taking the limit as Δt, $\Delta\omega$, $\Delta\lambda$, and ΔA go to zero. Then

$$I_\lambda \equiv \lim_{\substack{\Delta t \to 0 \\ \Delta\omega \to 0 \\ \Delta\lambda \to 0 \\ \Delta A \to 0}} \frac{\Delta E_\lambda}{\Delta t \Delta A \cos \theta \, \Delta\omega \, \Delta\lambda}. \tag{J.2}$$

or

$$I_\lambda = \frac{dE_\lambda}{dt \, dA \cos \theta \, d\omega d\lambda}. \tag{J.3}$$

The subscript λ has been added to remind us that intensity is a function of wavelength. Specific intensity is not really a constant because it can be a function of direction, wavelength, and perhaps time. The units of specific intensity (usually just called intensity) are ergs per second, per Angstrom, per square centimeter, per square radian.

An important point to note is that intensity can be defined at any point in space, not just on the surface of the star. The area ΔA could be an imaginary surface at any distance from the star, and the definition of intensity could proceed exactly as before. A second point to note is that intensity is independent of the distance from the source. Intensity is a measure of the energy flowing in a solid angle and this does not depend on distance. As an example, suppose that a star radiates evenly in all directions, that is, *isotropically*. A solid angle of one *steradian* (one square radian) then contains $1/4\pi$ times the total energy flow from the star. One steradian always contains this much energy no matter how far one is from the star.

Flux is defined as the *net* energy flow across an element of area per second per wavelength interval. For any given surface of area ΔA, we must sum all the energy flowing in and out of this surface from every angle. Figure J.2 illustrates this idea. Because we want the net energy crossing ΔA, inward and outward energy flows have opposite algebraic signs. Flux is then defined as

$$F_\lambda \equiv \lim_{\substack{\Delta A \to 0 \\ \Delta t \to 0 \\ \Delta\lambda \to 0}} \frac{\Sigma \Delta E_\lambda}{\Delta A \, \Delta t \, \Delta\lambda} \tag{J.4}$$

or

$$F_\lambda = \frac{\int dE_\lambda}{dA \, dt \, d\lambda}. \tag{J.5}$$

Solving Equations J.3 for dE_λ and substituting into Equation J.5 results in

$$F_\lambda = \int_{\text{all angles}} I_\lambda(\theta) \cos\theta \, d\omega = 2\pi \int_0^\pi I_\lambda(\theta) \sin\theta \cos\theta \, d\theta. \tag{J.6}$$

At the surface of a star, the integration can be broken into two parts, the flux leaving the star and the flux directed inward, or

$$F_\lambda = 2\pi \int_0^{\pi/2} I_\lambda(\theta) \sin\theta \cos\theta \, d\theta + 2\pi \int_{\pi/2}^\pi I_\lambda(\theta) \sin\theta \cos\theta \, d\theta. \tag{J.7}$$

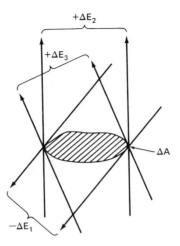

Figure J.2. Energy flow across ΔA.

In the second term, $I_\lambda(\theta)$ must be zero because at the surface of a star all of the energy is directed outward. Therefore,

$$F_\lambda = 2\pi \int_0^{\pi/2} I_\lambda(\theta) \sin \theta \cos \theta \; d\theta. \qquad (J.8)$$

If I_λ is independent of direction, then

$$F_\lambda = 2\pi I_\lambda \int_0^{\pi/2} \sin \theta \cos \theta \; d\theta \qquad (J.9)$$

or

$$F_\lambda = \pi I_\lambda. \qquad (J.10)$$

Keep in mind that this result applies to a rather special case and in general flux and intensity are not related so simply.

To illustrate the difference between intensity and flux, consider the following experiment (based partly on Gray,[2] page 103). Imagine that a telescope lens focuses an image of the sun onto a projection screen. Assume that the solar disk is illuminated uniformly, that is, no limb darkening. The screen has a small hole of area A_D that allows light to reach a photomultiplier tube. Figure J.3 illustrates the experiment. A_s is the area on the sun's surface that corre-

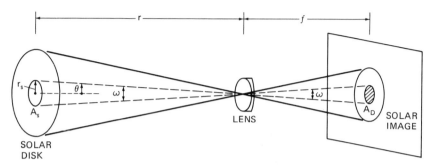

Figure J.3. Illustration to clarify difference between flux and intensity. See text.

sponds to A_D on the screen. In other words, the light entering the hole, A_D, was emitted from area A_s on the sun. Light emitted elsewhere on the sun is imaged to another portion of the screen. The only energy reaching the photomultiplier tube is that contained in the solid angle ω defined by

$$\omega = A_s/r^2 \tag{J.11}$$

where r is the distance between the lens and the sun. Because the output of the PM tube depends on this solid angle, this must be a measure of intensity. (Flux does not depend on solid angle.) If the distance to the sun could be slowly increased, the intensity measured by the photomultiplier tube would remain the same as long as the solar image is larger than A_D. To see this, note that

$$I \propto \frac{E_s}{A_s \omega}, \tag{J.12}$$

where E_s is the energy emitted each second by the surface element A_s into the lens. However, E_s is proportional to A_s for a uniformly emitting solar disk. Therefore,

$$I \propto \frac{1}{\omega} = \frac{r^2}{A_s}. \tag{J.13}$$

If we assume that the light rays pass through the center of the lens, and hence are undeviated, then

$$\frac{A_s}{r^2} = \frac{A_D}{f^2} = \omega \tag{J.14}$$

where f is the focal length of the lens. This last equation says that ω is determined by the size of our detector, A_D, and the focal length of our telescope. The projected area of the detector on the source is A_s. According to Equation J.14, ω is constant and Equation J.13 shows that intensity is constant.

Another way of obtaining the same result is to note that as the distance to the sun increases, A_s must increase because the angle at which the cone diverges from the lens is unchanged. If we assume, for the sake of simplicity, that A_s is circular, then

$$A_s = \pi r_s^2 \tag{J.15}$$

However, r_s increases with distance so that

$$r_s = r\theta \tag{J.16}$$

where θ is the angle subtended by r_s. Combining Equations J.15 and J.16, one finds

$$A_s \propto r^2 \tag{J.17}$$

Combining this with Equation J.13,

$$I \propto \text{constant.} \tag{J.18}$$

In other words, as the distance to the source increases, the area of the source imaged on the detector, A_s, increases in a compensating manner to keep the intensity constant. However, a transition occurs when the distance increases to the point where A_s equals the area of the disk of the sun. At this point, A_s has reached its maximum value and it no longer increases as the distance to the sun increases. The sun is now unresolved because the projected image is smaller than the PM tube opening. It is at this point that the photometer is no longer measuring intensity, but instead is measuring flux. The output of the PM tube is independent of ω, as long as ω contains the entire light source. As the distance between the telescope and the sun continues to increase, the output of the PM tube decreases because flux does depend on distance to the light source.

We can distinguish between two types of photometry. The surface photometry of galaxies is in fact a measurement of intensity. The procedure is to move the image of the galaxy across a small diaphragm opening. The data from this type of research specify a *magnitude per square arc second* at points across the visible surface of the galaxy. Stellar photometry, on the other hand, involves

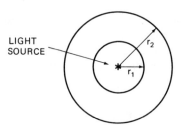

Figure J.4. Two concentric spheres.

unresolved point sources* and hence there is no specification of a solid angle, i.e., stars just have a "magnitude." We should note also that the use of a telescope or optical system can in no way increase the intensity reaching the detector. However, the total energy collected by the telescope depends on the area of the primary lens or mirror. This results in an increase in the flux passing through the focal point, which is a primary function of the telescope. When attempting to measure a faint star, the largest possible telescope should be used. When measuring an extended source (and therefore measuring intensity), the advantage of the large telescope is increased resolution. A small telescope can measure the intensity across the surface of a galaxy as well as a large telescope. However, in a small telescope, large regions may appear as an unresolved "blob," whereas in a large telescope, fine detail may be resolved and measured.

Flux obeys the familiar inverse square law of light. Consider Figure J.4, which shows a point light source surrounded by two transparent spheres of radii r_1 and r_2. If the light in the center is the only light source, then the same total energy that crosses the inner sphere per second must cross the outer sphere. The flux at each sphere is just the total energy radiated per second divided by the area of each sphere, that is,

$$F = \frac{E}{4\pi r^2} \qquad\qquad (J.19)$$

Thus the flux is inversely proportional to the square of the distance from the source:

$$\frac{F_1}{F_2} = \frac{r_2^2}{r_1^2}. \qquad\qquad (J.20)$$

*Distant galaxies can also appear as unresolved point sources.

The *luminosity* of a star is the total energy emitted per second at all wavelengths in all directions from the entire surface. We must therefore sum the energy contribution from each small element of stellar surface over all solid angles and all wavelengths. The geometry is the same as in Figure J.1. As in the previous discussion of intensity, the projected area, $dA \cos \theta$, must be used. The luminosity, L, is given by

$$L = \int \int \int I_\lambda (\cos \theta \, dA) \, d\omega \, d\lambda. \tag{J.21}$$

If I_λ is constant over the surface of the star, then

$$L = 4\pi R_*^2 \int \int I_\lambda \cos \theta \, d\omega \, d\lambda \tag{J.22}$$

where R_* is the radius of the star. By Equation J.6,

$$L = 4\pi R_*^2 \int F_\lambda^* \, d\lambda \tag{J.23}$$

where F_λ^* is the flux at the surface of the star. We demonstrate later that, to a good approximation, the above integral can be replaced by Stefan's law.

J.2 BLACKBODY RADIATORS

The description of the radiation leaving a star is an enormously complex problem, and there is no simple mathematical expression that accurately describes I_λ for a star. It would be extremely helpful to have a simple expression that at least approximates I_λ for a star. The *blackbody radiator,* a highly idealized radiation source described by theoretical physics, fulfills this need. A blackbody is an object that absorbs all radiation falling upon it. This object also emits as much energy as it receives and is therefore in an equilibrium state at some temperature. Note that a blackbody radiates and therefore need not appear black. For a blackbody, the intensity of the radiation it emits, I_λ, depends only on its temperature T and in the wavelength interval $d\lambda$:

$$I_\lambda(T) d\lambda = \frac{2hc^2/\lambda^5}{e^{(hc/\lambda kT)} - 1} \, d\lambda. \tag{J.24}$$

This expression is known as *Planck's law.* In this expression, T is the temperature in degrees Kelvin, h is Planck's constant (6.63×10^{-27} erg-seconds), c is the speed of light in a vacuum (3.00×10^{10} centimeters/second), k is the Boltzmann constant (1.38×10^{-16} erg/$°$K), and the wavelength is in centimeters. The units of I_λ are ergs per square centimeter per second per square radian per wavelength interval of one centimeter. Note that these are the units of intensity. By substituting all the constants, Equation J.24 takes on a more usable form of

$$I_\lambda(T)d\lambda = \frac{1}{\lambda^5}\left(\frac{1.19 \times 10^{-5}}{e^{(1.44/\lambda T)} - 1}\right)d\lambda \tag{J.25}$$

where λ is still in centimeters.

The continuum spectrum of most stars at least roughly approximates a black body spectrum. Figure J.5 shows the shape of the blackbody spectrum (a plot of Equation J.25) for two different temperatures. Note that the curves for different temperatures do not cross; a hot blackbody is brighter than a cool one at all wavelengths provided they are viewed from the same distance. The wavelength at which the curve reaches its maximum height, λ_{max}, is a function of temperature. To find this wavelength, it is necessary to solve

$$\frac{dI_\lambda}{d\lambda} = 0 \tag{J.26}$$

for λ, which then equals λ_{max}. The result, when T is in degrees Kelvin, is

$$\lambda_{max} = \frac{0.290}{T} \text{ centimeter.} \tag{J.27}$$

This result is referred to as *Wien's displacement law*. It is important to note that the constant in this equation applies to wavelength intervals only. That is, this equation cannot be used to find the frequency of maximum emission by substituting c divided by the frequency for λ_{max}. The constant must also be changed. That is, when T is in degrees Kelvin,

$$\nu_{max} = 5.88 \times 10^{10}\, T \text{ (Hertz).} \tag{J.28}$$

where ν_{max} is the frequency of maximum emission. Wien's displacement law is very useful for determining the temperature of a blackbody. It is simply a matter of measuring λ_{max} or ν_{max} to find the temperature. This technique can also be applied to stars because they radiate approximately as blackbodies.

Stefan's law is an expression that gives the total energy radiated per second per square centimeter per square radian *at all wavelengths*. Stefan's law is obtained by integrating Planck's law over all wavelengths. The result is

$$I(T) = \frac{\sigma}{\pi} T^4 \tag{J.29}$$

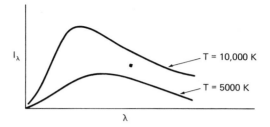

Figure J.5. Blackbody curves.

where $\sigma = 5.67 \times 10^{-5}$ ergs per square centimeter per Kelvin degree to the fourth power. $I(T)$ is simply the area under the curve in Figure J.5. For a blackbody radiator because I is independent of direction, Equation J.29 can be substituted into Equation J.10 to give the flux at its surface,

$$F = \sigma T^4. \tag{J.30}$$

This says that the total flux at all wavelengths depends solely on temperature. In this equation, F is related to F_λ by

$$F = \int_0^\infty F_\lambda \, d\lambda. \tag{J.31}$$

Equation J.30 can be substituted into Equation J.23 to yield an approximation for the luminosity of a star, that is

$$L = 4\pi\sigma R_*^2 \, T_*^4. \tag{J.32}$$

J.3 ATMOSPHERIC EXTINCTION CORRECTIONS

Figure J.6 shows the earth's atmosphere as a plane-parallel slab, i.e., the curvature of the earth is ignored. This is a valid approximation for stars that are more than $30°$ from the horizon. The relative loss of light flux dF_λ in traveling a distance ds in the earth's atmosphere is shown in Figure J.7. This loss must be proportional to F_λ (the more flux, the greater the absorption, in an absolute sense), to the absorption coefficient, α_λ (the fraction of flux lost per unit distance, in units of cm^{-1}), and the distance traveled through the atmosphere, ds. Stated mathematically,

$$dF_\lambda = -F_\lambda \, \alpha_\lambda \, ds. \tag{J.33}$$

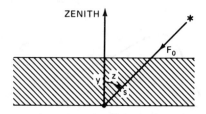

Figure J.6. Path Length is a function of Zenith angle.

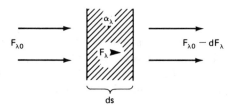

Figure J.7. Absorption of light.

The minus sign indicates that F_λ is decreasing, or being absorbed, with distance traveled. Equation J.33 can be rewritten as

$$\frac{dF_\lambda}{F_\lambda} = -\alpha_\lambda \, ds \tag{J.34}$$

and integrated over the path length, s, traveled in the atmosphere to yield

$$\ln{(F_\lambda/F_{\lambda 0})} = -\int_0^s \alpha_\lambda \, ds \tag{J.35}$$

or

$$\frac{F_\lambda}{F_{\lambda 0}} = \exp\left(-\int_0^s \alpha_\lambda \, ds\right) \tag{J.36}$$

where $F_{\lambda 0}$ is the flux at the top of the atmosphere and F_λ is the flux reaching the ground. Astronomers often define the *optical depth*, τ, by

$$\tau_\lambda = \int_0^s \alpha_\lambda \, ds, \tag{J.37}$$

as this term is dependent only on the absorbing material and the geometric orientation, not on the source of radiation. Then we can rewrite Equation J.36 as

$$\frac{F_\lambda}{F_{\lambda 0}} = e^{-\tau_\lambda}. \tag{J.38}$$

Note that if $\tau_\lambda = 1$, then the flux reaching the ground is $1/e$ of the incident flux on the top of the atmosphere.

To convert this flux ratio to a magnitude difference, we apply Equation 1.3 to yield

$$\begin{aligned}
m_\lambda - m_{\lambda 0} &= -2.5 \log (F_\lambda / F_{\lambda 0}) \\
m_\lambda - m_{\lambda 0} &= -2.5 \log (e^{-\tau_\lambda})
\end{aligned} \tag{J.39}$$

where m_λ and $m_{\lambda 0}$ are the apparent magnitude of the star at the earth's surface and above the atmosphere, respectively. Equation J.39 becomes

$$m_\lambda - m_{\lambda 0} = 2.5 \, (\log e)\tau_\lambda \tag{J.40}$$

or

$$m_{\lambda 0} = m_\lambda - 1.086 \, \tau_\lambda. \tag{J.41}$$

This equation can be placed in a more useful form if we show the variation of τ_λ with location in the sky. By Figure J.6

$$\cos z = y/s \tag{J.42}$$

or

$$s = y \sec z \tag{J.43}$$

and

$$ds = dy \sec z \tag{J.44}$$

where z is the zenith angle, y is the thickness of the atmosphere at the zenith, and s is the path length of the light. By Equations J.37 and J.44, the optical depth can be expressed as

$$\tau_\lambda = \sec z \int_0^y \alpha_\lambda \, dy. \tag{J.45}$$

The integral is simply the optical depth at the zenith, a constant factor. Thus, Equation J.41 becomes

$$m_{\lambda 0} = m_\lambda - 1.086 \sec z \int_0^y \alpha_y \, dy$$

or

$$m_{\lambda 0} = m_\lambda - k'_\lambda \sec z \tag{J.46}$$

where k'_λ is called the principal extinction coefficient and sec z represents the air mass, or the relative amount of atmosphere traversed. Air mass is often designated as X.

There are two different kinds of particles in our atmosphere that cause extinction. Each has different wavelength dependences. The major constituent are the molecules, where k'_λ varies as λ^{-4}. These particles are roughly the same size as the wavelength of light. Larger particles, like dust, are called *aerosols* and cause k'_λ to vary as λ^{-1} or λ^0. The relative fraction of each type depends on the atmospheric conditions and the zenith distance.

We have taken a simple approach to extinction. Our hypothetical case accounts for the wavelength dependence of the absorption, but we assume a plane-parallel atmosphere and filters with infinitely sharp bandpasses in order to obtain a magnitude at a specific wavelength. The actual case of a spherical earth is covered in Chapter 4. The bandwidth effect is discussed here and gives rise to a correction to the extinction known as second-order extinction.

Within a filter's bandpass, some wavelengths suffer more extinction than others. In general, blue wavelengths are absorbed and scattered more readily. An average extinction in the bandpass could be used, but then stars with rising flux toward the blue end of the bandpass (in general, hot stars) would systematically be given less extinction than is the real case, and those rising toward the red (cool stars) would be given more extinction and a fainter magnitude. In other words, using an average extinction introduces a systematic error in the magnitude determination, an error that is dependent on the color of the star and the air mass through which it is observed. Correcting Equation J.46 for this color-dependent term, we obtain

$$m_{\lambda 0} = m_\lambda - k'_\lambda \sec z - k''_\lambda c \sec z \tag{J.47}$$

or

$$m_{\lambda 0} = m_\lambda - (k'_\lambda + k''_\lambda c) \sec z \tag{J.48}$$

where k_λ'' is called the second-order extinction coefficient and c is the instrumental color index of the star.

Because atmospheric extinction is wavelength-dependent, the apparent color index of a star is also affected. Equation J.47 can be written with a subscript 1 or 2 for the two wavelengths. That is,

$$m_{\lambda 01} = m_{\lambda 1} - k_{\lambda 1}' \sec z - k_{\lambda 1}'' c \sec z \qquad \text{(J.49)}$$
$$m_{\lambda 02} = m_{\lambda 2} - k_{\lambda 2}' \sec z - k_{\lambda 2}'' c \sec z. \qquad \text{(J.50)}$$

Subtracting, we then obtain the color index

$$(m_{\lambda 01} - m_{\lambda 02}) = (m_{\lambda 1} - m_{\lambda 2}) - (k_{\lambda 1}' - k_{\lambda 2}') \sec z$$
$$- c(k_{\lambda 1}'' - k_{\lambda 2}'') \sec z. \qquad \text{(J.51)}$$

If we let the color indices c and c_0 be defined as

$$c = (m_{\lambda 1} - m_{\lambda 2})$$
$$c_0 = (m_{\lambda 01} - m_{\lambda 02}) = (m_{\lambda 1} - m_{\lambda 2})_0$$

and let

$$k_c' = k_{\lambda 1}' - k_{\lambda 2}'$$
$$k_c'' = k_{\lambda 1}'' - k_{\lambda 2}''$$

then

$$c_0 = c - k_c' \sec z - k_c'' (\sec z)\, c. \qquad \text{(J.52)}$$

In practice, the extinction coefficients can be determined by a few measurements of stars at various altitudes without any knowledge of α_λ or the actual physical processes of absorption. There are pitfalls in the determination of these coefficients because of their temporal and spatial variability. The practical details are presented in Chapter 4.

J.4 TRANSFORMING TO THE STANDARD SYSTEM

For observers at different observatories to be able to compare observations, observations must be transformed from the instrumental systems (which are all different) to the standard system. The main reason for this difference between photometer systems is that the equivalent wavelengths of observation are slightly different. The equivalent wavelength (λ_{eq}) is an average wavelength of observation weighted by the response function of the equipment, and is defined by

$$\lambda_{eq} = \frac{\int_0^\infty \lambda \phi(\lambda) \, d\lambda}{\int_0^\infty \phi(\lambda) \, d\lambda} \tag{J.53}$$

where $\phi(\lambda) = \phi_A(\lambda)\phi_T(\lambda)\phi_F(\lambda)\phi_{PM}(\lambda)$, as defined in Chapter 1. Small changes in the spectral response of the measuring equipment change λ_{eq}. This means that a magnitude determined by one instrumental system differs slightly from that found by a second system. For example, suppose you are measuring a hot star whose flux is rising very rapidly toward the blue. If your equivalent wavelength is slightly blueward of the standard system, your measured magnitude will be brighter than the accepted value. Because the difference in λ_{eq} is usually small, the magnitude on the standard system, M, can be approximated by a Taylor expansion in λ_{eq} about the instrumental magnitude, m_0. That is,

$$M = m_0 + \left(\frac{\Delta m_0}{\Delta \lambda_{eq}}\right) \Delta \lambda_{eq} + \text{higher-order terms.} \tag{J.54}$$

Figure J.8 illustrates this situation. Note that in this discussion the magnitudes are assumed to have already been corrected for atmospheric extinction. The term in parentheses is the slope of the star's continuum, which is proportional to the star's color or color index in that region. Any instrumental magnitude, $m_{\lambda 0}$, can be converted to the standard magnitude, M, by an expression of the

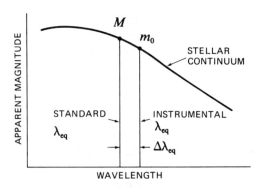

Figure J.8. Difference between the standard and instrumental equivalent wavelength.

form

$$M_\lambda = m_{\lambda 0} + \beta_\lambda C + \gamma_\lambda. \qquad (J.55)$$

β_λ and γ_λ are constants which are unique to the photometer in use and C is the standard color index of the star, near the wavelength in question.

The transformation of a color index (that has already been corrected for extinction) is found by applying Equation J.55 to each spectral region and forming the difference. That is,

$$(M_{\lambda 1} - M_{\lambda 2}) = (m_{\lambda 1} - m_{\lambda 2}) + (\beta_{\lambda 1} - \beta_{\lambda 2})C + \gamma_{\lambda 1} - \gamma_{\lambda 2}$$

or

$$C = c_0 + \beta_c C + \gamma_c \qquad (J.56)$$

where C is the color index on the standard system, c is the instrumental color index and β, γ, β_c, and γ_c are constants. If we define a constant, δ, by

$$\delta = \frac{1}{1 - \beta_c},$$

then

$$C = \delta c_0 + \gamma_c. \qquad (J.57)$$

For both the magnitude and color index transformations, we have assumed that the higher-order terms beyond a linear relation to the color index are negligible. This is not always the case. An example is the use of a "neutral" density filter that adds additional color dependence to the instrumental response. These situations are apparent when the coefficient determination is attempted, as departures from a linear dependence are evident. For these situations, the next higher-order term (quadratic in color) must be added to the procedure. As these conditions rarely arise, further treatment is not presented in this text. but you should be aware of the possibility.

REFERENCES

1. Aller, L. H. 1963. *The Atmospheres of the Sun and Stars*. New York: Ronald Press.
2. Gray, D. F. 1976. *The Observation and Analysis of Stellar Photospheres*. New York: John Wiley and Sons.

APPENDIX K
ADVANCED STATISTICS

Appendix K explains some of the finer points in statistics and their application to astronomy. The subject matter treated here is not essential for basic photometry, but is not covered elsewhere in this text and is given here to stimulate the interested to read further.

Much of the presented material has been drawn from elementary statistics texts[1,2,3] or from the astronomical literature.[4,5,6] You should know the meaning of the terms *matrix, determinant, derivative,* and *partial derivative* before you can make full use of this appendix.

K.1 STATISTICAL DISTRUBUTIONS

To introduce the idea of a probability distribution, assume that we are executing a coin toss. It is relatively simple to calculate the probability of tossing three heads and seven tails out of 10 tosses, but what is the probability of tossing n heads and $(m - n)$ tails out of m tosses? These numbers can be thought of as describing the function $p(n)$, where p is the probability that n of the tosses will be heads. Such a function is called a *probability distribution.*

If the index n varies between 1 and m, then we have included all possible events and the sum of these probabilities must be unity. That is,

$$\sum_{n=1}^{m} p(n) = 1 .$$

(K.1)

The two types of probability distributions extensively used in experimental data in photometry are the Gaussian, for experimental values, and the Poisson, for photon arrivals. You need not know the functional forms of these distributions to use the results that mathmaticians have derived from them, such as the standard deviation; but it is important to at least look at the shapes of the distributions.

The Gaussian (or normal) distribution is defined by Equation 3.10, rewritten here as

$$p(x) = \frac{1}{\sigma \sqrt{2\pi}} \exp\left[-\frac{1}{2}\left(\frac{x - \bar{x}}{\sigma}\right)^2 \right] \qquad (K.2)$$

This distribution is shown in Figure 3.1 and repeated in Figure K.1 for completeness. It has been shown to approximate errors of measurement very closely and therefore is the most widely known and used of all distributions.

Often, Equation K.2 is *standardized* when given in tables in the back of statistics texts. That is, the function is given with respect to the standardized normal variable, z, where

$$z = \frac{x - \bar{x}}{\sigma} \qquad (K.3)$$

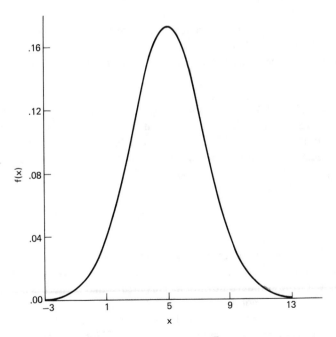

Figure K.1. Gaussian distribution for $\bar{x} = 5.0$, $\sigma = 2.3$.

then $p'(z)$ is tabulated where

$$p'(z) = \sigma p(z) = \frac{1}{\sqrt{2\pi}} e^{-z^2/2} \qquad (K.4)$$

This allows tables of the function to be given without having to list function points for every combination of σ and $\bar{x}$.

For approximating arrival rates of photons, the Poisson distribution is the most commonly used function. It is defined by

$$p\left(\begin{array}{c} y \text{ occurrences in} \\ \text{a given time unit} \end{array}\right) = \begin{cases} \dfrac{e^{-\lambda}\lambda^y}{y!}, \text{ for } \begin{cases} y = 0, 1, 2, \ldots \\ \lambda > 0 \end{cases} \\ 0, \text{ otherwise} \end{cases} \qquad (K.5)$$

where p is the probability of occurrence and λ is the mean arrival rate, the number of photons per second. This function looks much like the Gaussian, except:

1. The variance is given by $\sigma^2 = \lambda$.
2. It is a discrete distribution, not continuous like the Gaussian, because a photon either arrives or it does not arrive.
3. It is skewed to the right because there are no negative occurrences, that is, y is never negative.
4. As $\lambda \to \infty$, the Poisson distribution approaches the Gaussian distribution in form.

An example of the Poisson distribution for $\lambda = 5.0$ is given in Figure K.2.

Just as the standard deviation was defined for a Gaussian distribution, a similar "standard deviation" can be derived for the Poisson distribution. If Equation K.5 is substituted in a generalized form of Equation 3.6 (a messy proposition!), then the standard deviation of Poisson-distributed data is given by

$$\sigma_p = \sqrt{N} \qquad (K.6)$$

where N is the total number of observations. Note that this value is not the same as for the Gaussian distribution. In fact, no two distributions have the same value for the standard deviation. This means that if there is a bias in your sample so that it does not fit a Gaussian distribution curve, the standard deviation that you derive using Equation 3.6 is not the correct one for your sample! *You must be very careful to remove any chance of bias from your calculations.*

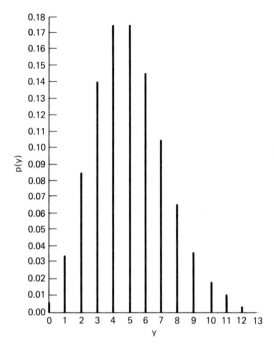

Figure K.2. Poisson distribution for $\lambda = 5.0$.

K.2 PROPAGATION OF ERRORS

If you use various experimental observations to calculate a result, and these observations each have uncertainties associated with them, then the error in the result will be a function of the errors of the individual observations. For example, if you want to calculate the density, or weight per unit volume, of a liquid in a container, you need to both find the volume of the container and its weight. It is not entirely obvious what the density error is if you know the volume to ± 0.1 percent and the weight to ± 1.0 percent. To find the resultant error, you need to propagate each individual error through the calculation and see how it affects the final result.

In a general form, assume that the function $f(x)$ is similar to that shown in Figure K.3. We can see that an error in the measurement of x, ϵ_x, causes a corresponding error, ϵ_f, in our evaluation of the function. Now

$$\frac{\epsilon_f}{\epsilon_x} = \frac{\Delta f(x)}{\Delta x} \cong \frac{df}{dx} = f'(x)$$

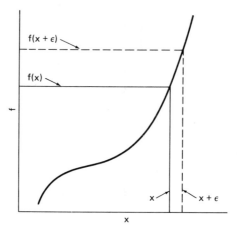

Figure K.3. Error in f(x) due to $\epsilon(x)$.

or

$$\epsilon_f = f'(x)\epsilon_x \qquad\qquad (K.7)$$

where $f'(x)$ is a shorthand way of expressing the derivative of $f(x)$, i.e., how fast it varies with a change in x.

We can extend Equation K.7 to functions of more than one variable:

$$\epsilon_F = \frac{\partial f}{\partial x}\epsilon_x + \frac{\partial f}{\partial y}\epsilon_y + \frac{\partial f}{\partial z}\epsilon_z + \cdots \qquad\qquad (K.8)$$

where $\dfrac{\partial f}{\partial x}$ is the partial derivative of f with respect to x, which means simply that we recognize f is a function of many variables, but we are evaluating the derivative with respect to x and hold the variations due to the other variables constant during the process.

Now

$$\sigma_F^2 = \frac{\displaystyle\sum_{i=1}^{N} \epsilon_f^2}{N} \qquad\qquad (K.9)$$

$$\sigma_f^2 = \frac{1}{N}\sum_{i=1}^{N}\left[\frac{\partial f}{\partial x}\epsilon_{x_i} + \frac{\partial f}{\partial y}\epsilon_{y_i} + \cdots\right]^2 \qquad\qquad (K.10)$$

which reduces upon expansion and removal of cross terms to:

$$\sigma_f = \left\{ \frac{1}{N} \left[\left(\frac{\partial f}{\partial x} \right)^2 \sigma_x^2 + \left(\frac{\partial f}{\partial y} \right)^2 \sigma_y^2 + \cdots \right] \right\}^{1/2} \tag{K.11}$$

that is, errors add in *quadrature*.

We seldom know the mathematical form of the function f. There are some examples in photometry, however, where Equation K.11 can be applied. The *UBV* transformation equations depend on the values of the zero points, the color terms, the extinction coefficients, and the air mass. By knowing the standard deviation in each of these parameters, you can calculate the expected deviation in the derived standard magnitudes and also see which terms are relatively unimportant.

K.3 MULTIVARIATE LEAST SQUARES

In Chapter 3, we considered the case of fitting a least-squares line to the function

$$f(x_i) = a + bx_i. \tag{K.12}$$

That is, by knowing the approximate $f(x_i)$ for several values of x_i, we could solve for the parameters a and b. This is simple linear regression in that the function $f(x)$ is dependent only in a linear fashion on one variable, x.

There are two ways that this result could be generalized: (1) $f(x)$ could have a nonlinear dependence on x, such as

$$f(x_i) = a + bx_i^2$$

or (2) the function f could be dependent on more than one variable, such as

$$f(x_i, y_i) = a + b_1 x_i + b_2 y_i. \tag{K.13}$$

Equation K.13 is known as *multiple linear regression* and is covered in this section. The nonlinear case can be found in Young,[1] Harnell,[2] and Bevington.[3]

Multiple linear regression is very important in photometry in solving the transformation equations. For example, substituting Equation 4.28 into 4.32 yields

$$V = \epsilon(B - V) + (v - k_v'X - k_v''(b - v)X) + \zeta_v, \tag{K.14}$$

which shows that V is a function of the star, the instrument, and the air mass through which the star is observed.

A mathematical representation of the regression equation is

$$\hat{y} = a + b_1 z_1 + b_2 z_2 + \cdots + b_m z_m \qquad \text{(K.15)}$$

where z_1, z_2, ... are *not* the individual values of one variable (z), but are independent variables. For example, a comparison with Equation K.13 gives $z_1 = x$, $z_2 = y$. Then we minimize the sum of the squares of the deviations, D:

$$
\begin{aligned}
D &= \sum_{i=1}^{n} (y_i - \hat{y}_i)^2 \\
&= \sum_{i=1}^{n} (y_i - a - b_1 z_{1i} - b_2 z_{2i} - \cdots - b_m z_{mi})^2
\end{aligned}
\qquad \text{(K.16)}
$$

where n is the number of observations. The procedure for minimizing D is the same as in the simple linear case, except that partial derivatives must be taken for $m + 1$ variables instead of just two. Setting these $m + 1$ partial derivatives to zero and solving, we obtain the following set of normal equations:

$$
\begin{aligned}
an &+ b_1 \Sigma z_{1i} &&+ b_2 \Sigma z_{2i} &&+ \cdots + b_m \Sigma z_{mi} &&= \Sigma y_i \\
a\Sigma z_{1i} &+ b_1 \Sigma z_{1i}^2 &&+ b_2 \Sigma z_{1i} z_{2i} &&+ \cdots + b_m \Sigma z_{1i} z_{mi} &&= \Sigma z_{1i} y_i \\
a\Sigma z_{2i} &+ b_1 \Sigma z_{1i} z_{2i} &&+ b_2 \Sigma z_{2i}^2 &&+ \cdots + b_m \Sigma z_{2i} z_{mi} &&= \Sigma z_{2i} y_i \\
&&&&&&& \text{(K.17)} \\
a\Sigma z_{mi} &+ b_1 \Sigma z_{1i} z_{mi} &&+ b_2 \Sigma z_{2i} z_{mi} &&+ \cdots + b_m \Sigma z_{mi}^2 &&= \Sigma z_{mi} y_i
\end{aligned}
$$

In matrix form,

$$
\begin{aligned}
A_{jk} &= \Sigma z_j z_k \quad \text{where } j = 0,n \text{ and } k = 0,n \\
N_j &= \Sigma z_{ji} y_i \\
B_j &= b_j \quad \text{where } B(0) = a
\end{aligned}
$$

then

$$A_{jk} B_j = N_j.$$

Removing subscripts,

$$\mathbf{A}\,\mathbf{B} = \mathbf{N}$$
$$\mathbf{B} = \mathbf{A}^{-1}\,\mathbf{N} \qquad\qquad \text{(K.18)}$$

Equation K.18 gives the coefficient vector B, providing that matrix A can be inverted. There are more elegant methods of solving the normal equations, for instance, by assuming they are separable, solving for $b_1, b_2 \dots, b_m$ and then back-substituting for the constant term b_0.

As an example, we solve Equation 2.10 for the zero-point, first-order extinction, and the transformation coefficient, that is a "full-blown" solution. If we rewrite Equation 2.10 by substituting Equation 2.7 to obtain

$$(B - V) = \zeta_{bv} + \mu(b - v)\,[1 - k''_{bv}X] - \mu k'_{bv}, \qquad \text{(K.19)}$$

We can see by correspondence that we have

$$y_i = a + b_1 z_1 + b_2 z_2$$
$$y_i = B - V$$
$$a = \zeta_{bv}$$
$$b_1 = \mu$$
$$z_1 = (b - v)[1 - k''_{bv}X]$$
$$b_2 = -\mu k'_{bv}$$
$$z_2 = X.$$

Then, writing the normal equations,

$$
\begin{aligned}
an &+ b_1\Sigma z_{1i} &+ b_2\Sigma z_{2i} &= \Sigma y_i \\
a\Sigma z_{1i} &+ b_1\Sigma z_{1i}^2 &+ b_2\Sigma z_{1i}z_{2i} &= \Sigma z_{1i}y_i \\
a\Sigma z_{2i} &+ b_1\Sigma z_{1i}z_{2i} &+ b_2\Sigma z_{2i}^2 &= \Sigma z_{2i}y_i,
\end{aligned}
\qquad \text{(K.20)}
$$

we obtain

$$
\begin{pmatrix}
n & \Sigma z_{1i} & \Sigma z_{2i} \\
\Sigma z_{1i} & \Sigma z_{1i}^2 & \Sigma z_{1i}z_{2i} \\
\Sigma z_{2i} & \Sigma z_{1i}z_{2i} & \Sigma z_{2i}^2
\end{pmatrix}
\begin{pmatrix}
a \\
b_1 \\
b_2
\end{pmatrix}
=
\begin{pmatrix}
\Sigma y_i \\
\Sigma z_{1i}y_i \\
\Sigma z_{2i}y_i
\end{pmatrix},
\qquad \text{(K.21)}
$$

a matrix equation, which can be solved by back-substitution or the use of minors. See Arfken[7] for more detail.

The transformation equations for V and $(U - B)$ can be solved in a similar manner. A subroutine to calculate the full treatment UBV least-squares solution can be found in Section I.5. You should be very wary of solving for both the color and extinction coefficients at once, as they interact with each other and bad data points are not obvious. We suggest using simple linear least squares for the color coefficients and a separate solution for extinction, as presented in Chapter 4.

K.4 SIGNAL-TO-NOISE RATIO

Each time a star is measured, there is an uncertainty in the value obtained. If systematic errors are ignored, the uncertainty can be defined as the *noise,* or the standard deviation of a single measurement from the mean of all the measures made on the star. The ratio of the value derived for the observed count rate to the uncertainty in that number is called the output *signal-to-noise ratio* (S/N).

If an idealized detector is considered, where no background is present and the only source of noise is from statistical fluctuations from the star, then the arriving signal is given by

$$S_{in} = \dot{C}_s t \qquad (K.22)$$

where S_{in} is the number of input photons to the detector in time t, $\dot{C}_s$ is the rate of photon arrival in photons per second, and t is the integration time, or the time required for the measurement (seconds). For a weak beam of photons, Poisson statistics are a good approximation to the statistical fluctuations of the beam. These statistics state that the noise, or standard deviation of the signal from the mean, is given by Equation K.6, or in another form,

$$N_{in} = S_{in}^{1/2} = (\dot{C}_s t)^{1/2}. \qquad (K.23)$$

The S/N calculated using Equations K.22 and K.23 tells us, in a sense, what fraction of the *arriving* signal is contributed by the noise. This ratio is given by

$$\left(\frac{S}{N}\right)_{in} = \frac{\dot{C}_s t}{(\dot{C}_s t)^{1/2}} \qquad (K.24)$$

or

$$\left(\frac{S}{N}\right)_{in} = (\dot{C}_s t)^{1/2}. \qquad (K.25)$$

One hundred total source counts would yield an S/N of 10. Because the noise varies as the square root of the signal, 10,000 total counts would be required to reduce the noise to one percent of the signal or equivalently, to have an S/N of 100.

K.4a Detective Quantum Efficiency

Very few photomultiplier tubes are perfectly efficient. In general, only a fraction, Q, of the incident photons are detected. The parameter Q can be thought of as the efficiency of detection of quanta or photons, or the *quantum efficiency*. Realizing this, the S/N (Equation K.24) for the output signal can be written as:

$$\left(\frac{S}{N}\right)_{out} = \frac{(Q\dot{C}_s t)}{(Q\dot{C}_s t)^{1/2}} \qquad (K.26)$$

$$\left(\frac{S}{N}\right)_{out} = (Q\dot{C}_s t)^{1/2}. \qquad (K.27)$$

Q is generally not known, but must be measured experimentally. Rearranging,

$$Q = \frac{\left(\dfrac{S}{N}\right)_{out}^{2}}{\dot{C}_s t}$$

$$Q = \frac{\left(\dfrac{S}{N}\right)_{out}^{2}}{\left(\dfrac{S}{N}\right)_{in}^{2}} \qquad (K.28)$$

Theoretically, Equation K.28 holds only for the case where the number of detected photons is just a simple linear fraction of the number of incident photons. We can generalize to the more common case by defining

$$DQE = \frac{\left(\dfrac{S}{N}\right)_{out}^{2}}{\left(\dfrac{S}{N}\right)_{in}^{2}} \qquad (K.29)$$

where DQE is the *detective quantum efficiency,* so called because it is a measure of how badly the actual detector deviates from a perfect detector. The actual detector or system performs as if it were an ideal detector with the input signal decreased by the factor DQE (≤ 1). The DQE of a system is always less than the quantum efficiency of the photocathode, as some electrons are lost in the dynodes and different detection systems weight the anode pulses differently. A typical photomultiplier system has a DQE of 2 to 4 percent.

So far we have discussed only shot or Poisson noise, the fluctuations inherent in the source itself. There are several other possible sources of noise, both in the sky and the actual detection system. All do not affect the output S/N in the same manner, and at a given source intensity, one noise component may be dominant or several may contribute. For faint sources, the source signal may be much smaller than the noise.

Listed below are the three major types of noise sources and how they affect the signal-to-noise ratio when they are dominant. Discussions of these sources can be found in other chapters.

1. *Noise dependent on the square root of the signal.*
   a. Photon shot noise, N_s, in the signal.

$$N_s = G(Q\dot{C}_s t)^{1/2}$$

Here Equation K.26 becomes

$$\left(\frac{S}{N}\right)_{out} = \frac{GQ\dot{C}_s t}{G(Q\dot{C}_s t)^{1/2}} = (Q\dot{C}_s t)^{1/2} \tag{K.30}$$

where G is the internal gain of the detector. Note that the S/N is proportional to the square root of the number of counts; increasing counts by a factor of 100 increases the S/N by only a factor of 10. By taking logarithms of both sides,

$$\log\left(\frac{S}{N}\right)_{out} = \tfrac{1}{2} \log (Q\dot{C}_s t) = \tfrac{1}{2} \log \text{(counts)}. \tag{K.31}$$

So plotting several readings of log (S/N) versus log (counts) gives a straight line slope ½.

2. *Noise linearly dependent on the signal.*
   a. Scintillation noise from the atmosphere.
      This noise source, N_{sc}, is a fractional modulation, m, of the incident beam, that is

$$N_{sc} = m \, Q \, \dot{C}_s t. \tag{K.32}$$

In other words, stars of all magnitudes vary by the same percentage. If a 10^m star is varying by 10 percent, then so is an 18^m star. Equations K.26 and K.31 then become

$$\left(\frac{S}{N}\right)_{out} = \frac{GQ\dot{C}_{sc}t}{GmQ\dot{C}_{sc}t} = \frac{1}{m} \qquad \text{(K.33)}$$

$$\log\left(\frac{S}{N}\right)_{out} = \text{constant} \qquad \text{(K.34)}$$

where the slope of the plot is zero.

3. *Noise independent of the signal.*

   a. Amplifier noise.

   Equations K.26 and K.31 become

$$\left(\frac{S}{N}\right)_{out} = \frac{GQ\dot{C}_s t}{N_{am}} \qquad \text{(K.35)}$$

$$\log\left(\frac{S}{N}\right)_{out} = \log G - \log N_{am} + \log(Q\dot{C}_s t) \qquad \text{(K.36)}$$

where N_{am} is the amplifier noise in *net equivalent photons,* that is, the number of incident photons that would be required to produce a noise signal the size of the amplifier noise. In this example, the slope of the plot equals 1.

   b. Background shot noise, N_b, such as from the sky.

$$N_b = G(Q\dot{C}_b t)^{1/2}$$

Our equations become:

$$\left(\frac{S}{N}\right)_{out} = \frac{GQ\dot{C}_s t}{G(Q\dot{C}_b t)^{1/2}} \qquad \text{(K.37)}$$

$$\log\left(\frac{S}{N}\right)_{out} = \log(Q\dot{C}_s t) - \tfrac{1}{2}\log(Q\dot{C}_b t) \qquad \text{(K.38)}$$

where $\dot{C}_b$ is the background count rate. Again, the slope is equal to 1. Each of these sources becomes dominant in different count regimes. For instance, bright sources have negligible background, sources near the horizon exhibit much more scintillation, etc. For count rates not dominated by one noise component, all contributors must be accounted for by adding the noise contributions in quadrature, i.e.,

$$N_{tot} = (N_s^2 + N_{sc}^2 + N_{am}^2 + N_b^2 + \cdots)^{1/2} \qquad \text{(K.39)}$$

so that

$$\left(\frac{S}{N}\right)_{out} = \frac{GQ\dot{C}_s t}{(N_s^2 + N_{sc}^2 + N_{am}^2 + N_b^2 + \cdots)^{1/2}}. \qquad (K.40)$$

A derivation of why uncorrelated noises (or standard deviations) add in quadrature is beyond the scope of this section, but can be described as taking the partial derivative of the total noise count function with respect to each of the contributors (source, sky, etc.) and noting that cross terms vanish (N_s is not dependent on N_b etc.).

A plot of the theoretical signal-to-noise ratio obtainable with $t = 1$ second, $Q = G = 1$, and $\dot{C}_b = 30$ counts per second for various sources (i.e., varying $\dot{C}_s$) is shown in Figure K.4. Note that for high count rates, the slope approaches ½ and for count rates near $\dot{C}_b$ the slope is approximately 1.

K.4b Regimes of Noise Dominance

This section examines three noise regimes as examples of signal-to-noise ratio considerations. These are:

1. *Background.* So far, only those cases where the background and source are uniquely known have been discussed. This is not normally the case, as the background is generally unknown and must be measured during

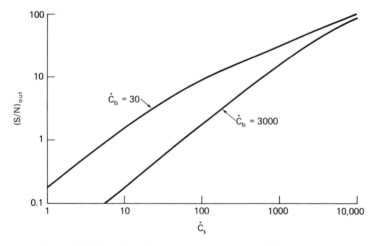

Figure K.4. Signal-to-noise ratio comparisons for differing sources.

part of the total observing time. For this case of first measuring source with sky background and then sky by itself, the noise or standard deviation from the mean is a combination of Poisson noise and background noise:

$$N = \{[\sqrt{(\dot{C}_s + \dot{C}_b)t_s}]^2 + [\frac{t_s}{t_b}\sqrt{\dot{C}_b t_b}]^2\}^{1/2}$$

$$N = \sqrt{\dot{C}_s t_s + \dot{C}_b t_s + \dot{C}_b t_s^2/t_b} \qquad (K.41)$$

where t is the amount of time spent measuring source or background and $\dot{C}_x$ is the count rate for a measurement, with subscript s referring to the source and subscript b the background. Also, the data are represented by:

$$\text{Total source counts} = S \pm N \qquad (K.42)$$

$$\text{Count rate for source (per unit time)} = \frac{S}{t_s} \pm \frac{N}{t_s} \qquad (K.43)$$

2. *Scintillation*. For brighter stars, the dominant noise source is scintillation. But if scintillation and background noises are both important for a source, one should realize that scintillation affects only the source counts and not the sky counts. The S/N for this case is:

$$\left(\frac{S}{N}\right)_{out} = \frac{(\dot{C}_b + \dot{C}_s)t}{\sqrt{\dot{C}_s t + \dot{C}_b t + m^2(\dot{C}_s t)^2}} \cdot \qquad (K.44)$$

As long as the source counts are low or the scintillation modulation, m, is small, the S/N takes on its previous appearance, Equation K.41.

3. *Amplifier noise*. In many cases, such as astronomical TV systems, both amplifier and photon shot noise are important. The S/N for this case is:

$$\left(\frac{S}{N}\right)_{out} = \frac{GQ\dot{C}_s t}{\{[G(\dot{C}_s t)^{1/2}]^2 + N_{am}^2\}^{1/2}}$$

$$= \frac{GQ\dot{C}_s t}{(G^2 Q\dot{C}_s t + N_{am}^2)^{1/2}}$$

$$\left(\frac{S}{N}\right)_{out} = \frac{Q\dot{C}_s t}{\left(Q\dot{C}_s t + \frac{N_{am}^2}{G^2}\right)^{1/2}} \qquad (K.45)$$

Note that the effect of the amplifier noise is decreased by the internal gain of the detector. The ratio is then added, much as a source of photons.

This noise-to-gain ratio can be thought of as the number of equivalent incident photons on the detector that would give shot noise of the same amount. In other words,

$$\frac{N_{am}}{G} = \text{amplifier noise referred to the input.}$$

We then see why amplifier noise, DC amplifier or pulse preamp, is not important for photomultiplier systems, because the noise-free gain in the photomultiplier tube is 10^6, which reduces the effect of amplifier noise to negligible levels.

K.5 THEORETICAL DIFFERENCES BETWEEN DC AND PULSE-COUNTING TECHNIQUES

There are two basic methods of detecting the output from a photomultiplier tube. DC techniques measure the feeble current generated by the incident photons while pulse-counting techniques measure the number of photons or pulses directly. Proponents of both sides have been arguing for decades over which technique, if either, is superior. The major area in which one may have an advantage over the other is in the signal-to-noise ratio. For this reason, the comparison between DC and pulse-counting methods is included in this chapter.

K.5a Pulse Height Distribution

Each dynode of a 1P21 photomultiplier tube has an average gain of about 5. However, statistically one dynode might have a gain of 4 one time, and 6 or even 10 the next. This means that the number of electrons collected at the anode is not constant, depending on which dynode deviates from the mean. This was shown earlier in Figure 7.2 for a typical photomultiplier tube output. The noise is given by N_{am}/G and is small for a photomultiplier tube but not negligible on other devices nor for larger dark currents. Typically the distribution of pulse sizes is called the *pulse height distribution,* shown for an idealized source in Figure 7.3.

The general features of such a distribution are readily seen. As x approaches zero, all pulses are a result of dark current or amplifier noise and the number of such pulses approaches infinity. After this initial peak, the next larger peak is a result of a photon liberating one photoelectron at the cathode. Other peaks occur at larger heights because more than one photoelectron is released by the photon or by cosmic ray induced electrons. Many photoelectrons may be produced if the cosmic ray strikes the photocathode at near grazing incidence. The

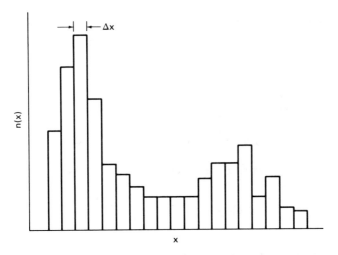

Figure K.5. Schematic pulse height distribution.

probability of more than one photoelectron being liberated by a photon is very small, and most of these higher energy events are caused by the extraneous noise sources such as cosmic rays at a rate of about two per square centimeter of cathode per minute. The shape of the distribution is not constant, but varies according to dynode voltages, temperature, wavelength, and cathode area.

K.5b Effect of Weighting Events on the DQE[10]

The primary theoretical difference between the two detection methods is in their weighting of photomultiplier pulses. The DC method gives the *average* current from the photomultiplier tube; therefore, a large pulse gives more current and is weighted more heavily, even though it signifies the arrival of only one photon just as a smaller pulse does. Pulse-counting techniques treat all pulses equally.

A schematic form of a pulse height distribution is shown in Figure K.5, where $n(x)$ is the number of detected incident photons which produce a pulse of height x.

$$S = Q\, n(x_1)\, \Delta x_1 + Q\, n(x_2)\, \Delta x_2 + \cdots \tag{K.46}$$

or, because $\Delta x_1 = \Delta x_2 = \Delta x_3$, and so forth,

$$S = \sum_{i=1}^{N} Q\, n(x_i)\, \Delta x. \tag{K.47}$$

In integral form ($\Delta x \rightarrow 0$),

$$S = \int_0^\infty Q\, n(x)\, dx. \tag{K.48}$$

Incorporating weighting factors, the equations become

$$S = w(x_1)\, Q\, n(x_1)\, \Delta x + w(x_2)\, Q\, n(x_2)\, \Delta x + \cdots \tag{K.49}$$

$$S = \sum_{i=1}^{N} w(x_i)\, Q\, n(x_i)\, \Delta x \tag{K.50}$$

$$S = \int_0^\infty w(x)\, Q\, n(x)\, dx. \tag{K.51}$$

The noise for unweighted signals is just

$$N = \sqrt{S}. \tag{K.52}$$

With weights, the noise equation is much more complicated. Because each bin in Figure K.5 can be thought of as a separate event, the total noise is given by adding in quadrature:

$$N = [\{w(x_1)[Q\, n(x_1)\, \Delta x]^{1/2}\}^2 + \{w(x_2)[Q\, n(x_2)\Delta x]^{1/2}\}^2 + \cdots]^{1/2} \tag{K.53}$$

In integral form,

$$N = \left[\int_0^\infty w(x)^2\, Q\, n(x)\, dx\right]^{1/2}. \tag{K.54}$$

Therefore, the output S/N for weighted events is given by

$$\left(\frac{S}{N}\right)_{\text{out}} = \frac{\displaystyle\int_0^\infty w(x)\, Q\, n(x)\, dx}{\left[\displaystyle\int_0^\infty w^2(x)\, Q\, n(x)\, dx\right]^{1/2}}. \tag{K.55}$$

From our definition of DQE, we have

$$DQE = \frac{\left(\dfrac{S}{N}\right)_{out}^{2}}{\left(\dfrac{S}{N}\right)_{in}^{2}} = Q \left\{ \frac{[\int w(x)\, n(x)\, dx]^{2}}{[\int w^{2}(x)\, n(x)\, dx]\, [\int n(x)\, dx]} \right\} \quad (K.56)$$

or

$$DQE = Q f \qquad (K.57)$$

where

$$f = \frac{[\int w(x)\, n(x)\, dx]^{2}}{[\int w^{2}(x)\, n(x)\, dx]\, [\int n(x)\, dx]}. \qquad (K.58)$$

So f is the factor that the unweighted DQE is modified by when weights are included. Two cases are involved:

1. *Weights equal to one, as in pulse counting* $(w(x) = 1)$. Then

$$DQE = Q \frac{[\int n(x)\, dx]^{2}}{[\int n(x)\, dx]\, [\int n(x)\, dx]}$$

This reduces to

$$DQE = Q \qquad (K.59)$$

for an ideal photomultiplier.
2. *Weights proportional to the size of the pulse, as in DC photometry* $(w(x) = x)$.
Then

$$DQE = \frac{Q\, [\int x n(x)\, dx]^{2}}{[\int x^{2}\, n(x)\, dx]\, [\int n(x)\, dx]} \qquad (K.60)$$

Some assumptions need to be made about the pulse height distribution before this equation can be solved. Typical trials include $n(x) = $ constant over a window, $n(x) = e^{-x}$, or $n(x) = $ Poisson distribution. These all lead to complicated reductions. Rather than show all three, we use the window function as an example. The pulse height distribution can be approximated by a box, i.e.,

$$n(x) = n_0, \; a < x < b$$
$$n(x) = 0, \; x < a \text{ or } x > b,$$

as shown in Figure K.6. Then

$$DQE = \frac{Q\left[n_0 \displaystyle\int_a^b x \, dx \right]^2}{\left[n_0 \displaystyle\int_a^b x^2 \, dx \right]\left[n_0 \displaystyle\int_a^b dx \right]}$$

$$= \frac{Q \, n_0^2}{n_0^2} \left\{ \frac{\left[\dfrac{x^2}{2} \Big|_a^b \right]^2}{\left[\dfrac{x^3}{3} \Big|_a^b \right]\left[x \Big|_a^b \right]} \right\}$$

$$= Q \left\{ \frac{\left[\dfrac{b^2 - a^2}{2} \right]^2}{\left[\dfrac{b^3 - a^3}{3} \right](b - a)} \right\}$$

$$= \frac{3}{4} Q \left\{ \frac{(b + a)^2 (b - a)^2}{(b^2 + ab + a^2)(b - a)(b - a)} \right\}$$

$$DQE = \frac{3}{4} Q \left\{ \frac{b^2 + 2ab + a^2}{b^2 + ab + a^2} \right\} \tag{K.61}$$

If the lower limit a is set to zero, then

$$DQE = \tfrac{3}{4} Q \tag{K.62}$$

or the DQE for DC photometry is about 25 percent less than that for pulse counting.

Other functions and experimental results give

$$0.5 \, Q \le DQE \le 0.8 \, Q$$

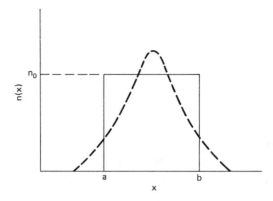

Figure K.6. Box window function.

for DC work. That is, pulse counting gives a better DQE in all cases, by as much as a factor of two. This advantage is greatest for weak signals and becomes much less for strong signals. In general, if the signal is larger than the noise, DC and pulse-counting methods are roughly equivalent, with perhaps 20 percent difference between the two techniques under good conditions. Because of a relatively narrow pulse height distribution, the 1P21 photomultiplier tube is slightly better for DC work than other types, such as the venetian blind tubes.

K.6 PRACTICAL PULSE–DC COMPARISON

In addition to the theoretical signal-to-noise comparison shown above, there are several practical comparisons that must be made when deciding which technique to use. It seems appropriate that, because we have discussed the theoretical differences, we list these observational considerations.

1. Pulse counting is relatively insensitive to amplifier drifts.
2. When high precision (less than 1 percent) is needed, pulse counting is better unless voltage-to-frequency conversion techniques are used with the DC amplifier.
3. When several measurements are to be added or a large number of observations are to be reduced, the data are much easier to handle when in digital form, obtained directly with pulse counting.
4. A digital system has a symmetric and sharp filter function, whereas DC methods have an RC filter, which tends to partially correlate readings, if a long time constant is used.

5. An analog system gives good real-time indication of sky conditions, difficult to obtain from digital methods.

6. Pulse counting provides discrimination against dark current. However, at the same time, some primary photoelectrons must be rejected. A better method to reduce dark current is to cool the photomultiplier tube.

7. Pulse counting is insensitive to leakage currents, but more sensitive to RF fields, such as generated by motors and relays in the telescope's environment.

8. Pulse counting can be performed at higher speed, DC is limited by the pen or meter movement. This advantage is negated if the DC signal is recorded on an instrumentation tape recorder and played back at a slower speed.

9. Pulse counting requires dead-time corrections that can be very significant for bright stars.

10. Complexity of instrumentation for the two methods is approximately the same.

K.7 THEORETICAL S/N COMPARISON OF A PHOTODIODE AND A PHOTOMULTIPLIER TUBE

This section is designed as an example of how two detectors can be compared on paper by their S/N characteristics. This calculation is also intended to be a fairly realistic comparison to help potential photometer builders decide between a photodiode or a photomultiplier as a detector. We have adopted the noise and quantum efficiency characteristics of the 1P21, and typical photodiode characteristics from the EG & G Electro-Optics catalog.[8]

Until now, the S/N discussion has assumed a pulse-counting photometer. However, a photodiode cannot be used for pulse counting because it lacks internal gain. The output of a photomultiplier consists of pulses, as seen in Figure 7.2, because each electron released at the photocathode is amplified by the dynode string by a factor of 10^6. Each detected photon produces a pulse that can be readily counted. Many of the noise sources within the photomultiplier produce smaller pulses at the output because they result from amplification by only part of the dynode string. It is easy to discriminate against much of the noise.

This is not the case for the photodiode because each detected photon contributes just one electron to the output current. There is no strong burst of electrons at the output when a photon is detected. The current produced by the photons looks identical to that produced by noise within the photodiode. This comparison assumes that both detectors are used with excellent quality DC amplifiers.

There are some minor modifications to be made to the S/N treatment for the DC case. Shot noise, whether for photons or electrical current, is a "white" noise. This means it is equally strong at all frequencies. The amount of noise depends on the bandpass of the amplifier. An amplifier that measures a frequency range from 1000 to 10,000 Hz detects much more noise than one that spans 1000 to 2000 Hz. Any equation for shot noise must include the width of the amplifier bandpass. For instance, photon shot noise is written as

$$N_s = G(2Q\dot{C}_s B)^{1/2} t \tag{K.63}$$

where B is the bandwidth (Hz). For pulse-counting photometry, the bandwidth has a very simple relationship with the integration time, t, namely,

$$B = \frac{1}{2t}. \tag{K.64}$$

For DC photometry, this relation is

$$B = \frac{1}{4\tau} \tag{K.65}$$

where τ is the RC time constant of the amplifier. Note that if Equation K.64 is substituted into Equation K.63, we get the same expression for photon shot noise used earlier. Also note that Equations K.64 and K.65 imply that

$$t = 2\tau.$$

Photon shot noise for the DC case is given by

$$N_s = G(2Q\dot{C}_s\tau)^{1/2}. \tag{K.66}$$

The noise sources that must be considered are the photon shot noise, shot noise from the sky background, amplifier noise, and detector noise. We ignore noise due to atmospheric scintillation because this is highly variable and a function of observatory location. Then by Equation K.40, we have

$$\left(\frac{S}{N}\right)_{out} = \frac{Q\dot{C}_s t}{\left[\left(\frac{N_s}{G}\right)^2 + \left(\frac{N_b}{G}\right)^2 + \left(\frac{N_{am}}{G}\right)^2 + \left(\frac{N_{det}}{G}\right)^2\right]^{1/2}} \tag{K.67}$$

where N_{det} is the detector noise. For a photomultiplier, this is given by the shot noise of the dark current. For the 1P21 at room temperature, N_{det} is about $2 \times 10^{-11} \, B^{1/2}$ amps or $1.3 \times 10^8 \, B^{1/2}$ electrons per second. If the tube is cooled to dry-ice temperature, N_{det} drops to 1.3×10^6 electrons per second. Persha[9] has recommended that photodiodes be used in a photovoltaic mode for astronomical photometry. In this case, there is no dark current but there is a thermal noise generated at the p-n junction given by

$$I_n = \left(\frac{4kTB}{R} \right)^{1/2} \qquad \text{(K.68)}$$

where k is Boltzmann's constant, T is the temperature (Kelvin), and R is the shunt resistance (ohms) of the photodiode. This resistance is also a function of temperature. According to the EG & G catalog, R approximately doubles for each 5 Celsius degree temperature drop. The largest shunt resistance now available is about 10^9 ohms at room temperature. The noise current for a photodiode is given by

$$I_n = 2.5 \times 10^4 \sqrt{B} \text{ electrons/second} \qquad \text{(K.69)}$$

at room temperature and

$$I_n = 413 \sqrt{B} \text{ electrons/second} \qquad \text{(K.70)}$$

at dry-ice temperature.

The amplifier noise for both detectors, referred to the amplifier input, is assumed to be $2500 \, B^{1/2}$ electrons per second. This is about the best that can be expected with present FET input amplifiers. We adopt an amplifier time constant of 1 second which fixes B at 0.25 Hz. The internal gain, G, for the photomultiplier is about 10^6 while for the photodiode, which lacks internal amplification, it is 1.0.

Using these various parameters, Equation K.67 becomes for the photomultiplier,

$$\left(\frac{S}{N} \right)_{out} = \frac{2Q\dot{C}_s \tau}{\left[2Q(\dot{C}_s + \dot{C}_b)\tau + \left(\frac{2500}{10^6} \right)^2 \frac{1}{4\tau} + \left(\frac{N_{det}}{10^6} \right)^2 \right]^{1/2}} \qquad \text{(K.71)}$$

and for the photodiode,

$$\left(\frac{S}{N} \right)_{out} = \frac{2Q\dot{C}_s \tau}{\left[2Q(\dot{C}_s + \dot{C}_b)\tau + \frac{(2500)^2}{4\tau} + \left(N_{det}^2 \right) \right]^{1/2}} \qquad \text{(K.72)}$$

The equations have been left in this form to illustrate how a high gain detector minimizes the effects of N_{am} and N_{det}. This advantage over the photodiode becomes evident in the calculations to follow.

The photon arrival rates, $\dot{C}_s$ and $\dot{C}_b$, are calculated for the B filter for various apparent magnitudes using Equation 2.33 with approximate corrections for the transmission of the atmosphere, telescope optics, and filter. A 20-centimeter (8-inch) diameter telescope is assumed. A sky background of twelfth magnitude was established from the known background at a dark site and scaled to a 0.5-millimeter diaphragm. This is a typical size for an active area of a photodiode. The quantum efficiencies at 4400 Å for the photomultiplier and photodiode are 0.10 and 0.60, respectively.

Figure K.7 shows the S/N, calculated from Equations K.71 and K.72 versus B magnitude for uncooled detectors. For very bright stars, the two detectors give comparable results. The reason for this can be seen in Equations K.71 and K.72. For very high photon rates, the S/N approaches a value of $(Q\dot{C}_s)^{1/2}$. Because $\dot{C}_s$ is the same for both detectors, the difference in S/N is set by their quantum efficiencies. In the high photon rate limit, the S/N of the photodiode should exceed that of a photomultiplier by a ratio of $(0.6/0.1)^{1/2}$ or 2.5. For all but the very brightest stars, the photomultiplier is clearly superior. This is a result of the amplifier and detector noise terms becoming important at low photon rates. These terms are not nearly as important for the photomultiplier because of its high internal gain. This more than compensates for the lower quantum efficiency of the photomultiplier.

The S/N curves become a little more meaningful if we consider an example. An 8.4 magnitude star produces a S/N of 100 with a photomultiplier tube and an amplifier time constant of 1 second. With this same time constant, this star would only produce a S/N of 4.5 with a photodiode detector. Because the S/N improves with the square root of the observing time, the observation with the photodiode would have to be 500 times the duration of the observation made with the photomultiplier to obtain the same accuracy. Finally, if we consider a S/N of 1 to be the detection limit, Figure K.7 shows that the photomultiplier can go almost four magnitudes fainter than the photodiode.

The situation improves if the photodiode is cooled to dry-ice temperature. The calculation proceeds as before except that the detector noise terms are reduced as discussed earlier. Figure K.8 shows an uncooled photomultiplier compared to a cooled photodiode. A cooled photodiode comes much closer to matching the performance of an uncooled photomultiplier tube. While the photodiode still appears to be inferior the uncertainties in the calculation are such that it is safest to say that they are roughly comparable. Figure K.9 compares detectors when both are cooled to dry-ice temperature. The photomultiplier has a superior S/N for stars fainter than fifth magnitude while the photodiode is

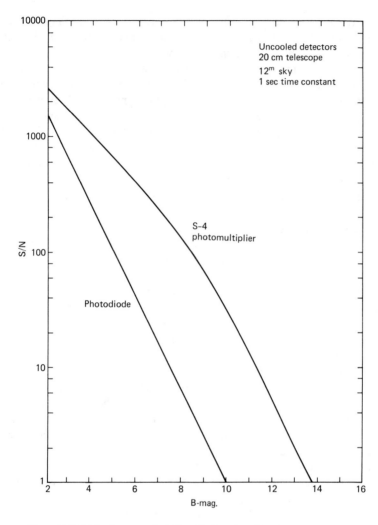

Figure K.7. S/N of an uncooled photodiode and an S-4 photomultiplier tube.

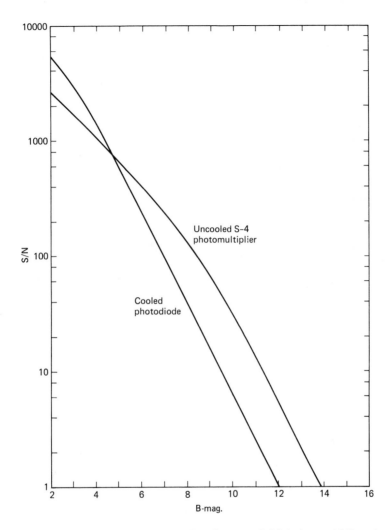

Figure K.8. S/N of a cooled photodiode and an uncooled S-4 photomultiplier tube.

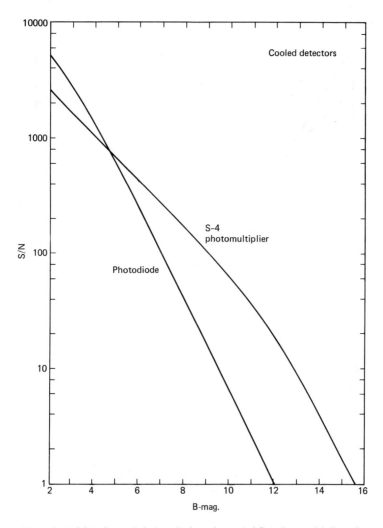

Figure K.9. S/N of a cooled photodiode and a cooled S-4 photomultiplier tube.

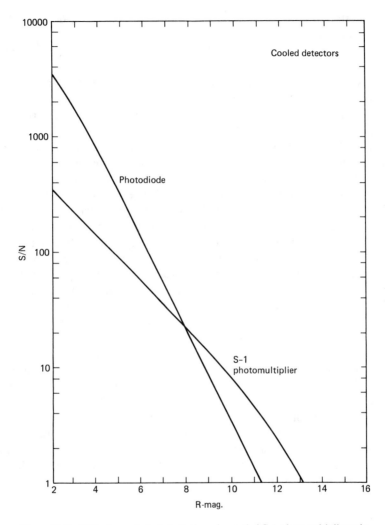

Figure K.10. S/N of a cooled photodiode and a cooled S-1 photomultiplier tube.

better for stars brighter than this. The photomultiplier has a detection limit about 3.5 magnitudes fainter than the photodiode.

Unlike the S-4 response of the 1P21, the photodiode has very high quantum efficiency in the near-infrared. The above calculation was repeated for the R bandpass (7000 Å) comparing the photodiode to an S-1 photomultiplier. Both detectors were assumed to be cooled. The superior quantum efficiency of the photodiode makes a significant difference in the infrared. An S-1 surface has a quantum efficiency of only 0.4 percent compared to the photodiode's 83 percent at 7000 Å. Figure K.10 shows that this difference makes the photodiode a superior detector down to the eighth magnitude, despite the higher internal gain of the photomultiplier. The curves would look much the same in the I bandpass (9000 Å) because the quantum efficiencies are nearly the same.

The above calculations are intended only as a rough comparison of these two detectors. The S/N curve for the photomultiplier has been checked at a few points with observational data and has compared well. Unfortunately, the authors have not had access to comparable empirical data for a photodiode photometer. However, we suspect that the theoretical calculation is not in large error. Figures K.7, K.8, K.9, and K.10 can be used to draw some general conclusions about detector selection. First, if you intend to use an uncooled detector, the photomultiplier tube is clearly the better detector. If you can design and build a cooling system, the photodiode will be only slightly inferior to an uncooled photomultiplier. A cooled photodiode offers the convenience of a single detector with sensitivity from the ultraviolet to the infrared. However, in general, the high internal gain of the photomultiplier makes it a superior detector overall. Finally, it should be noted that the photomultiplier has a potential S/N gain over the photodiode, which has not been included in these calculations. Because of its high internal gain, the photomultiplier can be used to photon count. By the results of Section K.5, this means an additional increase of as much as a factor of $\sqrt{2}$ in the S/N compared to the photodiode, which must use DC measuring techniques.

REFERENCES

1. Young, H. D. 1962. *Statistical Treatment of Experimental Data.* New York: McGraw-Hill.
2. Harnell, D. L. 1975. *Introduction to Statistical Methods.* 2d ed. Reading, Mass.: Addison-Wesley.
3. Bevington, P. R. 1969. *Data Reduction and Error Analysis for the Physical Sciences.* New York: McGraw-Hill.
4. Young, A. T. 1974. In *Methods of Experimental Physics: Astrophysics,* Edited by N. Carleton. New York: Academic Press, vol. **12A.**

5. Golay, M. 1974. *Introduction to Astronomical Photometry*. Boston: D. Reidel.
6. Meaburn, J. 1976. *Detection and Spectrometry of Faint Light*. Boston: D. Reidel.
7. Arfken, G. 1970. *Mathematical Methods for Physicists*. New York: Academic Press.
8. EG & G Electro-Optics Division, 35 Congress St., Salem, Mass. 01970.
9. Persha, G. 1980. IAPPP Com. **2**, 11.
10. Meaburn, J. 1976. *Detection and Spectrometry of Faint Light*. Boston: D. Reidel.

INDEX

Software for Astronomical Photometry

The authors of this book have written software intended to aid in the reduction of astronomical photoelectric photometry data from either a pulse counting or DC photometer system. This software is composed of a suite of 7 major programs, 4 utility programs and 6 standard star files. The major programs are:

1. DATA provides a means for entering the raw observational data and creating an output file for use by other programs.

2. STARLIST creates a file containing information about the observed stars which is used by several other programs.

3. INSTRU uses the files created by DATA and STARLIST to make an output file containing the heliocentric Julian date, universal time, air mass and instrumental magnitude for each filter of each star.

4. DIFF is for reducing differential photometry using an instrumental magnitude file created by INSTRU.

5. EXTINC a program that allows the user to select from four different methods of extinction coefficient determination.

6. COEFF computes the transformation coefficients to the standard photometric system.

7. CONVERT uses the coefficients in the TRAN.DAT file to convert the instrumental magnitudes found in the input file to standard magnitudes and colors.

The utility programs are:

1. JULDATE computes the Julian date from a given UT date or optionally computes the heliocentric time correction if the object's coordinates are entered

2. PRECESS will precess the coordinates of a star between any two epochs.

3. **DTIME** computes the dead time correction to the count rate entered at the keyboard. The dead time coefficient can be read from the **PARAM.DAT** file or it can be entered from the keyboard.

4. **SIDTIME** computes the local sidereal time from the UT date and time. The observer's longitude can be read from either the **PARAM.DAT** file or the keyboard.

The standard star files, from the appendices of *Astronomical Photometry*, in the **STARLIST** format are:

1. **PLEIADES.LST** contains the UBV data for the Pleiades cluster.

2. **M44.LST** contains the UBV data for the Praesepe cluster (M44).

3. **IC4665.LST** contains the UBV data for the cluster IC4665.

4. **1ORDER.LST** is the northern hemisphere first-order extinction table from Appendix A

5. **2ORDER.LST** is the second-order extinction table from Appendix B

6. **JOHNSON.LST** is a list of all of the Johnson UBV standards

7. **LANDOLT.LST** contains the 223 Landolt UBVRI Equatorial Standards.

All of these programs are designed to run on an IBM PC or compatible system, with or without a math co-processor chip. If a co-processor is present the computations will be greatly accelerated. The programs require no more than 128K of memory to run.

The output from most of the programs is in the form of an ASCII disk file. These files are read by the other programs and can be typed to the screen or printed by the user to record the various stages of the reduction process. Because these files are ASCII in form, they can be edited with a text editor if so desired. This is sometimes helpful to correct an input error that affected only one star in the file.

The programs are written in FORTRAN 77 and *both* source code and executable (compiled) programs are provided.

ORDER FORM

Please send me: ☐ *Astronomical Photometry Software*   **$39.95**

I wish to have this software in the following media

☐ Three (3) 360K 5.25-inch IBM-PC diskettes

☐ Two (2) 720K 3.5-inch IBM-PC diskettes

Handling[1]   **1.00**

TOTAL $_____

I wish to pay with:
☐ **Check** ☐ **Money Order**
☐ **Visa**   ☐ **MasterCard**   ☐ **American Express**

Card No._____

Card expiration date_____

Signature_____

Name (Please Print)_____

Street_____

City, State, ZIP_____

Willmann–Bell, Inc.
P.O. Box 35025
Richmond, Virginia, 23235
Voice (804) 320-7016 FAX (802) 272-5920

---

[1]Foreign orders: shipping charges are additional. Write for proforma invoice which details your exact costs for various shipping options.

Thinking Allegory Otherwise

Edited by Brenda Machosky

STANFORD UNIVERSITY PRESS

STANFORD, CALIFORNIA

Stanford University Press
Stanford, California

This book has been published with the assistance of The Stanford Fund, The Office of the Vice Provost for Undergraduate Education, and The School of Humanities and Sciences at Stanford University.

Essay One was originally published in *boundary2*, volume 3, no. 1 (Spring). Copyright, Duke University Press. Reprinted with permission.

Printed in the United States of America on acid-free, archival-quality paper

Library of Congress Cataloging-in-Publication Data
Thinking allegory otherwise / edited by Brenda Machosky.
    p. cm.
    Originates from a conference held at Stanford University in February 2005.
    Includes bibliographical references and index.
    ISBN 978-0-8047-6380-6 (cloth : alk. paper)
    1. Allegory—Congresses. I. Machosky, Brenda.
    PN56.A5T49 2010
    809'.915—dc22

                                        2009028684

Typeset by Thompson Type in 11/14 Adobe Garamond.

Contents

Acknowledgments

A collection such as this depends on the good will of many people and the generous support of many others. This collection is the sequel to a conference of the same name. Stanford University President John Hennessy provided financial support for the conference and this publication through The Stanford Fund. Generous funding was also provided by John Bravman, Vice Provost for Undergraduate Education, and Arnold Rampersad, Cognizant Dean of the Humanities. In the Office of the President, I would like to thank Jeffrey Wachtel, Senior Assistant to the President, for his support of this project. The Stanford Humanities Center, then under the direction of John Bender, provided an intellectually pleasant atmosphere for the original conference. My colleagues, Hans Ulrich Gumbrecht and Robert Harrison, encouraged this project and helped bring it to fruition. At Stanford University, this project has also received support from the Division of Literatures, Cultures, and Languages; the Departments of French and Italian, Comparative Literature, and English; The Philosophical Reading Group; The Program in Continuing Studies; The Introduction to the Humanities Program; and Interdisciplinary Studies in the Humanities. The conference and this book would not have proceeded so smoothly without the help of Monica Moore, Ruth Kaplan, and Ryan Zurowski. Thanks also to the reviewers, including Bruce T. Clarke, who provided insightful comments on the final organization and production of this collection. I am particularly grateful to Norris Pope and the editorial staff at Stanford University Press, who have provided kind and helpful guidance through this process. I owe especial thanks to the contributors of the volume. These scholars have made my editing job easy and pleasant. I appreciate their patience with me, their enthusiasm for this work, and their continued commitment to thinking allegory otherwise.

Contributors

JODY ENDERS is a past editor of *Theatre Survey* and is the author of numerous articles and four books on the interplay of rhetoric, literature, performance theory, law, and the theatrical culture of the European Middle Ages, among them *Death by Drama and Other Medieval Urban Legends* (Chicago, 2002, and winner of the Barnard Hewitt Award) and *Murder by Accident: Medieval Theater, Modern Media, Critical Intentions* (Chicago, 2009). She is Professor of French and Theater at the University of California, Santa Barbara.

ANGUS FLETCHER is Distinguished Professor Emeritus, CUNY Graduate School. Author of several books and articles on literary theory and history, he published *A New Theory for American Poetry: Democracy, Environment, and the Future of Imagination* (Harvard, 2004), which won the Truman Capote Prize. In 2007, Harvard published his book, *Time, Space and Motion in the Age of Shakespeare*. In 2008, he served as J. Paul Getty Research Professor, Los Angeles. Currently he is finishing a book on change and complexity as these occur in the arts and sciences, particularly focusing on the works of Joseph Conrad, Thomas Mann, Karel Capek, and J. G. Ballard.

BLAIR HOXBY, Associate Professor of English at Stanford University, is the author of *Mammon's Music: Literature and Economics in the Age of Milton* (Yale, 2002). His recent research has focused on early modern tragedy, opera, and allegorical drama. His forthcoming *Spectacles of the Gods: Tragedy and Tragic Opera, 1550–1780* reconstructs a set of deep assumptions and performance practices that cross national boundaries and makes the early modern period a distinct and meaningful time-section in the history of theater.

KAREN S. FELDMAN is Assistant Professor of German at University of California, Berkeley. Her book, *Binding Words: Conscience and Rhetoric in Hobbes, Hegel and Heidegger*, appeared with Northwestern in 2006. She has also published articles on philosophy and literary theory in *Journal of the History of Ideas, Philosophy and Rhetoric, Word & Image*, and *Angelaki*.

BRENDA MACHOSKY is an Assistant Professor of English at University of Hawaii West Oahu, where she teaches English, world literature, and drama. Her book *Faces of Allegory* is forthcoming with Fordham. She has published articles on allegory and literary theory in *SEL, Exemplaria*, and *Comparative Literature Studies*. Her current research focuses on allegory in postcolonial literature and other unusual places.

CATHERINE GIMELLI MARTIN teaches Renaissance literature at the University of Memphis. Her major publications include *The Ruins of Allegory: "Paradise Lost" and the Metamorphosis of Epic Convention* (Duke, 1998; James Holly Hanford Award winner, 1999); *Francis Bacon and the Refiguring of Early Modern Thought* (coedited with Julie Solomon, Ashgate, 2005), and *Milton and Gender* (Cambridge, 2004). She has also published numerous essays on early modern literature, science, and politics.

STEPHEN ORGEL is the J. E. Reynolds Professor in the Humanities at Stanford University. His most recent books are *Imagining Shakespeare* (Palgrave, 2003), and *The Authentic Shakespeare* (Routledge, 2002). He has edited *The Tempest* and *The Winter's Tale* in the Oxford Shakespeare and is the general editor, with A. R. Braunmuller, of the new Pelican Shakespeare.

JAMES J. PAXSON, Associate Professor of English at the University of Florida, is the author of *The Poetics of Personification*. He continues to work on the history and function of rhetorical "master tropes" in poetics and an account of cosmology for the forthcoming *Routledge Companion to Literature and Science*. He is an editor of *Exemplaria: A Journal of Theory in Medieval and Renaissance Studies*.

MAUREEN QUILLIGAN is the R. Florence Brinkley Professor of English at Duke University and former department chair. She is the author of books on allegory, on Spenser and Milton, and on writing by women in the Middle Ages and the Renaissance. She is currently at work on a book about royal female authority in sixteenth-century Britain and France.

DANIEL SELCER is Associate Professor of Philosophy at Duquesne University, where he specializes in early modern thought, connections between philosophy and rhetoric, and French poststructuralism. He is the author of *Philosophy and the Book: Early Modern Figures of Material Inscription*, forthcoming with Continuum Books (2010).

GORDON TESKEY is Professor of English at Harvard University. He is author of *Allegory and Violence* (Cornell, 1996) and of *Delirous Milton* (Harvard, 2006), which won the Milton Society of America's James Holly Hanford award. Gordon Teskey is editor of the Norton edition of *Paradise Lost*. He is writing on Spenser and Milton, as usual.

RICHARD WITTMAN is Associate Professor in the Department of the History of Art and Architecture at UC Santa Barbara. His book, *Architecture, Print Culture, and the Public Sphere in Eighteenth-Century France*, was published by Routledge in 2007.

Introduction

"A Protean Device"

BRENDA MACHOSKY

Embedded in museum displays, providing the structure for scientific thought, underlying the legal system, evading the hegemony of the idea, allegory is thriving in the twenty-first century. The call to "think allegory otherwise" initially led to a stimulating academic conference at Stanford University in February 2005. Some of the usual suspects were present, but there were also new voices, young scholars and academic veterans who were willing (and eager) to consider their work in an allegorical mode. The final result is this collection of essays, and our hope is to inspire broader and deeper engagements with this "protean device," as Angus Fletcher so aptly named it.[1] Even though the work contained herein has evolved and changed substantially since the conference, the title of the conference has been retained because "thinking allegory otherwise" remains the best descriptor of this limitless project.

Allegory is perhaps as old as language itself and certainly as variable as the languages and styles in which it has been written. The early readers of Homer allegorized the great epics. Philo of Alexandria adapted an allegorical system of interpretation for the Hebrew Bible. Augustine carefully explained the structure of allegory inherent in language. Aquinas differentiated the allegory of the theologians from the allegory of the poets. Dante countered Aquinas with a divine allegorical poem. In the medieval period, allegorical figures took the stage in mystery plays and pageants, adorned churches and monuments. De Lorris and De Meun, Chaucer, Tasso, Pizan—all produced fabulous works of allegory. Even during the Reformation, when icons were suspect, allegory maintained its presence. The Romantics tried to devalue allegory's particular system of representation, preferring the presumed coincident signification of the symbol, but allegory persisted. Walter Benjamin and Paul de Man challenged the Romantic view, and allegory became a formidable force in literary theory of the twentieth century. And allegory also continues to receive uninterrupted attention in the study of medieval and early modern works. Between occasional pinnacles, allegory has maintained a constant presence in artistic forms and humanistic study. All on its own, allegory inspires great works of literature and insightful commentary.

The powerful works of allegory can be so inspiring, in fact, that it is hard to wrest free of their influence. What person writing about allegory in English literature can avoid Spenser? In French, who can avoid *Le Roman de la Rose*? What allegorical theorist can ignore the Romantic judgment? This volume challenges such limits. Some of the greatest minds thinking about allegory in the past few decades were asked to think about it differently. And what of the great thinkers who haven't really thought about allegory? These scholars were challenged to think otherwise just by thinking about allegory. The results harness the excitement of a conference in presenting a variety of topics, not restricted to historical period or generic mode, in offering experimental ideas, in posing complex questions, in provoking further discussion and inspiring new work.

Angus Fletcher challenges the role of metaphysics in allegory by thinking about allegory without reference to ideas. Gordon Teskey reads the allegorical construction of colonialism and the ideology of the museum. Richard Wittman, an architectural historian boldly entering the fray, discovers allegorical structures in the architectural debates and broadsides of early modern Paris. Daniel Selcer reveals allegory in the performative aspects of diagrams in texts by Bruno and Galileo. Karen Feldman identifies an allegorical structure in philosophy by way of Hannah Arendt's *Life of the Mind*. James Paxson explores the place of allegory in contemporary scientific discourse. Literary texts also receive new treatment in the essays by Maureen

Quilligan (Christine de Pizan and Mary Wroth), Stephen Orgel (Spenser), Blair Hoxby (John Ford and Henry Purcell), and Catherine Gimelli Martin (Bacon and Milton).

In the opening essay, Fletcher's thinking primes us for a reconsideration of allegory in a variety of modes and serves as an apt introduction to the entire volume. Fletcher dives deeply into the problem of thinking allegory otherwise by thinking "Allegory without Ideas."[2] This seminal essay rethinks the allegorical tradition against what it has become and suggests a new "origin" with connections to ancient philosophy (Aristotle), medieval challenges to universalism (Ockham), and modern theories of nominalism (Quine). The essay is the sort of de/re/construction of which only a scholar of Fletcher's erudite breadth and freely roaming thought is capable.

In the first part, "Performing Allegory," only one of the three essays focuses on theatrical production as such. The drama is but one form in which allegory takes the stage. With her extensive knowledge of medieval theater, Jody Enders turns to the performance of the law in medieval France and articulates the ways in which allegory was embedded in the performance of capital punishment. Enders argues that the death penalty, especially in its medieval performances, is a supremely allegorical event in which criminals become signs of themselves, simultaneously literal and allegorical. Death penalty victims, in staging their own death, allegorize themselves. And Enders does not leave her observations in the medieval past. She forces us to consider the significance of the modern tendency to hide the images of a justice that imposes death. True to the promise in her title, "Back to the Medieval Future," Enders's realizations about the performative executions of the past point out the darkened allegory that continues to haunt the practice of capital punishment in the present.

In his essay on Galileo's *Massimi sistemi* and Bruno's *La Cena de le Cenari*, Daniel Selcer points out that performative allegory also plays a role in the written text. Selcer demonstrates that the drawing (or misdrawing) of Copernicus's diagram within the dialogues of Galileo's and Bruno's texts is itself a staging that takes place on the surfaces of the pages themselves, "a materialization of natural contemplation." Developing the implicit and explicit critiques and reconfigurations of allegory presented by both philosophers, Selcer shows that Galileo's text advocates a "script" of "naturalized allegory" in which the book of the universe is written, while Bruno claims that the field of philosophical contemplation is the only one in which the extreme tendencies of allegorical language can be controlled. Empirical data and mathematical order are shown to constitute a series of figures with which meaningful scientific discourse will correspond. The book of nature receives the allegorical text otherwise limited by Galileo to the sacred book. The allegorical nature of nature requires its readers to read allegorically. For both Galileo and Bruno, the philosophical-scientific text is a performance of allegory in which the authors, the characters, and the readers must participate.

Concluding the part on performance is Blair Hoxby's revised theory of allegory in baroque tragic drama. Counter to the claims of Walter Benjamin that the *Trauerspiel* or "tragic drama" is a demonstration of mourning and melancholy distinctly different from "tragedy" that induces a response of mourning, Hoxby argues that "tragic drama" uses allegorical modes in tandem with dramatic mimesis to create an experience of mourning. He challenges and expands Benjamin's notions of the genre by examining a conventionally "tragic drama," *The Broken Heart*, replete with the accoutrements of death so characteristic of Benjamin's view. However, through a detailed reading of Purcell's *Dido and Aeneas*, Hoxby also shows how the trappings of mourning are not essential to the form. This theatrical experience reconnects these dramas to ritual practices and the origin of drama itself. Thus Hoxby aligns the experience of tragic drama with seventeenth-century expectations about the pleasure of mourning.

Allegory has also been performed in more concrete media, particularly in public buildings and monuments, where figures or other conventional images are designed to express meaning. In the next part, Gordon Teskey and Richard Wittman expand the thinking of allegory in these other spaces. Teskey's study follows the Colonial Exhibition of 1931 through its ideological display and its current place in the recently opened Musée du Quai Branly. Teskey continues to acknowledge the violent capture of meaning constitutive of allegory, as thoroughly articulated in his book, *Allegory and Violence*. However, he also notes a fundamental change in the convention of allegory through the history of colonialism, as represented in the museum and in service of French nationalist ideology. Whereas the allegorical body has traditionally served to both bear and conceal meaning, in the modern context, especially (but not exclusively) of colonialism, the body bears its use value and serves to conceal an imperial ideology. Be it a diorama of "live natives" at work or the very locus of the exhibition in the working-class suburbs of Paris and the subsequent shifting frames of reference into which such images are forced, in modernity *work* itself becomes the work of allegory.

Likewise, Richard Wittman brings allegory into a new realm of consideration, the history of architecture. Wittman studies the architecture and city planning of eighteenth-century Paris—in practice and in writing. Most people are familiar with the allegories built into churches and other edifices through the time of the Renaissance. The Enlightenment mood of the eighteenth century, however, precluded complex allegorical figures and styles in favor of transparency and clarity. However, as conventional allegory disappeared from actual buildings, Wittman observes, it resurfaced in criticism of those buildings. Even more interesting, allegory became a determining feature in written proposals for buildings and monuments never intended to materialize. By means of a narrative discursive practice, allegory provided a way for architecture to express its meaning without a material edifice. In a way, allegory became the material of architectural theory.

The Renaissance is an epoch that cannot escape allegorical consideration, and thus the third section revisits allegory in this important period. Whereas Wittman's essay shows allegory as a means for an absolute abstraction from materiality, Maureen Quilligan's contribution establishes a materiality in works where allegory seemed mostly abstraction. In rethinking allegory in the Renaissance, Quilligan returns to Christine de Pizan's *City of Ladies* and the way in which Pizan literalizes the metaphor of her literary work. With a close reading and reworking of Teskey's argument in *Allegory and Violence*, Quilligan contributes a new and convincing argument in the long-standing discussion of the typically female gender of personifications and allegorical figures as materially and not merely metaphorically (or linguistically) gendered. In doing so, Quilligan also situates the female writers Christine de Pizan and Mary Wroth in a distinctive relationship against and within the patriarchal tradition of allegory.

Stephen Orgel, like Quilligan, discovers the fact of female agency within the patriarchal situations of sex and power in chivalric literature and art. In Spenser, and in a series of courtly images, Orgel shows that it is the women who are more typically active and the men passive. By considering "What Knights Really Want," Orgel thinks through allegory without writing about allegory. His essay is important for what it does not do. The essay does not construe knights as conventional allegorical signs. Knights, in general and as individuals, do not *mean* something else. Chivalry is likewise not a metaphor for some other ideal. However, in the figures of Spenser's knights, and in the women they love, Orgel reads a profound "message" about the tension between illicit sex and idealized love that underlies the chivalric tradition. Through a combination of textual and visual analysis, Orgel realizes that sex in Spenser, and in chivalry in general, is not a masculine action but a feminine one.

Catherine Gimelli Martin also revisits conventional views of Renaissance allegory and establishes a more complex understanding of the materiality of allegorical figures in Milton and Bacon. Walter Benjamin, Michel Foucault, and other modern theorists have shown how the status of knowledge changed radically in the seventeenth century. Martin's essay, together with Hoxby's on seventeenth-century tragic drama and Selcer's on Galileo and Bruno, explores the changes in the allegorical mode as expressions of this epistemological shift. Martin continues to think through the implications for particular allegorical figures in Milton's *Paradise Lost* and their ideological originals in Bacon's *Advancement of Learning*. As Quilligan shows how female agency is as material as it is metaphorical in Renaissance allegory, Martin reminds us that allegorical significance depends not merely on an absent meaning but on a material presence as well.

Each essay included here explores the significance of allegory's presence in all language, in the very being of language as such. The presence of allegory, in even the most ostensibly objective and straightforward language of sciences, forces us to think differently about allegory as such and to reconsider its essential value not only in our own language and forms of knowledge but also in our very way of being. Indeed, this ontological question is the driving force of the project to think allegory otherwise, and the concluding section brings allegory into dialogue with modern philosophical and scientific concerns. Karen Feldman argues that, as a form of metaphysical language, allegory constitutes the conditions of thinking and philosophy. Like Fletcher, Feldman points out that allegory provides the means for "imageless thought" (or thinking without ideas). She traces how the process of metaphorization makes "imageless thought" possible because figurality bridges the "two worlds" so essential to much of Western philosophy, but she also shows that this is not necessarily a hierarchical relation. This realization in turn challenges the oft-accepted view of allegory as a hierarchy, one privileging the signified, the meaning, over the sign or the figure. Nonetheless, allegory remains a slippery device. Feldman shows that while Hannah Arendt brings out the allegory of uncertainty in the history of philosophy, she does not fully realize the allegory of uncertainty within her own thought on figuration.

James Paxson concludes the volume with a challenge to the very realm that would seem most impervious to the threat of allegory, science. Paxson argues that most of the advancements in mathematical thinking, particularly in physics, depend on an implicit allegorical structure. He argues that by recognizing the role of allegory in scientific discourse and by not perceiving it as a "threat" to a scientific way of thinking, we may, in fact, gain a greater understanding of modern science. As Feldman demonstrated within philosophy, so Paxson argues that science itself will benefit by allowing for and realizing the presence of allegory in its theories and its evolution.

The collection proves that there is no going back to the old, established ways of thinking about allegory. And yet, it also manifests a realization about allegory that we should have known all along. The standard definition for "allegory" is to say one thing and mean another. Allegory has always demanded that we think otherwise. While the contributors to this volume faced a challenge in thinking allegory otherwise, the resulting essays demonstrate the facility and flexibility that this "protean device" really has and the pervasive power that it exerts in all language, not merely in the explicitly figural language of poetry and art but, far more interestingly, in the literal language of architecture, nationalism, philosophy, science, and even in the literal language of art and literature.

Those of us who work with allegory often feel defensive about the topic. There is a rumor, a perception, that allegory is passé, not as interesting as other modes of interpretation and theory. In fact, this collection, along with the books and articles and conferences about allegory that appear each year, proves that this perception really is just a rumor. The rumor perhaps reveals more about those who propagate it than about allegory as such. The rumor is perhaps an attempt to disempower an indisputable force in language of all kinds. Even in historical moments when it doesn't receive pronounced attention, allegory has always continued its work.

As part of its protean nature, allegory changes not only its form and its applications but even its name. Allegory is not always called allegory. This is what so many of the essays here prove. The thinking of allegory cannot be limited to the things that call themselves allegory. Self-identified allegory may provide clues about how allegory works; but, even then, as the essays that here revisit established allegories show, the ways of allegory challenge us to think otherwise. We hope that this volume will promote a continued conversation, a broader and deeper thinking of allegory. More than this, however, we hope that this collection will inspire more thinking otherwise, not only to think allegory otherwise, but that, in thinking allegory, thought will think itself in other ways.

Notes

1. Angus Fletcher, *Allegory: Theory of a Symbolic Mode* (Ithaca, NY, and London: Cornell University Press, 1964), p.1.

2. Angus Fletcher originally wrote this paper for a plenary session of the conference. The essay was first published in *Boundary2* (Spring 2006) and has been reproduced here by permission of *boundary 2*.

Allegory without Ideas

A N G U S   J .   S .   F L E T C H E R

I

As Renaissance authors used to say, allegory is the captain of all rhetorical figures of speech, and we might ask, Is it a ship of fools or a dreadnought? Certainly this "figure of false *semblaunt*" commands a large percentage of the world's symbolic activity, mainly because it permits the iconic rendering of power relations. Realism in fiction, history, and journalism may seek the inherent power connection of allegory, as we know from its structural properties, especially its demonic agency and cosmic range. The key to understanding how allegory works is to focus on its mode of agency, and here we find that from ancient times to the present, under varying guises, the demonic—not necessarily bad—is the embodiment of primordial agency; the *daimons* of Greek myth have a unique power to act without impediment, obeying a system of absolute, single-minded, purified intention. By

This essay is reprinted, with slight revisions. See Angus Fletcher, "Allegory without Ideas," in *boundary2*, volume 3, no. 1 (Spring), pp. 77–98. Copyright, Duke University Press. All rights reserved. Used by permission of the publisher.

radically simplifying purpose, the allegorist looks at life *as if* it were a game of getting and exploiting power. This confers on the method a vast general relevance, while other broad modalities do not have either this semiotic depth or this cultural—and significantly religious—usage. Even prophecy and typology in biblical interpretation lack the allegorical scope.

If iconologies of power are the issue, it must follow that we cannot understand the languages of politics and their rhetoric until we understand the allegorical method. It makes no difference what particular political order is in place; the defining allegorical structures will operate and will convert to the new situation, whenever a major political or cultural change of manifold occurs. Let us for reference purposes consider a rough rhetorical definition: Allegory is a method of double meanings that organizes utterance (in any medium) according to its expression of analogical parallels between different networks of iconic likeness. In setting up its correspondences between a certain story, let's say, and a set of meanings (the *significatio* of medieval exegesis), the method usually gives a vague impression of system. As rhetoricians ancient and modern perceived the process, a particular allegory will be either a composition or an interpretation based on a correspondence between images and agents (actions and the impressions they make) falling on one side of a wall of correspondence. Allegorical narratives, say a biblical parable or an Aesopian fable such as *Animal Farm*, lead us to imagine a set of meanings located on the other side of this hermeneutic wall. In political and cultural terms, these meanings lying on the other side of the wall comprise parts of the whole of an ideology—its commentary and interpretation.

Because allegory is a mix of making and reading combined in one mode, its nature is to produce a ruminative self-reflexivity. A large-scale allegory such as *The Divine Comedy* tends always to ruminate on its own levels of meaning, its own hermeneutic imperative, in a fashion we do not encounter, for example, with realism as in the novel or in historical writing. Self-reflection is obsessively an aspect of the allegorical method itself; that is, allegory works by defining itself in its enigmatic use. The motto of the mode might well be the line from Shakespeare's Sonnet 64, on time and the poet's destiny: "Ruin hath taught me thus to ruminate." The rumination focuses on symbolic activity occurring on both sides of an interpretive barrier. If my rather too solid wall metaphor holds, there is in allegory something odd about the wall; each side seems cognizant of the other's activity, but each needs to accept that a semiotic barrier of some kind intervenes between story and significance. For centuries it was common to think of allegory as the semiotic medium for enigmatic thoughts.

Two attributes of a basic ritual process—the traditional use of the interpretive guide—will illuminate this process, whereby interpretation is darkly enclosed within the boundaries of the fiction itself. Following this tradition of the interpretive guide, in *The Divine Comedy* Virgil and Beatrice accompany the narrator Dante; in *The Pilgrim's Progress* a variety of friends counsel Christian on the meaning of his journey. Thus, in *The Divine Comedy*, the poet is shown the enigmatic meaning of his travel though the other world, meeting strange or strangely familiar persons from history or vision. These encounters constitute Dante the narrator's experience of "the state of souls after death," and they create in the reader a powerful curiosity and desire to interpret each step of the mysterious journey. So also in John Bunyan's great Protestant work, Christian (and later his wife, Christiana, and their children) travels on a progress from temporal defeat to resurrection, and all along the way the story suggests ideas of trial, choice, hope, and fear attending that journey. Particular moments and events stem from a larger vision, in this case the virtually cosmic idea of a Christian life. Story and idea, both sides rather complex, are twinned along the journey. This ingemination, as a Renaissance poet would call it, amounts to a belief that creation and interpretation are doubles of each other; they need each other. If a poet writes an allegory, the resulting poem apparently invokes and then controls its own interpretation. In a modern science fiction novel, Walter Miller's *A Canticle for Leibowitz*, the interpretive guiding principle is inherent to the discovery of Leibowitz's banal shopping-list relic, a discovery made not casually but by a member of a desert religious order.

The principle of organization by which a story implies a set of parallel meanings will obviously not work with stories told merely for the sake of the plot; why should any tale as such correspond to anything except perhaps life itself? The story has to be structured to project repeatedly implied sets of oblique meanings. It then follows that ritual plays a central role in all allegorical compositions or readings.[1] In my own general theory of allegory, I have shown how such ritual spreads its effects widely, from an obsessive-compulsive psychic origin to the massed cultural inventions of sacred liturgical rituals or rituals of political rhetoric. Ritual seems to be one way to prevent excessive questioning of the wall metaphor to which I have referred, as if repeated actions could ease a hidden stress between the image and meaning. A skeptical view asks naturally for the grounding of such beliefs and practices, while to a great extent the unquestioning answer can usefully be that allegories flourish in the form of ritual interpretations. Given this ritual protection from skepticism, there seems to be no limit, either in religious history or elsewhere, to the number of adumbrations that may load discourse with extra meanings. Even when the plain sense of literal meaning conflicts with evolved doctrine of any kind, allegorical rituals employ methods of *accommodating* a privileged text to the system of ideas; another word for this accommodating art is *commentary*, and yet another, the broad term *interpretation*.

2

The interpretive dance of allegory is an ancient literary phenomenon, no doubt as old as the desire to convert speech and writing into "scripture," where sacred writ is accorded an authoritative status. In the sixth century B.C., it was possible to read Homeric epic as an allegory of physical forces, so that the apparent irrationality of the chthonic and Olympian gods was made into an acceptable allegorical parallel to nature's wildness. Much later, with the establishment of the Christian church, a quite different mode of accommodation developed into an elaborate semiotic system, whereby all events could be read as implying the omnipotent providence of God. The system of interpretation keeps on changing its court of appeal, usually slowly, but at times fast.

Medieval practice seems to be the most revealing stage to examine before attempting any reach into the strange kind of allegory I am proposing. Let us recall the most familiar tag from medieval Christian exegesis, the four-fold method, which is known to poets and theologians alike. Reams have been written—Henri de Lubac wrote four densely packed volumes—on this simple statement of policy, its origins in Judaism and early Christianity, and on the various ways allegory could be found in and around biblical texts, sermons, secular literature, and life in general. The interpretive method was encapsulated in four mnemonic lines:

Littera gesta docet;
Quod credas allegoria;
Quid agas moralia;
Quo tendas anagogia.

Loosely translating, we get:

> The letter teaches events, actions, and history;
> What you believe is the allegory;
> What you should do is the moral;
> Whither you leaning (your final purpose) is the anagogy.

Christian exegetes often reduced the fourfold to a dyadic set, with the first half being the literal sense of a text and items two, three, and four together constituting the "spiritual" interpretation of the letter. Augustine would have seen the method in that way, recognizing paradoxically that the literal is the most subtle part of the fourfold, for without a degree of grammar, utterance, and rhetoric, the letter could not function at all; because on the biblical view God created by speaking, no derived or original sacred text could be a pure grapheme, functioning as pure Derridean *différance*. Even so, while the chief mystery of language is packed into the first level—the literal—there is also, according to this patristic view, a standard efflux of extra meanings, those other three levels. Massive medieval texts, such as the *Cosmographia* of the twelfth-century author Bernard Silvestris, typically exfoliate their meanings in complex designs, all of them streaming from the fourfold sense of the text. The method descends especially from close readings of the works of Saint Augustine, for example, his treatise *On the Trinity*. The hermeneutic adventure has been fully documented and analyzed by modern scholars such as M. D. Chenu, Jean Daniélou, de Lubac, Jean Pépin, A. C. Charity, and, more recently, Jon Whitman, who, in his book on allegory, has reduced the wealth of issues to a manageable and analytically helpful conspectus.[2] The medieval fourfold system of reading is obviously the source of a rich semiotic because it can range from the most physical of senses to the most mysterious; if what is morally of concern (in the third level) is not understood as to its form of belief (second level), there will be a gap in the overall sense being conveyed, a kind of fragmentary loss of coherence. In fact, the four levels continuously modify each other as to meaning.

What is remarkable is that no exegetical scholar has given any weight to what appears to be the philosophical source of the fourfold system, that is, the theory of the four causes given in the *Metaphysics* and *Physics* of Aristotle. In Aristotle, all events and all change (as with natural motion, or kinesis) occur in relation to the four aspects, or "fashions," of causation, as the philosopher Jonathan Lear would say.[3] First, the material cause virtually states its own character because objects and events are composed in some sense materially, of matter, in one respect or another. Materiality is hence an initial type of causal efficacy. Second, things and events have a formal cause, in that the design of their changing gives a second essential attribute of their potential for change. Third, things and events have an efficient cause because they need energy and thrust to bring about their motion from a potential to actual state. Fourth, they possess a final cause, for any movement or change of state—materialized, formalized, and energized— still requires a goal or purpose, an end toward which their changing aspires. This famous tetrad directly parallels the medieval fourfold method of interpretation, and one can only suppose its neglect in the commentaries to result from a refusal of the secular aspect of the *Physics*.

The reason I stress this neglect is that it marks a failure to note the pre-Christian physical basis of the history of allegory. By neglecting to see that the allegorist's four levels of meanings are actually four levels of natural causation—admitting that here we deal with Aristotelian, pre-Galilean science— we fail to establish our next step in the historical account of the fortunes of allegory in the West. Lurking under the veil of hermeneutic obscurity, as the Bible and other texts were read, there had always been an Aristotelian implication, if it is correct that the four causes underlie the four levels of Christian exegesis. That supposition may be historically impossible to prove; its point—the strong analogy between the two systems of fourfold explanation—remains viable. We commonly say that Aristotle explains change in terms of four "causes"; but, as Richard Hope shows, in his translation of the *Metaphysics*, the words *aitia* and *aition* have many shades of meaning, perhaps best summed in the phrase "basic explanation."[4] This in turn leads to a sense of cause as "idea." The idea of a thing is in effect its cause, and, as idea, points us to the basic explanation of the thing being the way it is, not accidentally or contingently, but in essence. This sequence of relations in turn leads to the link between Aristotle (a fundamental Christian authority, of course) and the medieval allegory of the four levels of meaning. For each of these levels is an *aition* or system of *aitia*; and, in that respect, each level of interpretation is a "basic explanation," or, as Hope translates the key term, cause is the basic "explanatory factor" in reading the phenomenon of change correctly. A "level of meaning," finally, is a particular set of "explanatory factors," as, for instance, materials of which an object is made, or purposes to which its design contributes, and these factors in turn are accorded the status of ideas. In every case, the hermeneutic system is naturalized by virtue of its link to Aristotle's *Physics* and *Metaphysics* and anterior to those founding texts, the platonic theory of ideas. Given the embedded nature of the Aristotelian tradition, it is no wonder that on occasion exegetes might say there are more than four interpretive levels, as many as seven.

Rich with interpretive debate, this tradition opens up many doors, but behind them all there is a vision of the essential properties of being. Each of the four causes, or four levels, points to an essential (and only in that sense "natural") aspect of the Aristotelian reasons why things happen as they do. A deep essentialism animates this whole approach to meaning. If we say that the standard medieval interpretive system yields an allegory of ideas, we are also saying that it is an allegory of essences. Plato had imagined that the idea belongs to a realm of the unchanging, hence in a sense "eternal," and it has the aitiological power to generate change in things that need to change. The ideas toward which change points—say the events in a story— are points of unchanging essence, presided over by an ultimate unchanging essence, the final cause or *anagogia* of Christian destiny.

It is this resort to the finality of final causes that gives to Christian interpretation, say the account of doctrinal debates over science, even when extremely learned, such as Frederick Copleston's *History of Philosophy*, that strange willingness to assimilate all contradictions to the mysterious oneness and omnipotence of God, as if an essential property of the divine could resolve an earthly contradiction one has just noticed. One may feel better, but one has not resolved the contradiction.[5] Of course, such maneuvers tend to reinforce an impression of divine authority because mystery always suggests the touch of arbitrary power—like the King's Touch, on which magic belief the great medievalist Marc Bloch wrote a whole book. In medieval philosophy, it was no doubt inevitable that a thinker such as William of Ockham would sooner or later arise to question the allegory of ideas, and this questioning in fact leads to the steady building of a quite different tradition of allegory, which I wish now to examine, in brief and roughly.

3

Against the current of embedded Christian tradition, with its two-, four-, and sometimes sevenfold expansions, I want now to propose the peculiar, not to say uncanny, idea of an *allegory without ideas*. Most readers of fiction will say that allegory has too many ideas, especially if cataloged and ordered according to the medieval taxonomy. But even a modern allegory such as George Orwell's *1984* or Camilo Jose Cela's *The Hive* is likely to be seen this way; there is this idea, and that one, and that one, and so on. The average reader, schooled if at all on the traditional model or on a watered-down version of it, will be baffled by the thought of an allegory without ideas. How can that be? An allegory without ideas would at best seem to be a paradox, not unlike the Liar's Paradox—impossible, but logically and formally necessary. If interpretation yields ideas that are somehow "in" the text, then an allegory lacking them would not be interpretable, not even readable. Or so it appears at first. It seems hard to imagine a fiction that failed to yield a surplus of extra, other (*allos*) meanings. Fortunately perhaps, we know that "the liar" is a logically possible paradox of self-reference, however baffling, and so is an allegory without ideas. First, let us say that only with allegory, where the system of ideas is so important, could you even get their specific exclusion. With most literature, we are aware of overtones in the many different ways of understanding the stories told—a realistic novel such as *Anna Karenina* can elicit interpretation of its own social commentary, even though not an allegorical commentary. The fact that high symbolism of the post-Romantic era can inspire deep commentary does not suggest that it can become "symbolism without ideas," for the reason that in some basic sense it never had ideas, it had only a profound, implicit apprehension of "something far more deeply interfused," as Wordsworth wrote in "Tintern Abbey." If high realism (the nineteenth-century novel would give our examples) can express the things of this world, high symbolism—say Baudelaire, with all his religious yearnings—can express the feelings of our being. Both modes are secular in their inspiration, and neither is especially authoritarian and rigid in form. From them there is almost no way to subtract out the ideas, almost no way to produce the empty field on the other side of the wall. But with allegory, in theory, this is not the case. It is just that an allegory without ideas would be weird.

4

The platonic theory of ideas modulated into that system we know as the "realism" of the medieval philosophers and theologians—"realism," of course, because the ideas were the only ultimately unchanging reality, as permanent as the music of the spheres. On this foundation the allegory we usually take to be defining for the mode was built, and even in the case of modern works such as *1984* and *Animal Farm* and most of Karel and Josef Capek's plays and stories, this ancient idea-bound method is what the authors use. It is extremely powerful and will remain so, even though there will be continuing changes in the situation of allegorical thinking. Allegorical works such as *R.U.R.* and *The War with the Newts* reflect ideas of power as conditioned by twentieth-century combinations of war and industry; and, to the extent that such conditions are superseded, the allegory of power will correspondingly have to change. Yet any traditional allegory of power struggles will always look to a system of ideas where power is related to a platonic *idea of power.*

Nominalism, we recall, differs from realism chiefly in the following way. It questions the possibility of universals, those abstract entities that we identify with various modes of platonic form (the idea, the *eidos* of ancient Greek). No matter how different any particular thing or species may be, it can, under the umbrella of a universal idea (such as "tree"), be represented for us in all its essential character. Any given tree that I am pruning will be one that I see and touch, and hence the truly universal idea of the tree will rise above any sense perceptions involved in my pruning work or the tree's resulting appearance. Contingency, individuality, concreteness of the given thing will disappear into the perfection of the universal idea. This famous platonic notion is by no means dead; Bertrand Russell, Gottlob Frege, and Kurt Gödel were all, as mathematicians, inclined to accept the platonic view of the absolute perfection and extrahuman aspect of ideas and, in this respect, were opposed to the constructivist mathematical thinking of Luitzen Brouwer. For present purposes, to bring the ideal character of ideas down to Earth, the examples of number and geometric forms serve well enough—they simply do not change: "Three" is not "fairly close to three" on Tuesday or "threeish" over the weekend. Geometric figures do not change in the manner of the real objects they are used to demonstrate in physics. It seems impossible to imagine their changing or melting like a lump of butter. Triangles thus indeed seem to share in a kind of eternal stability, even permanence, residing in a platonic heaven of unchanging forms. To raise questions about such absolutist thinking, Jane Austen composed the famed ironical opening sentence of *Pride and Prejudice*: "It is a truth universally acknowledged, that a single man in possession of a good fortune must be in want of a wife."

The trouble with natural mutability is what Ockham noticed in a variety of ways, and he came to argue for the *constructing* power of the analytic mind. He saw that if experience showed us only the grounds for an allegorical "system of ideas," perhaps all would be well, but some universals are like the color blue, in which all sorts of different, individual, singular blue things and appearances seem to share. The moment one thinks seriously about what might be called degrees of universality, one begins to fret over the defining edges of the concepts that appear truly or really universal or, as a platonist might say, really real. How and wherein is it a universal observation if I measure a gallon of water? What is the relation between a particular instance of something, say a slice of Brie, and its genus, *le fromage*, in general?

Long before Austen delighted her property-minded readers, Ockham (ca. 1300–1350) introduced the radical principle that universals were in fact not eternal realities but were constructions of human thought, concepts in the mind. He argued for the *constructing* power of the analytic mind. Because no medieval Christian member of the church could very well escape the field of allegorical vision, we may say that Ockham was subverting the chief technical support of Christian theology, namely, our ability to substitute unquestioned human conceptions in place of the divine archetypes as imagined by religion.

On this view, as Roger Scruton says, universals were "brought into being by thought—specifically, that there is no more to the reality of universals than our use of general terms." Hence we get the term *nominalism*, "because the theory gives precedence to the name of the property over the property itself."[6] No longer is there an abstract platonic realm where universals live eternally free of all change. W. V. Quine summarizes the nominal dream this way: "Even the sophisticated Aristotelian principle that such permanent forms can live through their living instances, as immanent presence of the idea—even this principle now falls under the nominalist axe. When we say this tree is green, for a fact, then 'it is a fact about *us*.'" Quine goes on:

> Nominalism is in essence, perhaps, a protest against a transcendent universe. The nominalist would like to suppress "universals"—the *classes* of our universe—and keep only the concrete individuals (whatever these may be). The effective consummation of nominalism in this sense would consist in starting with an immanent (non-transcendent) universe and then extending quantification to classes by some indirect sort of contextual definition. The transcendent side of our universe then reduces to fictions, under the control of the definitions.[7]

We humans, then, in our defining powers, would become the masters of an immanent world, without recourse to any supreme fiction. In a philosophic universe where definitions are "contextual," they must in some general sense be relativistic procedures, and it was then asked by critics of nominalism, including Quine, whether the idea of "relation" and "relativity" is an eternal idea or not. Nominalism seems to envisage a world of endless qualification in speech and thought, so that no "classes" of things are even believed to be anything ultimately serious, until instanced by a concrete particular. One is reminded of the language machine in *Gulliver's Travels*, where in essence there had to be as many word-blocks, made of wood, as there were thoughts about anything.

There is no reason to suggest that the logic of such matters is simple, nor that ideas disappear entirely owing to the nominalist attack or scrutiny, but we do come to imagine a radical shift resulting from Ockham's approach to the real. If pushed to an extreme, one can imagine that sophisticated later poets such as Andrew Marvell were trying to evoke a world where the ideal green color may be imagined as such but where the more perfect rendering of greenness is only "the dawning of an aspect," as Ludwig Wittgenstein would later put it.[8] Green is an "accident," as the philosophers would say, but there is no platonic evergreen. Green as a living experience, the only green we know, if we think of it, belongs to the poets, whom Plato outlawed from the Republic. Marvell's poem "The Garden" seeks to express a broadly questioning view of these deep matters and leaves the reader with a sense that if there is to be an allegory of colors, it will have to doubt any ideal, perfect, eternal basis. To describe what Marvell is doing, we should use the idea of allotropes from chemistry rather than allegory as understood from the rhetoricians:

> Meanwhile the mind, from pleasure less,
> Withdraws into its happiness:
> The mind, that ocean where each kind
> Does straight its own resemblance find,
> Yet it creates, transcending these,
> Far other worlds, and other seas,
> Annihilating all that's made
> To a green thought in a green shade.[9]

What happens when we extend this annihilation to the field of allegory is that we must then rethink our wall between the literal and the higher-order interpreted "meanings," the *significatio* of medieval exegesis. If nominalist, then there will be no ideas in a strict sense, no meanings segregated to a "higher" place on the interpretive side of the wall. The so-called ideas of virtue and vice, good and evil, happiness and misery, fame and fortune will no longer be read as referring to universal notions. They will be mere functions of shared human speech and language, mere conventions, mere names and their grammar. The allegory without ideas could make no appeal to universals and hence could never legitimately establish belief in imagined higher values. Such surgically disformed allegory could never appeal to any hierarchic system defined in terms of the perfect. Furthermore, this allegory without ideas in the strict platonic sense, we might call it the Fregean mathematical sense, could not claim any serious degree of permanence in its meanings and interpretations, for as language changes with use, so does meaning, on the nominalist view.

You might think that allegory has never pretended to full permanence of meanings—after all, the *quo tendas* of the medieval distych, the "whither we are tending," implies an openness to change. Surely the poets and preachers have always been aware that values and ideas change, and hence presentations of their formal structures, their moral pleas, their anagogical visions, were always undergoing evolution over the millennia. But that is exactly the point. There is a deep internal conflict, or evasion, at the heart of an ambivalent allegorical procedure that seems to contradict itself, by its very operations. Yet allegory is the authoritarian mode of literature and art and discourse, and its claim to be able to project permanent truths is perhaps its chief traditional claim. Its employment of ritual forms reinforces this claim.

The central issue seems always to return to the "system of ideas" to which parabolic fictions allude. Granting that traditional allegories, whatever their languages and hermeneutic resources, simply believe in ideas and in something like philosophical realism, the poets and their interpreters do not often probe the logical consequences of believing in platonic ideas. True poets do not follow Rudolf Carnap into battle, trumpeting positive facts. Poetry is too lively, like a person of amiably loose morals. Like the rest of us, poets simply use ideas, the way Mozart uses fugal passages, a point much appreciated by those who have tried to build workable models of nominalism, only to find that by reducing all expression to a system of named concepts, you produce an infinite regress into a nightmare world of endless particulars—the opposite of the realist's productions of endless relations, relations of relations, and so on forever. In the ordinary world we live in, thankfully we have ideas; we use them to make general statements every minute of the day. We gain the platonic shortcut, if not to the truth at least to an effective and approximately ordered universe of discourse, where we use general ideas without worrying how they relate to their examples, their components. Following this custom, as rather old-fashioned moderns such as Orwell followed it, allegory adopts the pattern fixed by the wall between letter and meaning (allegorical signification, gloss, hyponoia, and the like). Because that is the old custom, we still tolerate its assumptions. But nominalism planted the seed of doubt; and, in certain periods of early modern literature and now more recently, the post-Romantic world gives way to what I am calling an allegory without ideas, partly for convenience but partly because there has at times arisen a belief that ideas in the strict sense are dangerous fictions, if imagined to have divine origin. The task of the critic will be to suggest how this shift, occurring on and off since the Middle Ages, has escaped from falling into nominalist hell. We are certainly not confident about ever reaching realist heaven.

5

Increasingly, with fits and starts, allegory after the late medieval period must be read as turning the ideas toward a vision of the secular. Ideas become the paradoxical tropes of historical events and conditions, and in this sense literature shares in Quine's version of the nominalist's "contextual" reading of ideas. Ideas for a cosmography have not broken free of their eternal implication; they are by no means entirely independent of their platonic source. Still, however, the change is occurring under the surface. A brief note on literary history will support this view. In France, Agrippa D'Aubigné writes *Les Tragiques*. Tasso rewrites his *Jerusalem Delivered* to become *Jerusalem Conquered*, so that while strengthening the ideality of his epic, he simultaneously reflects the acute pressures of the Counter-Reformation. In England, the tradition of the morality play weakens, despite leaving its imprint, for example, on the metamorphosis of the medieval Vice character, who becomes Marlowe's Mephistophilis or Shakespeare's Iago. Following the mid-sixteenth-century success of *The Mirror for Magistrates*, a strong new current of interest in local history seems to inspire the poet Samuel Daniel to write his *Civil Wars* and another major poet, Michael Drayton, to write *The Barons' Wars*. These revivals of chronicle, one of which—Ralph Holinshed's—profoundly altered Shakespeare's career, do not completely materialize the earlier interest in the platonic idea, but they do insist on its historical immersion. One could hardly imagine an English author more addicted to the medieval allegory of ideas than Edmund Spenser, and yet he conveys a strong sense of current political events and a general historicity colliding with archaic myth (the carrier wave of universals), as if to ensure that the epic poem be seen to *construct* its ideas (its guiding thematic classes of thought). In that way, Spenser, for all his medieval yearnings and leanings, is a modern, forcing his vast allegory to think more and more about current historical pressures, as his epic proceeds into its final three books. The great English drama of the public theater of course reflects material realities in all directions; one great Shakespearean scholar said that altogether the plays "wrote the history of his times."[10] A more critical example, however, is the intimate link of idea and current fact that animates virtually all the court masques of the period. Scholars, myself included, have shown that the masque expresses universal ideas of harmony and discord, but only in the context of courtly dynamics; and hence the idea is almost undermined by what was called the "antimasque." The latter was a rhetorical Jacobean device of dramatic irony, to be sure, but such burlesque irony is exactly what undermines the eternal perfection the allegorical idea had been imagined, since Plato, to possess.

For most recent readers, however, the movement toward an allegory without ideas comes with the middle of the seventeenth century. This was deeply understood by Walter Benjamin and was thus described, in many dimensions, by his book on the *Ursprung*, the explosive origins, of the German *Trauerspiele*. Among the many points Benjamin makes, none is more important than the way these "mourning plays" employ an imagery of ruins, for that in turn implies that allegory, as Benjamin saw, defies the older notion of the allegory of ideas. Those platonic universals could not change, but here ruin means the changing of everything believed to be most permanent. This point parallels A. O. Lovejoy's almost prophetic chapter on the temporalizing of the Great Chain of Being, where Lovejoy showed how the static, idea-supporting dream of the Platonistic tradition began to fall apart, sliding away from its atemporal perfection, as a new and largely scientific knowledge brought with it an awareness that the world is getting older, thus influencing old and hallowed models of fixity.[11] Reflecting the cultural shocks wrought by raison d'état, the *Trauerspiel* engages with history in a radical sense, through a focus on allegories of power, but throughout the baroque exploitation of this dramatic form there is everywhere a reduction of meaning to signs. Everything becomes emblematic, and each event is made into a fragment, to increase the feeling that the cohering beautiful ideas of the past are now being literally dismembered. Yet in spite of the fragmentary image, the overall effect of these plays remains "the very fluidity of time."[12] Benjamin pushes hard to show that allegory and symbol differ from each other profoundly, as temporal sequence in real time differs from the mystical, unifying, visionary "spot of time" so dear to the Romantics (thus giving rise to Paul de Man's famous essay, "The Rhetoric of Temporality"). A critical work so rich in observation deserves more than summary, however, so I shall point to only one thing about Benjamin's great essay.

In line with the period it considers, the war-torn seventeenth century, the apparently drifting but in fact controlled discussion of the *Trauerspiel* consistently suggests that the material context of action in these German allegories is intentionally made thinglike. Whereas an earlier vision might have shown the ideal version of courtly order, as Spenser does, this one shows the court as a material thing and framework for the significant themes of the work. Things and material conditions here become surrogates for what before would have been patently recognizable ideas. This is not political science but rather what one might call the coinage of a new materialized reality, as if the hard facts were all there is. These plays look forward to Heinrich von Kleist's dissections of false beliefs and empty ideals, but in themselves the plays enforce a belief that the realm of the ideal is not only empty but false to any truth we may hope to attain. Thus we get the famous remark, "Allegories are, in the realm of thoughts, what ruins are in the realm of things" (*GTD*, 177–178, 182). To take one example, which in my own research I found to have the same function that Benjamin finds, the picturesque is a newly invigorated mode, for it depends heavily on what Karl Borinski called "a picturesque field of ruins" (*GTD*, 178). It then follows from such usages that this new and odd allegory without ideas will depend heavily on inscriptions, dedications, and the like, all of which attempt to reduce the lively image to the static printed sign. The overall effect of these tragedies, as Benjamin saw them, was to fix the allegorical mode of attaining "other meanings" by reducing all truth to a radical materialism. Summing the subtle variety and scope of this critique, one must say that Benjamin, the great collector, saw that an allegory without ideas would have to be the expression of a collector's mania, which indeed the *Trauerspiele* are.

6

If this seventeenth-century *Trauerspiel* episode marks one stage along the way of a dispersed nominalism, another is the not unrelated development of a sfumato style in the Romantic approach to a literary absolute. Benjamin cites Novalis with approval, for Novalis perceived "a certain strangeness, respect, and bewilderment which shimmer through the writing" of the Baroque allegorists, and he furthermore perceived that now allegory will become indirect (with no clear division between the two sides of the hermeneutic wall), in fact is bound to approach the condition of music (*GTD*, 187). On the other hand, as Novalis also noted, "Scenes which are genuinely visual are the only ones which belong in the theatre. Allegorical characters, those are what people mostly see. Children are hopes, young girls are wishes and requests" (*GTD*, 191). Because natural scenes are coming more and more to have sublime and picturesque value, the Romantics make an effort to cloud the "scenes which are genuinely visual"—the staple of all older allegory. Romanticism at large makes an effort to fray the edges of clear ideas in allegory, as we see when Karl Solger debates with his friend Ludwig Tieck over the nature of allegory and its relation to symbol, claiming an important literary place for the mystical/obscure, even for the unconscious, as we might expect in a correspondence of 1818, when the sublime had long been a European passion.[13] Allegory, for Solger, should aspire to mysticism, but there is no doubt that as soon as irony comes to dominate the German critique of art and literature, the clear-eyed belief in fully established and presumably fixed "systems of ideas" ceases to work toward an allegorical modality of the medieval kind. Solger would say the depiction of God and his heaven in *Paradise Lost* is insipid rationalism, mere scheme, whereas he finds the formal Miltonic allegory of Sin and Death splendid—clearly because it seems to him mysterious and obscure. However we agree or disagree with these early judgments of Milton and his methods, of allegory and symbol in the light of Romanticism, we shall discover that the problem of allegory has become the question of the obscure. A Solger or Tieck, whose thought unquestionably derives from earlier meditations on the sublime and its link to allegory, can be shown to puzzle about mysticism, not just in the light of German pietism but because allegory had once possessed a numinous connection to the analogical, not to mention the medieval anagogical level, which it seemed, after the Enlightenment, to have lost.

Allegory was partly responsible for this loss, for it had relied too long on belief in unexamined universals, but the fact remains that allegory was yet another inevitable victim of a larger change in beliefs, yet one more victim of early modern science, which I take to be the philosophic heir to Ockham's nominalism. The question of gain and loss revolves around the fundamental notion that allegory deals in expressions of otherness because otherness itself infuses the parable and the fable with a contagion of whatever beliefs are dominant in the period at hand. In simpler terms, with allegory, the interpretation and the meanings on the hermeneutic side of our wall determine whatever we find or invent on the fable side of the wall. Here, interpretation determines creation. The Creation itself is interpreted, as the rabbis often claimed, before the world comes into being. This sounds oddly like a quantum mechanical experiment, but however we imagine it, we seem to be dealing with an enigmatic interaction between the real and the nominal.

7

Finally, turning to the most recent period, we are reminded that, in his discussion of allegory in "The Ideology of Modernism," Georg Lukács raises the question as to whether the nominalist drift arose by nature out of an inner tendency of transcendence or came about as "the product precisely of a rejection of these tendencies."[14] Taking the largest possible view, Lukács says that Benjamin had been asking how transcendent idealism (medieval realism, in effect) could not fail to destroy art itself. This ancient question keeps on recurring, to be sure. True also it is that for Benjamin, "the Baroque idea of history as the passion of the world . . . makes History significant only in the stations of its corruptions. Significance is a function of mortality—because it is death that marks the passage from corruptibility to meaningfulness." The Benjaminian theme of the ruin is read by Lukács as a "link between allegory and the annihilation of history."[15] In this context, Franz Kafka becomes a key figure, for his allegories deny any possibility of

historical change in the conditions of human life as progress toward freedom, as a Marxist would wish to anticipate. No doubt the central figure for
analysis should be Kafka, therefore, in the sense that his vision of almost
mystical impotence of the hero leaves us wondering if this is not a sort of
new-minted platonic idea. Of course, in logic and ontology, it cannot be
such, and yet there is an apocalyptic ideality in Kafka that disturbs Lukács,
as compared, let us say, with Thomas Mann.

How much a certain historical grit will rescue allegory from the medieval
model, and hence push it toward a more modern nominalism, will in part
depend on a precise understanding of the way allegory figures its meanings.
Allegory, unlike other modes, holds its meanings walled off from the source
or initial stage of its utterance. My wall metaphor stands for the method of
blocking and encapsulating meaning into strata or levels or schematic structures. Some ancients said that allegory is a "continued metaphor"; Cicero
called it a "continuous stream" of metaphors that flow (*fluxerunt*), while
it became an unexamined custom to think that allegorical elements are
carried forward on a thread of parabolic story.[16] If, like Longfellow in his
famous poem to the American Union, you continue a metaphor of the ship
of state, you present whatever parts of the ship, including its launching, that
may be ready to press into allegorical service. But this idea of "continued
metaphor" has always seemed wrong to me, if only because, while metaphors bring aesthetic life into expression, allegory is obsessively and at times
deliberately anesthetic.

If, as massive evidence from commerce, politics and religion suggests, allegory typically begins by striking the eye, in the long run its "advertising"
ends by anesthetizing the very sense it arouses initially. It must therefore
keep upping the ante. In this modality, image and idea are locked in a
deadly embrace. Nothing makes it easy to separate the couple, for image and
idea (the latter defined in either ancient Platonic terms or modern Lockean
psychological terms) are fundamental to all mental processes. Nevertheless, we may relate the intermixture to my present argument in the following way.

As noted at the outset, allegory is always involved in symbolisms of
power. Furthermore, this involvement takes the complex form of ritual sequence, such that its repetitions provide its rhythm, a pacing that in turn
dulls the mind and senses, by virtue of the noise implicit in the redundancy.
(Identical or strongly similar signals rapidly become hard to differentiate
from each other—the dulling effect.) Eventually this generalized anesthesia

stupefies the responder, so that a new problem arises—the sender of the message has to turn up the volume, in every way. An ancient branch of history shows this to be the case with religious propaganda; the faith only propagates when its authority is driven home with Pavlovian insistence.

If ritual repetition is most notable in religious practices, it occurs no less often nor with lower intensity in the propagation of massive secular consumerism; the secularity makes no difference because it is the repetition that counts, with the same need to constantly renew the faces, facades, and volume of the iconography. A spurious surface of variety tends to give allegory its claim to artistic skill, but underneath there is always the tendency toward controlled, ritual iterations, by which it happens that the mode can only reinforce stereotypes, slavishly imagining a world according to Flaubert's idiot savants, Bouvard and Pécuchet. We need, as it were, a new Flaubertian "dictionary of received ideas." Advertising today (as we see in media-driven "politics") wages semiotic war, forcing masses of people into secular addictions to buying and consuming. Iconography, in my strict sense, almost always triggers a need to consume the symbol.

Not accidentally does advertising always verge on symbolic terrorism, instilling a fear that one's implanted addiction will not be satisfied, except by rushing out to get the buyer's fix. Nor does our sophisticated, ironic, or cynical ability to see through doubtful advertising claims make much difference, for the ritual repetitions have already done their work; they have implanted half-truths at a deeper level, as if we had already been mesmerized. Promotional duplicities are of course familiar phenomena, but I want to link them to the machinery of ritual repetition. There is little virtue in holding the anesthetic effect at a comfortable academic arm's length. Forced gravitas is a big mistake. We need hardly be told that institutionalized religions have been practicing ad campaigns since the beginning of time.

The postmodern change in allegory, away from projecting transcendent ideas always subject to interpretation, toward a positivistic projection of material facts, as if they could adequately double for ideas, is not without its intricate developments. Brilliant authors—just think, for example, of A. S. Byatt or J. G. Ballard—have shown this. What we need always to reconsider is the underlying allegorical impulse to control symbols of power. This I have called "daemonic agency," and it has many faces. Although I am here claiming a postmodern turn in the history of allegory, the allegorical mode of action is always daemonic. Lest one need a reminder of this, consider a fountainhead, *Paradise Lost*, where Milton always uses the traditional term for the Daemons of his cosmic tale: In Book Five we learn that "Thrones, Dominations, Princedoms, Virtues, Powers" are what the Fallen Angels possess. But, as Satan at once tells them, they have become what they possess. Similarly, in *The Possessed* Dostoyevski later wrote the psychological story of this cognitive collapse; his novel is a vast parable of the way daemonic agents become possessed by what they possess. In Milton the Daemons, including good ones, the *eudaimonia*, including the Song of God, are finally simply called "Powers," while their personification depends directly on an enclosing cosmological belief system, a widespread illusion that daemonic energies (Milton's "Virtues") rightly constitute justified power and legitimate authority. The great literary allegories have always tried to attenuate this participation in the larger power game, by allowing their instructive fictions to be ambiguous in narrative line and verbal expression.

Nevertheless, the belief that allegory permits metaphoric continuation without losing the lively force of metaphor constitutes an important error. Despite arguments advanced by Victor Turner, ritual repetition will finally block the metaphoric function of seeing differences in sameness, a blocking that in turn must deny the claims of nature, expression, and natural philosophy. Hence the allegorist treads a fine, frustrating line. She will try to round off the corners of ritual. Along with unduly controlled ambiguity of language, allegory at its most useful and its most human always seeks to flex its main device of personification, which in a new direction postmodern allegory seeks through its strange and estranged nominalism, by rejecting what is left of the platonic, transcendental system of the ideas.

Channeled into the nominalistic worldview, this new allegory immediately takes the next nominalistic step beyond the concrete naming of concepts: It finds its *ideas* almost completely materialized into *things* such as robots, cyborgs, microdust, and the like. Things and objects, often unexamined, will serve like mercenary substitutes for the original transcendental syntax. Curiously, the move resembles certain thoughts of Bishop Berkeley, who wrote in one of his *Dialogues* that a certain understanding of objects is capable of "changing . . . ideas into things." For that to happen, the fiction must reshape the animistic trope of personifications, now appearing in a markedly new mode. This nominalistic allegory must occlude the older tradition, mockingly, paradoxically, as if it could find its new lexicon in a postmodern version of the Flaubertian dictionary.

When personifications cross in our minds from the literal to the figurative, they are the *figurae* of a passage between matter and spirit. That explains why Shakespeare created Wall, the most comically mysterious character in all his plays, when seeking to mystify the foolishly magical and weirdly concrete parabolic story of Pyramus and Thisbe. Much more could be said, and students of hermetic thought have indeed said much, about the question of passing between the esoteric and the exoteric, but what seems necessary is that there be some sort of magic agency to carry messages back and forth between letter and spirit. I mentioned Solger's Romantic sense of atmosphere before; in that light, looking ahead to the postmodern period, I would claim that when postmodern allegorical agency is fully personified and fully atmospheric, *it requires conspiracy.* Allegory on this basis must be a kind of conspiratorial agreement to employ secret meanings for public or semipublic meanings and communications.

This approach via atmosphere cannot fail to suggest the darker purposes of a Machiavellian theory of power, a central issue from which my remarks began. Not all allegories are fraudulent, but it is certain that all frauds are allegorical. When William of Ockham invented the nominalist method, he was inspired by his belief that the papacy was at that time engaging in fraud. He was a devout believer, so he came up with the idea that the platonic ideas are incredibly vulnerable to fraudulent uses. It seems that nominalist allegory must get rid of its ideas, in order that persons and actual behaviors be held accountable to those pondering the destiny of the Faith. Similar attitudes, if I read Ockham correctly, appear and reappear often in history, and they surface in some of our postmodern fiction, where many readers will have experienced a climate of universal duplicity allied with studiously cultivated public ignorance and anesthesia. The Ockhamite awareness of vulnerability to fraud is not, if we think of it, unfamiliar to the critical thinker of today. It is apparent that most modern advertising verges on deliberate fraud, while advertising is the demotic version of allegory, always "pushing the idea" of this product or that product, even when the product is a personified political agency, say an inherently mindless leader who needs grafting onto a higher model. Virtually all political spinning is of this order, and its allegorical aspect matters, because by analyzing its demonic agency, we get closer to what the politician is really up to.

Artists respond variously to this situation of a neorealist allegory pandemically spreading everywhere through universal corporate advertising. Authors such as Paul Auster question the Grand Narratives and fake Big

Ideas by limiting their stories to a kind of Kafkan parabolic minimalism where, to quote Kafka's parable on parables, the idea is to show that the incomprehensible is incomprehensible. But then, where and what could be the "idea" of such works? Perhaps there is none, and we are wrong to ask for one.

In our own period, we readily see that if one wants allegory without dubious ideas, one must go in for Chinese boxes, the famous mise en abîme, in order that the making of the story itself, the recursive pursuit of the pursuit, would be the moving ground of a different sort of otherness. Italo Calvino wrote this story in *If on a Winter's Night a Traveller*, where recursive structures lead the reader everywhere, if not quite nowhere. Let us suppose, then, that in good faith, and not like the perpetrators of allegorical fraud, we found in the Kafkan tradition an idea of otherness that is not "higher" but always "beyond," always receding before us. This looks like infinite regress because its plan is infinite progression, or processing, of parts of the story. Both the elegance of an Auster and the Parisian tonality of his fables accompany this sense that, finally, otherness of the horizon is an end in itself. In his *New York Trilogy*, or the more recent *Oracle Night*, Auster meets himself as not quite a person but rather as an intervening guide to his own interpretation—as a disembodied writing agency, author of his fiction, character in his fiction, voice on the phone who comes from a medium outside of fiction, name recalled from an Auster family history, entry in a lost notebook, and so on, all of these personae disappearing deeper and deeper into the recesses of origin. The disappearance, if we may call it that, is an excursion into the heart of naming itself. As with a quite different author, the Don DeLillo of *The Names* or *White Noise* or *Underworld*, where the ancient rhetorician's *underthought* or *hyponoia* becomes a fictive space, the compositional method approaches a secular, hermetic version of kabala. To give but one more example: José Saramago's *All the Names* intensifies the reification of the name, simultaneously mystifying it, by placing its hero in a rather Kafkan "Central Registry," where human identity becomes a function of "basic archivistic rules."[17] With all such authors we get a practicing imaginative version of nominalism that relies on narrative as a continuous definition of terms. The fable is intended to show what goes into creating or inventing the terms of any "higher" ontology because those terms no longer invent themselves according to a divine plan. We return to the stage when Ockhamite medieval philosophy, looking at the real world, saw that in a critical sense, every idea is also a name.

Clearly with the present age there is a need to dig into the depths of meaning, as if there were no readily available guarantors that the quest could ever be satisfied. If I. A. Richards were to rewrite his famous early book, today it would have to be called *The Unmeaning of Unmeaning*. My sense is that a real-world imperative always underlines the drive toward a nominalist attitude; and, perhaps besides the authors I have mentioned, it would be best to range this imperative with the Scholastically informed fictions and plays of Beckett, and more radically with the stories of J. G. Ballard. Ballard's work is not science fiction. It is an art of visionary extremism, in the sense that for him an ice age, a drowned or crystal world, a dried-out African continent, a civil war in Beirut are all scenes where actual events are so anomalous that they become mere names. He sees that when events are carried to monstrous extremes, there is no common realistic way to describe them—the scale is wrong—nor is there any "system of ideas" (with which we began this discussion) adequately in touch with what happens to give a higher order of understanding. Instead, there is only the task of rebuilding a frame of thought by exploring all the powers of naming. Naming is to be primordial, in literary history looking back to Daniel Defoe, as in J. M. Coetzee's *Foe*, or looking to a work such as William Golding's allegorical story of the first humans, *The Inheritors*, or to fantastic writing descended from the hyperdetailed surface of the nouveau roman and many earlier incarnations, mining the variations on the nominal grid (in our literature I think of Samuel Delany, to mention another intriguing author).

In this inherently nominalist world we now inhabit, actions must be shown to plunge so deep into bland semiosis that they lose natural connection to norms of action. They are soon so fully derealized and nominalized that Ballard might properly say, quoting his own titles, "This is the suburban running wild we have created. We are in the atrocity exhibition; this is crash; this is the terminal beach; these are the vermilion sands; this is the drowned world." As Benjamin's account of baroque allegory insists, the translation of thing to name through a semiotic process of last resort is the mark of the postplatonic allegory. The fictions exuding from our increasingly overnumbered world are bound to lose the two ends of the medieval allegorical scheme of meaning because while the platonic idea seems more and more doubtful, the mere things and common events of life are being dwarfed into nothingness. Doubt permeates both ends of the spectrum of realism and nominalism. Of course, we have an inchoate popular search for lost identity—people looking for their ancestors on the Internet—and for this reason it is clear we must honor those authors who have asked us to question the grounds of a questionable comfort discovered in the unexamined idea. Our allegory without ideas asks how the idea can be situated and placed in a sea of ambiguous and vague possibilities, for this strange allegorical style seeks to create the dreams descending from William of Ockham. Returning, then, to our initial concern, we find that the allegory without ideas systematically serves to represent power relations with what amounts to an increasingly secular, pragmatic, and materialist set of operations. This mode deliberately constructs its meanings. Despite any origins it may have in the magic of names, and hence in the religious worldview, the rhetoric of power seeks to parallel power itself and hence its production in a field of force; it gains strength by abjuring the eternal ideas, while its constructivist techniques give it greatly extended and enhanced naming powers. The mode begins to resemble a very hip ad campaign. For good or ill, the allegory without ideas makes possible an always more cunning manipulation of all the symbols of power itself, especially the most currently appealing symbols. By such means an ancient expressive technique makes contact with the shock of the new and is at once confused and stimulated by our age of omnipresent noise and chaos.

Notes

1. On ritual forms, see my *Allegory: The Theory of a Symbolic Mode* (Ithaca, NY: Cornell University Press, 1964), 195–199, 147–180. On power connections, see 41–66, 337–343.

2. Jon Whitman, *Allegory: The Dynamics of an Ancient and Medieval Technique* (Cambridge, MA: Harvard University Press, 1987).

3. Jonathan Lear, *Aristotle: The Desire to Understand* (Cambridge, U.K.: Cambridge University Press, 1988), 28–42.

4. Aristotle, *Metaphysics*, trans. Richard Hope (Ann Arbor: University of Michigan Press, 1960), 355. On the four causes, see 9ff., and on the "explanatory factor," see 88ff.

5. Frederick Copleston, SJ, *A History of Philosophy*, vol. 3 (New York: Doubleday Image, 1993), 62–69, 122–153.

6. Roger Scruton, *Modern Philosophy: An Introduction and Survey* (New York: Penguin, 1994), 89.

7. W. V. Quine, *The Ways of Paradox and Other Essays*, rev. ed. (Cambridge, MA: Harvard University Press, 1976), 202. Quine and Nelson Goodman found difficulties, foreseen by Bertrand Russell, in getting nominalism to work. Its operative relational entities turn out to be realist "ideas," after all.

8. Ludwig Wittgenstein, *Philosophical Investigations*, trans. G. E. M. Anscombe (Oxford, U.K.: Blackwell, 1999), 194, 206, 210, 212. Here Wittgenstein differentiates the gradual onset of emerging shapes from what he calls "continuous seeing." His example is the duck–rabbit illusion.

9. Andrew Marvell, "The Garden," stanza 6. See *Andrew Marvell*, ed. Frank Kermode and Keith Walker (Oxford, U.K.: Oxford University Press, 1990), 48.

10. This was a remark of the late Andrew Chiappe in a casual aside, one afternoon in the late 1960s at Columbia University.

11. A. O. Lovejoy, *The Great Chain of Being: A Study in the History of an Idea* (Cambridge, MA: Harvard University Press, 1936), chap. 9, 242–287.

12. Walter Benjamin, *The Origins of German Tragic Drama*, trans. John Osborne (London: Verso, 2003), 165. Hereafter, this work is cited parenthetically as *GTD*.

13. See the "Tieck–Solger Correspondence," in *German Aesthetic and Literary Criticism: The Romantic Ironists and Goethe*, ed. Kathleen Wheeler (Cambridge, U.K.: Cambridge University Press, 1984), 151–158.

14. Georg Lukács, *Realism in Our Time: Literature and the Class Struggle* (New York: Harper and Row, 1964), 40.

15. Lukács, *Realism in Our Time*, 41.

16. Cicero, *De Oratore*, ed. and trans. H. Rackham (Cambridge, MA: Harvard University Press, 1948), book 3, chap. 41, section 166. Compare Quintilian's *Institutes of Oratory*, book 9, chap. 2, section 46. The notion of continued metaphor is very hard to unfix.

17. José Saramago, *All the Names*, trans. Margaret J. Costa (San Diego, CA: Harcourt Brace, 1999), 141.

PART ONE

Performing Allegory

Memories and Allegories of the Death Penalty

Back to the Medieval Future?

J O D Y   E N D E R S

In 1495, in what is now the northern French city of Metz, an eighteen-year-old servant girl was burned at the stake in a most unusual way for having brutally murdered her newborn baby. As a large crowd gathers to witness both the death penalty in action and the special contraption crafted to add originality to the proceedings, her execution offers even today an unprecedented glimpse into the interplay between allegory, personification, forensic rhetoric, and memory, a nexus by which juridical culture makes meaning through the ultimate theatrical performative. The loquacious Philippe de Vigneulles, who was a historian, local politician, and frequent thespian in the rich theatrical life of Metz, tells the tale in his *Chronicles*. After some time at the pillory, the girl is moved to the scaffold:

> And there, a device had been fashioned that was out of the ordinary and unlike any other (*non pas à la coustume des aultre*): because this said girl was raised straight up against a large stake. And, first off, she had one of her hands cut off, and then the fire was lit and she was burned at the stake: but not so the fire would be allowed to consume her completely. Because, as soon as she was dead, they put out the fire, and she remained fully

upright, which was a hideous thing to behold. And *they put a wooden child in her arms, along with a painting of a child* (*Et lui mist on ung anffans de boix entre ces bras, avec ung aultres en pointure*).[1]

Just as one of the canonical functions of poetry is to make new again a tired old cliché or metaphor, so too, in 1495, did pictorialization, memory, theatricality, and the staging of a veritable drama of death remake, reanimate, reallegorize, as it were, that quintessential yet oh-so-dead metaphor of the law: *to make an example of someone*—and to do so in ways that lend new meaning to the term *legal representation*.

There might well have existed a Foucauldian spectacle of the scaffold long before the grisly early modern events that dot the critical landscape of *Discipline and Punish*.[2] Michel de Certeau might well have theorized that the law "writes itself on bodies" and "engraves itself on parchments made from the skin of its subjects."[3] Much earlier, with a metatheatrical vocabulary to match, Callistratus advocated a site-specific catharsis that attended the death penalty. In the great medieval compilation of legal teachings known as the *Digest of Justinian*, we read:

> The practice approved by most authorities has been to hang notorious brigands on a gallows in the place which they used to haunt, so that *by the spectacle* others may be deterred from the same crimes, and so that it may, when the penalty has been carried out, *bring comfort* to the relatives and kin of those killed in that place where the brigands committed their murders . . .[4]

And the rhetorical *artes memorandi* might well have trained generations of medieval legal theorists in large-scale allegorical habits of thought that ominously anticipate Friedrich Nietzsche's belief that "only what goes on hurting will stick" in the memory.[5] But none of it explains adequately the troubling thing that happened in 1495.

To my knowledge, the painting of the murdered child, which was allegedly placed in the dead mother's arms, has not survived; but, as we shall see, its iconographic traces were no longer necessary. Drawing on several stunningly visual fifteenth-century death penalty scenes, I argue instead that, once a cruel infanticide had already "burned the minds and scorched the memories"[6] of such a medieval community as Metz, it was paramount that the first (pictorial) image of murder be replaced by a second image of justice. As Plato had once urged in the *Laws*, it was the duty of the lawmaker to "persuade people that their notions of justice and injustice are illusory pictures."[7] Thus, what the lawmakers of Metz needed was *another picture* of the justice that they were endeavoring to disseminate through that supremely allegorical event that is the death penalty, an event that transforms criminals into signs of themselves in that proverbial theater of everyday life.[8] In Metz, they needed *two images*: a painting from the visual arts, not of *the* dead baby but *a* dead baby; and a prop from the world of theater—the wooden doll. In a cruelty that even Antonin Artaud could never have surmised, the doll doubles here as a prop from the theater of the law, where demonstrations are called *ostension* by Roman rhetoricians (and *exhibits* by contemporary attorneys).[9] Both doll and painting stand in as surrogates for all babies,[10] such that the legal community of medieval Metz produced an unforgettable *concrete allegory*, a representation that was simultaneously static and in motion, and a reified mise-en-scène that initiates us into the conflicted and conflictual world of medieval jurisprudence. Speaking of allegory involves speaking in riddles: *dynamic reifications, hypostatic motion, tangible abstractions* that one can see and feel and touch. It also means an irremediable interplay between what is literal and what is allegorical, such that the two apparent opposites seem, rather, to be synonyms.

In the theory and practice of the law, which is still rife even in the present day with allegorical thinking,[11] it was of the essence to reliteralize what had already been allegorized and theatricalized: legal representation. How law becomes allegory and theater and why it matters are questions that reveal a portentous tension between the seen and unseen, the literal and symbolic, the material and imaginary, stasis and motion, representation and not-representation—a tension that sends us hurtling back to a kind of medieval future.[12] In a contemporary American culture in which the secrecy or privacy surrounding the death penalty mitigates against the very allegorization that the Middle Ages staged so dramatically, those questions certainly take us straight to the heart of the eternal hegemonic efforts to theatricalize legal retribution as a means of manipulating the remembrance of things past, present, and future.[13]

In the *Rhetorica ad Herennium* of ca. 84 B.C., one of the most widely disseminated educational texts of the European Middle Ages, the Pseudo-Cicero defined allegory as "a manner of speech denoting one thing by the letter of the words, but another by their meaning" (*Permutatio est oratio aliud verbis aliud sententia demonstrans*).[14] Without dwelling on the odd resemblance of that definition to what most of us would call *irony*, suffice it to recall that one cannot address medieval allegory without bringing both law and theatricality into the picture of how things signify.[15] For one thing, in the learned milieus in which allegory plays out, forensic oratory served as the contextual frame not only for allegory but for the entire art of rhetoric. For another thing, *denotation* is not quite the same thing as *demonstration*; and *vive la différence*, which lies in the theatrics of visual culture. To paraphrase Stephen Greenblatt's oft-cited hypothesis about true versus false religion, one might say that "the difference between true and false legal politics is the presence of theater,"[16] a bodily medium that is present in ways that poems, novels, or paintings are not.

It is no coincidence, for instance, that, as his first example of the comparative properties of the trope of allegory, the Pseudo-Cicero looks to theatricality: "For when dogs act the part of wolves (*funguntur*), to what guardian, pray, are we going to entrust our herds of cattle?" (*RAH*, 4.46). In large part, that is because allegory constituted an extensive meditation about imitation, action, role playing, and appearances (deceiving or otherwise) in both the painting and the theatrical enactment of exemplary legal pictures, be it those of 1495, 2010, or beyond. As an important epistemological site of such "painting," the *ars memorandi* had long trained medieval jurists to understand crime and punishment by staging a mental scene, a personal psychodrama in which personifications (in the form of costumed characters) stood in for legal ideas, arguments, and dramatic plots of crime and punishment:[17]

> We ought, then, to set up images (*imagines*) of a kind that can adhere longest in the memory. And we shall do so if we establish likenesses (*similitudines*) as striking as possible; if we set up images that are not many or vague, but doing something (*agentes imagines*); if we assign to them exceptional beauty or singular ugliness; if we dress some of them with crowns or purple cloaks, for example, so that the likeness may be more distinct to us . . . (*RAH*, 3.37)

Even more relevant to the case under discussion is the fact that the psychic mise-en-scène that is memory also tended to focus as much on pictorial figuration as it did on deforming and disfigurement. Even in the lovely passage above, the Pseudo-Cicero goes on immediately to advise that images are also more memorable "if we somehow disfigure them (*deformabimus*), as by introducing one stained with blood or soiled with mud or smeared with red paint, so that its form is more striking. . . ." At the same time, however, he completes that sentence like so: "or by assigning certain comic effects to our images (*aut ridiculas res aliquas imaginibus adtribuamus*), for that, too, will ensure our remembering them more readily" (*RAH*, 3.37). That last point is of no small consequence in the various deathly denouements under discussion; for, although the inflammatory nature of infanticide makes for a compelling test case, the death penalty is scarcely the only medieval site for the disfiguring allegorization of punishment. Much as the Pseudo-Cicero described above the comic effects of mnemonic imagery, another spectacular— and infinitely less severe—punishment from Metz responded to what Philippe de Vigneulles dubs the "big joke" of 1511. When an unscrupulous German salesgirl came to market to sell pots of butter that turned out to be pots filled with "old breeches full of shit" (*dez vielle braye toutte brenoize*), she too was humiliated at the pillory for four hours. Surrounding her there were "seven of the pots hanging all around her"; they were literally—or is it allegorically?—rubbing her nose in it (*CPV*, 4: 99).

Rhetorical memory arts provided a translation program of sorts from thought to image by putting the law into theatrical action (whence my earlier characterization of such phenomena as *protodramatic*).[18] In an eerie twist on Richard Schechner's notion of twice-behaved behavior,[19] it seems that, if a medieval legal community sought to commit to the public memory a punitive act of justice, it was necessary to reallegorize it, to hypostatize the theatricality of an execution, to freeze the frame on the memory theater that had facilitated the allegorization in the first place by proposing motionless images, *imagines non agentes*, images that were no longer moving. A doll and a painting aid and abet the process; but so too does a charred corpse that is no longer a *tableau vivant* but a *tableau mourant* and, eventually, a *tableau mort* that could speak volumes, in silence, to all sorts of audiences—and not just to those who were able to conceive such things rhetorically because of their training at university.

It so happens, moreover, that another version of the execution of 1495, also by Philippe de Vigneulles, yields a fascinating depiction of just such *imagines*-no-longer-*agentes*. In his *Memoirs* or *Gedenkbuch*, Philippe states anew that the infanticidal mother was burned "not as others are burned"; but he makes a number of distinctions. The "little wooden baby" (*ung petit enffant de bois*) was placed not in her arms but next to her; and, above all, he adds that the body itself was placed upon a wheel for a panoramic view of a slightly different version of the image:

> As soon as she was dead, they put out the fire and her body was placed upon a wheel; and they put next to her *a little wooden child*; and, along with that, there was another large paper, attached to the aforesaid wheel, upon which *there was a painted child with his mother who was killing him* (*ung enffant en pointure et sa mère qui le tuoit*).[20]

In that sense, the execution of 1495 served as a phased, episodic progression of deadening the mnemonic *imagines agentes* during the imposition of the death penalty. We follow the unnamed girl's ordeal from a time when she is *still alive* during her four hours of humiliation at the pillory; when she *is dying*, as when her hands are cut off; and when *she is dead*, a charred corpse holding what seems, by comparison, to be a living doll or, at least, a doll who had once been alive enough for its mother to murder. This was a distorted mirror-image par excellence of the classic mnemonic technique of deploying visions, as Quintilian had once said, "whereby things absent are presented to our imagination with such extreme vividness that they seem actually to be before our very eyes" and whereby spectators come "face to face with the cruel facts (*in rem praesentem*)," such that a victim seems "not to have been murdered, but *to be being murdered* before their very eyes."[21] The Metz execution represents crimes absent through a variety of iconographic views of a moment of murder that was—with apologies for the mixed metaphor—*frozen* in time, but it does so with legally executed dead people who are present. If the *ars memorandi* was designed to "call the dead to life" (*defunctos excitare*), if rhetorical invention involved a prior imagistic conception of killing them first, and if medieval people were accustomed to living with the dead,[22] then the judicial community of Metz has brought the victim back to life simultaneously with bringing the living, dying, and dead criminal all the way back to death—and presumably all the way home to heaven (and not to the eternal damnation of hell), given the girl's "beautiful repentance at the end" (*Gedenkbuch*, 124).

Furthermore, despite Philippe's assertions to the contrary, the execution of 1495 was not the first Messin foray into such a process; nor would it be the last. Consider, for instance, that, in 1474, a murderer and adulterer had had both his hands cut off (one hand helping with the symbolic demonstration of the murder he had committed, the other "helping hand" providing a penalty for his theft of both the property and the wife of his employer). In the *Chronicles*, Philippe's lengthy narrative moves, with the occasional echo of Boccaccio, from a rape-by-impersonation, to a murderous conspiracy between a wife and her lover, to the actual murder of her husband, to the criminals' staging a false scene of the crime, to their dissemblance during separate police interrogations, and finally to the two spectacles of the scaffold of their two public executions. After the killers had been paraded through the city on the cart of infamy, the double execution took place on the Bridge of the Dead, where the former secretary of the rich merchant Dedier Baillat was the first to go: He "had his two hands cut off first, and then his head; and the explosive device (*pétal*) that he had used to inflict the fatal blow was attached so that it would hang high up next to the blade [presumably, with which the convicted killer had been decapitated] and next to the aforesaid head."[23] Similarly, approximately a decade after the events of 1495, when the time came to execute another young mother for infanticide, the community of Metz bore witness once again to the transmutation of another lengthy theatricalization into a more stable pictorial image. Philippe de Vigneulles assures us that the contraption devised for the ordeal of 1516 was also the first of its kind, this time boasting a phallic punning that is positively obscene. The better to concretize a denaturing and retributive rape by the justice system, there was

> a kind of chair with a hole in it that was suspended from up high, atop a large stake . . . . And then, the fire was lit, such that the flames cut right through the cords from which the contraption was suspended: thus, the chair started falling down, sliding down the length of the pole until it stopped about three feet from the ground, and remained thus until all was consumed (*CPV*, 4: 215–16).[24]

Far and away the most sinister feature of the events of 1495, though, was the legalistic spin on just what it meant to tender, anything but tenderly, the proverbial burnt offering. Philippe reports that the "scandal" had first broken "on the Friday before Palm Sunday, on the 10th day of April," when word spread through town that the serving girl "had conceived a child and she concealed it so well that she gave birth to it all alone" on Candlemas Eve. Upon giving birth, the "poor wretch" had taken it "by the feet and hit it against a wall, and killed it. And, having done that, she took it and threw it into a well," where the dead infant had remained until its mother transported it to a new hiding place in the outhouse.[25] But the child had floated in the well "from the day of Candlemas to the 10th day of April," a moment of the liturgical calendar of special significance in that Candlemas, which is observed on February 2 in the Latin rite, celebrated the purification of the mother after birth. According to the *Catholic Encyclopedia*, Mosaic law held that "a mother who had given birth to a man-child was considered unclean for seven days; moreover she was to remain three and thirty days 'in the blood of her purification.'" For a maid-child, however, "the time which excluded the mother from sanctuary was even doubled," a doubling that Philippe redoubles in his own narrative. If we trust his dates and numbers, then the infant appears to have been moved from the outhouse on the sixty-seventh day, or after the exact doubling of those "three and thirty days" in which the mother was to remain in "in the blood of her purification": Upon completion of the waiting period of forty or eighty days, and in accordance with the teachings of Leviticus 12:2–8, the mother was to "bring to the temple a lamb for a holocaust and a young pigeon or turtle dove for sin."[26] A holocaust is precisely what Metz justice had organized as the purifying catharsis of a public execution. The young mother does not appear to have brought a symbolic prop of her own but, instead, was forced to bear other symbols on her dead body; she was denied symbolic purification as she herself became a symbolic lamb to the slaughter in the pièce de résistance of 1495.[27]

In yet another account of the execution (this one reproduced in Jean-François Huguenin's 1838 compilation of several *Chronicles of the City of Metz*), we encounter an explicit allusion to the conscious practice of allegorization in everyday life: "And they put a wooden child in her arms along with *another painted one hanging around her neck in order to signify the crime* that she had committed (*en signiffiance du delit qu'elle avoit fait*)."[28] The macabre pun that emerges here, completely consistent with the narrative, is that, *on one hand*, it is difficult to imagine a more literal picture of synecdoche; while, *on the other hand*, a theatricalized legal penalty lays claim both to "death, really" and allegory in perpetuity. In both the person and the eradicated personhood of the convicted murderess of Metz, a community beheld a living, dying, and dead woman who was *not a doll* but who was *being made into one* in the name of the law. At the same time, they beheld a stick of wood that was reanimated as a living—and dying—victim, a piece of wood that now seems animate enough to have died and to be dying. Beyond the explicit allegorization, this was a literal enactment of the role of synecdoche itself in one of its most common applications within the larger metaphor of what the law does every day: proffer cases as bodily parts of the body of the state, which exemplify (through representational pictures of past actions) present and future visions of how the parts of a society must make up a civilized whole. When we then realize that the wooden doll that was used during the mortal performance at the scaffold was, in all likelihood, a Christ-doll,[29] the events of 1495 all come together in such a way as to shed new light on both personification and the allegorical erasure of personhood that accompanies the ultimate penalty that is death.

Important though it is to acknowledge that pictorialization, personification, and allegory are not exactly synonymous,[30] if an *ars memorandi* is foundational to the way that medieval justice literally *foresees* the enactment of trial and punishment, then the execution of 1495 obliges us to look not just at foresight but at hindsight or aftersight once a mnemonic process has come full circle. Perhaps the quest for innovation at the scaffold had been driven by what Harold Bloom much later termed the "anxiety of influence"; perhaps it had been inspired by long-standing counsel from rhetoricians about the importance of eyewitnessing in forensic rhetorical procedures of transforming suspicion or probability into fact and in raising and "exciting the dead" (*IO*, IV, 1.28).[31] But, once the curtain has fallen on the legal drama of 1495 and the malefactor is dead, standing in for, representing, incarnating all those of his or her ilk, the doll and the painting illustrate how a community reconsigns allegorical imagery (as newly stable picture) back to the memory, where, eventually, it might move again to generate something else from the ultimate stasis of death. With renewed apologies for the mixed metaphor, I submit that burning, petrifying an infanticidal mother's criminal body is like *freezing* the movement of human *imagines agentes*. Therefore, some kind of theoretical perspective must intervene, lest we face the disturbing notion that the same system that animates a wooden stick is what petrifies a living being.

Memory and allegory make the absent present and the dead speak; but, as we read in the *Ad Herennium*, so too does personification or prosopopoeia, which is more aptly translated as impersonation:

> Personification (*conformatio*) consists in representing *an absent person as present*, or in making a mute thing or one lacking form articulate, and attributing to it a definite form and a language or a certain behaviour appropriate to its character. . . . Personification may be applied to a variety of things, mute and inanimate. It is most useful in the divisions under Amplification and in Appeal to Pity. (*RAH*, 4.66; my emphasis)[32]

The execution of 1495 renders absent victims present as well as present criminals absent and permanently silent, except when their allegorization moves them toward a pictorial stasis that is generative nevertheless of revised pictures, literal *re-visions*. So, at this point, anyone seeking to comprehend such events is ensnared in the bizarre chiasmus that seems endemic to the subject of allegory. The criminal has become a kind of doubly absent presence in the form of a corpse standing in for a class . . . that is to be remembered as the individual malefactor is forgotten . . . in favor of the class that, dead or alive, she has come to symbolize. But, with a bit of critical alchemy that combines Derridean crypt, Girardian ritual, Roachian surrogation, and the empty tomb of the *Visitatio sepulchri*, it is unclear whether allegory arranges for a *doubly absent presence* or a *doubly present absence*.[33] In the end, even a theater historian must admit that, sometimes, action is not enough.

In his much understudied essay on "Interpreting Drama," Umberto Eco asks us to ponder the example of the drunken man who is picked up off the street and displayed moralistically outside a place like the Salvation Army. One need not be a theater historian to appreciate the relevance of his theory of ostension to the semiotics of theater and allegory alike. Eco notices that "the drunken man has lost his original nature of 'real' body among real bodies": He has become "a semiotic device; he is now a sign, something that stands . . . for something else . . . a physical presence referring to something absent." But, when arguing that such bodily display "de-realize[s] a given object in order to make it stand for an entire class," Eco comes about as close as one might imagine to the allegorical essence of mnemonics—or is it the mnemonic essence of allegory? It is a matter of bringing "things absent . . . before our very eyes" (*IO*, VI, 2.29), which is, for Eco, a type of ostension that is "the most basic instance of performance."[34] But it is also one of the most basic instances of how medieval death penalties make meaning allegorically. The drunk on display in front of the Salvation Army is a sign because he has been made into one by someone else, by some other moralizing authority, which suggests a coercive dimension that challenges some of the more interesting claims of postmodern theater phenomenology.

Bruce Wilshire contends, for example, that is impossible to stage oneself dying because the artist "cannot achieve the level of control of the subject matter necessary for such art" nor can that artist "stand outside himself as dying character and aesthetically frame and bound himself."[35] But what if he—or she—is made into an actor by the civic authorities who control the legal theater? From the Roman amphitheater to the early modern spectacle of the scaffold, early cultures had cultivated a coercive expertise in staging the deaths of others in such a way as to force the victims into spectacular allegorizations of themselves,[36] all of which raises a key question to anyone committed to thinking allegory otherwise: *Is it possible to personify a person?* A person is already a person; and yet, in a nightmarish take on Austinian pretense, the likes of which inspired Jean Baudrillard to study simulation in Borges, the human symbols that were legally ostended in 1495 were "not merely like but *distinctively* like the genuine article simulated."[37] Ultimately, what is as troublesome to art as it is to ethics in such morbid and pitiful medieval allegories of justice is that, when living and dying coopted bodies symbolize themselves, personification becomes a literal depersonification, the violent termination of personhood.

Once upon a time, Quintilian expressed his utter disgust with the lawyerly habit of "bringing into court a picture of the crime painted on wood or canvas (*in tabula*)." He objected that "the pleader who prefers a voiceless picture to speak for him (*mutam illam effigiem*) . . . must be singularly incompetent" (*IO*, VI, 1.32). Rhetorical pictures were meant to be speaking pictures; and allegorical performance, like the allegorical performativity of the death penalty, has a voice, regardless of whether one hears that voice on stage or off, or, following Augustine's own conception of memory, only silently but clear as a bell inside one's own mind in the company of one's God: "Though my tongue be quiet, and my throat silent, yet can I sing as much as I will" (*Confessions*, 1: 2.10). In 1495, there were two effigies of a dead baby—a wooden doll and a painting—plus a living criminal body that underwent a forced, spectacular metamorphosis into a dead-body-as-effigy. In the United States, where the vernacular makes room for such an expression as "burned in effigy" (a practice of protest that usually targets political persons and the regimes they *represent*), we may now have come back to the medieval future of the legal allegorization of death.

Of the extant accounts, one of the most interesting death penalties took place near the French city of Chartres in 1606; and it concerns the death sentence imposed on one Guillaume Guyard for having sodomized his (female) dog. Guillaume had been sentenced to be hanged and then "burned to ashes, along with the aforesaid bitch"; but because he had fled the jurisdiction, the sentence specified that that could happen only "if the aforesaid Guyard can be taken and apprehended in person (*en sa personne*)." If not, there was an allegorical alternative: "The sentence shall be executed in effigy (*exécuté par effigie*) *by means of a painting* that shall be placed and attached

to the aforesaid gibbet (*en un tableau qui sera mis et attaché*)."[38] Most reso-
nant of all here is the possibility of symbolizing, allegorizing, and enacting
not just death but a *death wish*.

What, then, do we wish allegory to do in the twenty-first century?

Granted, convicted murderers are no longer burned at the stake in the
contemporary United States; and, with the exception of films like Errol
Morris's *Mr. Death* (1999), the death penalty is all so euphemistic, so an-
tipictorial. Every now and then, there is a movie that imagines televising
the death penalty, such as *Witness to the Execution* (1994), or a lawsuit that
demands that such penalties be made visible to the public, such as *KQED
v. Daniel Vasquez* (from 1991).[39] But, for the most part, unless they are
journalists, clergy, or family members of either the victim(s) or the killer(s),
American citizens are not permitted access to capital punishment-in-action.
Does that mean that deaths silent and unseen are meant to be forgotten? Or
that we should remember the brutality of the crime and the pain of the victim but forget any American image of justice being done that is not mediated (by artists' renderings, journalism, or other audiovisuals from the Court
Television Network)? That we are meant to forget about the death penalty?
Or perhaps just about the conflict that surrounds it? Or is it, rather, that, we
are to seek symbolism and literalism elsewhere and otherwise?

In recent crimes of infanticide, the pictorials move so quickly to the
politics of abortion and to the so-called death sentences imposed on fetuses
that, compared to the graphic posters that challenge cultural opinions as
to whether aborted fetuses are living or not-yet-life, the medieval Messin
doubling in paintings and wooden dolls starts to look like child's play.[40]
Consider, for instance, the extreme literalism of the double death sentences
that constitute part of the theory and practice of radical Right-to-Lifers
who bomb abortion clinics illegally, enacting their latter-day *lex talionis* to
exact murder as the righteous penalty for what they believe to be a slaughter
of the innocents. And, beyond the inflammatory issue of abortion, infanticide is more likely nowadays to prompt a larger debate about postpartum
depression or psychosis; whereas medieval justice would have focused on
sin and redemption (and modern historians on the gendered, socioeco-
nomic lives of the serving classes). Meanwhile, widely aired imagery of the
American infanticides that scorched the collective memory—those notorious prom-queen moms who disposed of their children in toilets and trash
cans; the sequential, psychotically methodical murders by Andrea Yates of
her five children[41]—have directed our sights unceasingly to the pathos of

the victims, as evoked by the ubiquitous family photographs of the smiling Yates children.

In addition to the loss of Philippe's "beautiful repentance" (*Gedenkbuch*, 124) or of the *Digest*'s cathartic *solacio* at the scaffold,[42] something else has been lost as well. Medieval legal culture hyped its deadly visuals, and Philippe de Vigneulles recorded innovation after innovation at the scaffold, all designed to consign and reconsign allegories of justice to the collective memory: pictures of the living dead and the dead-no-longer-living. So it is a most curious thing that, when the United States, or one of its state governments, executes someone, medieval spectacle is replaced by an invisible rhetoric of exemplarity that recasts, in line with the symbol-making advent of modernity, contemporary punishments as *not cruel and unusual*. Needless to say, I am by no means singling out certain modes of execution as worthy recipients of our praise. Far from it. But, at the very least, there is an honesty that attends the theatrics of medieval cruelty that renders its modern descendants all the more bizarre, especially as mediated—literally—by the media.

If allegory is saying one thing and meaning another, then what are we to make of the fact that we actually see death all the time on television: in spectacles of terrorism that look more like snuff films, in such events as the airing of the Kevorkian-assisted suicide of Thomas Youk on *60 Minutes* in 1998, the endlessly reaired death screams of Nicole Brown Simpson during her call to 911, the attacks on the Twin Towers, or hostages pleading for their lives in Afghanistan or Iraq as a prelude to executions that are apparently shown by Al-Jazeera but not by U.S. news outlets.[43] What, moreover, are we to make of the U.S. government's authorization (in the person of Donald Rumsfeld) of the mass media dissemination on Al-Jazeera of the dead bodies of the sons of Saddam Hussein, Uday and Qusay? American networks carried the story and projected the images of the dead, supposedly as a point of information, the better to demonstrate to an American audience just what it is that a lawless people needs to *see* in order to believe.[44]

If pictorialization of punishment is for the so-called Third World, the message seems to be that, at least in part, barbarians need the concrete— not the allegorical or the symbolic—and that, above all, it is the United States that has the monopoly on symbol making, on allegorization. Showing not a symbol but an instantaneously recognizable dead body that is itself and itself only is perfectly consistent with the symbol-making needs of the projectors of the image: projectors who insist that such ocular proof is necessary only to a barbaric people in desperate need of the enduring freedom made possible by the infinite justice provided by those who read invasion as liberation. In that ultimate allegorization, even killing is not murder—it never is when authorized by the state. Instead, it is memorable justice, it is the reallegorization of an allegory that no one ever wanted to acknowledge in the first place.

We are not so far here from the advent of what Hans Robert Jauss called "the aesthetics of the *verisimile*," which constituted "a historical way [to] . . . resurrect and legitimize the here and now" while transforming the imaginary into the real (*QA*, 4–6; his emphasis). What looks like the opposite of allegory is the greatest allegory of all: the revisionary justice of revisionist history, as embraced by the Middle Ages as it is concealed today, and as medieval as it ever was.

APPENDIX

1. *La Chronique de Philippe de Vigneulles,* ed. Bruneau, 3: 337–338; my emphasis.

Une fille bruslée par justices.—En ce meisme tamps, le vandredi devant les Paulme, X^e jour d'apvril, advint en Mets une aultre esclandre. Car à ce jour fut accusée une josne fille, eaigée de XVIII ans, qui servoit Piéron des Mollin, le viez. Le cas fut telz que celle jonne fille, elle estant en cest eaige, avoit conceus ung anffans; et le cella tellement qu'elle l'enfanta toutte seulle. Puis la pouvre dollante, mal advisée, le print par les piedz et le frappait contre ung mur, et le tuay; et, ce fait, le gectait en ung puis qui estoit en la maison que ledit Piéron tenoit decost Saint Anthonne sus les mollin, là où il faisoient la servoize (car ledit Piéron estoit guernetier de la ville). Et y fut cest anffans depuis le jour de la Chandelleur jusques au Xe jours d'apvril. Auquelle jour les brasseurs qui bressoient la servoize en la dicte maison vollurent essaier ce qu'ilz n'avoient encor fait, c'est assavoir se l'yawe dudit puis seroit bonne à faire servoise; et, après la conclusion donnée, acomansairent à tirer de celle yawe. Mais incontinant ont veu l'anffans sur l'yawe, lequelle flottoit et négeoit. Dont il ont estés bien esbahis; toutteffois, il n'en ont fais aulcuns semblant, et ont délibérés de le celler tant que leur maistre Pierron seroit revenus de la pourcession. Mais, durant qu'il en devisoient, la fille les acoutoit; par quoy, incontinant qu'il ce/fussent pertis du lieu, elle ce desvallait au cellier, et, par une fenestre qui respondoit au puis, avec un rètez, elle print l'enffant, et le allait gecter en une courtoise. Et, quant ledit Piéron fut revenus, son nepveulx, le jonne Pierron, luy dist et contait comment en leur puis y avoit ung anffans; et, de fait, luy voult aller monstrer: mais il n'y trouvèrent riens. Et alors commencèrent à serchier par toutte la maison; et, à la fin, fut l'anffans trouvés dedans la corthoise. Incontinant la fille fut prinse et emmenée. Et, tantost le mardi après, elle fut mise on pillory; puis fut menée entre les deux pont. Et là on avoit fait ung angiens, non pas à la coustume des aultre: car la dicte fille estoit toutte droitte ellevée en hault et contre ung grant pal. Et, tout premièrement, olt l'une des mains couppées; et puis on bouttait le feu, et fut arse et brûllée: non pas que l'on la laissait consumer; car, incontinant qu'elle fût morte, on estindait le feu, et demourait toutte droitte, qui estoit hideuse chose à veoir. Et lui mist on ung anffans de boix entre ces bras, avec ung aultres en pointure.

2. Philippe de Vigneulles, *Gedenkbuch,* ed. Michelant, 124.

En celluy meisme temps par ung jour du grant mairdy de la grant semaigne de caresme, l'an iiij.xx et xv fut fait justice devant les pons de Mets d'une jonne fille eaigée de xiij ans, laquelle demouroit en l'ostel le gros Pieron des Mollins. Et fut la dite jonne fille menée au pillory depuis les x heures jusques aux ij heures, comme la coustume en est; et puis fut menée devant les pons et eust illec l'une des mains coupées et puis, celay fait, fut brulée et airse, non pas comme on art les aultres, car elle estoit haulte elevée, et incontinent qu'elle fut morte on estaindait le feu et fut mis son corps sus une rue; et luy mist-on emprès d'elle ung petit enffant de bois; et avoit encor avec cela ung aultre grant paipier, atachié à la dite rue, auquel avoit ung enffant en pointure et sa mère qui le tuoit. Et tout ce fut fait pourtant, que la powre jonne fille avoit esté engrossie d'ung mairchant estrangier et avoit tousjour nié à sa maitresse, qu'elle ne le seoit point; et une nuit qu'elle estoit en son lit, entour la chandelleur, devant qu'elle fut détruite, elle acouchait toute à par elle; mais avant que l'enfant fût du tout à monde, elle l'empougnait par la teste et le tirait dehors, puis le ruait en terre et le tuait, et le gairdait soubz son lit en des drapiaulz jusques au lendemain. Et le lendemain elle le ruait en ungne cisterne, qui estoit en ung cellier, où l'on ne tiroit guère souvent de l'yave. Mais de cop de fortune y eust un gairxon de léans, qui besoingnoit aulcune chose au cellier et voult regairder à la cisterne et le vit et le monstrait à ung sien compaignon; mais ils ne savoient au vray que ce fût. Cy le tirèrent

dehors et trouvirent que c'estoit ung enffant, et ainsy qu'ils le tiroient hors
de l'iawe, la fille vint au cellier et le print en son giron et le cuidait cacher
et s'en cuidoit fouir; mais incontinent fut acusée à justice et fut prinse et
brulée, comme vous aves oy, et souffrit grant tourment. Dieu luy pardont
ses faultes et nous les nostres, car elle eust une belle repentance en la fin.

3. *Les Chroniques de la ville de Metz,* ed. Huguenin, 604–605.

Le vendredi devant les palmes, qui fut le dixiesme jour d'apvril, on fist la
procession à Sainct Clement de la victoire heue contre l'entreprinse faicte
par le duc Nicollais de Loraine sus la cité; et à icelle y eult moult de gens,
car il faisoit beaul temps.

Ledit jour meisme, fut accusée une jonne fille, aigée de dix huict ans, qui
servoit le viez Pierron, clerc des ouvrages des mollins sus Muzelle, laquelle
estoit enceinte d'enffant; et, par seduction et temptation de l'ennemi
/ d'enffer, de la vigille de la Chandelleur qu'elle eult son mal d'enffant,
sans sonner mot ne appeller personne, elle enffanta toutte seulle et tira elle
meisme l'enffant hors de son ventre, comme elle le congneut et gehit à justice. Apres, ceste pouvre dollente, mal advisée print ledit enffant par les
piedz, le fraippa contre ung mur et l'assomma; puis, ce fait, le mist dessoubz
le chevet de son lict jusques au lundemain. Quant son maistre et sa maistresse estoient à l'eglise, elle print l'enffant et le pourta en une maison de
coste l'hostel St Anthoine sus Muzelle, en laquelle ladicte servante et sondit
maistre et maistresse estoient souvent, pourtant que en icelle on y vendoit
la servoise pour la cité et en estoit vendeur ledit Pierron et grainetier de la
ville, et gecta ledit enffant au puix de ladicte maison. Et y fut depuis le jour
de la Chandelleur jusques au dixiesme jour d'apvril, que les brasseurs de
servoise allont en ladicte maison et vouloient mettre du grant gervier pour
faire de la servoise. Et l'ung d'eulx se advisa et dist: Il y a ici ceans ung puix:
si l'yawe estoit bonne et nette, ce nous feroit ung grant plaisir; et y allont
veoir avec une chandoille et virent l'enffant qui estoit au dessus de l'yawe,
dont ilz furent bien esbahis. Toutesfois ilz conclurent qu'ilz n'en feroient nul
semblant, et le cellont tant que leur maistre fut revenu de la procession à
l'hostel. Mais durant qu'ilz en devisoient entre eulx, la servante les escoutoit
secretement. Et quant elle entendit que c'estoit de l'enffant qu'ilz devisoient,
qui estoit au puix, incontinent qu'ilz furent partis, elle se devalla au cellier
et par une fenestre qui respondoit au puix, pour estre plus pres de l'yawe,
avec ung ratel elle print l'enffant et le alla getteir en la cortoise de ladicte

maison. Et quant ledit Pierron fut revenu, son nepveu, le jonne Pierron, qui le servoit, luy dist et conta comment qu'ilz avoient veu ung enffant en leur puix et luy voult aller monstreir; mais ilz n'y trouvont rien. Si commencerent à cerchier par toutte la maison, et à la fin fut trouvé l'enffant getté en la cortoise et le tiront hors. De quoy ledit Pierron en avertit justice qui fist apprehendeir ladicte servante qui cogneust incontinent son cas. Et le mairdy elle fut mise au pillory, puis fut menée entre les deux ponts; et là on avoit fait ung engien, non pas à la coustume des aultres; car ladicte fille estoit toutte droicte, eslevée en hault contre ung grant pal et liée. Et eult premierement l'une des mains coppée; puis on boutta le feu, tant qu'elle fut arse et estouffée, non pas que l'on la laissast toutte consumer; car incontinent qu'elle fut morte on esteindit le feu; et là demeura toutte droicte; qui estoit chose hideuse à veoir. Et luy mist on ung enffant de boix entre ses bras avec ung aultre en peinture, pendu au col, en signiffiance du delit qu'elle avoit fait: et fut la main qu'on luy avoit coppée, clouée au pal où elle estoit attaichée.

4. Sentence pronounced by the Mayor of Loens de Chartres, 12 September 1606. Cited in E. P. Evans, *The Criminal Prosecution and Capital Punishment of Animals,* 296–297; his emphasis.

. . . Veu le procès criminel, charges et informations, décret de prise de corps, adjournement à troys briefs jours, les dicts trois deffaulx, le dict quart d'habondant, le recollement des dicts témoings et *recognaissance faicte par les dicts témoings de la chienne dont est question,* les conclusions dudict procureur, tout veu et eu sur ce conseil, nous disant que lesdicts troys deffaulx et quart d'habondant ont esté bien donnés pris et obtenus contre ledict Guyard accusé, attainct et convaincu. . . .

Pour réparation et punition duquel crime condempnons ledict Guyard estre pendu et estranglé à une potence qui, pour cest effet, sera dressée aux lices du Marché aux Chevaux de ceste ville de Chartres, au lieu et endroict où les dict sieurs ont tout droit de justice. Et auparavant ladicte exécution de mort, que ladicte chienne sera assommée par l'exécuteur de la haute justice audict lieu, et seront les corps morts, tant dudict Guyard que de la dicte chienne brûlés et mis en cendres, si le dict Guyard peut estre pris et apprehendé en sa personne, sy non pour le regard du dict Guyard, sera la sentence exécuté [*sic*] par effigie en un tableau qui sera mis et attaché à ladicte potence, et déclarons tous et chascuns ses biens acquis et confisqués à qui il appartiendra, sur cieux préalablement pris la somme de cent cinquante livres d'amende que nous avons adjugées auxdicts sieurs, sur laquelle somme seront pris les fraicts de justice. Prononcé et exécuté par effigie, pour le regard du dict Guyard les jour et an cy dessus. Signé *Guyot*.

Notes

1. *La Chronique de Philippe de Vigneulles*, hereafter *CPV*, ed. Charles Bruneau, 4 vols. (Metz: Société d'histoire de d'archéologie de la Lorraine, 1927–1933): 3: 338; my emphasis; and see also Bruneau's helpful biography of Philippe (1: i–xv). For the complete passage, which I reproduce as is (notwithstanding Philippe's bizarre orthography), see Appendix 1. All translations from the French are mine unless otherwise indicated. Bodily dismemberment (cutting off the hands) was a conventional medieval punishment to which we return below; and it is familiar to specialists of the medieval theater, e.g., in the symbolic dismemberment of the Croxton *Play of the Sacrament*. See David Bevington's edition of that play in *Medieval Drama* (Boston: Houghton-Mifflin, 1975): 754–788; at 772–773. Finally, while the subject lies beyond the scope of this study, the closest modern analog to this practice is to be found in the hideous U.S. legacy of the (extralegal) lynching; see, e.g., Harvey Young's superb—and supremely disturbing "The Black Body as Souvenir in American Lynching," *Theatre Journal* 57.4 (2005): 639–657.

2. Foucault, *Discipline and Punish: The Birth of the Prison*, trans. Alan Sheridan (New York: Pantheon, 1977): esp. chaps. 1 and 2.

3. De Certeau, *The Practice of Everyday Life*, trans. Steven Rendall (Berkeley: University of California Press, 1988): 140. *The law*, however, does not write or engrave; people do.

4. "Famosos latrones in his locis, ubi grassati sunt, furca figendos compluribus placuit, ut *et conspectu* dettereantur alii ab isdem facinoribus et *solacio* sit cognatis et adfinibus interemptorum eodem loco poena reddita, in quo latrones homicidia fecissent," *Digesta*, in *Corpus iuris civilis*, ed. T. Mommsen (Berlin, 1877): 2: bk. 48.19.28.15; my emphasis; trans. Alan Watson, *The Digest of Justinian*, hereafter *DJ*, eds. Theodor Mommsen, Paul Krueger; 2 vols. (Philadelphia: University of Pennsylvania Press, 1985).

5. Nietzsche, *The Birth of Tragedy and the Genealogy of Morals*, trans. Francis Golffing (Garden City, NY: Doubleday, 1956): 192. I discuss the medieval resonance of that passage in *The Medieval Theater of Cruelty: Rhetoric, Memory, Violence*, hereafter *MTOC* (Ithaca, NY: Cornell University Press, 1998), chap. 2.

6. Here I paraphrase Peter Brook, *The Empty Space* (Middlesex, U.K.: Penguin, 1972): 136; as ably discussed by Stanton B. Garner Jr., *Bodied Spaces: Phenomenology and Performance in Contemporary Drama* (Ithaca, NY: Cornell University Press, 1994): 161.

7. Plato, *Laws*, 2 vols., ed. and trans. R. G. Bury, Loeb Classical Library (1926; rpt. Cambridge, MA: Harvard University Press, 1942): 1: 663b–c.

8. While it is not our present focus, *justice* hardly seems the appropriate term for the punishment inflicted on a number of infanticidal mothers in Metz: Oftentimes, their offspring were stillborn, or they were the issue of rape. I discuss several such incidents in "Theater Makes History: Ritual Murder by Proxy in the *Mistere de la Sainte Hostie*," *Speculum* 79 (2004): 991–1016. On self-signification, I draw on Umberto Eco, "Interpreting Drama," in *The Limits of Interpretation*, 101–110 (Bloomington: Indiana University Press, 1990), to which we return shortly. On the theater of everyday life, see, in addition to de Certeau, Victor Turner, *From Ritual to Theatre: The Human Seriousness of Play* (1982; rpt. New York: PAJ, 1992): esp. 102–123; Alan Read, *Theatre and Everyday Life: An Ethics of Performance* (London and New York: Routledge, 1993); and Angus Fletcher on "symbolic action" in *Allegory: The Theory of a Symbolic Mode* (Ithaca, NY: Cornell University Press, 1964): chap. 3.

9. Folklorists also use *ostension* to denote what we call, in the vernacular, copycat crimes. See William Ellis, "Death by Folklore: Ostension, Contemporary Legend, and Murder," *Western Folklore* 48 (1989): 201–220. The theatricality of legal rhetoric is the subject of my *Rhetoric and the Origins of Medieval Drama*, hereafter *ROMD*, Rhetoric and Society, 1 (Ithaca, NY: Cornell University Press, 1992): esp. chaps. 1 and 2. For Artaud, I refer, of course, to *The Theater and Its Double*, trans. Mary Caroline Richards (New York: Grove Weidenfeld, 1958).

10. For the relevance of surrogacy to theater studies, see Joseph Roach, *Cities of the Dead: Circum-Atlantic Performance* (New York: Columbia University Press, 1996): defined at 2–3; and pioneered by René Girard in his groundbreaking *Violence and the Sacred*, trans. Patrick Gregory (Baltimore: Johns Hopkins University Press, 1977): esp. chap. 3.

11. Such canonical formulations as "*The State vs. John Doe*," where "The State" stands in for the community, are explored in *Law's Stories: Narrative and Rhetoric in the Law*, ed. Peter Brooks and Paul Gewirtz (New Haven, CT: Yale University Press, 1996). See esp. the editors' own contributions, Gewirtz, "Narrative and Rhetoric in the Law," 2–13; and Brooks, "The Law as Narrative and Rhetoric," 14–22.

12. Robert Zemeckis could hardly have anticipated the 23 million spins (as of fall 2006 on Google) on his *Back to the Future* (1985).

13. See the famous Augustinian mnemonic conflation of visions past, present, and future in *Confessions*, ed. and trans. William Watts, 2 vols., Loeb Classical Library (Cambridge, MA: Harvard University Press, 1950): 2: bk. 11, chap. 11.

14. [Cicero], *Ad C. Herennium*, hereafter *RAH*, ed. and trans. Harry Caplan, Loeb Classical Library (1954; rpt. Cambridge, MA: Harvard University Press, 1977): 4.46. On the availability in France of the *RAH* as early as the eleventh century, see Jules Alexandre Clerval, *Les Écoles de Chartres au Moyen-Âge du Ve au XVIe siècle* (Chartres, France: Selleret, 1895): 115–117.

15. In spite of such ambitious treatments of the subject as Wayne C. Booth's *A Rhetoric of Irony* (Chicago: University of Chicago Press, 1974); C. Jan Swearingen,

Rhetoric and Irony: Western Literacy and Western Lies (New York and Oxford, U.K.: Oxford University Press, 1991); and Hayden White, *Metahistory: The Historical Imagination in Nineteenth-Century Europe* (Baltimore: Johns Hopkins University Press, 1973), that literary mode has yet to receive the full critical treatment that it deserves in medieval studies. To this day, Martha Bayless's *Parody in the Middle Ages: The Latin Tradition* (Ann Arbor: University of Michigan Press, 1996) remains one of the few studies that even attempts it.

16. Greenblatt, *Shakespearean Negotiations: The Circulation of Social Energy in Renaissance England* (Berkeley: University of California Press, 1988): 126.

17. Drawing on the groundbreaking work of Frances Yates, *The Art of Memory* (Chicago: University of Chicago Press, 1966) and Mary Carruthers, *The Book of Memory* (Cambridge, U.K.: Cambridge University Press, 1990), I make that argument esp. in *MTOC*, chap. 2.

18. I coined that term in *ROMD*, 4–18.

19. See Schechner, *Between Theater and Anthropology* (Philadelphia: University of Pennsylvania Press, 1985): chap 2; and also, for theater's "re-production" and unrepeatability, see Walter Benjamin, *Illuminations*, ed. Hannah Arendt, trans. Harry Zohn (New York: Schocken Books, 1969): 220; also discussed by Read, *Theatre of Everyday Life*, 15.

20. *Gedenkbuch des Metzer Bürgers Philippe von Vigneulles aus den Jahren 1471–1522*, ed. Heinrich Michelant (Stuttgart, 1852; rpt. Amsterdam: Rodopi, 1968): 124; my emphasis. See below, Appendix 2.

21. Quintilian, *Institutio oratoria*, hereafter *IO*, ed. and trans. H. E. Butler, 4 vols., Loeb Classical Library (1920; rpt. Cambridge, MA: Harvard University Press, 1980): VI, 2.29; and 1.31; my emphasis.

22. The phrase from Quintilian appears in *IO*, IV, 1.28; in *MTOC*, 71–82, I argue that rhetorical theory calls for death as "preimaginative" mnemonic resurrection. See also Patrick J. Geary, *Living with the Dead in the Middle Ages* (Ithaca, NY: Cornell University Press, 1995).

23. "Le clerc eust premier les deux mains coppées, et puis la teste; et fut le pétal duquel il avoit fait le copt pandus et estaichiés en hault, contre la lance et a plus près d'icelle teste," *CPV*, 3: 34. Given that a *pétal* or *pétard* was a small explosive device (firecracker, bomb, mine, or the like), it is difficult to know what precisely would have been left to display next to the man's decapitated head. I thank Jack Talbott for his insight into French military history; and I treat this long narrative of over 1,000 words (3: 33–35) in an essay in progress entitled "Marital Rape and the Medieval Theater of Everyday Life." Compare also with the version in the *Chroniques de la ville de Metz, recueillies, mises en ordre et publiées pour la première fois: Le Doyen de S.ᵗ Thiébault.—Jean Aubrion.—Philippe de Vigneulles.—Praillon.—Annales Messines, etc., 900–1552*, hereafter *CVM*, ed. Jean-François Huguenin (Metz: S. Lamort, 1838): 413–414.

24. "Et estoit cest angiens en manier d'ugne chayre trouées, laquelle fut pandue en hault encontre ung grant paul. . . . et puis l'on alumait le feu, lequel couppait tantost la corde à quoy pandoit cest angiens: par quoy la chayre cheut en xaillant

et s'avallant au loing du paul jusques à trois piedz près de terre, et demourait ainssy jusques que tout fût consumés." One cannot help but make the transumptive rhetorical move to the contemporary, vulgar vernacular, which would have the woman being "screwed right back over" by the justice system.

25. As the site of infamy of countless antisemitic legends, the outhouse is one of the principal foci of my "Theater Makes History;" and it is well worth emphasizing here the logic of hiding a corpse in any locus (outhouses, charnel houses) where it would be overwhelmed by other stenches. See, of course, the exemplary work on medieval antisemitism by Miri Rubin, *Gentile Tales: The Narrative Assault on Late Medieval Jews* (New Haven, CT: Yale University Press, 1999); and David Nirenberg, *Communities of Violence: Persecution of Minorities in the Middle Ages* (Princeton, NJ: Princeton University Press, 1996). Regarding the events of 1495, there are significant variations even in the three accounts under discussion; but all involve dissemblance, concealment, and pretense. In the *Chronicles*, the body of the child is discovered in the well by a group of brewers, whom the girl overhears: She fishes the child out with a net and proceeds to hide the body in the outhouse, where it is eventually discovered by a search party. In the *Gedenkbuch*, the tiny corpse is discovered simply by happenstance, a *coup de fortune* by which a young boy happens to be in the cellar: He fishes out the child, after which he is apparently confronted by the girl, who takes the corpse and attempts unsuccessfully to flee. Compare the three accounts in Appendices 1, 2, and 3.

26. "Candlemas," *Catholic Encyclopedia*. For a literary perspective on the matter, see Peggy McCracken, "Engendering Sacrifice: Blood, Lineage, and Infanticide in Old French Literature," *Speculum* 77 (2002): 55–75.

27. In addition to the passage from the *DJ* cited above, the term *catharsis* has fascinating medical connotations of purifying purgation, which have been explored, e.g., by Andrzej Szczeklik, *Catharsis: On the Art of Medicine*, trans. Antonia Lloyd-Jones (Chicago: University of Chicago Press, 2005). The full connotations of *holocaust* as burnt offering are attested in Old French as early as the twelfth century.

28. *CVM*, ed. Huguenin (cited above, note 23): 605; my emphasis; see below Appendix 3.

29. See Christiane Klapisch-Zuber, "Holy Dolls: Play and Piety in Florence in the Quattrocento," chap. 14 of *Women, Family, and Ritual in Renaissance Florence*, trans. Lydia G. Cochrane (Chicago: University of Chicago Press, 1985). I thank Elina Gertsman for bringing that work to my attention.

30. W. T. H. Jackson, e.g., rightly stresses the debt of allegory to personification; but he insists that the latter is not the "decisive step" in allegorization, which occurs "when the personified abstractions become the only participants in the action or when the appearance of human beings is confined to the participation of the author himself or his *persona*" (*The Challenge of the Medieval Text: Studies in Genre and Interpretation*, ed. Joan M. Ferrante and Robert W. Hanning (New York: Columbia University Press, 1985): 160; his emphasis).

31. I make that argument in *MTOC*, 28–38. See also Quintilian on eyewitnessing (*IO*, IV, 2.123); Peter Burke, *Eyewitnessing: The Uses of Images as Historical*

Evidence (Ithaca, NY: Cornell University Press, 2001); and Bloom's *Anxiety of Influence: A Theory of Poetry* (Oxford, U.K.: Oxford University Press, 1975).

32. "Conformatio est cum aliqua quae non adest persona confingitur quasi adsit, aut cum res muta aut informis fit eloquens, et forma ei et oratio adtribuitur ad dignitatem adcommodata aut actio quaedam. . . . Haec conformatio licet in plures res, in mutas atque inanimas transferatur. Proficit plurimum in amplificationis partibus et commiseratione." Harry Caplan translates *prosopopoeia* as "personification" (*RAH*, 4.66) and notes that "representing an absent person as present would not today be regarded as strictly within the meaning of Personification" (398n). In his translation of Quintilian, however, Butler prefers to translate *prosopopoeia* as "impersonation," as do I (*ROMD*, 56–57): see, e.g., *IO*, VI, 1.25).

33. See Girard, *Violence and the Sacred*, chaps. 1–3; Peggy Kamuf's work on Derrida's *Fors* in *Fictions of Feminine Desire: Disclosures of Heloise* (Lincoln: University of Nebraska Press, 1982): xi; Anthony Kubiak's brilliant reading of the *quem quaeritis* trope in *Stages of Terror: Terrorism, Ideology, and Coercion as Theatre History* (Bloomington: Indiana University Press, 1991): 48–59; and Hans Ulrich Gumbrecht, *Production of Presence: What Meaning Cannot Convey* (Stanford, CA: Stanford University Press, 2003): esp. the (unnumbered) chapter, "Epiphany/Presentification/Deixis."

34. In addition to Eco, "Interpreting Drama," 102–103; my emphasis; see also, on the subject of derealization, Hans Robert Jauss's analysis of the work of Wolfgang Iser (esp. *The Fictive and the Imaginary: Charting Literary Anthropology.* [Baltimore: Johns Hopkins University Press, 1993]), in *Question and Answer: Forms of Dialogic Understanding*, hereafter *QA*, trans. Michael Hays, *Theory and History of Literature* 68 (Minneapolis: University of Minnesota Press, 1989): 10.

35. Wilshire, *Role Playing and Identity: The Limits of Theatre as Metaphor* (1982; rpt. Bloomington: Indiana University Press, 1991): 251; 268.

36. See Shadi Bartsch, *Actors in the Audience: Theatricality and Doublespeak from Nero to Hadrian*, Revealing Antiquity, 6 (Cambridge, MA: Harvard University Press, 1994): chap. 1.

37. See J. L. Austin, *Philosophical Papers*, ed. J. O. Urmson and G. J. Warnock, 2nd ed. (Oxford, U.K.: Clarendon, 1970): 214, his emphasis; and also Baudrillard on Borges in *Selected Writings*, ed. and trans. Mark Poster (Stanford, CA: Stanford University Press, 1988): 166–167.

38. E. P. Evans reproduces this text in *The Criminal Prosecution and Capital Punishment of Animals: The Lost History of Europe's Animal Trials* (1906; rpt. London: Faber and Faber, 1988): 296–297; and, for his English translation, 148; my emphasis. See also Appendix 4. One can only wonder about the content of the depositions from "those who testified on behalf of the bitch"; I discuss this bizarre legislation in "Homicidal Pigs and the Antisemitic Imagination," *Exemplaria* 14.1 (2002): 201–238.

39. For a brilliant analysis of that trial, see Wendy Lesser, *Pictures at an Execution: An Inquiry into the Subject of Murder* (Cambridge, MA: Harvard University Press, 1993): chap. 2.

40. The politics of abortion is not a purely modern concept, and its punishment was detailed in the *Digest of Justinian*. See, e.g., the explanation about the "bad example" set by "those who administer an abortifacient or aphrodisiac" (2: 48.19.38.5); and the death sentence of "a certain woman of Miletus [who] had . . . been condemned for a capital offense because . . . she herself aborted her own child with drugs" (2: 48.19.39).

41. I discuss both cases in "Theater Makes History."

42. For that *solacio*, see *DJ*, 2: 48.19.28.15; cited above, note 4.

43. See Mark Juergensmeyer on the "Theater of Terror," chap. 7 of *Terror in the Mind of God: The Global Rise of Religious Violence* (Berkeley: University of California Press, 2000). I discuss such incidents *Murder by Accident: Theater, Medievalism, and Critical Intentions* (Chicago: University of Chicago Press, 2009): 185–190.

44. "U.S. Releases Photos Said to Show Saddam's Sons' Bodies: Many Iraqis Want Proof That Uday, Qusay Were Killed," July 24, 2003. Retrieved on July 28, 2007, from: CNN.com.

THREE

The Mask of Copernicus and the Mark of the Compass

Bruno, Galileo, and the Ontology of the Page

DANIEL SELCER

> For the more distant the means of imitation from the imitated thing, the more marvelous the imitation will be.
>
> GALILEO TO CIGLO *(June 26, 1612)*[1]

In *Dialogo sopra i due massimi sistemi del mondo* (1632), Galileo mounts the stage of "the theater of the world" to defend and modify the position of Copernicus's *De revolutionibus* (1543).[2] On the second day of Galileo's dialogue, his filiation takes a particularly complex form. Salviati (the Copernican character) announces that he must tell Sagredo (the undecided character):

> That I act the part of Copernicus in our arguments and wear his mask. As to the internal effects upon me of the arguments which I produce in his favor, I want you to be guided not by what I say when we are in the heat of acting out our play, but after I have put off the costume, for perhaps then you shall find me different from what you saw of me on the stage.[3]

What exactly does it mean to wear the mask of Copernicus, and what differences can we expect when Salviati removes it? In Galileo's text they will involve better descriptions of the shape of the orbits of the planets; more precise measures of their sizes, speeds, and locations; the inclusion of an account of the moons of Jupiter, to be sure; all based on the radically more accurate observations made possible by Galileo's telescopes. From a scientific perspective, these are all important costume changes. But from a philosophical and rhetorical one, we might ask whether Galileo's Salviati ever removes his mask and inquire into its theatrical and allegorical character. If Galileo can take up and put down the mask of Copernicus, could another have worn it before him? Would this be the petrified death mask of a long-dead Polish mathematical astronomer (his *imago*), or would it be an emblem of "the general structure of the universe" Copernicus asserted that book to contained?[4]

This essay examines the mobilization of allegory in Galileo's *Dialogo*, comparing it with a slightly earlier dialogical defense of Copernicus in Giordano Bruno's *La Cena de le Ceneri* (1584).[5] I use these texts to explore the allegorical afterlife of a cosmological diagram produced by Copernicus (Figure 3.1)

Figure 3.1. Nicholas Copernicus, *De revolutionibus orbium cœlestium* (Nuremberg: Ioh. Petreium, 1543), fol. 9v. Shelf-mark fGC5 C7906.543d, by permission of Houghton Library, Harvard University.

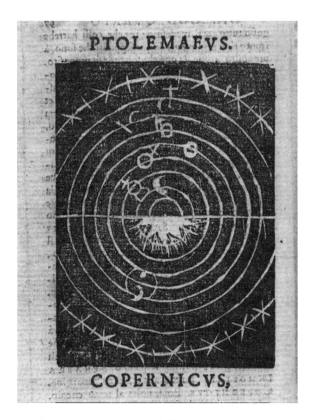

Figure 3.2. Giordano Bruno, *La Cena de le Ceneri* ([London]: [J. Charle-wood], 1584), 98. Shelf-mark STC 3935, by permission of Houghton Library, Harvard University.

then reproduced, transformed, and disfigured by Bruno (Figure 3.2) and Galileo (Figure 3.3).[6] I analyze the theatrical scenes for the inscription of this diagram in *Cena* and the *Dialogo*, arguing that they can be understood productively in terms of allegory and that neither the diagram nor these texts' dialogical forms can be reduced to mere ornamentation or illustration.[7] In his Piercean critique of both platonic realism and Husserlian phenomenology dealing with a related diagrammatic context (mathematics rather than cosmography), Brian Rotman emphasizes the corporeal and confrontational function of diagrams. "They are created and maintained as entities and attain significance only in relation to human visual-kinetic presence," he claims, and they "call attention to the materiality of all signs and the corporeality of those who manipulate them."[8] From a very different

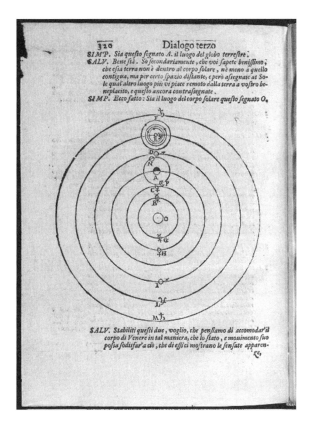

Figure 3.3. Galileo Galilei, *Dialogo dei massimi sistemi* (Florence: Gio Battista Landini, 1632), 320. Shelf-mark *90W-88, by permission of Houghton Library, Harvard University.

perspective, Reviel Netz's historical account of the practices surrounding the function of diagrams in ancient Greek mathematics denies the severability of diagram from proof and argues that "neither makes sense without the other" because "the diagram sets up a world of reference, which delimits the text" such that "each geometrical proposition sets up its own universe— which is its diagram." The diagram thus functions, Netz argues, as "the metonym of the [geometrical] proposition."[9] Like Rotman, I emphasize the process of corporealization inherent in the construction of scientific diagrams. I demonstrate that this embodiment—much more complicated than a simple act of cognitive representation—is central not only for diagrammatic signs and their manipulators, but also for what Netz calls their "material implementation" on the pages of the texts in which they are inscribed.[10]

Unlike Netz's reading of diagrams in ancient Greek mathematics, I propose that these early modern cosmographical diagrams are inseparable not only from the materiality of the book-apparatus in which they appear but also from the allegorical staging of their inscription on the page and the act of reading that inscription demands.[11]

In what follows, I begin with the scene of the reproduction of Copernicus's diagram in Galileo's *Dialogo*, examining it in relation to Galileo's implicit and explicit theories of allegory. I then take up the diagram's problematic prefiguration in Bruno's *Cena* and the discussion of allegory to which it is linked. I conclude by arguing that these scenes of dramatized diagrammatic inscription and associated theories of allegory exemplify a shift within philosophical and scientific discourse of the late sixteenth and early seventeenth centuries toward the materialization and naturalization of allegorical language. My focus is on the way that Bruno's and Galileo's texts frame their diagrams as products of dramatized conjunctions among the bodies of their characters armed with paper, ink, compasses, imaginary copies of Copernicus's *De revolutionibus*, and the pages of the texts in which they all appear. My problem is to describe the impact of allegory within philosophical discourse on what I will call the baroque ontology of the page.[12]

'LET THIS PAGE BE THE ENORMOUS EXPANSE OF THE UNIVERSE . . .'

The production of many of the diagrams located within the pages of the *Dialogo* are described in the text itself as Salviati, Sagredo, and Simplicio wield ink, paper, and compasses in an effort to develop their geometrical and cosmological positions. The story of one diagram they draw (the most famous in the book) is especially important both for the manner of its inscription and the way it locates Galileo's text in a particular iconographic and allegorical tradition. On the third day of the dialogue, Salviati sketches his familiar argument that not only Saturn, Jupiter, Venus, and Mercury have the sun as the center of their celestial rotation, but Earth does as well; furthermore, the moon orbits Earth and accompanies it in its annual rotation around the sun. Simplicio is puzzled by Salviati's position and proposes that he will "understand it better from the drawing of a diagram, which might make it easier to discuss." "That shall be done," Salviati answers,

But for your greater satisfaction and your astonishment, too, I want you to draw it yourself. You will see that however firmly you believe yourself not to understand it you do so perfectly, and just by answering my questions you will describe it exactly. So take a sheet of paper and a compass; let this page be the enormous expanse of the universe in which you have to distribute or arrange its parts as reason shall direct you.[13]

The diagram they draw (Figure 3.3), of course, is Galileo's modification of one that appears in Copernicus's *De revolutionibus* (Figure 3.1).[14]

The dramatic inscription of Galileo's diagram takes the form of an anamnetic exercise in figurative recollection. As in Plato's *Meno*, careful questioning by a philosopher elicits a grasp of concepts figured as already present in the mind of the one questioned, who by his own hand inscribes a diagrammatic figure that presents them coherently.[15] Indeed, Galileo's text frames the production of the diagram as the construction of a conceptual anteriority and thus as a process of figuration meant to call forth a form of understanding already possessed by Simplicio despite his denials. The *Dialogo* materializes this production of natural philosophical knowledge: This form of recollection requires not just mathematical reflection and observational acuity, but paper, ink, and a compass (Plato's Socrates, of course, must still have been equipped with sand and a stick of some sort). It also requires allegory, as Salviati establishes a series of signifying correspondences among discourses of different orders; the page is the enormous expanse of the universe, the circles are the celestial rotations, and the marks are particular planets. But if this scene is indeed allegorical, it is certainly rather flat compared to the figurative richness of other Renaissance literary, emblematic, and artistic allegories. Even in relation to the work of Galileo's contemporary cosmographer Kepler, it is all but tropologically void.[16] At the same time, the scene evokes precisely the anterior temporalization of a set of spatial relations that Paul de Man, for example, describes as the mark of the allegorical.[17] Further, the text's refusal to allow the diagram to stand as a mere illustration (as does its Copernican original) means that it is produced only through a series of activities undertaken by general personifications of particular systems of the world. Salviati wears the mask not only of Copernicus but also of Copernican cosmology; Simplicio wears that of the Ptolemaic system; and Sagredo in his indecision and contemplative openness wears the mask of the philosophically inclined reader of Galileo's text.

Yet what of Galileo's explicit accounts of the role of allegorical language in the pursuit of natural philosophy? Galileo famously rejects allegorical figuration as a basis for the expression of scientific truth, so in what sense can a positive and interpretively productive role for allegory be asserted of the *Dialogo*? Galileo in fact articulates three distinct *topoi* for the mobilization of allegory—what I will call the theological, poetic-aesthetic, and textual fields—associating each with a particular form of linguistic and conceptual catachresis. Theological allegory involves the extension of a series of metaphors from the scriptural to the philosophical sphere. Its misuse, Galileo argues, involves its mislocation. Theological allegory is acceptable (and even necessary) when scriptural language is framed as the metaphorical figuration of a natural world that it can neither contain nor express directly. To reverse this relationship (as did many early modern theologians) and claim that a true description of the natural world is one that allegorizes divine revelation, on the other hand, is to render theological allegory dangerous and mistaken. Poetic-aesthetic allegory, by contrast, structures literary texts and aesthetic objects in such a way as to render them receptacles of a meaning that transcends their direct signification or material instantiation. Galileo attacks such allegory on philosophical rather than stylistic grounds, insisting that it reduces words and images to structural bearers of allusion and obfuscation, thereby depriving art of its capacity to express concepts and narratives. Finally, textual allegory involves the conflation of literary works and the discourse of natural philosophical observation and demonstration or, more precisely, the subordination of natural philosophy to the domain of literature. Here, Galileo objects, observational acuity and theoretical systematization become nothing more than yet another trope in one more complicated rhetorical series. Most crucially, as we shall see, Galileo holds that such allegory leaves the world behind as it transforms natural philosophical thinking into textual research subordinated to practices of authorial legitimization.

In his frequent attempts to defend the Copernican hypothesis against charges of heresy, Galileo restricts the legitimate use of allegory to scriptural interpretation (and thus to the theological sphere), reserving an unqualified literality for accounts of natural phenomena based on sensory observation and demonstrative reasoning. In the face of suggestions that Copernicus must have intended his account of the structure of reality as a suppositional construct meant merely to save appearances, Galileo objects that only one who has never actually read the pages of *De revolutionibus* could hold such a position.[18] When it comes to charges of contradiction between biblical passages and the Copernican hypothesis, Galileo is nevertheless willing to frame himself as an unapologetic scriptural allegorian, arguing (implicitly in some texts and explicitly in others) from Augustinian principles distinguishing between literal and allegorical readings.[19] When biblical claims conflict with those of observational experience and rational investigation, Galileo holds, the words of scripture must be taken allegorically, whereas "in discussions of physical problems we ought to begin not from the authority of scriptural passages, but from sense-experiences and necessary demonstrations."[20] Galileo thus legitimates the discursive standing of theological allegory but only insofar as it is used to displace the literality of scriptural "truth" into the realm of allegorical signs so as to reconcile theology with the results of natural observation and rational proof. "To be accommodated to the understanding of every man" sacralized language can "speak many things which appear to differ from the absolute truth so far as the bare meaning of the words is concerned." Nature, by contrast, "is inexorable and immutable, never violates the terms of the laws imposed upon her, and does not care whether or not her recondite reasons and ways of operation are disclosed to the human understanding."[21]

Thus, as Eileen Reeves points out, while Galileo is willing to adopt the Augustinian allegorical framework, he reverses its semiological hierarchy such that slippery biblical passages now allegorize an immutable natural world. Natural phenomena are no longer "the visible index of scripture"; rather, scriptural passages "become a gloss on what Galileo saw as a more permanent text, the physical Book of the Heavens."[22] In other words, what Galileo gives with one hand he takes with the other. The condition for the legitimization of allegorical language is its restriction to the theological sphere. The first misuse of allegory—catachrestic theological allegorization—is thus the illegitimate displacement of allegorical interpretation from the discourse of theology to that of natural philosophy. This involves a practice of reading that extends allegorical language beyond its proper sphere and thereby mistakes the language of nature for a concatenation of signs ineluctably pointing to the veracity of scripture, while in fact only the reverse may be admitted. It is true that Galileo's willingness to describe his expositions of the Copernican model as necessary or empirical demonstrations rather than conditional hypotheses varied with the intensity of the political and cultural pressures arrayed against him. Nevertheless, he did not modify his position that in confrontations between scripture and natural observation, allegory was legitimate only for biblical interpretation.

The allegory of the theologians, as already noted, is not the only context for Galileo's engagement with the trope. The second sphere of allegory touched on by Galileo is the poetic-aesthetic, which he sees as involving a misguided approach that undermines the classical formalism of direct narrative and thereby explodes and obstructs the concepts it expresses, rendering them monstrous. In a classic interpretive text, Erwin Panofsky explored Galileo's express distaste for poetic and artistic allegory by examining Galileo's polemical contraposition of Tasso's metaphorics with the formal purity of Ariosto in *Considerazioni al Tasso*.[23] As Panofsky points out, in *Considerazioni* Galileo decries the manner in which Tasso's allegorical poetry unleashes meaning from rule-governed, deliberate linguistic construction such that it requires, as Galileo puts it, "the patching together of broken concepts that have no dependence or connection between them."[24] The reader is forced, in Panofsky's words, "to interpret everything as a recondite reference to something else," and indeed, Panofsky argues, Galileo's precise objection is that allegorical poetry is analogous to the distortion required for pictorial anamorphosis. Thus, in the poetic-aesthetic context, Galileo holds that allegory involves the exercise of illegitimate representational constraint by which "the current tale, openly and originally directly grasped, must accommodate itself to an allegorical meaning, obliquely seen and merely implied, which extravagantly obstructs the tale with chimerical, fantastic, and superfluous imaginings."[25] Galileo sees such a form of allegorization, of course, as anathema to the practice of natural philosophy.

Closely linked to his critique of poetic-aesthetic allegory and connecting it with the misuse of theological allegory is the critique of the category I identify as textual allegory. In a 1610 letter to Kepler, Galileo attacks allegorical misreaders who engage in a distortion of philosophical practice by mistaking philosophy for literature. He decries those who proceed as if "philosophy is a kind of book like the *Aeneid* or the *Odyssey*, and who seek truth not in the world or in nature, but in confrontation with texts."[26] This thematic is extended when, responding polemically in *Il Saggiatore* to the scholastic Oratio Grassi (with whom he had traded barbs over the Tychonian versus Copernican models), Galileo insists that philosophy is not "a book of fantasy by some writer, like the *Iliad* or *Orlando furioso*, productions in which the least important thing is whether what is written is true."[27] Galileo's attack on poetic-aesthetic allegory focused on Tasso's *Gerusalemme Liberata* while praising Ariosto's *Orlando furioso*, and the 1610 letter to Kepler initiates the attack on textual allegory by denouncing "textual confrontation" through explicit citation of the *Aeneid* and the *Odyssey*. On the other hand, in *Il Saggiatore* Galileo opposes natural philosophical and mathematical investigations to even those works of literature that *survive* his critique of poetic-aesthetic allegory. In the full critique of textual allegory, the classicist Ariosto is condemned along with the allegorically mannerist Tasso, and the supposedly historical *Iliad* is eschewed along with the fabulous and traditionally allegorically interpretable *Odyssey* and *Aeneid*. Thus the key to the problem Galileo identifies with textual allegory and what differentiates it from his critique of poetic-aesthetic allegory is not its reliance on fantasy per se but its faith in practices of legitimation that define truth through adherence to textual authorization. This form of allegory mobilizes a muddled interpretive framework that exchanges textual engagement with the philosophical contemplation of nature and thereby substitutes fiction for truth. To frame philosophy *in confrontatione textuum*, in other words, is to reduce truth to literary fantasy.

With regard to poetic-aesthetic allegory, both Panofsky and Dante Della Terza have suggested that Galileo's relationship to this form of rhetoric may be more complicated than it first appears. Panofsky points to the traces of Galileo's platonic commitment to the perfection of the circular movement of celestial bodies and his resistance to the more modern ellipses proposed by the (ironically) hermetic Kepler.[28] Complementing this observation, Della Terza proposes a distinction between the content of Galileo's polemic against Tasso's poetics and the intense stylistic residue the engagement with *Gerusalemme Liberata* leaves in Galileo's own rhetorical practices.[29] Galileo's enthusiasm for a specifically diagrammatic allegorical exercise in his 1588 lectures on the architecture of hell in Dante's *Inferno* could be added to this list of instances rendering problematic his condemnation of poetic-aesthetic allegory.[30] With regard to allegorical language involving a confrontation with texts and relying on the fallacy of authority, Galileo, as is well known, *does* frame the philosophical investigation of the cosmos as a series of *confrontatione textuum* in the most celebrated passage from *Il Saggiatore* where philosophy is figured as the careful practice of reading the grand book of the universe written in the language of mathematics.[31] While the famous lines regarding the book of the universe are sometimes too quickly assumed to oppose it directly to the scriptural language of the "divine book," it is clear (as I showed earlier) that Galileo primarily has in mind what he sees as the illegitimate practice of authorial legitimation through confrontation with texts.

What all three misuses of allegory share is a commitment to a hermeneutic of authorization through a confrontation with texts that insists that philosophical claims be indexed to an external allegorical framework, whether via a priority attributed to sacralized language (theological allegory), the chimerical obfuscation of oblique metaphor (poetic-aesthetic allegory), or the literary practice of legitimation by *auctores* favored by the scholastic Aristotelians (textual allegory). So what is it about the allegorical practice of reading the grand book of the universe that exempts it from Galileo's overarching critique of textual allegory as literary fantasy and poetic-aesthetic allegory as conceptual obfuscation? Galileo's overarching critique of allegorical discourse is that it demands the arbitrary imposition of unnatural conceptual and tropological correspondences that obstruct "the current narrative" of immediate data gleaned from experience and the observation of nature. Nevertheless, Galilean allegory proper will dispense with the chimerical and fantastic in favor of a different kind of connection between allegorical figuration and its meaning. Where the object of his critique is reliance on authorial legitimation, reading the book of nature allegorically will no longer mean imposing structures of similitude on experiential phenomena to interpret them according to a series of given textual categories and figures. Instead, this most unnatural of tropes will be naturalized, as the data of experience and its mathematical organization by reason constitute the well-ordered series of figures to which any meaningful discourse must correspond. The book of nature, in other words, will be the allegorical touchstone for Galileo's own *Dialogo*, and the task of the latter will be to bring its readers into conformity with the former. Galilean allegory proper (as opposed to the three forms of allegory he condemns) is thus not governed by acts of reading legitimized with reference to authority but by the allegorization of the activity of philosophical reading as such, realized through staging the materialization of natural philosophical contemplation in the dramatized inscription of Galileo's diagram within the pages of the *Dialogo* itself.

Reading Copernicus's *De revolutionibus*, we are presented with a static diagram whose structure corresponds to a set of claims about the celestial movements and their spatial relationships as described in the text. In Galileo's *Dialogo*, we are invited, along with Simplicio and Sagredo, to find our own ink and compass and to engage in the production of a parallel diagram, perhaps in the very margins of the book beside its printed instantiation, transforming the pages of our own copies into the enormous expanse of the universe.[32] Wearing the mask of Copernicus, Salviati mobilizes the reproduction and transformation of Copernicus's diagram, narrating the process of its inscription onto the pages of the text in which *he* is written and implicitly demanding that Galileo's readers produce it yet again. By mobilizing an immobile diagram of the movement of the planets around the sun, the *Dialogo* ensures that not only the *claims* of the Copernican thesis will be propagated but that the *image* of that system and the anamnetic process by which its readers both grasp and produce the Copernican structure of the universe will function as an interpretive key to unlock the emblematic codes of its cosmology.

THE MARK OF THE COMPASS

As Arielle Saiber has pointed out, Bruno's *Cena* hyperbolically insists on the identity of reading and diagrammatic visualization from the start, as Bruno instructs his readers in the prefatory epistle "you are to read and visualize [*leggete e vedrete*] what I have to say."[33] Unlike Galileo's scene of diagrammatic construction, Bruno's is neither pedagogical nor anamnetic but polemical. It stands, nevertheless, as equally self-referential, performative, and allegorical, though in a thoroughly puzzling way. Like Galileo's text, *Cena* is cast in dialogical form. Teofilo (who, like Salviati, wears the mask of Copernicus) narrates another conversational drama, recounting to Smitho (a hilariously generic Englishman) the travails of a character named the Nolan at an Ash Wednesday banquet in London where he debates a pair of Oxford dons ("Il Nolano," of course, is an author-metonym for Bruno of Nola). In the fourth dialogue, the Nolan demolishes various objections to the Copernican hypothesis raised by an Oxford pedant, Doctor Torquato, and presents elements of his own differences from Copernicus (his commitments to the infinity of the universe, the similarity of the stars to our Earth, their "ensouled" nature, and so on). The infuriated Torquato subsequently calls for paper and an inkpot, insisting that he will teach the Nolan the right way to understand Ptolemy and Copernicus. The diagram he produces (its inscription is described step by step in the text, as with Galileo) is a double one, displaying in one and the same figure the Ptolemaic and Copernican systems, the former above the centerline and the latter below it. When Torquato finishes, the Nolan peers at the diagram and scornfully says, "This man wanted to teach me as Copernican doctrine a thing

Copernicus himself did not intend; and he would have preferred having his throat slit rather than to say or write it."[34] The problem with Torquato's diagram, the Nolan sarcastically explains, is that it places the mark meant to stand for Earth in the center of the epicycle on the circumference of the third sphere, rather than on the circumference of the epicycle of the moon.[35] Torquato will not admit that he has made a mistake, so the other guests at the banquet call for a copy of Copernicus' *De revolutionibus* to be brought in.[36] As they examine the page with Copernicus's diagram, Teofilo relates, "The Nolan burst into laughter and told them that the point [which Torquato thought was Earth] was only the mark of a compass left when drawing the epicycle of the earth and the Moon, which is one and the same."[37] He admonishes, "If you really want to know where Earth is according to Copernicus' theory, read his own words."[38] They read the text before them and find that the Nolan is correct, at which point Torquato leaves the banquet in disgrace.

There are a number of elements in this scene that render Bruno's text deeply fascinating and problematic, the least of which is that the actual diagram printed in *Cena* in 1584 is *not* exactly the diagram constructed by the characters in the dialogue (Figure 3.2). Aside from lacking various labels and signs that Teofilo describes Torquato as adding, more importantly, it substitutes the Nolan's "correction" for Torquato's "error": Earth and the moon are depicted as circling one another on an epicycle whose center is located on the third celestial sphere (this can be seen in the complex of figures inscribed below the centerline). Far stranger are the conditions of the Nolan's triumph over Torquato and the subsequent emendation of the printed diagram: *Torquato is right and the Nolan is wrong!* If, as the dialogue invites us to do, we were to fetch our own copy of *De revolutionibus*, we would find that Copernicus *does* place Earth on the circumference of a celestial sphere and sets the moon in an epicycle around it, just as Torquato claims.[39] The point described by the Nolan as the mark of Copernicus's compass is just what we know it to be today: Earth orbiting the sun, with the moon orbiting it in turn. Neither the language of Copernicus's text nor the diagram printed with it (Figure 3.1) matches the Nolan's triumphant description and the diagram printed in *Cena*. Astonishingly, on the autograph manuscript page of *De revolutionibus* containing the earliest extant version of the diagram in question (a page Bruno certainly never saw) something that may be the physical mark left by Copernicus' compass *is* clearly visible, though only in the location of the sun at the center of the whole apparatus of the celestial spheres.[40] It is as if the Nolan's error has been answered not only by the reader who accepts his invitation to carefully consult a copy of *De revolutionibus*, but *avant la lettre* by the conjunction of Copernicus's page and the mechanical tool of its inscription.

Things become even odder when we remember that the whole banquet described by Teofilo in *Cena* is a revenge drama written by Bruno in response to his humiliating treatment at Oxford in 1583 (the year before the publication of his book). While details of the historical event remain murky, in the pages of *Cena* Frula (a companion of Teofilo) relates that during the public disputation with the Oxford doctors of theology, the Nolan "answered their arguments and . . . fifteen times, for fifteen syllogisms, the poor doctor whom they put before the Nolan on this grave occasion . . . felt like a fish out of water."[41] In response, Frula relates, the resentful dons cravenly cancelled Bruno's public lectures on the immortality of the soul and its cosmological consequences. As one historian of the actual event has discovered, the real reception of the Oxford dons to Bruno's lectures was just as dripping with vitriol as Bruno's own prose. Robert McNulty cites an account by George Abbot, Master of University College, who scornfully described Bruno as

> that Italian Didapper who . . . stripping up his sleeves like some juggler, and telling us much of *chentrum* and *chirculus* and *churcumferenchia* . . . undertook among very many other matters to set on foot the opinion of Copernicus that the earth did go round, and the heavens did stand still, whereas in truth it was his own head which rather did run round and his brains did not stand still.[42]

Abbot further recounts discovering that Bruno's lectures were lifted verbatim from Ficino's *De vita coelitus comparanda* and having the rest of them cancelled for this plagiarism. The strange thing here is that it is all but impossible to imagine how a verbatim recitation or even a rough paraphrase of Ficino's text could be used to defend the Copernican hypothesis because the work in question is devoted to a description of the astrological powers of the planets and their images in no way arranged according to the Copernican system. On the other hand, *De vita* does contain discussions of the astrological powers Ficino attributes to the images of the stars and planets, even including a chapter entitled "How to Construct a Figure of the Universe."[43]

With Bruno we first have an initial historical event in which a defense of Copernicus is undercut by charges of plagiarism that were probably false.

Second, we have a narrative recasting of this event in a conversation between Teofilo and Smitho that stands as the allegorical framework in which Bruno defends the Copernican hypothesis and develops a theory of the relationship between metaphorical figures and the discourse of truth (something I will discuss shortly). Third, we have the allegorical redramatization of the historical event in the metaphor-laden Ash Wednesday banquet described by Teofilo, where the Nolan, if only in the pages of *Cena*, triumphantly vanquishes the Oxford dons by demonstrating that they have only been glancing at the diagrams of Copernicus's book and not seriously reading its text. Finally, we have the odd fact that the Nolan provides *neither* a true account of the Copernican thesis *nor* an accurate reproduction of its diagram but instead constructs an argument based on little more than a glance at the images in Copernicus's book, one whose precision is nevertheless confirmed (within the dialogue) through a dramatized consultation with a copy of *De revolutionibus* itself.

Does it make sense to say that this diagram and the argument surrounding it function allegorically? This is certainly the tack taken by most commentators on *Cena*, who have tended (under the influence of Francis Yates) to emphasize the ineluctably hermetic nature of Bruno's philosophical thought, insisting, as do Edward Gosselin and Lawrence Lerner, that the diagram is "a grand metaphor or hieroglyphic for his insights into the fundamental nature of the universe" and "an iconographic device to lead the reader towards deeper insight."[44] It is certainly true that *Cena* is shot through with references to the hermetic tradition (as is *De revolutionibus*) as well as explicit attempts to differentiate the position of the Nolan from that of Copernicus. But insofar as questions about how to read Bruno's diagram circle around the dichotomy of a hermetic, prophetic Copernicanism versus a natural philosophical one, I think they remain uninteresting. It is more productive, I propose, to ask how this particular tropological assemblage of the visual, the literary, and the philosophical—Copernicus's diagram and its reconstruction, propagation, and in Bruno, its deformation—*functions* allegorically.[45] We can then approach Bruno and Galileo as allegorical *readers* (and misreaders) not of Copernicus the astronomer, but of Copernicus's book *De revolutionibus* and its diagram. In this vein, I propose that the hermetic interpreters of Bruno are right to take his diagram to be an allegorical hieroglyph but that rather than simply assuming this means excusing its inaccuracy with a gesture toward hermetic mysteries, it makes more sense to investigate the status and function of the hieroglyphic and the allegorical in the pages of *Cena*.

Immediately preceding the construction of the diagram, Teofilo and Smitho engage in an important discussion of metaphor and allegorical language. Smitho raises the standard theological objection to the Copernican thesis: Its propositions contradict scripture. Teofilo responds by drawing a distinction between two types of texts, those that deal with "demonstrations and speculations about natural matters, as if with philosophy" and those that "direct the practice of moral actions through laws."[46] Because scripture belongs to the latter category, all of its claims bearing on natural philosophy are, Teofilo argues, quite simply irrelevant. Just as Galileo will later reject scriptural authority in favor of reading the grand book of the universe, Teofilo holds that justifications by way of biblical reference have no place within natural philosophical discourse. In a move quite different from Galileo's critique of theological allegory, however, Bruno's Teofilo proposes that it is precisely their amenability to allegorical interpretation that makes sacred texts unsuited to ground claims about the natural world because they admit of an infinite range of interpretations and are structured by unstable metaphors.[47] The allegorical interpretation of sacred texts is a mistake from the start, he argues, despite the sense in which they seem to demand it. Because their aim is the direction of moral action, sacred words should be interpreted, as Smitho puts it, "according to the common understanding."[48] When it comes to passages in these texts that appear to make claims regarding natural things we ought not resort to allegorical interpretation, he exhorts, but simply remember that their objects have nothing at all to do with the truths of the natural world. In fact, it is the allegorical interpretation of sacred (and thus moral rather than philosophical) texts that leads contemplation awry, such that "parrots of Aristotle, Plato, and Averröes, by means of whose philosophy they have promoted themselves to theologians, say that all these statements [in scripture] have a metaphorical meaning so that by virtue of their metaphors they extract any meaning they please, through jealous preference for the philosophy on which they were raised."[49]

We might have expected Bruno to make a more familiar move by aligning allegorical interpretation with religious texts and literal reading with philosophy, a strategy (like Galileo's) traceable to Augustine. He would thereby easily sidestep Smitho's objection because biblical passages that deny Earth's movement could be allegorically recoded to support (or at least not to conflict with) the theses of Copernicus and the Nolan. But Bruno is doing just the opposite when Teofilo establishes his "distinction between truth and metaphor," claiming, "We should not take as metaphor what has not been said metaphorically or on the contrary to take to be true what has been said as a simile."[50] The first element of his position is that allegorical readings of sacred texts undermine the distinction between metaphor and truth, and so such texts ought to be read literally. The second is that they must be rigorously confined to their proper sphere—the laws of practical morality—and kept at arm's length from explications of truths of the natural world. If, within this dyad of sacred moral discourse and profane philosophical truth, allegorical reading has been delegitimated as an interpretive practice for moral discourse, it is only with the language of philosophical contemplation—where the common meaning of words has been left behind and "special understanding" is present—it is only here, *within the discourse of truth*, that one can legitimately wield metaphor and allegory.[51]

Where in his explicit critique of theological allegory Galileo would deny that allegorical language has any role within philosophical discourse and insist that it be restricted to the theological sphere, in Bruno's *Cena* allegory is denied entirely to theology and restricted to philosophy. However irreconcilable this move is with Galileo's, each is meant to accomplish the same goal: to avoid the reduction of philosophical claims to mediated articulations of religious dogma. The difference is that rather than delimit philosophical language within the space of literality, Bruno's text frames it as the only legitimate field in which allegory can function without distortion. Where for Galileo the philosophical language of truth would require the careful circumscription of its claims to guard against theological prejudice, poetic-aesthetic chimeras, and textual practices of authorization, for Bruno the truth-function of philosophical discourse is the condition for the legitimation of allegory as such. This is not to say that allegorical interpretation and the language of truth collapse entirely in *Cena*. Rather, it is only within the precisely delimited sphere of philosophical contemplation that one can rigorously distinguish between them and thus use the languages of both truth and allegory legitimately. Bruno's precise critique of the platonic, Aristotelian, and Averröist "parrots" is not that they use allegory as such but that they *destabilize* its metaphors by drawing them from sacred rather than philosophical texts. The only *stable* allegories in the position Bruno develops are constructed within the sphere of the philosophical contemplation of nature.

THE ONTOLOGY OF THE PAGE

Without, I hope, engaging in my own version of the fallacy of appeal to authority that Galileo denounced in his critique of textual allegory, I will conclude by demonstrating that the complex relationships between philosophical and allegorical language framed by the *Dialogo* and *Cena* can be productively understood within the broader framework of the epistemological and rhetorical transitions that mark the end of the Renaissance, as described theoretically by Walter Benjamin and Michel Foucault. I argued above that Galileo's critical stances toward theological, poetic-aesthetic, and textual allegory shared a single ground: the refusal to allow philosophical contemplation to be governed by a hermeneutic structure of authorization that would bind it to an allegorical framework outside of and prior to sensory observation and natural reason. The scene of diagrammatic construction in the *Dialogo*, I proposed, does not abandon allegory as such in the face of this resistance. Instead, Galileo's text restructures it first, as the *naturalized allegory* of the experiential and mathematical script in which the book of the universe can be read, and second, as the *allegorical naturalization* of the activity of such philosophical reading itself as the readers of the *Dialogo* are wrenched into the material process of the text's diagrammatic construction. A rhetorically and philosophically significant result is that the allegorization at work in Galileo's discourse no longer involves the assumption that there are natural structures of resemblance linking allegorical figures to allegorized meanings.

Despite his reversal of Galileo's critical locus for allegory vis-à-vis philosophical and theological language, Bruno's concern with the instability of allegorical discourse—or at least Teofilo's concern within the pages of *Cena*—turns on a similar displacement. In Bruno's text, the problem with allegorical language when mobilized outside the sphere of philosophical contemplation is that it is infinitely interpretable, exploding into a multiplicity of possible meanings. Every scriptural, poetic-aesthetic, or textual allegorical figure can be framed so as to resemble any other, and thus allegorical language immediately spins out of control. This use of allegory reduces claims to explicate natural laws and structures to polemical weapons wielded in the service of dogmatic and arbitrary images of the real, such as that which insists that Earth does not move and the universe is finite. For Bruno, allegory can be mobilized coherently only within the discursive sphere of philosophical truth, based on the experiential observation of nature and rational demonstration. As in Galileo's text, the dramatization of the construction of a cosmological diagram materializes the process of natural philosophical contemplation as an act of philosophical reading, with the difference that the copy of Copernicus's *De revolutionibus* that enters Bruno's stage does not, in fact, resemble the diagram his text claims to reproduce.

Much later, Benjamin, too, was interested in the baroque tensions between the endless interpretability of allegorical figures and their necessary stabilization (though with an emphasis on the historical entirely lacking in Galileo and Bruno). On one side of Benjamin's "antinomies of the allegorical," "Any person, any object, any relationship can mean absolutely anything else" rendering allegorical language ineluctably secular and conventional.[52] On the other hand, the fragmentary images arranged by allegorical signification derive thereby an expressive power "which makes them appear no longer commensurable with profane things" and transforms them into sacred language.[53] One result of this antinomy is the mutation of the language of sacred texts and their images into complex hieroglyphs that guarantee the stable signification of allegorical script. For Benjamin, the German baroque *Trauerspiel* theater is a unique (or more precisely, "extreme") manifestation of these antinomies insofar as what it presents is the *failure* of the hieroglyphic character pushed to its limit. The object of its hieroglyphic sacralization is the decay and finitude of profane and secular history, figured nevertheless as an eternal dialectic of the transience and death that belong to the sphere of becoming.[54] With the explosion of allegorical figuration, the rise of the sense that its images are expressions of convention, and the concomitant vision of secular history as sacralized and eternal finitude— that is, at the extreme limits where its coherency disintegrates—the very *idea* of baroque allegory begins, for Benjamin, to become legible.

Foucault analyzed a similar transitional phenomenon when he described the move beyond a Renaissance episteme dominated by systems of natural similitude and resemblance and obsessed with deciphering the signatures of the world as a form of sacred hieroglyphics.[55] Bruno, of course, is still committed to the hermetic system of natural magic that expresses itself in terms of sympathy and antipathy, analogy, emulation, and symmetry. Unlike the central texts in Foucault's archaeology of late Renaissance similitude (works by Paracelsus, Oswald Croll, and Giovani Della Porta figure most prominently), Bruno's *Cena* insists on stabilizing signatures and limiting the legitimate mobilization of the structures of resemblance that make allegory possible. In this we can see the kernel of the critique of resemblance that undergirds—again on Foucault's reading—the shift to the episteme of representation in the seventeenth century. For Bacon, Descartes, Arnauld, and others, the resemblance that was to guarantee the validity of allegorical discourse delegitimates itself in the moment of its triumph as the hypostatization of similitude. Where every object, phrase, figure, and trope resembles every other, similitude itself becomes the danger against which philosophical thinking must guard. Where every figure is both the potential subject and object of allegorization with respect to every other, the very resemblance that renders allegorization possible must be carefully circumscribed within the domain of error. Here "Language is no longer one of the figurations of the world, or a signature stamped upon things from the beginning of time," Foucault writes. "It is the task of words to translate truth if they can; but they no longer have the right to be considered the mark of it."[56] Foucault's description of this epistemic shift has been challenged, of course, both with regard to the completeness of his account of the Renaissance episteme (it relies too heavily on texts that function as remnants of late neoplatonism while ignoring late Aristotelian positions) and the decisiveness of the turn away from similitude in early modernity (the category continues to function productively for many philosophers of the seventeenth century).[57] Nevertheless, neither of these forms of critique effectively touches on Foucault's claims regarding the nature of a general shift away from similitude itself, even if they demonstrate that it is not as complete as Foucault proposes.

Bruno and Galileo make somewhat different moves, the essence of which are nevertheless captured by Benjamin and Foucault. As in the accounts of baroque language by this pair of twentieth-century philosophers, the work of these early moderns clearly acknowledges the difficulty inherent in the allegorical mobilization of an infinitely metaphorical discourse. In attempts to reconcile the language of truth regarding the nature of the world with given and established figures of sacred script, they discern allegory dismantling its own power to evoke and communicate truth. The Galilean alternative is that allegory used correctly does not obscure the relation of similitude between figure and concept because it dispenses with that relation altogether by collapsing the practice of philosophical reading into the activity of philosophical inscription. When Salviati takes up the Copernican mask, the *Dialogo* does not assume a series of given authorial figures of reference to which truth claims about the natural world must correspond.

Instead it leaves behind the logic of authorization altogether by weaving its readers into the fabric of its textual construction. For Bruno, only within the bounds of a secularized discourse of philosophical contemplation can allegory be stabilized and put to work in the explication of nature. Rather than turn its back on the allegorical possibilities of language in the name of establishing a firm and lasting foundation for the sciences, Nolan discourse instead inscribes them on the surface of the pages of the Copernican book of the world. In *Cena*, allegory finds its proper and stabilized home within the domain of philosophical truth. Does this mean, finally, that we can rescue the errors of Bruno's cosmological diagram by rendering them allegorical? It certainly does not. If anything, these errors present a moment of the *failure* of the allegorical to accomplish its own legitimation within the limits of philosophy. It does mean that when we read the *Cena* diagram in its becoming, locating its pre- and posthistory in the texts of Copernicus and Galileo, we find in Bruno's text a ground for understanding the place of allegory within baroque natural philosophical discourse.

Notes

1. EN XI, 341. The following abbreviations are used throughout the essay:
   EN: Galileo Galilei, *Le opere di Galileo Galilei*, ed. Antonio Favaro, nuovo ristampa della Edizione Nazionale, 20 vol. (Florence: G. Barbèra, 1968).
   D: Galileo Galilei, *Dialogue Concerning the Two Chief World Systems*, trans. Stillman Drake (Berkeley: University of California Press, 1967).
   C: Nicholas Copernicus, *Opera omnia*, ed. Polish Academy of Sciences, 2 vols. (Warsaw: Officina Publica Libris Scientificis Edendis, 1973–1975).
   R: Nicholas Copernicus, *On the Revolutions*, ed. Jerzy Dobrzycki, trans. Edward Rosen, vol. 2 of *Complete Works*, ed. Polish Academy of Sciences (London: Macmillan, 1973).
   B: Giordano Bruno, *Le Souper des Cendres* [*La Cena de le Ceneri*], ed. Giovanni Aquilecchia, trans. Yves Hersant, vol. 2 of *Oeuvres complètes* [critical edition of the original Italian text with French translation] (Paris: Les Belles Lettres, 1994).
   A: Giordano Bruno, *The Ash Wednesday Supper*, ed. and trans. Edward A. Gosselin and Lawrence S. Lerner (Toronto: University of Toronto Press, 1995).
2. EN VII, 29; D, 5.
3. EN VII, 157–158; D, 131.

4. C II, 5; R, 5.

5. This essay is not as directly concerned with establishing the lines of historical influence among these texts as it is with investigating the genealogical and textual traces of what I am proposing is an allegorical genre of the cosmological diagram. For more direct examinations of the philosophical-historical influence of Bruno's dialogue on Galileo's, see Giovanni Aquilecchia, "Possible Brunian Echoes in Galileo," *Nouvelles de la République des Lettres* 1 (1995): 11–18, and Hilary Gatti, "Giordano Bruno's 'Ash Wednesday Supper' and Galileo's 'Dialogue of the Two Major World Systems,'" *Bruniana e Campanelliana* 3.2 (1997): 283–300.

6. While it is extremely unlikely that Copernicus actually carved the woodcut used for printing the diagram in 1543, the image is based on the hand- and compass-drawn diagram in his autograph manuscript. The autograph manuscript (located in the Jagiellonian Library in Krakow) is reproduced in several facsimile editions, including C I, 9v.

7. In philosophical discourse, interrogation of diagrammatic reasoning has tended to focus on (a) the function of diagrams as visual modes of logical representation in relation to symbolic and linguistic systems or (b) the possible role of diagrammatic thinking in internal cognitive representation. The most notable work for the former approach is Sun-Joo Shin, *The Logical Status of Diagrams* (Cambridge, U.K.: Cambridge University Press, 1994). For the latter, see Michael Tye, *The Imagery Debate* (Cambridge, MA: MIT Press, 1991) and the essays collected in *Imagery*, ed. Ned Joel Block (Cambridge, MA: MIT Press, 1981). Thus, the bulk of philosophical interest in diagrams has been restricted to central topics in the disciplinary node involving philosophy of mind, logic, cognitive science, and information theory. The work of Mark Greeves is a notable exception, in that while continuing to focus on the role of diagrams in logical representation he also insists on framing those functions with respect to the history of philosophical mathematics (Mark Greeves, *The Philosophical Status of Diagrams*. Stanford, CA: CSLI Publications, 2002). Recently, John Mullarkey has begun to map the terrain in which a form of "diagrammatology" may be articulated at the post- or anti-Derridean end of the late twentieth century French philosophical tradition, particularly with respect to the work of Gilles Deleuze, Alain Badiou, Michael Henry, and François Laruelle (with a more marginal engagement with Bruno Latour). See especially Mullarkey's promissory chapter "Thinking in Diagrams" in his *Post-Continental Philosophy: An Outline* (London: Continuum, 2006), 157–186. Forthcoming work by literary historian John Bender and art historian Michael Marrinan is likely to open the field of debate more broadly by considering diagrammatic reasoning in relation to cultural history and the theoretical discourses of a broader swath of humanistic disciples.

8. Brian Rotman, "Thinking Dia-Grams: Mathematics, Writing, and Virtual Reality," *South-Atlantic-Quarterly*, 94.2 (Spring 1995): 401.

9. Reviel Netz, *The Shaping of Deduction in Greek Mathematics* (Cambridge, U.K.: Cambridge University Press, 1999), 26, 31, 32, and 37.

10. Ibid., 12.

11. While thus entirely sympathetic with the constellation of theoretical problems and objects Walter Ong arranges in "From Allegory to Diagram in the Renaissance Mind: A Study in the Significance of the Allegorical Tableau," *The Journal of Aesthetics and Criticism* 17.4 (1959): 423–440, my approach is quite different. For a powerful essay exploring the strategies by which Galileo's *Sidereus Nuncius* stages the moment of its reception as a text and uses its illustrative practices to frame cosmological structures as its visual analogues, see Elizabeth Spiller, "Reading through Galileo's Telescope: Margaret Cavendish and the Experience of Reading," *Renaissance Quarterly* 53.1 (Spring 2000): 192–221. On the relationship between Galileo's work and artistic rather than textual forms of depiction, see Eileen Reeves, *Painting the Heavens: Art and Science in the Age of Galileo* (Princeton, NJ: Princeton University Press, 1997). For an overview of the most important work on Galileo's use of and engagement with images, see Horst Bredekamp, "Gazing Hands and Blind Spots: Galileo as Draftsman," in *Galileo in Context*, ed. Jürgen Renn (Cambridge, U.K.: Cambridge University Press, 2001), 153–187 and—more extensively—Bredekamp's recent *Galilei der Künstler: Die Zeichnung, der Mond, die Sonne* (Berlin: Akademie Verlag, 2007). A forthcoming book by Bredekamp and a group of art historians, art conservators, and conservation scientists focuses on the images associated with the *Sidereus Nuncius* and may contribute to reconfiguring the terms of this debate.

12. My thanks to Harry Berger for suggesting this phrase.

13. EN VII, 350; D, 322–323.

14. As Owen Gingerich discovered in the course of his exhaustive survey of the extant copies of *De revolutionibus*, Galileo owned a copy of the 1566 second edition, specifically one that is now at the Biblioteca Nazionale Centrale in Florence. Gingerich reports that while in his copy Galileo carried out the textual censorship required by the 1616/1620 Decree of the Holy Congregation, the passages in question are only lightly crossed out and still clearly legible (Owen Gingerich, *An Annotated Census of Copernicus' 'De Revolutionibus.'* Leiden: Brill, 2002, 122).

15. Plato, *Meno*, 82a–85e in *Laches, Protagoras, Meno, Euthydemus*, trans. W. R. M. Lamb, Loeb Classical Library 165 (Cambridge, MA: Harvard University Press, 1990), 304–321.

16. On Kepler as a rhetorician, see Fernand Hallyn, *La Structure poétique du monde: Copernic, Kepler* (Paris: Éditions de Seuil, 1987), and specifically as an allegorist, see James Paxson, "Kepler's Allegory of Containment, the Making of Modern Astronomy, and the Semiotics of Mathematical Thought," *Intertexts* 3.2 (Fall 1999): 105–125.

17. Paul de Man, "The Rhetoric of Temporality," *Blindness and Insight* (Minneapolis: University of Minnesota Press, 1983), 187–228.

18. Galileo to Dini (March 23, 1615), EN V, 299–300.

19. For a direct account of Galileo's indebtedness to Augustine on this issue, see Eileen Reeves, "Augustine and Galileo on Reading the Heavens," *Journal of the*

History of Ideas 52.4 (Oct.–Dec., 1991): 563–579. For a more general account of the intertwining of rhetorical and scientific discourse in Galileo's work, see Jean Dietz Moss, *Novelties in the Heavens: Rhetoric and Science in the Copernican Controversy* (Chicago: University of Chicago Press, 1993).

20. *Lettera a Madama Cristina di Lorena Granduchessa di Toscana*, EN V, 316; *Letter to the Grand Duchess Christina* in *Discoveries and Opinions of Galileo*, trans. Stillman Drake (New York: Random House, 1957), 182.

21. EN V, 316; *Discoveries and Opinions*, 182. Cf. Galileo to Castelli (December 21, 1613), EN V, 282.

22. Reeves, "Augustine and Galileo," 571–572. See also Ernan McMullin, "Galileo on Science and Scripture," in *The Cambridge Companion to Galileo*, ed. Peter Machamer (Cambridge, U.K.: Cambridge University Press, 1998), 271–347.

23. Erwin Panofsky, *Galileo as a Critic of the Arts* (The Hague: Martinus Nijhoff, 1954). Galileo's *Considerazioni al Tasso* can be found at EN IX, 59–148.

24. EN IX, 63. Galileo writes, "*rappezando insieme concetti spezati e senza dependenza e connessione tra loro.*" See also *Postille all'Ariosto*, EN IX, 149–194 (Panofsky, *Galileo as a Critic*, 13). Panofsky also argues that Galileo's general aesthetic stance involves a conscious rejection of Mannerist painting. For a reassessment of Panofsky's position in light of later research on the nature and origin of Galileo's images, see Bredekamp, "Gazing Hands and Blind Spots," 184–187. On Panofsky's account of the exemplarity of Ariosto and Tasso, see Reeves, *Painting the Heavens*, 18–22.

25. EN IX, 130.

26. Galileo to Kepler (August 19, 1610), EN X, 423.

27. EN VI, 232; *The Assayer* in *The Controversy of the Comets of 1618: Galileo, Grassi, Guiducci, Kepler*, trans. Stillman Drake and C. D. O'Malley (Philadelphia: University of Pennsylvania Press, 1960), 183, translation modified.

28. Panofsky, *Galileo as Critic*, 20–31.

29. Dante Della Terza, "Galileo, Man of Letters," in *Galileo Reappraised*, ed. Carlo L. Golino (Berkeley: University of California Press, 1966), 6–7. See also Mario Biagioli, "Galileo the Emblem Maker," *Isis* 83.2 (June 1992): 195–217.

30. *Due lezioni all'Accademia Fiorentina circa la figura, sito e grandezza dell' Inferno di Dante*, EN IX, 29–58.

31. "Philosophy is written in this grand book—I mean the universe—which stands continually open to our gaze, but it cannot be understood unless one first learns to comprehend the language and interpret the characters in which it is written. It is written in the language of mathematics, and its characters are triangles, circles, and other geometrical figures, without which it is humanly impossible to understand a single word of it; without these, one is wandering about in a dark labyrinth." EN VI, 232; *Controversy of the Comets*, 183–184.

32. Gingerich notes that while Galileo made no technical annotations in his copy of *De revolutionibus*, a later reader of the same copy performed exactly the type of marginal reproduction of Copernicus' diagrams I am arguing Galileo's own text demands (Gingerich, *Annotated Census*, 122).

33. B, 13; A, 69. Arielle Saiber, *Giordano Bruno and the Geometry of Language* (Burlington, VT: Ashgate, 2005), 119. Saiber deals with diagrams in other texts by Bruno in *Bruno and Geometry*, 48–60, as well as in "Ornamental Flourishes in Giordano Bruno's Geometry," *Sixteenth Century Journal* 34.3 (2003): 729–745. Other work on Bruno's diagrams includes Mino Gabriele, *Giordano Bruno: Corpus iconographicum: Le incisioni nelle opere a stampa* (Milan: Adelphi, 2001), and Cristoph Lüthy, "Bruno's *Area Democriti* and the Origins of Atomist Imagery," *Bruniana e Campanelliana* 4 (1998): 59–92, though neither provide a sustained treatment of the diagrams in *Cena*.

34. B, 227; A, 192.

35. What Bruno refers to as "the third sphere" is the fully visible semicircle third from the sun in the lower "Copernican" half of his diagram (Figure 3.2). The two central semicircles of the upper "Ptolemaic" half are eliminated in the textual description of the lower half of the diagram, even while one of them remains visible beneath the flames of the sun in the woodblock print. In Copernicus's diagram, the corresponding sphere is labeled "*V. Telluris cum orbe Lunari annum revolutio*" but is referred to in the text as "the series's fourth place" [*quartum in ordine*], i.e. the fourth place in the series of mobile planetary spheres contained within the immobile sphere of the fixed stars (Figure 3.1; C II, 20; R, 21). In Galileo's diagram, the same sphere is labeled "A" with the Moon's epicycle marked as "NP" (Figure 3.3).

36. Presumably, Bruno has in mind his own copy of *De revolutionibus*, a second edition like that possessed by Galileo. Gingerich reports that Bruno owned the copy now in the collection of the Biblioteca Casanatense in Rome, named for the head of the Inquisition that ordered Bruno to be burned at the stake (Gingerich, *Annotated Census*, 115). This copy contains no annotations by Bruno, and while he reproduces Bruno's "bold signature," Gingerich elsewhere significantly claims that there is "no evidence that he actually read the book" (Owen Gingerich, *The Book Nobody Read: Chasing the Revolutions of Nicolaus Copernicus*. New York, Walker & Co., 2004, 64–65).

37. B, 227–229; A, 192. For a brief account of the history of Bruno's clearly metaphysical fascination with the compass, see Saiber, *Bruno and Geometry*, 136.

38. B, 229; A, 192.

39. Copernicus's statement is "The annual revolution . . . contains the earth, as I said, together with the lunar sphere as an epicycle" (C II, 20; R, 21). For an overview of Bruno's misreading and the various proposed interpretations of its origin, see Ernan McMullin, "Bruno and Copernicus," *Isis* 78.1 (March 1987): 55–74.

40. C I, 9v. In the critical notes to his translation of *De revolutionibus*, Rosen explicitly identifies the apparent circle at the center of the manuscript diagram as "the mark left unintentionally by the fixed, blunt foot of the compass with which Copernicus drew the circles in this diagram" (R, 359n20). The status of this mark remains a question, however, since a full examination of the various available facsimiles of the autograph present highly contradictory evidence with respect to it.

In collaboration with paper conservator Theresa Smith, I am currently engaged in a project examining the implications of these contradictions.

41. He felt like a *"pulcino entro la stoppa,"* more literally "a chick on a leash" (B, 215; A, 186–187).

42. George Abbot, *The Reasons Which Doctor Hill Hath Brought Forth for the Upholding of Papistry* (Oxford, 1604), fols. 4v–5r, cited in Robert McNulty, "Bruno at Oxford," *Isis* 13.4 (Winter 1960): 302–303, with the typography and spelling modernized here. See also Ernan McMullin, "Giordano Bruno at Oxford," *Isis* 77.1 (March 1986): 85–94, as well as Hilary Gatti, *Giordano Bruno and Renaissance Science* (Ithaca, NY: Cornell University Press, 1999), 43–46.

43. Marsilio Ficino, "De fabricanda universi figura," *De Vita Coelitus comparanda, De Vita libri tres . . .* , vol. 1 of *Opera Omnia* (Torino: Bottega d'Erasmo, 1962), 519–572.

44. Gosselin and Lerner, Introduction to A, 27–28 and 198n56. The critical introduction to their translation of *Cena* remains a touchstone for many contemporary Anglo-American readings of the work. This interpretation of Bruno as a hermetic mystic rather than a natural philosopher committed to a form of revised Copernicanism can be traced back to Francis Yates, "Giordano Bruno's Conflict with Oxford," *Journal of the Warburg Institute* 2 (1938–1939): 227–242, as well as her influential *Giordano Bruno and the Hermetic Tradition* (Chicago: University of Chicago Press, 1964).

45. I agree with Gatti in rejecting Yates's hermetic explanation of Bruno's error (and indeed with her more general critique of the "hermeticized" presentation of Bruno as such), though for different reasons than those she presents (Gatti attempts to harmonize Bruno's explanation with several arguments from Book 3 of *De revolutionibus*) (Gatti, *Renaissance Science*, 64–71). For another argument emphasizing the importance of the literary and rhetorical context of *Cena* over and against hermetically inclined interpretations, see Adi Ophir, Introduction to B, esp. xx–xxxix.

46. B, 191; A, 177.

47. B, 201; A, 181. Bruno writes of judging whether metaphors are *"costante."*

48. B, 193; A, 178.

49. B, 201; A, 181.

50. B, 197; A, 180.

51. B, 195–197; A, 179. Teofilo speaks of *"il particular intendimento"* at work in philosophical thought.

52. Walter Benjamin, *Ursprung des deutschen Trauerspiels* (Frankfurt am Main: Suhrkamp, 1990), 152; *The Origin of German Tragic Drama*, trans. John Osborne (London: Verso, 1998), 175.

53. Benjamin, *Ursprung*, 153; *Origin*, 175.

54. Benjamin, *Ursprung*, 144–145; *Origin*, 166.

55. This description of the episteme of the late Renaissance appears in the second chapter of *Les mots et les choses*, where Foucault's analysis of "signatures" derives

primarily from an engagement with Oswald Croll's *Tractatus de signaturis internis rerum* in *Basilica Chymica* (Geneva: Samuel Chouce, 1658 [c. 1590]) (Michel Foucault, *Les mots et les choses*. Paris: Gallimard, 1966, 32–59). Foucault's third chapter analyzes the break with this structure and the rise of an episteme of representation in the early seventeenth century (Ibid., 60–91).

56. Ibid., 70; *The Order of Things*, trans. Alan Sheridan (New York: Vintage Books, 1973), 56.

57. On the first of these criticisms, see Amos Funkenstein, *Theology and the Scientific Imagination: From the Middle Ages to the Seventeenth Century* (Princeton, NJ: Princeton University Press, 1987), 28–37; and George Huppert, "Divinatio et Eruditio: Thoughts on Foucault," *History and Theory* 13.3 (Oct. 1974): 191–207. On the second criticism, see André Robinet, "Leibniz: La Renaissance et l'Âge Classique," in *Leibniz et la Renaissance*, ed. Albert Heinekamp, Studia Leibnitiana Supplementa 13 (Wiesbaden: F. Steiner, 1983), 32–36.

FOUR

The Function of Allegory in Baroque Tragic Drama

What Benjamin Got Wrong

BLAIR HOXBY

In *The Origin of German Tragic Drama* (1928), Walter Benjamin character-izes mourning, melancholy, and the allegorical way of seeing as points of a single constellation: the *Trauerspiel*. Although *Trauerspiel* literally means "mourning play," Benjamin applies the term to most tragic drama from Shakespeare to Schiller to differentiate it from the tragedy of ancient Athens (*Tragödie*). Attic tragedy is grounded in myth, and its hero, says Benjamin, is always the same. "In tragedy pagan man realizes that he is better than the gods, but this realization strikes him dumb, and it remains unarticulated." The "sublime element of tragedy" is "the paradox of the birth of genius in moral speechlessness, moral infantility."[1]

According to Benjamin, Shakespeare, Calderon, and their contempo-raries in Germany did not write tragedies. They wrote *Trauerspiele*, which sprang from different historical circumstances and yield a different truth when subjected to critical pressure. *Trauerspiele* are grounded in history rather than myth. They are earthbound and corporeal. They cling to life. Their central characters are the tyrant and martyr, who embody the myster-ies of absolute will and hapless subjection and who often appear on stage as different aspects of the same sovereign ruler. Their true roots cannot be found in Attic tragedy, or even in Aristotle's *Poetics* (the authority that seems to have exercised such an influence on baroque dramaturgy), but in the mystery cycles and the revival of Senecan tragedy in a Christian culture. Their favored mode of expression is ranting, talking, and lamenting. They require an audience to behold their memorabilia of grief, but they are not intended to induce a *response* of mourning; rather, they are plays directed at the permanently mournful—the melancholy.[2] Their characteristic stage property is the corpse. For it is only in death, says Benjamin, that the body "comes properly into its own": "the allegorization of the physis," or the natural, "can only be carried through in all its vigour in respect of the corpse. And the characters of the *Trauerspiel* die, because it is only thus, as corpses, that they can enter the homeland of allegory."[3]

Benjamin's conception of baroque allegory is heavily reliant on the historical narrative told by Karl Giehlow.[4] According to Giehlow, medieval allegory was Christian and didactic. In the Renaissance, on the other hand, the neoplatonists who attempted to decipher the hieroglyphs of the Egyptians believed that the pictorial writing of the ancients might hold the keys to the book of nature. Egyptian priests "must have wanted to create something corresponding to divine thought," concluded Marsilio Ficino, "since divinity surely possesses knowledge of all things, not as a changing idea, but as the simple and fixed form of the thing itself." That meant that hieroglyphs were "an image of divine ideas."[5] Guided by ancient allegorical commentators, the authors of neoplatonic allegories ransacked the classics for myths and images because they believed that these held the secrets of the supersensible world. But as emblem books were published at a prodigious rate from the sixteenth through the eighteenth centuries, the result was not a mastery of the book of nature; it was a chaos of codes. Egyptian, Hebrew, Greek, and Christian signs were combined and recombined in ever more remote and obscure allegories. Eventually, Giehlow maintains, "one and the same thing [could] just as easily signify a virtue as a vice, and therefore more or less anything."[6] This is the state of allegory in the *Trauerspiel*, says Benjamin: "any person, any object, any relationship can mean absolutely anything else."[7]

Benjamin does not conceive of allegory as a rhetorical figure or dramatic device used to induce an affective or cognitive response in the audience. Instead, he thinks of it as a state of vision produced by the clash of pagan naturalism and Christian spiritualism during the Middle Ages and the

Counter-Reformation. Or, alternatively, he describes it as a way of seeing engendered by melancholy. Although he offers a desultory historical account of the origin of that melancholy in the German poets who concern him most (Lutheranism deprived all human actions of value and made the "scene" of human existence "appear like a rubbish heap of partial, inauthentic actions"), he makes no special effort to explain the fact that the greatest masters of allegorical drama were Catholics like Don Pedro Calderón de la Barca—presumably because his more settled conviction is, as Howard Caygill explains, that "Melancholy is in the world and the creature, not necessarily in the gaze of man: human melancholy . . . is but an aspect of a general ontological melancholy, not its source and privileged center."[8]

If a cause for that ontological melancholy can be located in Benjamin's thought, it must be the inadequacy of our fallen tongues, which he imagines to be the mere ruins of a divinely dictated language that consisted only of proper names. As humans gaze at nature with the eye of melancholy, they try to read what they can no longer name with that divine language, and they impute allegorical significance to the lifeless objects they behold. For a time, they may accept these as a "key to the hidden realm of knowledge," but the gulf between sign and signified inevitably reasserts itself. As a result, the "disconsolate every day countenance" of the "banal object" reemerges, and we abandon the "exhausted emblem" in disappointment.[9]

Benjamin does not imagine himself as a historian of *mentalité* or a literary critic. He asserts that he is writing a form of criticism that will yield a philosophic truth by "mortifying" an artistic form; whereas Romantic critics imagined their objective to be "awakening the consciousness in living works," Benjamin describes his as "the settlement of knowledge in dead ones."[10] The knowledge that the *Trauerspiel* yields to Benjamin is not, however, what we might expect either from its macabre imagery or his own morbid preoccupations:

> Ultimately in the death-signs of the baroque the direction of the allegorical reflection is reversed; on the second part of its wide arc it returns, to redeem. . . . Allegory, of course, thereby loses everything that was most peculiar to it: the secret, privileged knowledge, the arbitrary rule in the realm of dead objects, the supposed infinity of a world without hope. All this vanishes with this *one* about-turn, in which the immersion of allegory has to clear away the final phantasmagoria of the objective and, left entirely to its own devices, re-discovers itself, not playfully in the earthly world of things, but seriously under the eye of heaven. And this is the essence of

melancholy immersion: that its ultimate objects, in which it believes it can most fully secure for itself that which is vile, turn into allegories, and that these allegories fill out and deny the void in which they are represented, just as, ultimately, the intention does not faithfully rest in the contemplation of bones, but faithlessly leaps forward to the idea of resurrection.[11]

Benjamin, at this point in the *Origin*, is not explaining the way that baroque audiences understood the emblems of the *Trauerspiel*. He is interpreting its ruins and corpses as Kabbalists read the Torah of the Exile—to divine its opposite, the Torah of Redemption.[12] He is reading the *Trauerspiel* for its message of consolation, however fleeting.

Benjamin's *Origin* is a difficult work to refute or correct because it contains so many unstated assumptions, hermetic pronouncements, and contradictory assertions that any positive claim ascribed to it can be disputed with a contradictory statement found elsewhere in the text. But I would nevertheless insist that Benjamin's idea of tragedy underrates the centrality of mourning as a motive and theme of Attic drama and fails to account for works like the *Ajax*, the *Philoctetes*, or the *Trojan Women*—no doubt because they resemble their supposed antithesis, the *Trauerspiel*, and because recognizing their existence might undercut Benjamin's claim that the baroque era has more in common with the Middle Ages than it does with the ancient world or the Renaissance.[13] My concern in this essay, however, is not Benjamin's idea of classical tragedy but how allegory functions in baroque tragic drama.

I would like to approach this question only after dispensing with some of Benjamin's most intractable assumptions: that our tongues are the relics of a divine language whose loss makes nature mourn; that melancholy pervades nature and humanity; and that the allegories of the *Trauerspiel* can be understood only "from the higher domain of theology."[14] We need accept none of these assumptions if we investigate the function of allegory as students of theater and ritual, accepting as an alternative starting point Victor Turner's model of the relationship that exists between social dramas and the dramas that are performed in theaters.

Social dramas are actual social conflicts that often unfold through the four stages of breach, crisis, redressive process, and reintegration or schism.[15] If the theater may be said to hold a mirror up to them, it is the third stage, with its wars, judicial deliberations, divinations, sacrifices, rituals of affliction, and life crisis rituals, that preoccupies tragedy. Although many of the redressive processes that may be dramatized in the theater are not rituals (or, like revenge killings, are not *simply* rituals), those that are often take the form of rites of passage that comprise three stages: rites of separation (which communicate society's deepest values through the exhibition of sacred symbols, the imparting of instructions, or the enactment of myths); rites of limen (which rely on the ludic or fanciful deconstruction and recombination of familiar cultural configurations); and rites of reaggregation (which reestablish lines of authority or seal communal bonds).

I introduce this model because Benjamin is careful to deny that *Trauerspiele* "cause mourning." He instead imagines them as doleful visions that afford "the only pleasure that the melancholic permits himself"—"allegory."[16] I maintain, in contrast, that the primary function of allegory in baroque tragic drama is to create a theater of the limen, a space betwixt-and-between the living and the dead, a world of dying and mourning. The pleasure that baroque tragic drama delivers is remembrance amid grief.

The eminent philologist Daniel Heinsius says as much in his authoritative guide to the *Poetics* and to tragedy in general. "Not every pleasure is to be sought from tragedy but the one proper to it," he writes in 1611. Although tragedy "moves either horror or pity or both," and although "those emotions in themselves properly beget sorrow, . . . the imitation of them breeds pleasure." This paradox, says Heinsius, may be explained by an observation found in Aristotle's *Rhetoric*, "that there is pleasure in grief and mourning, as when we mourn the dead":

> For grief has its origin in the person who is gone, but pleasure arises from remembrance of the person that was—from his deeds, from his sayings, things that we vividly recall. Hence by (as it were) divine inspiration in the poet, Andromache says, when she mourns her spouse, that the greatest pleasure had been taken from her, for she had not received his last words and behests to keep in mind night and day, and Lucan's Polla continuously gazed on the face of the man whom she mourned unceasingly.[17]

Heinsius's commentary invites us to read *Trauerspiele* and other forms of early modern tragic drama as plays that were consciously crafted to afford audiences the pleasure occasioned by grief. We should not be surprised, therefore, to see them appropriate the forms and ceremonies of mortuary rites and funerary memorials.

When we consider *Trauerpsiele* as liminoid plays of mourning, their allegory no longer seems to be arbitrary, horizontal, and binary, as Benjamin characterizes it. In fact, what is most important about the allegory of baroque tragic drama is not its status as *allegory* at all but its inseparability from the mimetic surface of the drama. If we imagine the relationship between mimesis and allegory in plastic terms, we can say that the characters and properties of baroque tragic drama are like those theriomorphic figures who, with their dual natures as beast and human, mortal and god, tend to make their appearance in liminal rites. Or if we express the relationship in temporal terms, we can say that the mimetic surface looks lovingly back to the life of the flesh and the community of the living, while the allegorical depth looks impatiently forward to the company of the dead and a final revelation. The tension between surface and depth, nostalgia and anticipation leaves the audience neither here nor there but in the transitional space betwixt and between. If handled differently, such a tension could be exploited to initiate participants into a mystery like marriage rather than death, but in baroque tragic drama its function is to induce a response of mourning.

To make my case, I want both to meet Benjamin on his own ground and to conjoin territory to this investigation of tragic allegory that he would have considered alien. Although Benjamin considers *Hamlet* (1601) to be the greatest example of the *Trauerspiel*, he also maintains that derivative and decadent works of art often reveal the most about the nature of a genre, and because I agree I want to focus on a series of tragic dramas that meditate on Hamlet's dialogue with the grave-diggers: Henry Chettle's *Tragedy of Hoffman* (1603?), Thomas Middleton's *Revenger's Tragedy* (1606) and *Lady's Tragedy* (1611), and John Ford's *Love's Sacrifice* (1628). The capstone of this series is Ford's *The Broken Heart* (1629–1633), a tragedy that conforms closely to Benjamin's description of the *Trauerspiel*. It assigns the role of the tyrant to an honorable but erring brother who condemns his sister to a "resolved martyrdom" (3.2.84) of "tortures," "agonies," "miseries," and "afflictions" (4.4.34–35).[18] It features patient women who impose rules of physical self-denial on themselves so extreme as to guarantee death. It invites us to listen to the agonies of the saints, however much their groans may be transmuted into artful and ritualized expressions of pain and grief. It identifies the world with the stage and the stage with the world. It associates tragedy with the Dance of Death and other games of lamentation. It kills its characters so that it may use their corpses as stage properties. And it assumes a deep, if mysterious, relationship between mourning, melancholy, and the allegorical way of seeing. *The Broken Heart* permits us to examine the function of allegory in a play that is as close to "mortuary art" as Benjamin could desire.

I want to pair *The Broken Heart* with a work that Benjamin would not have considered a *Trauerspiel*: Nahum Tate and Henry Purcell's *Dido and Aeneas* (1684–1689). This pairing permits us to test Benjamin's claim that the *Trauerspiel* bears no comparison to musical tragedy or opera, and— because they are present in *The Broken Heart* and absent from *Dido and Aeneas*—it encourages us to ask whether the skulls, corpses, and ruins on which Benjamin dwells are really essential to the resonance of mourning.

WE WHO WERE LIVING ARE NOW DYING WITH A LITTLE PATIENCE

Benjamin writes as if the deaths that occur in *Trauerspiele* were an unimportant preliminary to the production of inanimate stage properties. But what is more striking about these plays is their determination to make the living dwell with the dying—with those who are neither fully alive nor completely dead and forgotten.

Hamlet must share the stage with the ghost of a father "Doomed for a certain time to walk the night/And for the day confined to fast in fires" (1.5.10–11), with the guts of a counselor being eaten by "a certain convocation of politic worms" (4.3.19–20), with the shell of a girl whose wits are distracted, and then with the corpse of the same girl, denied the full rites of burial.[19] Hoffman lives in a cave by the shore, where he keeps the "bare anatomy" of his father suspended in a tree. When the son of his father's killer comes into his power, Hoffman exacts a mimetic revenge: He places a burning crown on the victim's head so that his brains boil, his sinews shrink, his blood dissolves, and his nerves and tendons fail. He then pares the flesh from the bones and chains the skeleton next to the "dead remembrance" of his "living father" (1.1.8), whom he addresses in the second person like one of the living.[20] Nor is Hoffman the only one to treat these anatomies as if they were not quite inanimate: Lucibella, who is herself suspended between life and death (because she has been stabbed and is mad with grief), addresses them as "leane porters" (5.1.1948) and "staru'd ghosts" (5.1.2070–2071). The Vindice of *The Revenger's Tragedy* also lives with a reminder of the wrong done to him—the "sallow picture" of his "poisoned love," a "shell of death" (1.1.14–15).[21] Not only does he address this relic as "thou" and "madam," he deceives the lecherous Duke into making a fatal attempt on it: What the Duke takes for a masked lady is in fact the skull of his victim smeared with poison.

To be sure, there are moments in these plays when a character interprets a skull as a memento mori, and if he is given to melancholy like Hamlet or Vindice, he may indulge in an interpretive excess that makes us acutely aware of his willfulness as an allegorist. But such moments are isolated and can scarcely justify the presence of so many characters and properties on stage that are neither wholly alive nor fully dead and gone. These have another and more crucial function: They present death not as an instantaneous event but as a transition that has a duration of its own; and, as such, they transform a binary opposition into a rite of passage whose stages can be marked by rites of separation, transition, and incorporation.

We might expect that rites of separation would be the most important component of funeral ceremonies; but, as Arnold van Gennep observed almost a century ago, the transition rites of death rituals "have a duration and complexity sometimes so great that they must be granted a sort of autonomy."[22] In some societies, the liminal period of death is thought to begin when victims breathe their last and to end when the flesh has fallen from the bones or the liquid has drained from their bodies. Until then, mortals are considered neither alive nor finally dead, and their spirits may lurk near their remains or haunt their kin. The end of the liminal period is often marked by a reprocessing or reburial of the remains.[23]

Even in early modern England, where this sort of reburial was not practiced, death was not imagined as an instantaneous event that terminated with the last breath of the victims.[24] In his final sermon, which he delivered from the pulpit while wrapped in his own winding sheet, John Donne could ask, "Is that dissolution of body and soule, the last death that the body shall suffer?" And he could reply, "It is not. Though this be *exitus a morte*, it is *introitus in mortem*: though it bee an *issue from* the manifold *deaths* of this *world*, yet it is an *entrance* into the *death of corruption* and *putrefaction* and *vermiculation* and *incinceration*, and dispersion in and from the *grave*, in which every dead man dyes over againe."[25]

In medieval and Renaissance England, the desire to distinguish between the natural and the political bodies of the king, the former "subject to all infirmities that come by Nature or Accident" and the latter "utterly void of Infancy, of old Age, and other natural Defects and Imbecilities, which the Body natural is subject to," led to the use of effigies in royal funerals.[26] At the death of Elizabeth I in 1603, her natural body was left to lie in state, where she was attended by her Council and served "as though she were not wrapped in many a fold of cere-cloth, and hid in such a heap of lead, of coffin, of pall, but walking as she used to do at this season, about the alleys of her garden."[27] The focal point of her funeral procession was not, however, her corpse but a lifelike effigy that was "crowned in her Parliament Robes" and set atop the "balmed and leaded" corpse.[28] When onlookers "beheld her statue and picture lying upon the coffin set forth in Royall Robes," reports John Stow, there was "a generall sighing and groning, and weeping," the like of which had "not beene seene or knowne in the memorie of man."[29] Historians have wondered whether this could be true, for the popularity of the queen had declined by her death, but grief was not simply a private and spontaneous effusion in early modern England; it was a public and scripted performance of proper feeling.

By the time of James I's funeral, it was his effigy that lay in state for a month, attended by courtiers and provided with food. The funerals of the Roman emperors served as a precedent for this observance. After the corpse of Septimius Severus was interred, for example, his followers laid out his effigy on a bed in the imperial palace, where he was surrounded by senators and matrons. The emperor's physicians visited the effigy each day and declared him to be sicker and sicker until, after a week, they pronounced him dead. They then carried the effigy to the old market place, where Roman magistrates rendered up their offices, and thence to a pyre on the Campus Martius.[30]

The care lavished on these effigies underlines the importance of protracting the liminal period of dying to give scope to mourning. Baroque tragic drama strives for a similar effect by representing death not as a discrete event but as a transformation that unfolds through time and that may continue after characters have breathed their last. In *The Lady's Tragedy*, for example, the dead Lady is disinterred by the Tyrant, who is determined to vent his lust on her corpse even though he could not possess her living body: Her spirit continues to walk the stage costumed, like the corpse, in black velvet and a crucifix. Only upon her reinterment does the play treat her as fully dead. In *Love's Sacrifice*, on the other hand, Fernando protracts the liminal period of dying by anticipating his own suicide. For a time, he lives with the dead in a sepulchre, wrapped in a winding sheet.

But perhaps no English *Trauerspiel* is more single-mindedly committed to representing death as a process than *The Broken Heart*.[31] Ithocles sets the tragic action in motion by forcing his sister Penthea to marry the jealous old nobleman Bassanes rather than the man she loves, Orgilus. She dies of grief, and Orgilus takes his revenge by inviting Ithocles to sit opposite her corpse in a mechanical chair that renders him incapable of defending himself. As the court revels unaware of these terrible events, messengers bring the princess Calantha terrible news: The king, her father, has died of old age, her companion Penthea has starved, and her bethrothed Ithocles has been murdered. She orders the execution of Orgilus, makes preparations for her own coronation as queen, marries the corpse of Ithocles, and dies of a broken heart, thus fulfilling the prophecy,

> *When youth is ripe, and age from time doth part,*
> *The lifeless trunk shall wed the broken heart.* (5.3.99–100)

What such a bare outline cannot begin to express is how protracted the play's deaths are. Penthea begins to die the moment she is "buried" in a "bride-bed" (2.2.38), but we watch her waste away, lose her ability to menstruate, go mad, and die over the course of three acts that prove the contention of her "deathful air": "Love's martyrs must be ever, ever *dying*" (4.3.155, 153; my emphasis). Left to choose the manner of his own execution, Orgilus elects to bleed to death slowly, thus reducing a vital masculine body to a "bloodless" corpse (5.2.158). And even Ithocles, who dies quickly enough from his wounds, continues to be dressed and addressed as one of the living. All these characters project a special theatrical power because they have left the profane world and entered a world of the dying that lies close to the core of social value and theatrical meaning.[32]

Because the early modern tragic stage was routinely draped with the black cloths employed for funerals, its trappings would have primed the audience to assume the role of mourners.[33] But the play's penchant for paradox and chiasmus—so nicely exemplified by Donne's title, "Against the Dying Life, and Living Death of the Body"—would have reinforced the audience's impression that they were sharing a liminal space with the dying. *The Broken Heart* bristles with contradictions like "earthly immortality" (2.2.88) and "desires infinite, but hopes impossible" (3.2.49). It asks unanswerable questions like, "Can you grasp a sigh?" (3.1.5). And it confuses life and death, womb and tomb, cure and bane, dream and reality: "I could wish/That the first pillow whereon I was cradled/Had proved to me a grave" (3.2.36–38), "That remedy/Must be a winding sheet "(3.4.31–32), "I've slept/With mine eyes open a great while" (4.2.73–74).

The play's perfect balance between mimesis and allegory, representation and memorial is another ludic deconstruction and recombination that holds the audience in the transitional space occupied by the dying and the mourning. For even as Ford asks the audience to see and hear the actors on stage as embodied presences, he transforms them into markers for something other or beyond.[34] He does so by unleashing the emotive force of what Aby Warburg calls *Pathosformeln*, or formulas of pathos, even as he subjects these formulas to the violence of allegorical interpretation.[35] His play is punctuated, in other words, by dramatic moments when the unmediated, mimetic energy of the actors seems to fight with only partial success against being seen *through*.

Such a tension between mimesis and allegory, pathos and emblem, is sustained by a good deal of Renaissance and baroque art. Take, for example, Lucas Furtenagel's *The Burgkmaier Spouses* (1529). The flesh of the aging couple is rendered in lifelike detail, and the expressive force of their countenances conveys all the pathos of aging, but the death's heads visible in a convex mirror also imply that this couple can see the skull beneath the skin and the death that will meet them after life (Figure 4.1). In their own eyes and in the eyes of the viewer, they possess a double nature (both alive and dead) and they occupy two times (both now and hereafter). An engraving in Andreas Vesalius's *De Humani Corporis Fabrica* (1543) is likewise haunting because the skeleton assumes the posture of a contemplative man even as the skull he looks at seems to transfer its emblematic significance to his bones, wrestling a formula of pathos into submission and transforming it into a memento mori (Figure 4.2).

In *The Broken Heart*, Penthea weeps and hangs her head because "the Demission or *hanging down of the Head* is the Consequence of *Grief* and *Sorrow*."[36] We see three examples of demission in Pieter Paul Rubens's *Entombment* (Figure 4.3)—a gesture to which Penthea herself draws attention:

There's not a hair
Sticks on my head but like a leaden plummet
It sinks me to the grave. (4.2.76–78)

Penthea's own words also invite us, however, to compare her to that emblem of saintly affliction, the palm tree exercised by plumb weights: Virtue grows beneath weights (Figure 4.4). Penthea's death is marked by a similar tension between theatrical presence and allegorical interpretation. It is announced

Figure 4.1. Lucas Furtenagel, *The Burgkmaier Spouses* (1529) (*Der Maler Hans Bugkmair und seine Frau Anna*, geb. Allerlai). Kunsthistorisches Museum, Wien oder KHM, Vienna.

by a dirge heard offstage, whose affective force depends on music's power to sway the passions, yet we can scarcely fail to notice that at the moment of her death, Penthea is reduced to the meaning of her name, "Complaint." Orgilus's insistence on standing up as he bleeds to death suggests that he knows the theatrical power of a stance, but he also transforms himself into an

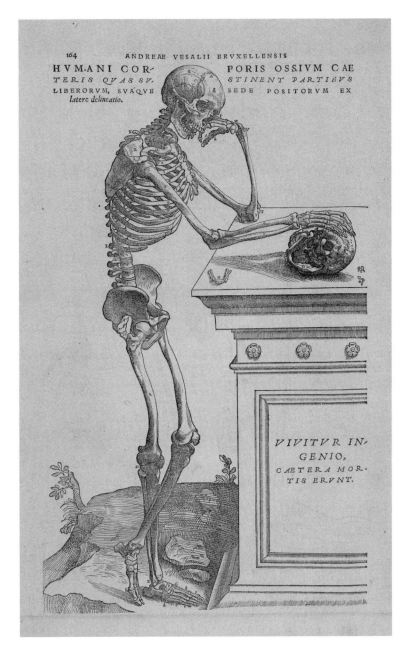

Figure 4.2. Andreas Vesalius, *De Humani Corporis Fabrica*, plate 22. In an earlier version of the plate, the tomb featured the motto, *Vivitur ingenio, caetera mortis erunt*, "Genius lives on, other things are mortal." Courtesy of Harvey Cushing/John Jay Whitney Medical Library, Yale University.

Figure 4.3. Peter Paul Rubens, *The Entombment* (c. 1612). Oil on canvas, 131 × 130 cm. The J. Paul Getty Museum, Los Angeles.

emblem when he provides a motto for the spectacle: "Revenge proves its own executioner" (5.2.147). This is characteristic of a play that is careful to provide a physiological explanation of its heroine's death—her heart breaks because she refuses to weep and thus to vent the fluids congregating morbidly around her heart—yet expects us to remember that broken hearts are a part of the emblem tradition (Figure 4.5).[37] We can never be sure when to see the characters' stage actions as *Pathosformeln* and when to view them as emblems. They possess the double nature and duple time of the body of Christ in Rubens's *Entombment*, which is both a luminous corpse disfigured with blood and, as the wheat beneath him on the tomb/altar indicates, a sacrament—the elevated body and blood of Christ. The corpse of Ithocles

Figure 4.4 Palm tree exercised by leaden plummets. Detail from the engraved frontispiece to *Eikon Basilike* (1649). Courtesy of Beinecke Rare Books Library, Yale University.

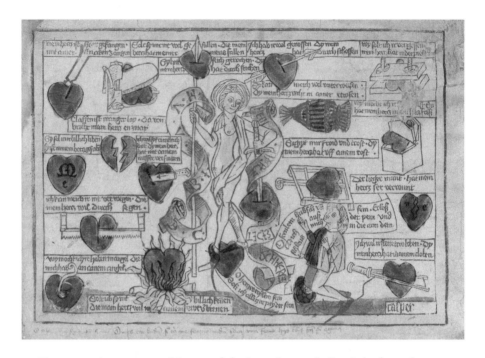

Figure 4.5. Anonymous, *Venus and the Lover* (c. 1485). Single leaf woodcut, colored, by Master Caspar, 25.7 × 36.5 cm. Regensburg, Germany. Inv. 467-1908. Photo: Joerg P. Anders. Kupferstichkabinett, Staaliche Museen zu Berlin, Berlin, Germany. Photo Credit: Bildarchiv Preussicher Kulturbesltz/ Art Resources, NY.

is the most memorable example of this effect in the play. It is dressed in the trappings of royalty like an effigy, yet it is a natural body: It thus conflates the corruptible and imperishable aspects of the self that were distinguished in royal funeral ceremonies and transi-tombs (Figure 4.6).

By providing an allegorical gloss on the name of each of his characters in the frontmatter, Ford invites us to interpret his entire play not only as an imitation of an action but as a dramatic allegory. In the theater, however, it is the play's memorable triumphs and funerals-as-triumphs that seem to solicit allegorical interpretation most urgently. Much as the pageant wagons of Petrarch's *Trionfi* supersede each other in a meaningful progression from Love, through Chastity, Death, Fame, and Time, to Eternity, the triumphs of *The Broken Heart* tell their own stories when viewed in sequence. Penthea's life unfolds like a pageant led by Love, Chastity, Death, Memory, and Truth, while Ithocles enjoys "triumphs" as a conqueror, a sacrifice, and

Figure 4.6. Tomb of Bishop Thomas Bekingham (c. 1451), Wells Cathedral. By permission of the Chapter of Wells Cathedral.

a corpse. Always we see and hear of progresses, chariots, and triumphs, and we witness characters, and particularly Ithocles, seated or carried in seats (Figure 4.7). Dramatic action is carefully balanced against allegorical pageant to produce a sacred theater of the limen.

As they approach their ends, the characters of *The Broken Heart* see their actions from the detached perspective of a theater audience. Bassanes, for example, speaks of Orgilus as if he were a puppet sent to torment him and praises his grizzly suicide as a "majestical" "pastime" (4.3.106, 105). He perceives even Calantha's death as a part she has played (5.2.96). But it is Penthea who states the theme most fully:

On the stage
Of my mortality, my youth hath acted
Some scenes of vanity, drawn out at length
By varied pleasures, sweetened in the mixture,
But tragical in issue. (3.3.15–19)

Figure 4.7. A Roman corpse being displayed during a funeral oration. Thomaso Porcacchi, *Funerali antichi de diversi populi et nationi* (Venice, 1574), Plate 8, page 59. Engraving by Girolamo Porro. Houghton Library, Typ 525.74.707 (A), Harvard University.

Penthea, in other words, approaches the state of mind at which René Descartes believed great souls would arrive when they considered themselves as imperishable souls inhabiting vulnerable and short-lived bodies:

> For, on the one hand, considering themselves as immortals and as capable of receiving very great contentment, and, on the other hand, considering that they are joined to fragile mortal bodies, which are subject to many infirmities and which will inevitably perish in a few years, they do everything in their power to render Fortune favorable in this life, but they nevertheless esteem it so little in relation to Eternity that they come close to considering events as we do plays. And just as the sad and lamentable stories we see represented in the theater often give us as much recreation as cheerful ones do, even though they bring tears to our eyes, so the greatest souls I speak of derive satisfaction within themselves from everything that happens to them, no matter how upsetting and unbearable; and thus, feeling pain in their bodies, they apply themselves to bear it patiently, and the proof of their strength which they get in this way is pleasant to them.[38]

Calantha smiles in death to crack her heart, it is true, but the proof of her own strength may also be pleasing to her.

If the tension between mimetic energy and allegorical signification helps to plunge the audience into the betwixt-and-between world of the dying and the mourning, it also helps them to put the fragility of their own bodies and the permanence of eternity into perspective so that they may know when to rejoice, sorrow, or commiserate in due measure. Such a habit of proper feeling could be formed by watching tragedies, said Heinsius, because:

> Just as anyone who with long practice has readied himself for performance, properly executes a given art, so by a certain conditioning to the objects by which the passions of the soul are stimulated, their mean is induced. . . . This is what the things exhibited in the theater must answer to, because it is a kind of training hall of our passions which (since they are not only useful in life but necessary) must therefore be readied and perfected.[39]

The allegory of *The Broken Heart* is not a melancholy indulgence, it is a dramatic device intended to generate a response of mourning even as it tempers that response by means of the split-consciousness of Fortune and Eternity that Descartes describes.

WHEN I AM LAID IN EARTH

I want to turn now to *Dido and Aeneas* (1684–1689) so that we can consider the affective function of the struggle between representation and memorial in a drama whose allegorical properties are far removed from the skulls, anatomies, and ruins that lead Benjamin to describe allegory as a mortuary art. Although Naham Tate's libretto retells Book 4 of the *Aeneid*, it values affective bonds, passive suffering, and elegiac recollection more highly than the Virgilian values of piety, labor, and empire. By introducing a coven of witches who send a spirit in the guise of Mercury to instruct Aeneas to leave Carthage, it undermines Virgil's claims that Rome was fated to sway the world and that the cause of empire requires personal sacrifice. And by declining to have Dido curse her faithless lover and then stab herself with his sword on their bed, it quickens our sympathy for a wronged queen, implying that her suffering, which is caused by the indubitable passions of her soul and is sufficient to break her heart, is in some sense better founded,

more real, more true than the life of action to which Aeneas heads—
founded, as it is, on an illusory imperative.

Although *Dido and Aeneas* draws on many musical and theatrical traditions, including the Stuart masque, Italian opera, French chamber opera,
and Sir William Davenant's spectacular, operatic production of *Macbeth*,
its most important model is the *Venus and Adonis* (1682) of Henry Purcell's
teacher John Blow, a fully sung masque that, like *Dido and Aeneas*, opens
with an allegorical prologue, unfolds in three acts with allegorical dances,
and concludes with a chorus that laments the untimely and passive death
of its hero. The basic dramatic unit of both works progresses from recitative
through air, chorus, and dance. But Purcell lends a greater sense of structure
and momentum to his opera by introducing three ground basses that define
the key centers of the acts (C minor, D minor, and G minor) and that direct
all the tragedy's lines of sight toward a single terminus.[40] Because I want to
focus on the tension between mimetic energy and emblematic significance
that builds as the opera's music and dance converge on Dido's final lament,
I propose to follow three key elements through the action.

The first is Purcell's use of modal affects or key feelings to express particular passions or to signal dramatic relationships. In the sixteenth and
seventeenth centuries, music theorists and composers expended a great deal
of effort trying to revive the eight ancient modes of music, which were
thought to have had the power to arouse and assuage the soul at will. These
ancient modes were supposed to have operated directly on the soul, without
depending on conventional associations or emblematic meanings, but as
baroque theorists published various schemes of what were sometimes called
the character (*ethos*) or energy (*energeia*) of the modes, particular modes
did take on conventional associations and invite allegorical interpretations.
Although Purcell left no written scheme codifying his own practice, his
selection of modes (which I shall henceforth refer to as our modern keys)
is systematic.

The second element I want to focus on is Purcell's use of ground basses.
By the time Purcell was writing, something like a musical rhetoric of the
passions had already been established by composers like Monteverdi and
Cavalli working in the opera houses of Venice. One of Monteverdi's most
widely admired expressions of grief was his ostinato bass with a descending minor tetrachord.[41] In his "Lament of the Nymph," the insistent and
repetitive downward pull of the bass line suggests an emotional distress that
borders on distraction; it gives the passions a musical embodiment that is

distinct from the voice, which struggles for its own autonomy; and it drags the Nymph relentlessly down to despair and death. This bass had already served as an emblem of lament in Cavalli's *Egisto* (1642) and numerous other operas and cantatas by the mid-seventeenth century, so by the time Purcell used it in the 1680s, it was a musical device balanced on the knife's edge of mimetic energy and allegorical significance.

The final element I shall follow is the dances that punctuate the action of *Dido and Aeneas*. One group of dances exhibits the virtues of the sexes and doubles the courtship plot. In the Renaissance, dance was thought to inculcate the virtues proper to the sexes in the kinesthetic memories of the dancers, teaching men to be "fiers, hardy, stronge in opinion, couaitous of glorie, desirous of knowledge, [and] appetiting by generation to bryinge forth [their] semblable" and training women to be "milde, timorouse, tractable, benigne, of sure remembrance, and shamfast."[42] Although dance was thought to be a somatic expression of the soul, its scripted bodily motions also bore within themselves "wonderfull figures or as the grekes do calle them *Ideae*."[43] The allegorical character of court dances was most clearly displayed in masques, which, by bringing dancing Cupids on stage, often invoked the Orphic and neoplatonic myth that Primal Love first taught the starry quires how to dance: To dance in a masque was to instantiate the harmony of the cosmos in court and to tune one's soul to the heavens. But the belief that men and women were microcosms of the universe who might attune themselves to its spiritual influences by manipulating occult resemblances, or by performing the motions proper to celestial bodies, also invested such figured dances with all the mysterious potential of magic— whether benign or demonic.[44] The remaining dances of *Dido and Aeneas* exploit both the light and the dark side of this neoplatonic model of dance: They put allegory into action.

I would like to begin with Act 1 because the music for the allegorical prologue to *Dido and Aeneas* is lost. The action commences with a French overture whose fugal second section in C minor immerses the audience in the atmosphere of anxiety and depression oppressing Dido's court. Its chromaticism and the eighth notes of its canzona suggest that Dido's love is obsessive and destructive, and the insistent descent of its bass imparts a downward momentum to the action before it has even begun.

In the first words of the drama, Dido's confidente Belinda and the chorus try to lift Dido from C minor into the regal and tranquil key of C major, singing, "Shake the clouds from off your brow" and "Banish sorrow, banish care."[45] Dido confides in recitative written over an ostinato bass that resembles that of a chaconne in a minor key, "Ah! Belinda, I am press'd,/ With torment not to be confess'd." After the descending bass has been stated nine times, she lifts into a miniature da capo aria whose melody begins as a quotation from the ground, "Peace and I are strangers grown,/I languish till my grief is known,/Yet would not have it guess'd." When she arrives at, "Yet would not," she reaches up for the C major to which all her court has been trying to direct her, only to subside back into C minor. Her feeling is so full that an instrumental accompaniment must complete the statement of her passion. Belinda and the Second Woman extol the virtues and attractions of Aeneas, and the queen confesses that her heart, though "with storms of care oppress'd," "Is taught to pity the distress'd." Singing in C major and parallel thirds, Belinda and the Second Woman enjoin Dido to fear no danger.

When Dido and Aeneas meet for the first time, he asks in the bold and confident key of G major, "When, Royal Fair, shall I be bless'd?," and Dido, beginning the music's descent through A minor to E minor, responds, "Fate forbids what you pursue." After Aeneas responds quite falsely, "Aeneas has no fate but you!" the Chorus, representing the force of desire, intrudes with an air ("Cupid only throws the dart") whose affecting dissonances on words like *dart* and *heart* are intended to express the paradox that love is an agreeable pain. If Dido can be said to "accept" the advances of Aeneas at any time during the drama itself, it is between Belinda's observation, "her eyes/ Confess the flame her tongue denies" and the choral air that concludes, "Let the triumphs of love and beauty be shown./Go revel, ye Cupids, the day is your own." The only thing that occurs in the interim is a chaconne, a dance that was thought to have originated in Spain or Africa and that still retained some overtones of the erotic and exotic despite being used as a courtly dance appropriate for weddings. With the triumph of the Cupids that ends the act, G minor, the key in which Dido will die, intrudes with tragic irony.

Act 2 consists of three scenes. In the first, the Sorceress and her wayward sisters plot the destruction of Dido. As they sing in C major, they emphasize their resemblance to Dido's courtiers: Both groups are driving her to her doom, an irony that is emphasized if the same singers appear in both roles. As they sing in G minor, they identify themselves as agents of Dido's death. The echo dance that the Furies perform after the wayward sisters withdraw into their cell to cast their spell is the opera's most remarkable representation of the demonic potential of neoplatonic allegory. Ficino said that music, in its "airy and rational motions" was a "most powerful imitator of things."[46] The musician projected song ("this potent phantasm") into the world, where it immediately provoked the singer and the audience to "act out" the things it presented. This is the same theory that underwrote the attempts of court masquers to capture the gifts of the stars through dance. Purcell's echo dance stages this process by playing a measure that represents the charms being cast by the wayward sisters concealed backstage in their cell, and then repeating it, with slight variations, so that we can see the result of their spells enacted on the forestage by the dance of the Furies—though there is always just a little something lost in the translation. According to some scores, six of the Furies should sink down and another four should fly up at the end of the echo dance. The dance reinforces our brooding sense of the destructive potential of the universe's malign forces—even when they are not visible on stage. In the second scene, when Dido and Aeneas go hunting, their courtiers sing of Acteon and Adonis, hunters whose violent but passive deaths were attributed to their passions by Ovid's moralizers. The music insists on the application of the stories to Dido by introducing a vocal ground bass to narrate the death of Acteon—a setting reserved in Acts 1 and 3 for the laments of Dido herself. Then in the third scene, an elf appears in the guise of Mercury to tell Aeneas he must forsake Carthage to restore Troy.

Act 3 commences with Aeneas' sailors deciding to "Take a boozy short leave of your nymphs on the shore,/And silence their mourning/With vows of returning/But never intending to visit them more." As Curtis Price has observed, the inner couplet of both the air and the chorus is set over a descending tetrachord that anticipates Dido's final lament.[47] Beginning on the note C, the sailors lead to a strong cadence in G minor—a foreshadowing of Dido's doom. This anticipation of Aeneas's leave-taking demystifies the hero's official line. Now the wayward sisters seem to be allied with the chorus of sailors as they delight in Dido's impending death, just as they were allied with the courtiers of Carthage when they incited her passions. The sailors' jovial dance brings the opera's series of courtship dances to a harsh, parodic close. It has an effect that is similar to the jesting of the clown who brings Cleopatra's asp in the last act of Shakespeare's *Antony and Cleopatra*: It isolates the tragic heroine and defines the rhetoric, the music, the bodily deportment appropriate to her as distinct, other, higher. When Aeneas appears to take his leave, the queen's charge that he is a "deceitful crocodile," a "hypocrite," and a "murderer" shakes his resolve, but Dido then reverses herself and bids him fly to his empire lest she dispose of her life violently. Her threat has the convenient effect of discharging Aeneas from most moral responsibility for her end, and it also permits her to die more peacefully of a broken heart.

Once Aeneas has taken his leave, Dido is left alone to sing her own threnody, "Now I am laid in earth." Her voice is supremely expressive as she intones her final injunction, "Remember me, but ah! forget my fate," especially as she sings that preverbal expression of grief, "Ah," then reaches up for the royal key of C major in a final assertion of regal dignity, then collapses into G minor, the key of death in the opera.[48] The ostinato bass, which reasserts itself during her final lament, lends a sense of tragic inevitability and momentum to the action. Because it is based on a chaconne, a dance especially associated with weddings in the French musical tradition and probably used to figure her initial acceptance of Aeneas in the opera, it depicts Dido's decease as a marriage to death.

Once Dido has died of a broken heart, the chorus sings its beautiful, communal expression of grief, "With drooping wings you Cupids come/ To scatter roses on her tomb." In an ending that is omitted in most modern productions, cupids then descend from the clouds and dance about her tomb. The descent of the cupids is a gesture of piteous condescension that appears sharply different from both the cupids' triumphing dance in Act 1 and the aggressive upward flight of the Furies in Act 2. The cupids' dances have been recurring throughout the play like the ostinato bass that provides the underpinning for Dido's lament, and they serve a similar function: they lend a sense of tragic inevitability to the action, they commemorate her death with a conflated wedding revel and funeral ceremony, and they turn Dido's sacrifice into a ludic lamentation. The way in which the members of the final chorus echo each other is itself an echo of the dance of the Furies. It seems to communicate grief in waves through the community of mourners and out into a wider world connected by invisible sympathies. The dance of the cupids, which is also a dance of the cosmos, then reabsorbs the scattered individual.

Dido and Aeneas spares no pains to generate a response of mourning, a response that depends, I would argue, on its balancing of mimetic energy and allegorical significance, its insistence on the vital *presence* of Dido in a world of shadowy signs and occult resemblances. Yet it also careful to provide the *pleasure* of grieving, which arises from our remembrance of the dead. In *The Broken Heart*, that pleasure is produced when Penthea asks Calantha to be her "executrix" so that she may "dispose/Such legacies as I bequeth impartially" (3.5.37–38) and when Calantha lays down conditions for a marriage that are really her last will and "testament" (5.3.53). In *Dido and Aeneas*, it is produced by Dido's repeated injunction, "Remember me, but ah! forget my fate." As Lord Kames observed in his analysis of the passions, "Grief is a most painful passion or impression, yet it is the farthest of any thing from being mixed with any degree of aversion. On the contrary, we cling to the object which raises our grief, and love to dwell upon it."[49] No one could wish the lament of Dido or the dirge of the chorus any shorter.

In the *Origin*, Benjamin extracts passages from *Trauerspiele* and arranges them as if they were so many leaves from the Sybil portending a truth that can only be perceived "from the higher domain of theology." We can better understand how *The Broken Heart* and *Dido and Aeneas* function as dramas of mourning if we interpret them as theatrical representations that, by appropriating the forms of mortuary rituals, dilate our exposure to the dying and transform us into a community of mourners who inhabit the shadowy borderland between life and death—a limen that, as I have tried to suggest in my reading of *Dido*, we can enter even without the aid of corpses and ruins on stage. This approach not only accounts for the cognitive and affective function of one of the most salient characteristics of baroque tragic drama—its yoking of mimetic energy to allegorical significance—it respects the seventeenth century's own account of the pleasure that audiences sought from tragic representations: "the pleasure in grief and mourning, as when we mourn the dead."

Notes

1. Walter Benjamin, *The Origin of German Tragic Drama*, trans. John Osborne, intro. George Steiner (London and New York: Verso, 1998), p. 110, quoting his own "Schicksal und Charakter," p. 191. On Benjamin's conception of tragedy, which is deeply influenced by those of Florens Christian Rang, Franz Rosenzweig, Friedrich Nietzsche, and Max Scheler, see Benjamin, *Origin*, esp. pp. 106–118; Ferenc Fehér, "Lukacs and Benjamin: Parallels and Contrasts," *New German Critique* 34 (1985): 125–138; Bernd Witte, *Walter Benjamin: An Intellectual Biography*, trans. James Rolleston (Detroit, MI: Wayne State University Press, 1991), p. 78; Steiner, introduction, p. 16; and Carrie L. Asman, "Theater and Agon/Agon and Theater: Walter Benjamin and Florens Christian Rang" *MLN* 107 (1992): 606–624.

2. Benjamin, *Origin*, esp. pp. 62, 69–74, 119–138, 182, 198, 217–218.

3. Benjamin, *Origin*, p. 217. On Benjamin's idea of the *Trauerspiel*, also see his "*Trauerspiel* and Tragedy" and "The Role of Language in *Trauerspiel* and Tragedy," both in *Selected Writings*, Vol. 1 (Cambridge, MA: Belknap Press of Harvard University Press, 1996), pp. 55–61; Richard Wolin, *Walter Benjamin: An Aesthetic of Redemption* (New York: Columbia University Press, 1982), ch. 3; John McCole, *Walter Benjamin and the Antinomies of Tradition* (Ithaca, NY: Cornell University Press, 1993), ch. 3; Max Pensky, *Melancholy Dialectics: Walter Benjamin and the Play of Mourning* (Amherst: University of Massachusetts Press, 1993).

4. Karl Giehlow, "Die Hieroglyphenkunde des Humanismus in her Allegorie der Renaissance besonders der Ehrenpforte Kaisers Maximilian I. Ein Versuch," ed. Arpad Weixlgärtner, *Jahrbuch der kunshistorischen Sammlungen des allerhöchsten Kaiserhauses* 32 (1915), also available in Italian translation as *Hieroglyphica. La conoscenza umanistica dei geroglifici nell'allegoria del Rinascimento. Una ipotesi*, ed. Maurizio Ghelardi and Susanne Müller (Turin: Nino Aragno Editore, 2004).

5. Giehlow, "Die Hieroglyphenkunde," p. 23, quoted in Benjamin, *Origin*, p. 169.

6. Giehlow, "Die Hieroglyphenkunde," p. 127, quoted in Benjamin, *Origin*, p. 174.

7. Benjamin, *Origin*, p. 175. For somewhat different accounts of the historical development of allegory, see Gombrich, "Icones Symbolicae: The Visual Image in Neo-Platonic Thought," *Journal of the Warburg and Courtauld Institutes* 11 (1948): pp. 163–192; and Blair Hoxby, "Allegorical Drama," in *The Cambridge Companion to Allegory*, ed. Rita Copeland and Peter Struck (Cambridge, U.K.: Cambridge University Press, 2009).

8. Benjamin, *Origin*, p. 139; Howard Caygill, "Walter Benjamin's Concept of Cultural History," in *The Cambridge Companion to Walter Benjamin*, ed. David S. Ferris (Cambridge, U.K.: Cambridge University Press, 2004), p. 88.

9. Benjamin, *Origin*, pp. 184–185.

10. Benjamin, *Origin*, p. 182.

11. Benjamin, *Origin*, pp. 232–233.

12. See esp. Wolin, *Walter Benjamin*, ch. 3.

13. The importance of these plays to the conception of tragedy in the seventeenth century will be one of the themes of my forthcoming *Spectacles of the Gods: Tragedy and Tragic Opera, 1550–1780*.

14. Benjamin, *Origin*, p. 216.

15. See esp. Victor Turner, *From Ritual to Theatre: The Human Seriousness of Play* (New York: PAJ Publications, 1982); and Turner, "Are There Universals of Performance in Myth, Ritual, and Drama?" in *By Means of Performance: Intercultural Studies of Theatre and Ritual*, ed. Richard Schechner and Willa Appel (Cambridge, U.K.: Cambridge University Press, 1990), pp. 8–18.

16. Benjamin, *Origin*, pp. 119, 185. Benjamin does not distinguish clearly between *mourning* and *melancholy*, but I take his uses of the words *mournful* and *mournfulness* on p. 119 to refer to a permanent affect that is a species of melancholy. In keeping with Renaissance usage, I, on the other hand, will employ the word

mourning to refer to the conscious display of a temporary grief that seeks comfort in the midst of tribulation and heaviness and use the word *melancholy* to refer to a protracted affective state of grief or dullness whose origin may be ascribed to a predominance of black bile in the blood, the influence of the planet Saturn, or anxiety about religious salvation, and whose symptoms may range from lethargy to furious ire.

17. Daniel Heinsius, *De Tragoediae Constitutione, On Plot in Tragedy* (1611), trans. Paul R. Sellin and John J. McManmon (Northridge, CA: San Fernando Valley State College, 1971), p. 47.

18. All quotations are from John Ford, *The Broken Heart*, ed. Donald K. Anderson Jr., Regents Renaissance Drama Series (Lincoln: University of Nebraska Press, 1968).

19. All quotations are from *Hamlet*, ed. A. R. Braunmuller (New York: Penguin Books, 2001). For a reading of *Hamlet* that emphasizes the liminal qualities of purgatory, see Stephen Greenblatt, *Hamlet in Purgatory* (Princeton, NJ: Princeton University Press, 2001).

20. All quotations are from Henry Chettle, *The Tragedy of Hoffman*, ed. Harold Jenkins (London: Malone Society, 1950).

21. All quotations are from Thomas Middleton, *The Collected Works*, gen. eds. Gary Taylor and John Lavagnino, 2 vols. (Oxford, U.K.: Clarendon Press, 2007).

22. Arnold van Gennep, *The Rites of Passage*, trans. Monika B. Vizedom and Gabrielle L. Caffee, intro. Solon T. Kimball (Chicago: University of Chicago Press, 1960), p. 148.

23. Robert Hertz, *Death and the Right Hand*, trans. Rodney and Claudia Needham, intro. E. E. Evans Pritchard (Aberdeen, U.K.: Cohen & West, 1960), pp. 9–86; Richard Huntington and Peter Metcalf, *Celebrations of Death: The Anthropology of Mortuary Ritual* (Cambridge, U.K.: Cambridge University Press, 1979), pp. 61–92.

24. Clare Gittings, *Death, Burial, and the Individual in Early Modern England* (London: Croom Helm, 1984), esp. pp. 19–23.

25. John Donne, "Death's Duell, or, a Consolation to the Soule, against the Dying Life, and Living Death of the Body, 25 February 1631," in *Selected Prose*, ed. Neil Rhodes (Harmondsworth, U.K.: Penguin Books, 1987), p. 315.

26. Edmund Plowden, *Commentaries or Reports* (London: S. Brooke, 1816), 221a; see Ernst H. Kantorowicz, *The King's Two Bodies: A Study in Mediaeval Political Theology*, new pref. by Chester Jordan (Princeton, NJ: Princeton University Press, 1985).

27. *Calendar of State Papers Domestic* 10 (1603–1607), 22, quoted in Jennifer Woodward, *The Theatre of Death: The Ritual Management of Royal Funerals in Renaissance England, 1570–1625* (Woodbridge, U.K.: Boydell Press, 1997), p. 116.

28. Henry Chettle, "The Order and Proceeding at the Funerall of the Right and Mighty Princesse Elizabeth Queene of England, France, and Ireland from the

Palace of Westminster, Called Whitehall: To the Cathedrall Church of Westminster. 28th April 1603," quoted in Woodward, *Theatre of Death*, p. 87.

29. John Stow, *The Annales* (1615), p. 815, quoted in Woodward, *Theatre of Death*, p. 88.

30. Herodian provides the fullest account of the funeral of Septimius Severus. Politian published his Latin translation of Herodian in 1493. French translations appeared in 1541 and 1546. Nicholas Smith published his English translation, *The History of Herodian, a Greeke Author, Treating of the Romayne Emperors* in 1550; the funeral is described on fols. xlvi–xlvii. See Ralph Giesey, *The Royal Funeral Ceremony in Renaissance France* (Geneva: E. Droz, 1960), pp. 147–151, 170. Many books on the burial customs of ancient and foreign peoples were published in the sixteenth and seventeenth centuries. Representative examples include Thomaso Porcacchi, *Fvnerali antichi de diuersi popoli, et nationi: forma, ordine, et pompa di sepolture, di essequie, de consecrationi antiche et d'altro* (Venice, 1574); Claude Guichard, *Fvnerailles, & diuerses manieres d'enseuelier des Rommains, Grecs, & autres nations, tant anciennes que modernes* (Lyon, 1581); Anon., *Of the Antiquity of Ceremonies Used at Funerals in England* (London, 1599); Jan Meursius, *De funere liber singularis, in quo Graeci et Romani ritus* (Hague, 1604); Johann Kirchman, *De funeribus Romanorum* (Hamburg, 1605); Richard Braithwait, *Remains after Death: . . . including divers memorable observances* (1618); and Francesco Perucci, *Pompe funebri de tutte le nationi del mondo: raccolte dalle storie sagre et profane* (Verona, 1639). For some suggestive remarks about the cultural function of effigies, see Joseph Roach, *Cities of the Dead: Circum-Atlantic Performance* (New York: Columbia University Press, 1996), pp. 36–41; and "Celebrity Erotics: Pepys, Performance, and Painted Ladies," *Yale Journal of Criticism* 16 (2003): 211–230.

31. Critical interpretations of *The Broken Heart* include R. J. Kaufmann, "Ford's 'Waste Land': *The Broken Heart*," *Renaissance Drama*, n.s. 3 (1970): 167–187; Ronald Huebert, *John Ford: Baroque English Dramatist* (Montreal: McGill-Queen's University Press, 1977); Dorothy Farr, *John Ford and the Caroline Theatre* (London: Macmillan, 1979), pp. 79–104; Michael Neill, "Ford's Unbroken Art: The Moral Design of 'The Broken Heart,'" *MLR* 75 (1980): 249–268; Anne Barton, "Oxymoron and the Structure of Ford's *The Broken Heart*," *Essays and Studies* 33 (1980): 70–94; Verna Ann Foster and Stephen Foster, "Structure and History in *The Broken Heart*: Sparta, England, and the 'Truth,'" *English Literary Renaissance*, 18 (1988): 305–328; William Dyer, "Holding/Withholding Environments: A Psychoanalytic Approach to Ford's *The Broken Heart*," *English Literary Renaissance* 21 (1991): 401–424; Lisa Hopkins, *John Ford's Political Theatre* (Manchester, U.K., and New York: Manchester University Press, 1994); and Michael Neill, *Issues of Death: Mortality and Identity in English Renaissance Tragedy* (Oxford, U.K.: Clarendon Press, 1997), pp. 354–374.

32. Victor Turner, *The Forest of Symbols: Aspects of Ndembu Ritual* (Ithaca, NY: Cornell University Press, 1967), pp. 93–111.

33. E. K. Chambers, *The Elizabethan Stage*, 4 vols. (Oxford, U.K.: Clarendon Press, 1951), 3:79; M. C. Bradbrook, *Themes and Conventions of Elizabethan The-*

atre, 2nd ed. (Cambridge, U.K.: Cambridge University Press, 1980), pp. 16–17; Neill, *Issues of Death*, pp. 282–283.

34. On "the production of presence," see Hans Ulrich Gumbrecht, *Production of Presence: What Meaning Cannot Convey* (Stanford, CA: Stanford University Press, 2004).

35. Aby Warburg, *The Renewal of Pagan Antiquity*, intro. Kurt W. Forster, trans. David Britt (Los Angeles: Getty Research Institute for the History of Art and the Humanities, 1999), pp. 89, 271, 553–558; Matthew Rampley, *The Remembrance of Things Past: On Aby M. Warburg and Walter Benjamin* (Weisbaden: Harrassowitz Verlag, 2000), pp. 125–150. On the violence of allegory, see Gordon Teskey, *Allegory and Violence* (Ithaca, NY: Cornell University Press, 1996).

36. [Thomas Betterton,] *The History of the English Stage* (London: Printed for E. Curll, 1741), p. 65.

37. Michael Neill reproduces this image in his critical interpretation of Ford's *'Tis Pity She's a Whore*, "'What Strange Riddle's This?': Deciphering *'Tis Pity She's a Whore*," in *John Ford: Critical Re-Visions*, ed. Michael Neill (Cambridge, U.K.: Cambridge University Press, 1988).

38. René Descartes, *Oeuvres des Descartes*, ed. Charles Adam and Paul Tannery, new ed., coed., Centre National de la Recherche Scientifique, 12 vols. (Paris: Librarie J. Vrin, 1957–1968), 4:202–203; my translation.

39. Heinsius, *De Tragoediae Constitutione*, p. 12.

40. My understanding of the score of *Dido and Aeneas* has been particularly enriched by Robert Etheridge Moore, *Henry Purcell & the Restoration Theatre* (Cambridge, MA: Harvard University Press, 1961), ch.2; Curtis Price, *Henry Purcell and the London Stage* (Cambridge, U.K.: Cambridge University Press, 1984), ch. 5; and Peter Holman, *Henry Purcell* (Oxford, U.K.: Oxford University Press, 1994), pp. 194–201.

41. See Ellen Rosand, "The Descending Tetrachord: An Emblem of Lament," *Musical Quarterly* 65 (1979): 346–359; Gary Tomlinson, "Madrigal, Monody, and Monteverdi's 'Via Naturale all Immitatione,'" *Journal of the American Musicological Society* 34 (1981): 60–108; Nigel Fortune, "Monteverdi and the *seconda prattica*," in *The New Monteverdi Companion*, ed. Denis Arnold and Nigel Fortune (London: Faber and Faber, 1985), pp. 192–197; and the special issue on laments that appeared in *Early Music* 27 (1999).

42. Sir Thomas Elyot, *The Boke Named the Governour* (1531), fol. 82v–fol. 83r.

43. Elyot, *The Boke Named the Governour*, fol. 84r.

44. The magical quality of court masques remains contested. For arguments against it, see for example, D. J. Gordon, *The Renaissance Imagination*, ed. Stephen Orgel (Berkeley: University of California Press, 1975), p. 21; and Stephen Orgel, *The Illusion of Power: Political Theater in the English Renaissance* (Berkeley: University of California Press, 1975), pp. 55–57. On the other hand, Orgel's coauthor Roy Strong stresses the compatibility of neoplatonism and magic in his *Art and Power: Renaissance Festivals 1450–1650* (Woodbridge, Suffolk, U.K.:

Boydel Press, 1984). See also Thomas M. Greene, "Magic and Festivity at the Renaissance Court: The 1987 Josephine Waters Bennet Lecture" *Renaissance Quarterly* 40 (1987): 636–659.

45. I follow the text and score printed in *Dido and Aeneas: An Opera*, ed. Curtis Price, Norton Critical Scores (New York and London: Norton, 1986).

46. See Marsilio Ficino, *Three Books on Life*, ed. and trans. Carol V. Kaske and John R. Clarke (Binghampton, NY: Medieval & Renaissance Texts & Studies, 1989), pp. 358–359.

47. Price, *Henry Purcell and the London Stage*, p. 254.

48. Curtis A. Price, "*Dido and Aeneas* in Context," in Purcell, *Dido and Aeneas: An Opera*, p. 36.

49. Lord Kames, *Essays on the Principles of Morality and Religion* (Edinburgh: R. Fleming, for A. Kincaid and A. Donaldson, 1751), p. 10.

PART TWO

Allegory in Place

FIVE

Colonial Allegories in Paris

The Ideology of Primitive Art

GORDON TESKEY

The center of Paris is bounded on the east and the west by two "woods," in the manicured, French sense of the word—all that remain of the ancient forests, Lanchonia Silva and the Forêt du Rouvre, now the Bois de Vincennes and the Bois de Boulogne. The river runs between them from east to west, passing to the south of the Bois de Vincennes on its way into the city and, as it leaves the city, turning north to embrace with its right bank the far side of the Bois de Boulogne. The westerly flow of the Seine is an emblem of how Paris works: Following ancient patterns, those who supply labor and goods live upstream from those who receive and consume. On the coat of arms of the city is a ship with the motto, *fluctuat nec mergitur*: "It goes with the flow, so as not to sink." Until the Luftwaffe bombed it, there had long been a huge wine market on the upstream right bank at Bercy, near the Bois de Vincennes, whence casks were floated on barges into the city and unloaded at various points, the best wines last.[1] Today, the ring-road tunnels beneath the Bois de Vincennes; and, beyond it in industrial Bercy, trucks unload in vast warehouses goods destined for the city. In Paris, luxury, power, and magnificent display flow inexorably downstream, to the west, from the Bois de Vincennes to the Bois de Boulogne.

With its elegant avenues and palatial hideaways for the likes of the Duke and Duchess of Windsor, or Princess Di and Dodi Fayed, the Bois de Boulogne is in the westerly part of the aristocratic sixteenth arrondissement, formerly the suburb called the Faubourg Saint-Honoré.[2] The Elysée Palace, where the president is lodged, is on the Rue du Faubourg Saint-Honoré, as are many of Paris's most elegant shops—there, and on the adjacent Place Vendôme, neighboring the Ritz Hotel. The association of west Paris with conspicuous luxury began in the Renaissance, when the unpopular, fiercely aristocratic second queen of Henri IV, Marie de Medici, disgusted by the rowdy populace around the fortress of the Louvre, extended the royal prospect westward from the Tuileries gardens, planting along the right bank of the Seine the treed alleys of the Cours-la-Reine and beside them the vast gardens that would become the Avenue des Champs Elysées, the Elysian Fields, the most elegant street in the world. In the days of Marie's grandson, Louis XIV (who was born to the west of the city, in the great château of Saint Germaine-en-Laye), the nobles would travel still farther west, taking the Rue du Faubourg Saint-Honoré out of the city on the way to Versailles.

The Bois de Vincennes is at the other, east end of Paris, in the now hip but once unfashionable working-class twelfth arrondissement, which occupies the southern portion of the old Faubourg Saint-Antoine, cradle of the revolutionary mob. It seems right that while he was traveling eastward, on the road to Vincennes, Rousseau would conceive the *Social Contract*. Although it was once a royal hunting preserve, the Bois de Vincennes, with its vélodrome and its zoo, has long been associated with the people; Saint Louis is said to have rendered popular justice there, under an oak. It was favored for hunting and also less vigorous sports by Marie de Medici's much more popular husband, Henri de Navarre, the first of the Bourbon kings, who in 1594 ended the decade-long Wars of Religion and won the capital by renouncing his Protestant faith, quipping, "Paris is well worth a mass"—"*Paris vaut bien une messe.*" He appears in Spenser's *Faerie Queene* as Sir Burbon, the knight of the unfaithful Flourdelis (France). In trying to win her back, Sir Burbon shamefully abandons the shield of true religion given him by the Redcross Knight: "That bloudie scutchin being battered sore,/I layd aside, and have of late forebore,/Hoping thereby to have my love obtained."[3] The real Henri had little trouble in that department.

To the north of the twelfth arrondissement, farther from the Seine, to which it is connected by the canal Saint Martin and the Arsenal Basin, is the eleventh arrondissement, the center of the old Faubourg Saint Antoine, which at the time of the Revolution was outside the city walls, eastward from the heavily fortified Porte Saint Antoine. The most imposing part of those defenses was the eight-towered fortress of the Bastille, which was built to guard Paris's vulnerable east flank and did so until its capture and dismantling in 1789, the only time it was ever attacked. The Place de la Bastille is still the main rallying point for Paris's regular demonstrations and strikes, as it was for rejoicing in 1981, after the election of François Mittérand's socialist government. In solidarity with their electoral base, the socialists rowed, as it were, upstream against the current of power by developing east Paris, building the immense Omnisports Palace and new edifices for the Radio and Television Commission and the Ministry of Economy and Industry. Across the river from these, in the neglected and still more proletarian thirteenth arrondissement, there rose like an apparition the stern ziggurat and towers of the Bibliothèque Nationale de France-Francois Mittérand, to give the new national library its full honors. In the Place de la Bastille itself, on its east side, another vast structure was raised: the Opéra de la Bastille, the socialists' answer to the temple to bourgeois luxury raised during the Second Empire. The building in which the new opera is housed exemplifies how out of place in east Paris official display feels. No one seems to pay much attention to its impassive, stealth-bomber surfaces, not out of dislike but from simple inability to register its presence. All eyes are drawn instead to the great column at the center of the Place de la Bastille commemorating the victims of the July Revolution of 1830 and surmounted by a winged, allegorical statue, the "Genius of Liberty." Or they are drawn easily past the opera into the lively neighborhood of the Rue de la Roquette, with its outdoor markets; its long-established African and Arab communities; its ateliers of artists, musicians, and fashion designers; and its youth-culture paradise of motorcycle repair shops, grungy bar-cafés, and loud bands.

Yet it was in the extreme east of Paris, in 1931, at the entrance to the Bois de Vincennes, in what it would be a joke to call a run-down neighborhood, that France's Third Republic (1870–1939) staged one of its most impressive official displays: the *Exposition Coloniale*. The grand exhibitions of the past, so important to the ideological work of official French culture, and in particular to that kind of ideological work called *allegory*, had always been held in west Paris. Of course, the French royalty, like most European monarchs and princes, followed the Italians in designing vast public allegories—notably in the famous royal entrances of the much-traveled Catherine de' Medici—to embody and nourish the ideological forms of their power. Revolutionary France was remarkable for her use of what we may call festive allegory, in which real people are employed as signifiers of abstract ideas. At the height of the Terror, there were huge allegorical processions on the Champ de Mars to the west of the city to honor the Goddess of Reason and the Supreme Being.

By the centenary of the Revolution, which the Third Republic celebrated with the *Exposition Universelle* of 1889, the Supreme Being was Technology, enshrined in a vast Hall of Machines, sustained by a "Fairy of Electricity" and symbolized by the Eiffel Tower itself, also situated in the west, uniting the earth with the sky. The *Exposition Universelle* of 1900, on the Champs Elysées, deployed allegorical figures in still greater profusion, for example on the new triumphal bridge dedicated to Tsar Alexander III, which opened a line of sight between the Invalides on the left bank of the Seine and, on the right bank, the astonishing metal and glass structures of the Petit Palais and the Grand Palais, raised for the occasion. The latter is surmounted by spectacular allegorical chariots, executed by the sculptor, Georges Recipon: "Harmony Overcoming Discord" and "Eternity Overcoming Time." Time with his scythe and Discord with her immense, withered dugs, her contorted visage and her snaky hair, are in the purest iconographical tradition going back to classical times. Likewise, Harmony recalls the classical Apollo and Eternity Apollo's sister, Athena. The magnificent horses drawing the chariots have the sharp, swift lines of the horses from the Parthenon—on display then, as now, in the British Museum. Nothing less classical in idiom would be acceptable on the Avenue des Champs Elysées. But in east Paris a new kind of allegorical imagery—an imagery of the teratological and the exotic, reminding us of the Africa of Conrad and the South Seas of Melville—was to enlarge the language for allegorical expression in the modern world.

The Colonial Exhibition had been decided on as early as 1920, soon after the Pyrrhic victory of World War I, and was intended to assert the defining role of the Third Republic as an apostle of Enlightenment and of universal exchange going forth on the oceans of the world. The Avenue Daumesnil and métro line number 8 had to be extended just to reach the exhibition;

the Bois de Vincennes was engrossed within the city of Paris; and the name of the Porte de Picpus was changed to Porte Dorée, "Golden Gate," suggesting an opening out to the rest of the world. Beautifully designed stamps and posters were issued, showing pith-helmeted French officers in exotic locations and also showing the colonial subjects in traditional costumes or in the uniforms of the French overseas forces: elegantly mysterious Southeast Asians, tamed but still savage-looking South Pacific islanders, stately Arabs on camels, and benevolent, towering black Africans near mud buildings in the western Sahara. In all these pictures on posters and stamps, the French flag, the *tricouleur*, is flying somewhere in the background.

On the grounds of the exhibition itself, around the Lac Dausmesnil within the Bois de Vincennes, pavilions to French colonies in Asia, Africa, and Polynesia were raised, the most impressive ones to the colonies to which France was most strongly committed: Morocco, Algeria, French West Africa, and Indochina, with a full-scale reproduction of the vast Cambodian temple of Angkor Vat. The other colonial powers were present, as well: Italy, Portugal, Holland, Belgium, Denmark, and the United States. Two miniature railways conducted visitors around the exhibition, and at its eastern extremity there was a new kind of zoological park, one in which the animals, separated from the spectators by invisible ditches, could be viewed in reconstructions of their natural habitats, or what were supposed to be their natural habitats: Lions roared not from a savannah but from a rocky eminence, to the delight of the crowds (perhaps the lions' feet hurt). Something on the order of 300,000 tickets were sold in the first seven months of the exhibition.

The exhibition's one permanent structure, the Musée Permanent des Colonies, as it was then called, thus distinguishing it from the temporary pavilions of the Colonial Exhibition, was designed by celebrated architect Albert Laprade and is still considered a landmark of modern French architecture, especially for its revolutionary *technique d'éclairage zénithale*, lighting the space from above, instead of through windows. After the exhibition closed it was simply the Musée des Colonies. That name would eventually be changed, in deference to the inhabitants of those colonies, who had been accorded limited French citizenship in 1946, to the Musée de la France d'Outre-Mer, "Museum of Overseas France," in keeping with the official alteration in that year of the name of the ministry in charge of the colonies. The colonies were no longer colonies—and this was especially true of Algeria—but "Overseas France."

The Musée des Colonies is decorated on the exterior by an immense, allegorical bas-relief by Alfred Janniot and assistants, depicting spectacular scenes from the French colonies throughout the world—most famously, a hippopotamus hunt. It covers the entire façade and wraps around some distance onto the sides of the building. At about 1,000 meters square, it is, I believe, the largest bas-relief in existence, a gigantic fresco in stone, as it has been called. The interior of Laprade's museum is finished entirely in colonial materials, design, and décor, including rhinoceros-tusk door handles, gleaming tropical woods such as teak, and floor tiles of African and Arabic design. To bring in the light from above, the grand ceremonial hall, the *Salle des Fêtes*, is crowned by a gorgeous pagoda-like lunette with a blue wave pattern, providing layers of indirect light that illuminate the hall evenly and without glare. The decoration of the walls bathed in this light are the original occasion for this essay: a cycle of allegorical paintings by Pierre Ducos de la Haille and his students from the Ecole des Beaux Arts in the outmoded but demanding and resilient medium of true fresco, a technique, which by that date had been all but lost, for painting on wet plaster applied to the wall. The frescoes, usually referred to as "colonial allegories," were executed between 1929 and 1931 and are on the subject of France in her relations with the continents of the globe: Europe, Asia, Africa, Polynesia, and America.[4]

The questions that first prompted me to write about the frescoes, which I had referred to but not seen when I wrote *Allegory and Violence*, were simple but, to me, intriguing. How is a highly traditional, originally medieval mode of expression, allegory, put into the service of the ideology of global, colonial power in the modern age? What is at work in the allegorical representation of the bodies of colonial subjects? A short time after these frescoes were made, from 1933 to 1939, Walter Benjamin was in Paris working in the Bibliothèque Nationale on the *Arcades Project* and arguing—*showing* would perhaps be the better word—that the sumptuous, glassed-in arcades of nineteenth-century Paris (many of which have today been restored), with their diminutive, elegant shops, are modern versions of older allegorical forms of expression. In the Paris arcades, the luxury commodity replaces the allegorical sign. It was Benjamin's insight that the overdetermined character of the sign in medieval and Renaissance allegory (the sign means what it says, but it also means something more, something mysterious that participates in the system as a whole) bears a striking resemblance to Marx's famous analysis in *Capital* of the fetish of the commodity. Benjamin took this similarity to be more than accidental: It was historical. The ideology of princely power in Renaissance allegory is given a total form in gigantic, allegorical works such as Dürer's *Triumph of the Emperor Maximilian* or Giulio Romano's *Palazzo Te* or Spenser's *Faerie Queene*. In modern, capitalist societies, however, ideology and capital power become entirely blended in the presentation of commodities in circumstances like those of the Paris arcades, more broadly, in what we call *advertising*. Benjamin's startling insight was that modern, commodity culture does not need to produce allegories in the old way, at vast expense and for a privileged few, because allegory has become incorporated in the total, economic structure of capitalist, commodity culture. Observing and buying luxury commodities in the Paris arcades afforded a sacramental experience of entering into a larger system of rich and mysterious meaning. In the democratizing of the experience of allegory, coveting replaces reading and purchasing replaces interpretation. Seen in this light, the colonial allegories of Pierre Ducos de la Haille were long out of date, even as they seemed to speak to France's high destiny as an economic, colonial power. But one striking thing about the allegorical character of the commodity culture of which Benjamin speaks is its almost total occlusion of the body. In the colonial allegories, by contrast—and I refer to Janniot's great bas-relief as well as to Ducos de la Haille's frescoes— the body is spectacularly on view.

On this issue of the spectacle of the body, it is noteworthy that actual people, not just representations of them, were also on display for the crowds at the Colonial Exhibition, in cultural dioramas like those that appeared in earlier exhibitions in Paris and London (one of which inspired W. S. Gilbert to write *The Mikado*), dioramas that were not so different from the Paris arcades. There were even preparations for a group of so-called "cannibals"— *anthropophages*—to be viewed in the zoological park, near the roaring lions. But at the last moment these unfortunate people, who had been transported to Paris from the South Pacific under shockingly false pretenses, were excluded from the Colonial Exhibition as inconsistent with its higher view of humanity. Unaware of these expectations, and lacking any experience with anthropoghagy, unless the Roman Catholic mass may be counted (a great attraction for them was that they would be allowed to worship at the cathedral of Notre Dame, of which they had heard so much at school), they expected to perform their traditional dances a few times daily and practiced them for months on the long voyage to Marseilles. They were promised warm clothing for the rest of the time, suitable for going around Paris and spending the pay they were also promised. They were instead put on display in the Bois de Boulogne, where in cold, sometimes freezing weather, wearing only their traditional clothes, they were forced to perform all day long as subhuman savages, roaring and tearing at joints of raw meat. Some were shipped off to zoos in Germany, to replace crocodiles that had died in transit from Egypt. But that is another story, a good one.[5] Suffice it to say that the public display of exotic peoples in their cultural environments, weaving baskets and fashioning weapons, holding ceremonies, and so on, goes back to the mid-nineteenth century in Paris, when anthropology was accorded recognition as a science and public education in this new science became the justification for what degenerated, in the Bois de Boulogne's Jardin d'Acclimatation, into something like circus—bad circus.

When you come up out of the Porte Dorée métro station today you see the first of two monuments that remain from the Colonial Exhibition: an impressive, gold statue on a marble plinth, the personification of "France Colonizing"—*la France Colonisatrice*. It is situated on a large traffic island at the entrance to the Bois de Vincennes. From under the plinth, which bears the ship-symbol of Paris, a stream rushes forth to flow over a series of marble cascades and pools lined by palm trees (a surprising sight, in Paris), signifying the benefits of French culture flowing out to her colonies on the oceans of the world. The statue itself is fashioned after the goddess Athena, complete with helm, shield, and serpent. She supports on one extended palm a small, winged *daemon*, or "genius of plenty," who in turn holds a cornucopia. The allegorical message is expressed in iconographical language as traditional as that of Georges Recipon's chariots on the Grand Palais: *La France Colonisatrice* gathers material goods to herself from the whole world but returns benefits in greater abundance.

The golden statue used to stand on the steps of the other monument of the Colonial Exhibition, which is a little further on, to the left, just inside the Parc de Vincennes and set back a little from the Avenue Daumesnil: the Colonial Museum itself, "the summit of colonial art," as Dominique Jarrassé has described it.[6] From photographs, one can see why the statue was moved: Its classical style is inconsistent with wilder and more exotic imagery of the museum, especially of the exterior. A broad staircase leads up to a portico, which extends the full length of the building, supported by slender, segmented columns that suggest the boles of palm trees, behind which, covering the façade and, as I mentioned, wrapping around onto the sides, is Janniot's bas-relief representing France and her colonies throughout the world, but representing them in terms of the actual, raw materials they supplied to the metropolitan center. Around the main entry a personified France and her port cities appear, traditionally draped, as in medieval allegory. But they are flanked by gigantic elephants to the right (far exceeding life size) and, to the left, the hippopotamus hunt I have mentioned, the vast, yawning animals pursued at a run by magnificent black Africans with spears, while still more magnificent black African women are engaged in various laborious tasks which put them in interesting postures. (Photographs show that Janniot worked with live naked models at the site, shielded from view by canvas curtains.) Such scenes are brilliantly juxtaposed to a background that is a map of the world, showing the French colonies and naming the raw materials (the words are actually carved in the stone) those colonies supplied: gold and silver, of course, and ivory, of course, but also tin, lead, iron, manganese, coal, phosphates, graphite, leather, rubber, wood, cereals, silk, fruits, sugar cane, and cocoa.

"While the public expected dreamlike exoticism," Jarrassé writes, "it was necessary also to show it an empire that works, that produces goods, and that provides a profit on France's investment . . . but there must be no economic benefit to France without something returned, without a social gain for the colonized and, at the same time, a recognition of the indigenous culture of the colonized."[7] That second gain—recognition of the indigenous cultures—was expressed in the pavilions and the colonial museum itself, as something picturesque, exotic, teratological, and allegorical. But for the general public, and for most of the politicians of the Third Republic, the first gain was far more important. It was the shining forth (*rayonnement*) to the "inferior" peoples of the globe—so they were called in contemporary newspaper accounts—of European, enlightenment culture. The idea goes back to one of the great liberal figures of the Third Republic, Jules Ferry, who in an 1885 speech to the National Assembly promoted colonialism in Tunisia, Madagascar, the Congo, and Tonkin as a moral project: "The superior races have the duty to civilize the inferior races."[8]

While Alfred Janniot's bas-relief for the Musée des Colonies emphasized the material benefits France's colonies brought her, the colonial frescoes in the Great Hall were to emphasize the spiritual and cultural benefits France brought to her colonies, a structure familiar from the palaces, chateaus, and enclosed gardens of medieval French allegory, or the houses and castles of Spenser's *Faerie Queene*. The principle is a classically allegorical one. As with the Sileni mentioned by Alcibiades in the *Symposium* and explicated by Erasmus, an allegory is like an ugly statue of the satyr Silenus, which when opened reveals a beautiful god within. There is meant to be a sharp contrast in sense, almost a reversal, between exoteric display and esoteric disclosure, between what anyone may observe on the façade of this building without and what the adept will see on the interior walls, in the protected spaces of the building's *penetralia*. We shall see that the counterparts in Pierre Ducos de la Haille's frescoes to those raw materials on Janniot's bas-relief are the sails of the French trading-ships, the caravelles, bringing the light of French civilization to every corner of the globe.

Another feature typical of allegory appears on the west exterior wall of the museum, around to the left as one faces the building, where the bas-relief ends. It is a roll of 160 names of the heroes of the "colonial epic"— *l'épopée coloniale*—who are thanked in language that recalls the inscription over the Pantheon, where France's greatest heroes rest, making this building a sort of colonial pantheon: "A thankful France to her sons, who have extended the empire of her genius and made her name to be adored beyond the seas" ["*A ses fils qui ont étendu l'empire de son génie et fait aimer son nom au délà des mers, la France reconnaissante*"]. Many such lists appear in allegorical works, for example, in the dungeon of the House of Pride in Spenser's *Faerie Queene*, which contains all the famous conquerors of history, "Like carkases of beasts in butchers stall":

All these together in one heape were throwne,
Like carkases of beasts in butcher's stall.
And in another corner wide were strowne
The antique ruines of the *Romaines* fall:
Great *Romulus* the Grandsyre of them all,
Proud *Tarquin*, and too lordly *Lentulus*,
Stout *Scipio*, and the stubborne *Hanniball*,
Ambitious *Sylla*, and sterne *Marius*,
High *Caesar*, great *Pompey*, and fierce *Antonius*.

(*The Faerie Queene I. v. 49*)

One is startled to see that this list of heroes from this *épopée coloniale* begins with Godefroy de Bouillon, 1058–1100, the leader of the first crusade, and that it contains Saint Louis, that addict of crusading, as well. Names more familiar to France's colonies follow, among them Cartier, Champlain, Richelieu, Colbert (for the reorganization of the navy under Louis XIV), Talon, Frontenac, Montcalm, de la Vérendreye, Tallyrand, and on to the modern generals, explorers, scientists, colonial administrators, ethnographers, doctors and engineers, including, of course, Ferdinand de Lesseps, for the "piercing" of the Suez canal. There is one woman, Anna Marie Javoukey, 1779–1851, teacher and renderer of unspecified "assistance" to the colonies. I will confess to being thrilled at this roll call of famous and not-so-famous names going down the centuries from the Middle Ages to modern times, punctuated throughout with such evocative place names: Brazzaville, Djibouti, Western Sahara, the kingdom of Tonkin, Mauritius, Niger, Dahomey, Tunesia, Melanesia, Tombouctou in the Sudan. With the intense traffic at one's back, peering through an ugly fence and through litter entangled in the ragged tree branches, one can still experience the intoxication of the day, the feeling of being embarked on a high enterprise that began almost with the origin of France herself, leading humanity into the future. It feels as if the dream of globalization, of universal harmony amid the greatest possible diversity, has its origin here.

The principal tableau of Pierre Ducos de la Haille's frescoes in the Great Hall shows France, with a muscular Europe in a toga beside her, holding the dove of peace and receiving tribute from the continents of the globe in return for French enlightenment, French liberty, and French cultural forms. Asia and Africa ride toward France on their respective species of elephant while Polynesia and America are borne on fabulous sea horses with webbed front feet and serpentine tails, rearing from the waves. Polynesia is a voluptuous South Seas odalisque, reclining on her steed, her black curling tresses cascading about her. America's hair is cut in a short, sensible bob, and she seems to head toward Polynesia instead of France, in a scene of inadvertent sexual threat, brandishing a skyscraper that rises from her lap. Ducos de la Haille was taken to task about that skyscraper, which seemed to suggest, among other things, that Manhattan is or ever was a colony of France. But the artist was immovable, and rightly so. France did have a remarkable—and comparatively bloodless—colonial history in North America, and Manhattan symbolizes the height of North American civilization. Manhattan is also the symbol of the future. The skyscraper articulates a secondary theme inherent to the tradition of allegories of the continents, especially that of Giambattista Tiepolo, in Würzburg: the temporal narrative of human progress from Earth-bound primitivism to the highest stage of civilization, which touches the sky with its buildings and, like the Eiffel Tower, sends electronic signals around the planet.

On the other walls of the *Salle des Fêtes* are beautiful genre scenes, interspersed with personifications (Commerce, Arts and Industry, and so on), in which the exotic peoples of the French colonies in Indochina, Africa, and Polynesia receive the benefits of French culture and enlightenment. There are scenes of surveying in Southeast Asia, of medical science being imparted to the people of Polynesia, of archeologists at work, of Chinese laborers loading ships, and of religion being taught to black Africans by a missionary who frees them from their chains, a deft conflation of manumission from literal slavery and from the spiritual abjection of idolatry.

The heroic representations of the virtues, interspersed throughout the scenes from the colonies, are there to show what makes the colonial project possible: Liberty, Justice, Labor, and Culture. Justice with her Herculean arms might have been better termed "Enforcement." Following iconographic tradition, she is blindfolded and holds a sword in one hand, although its point is planted in the earth, and she has no balances, which might have implied a judicious weighing in the balance of the claims of the colonial other. Instead, she grasps by the throat a huge python, the body of which arches over her shoulder and winds around her back to grasp the sword with its tail. The wisdom of the serpent urges restraint, but not a fair hearing. Behind her is a huge American buffalo; and behind it, filling the background as they come over the horizon on a limitless sea, are the billowing sails of the French caravelles.

Only gradually does one notice that these beautiful sails are everywhere in the background, coming toward us from all directions on a continuous blue ocean encircling the pictorial space. Those sails on the ocean are the freest, the most delightful part of the design, promising release from the crowded jungles and docks of the colonial scenes into open spaces beyond. But the sails are all coming toward us, as if the open spaces that attract us were being folded into the colonial allegories from which we have been promised a temporary, aesthetic escape. Where do they come from? Obviously, from France. But I am unable to say how many times I had visited the *Salle des Fêtes* before I noticed that, in the principal tableau of France and the continents, the dove of peace that France holds is multiplied in the foliage above her into many doves and that these are implicitly transformed into the sailing ships on the ocean behind her. Thus, in Ducos de la Haille's iconographical design, the dove that France holds in her hand as an offering of peace multiplies and metamorphoses into all the ships we see on the ocean that encircles the globe.

I said that Ducos de la Haille's genre scenes are beautiful, which they are. It is always a pleasure to watch others doing physical labor from which one is free. But those scenes are also disturbing because, in a mysterious sense, all the happy bodies we see feel as if they are imprisoned. Such representations of the body are often governed by what in *Allegory and Violence* I called *capture*, the principle underlying personification. Allegorical capture gives us the sense that a living body, such as that of Francesca da Rimini in Dante's *Inferno*, has been confined to an alien structure of meaning, one in which the human person has been reduced to performing the function of a sign in a system of signs—or partly so. Dante's genius as an allegorical poet is in his ability to have characters resisting their reduction and speaking against it, so that the reduction is never complete but is always a struggle. His characters are like caryatids that push upward against the immense weight of the meaning that is bearing down on them and of which they are the captive signifiers. But in its struggle to assert itself against an overbearing meaning, this humanity is thrown into sharper relief than it would be were it not under such hostile pressure. On the other hand, the meaning exerting this pressure is also thrown into relief because it is not static signification but meaning at work, meaning bearing down against a contrary force, which is human subversion. The violence is directed both ways, as in an *agon*, a contest, each contestant striving to master and transform the other. Although meaning in Dante's *Commedia* is less readable than meaning is in the simpler kind of allegory that follows in the tradition of the *Roman de la Rose*, where characters bear their labels unresistingly, such meaning is deepened by the struggle to assert itself against a humanity that is other with respect to it, and that subverts it. The allegory shines because of this violence, not in despite of it.

The analysis I have just given of the struggle in the allegorical personification between meaning and humanity is important for understanding the surging force of human and animal bodies in the colonial allegories of the *Musée des Colonies*. In the first place, the meaning of a body is the work it can do: loading ships, digging mines, bearing loads. In the second place, as we saw when we observed the similarity between the allegorical sign and the commodity, the meaning of a body is its contribution to the global system of the allegory in which material goods are exchanged for cultural forms—exchanged at a distance. The resistance against this meaning, pushing upward, as it were, is often the sexual allure of the bodies portrayed and the equally incidental allure of the exotic worlds in which those bodies live, apparently so joyously and freely. We see the athletic, working breasts and laboring torsos of dark-skinned people engaged in such energetic tasks as a hippopotamus hunt, or riding on elephants, or bearing goods in a procession, or, as I said, loading ships and digging mines. Anticipating the global tourism industry, and especially tourism of the kind described in Michel Houllebecq's *Platforme*, we want to enter an exotic world of imaginary freedoms with the exotic bodies that live there. We do not want to bring them home with us as servants or to settle them in the suburbs of our cities. We want them to work where they are, fulfilling the colonial allegory while we stay at home to receive what they produce. But we also want to go where they are so they can put down their work for our sake, long enough to show us their world and themselves. I am not speaking just of what passes through the fantasies of the viewer of these allegories, although I am certainly speaking of that. I am also speaking of how the allegories are actually made and of what inspires the makers, as Dante was inspired by the story of Francesca da Rimini's adultery, creating a character who is sexually attractive to us because she is to him. So it is with the illustrators, painters, and sculptors of the Colonial Exhibition. They have an allegorical task to fulfill, but they also want to make alluring art, and this allure, which draws on our proclivity to sexual fantasies and unproductive travel, is subversive of the global ideological scheme the colonial allegories were expected to promote.

The formal opening of the Colonial Exhibition, performed by the president of France, Gaston Dommergue, took place on May 6, 1931, in the ceremonial hall of the Museum of the Colonies. The principal harangue was delivered by the director of the colonial exhibition, one of the great architects of France's colonial adventure, Louis Hubert Gonsalve Lyautey, *Maréchal de France*, resplendent in full marshal's uniform, complete with kepi, a visual reminder of what the exhibition was supposed to help the French forget: the generals of the Great War. Lyautey had served most of the war in Morocco, not on the Western Front, but he was minister of war in 1916–1917. To say the least, Lyautey was a complicated figure, a model, in part, for Proust's homosexual reactionary, the baron de Charlus. Educated at the elite Ecole Polytechnique and the still more elite Ecole Militaire de Saint-Cyr, Lyautey was a military man, a Catholic conservative, and also, astonishingly for the time, a monarchist—convictions that gave him, as he recognized, a spontaneous sympathy with and understanding of the deeply religious and hierarchical character of Arab culture. But in contrast with his conservative tendencies, Lyautey was probably pro-Dreyfus, or he was at least contemptuous of the populist anti-Semitism whipped up by the anti-Dreyfusards, and he was certainly, as I said, homosexual and not especially secretive about it. In a still more striking departure from the attitudes of many of his class and convictions, Lyautey translated Hitler's *Mein Kampf* so the French could see what the Führer had in store for them (Hitler tried to block its publication). Lyautey acquired deep knowledge and appreciation of the colonized cultures in which he served for most of his career, not only that of Moslem North Africa, in particular Morocco, where he was interred for a time, in Rabat, before being brought to the Invalides.[9] But he was not lacking in ruthlessness either, as we shall see. Lyautey's opening address at the Colonial Exhibition was the perfect expression of the dream of world-wide French empire. The purpose of the exhibition, he said, is to show "that there are for our civilization other fields of battle, that the nations of the twentieth century can now rival one another not in the quest for military domination but in the works of peace and of progress."[10]

Another reason to hold the Colonial Exhibition in east Paris, a reason Lyautey acknowledged only in private, was that the working-class populace of east Paris was voting for the communists. (The communists and the surrealists nobly joined forces to mount a sparsely attended counterexhibition on the evils of colonialism.) The Colonial Exhibition would be a way of enlisting the working classes' patriotic sympathy for the colonial project and their material interest in it. Lyautey had initially opposed the location of the Colonial Exhibition in east Paris for the reasons we have seen: East Paris is a place of no honor, and west Paris is where the Third Republic had held its great exhibitions of the past, leaving in their wake, so to speak, the Eiffel Tower and the palaces on the Champs-Elysées. But once the decision was taken for east Paris, Lyautey spoke of the project in a private letter with the enthusiasm of a civil engineer, which is what he was by training: "Is not the east of Paris a region of which it is commonly said that it is lost to communism? It may be worthwhile to cultivate our new, green shoots of colonialism [*nos pousses coloniales*] in the midst of this populist area . . .

I rejoice, for my part, to behold this population and to enter into discussion with it [*de voir cette population et de causer avec elle*]. I am convinced that the exposition could be a great influence for social peace in this region of Paris."[11]

Lyautey goes on in this letter to say that he is fired with the ambition to bring about this "social peace" by the "Haussmanization" of the area in a manner that would be "at once up-to-date and total," treating the region as a "tabula rasa."[12] He had done so before with the Moroccan capital, Rabat, razing its labyrinthine Souk and laying the avenues out in the form of a modern French city. The term *Haussmanization* refers to the later nineteenth-century transformation of the Paris of the Second Empire by Baron Georges Eugène Haussmann, who bulldozed the medieval buildings, narrow streets, and old parishes of the city to make room for the grand avenues that not only beautified Paris and let in the light but also made it possible for troops to be transported rapidly from one neighborhood to another and for artillery to have a clear field of fire. It was accomplished at enormous cost to the working classes, many of whom were forced out of the city to the east, where Lyautey now proposed to assist them by means of another displacement. As the reference to "social peace" makes clear, the authorities did not forget that public unrest and, occasionally, insurrection, come to Paris from the east.

I said that the Colonial Exhibition was intended to assert a defining role for the Third Republic after the disaster of the Great War. But this role was not new. The achievements of the Third Republic as a colonial power over the nearly seventy years of its existence, in the exploration, conquest, and administration of very distant lands and peoples, were determined and impressive. It was not called "the conquering republic" for nothing. By the 1930s, to judge by the sheer extent of her territorial possessions, France had reached her apogee as a colonial power. Nothing seemed more certain than that she would go from strength to strength, consolidating her access to the raw materials and huge markets within her vast territories by conferring on the populations resident in those territories—populations outnumbering by many times that of France itself—the benefits of French law, language, and culture—and at length of limited French citizenship. Colonization would drive the transformation of France from what was still largely an agricultural society (a major reason for the military defeats she had suffered at Germany's hands) into a modern, industrial economy operating on a global scale. Had she not already realized the dream of the Emperor Charles V—

the Holy Roman Emperor during Spain's conquest of Mexico and Peru—of commanding an empire on which the sun never set?

It was to set sooner than anyone at the time could imagine. Within three decades, after another world war brought down the Third Republic and the long-drawn-out agonies of Indochina and Algeria brought down the Fourth, the French dream of an empire lay in ruins. Colonialism was condemned by intellectuals on the political left, following Sartre, as a long series of rapacious thefts and crimes against humanity, which is to be expected in the early stages of global class struggle and the vindication of international communism, of which the Indochinese, Algerian, and Cuban revolutions were models. This was delusional, but not so delusional as the dream of the political right, the same one that animated the Colonial Exhibition: that it would be possible to make loyal French subjects out of colonial subjects, despite the impossibility of ever giving them more than limited citizenship if France itself was to survive. As Raymond Aron saw, there could never be a France *outre-mer*, a France beyond the seas, of any size or significance. The independence of the former colonies was therefore both desirable and inevitable, though likely to be a catastrophe for them, as has proven to be true. When the dream of France beyond the seas lay in ruins, it left in its wake the intractable problems associated with the second and third generations of immigrants from the colonies, crowded into the desperate, periodically incendiary high-rise suburbs surrounding the cities: the *bandes de misère,* or "rings of misery," as they are called. France beyond the seas had imploded. Almost half a century later, France's colonial history is still a subject of bitter debate, and the social problems left behind by that history are greater now than they were immediately after the collapse. The mood in the *banlieue* is reflected in the words of the rapper, N.A.P.: "*Écoute l'histoire de Renoi, Rabza, qui ont grandi dans tes poubelles*" ("Hear the story of Kalb [Black] and Bara [Arab], who grew up in your garbage cans").[13]

After the collapse of the ideology of the colonial project, the history of the Colonial Museum, the building generally referred to now as the Palais de la Porte Dorée, is interesting and instructive to follow. In 1960, at the beginning of the Fifth Republic, and at the instigation of President de Gaulle's minister of culture, André Malraux, the Colonial Museum became the Musée Nationale des Arts d'Afrique et d' Océanie. Making a trenchant, if not easily tenable distinction, Malraux took the African and Oceanic collections from the Louvre and sent those of chiefly ethnographic interest to the

Musée de l'Homme at the Trocadéro, while selecting for the new museum works that merited analysis in the aesthetic language of abstract forms and plastic values and that seemed, in the light of such analysis, to rise above the primitive circumstances of their production to achieve universal value. With Algerian independence, the collapse of the Fourth Republic, and the return of General de Gaulle, a museum of the colonies hardly went with the spirit of the times. But the material loss of France's colonial possessions could now be reconceptualized as an aesthetic gain for the cultural heritage of mankind. Visitors to the museum were instructed in the circumstances of the works' origins in Polynesia and Africa, as they were also in the history of French colonialism, which was still presented in a positive light. They were also informed of the influence of these works on the great modern artists, from Gauguin to Giacometti and Picasso.[14]

As was to be expected, the museum fell into greater obscurity and disapproval after 1968. But its end was assured only later, when a fever pitch of indignation was reached on March 15, 1990, in a manifesto published in the left-wing newspaper *Libération*, signed by nearly fifty eminent artists, authors, and anthropologists, including Michel Leiris, Maurice Blanchot, Yves Bonnefoy, Hélène Cixous, Henri Cartier-Bresson, Jean-François Lyotard, Philippe Lacou-Labarthe, and Jean-Pierre Vernant, attacking the Musée des Arts Africains et Océaniens, as it was also called, for sequestering the so-called primitive arts in east Paris—a place, as we have seen, of no honor—and urging their return to the Louvre.[15] The author of this document was the fascinating, shadowy figure of the late Jacques Kerchache (d. 2001), a great collector and champion of "primitive" or "First Peoples'" arts (the first term is assumed to be derogatory; the second is almost meaningless). He had been jailed in Africa for attempting to export art illegally, and that was just one of the swashbuckling adventures he made no attempt to conceal: On the contrary, he gloried in what was intended to be an unflattering characterization of him as "the French Indiana Jones." He was a personal friend of the French president, Jacques Chirac, in whom he found a fellow enthusiast for primitive arts, and he used his influence with the president to discredit the ethnologists at the Musée de l'Homme, whose scholarly concerns—with provenance, culture, ritual context, and the like, and of course publication—he regarded as a distractions from the pure aesthetic values embodied in the masterpieces of primitive art.[16] This is the man who was the animating force of a new museum of primitive arts to replace both the Musée de l'Homme and the Musée des Arts Africains et

Océaniens: the Musée du Quai Branly, the theater of which is devoted to his name. Kerchache was the purest expression of André Malraux's noble intention to treat at least some of the religious artifacts of Africa and Oceania as being as worthy of veneration as the masterpieces of European art. He was also the purest expression of the confusions into which an unhistorical, decontextualized aestheticism can lead.

For example, one of the more interesting tendencies of those in the debate who favor the aesthetic independence of the works of art from their cultural and ritual contexts is to transfer human qualities and rights from the makers of the works of art to the works of art themselves and to become indignant on behalf of those works. These great masterpieces have been subjected, because of racist aggression against them, to an humiliating displacement from the Louvre, their rightful home, to the nowhereland of east Paris. I do not exclude myself from those who take very great pleasure in contemplating these works aesthetically—as no doubt some ethnographers do. But it is important to be aware of the danger of attributing to the works human qualities—and, more to the point, human rights—that allow those works to be substituted symbolically for *real people*. The height of absurdity is reached when the manifesto in *Libération* proclaims, "Masterpieces throughout the world are free and equal." We saw that in 1930, at the colonial exhibition, actual persons were being presented allegorically, as works of art. Now, in 1990, the rights of persons were being accorded to works of art: Masterpieces are born free and equal. Five years later, on November 14, 1995, President Chirac, standing under the Louvre pyramid, would announce the return to the Louvre, in the Pavillion des Sessions, of a selection of 100 especially magnificent works of primitive art—in the literature the word *primitive* is both condemned and employed. The Pavillion des Sessions contains a truly magnificent display of primitive arts from around the world, although especially from Africa, curated entirely by Jacques Kerkache. Due largely to Kerkache's influence, the Musée des Arts Africains et Océaniens and the Musée de l'Homme at the Trocadéro were closed (in the latter case, not without a struggle) and a new museum planned in which the works could be displayed in the spirit of the exhibition at the Pavillion des Sessions.

The Musée des Arts Africains et Océaniens closed officially in 2003. The works of African and Oceanic art were removed to a "worksite" or *chantier du musée* underground in the thirteenth arrondissement, near the Bibliothèque

Nationale, for elaborate restoration and cataloguing and in preparation for their transfer to a new museum, the existence of which I first learned in the winter of 2004, during a riverside walk on a winter night in west Paris on the Quai Branly. Meditating at the time on Pierre Ducos de la Haille's frescoes, and only vaguely wondering what became of the works of African and Oceanic art that used to be in the same building, I was startled to come on a large work site with signs advertising a museum of primitive arts, legible in the lights blinking overhead from the Eiffel Tower. But the building that housed the Musée des Arts Africains et Océaniens remained open, under the name the Palais de la Porte Dorée or, more simply, Aquarium, for that is what it also was from the beginning, on its lower level, where fish species from the colonies were displayed. The association of the Palais with France's colonial past continues to make it a political football. During France's intense bid for the Olympics, the Great Hall held displays celebrating French athletes—many of whom are descended from former colonials, a point not missed in the displays—and there were plans, since shelved, for an elite sports facility to be built in the Bois de Vincennes. To honor Albert Laprade's innovations, the Palais was briefly destined to be a museum of modern architecture—long enough for the books to be brought into the bookstore and then carted away. In January 2007, after an elaborate architectural redesign of the interior (not all of it happy), the Palais opened the Cité Nationale de l'Histoire de l'Immigration, a project Jacques Chirac had envisaged since his reelection in 2002 and which he announced in 2004. Not only do the exhibits in the Cité de l'Immigration celebrate the contributions of immigrants to French culture: They practically assert that immigrants—very, very broadly defined for the purpose—are the creators of French culture in its totality. The model of *rayonnement* in the frescoes in the Great Hall below the Cité de l'Immigration has been reversed: France is now a destination for oppressed peoples around the world (none of whom have been oppressed by the French, of course), who bring cultural enlightenment with them. Even that great definer and utterly ruthless savior of Renaissance France, Catherine de' Medici, was an immigrant, after all. While it is true that these very favorable representations of France's treatment of foreigners do not forget what the Vichy government—and the French who collaborated with it—did to the Jews in World War II, it is as if the dark side of French colonialism never occurred, an astonishing omission in that place. In this respect, for all its political correctness, or, I suppose, because of it, the Cité de l'Immigration is as ideologically blind as the Colonial

Exhibition itself. As a cultural institution it remains a political statement to a degree that is unusual even in France. It is no doubt partly for this reason that the future of the Cité de l'Immigration is most uncertain under President Sarkozy, who has rather different ideas about the contribution of immigrants to French culture.

There is then another story to be told about the works of African and Oceanic art that were removed from the Musée des Arts Africains et Océaniens and from the Musée de l'Homme for eventual inclusion—downstream—in the new museum, which opened in June 2006. In the manner of French presidents, the new museum is Jacques Chirac's monument to his presidency, as the Pompidou Center is to Georges Pompidou and the National Library to François Mittérand. This is the sumptuous and prudently named Musée du Quai Branly (not a word about "primitivism" or "First Peoples"), an extraordinary building designed by France's most famous architect, Jean Nouvel, whose other great work along the Seine is the Institut du Monde Arabe. The Musée du Quai Branly is no less an ideological statement than was the Musée des Colonies, even if the passage of time has yet fully to unveil the extent to which this is so. But here, at the end of this story, as a way of rounding it off, we may note the symbolic location of the Musée du Quai Branly far downstream from the Bois de Vincennes, in west Paris, under the Eiffel Tower, where, as we saw at the outset, luxury and official display are at home.

Notes

1. Thirza Vallois, *Around and about Paris*, 2nd ed. vol. 2 (London: Iliad, 1998), p. 178. I am more indebted to Vallois's superb, three-volume walking guide to Paris (1995–1998) than this one reference indicates. I suspect that about three-quarters of the factual information in this essay about Paris and its history comes either from Vallois or from following up on things seen during the countless walks I took with her volumes in hand. Other information about Paris comes from the most recent edition of the *Guide Bleu de Paris*, the Bibliothèque Nationale, and the Bibliothèque de la Ville de Paris. Except for the works cited below, a great deal of information about the museums discussed in this essay and the public debates swirling around them come from sources too numerous too document or even, admittedly, after five years of immersion in the subject, to recall. These sources include newspaper articles; public notices on the history of Paris; television programs on the French cultural channel, *Arté*; websites, including that of the new *Musée du Quai Branly*, before and after its opening; documents such as the news bulletin of the twelfth arrondissement; posters and stamps seen in bookstores, especially

L'Harmattan, on Boulevard Saint Germain; old maps in the Louvre; official information and notices at the museums themselves; and numerous documents and objects, including a model of the entire Colonial Exhibition, at the Palais de la Porte Dorée, where I benefited from the many courtesies of the staff. I express my thanks to them here.

The occasion of this essay was a single reference to the Musée des Colonies in my *Allegory and Violence* (Ithaca, NY: Cornell University Press, 1996), p. 117, which Brenda Machosky urged me to follow up for a lecture at the conference on which the present volume is based. I thank Professor Machosky for her patience with the many evolutions of this essay since it was originally given as a lecture. Special thanks are due to my learned friend, Dr. Uta Kriesten, a proud resident of the twelfth arrondissement, who cheerfully fulfilled many requests to verify information and in the course of doing so found more. I wish also to thank Penelope Fletcher-Lemasson, at whose bookstore, The Red Wheelbarrow, on Rue Saint Paul, I found Thirza Vallois's volumes and where I also had invaluable conversations on the subject of this essay with the many foreign and French Paris aficionados who find their way daily to the Red Wheelbarrow Bookstore.

2. The arrondissements are the administrative regions of Paris that spiral outward from the center, the Isle de la Cité. A faubourg, or "false town," is the old word for a suburb, an area outside the old city walls. On old maps the large faubourgs enclosing Paris on the east and west respectively are the Faubourg Saint Antoine and the Faubourg Saint Honoré. The modern word for a suburb is *banlieue*, an administrative region having the right of *ban* or proclamation.

3. *The Faerie Queene* V.i.54

4. Catherine Bouché, "Allégories Coloniales," *L'Objet d'Art* (April 1988): 88–97.

5. The authoritative historical account is by the historian Joël Dauphiné, *Canaques de la Nouvelle-Calédonie à Paris en 1931: De la Case au Zoo* (Paris: L'Harmattan, 1998). An entertaining, though historically inaccurate, novel about this episode is Didier Daeninckx's *Cannibale* (Lagreasse: Verdier, 1996). In this softened and almost charming account, the Kanak "cannibals" are lodged, as promised, on the grounds of the Colonial Exposition and perform there. But they are more or less imprisoned. A couple of them escape into Paris and have fish-out-of-water adventures, which turn darker when the girlfriend of one is among those who are transported to Germany.

6. "Un Programme Idéologique et Didactique," in Germaine Viatte and Dominique François, *Le Palais des Colonies: Histoire du Musée des Arts d'Afrique et d'Océanie* (Paris: Réunion des Musées Nationaux, 2002), pp. 87–88.

7. Ibid., p. 87.

8. Cited in *Le Monde*, Saturday, January 21, 2006, "Dossier" vii. This is an eight-page insert on France's colonial history and on what is still a very heated debate over it.

9. See the article on Lyautey in the French *Wikipedia*.

10. Quoted in Germaine Viatte and Dominique François, *Le Palais des Colonies: Histoire du Musée des Arts d'Afrique et d'Océanie* (Paris: Réunion des Musés Nationaux, 2002), p. 24.

11. Ibid., p. 27.

12. Ibid., p. 28.

13. From the song, "Si loin, si proche," on the album, *La Fin du monde*, High Skills/B.M.G, 1998. In the argot code-language, Verlans (i.e., *envers*, backward), *renoi* and *rabza* are, respectively, *Noir* (Black) and *Arabe*.

14. Jobic Lemasson, personal communication.

15. Jacques Kerchache, *Pour que les Chefs d'Oeuvre du Monde Entier Naissent Libre et Egaux*. Reproduced on the website for the Musée du Quai Branly (quaibranly.fr/kerchache).

16. See Bernard Dupaigne, *Le Scandale des arts premiers: La Véritable Histoire du Musée du Quai Branly* (Paris: Mille et Une Nuits, 1986). Dupaigne was director of the laboratory of ethnology at the Musée de l'Homme from 1991 to 1998, and he is the author of numerous works on Afghanistan and central Asian nomads. This fascinating polemic is written in a tone of cold outrage, but its account of events by an insider is scrupulously and extensively documented—it is far and away the best documentary source for anyone studying the evolution of the Musée du Quai Branly—and its portrait of Jacques Kerchache, the man who calumniated him and his colleagues, and, as he reports, destroyed the Musée de l'Homme, is surprisingly sympathetic in its portrait of a man he clearly regards as a sociopath. For an English account of these events, see Sally Price, *Paris Primitive: Jacques Chirac's Museum on the Quai Branly* (Chicago: University of Chicago Press, 2007).

SIX

Monuments and Space as Allegory

Town Planning Proposals in Eighteenth-Century Paris

RICHARD WITTMAN

I

Examples of allegory in the architecture of the premodern period are abundant. From antiquity through the Renaissance and Baroque periods, architecture was understood as a practice of symbolic representation. Its key forms all had multiple meanings. The central element of the classical system, the column, carried with it the idea of a tree. This enabled temples to be experienced as an allegory of the sacred groves where the gods had once been worshipped. Columns were also identified with the human body; thus the many medieval church choirs that were supported on two rows of twelve columns were legible as allegories of the Church, supported by the twelve apostles with twelve prophets behind them. The different orders of columns—Tuscan, Doric, Ionic, Corinthian, and Composite—not only symbolized different human types but also carried specific associations that could open up allegorical meanings in the architectural spaces they articulated. To take an example at random, all but four of the interior columns at the Lateran baptistery in Rome are Corinthian, while the other four, which frame the entry and exit, are Composite. The Composite order, invented in ancient Rome, was explicitly associated with victory; the most famous examples appear on the triumphal Arch of Titus in Rome. Their use here effectively transformed the ceremony of baptism into an allegory of one's triumphal entry, first, into the Church (with the church here acting as a symbol of the Church), and thence a second triumphal entry into paradise.[1] One could multiply such examples ad infinitum.

To speak of allegory in the public architecture of the French Enlightenment, however, is a more surprising prospect. Most architects and theorists during this period were striving desperately for clarity and even transparency of meaning. Thanks in part to the press and the development of architectural criticism, architects were increasingly aware that they were addressing an unprecedentedly broad and heterogeneous public, one in which classical erudition was ever rarer.[2] In such circumstances, the symbolic language of classical architecture often seemed irrelevant. In 1783 the playwright and journalist Louis Sebastien Mercier addressed the following questions to architects: "Why always columns in architecture? Why always the same entablature? Why always the same compositions eternally repeated? Those columns recall tree-trunks; excellent. That entablature recalls beams; wonderful. But I'm seeing it now for the thousandth time. Can't you imagine something else?" He added that, nowadays, when a peasant visits the big city and passes by a recently constructed bourgeois house, he imagines that it's a temple; before you know it he's on one knee looking around the front door for the holy-water stoup.[3] Eager to salvage architecture's attenuated public vocation, theorists became preoccupied with questions of architectural expression. The concept of "character" came to the fore: How could a building signal its purpose and nature in a legible fashion that transcended the vagaries of culture and education within the public? In the latter part of the century, it was Edmund Burke's analyses of the psychological effects produced by different perceived phenomena that most piqued the interest of architects, who began to dream of an irresistibly expressive architecture based on contrasts of light and shade, terrifying size, pure geometries, and so forth. What possible place could allegory—a rhetoric of *concealed* meaning—have in architecture at a time like this?

The development of architectural criticism had accelerated in France after about 1740, as pamphlets and articles in the periodical press introduced an expanding reading public to various kinds of occasional writing on architecture and the city. Much has been said in recent years about the ways in which art criticism, theater criticism, music criticism, and literary criticism were used during the eighteenth century as vehicles for thinly veiled political commentaries that would have been illegal on their own terms. Criticism associated with the biannual Salon exhibition of paintings by members of the Royal Academy is one of the best-known examples of this. Central to the discourse of Salon criticism was the notion of the Academy as a mirror of the feudal politics of monopoly, exclusion, and privilege. This enabled radical art critics to attack the degeneracy of academic art as a way of proclaiming the corruption of the aristocratic regime. The frequent use of erudite classical allegories in academic history paintings was a major target, attacked by critics as a mirror of the ruling elite's effeteness, penchant for dissimulation, and contempt for the ordinary person.[4]

The irony, of course, is that the very mode of criticism being used here was itself allegorical: For, in these sorts of texts, the academy stood for feudalism, the artists stood for the apparatchiks who served the regime, the exhibition itself stood for the public domain, the Salon public stood for the larger public, and finally the art critic stood for the patriotic citizen who exposed the moral bankruptcy of the regime to his or her fellow citizens.[5] One obvious benefit of submerging all this allegorically, in what were ostensibly works of art criticism, was that it made censorship difficult. The regime was very sensitive to charges of despotism and did what it could to preempt them by fostering a lively, if tightly policed, cultural life. Tightening the controls on something as seemingly harmless as art criticism would have exposed the artificiality of that cultural life—as the regime usually discovered whenever it *did* try to censor art criticism.[6]

A similarly allegorical framework for criticism existed in the domain of architecture and town planning as well. The critic La Font de Saint-Yenne provides us with a superb example in his 1747 discussion of the new facade of the parish church of Saint-Sulpice in Paris (Figure 6.1).[7] La Font was normally a partisan of muscular classicism, and one would have expected him to appreciate this powerful façade; but instead he attacked it, and with startling venom. He expressed satisfaction that it was partly concealed from view by a preexisting building; he scathingly ridiculed the huge expense that had been lavished on it; he decried the fact that "an infinity" of excellent French architects had been bypassed for its design, in favor of a foreigner—the Italian Servandoni—who, La Font hissed, was not even an architect but a mere stage-set decorator (which was true). He concluded: "Who will be able to believe their eyes when they see the license & false

Figure 6.1. Servandoni's facade for Saint-Sulpice in Paris. Bibliothèque Nationale de France.

Ultramontane taste triumphing so pompously throughout this Edifice?" This was very politically loaded language: By 1747 the word *ultramontane* referred unmistakably to those forces within the upper clergy and aristocracy who approved of King Louis XV's attempts to enforce the papal bull

Unigenitus in France.[8] This notorious bull excluded from communion and Christian burial all persons unable to prove themselves free of the taint of Jansenist theological leanings. The Jansenist heresy was popular in Paris and in other parts of France, and the Paris Parlement—which contained many influential Jansenists—aggressively took up the Jansenist cause against the crown. The long series of crises this caused together constitute the central political conflict of the French eighteenth century. This was in part because the Parlement managed to frame the conflict as a constitutional issue: Did the king owe his power to God alone, and was he thus empowered to act on the pope's orders, very much against the public will? Or was royal authority conditional, and did the nation, through Parlement, have a right to steer and restrain the crown?

So why did La Font de Saint-Yenne level a charge of false ultramontane license and theatricality at this specific façade? Because the parish and seminary of Saint-Sulpice was a principal stronghold of the anti-Jansenist position in the French capital—and because La Font himself was a pious and politicized Jansenist. The priest who had sponsored the work at Saint-Sulpice was a rabid anti-Jansenist noted for his labors to purge his parish of the heresy. His brother was the powerful archbishop of Sens, who has been called by one recent historian "the chief scourge of Jansenists in the first half of the eighteenth century."[9] As for the charge of "theatricality," this was common in Jansenist attacks on the Jesuits and on the aesthetics of the Roman Church generally.

And so, with his use of the word *ultramontane*, La Font would immediately have evoked the whole Jansenist controversy to his readers, inviting them to see an allegorical dimension to his criticism of the façade. In this submerged narrative, the parish of Saint-Sulpice would represent the anti-Jansenist position; the construction of a theatrical façade at the center of Paris by an ultramontane architect would parallel the application of a papal bull to the edifice of French law; while the unjust neglect of good French architects would parallel the crown's betrayal of the nation into the foreign hands of the pope.

Another way that political content was introduced allegorically into architectural writing was in the form of proposals for urban monuments. These texts were typically pamphlets or articles in literary periodicals that suggested a project for Paris in which one or more monuments, streets, or plazas would occupy, destroy, or reframe significant sites or buildings or even establish meaningful dialogues between monuments. These proposals were published, with few exceptions, in the full knowledge that they would never be constructed; their purpose, rather, was entirely discursive. For instance, in January 1776, just three weeks after a fire had severely damaged the Palace of Justice in Paris, the architect Perrard de Montreuil published a proposal for its reconstruction.[10] The palace was the courtroom complex where the Parlement of Paris met. They were the most important of the various Parlements of France, with whom, as noted, the crown had been involved in a long, hard struggle regarding whether the king's authority was absolute or not. In 1771, that struggle had come to a head: Following the plans of his chief minister, Louis XV abolished the Parlements altogether. The move was deeply unpopular. The ousted parliamentarians launched a publicity offensive that accused the crown of despotism. The crown hired pens to respond, and before long an unprecedented battle to win over public opinion had erupted.[11] In 1774, after more than two years of this, Louis XV died. The much milder Louis XVI assumed power and almost instantly caved in to pressure to reinstate the Parlements and to dismiss the ministers who had been responsible for their suppression. Spontaneous celebrations erupted in Paris and the provinces, with many revelers willfully portraying the event as a royal acknowledgment of the sovereignty of public opinion.[12] It was at this point, right after the Paris Parlement had resumed its duties, that fire destroyed the Parlement's quarters at the Palace of Justice.

As its accompanying text made clear, Perrard de Montreuil's project (Figure 6.2) was an allegorical commentary on these recent events. The text opened with a reference to the Palace that had burned—a vast, rambling warren of dead-end corridors and misshapen rooms that had accreted over several centuries. Perrard remarked how astonishing it was that, for so many centuries, those coming in search of justice had been confronted, on their arrival, with the image of a labyrinth. It was astonishing not only because it was inappropriate but because it so accurately reflected the character of the legal system that had grown up in France over the centuries. In explaining why even the repairable parts of this building ought to be demolished, Perrard declared: "Let us efface, by our writings, by our institutions, and by our monuments, the reigns of Louis IX, of François I, of Louis XIV, & of Louis XV."[13] So it wasn't just a building that he dreamed of sweeping away; it was the entire heritage of those several kings who in succession had built the building.

As for the new complex, Perrard explained that it would be clear and logical, rigorously symmetrical, and splendid in its architectural decor. The

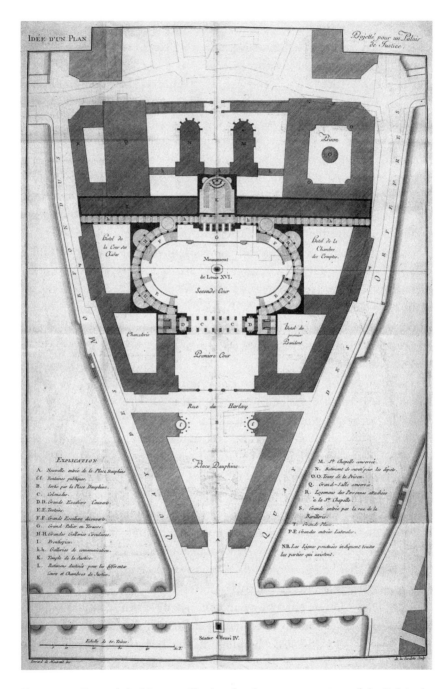

Figure 6.2. Perrard de Montreuil's plan for the reconstruction of the Palais de Justice (1776). Bibliothèque Historique de la Ville de Paris.

Louis XVI statue at its center was to stand before the great central court-room, which Perrard called the Temple of Justice and planned to outfit with a massive classical façade. The king would be shown gesturing toward these new buildings as he surrendered the book of laws to Themis, the goddess of justice, who would be smiling her approval at him. A bas-relief on the pedestal would show the king signing the recall of the Parlements while Minerva, goddess of wisdom, whispered in his ear. The statue would face to the west, looking through a screen of columns and across another court, through a widened Place Dauphine, and toward the older statue of King Henri IV standing on the Pont Neuf.[14] Everything about this king was sub-missive: Having surrendered the book of the laws to the goddess of justice, he was just another supplicant at her temple. But the reference to Henri IV was key, for a popular cult had developed around Henri IV during this period. He was remembered as a benevolent and selfless king who had loved Paris, rebuilding it in the wake of the Wars of Religion, in contrast to his descendants, who had abandoned it for Versailles. On the death of the detested Louis XV, a wave of Henri IV nostalgia had overtaken Paris— ruff collars and balloon sleeves came briefly into fashion; on the day Louis XVI was crowned, someone placed a placard on Henri's statue that said "*Resurrexit.*"[15] The connection hinged on a parallel between Louis's resolu-tion of the Parlements crisis and Henri's ending of the Wars of Religion.

In sum, Perrard's project was allegorical: The labyrinthine old building stood for the corrupt and oppressive heritage of the Old Regime; the act of destroying it signaled a desire to sweep away that heritage; the construction of a clearly organized, symmetrical new temple for justice pointed toward the inauguration of a more open, more rational, more equitable society gov-erned by the rule of law; while the erection of a new royal image at the monument's center expressed a longing that a new conception of kingship might emerge, one in which the king, under the watchful eye of his new model, Henri IV, submits to the law and to public opinion.

2

Is there anything more to be said about these allegories beyond the obvious point that they enabled their authors to publish on controversial political matters without being censored? There is, if one places them in the larger context of architecture's changing and increasingly problematic place in the public sphere during the eighteenth century. The expansion of the architectural public during this period provoked much anxiety concerning the relevance of architecture as a public art. At the heart of these anxieties was an implicit sense that architecture, as the ultimate site-specific art form, had lost its purchase in a new kind of spatially exploded, nationally scaled public sphere. This was a public sphere that no longer referred primarily to the embodied experiences of communities dwelling in specific places but was constituted rather by the circulation of printed matter across great distances among anonymous strangers. The resort to allegory—to recasting the meaning of buildings and urban places in terms of hidden stories, skillfully told in print by the knowing critic—was in fact but one facet of the much broader compulsion during these years to translate the spatial fixity and implicit, poetic expressivity of architecture into the more explicit and more widely communicable format offered by print.

The large-scale public discourse on architecture that began in the 1740s erupted after the young Louis XV had decided to take the reins of government personally, after two decades of rule by an unpopular prime minister, Cardinal Fleury. Under Fleury, the state had sponsored hardly any major public buildings in Paris. This neglect weighed heavily on patriots who had been raised on Latin classics and the glories of Rome, and it fed a creeping nostalgia for the grand projects of the early years of Louis XIV's reign, before his move to Versailles. The other main legacy of Cardinal Fleury's time in power was an increasingly politicized Parisian populace, the result mainly of his battles with Parlement over the Jansenist heresy. All of which meant that Louis XV's decision to assume command of the government in 1743 immediately sparked intense maneuvering among various factions who hoped to advance their agendas in his government's crucial first years. And it was in writing about architecture and especially town planning that several insurgent critics, nearly all of them pro-Parlement and pro-Jansenist, found an unexpectedly effective polemical instrument.

Two images dominated the early years of debate, from about 1747 to 1755. The first was the east wing of the royal Louvre Palace. Like Paris itself, the Louvre had been largely abandoned by the monarchy when Louis XIV had moved the royal court to Versailles in the late seventeenth century. The most visible and potentially magnificent part of the palace, the Louvre colonnade, stood incomplete as an unroofed shell (Figure 6.3). The symbolism of this impending ruin fit neatly into the thematic of the crown–Parlement disputes: What could speak more clearly of the crown's turn away from the

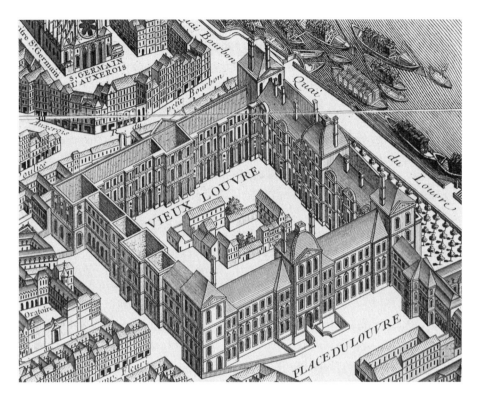

Figure 6.3. The Cour Carrée of the Louvre, as depicted in the Plan de Turgot of 1739. Bibliothèque Historique de la Ville de Paris.

nation than the abandonment of the royal palace in the principal city of the realm? Thus polemicists began representing the empty Louvre as a tragic image of royal desertion and neglect. The pro-Parlement critic Louis Petit de Bachaumont wrote and circulated a song, set to a popular tune, which told of a jolly family of commoners going down on a feast day to the Louvre to shout *"Vive le roi!"*—and wondering why the king won't come to the window to acknowledge their cheers.[16] Patriotic appeals for the restoration and completion of the palace soon began appearing in print, several of which expressed the hope that the monarch would then return there to dwell—in other words, that he would descend from the Apollonian fantasies of Versailles and return to governing as French kings once did, that is, in contact and cooperation with the nation (as represented by the Parlement).

The second image dear to the architectural polemicists of the late 1740s was closely related to the first: It was that of the king himself, cast in bronze.

In 1748 the municipal authorities in Paris had announced their intention to build a square in Paris centered on a statue of the king, though neither the design nor even the site were specified.[17] Into that vacuum rushed dozens of proposals, composed by architects, critics, retired military men, men of letters, and more.[18] In several of these, the sculpted image of the king became a pointed proxy for the missing royal presence. Visibility was stressed again and again: In one proposal, the royal statue was to stand exposed on a bridge at the center of the city, with streets radiating out all the way to the city walls so that the bronze king could be, as it were, visually present everywhere at once. And several writers slyly proposed placing the royal image at the restored Louvre palace itself.[19]

No text did more during these years to announce this transformation of the cityscape into a political allegory than a little book entitled *L'Ombre du Grand Colbert*, published in 1749 by the same La Font de Saint-Yenne who, two years earlier, had written about Saint-Sulpice.[20] This text took the form of a dialogue among the royal palace of the Louvre, the city of Paris, and the spirit of Louis XIV's great controller general, Jean-Baptiste Colbert. In La Font's hands, these three characters became a family, transforming the plight of the city into a bourgeois family drama: The Louvre became an unjustly neglected son, the city of Paris became a long-suffering yet fiercely loyal mother, and Colbert, fondly remembered for his efforts to embellish Paris, became the dear departed family patriarch, back on a visit from the afterlife. The book opened with the Louvre plaintively asking his mother, Paris, why he had been so neglected and abused. Paris tries to reassure him, but before long she is pining for Colbert, who she knows would have made both her and her son into marvels of the universe had he only lived longer. Colbert's ghost then appears from the underworld. He is greeted on bended knee. Colbert, however, is shocked by what he sees. To Paris he says, "Eh! who are you?" Paris responds, "O humiliating question!" and pours out her tale of woe and neglect. Colbert sputters in outrage and disbelief.[21] He then goes to visit the Louvre, his son. Seeing the building largely abandoned, its most famous facades hidden by shacks and parasite buildings, he becomes apoplectic and flees back to the underworld, to "the eternal oblivion of the dishonor of my nation"—a moment captured in the vivid frontispiece that accompanied the second edition of the book (Figure 6.4). Alone again, the Louvre turns desperately to Paris, tells her that she is his only hope for redemption, and begs her to save him. Paris swears that she will do what she can and will not remain silent.[22]

Figure 6.4. The frontispiece of La Font de Saint-Yenne's book, *L'Ombre du Grand Colbert* (1752). © cliché publié avec l'autorisation gracieuse de la Bibliothèque de l'Institut national d'histoire de l'art, bibliothèque (collections Jacques Doucet).

Jürgen Habermas has argued that the eighteenth-century public's understanding of its use of reason in the political sphere grew out of the private experiences of the conjugal family's intimate domestic sphere—the sphere of marriage and the family. This occurred, he argues, in the ostensibly apolitical literary public sphere, where novels and so forth provided an occasion for members of the book-reading public to reflect on matters common to their own scattered "subjectivities," matters such as love, marriage, the family, and individual psychology. This offered a training ground for a critical public reflection, one that accustomed the bourgeoisie to trust the authority of its own judgment.[23] In a later phase, explicit political content was increasingly brought to the attention of the bourgeois public via such dramas. Thus Voltaire, for instance, took to publishing sentimental, embellished accounts of contemporary court cases in which, typically, well-meaning, innocent, ordinary people were in danger of being victimized by powerful and privileged interests. Such works translated political abstractions into highly accessible personal dramas, in which any ordinary person could have a clear sense of what was at stake.[24] This was the strategy underlying La Font's dialogue as well, which also packaged political ideas in dramatic, familial terms that were more amusing than connoisseurial criticism and less foreboding than a political essay.

But this only leaves a larger question hanging: Why the recourse to narrative in the first place? Granted, one cannot publish and circulate a building. But why not describe it or engrave it to bring it to the attention of the reading public? For that is the one thing that all these different architectural allegories and narrations do not do: They do not describe appearances.

Somewhere in the background to La Font's dialogue lies a text published in 1733, entitled *Architecture des Églises Anciennes et Nouvelles*, by an obscure writer named H. LeBlanc. In one part of this work, LeBlanc had compared the facades of Saint Peter's Basilica in Rome, Saint Paul's Cathedral in London, and Reims Cathedral in northern France. He had summarized his sense of how the façades related to the viewer by writing that "the façades of Saint Peter's and Saint Paul's say to your eyes: stay outside and admire us, rather than come in the Church. The Portal of Reims on the other hand says: come in the Church rather than admire me."[25] Here, even before La Font's dialogue, we see architectural expression assimilated to a spoken narrative. A year later, in 1734, a reply to LeBlanc's pamphlet was published in the court periodical, the *Mercure de France*, by the famous military engineer Amedée-François Frézier. Frézier—who was participating in this dis-

embodied conversation from a military outpost on the German border—
lamented that LeBlanc's claims could be contested only in their own terms:
"If one really must adopt the language of Fables in which inanimate objects
can speak, here, according to me, is the invitation offered by Saint Peter's."
And then he went on to provide an alternative narrative.[26] What was the
logic of this rhetorical move, in which words were used not to describe architectural form but as a substitute for architectural expression itself?

Public architectural discourse in France had been occurring at a relatively modest level when Le Blanc and Frézier were conducting their dis-
pute. But when La Font de Saint-Yenne was publishing, a decade and a half
later, it had begun to erupt into a far broader phenomenon. More books,
pamphlets, and periodical articles on architecture and the Paris cityscape
were to appear between 1748 and 1755 than during the whole of the preceding half-century.[27] But in a larger sense, these publications were but a facet
of larger changes that had been occurring for 150 years, in government,
religion, the economy, and cultural life; changes whose cumulative effect
was to amalgamate what had long been a fragmented, heterogeneous, par-
ticularistic culture in France, leaving in its place a comparatively unified,
normative, and national one. Administrative innovations from the royal
center were replacing local power structures; the authority of the state was
being imprinted on the natural order in the form of road networks, frontier
fortresses, and canals; the Counter-Reformation Church was becoming far
more vigilant toward unsanctioned religious practices on the local level;
integrated commodity markets were developing inexorably, requiring of individuals an awareness of events well beyond the spatial orbit of their daily
life; and, finally, traditional popular culture was gradually succumbing in
the face of printed imagery and literature.[28] By the eighteenth century, the
cumulative power of these and other developments had begun to effect a
broad epistemological revolution, whereby the thoughts and experiences by
which people constituted their attachment to a social commonality were directed away from the life of some localized community, gathered physically
in a specific place, and turned instead toward the life of a national culture
that extended across the whole of French territory. I am not speaking here of
the peasantry, of course, but the shift did become broad enough in the eighteenth century to finally have a decisive effect on politics and culture.[29]

This dispersed national community to which the imagination now turned
did not dwell in a discrete place but rather assembled in the abstract, via
discourse. Its concept of time was also new; for as Benedict Anderson has

pointed out, printing helped engender within early mass reading publics a sense of *simultaneity* that was distinct from the lived time of embodied experience. The knowledge that thousands of others are reading the same thing as you, around the same time, helps generate the confidence of community even within what is in fact disaggregation, solitude, and anonymity. This was crucial in enabling people to think of these dispersed groups *as communities*.[30] With these transformations in the normative view of space and community, the possible horizons for architectural experience were also disrupted. Space and community are, after all, very basic components of architectural experience. One can look at a photo or read a description of a distant building, but those are secondary levels of experience that refer to a primary level, which involves the presence of your body at the space of the building. As for community, or social experience more generally, architectural meaning was grounded for most of Western history in those webs of belief and expectation and prejudice that permit social groups to cohere. The classical tradition in French architectural theory used rhetorical terms like *bienseance* or *convenance*, which translate roughly to "decorum" or "propriety," to articulate how a community drew forth meaning from the forms of a building; Without that community of reception, with its shared assumptions about the nature of the good, the forms could only remain mute.[31]

So what kind of architectural experience could be available to a community that gathered, as a community, not in a place, nor at a given moment, but rather in the abstract, via the perpetual, private consumption and production of printed matter and other cultural goods? Already in the early eighteenth century, some people seem to have intuited that, at the least, such a public would have different possibilities for architectural experience than people in traditional communities. An example is found in an early eighteenth-century manuscript by a writer called Jean Pagès.[32] Pagès was an obscure amateur historian who had spent virtually his entire life in Amiens, in northern France. Pagès adored Amiens, and no part of it more than the magnificent Gothic cathedral that dominates the town. In his desire to understand that great building, Pagès had turned to the growing theoretical literature that had begun to appear with the foundation of the Royal Academy of Architecture in the late seventeenth century. In 1709, Pagès composed a dialogue in which two spectators, a local man from Amiens and a visitor from Paris, walked around and discussed the cathedral. Their conversation thematized the distinction between two ways of knowing the cathedral, one that stemmed from a local experience of the building as the memorial center of an ancient community and the other that stemmed from books in which buildings were understood as aesthetic objects. Not surprisingly, the text suggests that the insider's experience is more intense. Pagès's two characters repeatedly encounter aspects of the cathedral that lead the local man to thoughts about God, or about his community and what binds him to it, but that are experienced as curiosities or items of historical interest by the Parisian visitor. At the heart of Pagès's parable were two modes of communication, architecture and printing. And if for Victor Hugo a century later these emblematized two different paradigms for intellectual production, one could argue that in Pagès's text, architecture and printing were reflective of distinct spatial constructions of community: architecture, which reflects an embodied community that gathers in a real place; and printing, which assumes an anonymous community of disembodied discussion, gathered only in a virtual sense.

Thus Pagès's two characters, and the two modes they embody, point to the ways in which a dispersed public, by its very structure, opens gaps in the traditional economy of collective architectural experience, gaps that it tends to fill by the most effective means it possesses: verbal representations. For the dispersed public can only experience *as a public* that which is distributed to its members individually; that which has been rendered clear enough, and durable enough, to retain some communicative efficacy uniquely as a copy or representation, lacking the aura of the original object. The model for such clear and durable distributability was, of course, the word.

With this in mind, it becomes possible to understand the manner in which the word jumped from describing architectural form to being a substitute for architectural expression itself—as drama, as dialogue, as political allegory—as related to the pervasive anxiety that gripped contemporary architectural theorists, who yearned to imagine a new and more powerful basis for architecture communication. For the evidence was mounting during these years that the means of expression proper to architecture lacked purchase within the new kind of placeless public sphere constituted by print. Unlike the traditional spectator, whose experience is embedded in a specific social role tied to a physical place (like Pagès's local man), the reader's judgment occurs in the privacy of the mind, where one is alone and free amid an imagined community of other readers. Thus the reader is reputed to judge free of coercive, socially inflected communal frameworks—without which the mute forms of architecture could signify little more than themselves. Not for nothing did eighteenth-century French architectural thought culminate in a rash of bizarre experiments in expression, all in one way or another rooted in despair about the capacity of form to carry public meaning. There were logorrheic monuments slathered in text; there were gargantuan buildings that targeted the mechanics of perception through sublime effects; and there were utopian fantasies about "architecture parlante," a "speaking architecture."[33]

Projects like these were foreshadowed earlier in the century by the allegorical modes we have been considering, all of which represent different aspects of what I would pinpoint as *the* great architectural anxiety of the eighteenth century: namely, that the public domain had changed in some fundamental way that, quite literally, took the ground out from under architecture's ancient vocation as the human artifact that most prestigiously and most legibly shaped the common spaces of social experience. Politically allegorical architecture criticism, in sum, was a way of making the social meanings of the built environment publicly available for a dispersed, anonymous, temporally disaggregated public—one that was outgrowing the traditional space-time of architecture but that still credited the traditional claim of the monumental to articulate shared beliefs and aspirations.

Notes

1. John Onions, *Bearers of Meaning: The Classical Orders in Antiquity, the Middle Ages, and the Renaissance* (Princeton, NJ: Princeton University Press, 1988), 62–63.

2. The context of print culture and social change evoked here, as well as my larger argument about architecture and print, is drawn from my book, *Architecture, Print Culture, and the Public Sphere in Eighteenth-Century France* (London: Routledge, 2007). See also my article, "Architecture, Space, and Abstraction in the Eighteenth-Century French Public Sphere," *Representations* 102 (Spring 2008), 1–26.

3. Louis-Sebastien Mercier, *Tableau de Paris* (Paris: Mercure de France, 1994), vol. 1, 389–392, and vol. 2, 836–839 (first published 1781–1788).

4. Thomas Crow, *Painters and Public Life* (New Haven, CT, and London: Yale University Press, 1985); Bernadette Fort, "Voice of the Public: The Carnivalization of Salon Art in Prerevolutionary Pamphlets," *Eighteenth Century Studies* 22:3 (Spring 1989): 368–394; Richard Wrigley, *The Origins of French Art Criticism* (Oxford, U.K.: Clarendon Press, 1993).

5. Fort, "Voice of the Public," 370–371.

6. Wrigley, *Origins of French Art Criticism*, 151–152.

7. Étienne de La Font de Saint-Yenne, *Réflexions sur quelques causes de l'état présent de la peinture en France* (The Hague: J. Neaulme, 1747), 137–139.

8. Dale Van Kley, *The Religious Origins of the French Revolution from Calvin to the Civil Constitution, 1560–1791* (New Haven, CT: Yale University Press, 1996), 34–37, 73, and 140.

9. Charles Hamel, *Histoire de l'église Saint-Sulpice* (Paris: V. Lecoffre, J. Gabalda, 1909), 193–194; Van Kley, *Religious Origins*, 81.

10. François-Victor Perrard de Montreuil, *Nouveau Palais de Justice, d'après les plans de M. Perrard de Montreuil* (Paris: P.-G. Simon, 1776).

11. Durand Echeverria, *The Maupeou Revolution: A Study in the History of Libertarianism, France, 1770–1774* (Baton Rouge: Louisiana State University Press, 1985).

12. John Hardman, *French Politics, 1774–1789: From the Accession of Louis XVI to the Fall of the Bastille* (London and New York: Longman, 1995), 32–44.

13. Perrard de Montreuil, *Nouveau Palais de Justice*, 10.

14. Perrard de Montreuil, *Nouveau Palais de Justice*, 14–15.

15. Charles Brenner, "Henri IV on the French Stage in the Eighteenth Century," *Publications of the Modern Language Association of America* 46 (1931): 540–553.

16. [Louis Petit de Bachaumont], *Chanson sur la colonnade du Louvre, sur l'air: Allons la voir à S. Cloud, cette belle incomparable*, n.p. [Paris]: n.p., n.d. [1755].

17. On June 27, 1748, the Paris Bureau des Marchands officially requested permission from Louis XV to build the square, although this was likely a formality consecrating a decision already taken by the crown (Richard Cleary, *The Place Royale and Urban Design in the Ancien Régime*, Cambridge, U.K., and New York: Cambridge University Press, 1999, 212).

18. Some were submitted to the government in manuscript form (many can be found at the Archives Nationales [01 158 –{228–321}]), but most were published as pamphlets or in contemporary periodicals such as the *Mercure de France*.

19. See the proposals gathered in *Lettres de divers auteurs sur le projet d'une place devant la colonnade du Louvre, pour y mettre la statue équestre du roi*, ed. Jean-Baptiste de La Curne de Sainte-Palaye (Paris: 1749).

20. Étienne de La Font de Saint-Yenne, *L'Ombre du Grand Colbert, le Louvre et la ville de Paris, dialogue* (The Hague: n.p., 1749).

21. La Font de Saint-Yenne, *L'Ombre*, pp. 6–9, 23.

22. La Font de Saint-Yenne, *L'Ombre*, pp. 153–170.

23. Jürgen Habermas, *The Structural Transformation of the Public Sphere* (Cambridge, MA, and London: MIT Press, 1989), 43–51.

24. Sarah Maza, *Private Lives and Public Affairs: The Causes Célèbres of Pre-Revolutionary France* (Berkeley, Los Angeles, and London: University of California Press, 1993), esp. 10–17.

25. H. Le Blanc, *Architecture des églises anciennes et nouvelles* (Paris: Le Gras, Pissot, & Briasson, 1733), 26–30.

26. Amedée-François Frézier, "Lettre de M. Frézier, Ingénieur en Chef de Landau, à M. D. L. R. touchant les Observations de M. le Blanc sur le gout de l'Architecture des Eglises anciennes et nouvelles," *Mercure de France* (July 1734): 1501–1503.

27. This claim is based on a systematic survey of European library catalogs and seventeenth- and eighteenth-century periodicals. See *Architecture, Print Culture, and the Public Sphere*, chapter 1.

28. See Robert Muchembled, *Popular Culture and Elite Culture in France 1400–1750* (Baton Rouge and London: Louisiana State University Press, 1985), 11–180; Natalie Davis, "Printing and the People," in *Society and Culture in Early Modern France: Eight Essays* (Stanford, CA: Stanford University Press, 1975), 189–227; Jean Delumeau, *Catholicism between Luther and Voltaire: A New View of the Counter-Reformation* (London and Philadelphia: Burns & Oates and Westminster Press, 1977); John Bossy, "The Counter-Reformation and the People of Catholic Europe," *Past and Present* 47 (May 1970): 51–70; Chandra Mukerji, *Territorial Ambitions and the Gardens of Versailles* (Cambridge, U.K., and New York: Cambridge University Press, 1997), 1 and passim.

29. Eugen Weber, *Peasants into Frenchmen: The Modernization of Rural France, 1870–1914* (Stanford, CA: Stanford University Press, 1976).

30. Though his focus is on a later period, Benedict Anderson offers suggestive ways of thinking about this (*Imagined Communities: Reflections on the Origin and Spread of Nationalism* [London and New York: Verso, 1991], 22–36).

31. On these terms, see Werner Szambien, *Symétrie, goût, caractère* (Paris: Picard, 1986), 92–98, 167–173.

32. Jean Pagès, "L'Auguste Temple, ou Description de l'Eglise cathédrale de nôtre Dame d'Amiens," (1708, with later interpolations through 1723), in volume 1 of Pagès's "Notices historiques sur la ville d'Amiens" (Bibliothèque communale d'Amiens, ms 829 E [10 volumes]). The nineteenth-century publication of Pagès's text is abridged and suppresses its dialogue format (Jean Pagès, *Manuscrits de Pagès, Marchand d'Amiens. Ecrits à la fin du 17e et au commencement du 18e siècle*, volume 5, Amiens: A. Caron, 1862). On Pagès see: Richard Wittman, "Local Memory and National Aesthetics: Jean Pagès's Early Eighteenth-Century Description of the 'Incomparable' Cathedral of Amiens," in *Monuments and Memory, Made and Unmade*, eds. Robert S. Nelson and Margaret Olin (Chicago and London: University of Chicago Press, 2003), 259–279; and Wittman, *Architecture, Print Culture, and the Public Sphere*, chapter 2.

33. One manifestation of this was sensationalist architectural theory. See [Jean-François de Bastide], "La Petite Maison," *Le Nouveau Spectateur* 2 (1758): 361–412 (later published separately, as *La Petite Maison* [Paris: L. Cellot, 1762]); Nicolas Le Camus de Mézières, *Le génie de l'architecture; ou, l'analogie de cet art avec nos sensations* (Paris: Author and Benoit Morin, 1780); and Pierre-Joseph Antoine, *Série des colonnes* (Paris: Alexis Jombert jeune, 1782). Although neither discusses Antoine's book, see Remy Saisselin, "Architecture and Language: The Sensationalism of Le Camus De Mézières," *British Journal of Aesthetics* 15 (1975): 239–253; and Robin Middleton, "Introduction," in Nicolas Le Camus de Mézières, *The Genius of Architecture, or, The Analogy of that Art with our Sensations* (Santa Monica, CA: Getty Center for the History of Art and the Humanities, 1992), 17–64.

PART THREE

Revisiting Allegory in the Renaissance

SEVEN

Allegory and Female Agency

MAUREEN QUILLIGAN

Why do allegorical personifications so often have female gender? Does it have anything to do with actual female agency? Is it simply a question of linguistic convenience having to do with the fairly arbitrary rules of gender in Latin and therefore in most romance languages? Or are there more interesting answers to be found to these questions?

In a recent study of the underlying theological purposes of the use of female personifications in a vast range of medieval texts, Barbara Newman argues that the feminine gender of personifications allowed medieval writers a freedom to discuss religious concepts that would have been transgressive had they been predicated of the male trinity. For example, the three daughters of God that Christine de Pizan animates in the *Livre de la Cité des Dames* are female, according to Newman, because talk about the actual Trinity was too dangerous, and so it became convenient to talk about imaginary daughters instead. According to Newman, the positing of the existence of the many daughters of God enabled a far wider discursive space in which medieval writers could freely consider the nature of God: "It was much safer to theologize about them, than about the Trinity."[1] The daughters of God (Nature, Holychurch, Poverty, and so on) allowed discussion of religious experiences that did not fall within recognizable church doctrine; they also provided means for safely analyzing conflicts within divinity, similar to the power of personification to analyze human conflicts. Female personifications were theologically convenient.

Gordon Teskey's analysis in *Allegory and Violence* posits a far more compelling if also more problematic reason for the gender of personifications in allegorical narrative. For him, their gender specifies the peculiar kind of female agency that haunts any allegory. Because Teskey's purview includes more literary history than that of the Middle Ages, his argument on the face of it may have more purchase on Renaissance practice than Newman's. But Teskey's argument also seems to be able to account for the real power of Newman's thesis and thus, I think, deserves careful consideration.

Teskey argues that personification is a trope by which abstractions, figured as masculine in Western philosophy, must take on the material agency of embodied nature, often imagined as feminine in the same philosophical tradition; the rhetorical figure of personification thus requires a violent appropriation of female materiality by male abstraction for the philosophical abstraction to gain narrative agency. Teskey's important insight is that the "trace" of this violent and fully completed *raptio* lies in the characteristic predication of the feminine gender to refer to most personifications. Thus Justice becomes a woman who engages in just actions; Boethius's Philosophy is a woman who carries books. In *Le Roman de la Rose*, Lady Reason is a woman who offers reasonable arguments. The violence is completely hidden, and the operation of personification looks perfectly pacific. According to Teskey, however, occasionally we can see this process of *raptio* or "capture" caught half way, and there the violence is fully on display.

Two such moments are Francesca da Rimini's lament in Dante's *Commedia* and Amoret's torture in Book III of Spenser's *Faerie Queene*; both episodes reveal a similar violence in the figure of "capture," where allegory makes clear the epistemological "rape" that is at the heart of the trope of personification. According to Teskey, neither Francesca nor Amoret are full-blown personifications because the philosophical process of the nonetheless violent transformation is incomplete, and we are thus treated to scenes that reveal the violence of the allegorical process itself:

> In the more powerful allegorical works this prevenient [sic] violence is
> unexpectedly revealed at moments that are so shocking in their honesty

that they are consistently misread as departures from allegorical expression. Such moments literalize a metaphor from Neoplatonism, the moment of raptio, or "seizing," in which Matter perversely resisting the desire of the male, must be ravished by Form before being converted and returned to the Father. We are confronted with a struggle in which the rift between heterogeneous others is forced into view. The woman continues forever to resist being converted into an embodiment of the meaning that is imprinted on her.

Both of the proof texts for his argument, the conversation with Francesca da Rimini in Dante's *Commedia* and the torture of Amoret in Spenser's *Faerie Queene*, are crucial moments in canonical texts. Perhaps more importantly for understanding the historical engagement of the trope of personification with actual female agency, they are also moments that two separate female authors (one medieval and one Renaissance) chose to revise with articulate and self-conscious protofeminist purposes. Teskey's discussion of the gender of personification takes on a special relevance to any consideration of allegory and female agency because of the remarkable coincidence by which Christine de Pizan and Mary Wroth chose to revise his two proof texts.[2] While I do not intend the following argument to be a wholesale endorsement of Teskey's point that allegory depends on what he calls an "allelophagic" desire for mutual engulfing, I do think that his accounting for the prevalent female gender of personifications in allegorical narrative in terms of of the nature of neoplatonic philosophy is far more interesting than the less forceful cause (which I have relied on elsewhere) based on the grammar of certain classes of nouns in romance languages.[3] At the very least, Christine de Pizan and Mary Wroth witness the interesting canniness of Teskey's choice of proof texts. If he can unknowingly select two episodes in major canonical texts that were already tabbed some 600 and 400 years ago by two female writers as interesting moments they might wish to revise in specifically gendered terms, his theoretical inquiry may well have opened up some interesting connections between gender and allegory.

Teskey's invocation of Dante and Spenser episodes aims to make a point about the theoretical nature of allegory as a genre, which remains the same through all of its historical periods. By juxtaposing Christine's rewrite of Dante with Wroth's rewrite of Spenser, I hope to be able to see not only what remained the same in allegorical technique but also what changed from the Middle Ages to the Renaissance. If we keep in mind Joan Kelly Gadol's famous question—Did women have a Renaissance?—we may be able to see how Christine's revisions of Dante and Wroth's rewriting of Spenser elucidate very different potentialities in the genre of allegorical narrative, and so we can begin to gauge the changes in the genre from one historical period to the next. Christine's rewrite of Dante in 1405 revivifies allegory by literalizing the feminine gender of personification; Christine's revisions of Dante form a major contribution to the creation of the canon of texts for Western medieval literature and for the very institution of literature itself. Her revisions are foundational for the place of Dante within French literature and literature more broadly. Wroth's revisions of Spenser in 1621 indicate allegory's changing use as a narrative genre, heralding the beginning of narrative techniques, which respond to the changing economic substratum of society, an evolution to which Wroth pays due attention with her ironic imitations of Cervantes's *Don Quixote*.

Paul Alpers was one of the first to note that the stanza of Amoret's torture was a central moment for Spenser's poetic:

> And her before the vile Enchaunter sate,
> Figuring straunge characters of his arte,
> With liuing bloud he those characters wrate,
> Dreadfully dropping from her dying hart,
> Seeming transfixed with a cruell dart,
> And all perforce to make her him to love,
> Ah who can love the worker of her smart?

Teskey agrees that the moment is pivotal and summarizes: "In a literary genre concerned more than any other with the metaphysical implications of gender, such moments are infrequent. It is more broadly characteristic of allegory—though by no means more true of it—for violence such as this to be concealed so that the female will appear to embody, with her whole body, the meaning that is imprinted on her." Engaged with the metaphysical implications of gender and not merely responding to grammatical structures, as Teskey insists, allegory would thus appear to be a genre most conducive to investigations into the problematic exercise of female agency.

Teskey points to the importance of Amoret's act of resistance, and that she *cannot* be made to represent an allegorical character beyond herself. If Teskey is right, it makes sense that readers have found it difficult to specify the exact label for the scene of Amoret's torture. While Amoret cannot be guilty herself of the transgressions for which we see her being punished, it is equally difficult to see how Spenser can escape the guilt that Busyrane exhibits in this shocking and writerly torture.[4] As Harry Berger has succinctly put it, the "busy-reign of the male imagination becomes busier and more frenzied as the feminine will recoils in greater disdain or panic."[5] Teskey's point about the gender question here is that by envisioning Amoret's torture Spenser is only being honest about the machinery of his genre. Busyrane is not at fault in this scene; allegory is. Allegory—at least here—is held responsible for its necessary (and violent) appropriation of a female gendered materiality.

In Teskey's formulation, "material in allegory [is] that which gives meaning a place to occur but which does not become meaning itself" (p. 19). Such an argument about allegory—that makes women to be the material site of meaning when they can have no access to that meaning—situates allegorical processes within a problematic for female agency very similar to that which Claude Levi-Strauss exposed by saying that men use woman as signs in the semiotic system of kinship—predicated on the "traffic in women"—but that women cannot speak for themselves in that system.[6] Such a curious congruence between modern anthropological theory and Renaissance philosophy helps to reinforce Teskey's insistence on the philosophical importance of Spenser's scene and to lend greater weight to his formulation that the force of gender difference subtends agency in philosophical narratives. As we shall see, the parallel also points to another odd congruence between Levi-Strauss' understanding of the laws of kinship structure and the proof texts Teskey chooses for his discussion of female agency in allegorical narrative.

Importantly, Teskey neglects to consider an important element of Spenser's scene (he is not writing a commentary on Spenser's poem). Amoret is not the *only* female agent in Spenser's scene. Britomart's presence makes all the difference. The difference may not be due so much to the change from Dante's Middle Ages to Spenser's Renaissance as to the fact that Spenser was "shadowing" with Amoret's sister, the armed warrior Belphoebe, one part of the nature of the actual female ruler who had immense agency over Spenser as a subject of her realm.[7] Because Britomart—progenitor of Elizabeth I—is present in the scene, Amoret's situation is very different from that of Dante's Francesca, where instead of a female in full battle dress who makes oblique reference to a major female agency outside the text, there is a doubled male poetic tradition in the persons of Virgil and Dante. Spenser explicitly tells us that Book III, with its climactic scene of Amoret's torture and release by

Britomart, aims to elucidate Elizabeth I's peculiar brand of chastity. Her presence as first reader of the text contextualizes its narrative as part of what Louis Montrose has recently called "the Elizabethan imaginary," a set of cultural codes that aimed to adjust to the anomalous power Elizabeth, as woman, held in a patriarchal society.[8] Britomart's bizarre contextualization in Spenser's text by strange incest narratives also point to an uncanny congruence between the issue of gender in this allegory and Levi-Strauss' arguments about incest. In Book V Britomart dreams of coupling with her beloved under the guise of Isis and Osiris, incestuous brother and sister.[9]

While Francesca exercises a most important agency, Paolo does not. She speaks. He does not. And indeed Francesca speaks to resist the justice of the punishment meted out to her and her partner, so she speaks for him. As with Spenser, Teskey again tends to slide by a problematic part of the gender issue he uncovers in his discussion of Francesca's objections. While he notes that, as with Spenser's insistence on Amoret's resistance, Dante lays bare the workings of allegory in the Paolo and Francesca scene, Teskey also mentions the pivotal importance of Semiramis: "In reading the episode it is of some importance not to mistake which sin is reaching out to Francesca to make her its mask. Given the authority with which the word *lust* has been applied to her, it should be noted that the word *lussuria* is used in the canto only to characterize Semiramis, a rather special case" (p. 26). Teskey thinks Semiramis's "special" nature—that she is guilty of incestuous lust, while Francesca is guilty only of acting on her desire—allows Francesca legitimately to complain against the punishment given her.

While Semiramis may indeed be a special case in notions of female lust, the extremity of the case of mother–son incest may not be so easily cordoned off from other exertions of female agency and desire. Just as Spenser places Britomart and her incest-haunted desire within the scene with Amoret, so Dante's episode also includes it. This congruence, unremarked by Teskey, is important. In her now classic article critiquing Levi-Strauss, Gayle Rubin has built on Levi-Strauss and importantly argued that the incest taboo is constructed to interdict *any* sort of active female desire, not merely desire for a close family member.[10] *Any* fully active female desire is as threatening to the proper traffic in women as Semiramis's trammeling of the law against mother–son incest, because any desire that does not simply follow the prescriptions of the men who do the trading threatens to halt the exchange. Incest is thus the special case that authorizes the suppression of all active female desire; the laws of exchange require a quiescent female desire that

will passively follow the path for the traffic chosen by males. Any active female desire is tantamount to incest itself and thus any exhibition of female
agency will naturally signal this extreme limit case. At least, both Dante's
and Spenser's proof texts do so, quite noticeably. It is not just Christine de
Pizan who witnesses Semiramis's importance in Dante's text.

As if to prove that Semiramis's position in the first circle of hell is no
mere accident by association, Boccaccio made her the first famous pagan
woman he discussed in the *De Claris Mulieribus*. For Boccaccio, she is famous both for her great achievements and also for the great sin of incest that
stained everything she did. When Christine thus chooses to make Semiramis one of the first stories she tells in her own book about famous women,
specifically making hers the first foundation stone in the building of the
allegorical City of Ladies, she not only imitates her immediate precursor
Boccaccio, she also reinvests Dante's Semiramis with a discursive power
Dante denigrates in her. Dante has Francesca condemn the book Paolo and
Francesca have been reading, just as Christine herself condemned the im-
moral sexuality of Jean de Meun's *Roman de la Rose*. Christine would thus
have found Dante's strictures about reading the wrong literature as central
to her own way of assessing literature. (In her letters against the *Rose*, she
counseled her readers to read Dante rather than Jean.[11])

Christine's defense of Semiramis depends on the specific literary terms
of Dante's denegration. According to Dante, Semiramis is evil because she
"libito fe licito in sua legge" (she made lust licit in her laws). In contrast,
Christine reverses these terms in her exoneration of Semiramis because,
when she had sexual intercourse with her son, "adonc n'estoit encore point
de loy escripte" (there was as yet no written law).[12] While Dante's Semiramis decrees her own law, Christine's lives before a written one. Christine's
emphasis on the written nature of the law speaks not only to the legal rami-
fications of the elementary structure of kinship as Levi-Strauss terms incest,
but also to the fascinating violence of the written, the violence itself enacted
in the reading Francesca and Paolo undertake.[13] Christine's Semiramis not
only responds to Dante's argument against the Babylonian queen, she also
situates herself outside the institution of literature, importantly prior to it.

This is not to argue that Christine denigrates literature or writing itself;
indeed she is trying to bring an oral tradition into the realm of letters, correcting the erroneous version passed on by the misogynist, male-authored
textual transmission. Christine is also clearly interested in Dante's Semiramis because she is twinned with Dido, another lustful queen, but one

who also built a city. Her choice to begin building her city with Semiramis is thus profoundly bound up with the fundamental nature of the empire-founding agency of women, and Christine duly tells Dido's story later in her text. Francesca is, for her part, a mere reader of Arthurian romance, that is, the reader of a story where a queen's infidelity destroys a kingdom. Augustine had gone notoriously astray in his pity for Dido; Dido's creator also stands before Francesca as one of her accusers in Dante's hell. Dante's scene is thus profoundly associated with the power reading and writing have in deciding the kinds of cities one is going to build. Like Augustine himself, who turns away from Virgil, Christine critiques her own precursor Dante when she rehabilitates Semiramis.

While Christine is, as I hope I have here suggested, an inspired and profoundly nuanced reader of Dante, whom she imitates in myriad subtle ways in other texts, she also understands that, to found a female tradition of authority, she will have to stand outside the tradition of male *auctores*. Dante's turn away from Virgil to Beatrice, a Christian woman, reenacts the step taken by Augustine, but Christine needs to take it, as she does here, at the outset of her narrative, not midway through. Hence her insistence on the *written* nature of the law before which Semiramis lives. As I have elsewhere argued in greater detail, Christine accentuates the unscripted, oral quality of the female authorities she follows in her building of the city.[14] Dante's Semiramis stands for the illicit law opposed to the one that decrees the architecture of hell down which Vergil and Dante scramble in the Inferno. Christine takes the illicit "*legge*" Dante associates with Semiramis and gives to it her own legitimacy, making it provide the foundation, literally so, in terms of her own architectural metaphor, for an alternate, unwritten tradition of female authority. That the walls of the city are circular may also be further testimony to her conscious troping of Dante's structure.

The canniness of Teskey's reasoning about Francesca's resistance to the "imprinting" of the word *lust* is thus strangely anticipated by Christine's defense of Semiramis's relationship to the written. Amoret is absolutely engaged in resisting Busyrane's bloody script; Christine's revision of the Francesca episode makes the inherent violence of that same writing quite clear. Semiramis does not know the written law that would condemn her; Francesca, a mere girl and a reader, resists that law and in the process speaks for the two queens whom Dante renders silent. Compared to Dido and Semiramis, Francesca is a nobody; she builds no city, wins no battles, rules over no kingdoms. She is a far easier mark. Compared to the fully embodied personification of lust, however, Francesca has a compelling tragic story that lures us to a sympathy Augustine was wrong to feel for Virgil's queen. However mild, private, timid, and domesticated Francesca's romantic sexual desires may seem in comparison to Semiramis's and Dido's heroic accomplishments, even she cannot be silenced utterly. She is doubtless there to silence them, speaking as she does *for* them (would Dante's Dido have had something more to say than Virgil's did?); but even she makes a compelling case for herself.

Christine makes an even more compelling case for Semiramis, even though Semiramis does not speak for herself. Instead, Lady Reason narrates her story to Christine herself, named (as Dante is) as the author of the text the reader reads. If we may, for a moment, compare the disposition of the scenes in Dante and in Christine with respect to their dramatis personae: (1) Francesca speaks to Dante and Virgil; (2) Lady Reason speaks to Christine about Semiramis. As such a comparison makes clear, Lady Reason stands in the place of the primary narrator. What we have, in broad outline, is Christine's replacement of Francesca as speaker for female agency with her own Lady Reason, a personification. In Teskey's terms then, Christine privileges the full fledged personification Lady Reason over Francesca, the figure of "capture" who still exercises some rudiment of materialized female agency. Seen from this perspective, Christine's rewrite proves Teskey wrong when he argues that the figure of capture speaks for the repressed female materia as a personification can never do; either that, or it demonstrates that Christine is an allegorist who chooses not to show the violence allegory does to feminine *materia*, another instance, Sheila Delaney might say, of her remarkable conservatism. Christine's current standing among allegorists, certainly not as high as Spenser's or Dante's, suggests that perhaps she is less "strong" than they, who can risk the revelation of allegory's prevenient violence. As I very much hope to help adjust her standing in the canon (which she did so much to create, especially Dante's position within it) I do not think such an option is the one to select. Instead, we need to see what further purposes the Semiramis episode serves in Christine's intervention into the canon of allegorical literature.

In the *City of Ladies*, Lady Reason is a direct answer to Jean de Meun's Raison. Christine had already privileged Dante over the *Roman de la Rose*; she specifically names Dante, but refers to Jean's poem by its title, thus denying him the status of *auctor* while conferring that status on Dante. She specifically explains that Jean's poem is the text that most needs to be critiqued in its misogyny. In a direct rewrite of the interview between Amant and Raison in the *Rose*, Lady Reason tells Christine that those who have attacked women "*ce ne vint onques de moy*" ("have never originated with me [Reason]") (p. 643; p. 18). Such a specific attack on the authority of Jean's figure, Raison, allows the gender of the figure in Christine's text to assume a literalness that recuperates some of the materiality lost to the abstraction in the process of personification. The position of a "real" human female Christine, author of the text and possessor of the same ontological space as Dante and Virgil in the *Commedia,* revivifies the personification in ways that are not entirely available in a male-authored text; or, at least, a text that does not make the question of gender difference so specifically a focus in the conversation between the two interlocutors. Because Christine's critique is leveled at a mindless tradition of the empty citation of literary authorities, which contrasts to the evidence presented by Christine's own physical female body, the text negotiates the interstice between materiality and literary abstraction as its specific overt topic:

> *Autres, pour monstrer que ils on biaucoup veu*
> *d'escriptures, se fondent sur ce qu'ilz ont trouvé en*
> *livres et dient après les autres et aleguent les autteurs.* (p. 643)
> Others, in order to show they have read many authors, base
> their own writings on what they have found in books and
> repeat what other writers have said and cite different authors. (p. 18)

Lady Reason's understanding of Semiramis's transgression of an as-yet-to-be-written incest taboo stands outside the textual tradition mindlessly handed down by men. Before Reason narrates Semiramis's story, she helps Christine to carry away all the dirt of misogynist opinion left lying all over the "field of letters." All allegorical narrative proceeds by means of such literalizing of the metaphors inherent in the trope of personification; literalizing the gender of such figures is another version of the wordplay generic to allegorical narrative.[15] Christine even plays with her own name as the feminine form of Christ when Lady Justice narrates the story of Saint Christine, who receives her name directly from Jesus. Justice emphasizes the violence of this story—the longest of the saints' lives narrated in this section, specifically the excision of Saint Christine's tongue, so that she is able to spit a piece of it into her torturer's eye, blinding him. As such a grisly detail implies, female personifications understand the violence done to material bodies—both male and female.

The vast testimony Barbara Newman has amassed to demonstrate the widespread theological instrumentality of female personifications throughout a number of centuries underscores the need for "safety"; her argument implicitly assumes that violence does, in fact, threaten somewhere in the arena of theological debate that the daughters of God enabled writers to evade. To say, as Newman does, that the goddesses provide "safe" havens is another way of saying that no violence will happen in the landscapes they populate, an argument that bears at least a remote relationship to Teskey's own formulation. Teskey's fundamental point is that we do *not* ordinarily see the violence of personification except in those few strange places where the greatest allegorical poets allow us to view its mechanisms stripped bare in the moment of incomplete "capture"; the rest of the time, the medieval narratives operate with just the efficient analytical "safety" Newman so beautifully describes in the many texts she elegantly surveys. It is important to remember that very existence of the Trinity owes its own special internal dynamic between the Father and the only begotten Son to the female materiality the Son borrows from His human mother so that he may, in fact, be able to suffer a violent death on the cross. It may be impertinent to argue that while the Logos is far more than a mere personification, the violence done His materiality is one of the most crucial elements of His Passion. To say, then, as Newman does, that the theological nature of the goddesses in medieval literature guarantees their distance from the violence that would threaten any discussion of the actual male Trinity itself calls attention to the miraculous disruption of normative human relations required by the very theology of the Incarnation and Passion. The violence of the Passion allows the Christian revision of Old Testament written law. Teskey and Newman are not, finally, in essential disagreement about the profound philosophical and theological difficulties allegorical personifications manage, in their normal workings, to evade.

In Teskey's second scene of "capture" the violence is impossible to forget: Amoret's heart is withdrawn from her chest cavity and placed in a bowl of blood:

> At that wide orifice her trembling hart
> Was drawne forth, and in siluer basin layd,
> Quite through transfixed with a deadly dart,
> And in her bloud yet steeming fresh embayd. (3.12.21)

It is this "wound" that the female warrior Britomart makes disappear; she forces Busyrane to reverse his verses:

> The creull steele, which thrild her dying hart,
> Fell softly forth, as of his owne accord,
> And the wide wound, which lately did dispart
> Her bleeding brest, and riuen bowels gor'd,
> Was closed vp, as it had not been bor'd,
> And euery part to safety full sound,
> As she were neuer hurt, was soone restor'd'
> Tho when she felt her selfe to be unbound
> And perfect hole, prostrate she fell vnto the ground. (3.12.38)

Such an undoing of sadistic art has at times been read as playing on the image of the postcoital detumescent penis. If so, the genital terms can be seen aptly to literalize the Neoplatonic metaphor of *raptio*, which Teskey argues subtends the scene. Similarly, readers have also noticed that being rendered perfectly "hole" does not mean that Amoret is no longer penetrable; though virginal, she is still capable of intercourse, that womanly potential being indeed her characteristic quality.[16] But what no readers have remarked is that the horrifyingly large and gaping wound that closes up to a normal "hole," from which formerly protruded a large and detached bloody object, very accurately mimes the gory actualities of childbirth. In childbirth, an internal body part does seem to be torturously extruded from the female vagina, which, rather startlingly, then returns to its former state and without a death-dealing amount of pain. (In this context it is perhaps important that the stanza does not describe the heart's reinsertion into the body but simply the closure of the opening, as if the point is not to reinsert the pulsing organ but simply to close the "wide wound.") If such a suggestion is not wildly off the mark, it more fully fleshes out, as it were, the bare theoretical frame of Teskey's argument. Amoret's materiality not only resists being turned into an abstraction, that materiality also reenacts the original function of *materia*, parturition itself. Amoret's experience of a horrific fantasm of childbearing radically contrasts with her own painless birthing by her mother Chrysogone in the Garden of Adonis, which as a landscape in and of itself represents the cosmological purpose of corporeal generation. The narrative of Book III continues to circle back onto this essential issue of female chastity.[17]

To suggest this new understanding of one aspect of Amoret's "torture" is not fundamentally to revise our traditional interpretation of what Busyrane is attempting to do to her or why. It may serve instead as one more way of seeing his attempt to textualize Amoret's experience; that is, to turn Amoret's physical, material experience into a poetic text by borrowing her fecund, bodily based creativity to make poetry of his own. To see the healing that Britomart helps to achieve as one that images what happens to the female body at the moment of giving birth is, however, to see in a new and useful way what it is that Britomart learns from attending on Amoret. This moment of magically self-healing physical protrusion (this bloody creativity) is precisely where Britomart's own heroically erotic energies are leading her. (We are given another brief glimpse of this moment of parturition in Book V when Britomart dreams of giving birth to a lion in Isis Church.)[18]

When Wroth rewrites Spenser's scene, she is clearly more interested in switching the genders of the protagonists than in commenting on the underlying issue of childbirth. In Spenser's scene, the enchanter Busyrane is a sadistic sonneteer, who writes strange characters with Amoret's heart's blood. In Wroth's variation on this episode, the poet Pamphilia is the rescuer, not the torturer, and the torture victim is Amphilanthus, a character based on her own beloved first cousin, William Herbert, the third Earl of Pembroke, and therefore male. The torturers are icons of female sexual predatoriness, rivals to the heroine. While the fact that the victim is male means that Wroth is unable to consider the issue of childbirth embedded in the heart of Spenser's episode, the names of the characters Wroth has chosen to give the torturers are very suggestive. Musalina, although she is a fully developed character in the text and one of the heroine's main rivals for the beloved Amphilanthus, has a name that allies her with the muses. She may thus name the problem of Petrarchan discourse overtly addressed in Spenser's scene, where the process of torture is also the process of writing. The other torturer is Lucenia, who, like Musalina, is a fully developed character in the fiction and who, therefore, is more than merely her name. But like Musalina, her name has a quite specific resonance; Lucenia recalls Saint Lucena, who was the Roman saint of childbirth. If such an allusion were intended by Wroth (and one wishes that it were clearer that it was: Wroth's character Lucenia has nothing immediately discernable to do with children or childbirth elsewhere in the text), then it would be possible to claim that Wroth, as a female reader of Spenser's text, had, in fact, intuited the physiological events implicit in the scene of Amoret torture. Wroth did in fact herself give birth to two illegitimate children fathered by William Herbert, the man on whom Amphilanthus is modeled. Musalina and Lucenia might well then refer obliquely to the two most compelling reasons Amphilanthus/Herbert might have for remaining loyal to Pamphilia/Wroth: Wroth's expertise in poetry and her also having given birth to Herbert's children.[19] The location of the scene of torture is a ring of stones reminiscent of Stonehenge, which was an easy ride from the Earl of Pembroke's seat at Wilton. The details of the scene are thus tied quite closely to Wroth's own relationship with her first cousin.

Wroth's rewrite of Spenser poses another immense contrast: Britomart succeeds in her rescue of Amoret from torture, while Pamphilia fails:

> Pamphilia adventured, and pulling hard at a ring of iron which appeared, opned the great stone, when a doore shewed entrance, but within she might see a place like a Hell of flames, and fire, and as if many walking and throwing pieces of men and women up and downe the flames, partly burnt, and they still stirring the fire . . . the longer she looked, the more she discernd, yet all as in the hell of deceit, at last she saw Musalina sitting in a Chaire of Gold, a Crowne on her head, and Lucenia holding a sword, which Musalina took in her hand, and before them Amphilanthus was standing, with his heart ript open, and Pamphilia written in it, Musalina ready with the point of the sword to conclude all, by razing that name out, and so his heart as the wound to perish. (p. 494)[20]

Wroth's rescripts Spenser's already literalized set of conceits in Amoret's torture by having the written name "Pamphilia" visible on Amphilanthus's fleshly heart. The detail is authorized by Spenser's own practice in the first poem of the *Amoretti*, where his beloved reader is asked to read what has been written by tears in "heart's close bleeding book."[21] The bits and pieces of burnt male and female lover's flesh derive from the dismembering tradition of the Petrarchan blazon, which is clearly one influence on this baroque scene of torture.[22] But what is most striking about Wroth's revision of Spenser's scene is that the moral values are completely reversed. Pamphilia tries vainly to come to Amphilanthus's rescue, but she is unable to do so, not because she may, like Scudamour, be implicated in some way in causing the torture, nor because she has no powers of aggression (nothing comparable to Britomart's magic—and some have thought phallic—lance), but because only *false* lovers are able to enter such an arena. All-loving Pamphilia is too true and constant (read "chaste") to pass through the flames:

so with as firm, and as hot flames as those she saw, and more bravely and truly burning, she ran into the fire, but presently she was throwne out again in a swound, and the doore shut; when she came to her selfe, cursing her destinie, meaning to attempt again, shee saw the stone whole, and where the way into it was, there were these words written:

Faithfull lovers keep from hence
None but false ones here can enter:
This conclusion hath from whence
Falsehood flowes, and such may venter. (p. 494)

Britomart had ignored the script over the doors in Busyrane's palace and had gone in a "bold Britonesse." Pamphlia has all the courage necessary to do the same. The problem is that the enchanted site rejects her because of her very virtue. This site is the polar opposite of another enchanted place, the palace of Venus on Cyprus, where Pamphilia has already shown her heroism. There, by the power of her virtue constancy, Pamphilia is able to open the doors to the castle and to free the lovers. She is, however, unable even to remain for long within this "hell of deceit." It is as if Poverty, or Chastity itself, were trying to enter Deduit's Garden of Love in the *Roman de la Rose*. Such virtues must remain arranged as statues on the outside of the garden wall, decorating it, but incapable of entering it. As Wroth's contrasting sites attest, her use of landscape allegory insists on the defining character of the moral virtue of constancy (the titular virtue for the incomplete seventh book of Spenser's epic). Pamphilia is the heroine of the *Urania* because she is the truest, most constant lover, the most all-loving. Wroth's huge romance, then, rewrites Spenser's satirical Squire of Dames dilemma as well as the constancy test of the Argalus and Parthenia episode in the *Arcadia*.[23] One might also say that Wroth rewrites the "Mutabilitie Cantos" as well, insisting by doing so that the female is the principle not of Mutabilitie, but of Constancy. As we see in the repeat of the Amoret-torture scene, when it is Pamphilia's (and not Amphilanthus's) chest that is torn open, Pamphilia's experience in the earlier scene in Venus's palace remains central to the Wroth's manipulation of Spenser's allegorical techniques.

The scene of the enchanted castle on Cyprus is the climax of Book I of the *Urania*. It is also the scene selected to be portrayed on the title page of the printed volume (Figure 7.1). It is clearly an important moment in the text, and thus its links to the episode that rewrites Amoret's torture are key to what Worth aims to accomplish in her use of personification. When

Figure 7.1. Title page of Mary Wroth's 1621 *The Countess of Mountgomeries . . . Urania.* Reproduced by permission of The Huntington Library, San Marino, California.

Pamphilia releases the prisoners in the Castle of Love on Cyprus by giving to Amphilanthus the key that the statue of Constancy has just given to her, the personification of Constancy as represented in the statue on the bridge disappears into Pamphilia's breast:

> Both then at once extremely loving, and love in extremity in them, made the Gate flie open to them, who passed to the last Tower where Constancy stood holding the keyes, which Pamphilia tooke; at which instant *Constancy* vanished, as metamorphosing her self into her breast; then did the excellent Queene deliver them to Amphilanthus, who joyfully receiving them, opened the Gate. (p. 169)

Here, it is almost as if, to use Teskey's formulation, the allegorical abstraction Constancy has effected a "capture" of Pamphilia, transforming her irremediably. It seems to be on the basis of this moment that Pamphilia later says that she must become of a different "constitution" for other thoughts to fall into her breast so that she would become able to love someone other than Amphilanthus. Like Amoret's, Pamphilia's breast later becomes the site of her own baroquely imagined torture; Constancy's transformation into that breast allows us to see how carefully Wroth prepares her rewrite of Spenser. Her series of scenes seem almost explicitly to address Teskey's understanding of what is at stake in the negotiations of female authority with allegorical personifications. The mediating text in the first disenchantment episode is Ovid's *Metamorphosis*; it is again recalled in Constancy's "metamorphosing her self" into Pamphilia's breast. It appears first in the description of the statue of Venus, which is compared to Pygmalion's masterpiece. (Wroth rewrites Ovid constantly in the *Urania*, regendering, as Roberts points out, Ovid's tale of Arethusa and Byblis.[24])

To recall the myth of the transformation of Pygmalion's statue into a real woman is to move in reverse along the path Teskey calls the "half way process" of capture, that is, the movement is away from abstraction toward materiality. This is also true of the relationship between Constancy and Pamphilia: Constancy vanishes, transformed into the breast of a real woman, almost as if Wroth herself might be meditating on Shakespeare's rewrite of the Pygmalion myth in *The Winter's Tale*—where the statue can move because it has always been a real, aging, female body. In each of these rehearsals what gets insisted on is that the woman is real, the artwork is not.[25] Pamphilia is half-captured, not by constancy, but by love. This very half capture has made her into a poet. She is not the dead and lifeless work of art but the artist who creates poetry out of her sufferings as a constant woman. When we hear Pamphilia and Urania debate the problems surrounding "this word constancy" as Urania derisively terms it, she gives Pamphilia the opportunity to articulate her own ontological status in relation to the term.

Urania criticizes Pamphilia for loving her brother Amphilanthus, but not because theirs is an unsuitable match between first cousins (although Urania has just been cured of a parallel attachment to Pamphilia's brother by Amphilanthus's ministrations in Saint Maura); Urania's point is rather that Pamphilia deserves someone better than her inconstant brother. (Although apparently acceptable, an official union between the two is never contemplated by anyone, even though both principals are unmarried and later—in the manuscript continuation—freely marry others.) Because Amphilanthus has been constantly inconstant to her, so Urania reasons, Pamphilia too should be allowed a change in her affections. Urania argues against Pamphilia's obstinate refusal to do so:

> 'Tis pitie said Urania, that ever that fruitlesse thing Constancy was taught you as a vertue, since for vertues sake you will loue it, as having true possession of your soule, but understand, this vertue hath limits to hold it in, being a vertue, but thus that it is a vice in them that breake it, but those with whom it is broken, are by the breach free to leave or choose againe where more staidnes may be found. (p. 470)

Urania does not, of course, specifically single out herself as a happy instance of those who find greater contentment in change, although Amphilanthus did save her a period of sorrow by pitching her over the cliff, thereby drowning out memories of her unsuitable love. For her part, Pamphilia insists on the willful activity of her desire, irrespective of anything Amphilanthus might or might not do to deserve her devotion. Pamphilia's position seems at first glance to be quite masochistic; however, on closer scrutiny of its specific terms, it demonstrates rather that she has a will of her own and that she exercises full command over it to institute her own active desire as her possession of herself. Urania charges her with something like having been captured by the abstraction "constancy," which has taken "possession" of her. Pamphilia insists that her virtue is her own:

> To leave him for being false would shew my love was not for his sake, but mine owne, that because he loved me, I therefore loved him, but when hee leaves I can do so to. O no deere Cousen I loved him for himselfe, and

would have loved him had hee not loued mee, and will love though he dispise me. . . . Pamphilia must be of a new composition before she can let such thoughts fall into her constant breast, which is a Sanctuary of zealous affection, and so well hath love instructed me, as I can never leave my master nor his precepts, but still maintaine a vertuous constancy. (p. 470)

As paradoxical as it may sound, Pamphilia's point is really that if she loved Amphilanthus only as a return for his loving her, her desire would have its origin in the male's desire; then female desire would remain a mere reflective repetition of male desire. To locate an active desire in her female self, she needs her own will to be autonomous. While she appears to depend on him, taking her identity from loving him constantly, she in fact insists on an identity impervious to any action he might take. Her constancy is, finally, an act of willful self-definition. She "will love though he despise" her. The "master" whose instructions she follows is love itself, the Amor of an older tradition of love poetry, not the boy Cupid but a mature Lord of Love such as the one who instructed Amant in the *Roman de la Rose*. Pamphilia defines herself by the constant breast she maintains—and the anatomical location of the "sanctuary" she celebrates here is the same place where Amoret's torture takes place, and, consequently, Wroth's rewritings of that scene of torture.

Pamphilia's tenacity derives not merely from a biographical choice clearly made by Wroth herself in her illegitimate alliance with her inconstant cousin William Herbert. Rather this pivotal conversation between the two lead female characters in her narrative has deeply embedded connections to Wroth's rewrite of Spenser's allegory in *The Faerie Queene*. When Pamphilia remarks that she cannot let thoughts of a new lover "fall into her constant breast" until she is of a new composition, she borrows for herself the authority of a personification without, I would like to suggest, sacrificing her own female agency.

The ultimate revision of the moment of torture—which again insists on the unreality of the artwork in contrast to the living woman—is the vision Amphilanthus has of Pamphilia in the Hell of deceit. Already replicating the scene in which Pamphilia sees Amphilanthus being tortured by women (with his heart ripped out of his chest cavity and Musilina trying to erase Pamphilia's name from its surface), Amphilanthus's vision is a return to the original gender arrangements of Spenser's scene in which Amoret is tortured by Busyrane:

A Ring of iron hee then saw, which pulling hard, opened the stone; there did he perceive perfectly within it Pamphilia dead, lying within an arch, her breast open, and in it his name made, in little flames burning like pretty lamps which made the letters as if set round with diamonds, and so cleare it was, as hee distinctly saw the letters ingraven at the bottom in characters of bloud; he ran to take her up, and try how to uncharme her, but he was instantly throwne out of the Cave in a trance, and being come again to himself, resolving to dye, or to release her since he found her loyalty, he saw these words onely written in place of the entrance.

This no wonder's of much waight,

'Tis the hell of deepe deceite. (pp. 655–656)

Pamphilia here seems to have been turned into a dead icon of "loyalty," as if the "capture," in Teskey's sense, had been total. Here too we get fully literalized, the "characters of blood" in Busyrane's kind of writing. The narrative itself, however, undercuts this vision; it is not, finally, "of much weight," for the vision is a false one, of "deep deceit." It is not that Pamphilia is not false but that she is not dead. She is, in fact, alive, whole, and still loving of Amphilanthus. If only inconstant lovers can be "in" the hell of deceit, the place is capable of offering only deceitful visions. What Amphilanthus sees is a false vision, rather like the false vision created by Archimago that leads the Redcrosse Knight astray in Book I of *The Faerie Queene*. Through its falsity, however, Amphilanthus understands the truth, that Pamphilia is constant. Her constancy, however, is not a dead thing but fully agented. A few paragraphs after this vision, Pamphilia appears in the narrative, unharmed in any way. Amphilanthus may imagine Pamphilia constant and dead; but she is, in fact, quite alive.

The conclusion of the first enchantment in Book I had hinted at Pamphilia's freely chosen agency, for there the force named by another term takes the place of Constancy in effecting the happy outcome. The narrator explains how the prisoners in the Tower of Love are finally released:

[Pamphilia and Amphilanthus] then passed into the Gardens, where round about a curious Fountaine were fine seates of white Marble, which after, or rather with the sound of rare and heavenly musick, were filled with those poore lovers who were there inmprisoned, all chain'd one unto another with linkes of gold, enameled with Roses and other flowers dedicated to *Love:* then was a voice heard, which delivered these wordes:

"Loyallest, and therefore most incomparable Pamphilia, release the Ladies, who must to your worth, with all other of your sexe, yeeld right preheminence: and thou Amphilanthus, the valliantest and worthiest of thy sex, give freedome to the Knights, who with all other must confessee thee matchlesse: and thus is *Love* by love and worth released." (p. 170)

Wroth may well be punning on her own name in insisting on the "worth" that pairs with love to release the prisoners. Because "worth" is predicated of her preeminence among women, we are invited to see Wroth's authorial character present in Pamphilia's achievement. Paradoxically, Pamphilia's "worthiness," like Stella's "richness" in Sidney's sonnet cycle, is declared by the husband's name. (Like Bess of Hardwick's initials "ES," Wroth's name further signifies her identity as a widow, on which rests at least some of her free agency.)

Within the fiction of the romance, Pamphilia is as famous for her poetry as is Amphilanthus. When she complains of his infidelity and insists in poem after poem on her own constancy, she borrows the authority of the personification of the virtue, but she bases her own agency on her refusal to respond to the fluctuating demands of male desire. Hers is an active volition that is to be distinguished from the personified abstraction she not so much refuses to become (like Dante's Francesca), in Teskey's formulation, but that she contains within herself to make it a defining characteristic of her own will.

What Wroth has done then is to reformulate a transgressively active female desire, dressing it up in a traditional female virtue, patient constancy. Out of this maneuver, she creates Pamphilia's authority, institutionalized in the poems of the sonnet cycle appended to the Urania. In the process she adjusts the terms of romantic fiction in the direction of the ironic realism Cervantes opened up as a possible avenue in *Don Quixote*. In her edition of the Urania, Josephine Roberts outlined Wroth's debts to Cervantes as one of the most important influences on her work.[26] A signal moment Roberts mentions is Wroth's revision of Spenser's use of Una's emblematic lamb in Book I of *The Faerie Queene*; Wroth gives Urania a lamb; but, rather than see it as a symbol of innocence and purity, Urania cooks it for supper. As Roberts puts it: "Wroth's sudden shift from Lamb of God to lamb chops reveals a rupture between the world of high idealism and that of hard, pragmatic circumstance" similar to the juxtaposition of the two in Cervantes' book (p. xxiii).

The very frontispiece to the romance indicates the importance of Cervantes, for in the upper-right-hand corner of the landscape there is an odd windmill; the climactic scene of disenchantment when the statue of

Constancy metamorphoses into the living breathing Pamphilia, then, includes a visual signal of its Cervantean context.[27] The picture is of the moment just before the female artist may be said to master the personification,
when Amphilanthus and Pamphilia walk toward the statues on the bridge.
This artist can even have a conversation with another woman about the
virtue at hand, rejecting the possibility that she has been possessed by it.
Wroth thus avails herself of the full panoply of allegorical techniques to display the sumptuous and violent elegance of the personified virtue she masters and makes the fuel of her art. In the process she reinvests the violence of
the allegorical process of personification, reversing (just as Britomart forces
Busyrane to undo) the masculinist falsity of vision to reveal an ironic perspective on the possibilities of romance narrative.

This irony is far more subtle than Sancho's being tossed in a blanket for
nonpayment of inn bills because Don Quixote thought they were staying
as guests of a great lord in a chivalric castle of his reading-maddened imagination. Typical of Wroth's irony is a scene in which Musalina, Lucenia,
and Amphilanthus again figure centrally: The scene plays out the issue of
woman's constancy with the irony characteristic of Wroth's wry narrator.
A nameless country girl complains to the three courtiers about losing her
love to a grand Lady, which proves the natural inconstancy of men. Wroth
allows the country girl to comment on the great change in social attitudes
toward the relative values placed on male and female virtue; it is a change
that Wroth's narrative, in effect, is helping to bring about:

> For believe it, the kindest, lovingst, passionatest, worthiest, loveliest,
> valientest, sweetest, and best man, will, and must change, not that he, it
> may be, doth it purposely, but tis their naturall infirmite, and cannot be
> helped. It was laid to our charge in times passed to bee false, and chang-
> ing, but they who excelle us in all perfections, would not for their honours
> sake, let us surpasse them in any one thing, though that, and now are
> much more perfet, and excellent in that then wee, so there is nothing left
> us, that they excel us not in, although in our greatest fault. (p. 440)

Roberts cites a similar sentiment on the part of the narrator, who comments
in passing about some nameless gentleman: "But being a man, it was necessary for him to exceede a woman in all things, so much as inconstancie was
found fit for him to excelle her in, hee left her for a new" (p. lviii). Engaged
in the philosophical debates about women that were popular in the opening decades of Jacobean rule, Wroth (like Christine before her) shapes al-

legorical technique to her own ends in the defense of women. In the process she participates in the inception of a radically different kind of narrative, hospitable to enchantments but also able to scrutinize with wry irony the romantic assumptions of chivalric myth.

Clearly empowered by the gendered forces contending within the allegorical figure of personification, Christine and Wroth both revisit its violent workings to provide forceful narratives about the agency of women. Christine writes at one moment when allegorical narrative was at its most powerful; her move is thus to intervene in its canonical lists of texts, aiming quite specifically to insert her own female authority and within that canon. Writing at a far different moment, just before allegorical narrative turns into the "ruin" Walter Benjamin held it to be in the baroque period,[28] Wroth stages the relationship between a female protagonist and the virtue she embodies so that the woman takes on the authority of the personification, not, as Teskey has it, the reverse. In the process, Wroth allows a wonderfully parodic irony to pervade the wit of her text, commenting on the earlier allegorical tradition and showing how personification allegory works before it disappears within the narrator's specific authorial agency.

Notes

1. Barbara Newman, *God and the Goddesses: Vision, Poetry, and Belief in the Middle Ages* (Philadelphia: University of Pennsylvania Press, 2003), p. 39.

2. Gordon Teskey, *Allegory and Violence* (Ithaca, NY: Cornell University Press, l996). pp. 18–19.

3. *The Allegory of Female Authority: Christine de Pizan's "Livre de la Cité des Dames"* (Ithaca, NY: Cornell University Press, 1983), pp. 23–27.

4. Susan Frye, *Elizabeth I: The Competition over Representation* (Oxford, U.K.: Oxford University Press, 1993), pp. 124–135, argues for Spenser's complicity in Busyrane's rape of Amoret.

5. Harry, Berger, *Revisionary Play: Studies in Spenserian Dynamics* (Berkeley: University of California Press, 1988), p. 179.

6. Claude Levi-Strauss, *Elementary Structures of Kinship* (London: Eyre and Spottiswode, 1969), p. 496.

7. Spenser displays the kind of power such a female ruler has in the episode of Malfont, the bad poet, whom Mercilla punishes by having his tongue nailed to a post in Book V.

8. Louis Montrose, *The Subject of Elizabeth: Authority, Gender, and Representation* (Chicago: University of Chicago Press, 2006), pp. 3–5; and Louis Montrose, "Spenser and the Elizabethan Political Imaginary," *ELH* 96 (2002): 907–946.

9. See my *Incest and Agency in Elizabeth's England* (Philadelphia: University of Pennsylvania Press, 2005), pp. 152–163.

10. Gayle Rubin, "The Traffic in Women: Notes on the 'Political Economy' of Sex," in *Toward an Anthropology of Women*, ed. Rayna Reiter (New York: Monthly Review Press, 1975), 157–210.

11. See *"La Querelle de la 'Rose'": Letters and Documents*, North Carolina Studies in Languages and Literatures (Chapel Hill: University of North Carolina Department of Romance Languages and Literatures, 1978), p. 138; *Le débat sur le "Roman de la rose,"* ed. Eric Hicks (Paris: Honoré Chanmpion, 1977), pp. 141–142.

12. The *Livre de la Cité des Dames* of Christine de Pizan: A Critical Edition, ed. Maureen Curnow, 2 vols. (PhD. Diss, Vanderbilt University, 1975); Earl Jeffry Richards, trans., *The Book of the City of Ladies* (New York: Persea Press, 1982), p. 40.

13. Jacques Derrida analyzes the violence writing does to an oral society in his discussion of girls divulging to Claude Levi-Strauss the names of their tribe, *Of Grammatology*, trans. Gayatri Spivak (Baltimore: Johns Hopkins University Press, 1976), pp. 101–140.

14. *Allegory,* especially pp. 79–81.

15. *Allegory*, p. 26.

16. Jonathan Goldberg, *Endlesse Work: Spenser and the Structures of Discourse* (Baltimore: Johns Hopkins University Press, 1981), p. 11, discusses Amoret's penetrability. For an immensely intelligent critique of Teskey from the point of view of Spenser's more positive delineations of allegorical meaning and female agency, see Katherine Eggert "Spenser's Ravishment: Rape and Rapture in *The Faerie Queene*," *Representations* 70 (2000), 1–26.

17. Eggert discusses the potential pleasure in Chrysogone's impregnation and Acrasia's sexuality, as well as the possible "rapture" when Amoret's falls free of her bonds after Britomart forces Busyrane to "reverse" his verses, p. 14.

18. For a fuller discussion of the thematics of childbirth in Britomart's narrative, see my *Incest and Agency*, pp. 136–163.

19. Wroth was famous for both, the twin accomplishments being an important focus of a poem by Lord Herbert of Cherbury: "While other poets can produce 'feet' Wroth is able to add toes to them." See Josephine Roberts, *The Poems of Lady Mary Wroth* (Baton Rouge: University of Louisiana Press, 1983).

20. Josephine Roberts, ed., *The First Part of the Countess of Montgomery's Urania* (Binghamton, NY: Medieval and Renaissance Texts and Studies, 1995); all citations are to this edition, subsequently cited in the text.

21. Compare Ferdinand's baroque keen in *The Duchess of Malfi* that the image of his sister's making love to another man will "stick" in his memory, "Till of her bleeding heart I make a sponge/To wipe it out."

22. What Wroth has done is to literalize not only the "flames" of passion that "burn" a lover's heart but also the elaborately celebrated body parts from the tradition of the blason Spenser himself mocks, for instance, in the scene with Serena and the cannibals in Book VI of *The Faerie Queene* (VI, ix, 39). For a discussion

of the blason as implicit dismemberment, see Nancy Vickers, "Diana Described: Scattered Woman and Scattered Rhyme," *Critical Inquiry* 8 (1981), 265–279.

23. The story of Argalus and Parthenia, the first new story Sidney interpolated into his revised *Arcadia*, tests male versus female constancy. The story of Parthenia's disfigurement may be a reference to Sidney's own mother's tragic facial scarring by smallpox; her case was so severe that Lady Sidney secluded herself from court. Parthenia's magical healing may represent the son's wish to erase his mother's pain—as well as, of course, to provide the exemplary test case of Argalus's constancy, when he refuses to accept a perfect look-alike who is not in fact Parthenia herself. For an argument assuming this familial referentiality in the Argalus episode, see Margaret Hannay, *Philip's Phoenix: The Countess of Pembroke* (Oxford, U.K.: Oxford University Press, 1990). The possibility that Sidney's episode is a familial roman à clef (a possibility that could have been assumed, if anywhere, within the Sidney family) would have provided added authority for Wroth's autobiographical account of her own experiences in the story of Lindamira in the *Urania*, especially as her story begins with an apparent description of her parents'— Robert Sidney and Barbara Gamage's—courtship. For a discussion of the parallels see Roberts, pp. 30–31.

24. Roberts, p. xxxiii.

25. Lori Humphrey Newcombe argues that Ovid suggests that Pygmalion may have regretted the loss of his masterpiece in "'If that which is lost be not found': Monumental Bodies, Spectacular Bodies in *The Winter's Tale*" in *Ovid and the Renaissance Body*, ed. Goran V. Stanivukovic (Toronto: University of Toronto Press, 2001), pp. 239–259.

26. Roberts, pp. xx–xxv.

27. *Incest and Agency*, pp. 185–191.

28. Walter Benjamin, *The Origin of German Tragic Drama* (London: Verso, 1998).

EIGHT

What Knights Really Want

STEPHEN ORGEL

Spenser's knights never seem to want what they're supposed to want, a life of action and glory on the battlefield, but keep being distracted by the temptations of art, or love, or a life of ease. I begin with a primal scene of knightly distraction: Near the end of Book 3 of the *Faerie Queene*, Britomart in the House of Busirane admires a series of tapestries depicting the loves of the gods and the universal triumph of Cupid—the embodiment of love is not Venus but Cupid, and not the modern innocent cherub, but something more like Figure 8.1, the lascivious prepubescent hustler of Caravaggio's outrageously seductive embodiment of victorious desire. The tapestries constitute a compendious repertory of rampant desire, and though there is a certain amount of moralizing about what a miserable experience love really is, the divine participants do generally get what they want. The human objects of their desire fare less well, but they are, on the whole, willing participants in the various rapes and abductions—thus Ganymede is not urged to resist and preserve his chastity (clearly already lost in Michelangelo's version, Figure 8.2) but merely to hold on tight; Leda, as in Figure 8.3, only pretends to be asleep as Jove "did her invade,"

Figure 8.1. Michelangelo Merisi da Caravaggio, *Amor as Victor* (1602). Oil on canvas, 156 × 113 cm. Inv. 369 Photo: Joerg P. Anders. Gemaeldegalerie, Staatliche Museen zu Berlin, Berlin, Germany. Photo Credit: Bildarchiv Preussicher Kulturbesltz/Art Resource, NY.

Figure 8.2. Michelangelo Buonarroti. GANYMEDE. Black chalk on off-white antique laid paper; wings of eagle incised with stylus and damaged, parts then retouched; actual: 36.1 × 27 cm (14-3/16 × 10-5/8 in.) Harvard Art Museum, Fogg Art Museum, Gifts for Special Uses Fund, 1955.75. Photo: Allan Macintyre © President and Fellows of Harvard College.

Figure 8.3. Michelangelo Buonarroti (after), *Leda and the Swan*. National Gallery, London, Great Britain. Photo Credit: Alinari/Art Resource, NY.

> . . . yet twixt her eielids closely spyde
> How towards her he rusht, and smiled at his pryde; (3.11.32.8–9)[1]

Daphne, here in Figure 8.4 by Bernini, in perhaps the most startlingly revisionist moment, is faulted for her refusal to be a party to her rape by Apollo: "Lesse she thee lov'd, then was thy just desart" (3.11.36.8). This is Spenser at his most Italian: Ariosto had similarly condemned Daphne to the hell of ungrateful women: "Here Daphne lies that now repents her shunning/ Of Phebus whom she scapt with overrunning," in Harington's translation (34.12).

Spenser's voice in describing the tapestries is resolutely amoral. What is more surprising is that Britomart's reaction, too, is aesthetic rather than moral; she admires and wonders, "Ne seeing could her wonder satisfie" (3.11.49.7). The tapestries, after all, are a celebration of lechery, but the Ovidian exempla do not cause her to trash them as Guyon destroys the

Figure 8.4. Gian Lorenzo Bernini, *Apollo and Daphne*, 3/4 view. Prerestoration. Galleria Borghese, Rome, Italy. Photo Credit: Scala/Art Resource, NY.

art of the Bower of Bliss. Perhaps more to the point, they do not cause her to burn in unsatisfied desire, which presumably is the reaction they are intended to elicit. What does provoke that reaction, however, is the sight of Amoret and Scudamore in each other's arms in the original ending of Book 3:

> So seemd those two, as growne together quite,
> That *Britomart* halfe envying their blesse,
> Was much empassiond in her gentle sprite,
> And to her selfe oft wisht like happinesse,
> In vaine she wisht . . . (3.12. 46.5–9)

"Much empassioned"—she has, after all, been wounded by Busirane, even though she has emerged victorious. The 1596 ending, in which Scudamore has already departed when Britomart emerges with Amoret, spares Britomart the pains of frustrated desire but, in a characteristically Spenserian economy, replaces it with Amoret's frustrated desire.

In most of the tapestry's examples, lust is the property of a masculine subject, of which women, or occasionally boys, are the object. The difference between Busirane's pictures and Spenser's poem, however, is the complicity of the objects of lust: The image of Florimel and the Foster, the chaste, endangered heroine and the lustful attacker, reappears in various forms throughout the *Faerie Queene*, including at the center of Busirane's own palace in the person of the captive, wounded, but definitively uncompliant Amoret. Spenserian rapists are invariably failures, and even enchanters cannot compel love. Only the divine lechers depicted in works of art get what they want. But even their success has unwanted consequences: Love both humanizes and unmans them—Mars himself "did shreek,/With womanish teares, and with unwarlike smarts,/Privily moystening his horrid cheek" (3.11.44.5–7).

The Ovidian exempla reflect significantly on Gloriana's knights, for whom eroticism constitutes the prime temptation to give up their quests and renounce the life of action. At the very beginning of the *Faerie Queene*, the Redcross knight is deflected from his pursuit of the dragon of Original Sin and the liberation of Adam and Eve by Archimago's simple stratagem of substituting Duessa for Una, a sexually provocative woman "clad in scarlet red" for a cool and virtuous one in black and white who hides her face under a veil. At the poem's end, Calidore gives up the quest of the Blatant

Beast in favor of Pastorella—pastoral love, reversing the Virgilian topos, constitutes the end of epic. In this case there is no suggestion that Pastorella is anything less than virtuous; but she implicates the erotics of the poem in a large structural ambivalence because all the quests are ultimately quests for love; the projected end of all the poem's adventures is marriage beneath the benevolent aegis of the Fairy Queen. Even Guyon, the only one of the knights not provided with a lady, serves Gloriana; and how far the queen's service extended was always an open question, as the recurrent rumor that Elizabeth had had a child by Leicester indicates. Duessa may deflect the Redcross Knight from Una, but both women represent the end of knightly action; and when the Redcross Knight bolts from his wedding party declaring that he won't be ready to go to bed with Una for another seven years, he is making clear just how conclusive an ending love constitutes. It doesn't really matter whether the woman is good or bad, a lecherous mistress or a chaste wife. In Spenser's celebration of his own marriage, the *Epithalamion*, he assures the success of his love by analogizing himself to Jove; but even within sight of the altar, the king of heaven remains the irresistible polymorph of Busirane's tapestries: Spenser's analogy for his bride is not the regal Juno, who after all is patron of marriage, but Maia or Alcmena; the divine, the poetic, model for wedlock is rape, or adultery. Or, alternatively, total disaster: The bride is also compared to Medusa, the beautiful Gorgon transformed by the experience of love into the monster whose very look causes impotence.

In fact, in Spenser's England, removing one's armor and opting out of the chivalric life is always an ambiguous matter; the temptation to effeminacy is on the one hand very bad and dangerous, but it can also, paradoxically, represent everything one wants, the highest good. Lord Herbert of Cherbury in Figure 8.5 reclines in a wood, while his discarded armor is hung on a tree by a squire whose head is completely obliterated by the extraordinary red plume of his master's helmet. Herbert retains only his shield, which depicts his heart in flames and the motto *Magica Sympathiae*, "sympathetic magic," as he ascends, with his heart, from the world of action to that of contemplative philosophy.

Or so I assume: There is no evident love interest in the picture, though the flaming heart must at least analogize what Herbert really wants, the passion of love. It is surely to the point that this is the principal mode of desire, even of the most passionately chaste and holy desire, such as that of Ber-

Figure 8.5. Isaac Oliver, *Edward Herbert, First Lord of Cherbury.* Powis Castle, The Clive Collection (The National Trust). © NTPL/John Hammond/Powis Estate Trustees.

nini's Saint Teresa in Figure 8.6, about to be entered by the shaft of divine love. Donne goes so far as to demand to be sodomized by the very physical God who has been battering his heart: "I/Except you'enthrall mee, never shall be free,/Nor ever chast, except you ravish me" (Holy Sonnets 10).[2] The paradox is embodied in the trope itself: Lust is a consuming passion, but the rapist is thereby represented as acted on, not acting. Bernini's Apollo in the *Apollo and Daphne* is definitively the aggressor, but in Spenser's account of the inner life of the pair, the woman is the active and destructive one: "Fayre *Daphne Phœbus* heart with love did gore" (2.12.52.5).

Still, the problem with knights who undress is not that they are becoming amorous. Figure 8.7 is Captain Thomas Lee without his trousers. This is not an announcement of the abandonment of his military career for an

Figure 8.6. Gian Lorenzo Bernini, *The Ecstasy of Saint Teresa*. Close-up. Cornaro Chapel, S. Maria della Vittoria, Rome, Italy. Photo Credit: Scala/Art Resource, NY.

amatory, or even for a hermetic life—though he seems absurdly vulnerable, he is nevertheless amply furnished with shield, helmet, and weapons; what he wears, all the art historians assure us, is Irish military dress (a similarly costumed figure appears in Boissard as "Hibernus Miles," an Irish soldier),

Figure 8.7. Marcus Gheeraerts II, *Portrait of Captain Thomas Lee* (1594). Tate Gallery, London, Great Britain. Photo Credit: Tate, London/Art Resource, NY.

Figure 8.8. Hans Holbein The Elder, *An Allegory of Passion* (c. 1532–1536), medium size. The J. Paul Getty Museum, Los Angeles.

and it is seriously claimed that Lee has removed his pants so that they won't get dirty in the Irish bogs—the ultimate pastoral motive. This may, of course, reflect on Spenser's sense of his own exile in Ireland while he was writing the poem—all Spenser's knights are, in a sense, Irish. In any case, Captain Lee is certainly not preparing for sex. Potential rapists in Spenser, as in Holbein's allegory of Desire in Figure 8.8, tend to be chronically on the run, and on horseback, and to remain there until they are unhorsed by other men, not by catching their prey. Unarmed knights like Lord Herbert, in fact, constitute in themselves a temptation: Britomart removing her helmet to reveal her hair is of course a special case, but men in various degrees of nakedness are represented throughout the poem not as a threat to women but as their prey; and here it is worth looking closely at both what men want from the women they lust after and what women want from the men they have succeeded in captivating.

Consider Cymochles in the Bower of Bliss. Acrasia provides for his entertainment (2.5.28) with both loose ladies and lascivious boys—Bronzino, in Figure 8.9, is our touchstone now, though the boys stop being mentioned almost at once: Perhaps those inviting rear ends really are more than Spenser can handle. Cymochles initially seems in his element, "given all to lust and loose living," and the dissolute damzels "every of them strove with most delights,/Him to aggrate and greatest pleasures shew" (33)—but "show" turns out to be the operative concept: Instead of an endless series of infinitely inventive lovers producing countless wonderful orgasms, Cymochles wants no action at all:

> He, like an Adder, lurking in the weedes
> His wandring thought in deepe desire does steepe,
> And his frayle eye with spoyle of beauty feedes;
> Sometimes he falsely faines himself to sleep,
> Whiles through their lids his wanton eies do peepe,
> To steale a snatch of amorous conceipt,
> Whereby close fire into his heart does creepe:
> So, he them deceives, deceivd in his deceipt,
> Made dronke with drugs of deare voluptuous receipt. (2.5.34)

What is the point of the deception; why all the lurking? The sex workers are only out to please him: Surely this is a case where the knight really can have anything he wants. So is this what knights really want? To be able to look secretly from a distance at half-naked women and lascivious boys while pretending to be asleep? Who's doing what to whom? Adders do, after all, eventually strike; but by the stanza's end Cymochles is no adder, "deceivd in his deceipt,/Made dronke with drugs . . ."

As a matter of fact, Cymochles is uncharacteristic in that he at least remains awake, only pretending to be unconscious. For the most part knights who fall for seductive ladies simply fall asleep: Here, in Botticelli's *Mars and Venus* (Figure 8.10), we are obviously witnessing the pair after their

Figure 8.9 Agnolo Bronzino, *Cupid, Venus, Folly and Time. An Allegory with Venus and Cupid* (c. 1540–1550). Inv. NG651. National Gallery, London, Great Britain. Photo credit: Art Resource/National Gallery, London, Great Britain.

lovemaking is over. Mars is exhausted, and Venus takes the opportunity to disarm him. The Samson and Delilah story preaches a similar moral. But Acrasia actually takes her sexual pleasure while her lover is sound asleep, as Van Dyck's Armida does with Rinaldo in Figure 8.11,

Figure 8.10. Sandro Botticelli, *Venus and Mars*. National Gallery, London, Great Britain. Photo Credit: Art Resource, NY.

Figure 8.11. Sir Anthony Van Dyck, Flemish, 1599–1641. *Rinaldo and Armida,* 1629. Oil on canvas, 93 × 90 in. The Baltimore Museum of Art: The Jacob Epstein Collection BMA 1951.103.

. . . greedily depasturing delight:
And oft inclining downe with kisses light,
For feare of waking him, his lips bedewd,
And through his humid eyes did sucke his spright,
Quite molten into lust and pleasure lewd. (2.12.73.4–8)

Spenser says this scene takes place "after long wanton joys," but how much better than "quite molten into lust and pleasure lewd" does sex get when you're awake?

In most versions of the Venus and Adonis story, as in Titian's in Figure 8.12, Adonis is a singularly active youth, though in Shakespeare and Titian the action extends to hunting but not to sex. But when Spenser's Venus seduces Adonis, he is asleep at least half the time: "him to sleepe she gently would perswade,/Or bathe him in a fountaine by some covert glade." The other half, when he is awake and with his clothes off,

Figure 8.12. Titian (Tiziano Vecellio), *Venus and Adonis*. The Jules Bache Collection, 1949 (49.7.16). The Metropolitan Museum of Art, New York, NY, USA. Image Copyright © The Metropolitan Museum of Art/Art Resource, NY.

> . . . whilst he bath'd . . . ,
> She secretly would search each daintie lim,
> . . . And ever with sweet Nectar she did sprinkle him.
> So did she steale his heedless hart away,
> And joyd his love in secret unespyde, (3.1.35–7)

which in the context seems to mean unespied by him. Why all the secrecy? Lust so configured is essentially a solitary activity, with its object unaware or simply insensible. Even in the Garden of Adonis, freed from the dangers of traditional masculine activity, with the boar safely "emprisoned for ay," Adonis remains the passive partner:

> There wont fayre *Venus* often to enjoy
> Her deare *Adonis* joyous company,
> And reape sweet pleasure of the wanton boy:
> There yet, some say, in secret he does ly,
> Lapped in flowres and precious spycery . . .
> But she her selfe, whenever that she will,
> Possesseth him, and of his sweetnesse takes her fill. (3.6.46)

It would appear, therefore, that when Malecasta, after her extended flirtation with Britomart, creeps into bed with her sleeping houseguest, she really does get what she wants:

> . . . to her bed approaching, first she proov'd,
> Whether she slept or wakte, with her softe hand
> She softely felt, if any member moov'd . . .
> Which whenas none she fond, with easy shifte,
> . . . by her side her selfe she softly layd,
> . . . ne word she spake,
> But inly sigh'd. (3.1.60)

Britomart then awakes, but surely too late: That inward sigh reveals that Malecasta has already satisfied her lust—she has, in fact, got what all the other unchaste ladies in the poem want, a sleeping lover. Britomart, now wide awake, "to her weapon ran, in minde to gride/The loathed leachour," and the other knights enter to find her holding her "avenging blaed" over her swooning and utterly unthreatening hostess (3.1.62–63).

If the scene were in Ariosto, it would be comic, and the knights would dissolve in laughter; but Spenser isn't out for laughs. Britomart's militant outrage indicates not simply that Malecasta has mistaken her quarry, but that something sexually dangerous has in fact happened, something that ends with Britomart pierced by Gardante's arrow, so "That drops of purple blood thereout did weepe,/Which did her lilly smock with staines of vermeil steepe" (65). This sounds like a defloration; and surely it implies at the very least that some kind of innocence is gone—Britomart *is* wounded and stained, as she is to be again by Busirane. Earlier in the book, in one of Spenser's zanier moments, Britomart is praised for not accompanying Guyon and Timias in aid of the distressed Florimel: "fair *Britomart*, whose constant mind/Would not so lightly follow beauties chace,/Ne reckt of Ladies Love, did stay behynd" (3.1.19). In light of her panic (or of Spenser's) at finding Malecasta in bed with her, perhaps the point really is just what it seems so anachronistically to be: She is being praised for the fact that she "ne reckt of Ladies Love," for not being lesbian, as if this were something unusual in the poem. But if ladies' love isn't a problem for her, why the panic, and why the wound?

The only dramatically significant one of the very few women in Spenser who actually want and get genital sex with men who are awake is Hellenore, in Book 3, Cantos 9 and 10. (Radigund says she wants it, but it doesn't get her anywhere; it only produces a sleeping lover for her maid.) It is certainly made clear that the problem with her husband Malbecco is not primarily that he is old, ugly, horrible, jealous, and a miser, but that he does not satisfy her sexually; and her ultimate retreat, via Paridell, to a community of satyrs is represented as an arrangement that really does make her happy. This is the closest Spenser comes to a scene of genital sex: As Malbecco watches, Hellenore

> . . . emongst them lay,
> Embracèd of a *Satyre* rough and rude,
> Who all the night did minde his joyous play:
> Nine times he heard him come aloft ere day,
> That all his hart with jealousy did swell. (3.10.48.2–6)

(This is an earlier sexual use of *come* than the OED's earliest citation, from one of Percy's ballads, c. 1650: s.v. 17.)

Malbecco undertakes to reclaim his wife with some powerful Spenserian rhetoric—the same rhetoric, indeed, with which Malecasta and Acrasia have been condemned:

Tho gan he her perswade, to leave that lewd
And loathsom life, of God and man abhord,
And home returne, where all should be renewd
With perfect peace, and bandes of fresh accord . . .
But she it all refused at one word . . .
But chose emongst the jolly *Satyres* still to wonne. (3.10.51)

This is a remarkably unambiguous conclusion. I suggest, however, that, as the classical and Italian names, the fabliau form, the satyrs, and especially the uniqueness of the sex in the poem make clear, for Spenser it constitutes a foreign and basically unworkable solution to an English problem—find yourself a sexually active man who likes going to bed with you; or if you are a man, find yourself a woman or a lascivious boy who doesn't put you to sleep. Isaac Oliver provides a striking parallel in the astonishing drawing in Figure 8.13, unique in both his oeuvre and in Elizabethan England: active men (those jolly satyrs) and women being pleased. The native English

Figure 8.13. Isaac Oliver, *Nymphs and Satyrs,* c. 1605–1610. The Royal Collection © 2009, Her Majesty Queen Elizabeth II.

Figure 8.14. Isaac Oliver, *Allegory of Unchaste Love.* Statens museum for Kunst, Copenhagen. Photo Credit: SMK Foto.

solution is depicted in this equally extraordinary, and equally unique, Oliver miniature in Figure 8.14. In the background, men pursue a life of action: Hunters spear a boar and shoot ducks; a falconer's hawk catches a cormorant on the wing. In the courtly erotic scene in the right foreground, however, it is the women who are active, while the men are languid and passive: This is love in the Bower of Bliss. In the left foreground, in contrast, three soberly dressed women, a lady and her two maids, are chaperoned by a man. Their dress identifies them as city folk, not courtiers; and they observe the erotic scene, of which they seem to disapprove.

But can we really tell the good women from the bad? The courtesans are clearly licentious, with bare breasts and filmy garments, their clothing a striking contrast to that of the city women: The mistress in the left foreground wears a sober black overgarment with a high neck, white ruff and lace cuffs, a russet skirt, a black hat. But now look at the lady engaged in the love scene immediately behind the moralizing group: black overgarment, high neck, white ruff and lace cuffs, russet skirt, black hat. She is indistinguishable in dress and features from the standing moralist—as indistinguishable as Florimel is from the False Florimel: Are they, perhaps, even the same person? When this picture was most recently exhibited in London, at the *Dynasties* exhibition at the Tate in 2002, the art historians had finally noticed this subversive little pair. The catalogue entry suggests that "the embracing couple on the ground . . . may be a mother and son, who represent maternal love." But this is surely pure desperation: The only reason to call this maternal love is that art history believes that women dressed in black cannot be interested in sex. But the courtesan gestures back toward the city lovers: Look, they do it, too—*Così fan tutte.*

What do knights really want? The standard Spenserian temptation is to abandon chivalric action in favor of sex; but sex turns out to be not another kind of action, the rampant potency of Paridell and the satyrs, but utter passivity: The ideal is to be doted on while sleeping, or worse, feigning sleep. This is obviously why Spenserian eroticism is so bad and disabling, and so central a model for the corruption of chivalry; the question, however, that goes to the heart of Spenser's psychopathology, is why it should be a model of sex.

Notes

1. Quotations from *The Faerie Queene* are from the edition of A. C. Hamilton (Longman, 2007). The letters *u* and *v* have been normalized.

2. The text is that of Helen Gardner, *Divine Poems of John Donne* (Oxford, U.K.: Clarendon Press, 1964).

NINE

Eliding Absence and Regaining Presence

The Materialist Allegory of Good and Evil in Bacon's Fables and Milton's Epic

CATHERINE GIMELLI MARTIN

As most allegorists have long been aware, Walter Benjamin's most signal contribution to the theory of allegory was to reject the German Romantic aesthetics of the symbol followed by most mainline English critics from Coleridge onward. In this enduring Romantic and post-Romantic tradition, the symbol had been to allegory as presence is to absence: As the symbol's inferior mental "supplement," the allegorical sign pointed toward an essential "Being" it did not share. The symbol, by contrast, actually partook of its transcendental object either aurally, visually, or both. Benjamin's reversal of this logocentric assumption not only anticipated Derrida's famous critique of Rousseau's elevation of "ineffable" speech over the written sign in *Of Grammatology*, but at the same time recuperated the "fallen," post-sacramental sign system of "ruined" allegory. This late allegorical mode was the by-product of Protestant iconoclasm's gradual subjection of all visible signs of transcendent truth to the skepticism with which they regarded the Catholic miracle of transubstantiation. Among English writers, Benjamin found this skepticism most clearly epitomized in Shakespeare, especially in *Hamlet*. Here the tragic hero embarks on a famously failed quest for tangible proof of his father's murder, a quest that Stephen Greenblatt directly links to the loss of transubstantiation.[1] More generally, Hamlet's inability utterly to separate guilt from innocence in Claudius, his possible accomplices, himself, or even his murdered father recapitulates the linguistic divide that Shakespeare and his contemporaries linked to the original fall of man. Foreshadowing the second fall of language at Babel, Adam's lapse not only initiated a tragic divorce of words from things but, as Donne famously lamented, made the first marriage "our funeral."

Yet other seventeenth-century thinkers took a considerably less pessimistic approach to the fall, one that virtually erased the unbridgeable gulf that Donne's *First Anniversarie* places between Adam's pre- and postlapsarian condition.[2] Francis Bacon's reinterpretation of Genesis influenced an entire new generation who would argue (as Milton does in his *Areopagitica*) that our exile from Eden is ultimately reversible, that the dividing line between guilt and innocence has always been "fruitfully" ambiguous, and that slippery verbal signifiers are neither fatal nor limited to postlapsarian existence.[3] Truth rightly has "more shapes then one," and her temple—which Milton claimed was rapidly being rebuilt in England—is not ideally seamless.[4] *Paradise Lost* continues this linguistic line of thought by refusing to identify closure with Eden or confusion exclusively with Chaos or hell. As Victoria Kahn observes, the poem not only inverts the traditional opposition between paradise and open-endedness but makes the boundless sphere that "Christianity has traditionally marked with the fall" into the essence of Eden. This inversion is the ultimate result of Milton's "free will" argument, which both Kahn and Blair Hoxby directly link to Bacon's promotion of the free circulation and testing of new ideas as the only remedy for humankind's impaired "estate."[5] Yet Milton critics still tend to ignore how radically this reversal of older assumptions about openness and closure erases the old gap between presence and absence in the "ruined allegory" of *Paradise Lost*, which additionally alters its representation of good and evil.[6] Clinging to the standard assumption that Milton's Sin is a metaphysical "nothing" as in Saint Augustine (where sin is the mere "privation" of the good) further obscures how Bacon's revival of animist materialism contributes to these alterations. Even critics who focus on the new materialism fail to perceive how animism radically transforms Milton's Sin and Death. Gaining a complex dynamics and a genealogy utterly lacking in Spenser's Errour, they share many key characteristics with the allegorical personae who in both Bacon's *Advancement of Learning* and *The Wisdom of the Ancients* not only symbolize physical forces but often "embody" the living presence of matter. Yet Stephen Fallon is hardly alone in confining Milton's atomism to the material world created by God and consigning degenerate "beings" like Sin and Death to nonentity.[7]

In what follows, we will see that Sin and Death's effects on the real world are every bit as real and lasting as they are in ours, where evil (pain, fear, loss, and so forth) is no mere "nothing" with no lasting consequences. In failing to return to the absence out of which the traditional Christian God creates everything, Sin and Death inhabit a complex amalgam of presence and absence in an epic where not even "the Spirits damn'd/Lose all thir virtue." Here evil not only partakes of the good, but good can be distinguished from "close ambition varnish'd o'er with zeal" only by trial and error (*PL* 2.482–485).[8] In essence, this means that *Areopagitica*'s "mixed" description of our postlapsarian state also applies to the prelapsarian worlds of heaven and Eden:

> Good and evil we know in the field of this World grow up together almost inseparably; and the knowledge of good is so involv'd and inter-woven with the knowledge of evill, and in so many cunning resemblances hardly to be discern'd, that those confused seeds which were impos'd on Psyche as an incessant labour to cull out, and sort asunder, were not more intermixt. It was from out the rinde of one apple tasted, that the knowl-edge of good and evil as two twins cleaving together leapt forth into the World. And perhaps this is that doom which the *Adam* fell into of know-ing good and evil, that is to say of knowing good by evil. As therefore the state of man now is; what wisdom can there be to choose, what conti-nence to forbeare without the knowledge of evill? (*CPW* 2:514)

Although Satan has no prior knowledge of evil when he first consorts with Sin in heaven, his experience of her "cunning" resemblance to truth and beauty is essentially the same as Adam's because Milton never argues here or elsewhere that good can *only* be known by evil, as the medieval theory of the "fortunate fall" taught.[9] On the contrary, while the "twins" of sinful and innocent desire are eerily similar, they are ultimately distin-guishable by the light of reason alone. Reason is thus "but choosing" the less sinister course of trusting one's Maker, who in turn entrusts his crea-tures with the gift of free will. Without it, God would have created "a meer artificiall *Adam*," not an independent subject "free . . . [to seize] a provok-ing object, ever almost in his eyes; [for] herein consisted his merit, herein the right of his reward, the praise of his abstinence" (*CPW* 2:527). *Paradise*

Lost illustrates Milton's ongoing belief that both freedom and right reason can be maintained only by refusing to turn the "provoking object" into an idol. Eve fails this test not merely by eating an apple but by turning it into an idol of power she cannot live without. Kenneth Gross usefully defines this all-too-human tendency as the "ironic twin" of rational or provident choice, a selfish desire "to subject a life *other* than its own to the reductions of idolatry," or objectification. Its positive twin, the opposite of turning living things into reified objects, consists in endowing dead things with psychic life and thereby emulating a Creator for whom all life is a "thou," not an "it" or an object. Gross's analysis clearly draws both on Martin Buber and on Bacon's most undisputed philosophical heir, Giovanni Battista Vico, in explaining Spenser's understanding of idolatry, and it is equally clear that Milton is indebted to both Bacon and Spenser. All three show that no "single act of iconoclasm [can] ever finally cut off the proliferating magical error of idolatry."[10]

Nevertheless, Bacon's *Advancement of Learning* more profoundly influenced Milton than Spenser because it alone questions and revises the traditional interpretation of Adam's fall. Disconnecting it from "knowing" in the simple biblical sense of aspiring to forbidden knowledge, Bacon actually argues that God's "commandments or prohibitions were not the originals of good and evil" at all. The causes of Adam's transgression were more complex than that because both sin and innocence are contingent on what knowledge *means* to the seeker. In itself, "natural knowledge" was never forbidden, so God's interdiction on the apple must have constituted a test of obedience, not a decree of perpetual ignorance. By failing this test Adam and Eve chose "to make a total defection from God, and to depend wholly upon" themselves, thereby gaining a forbidden and unfortunate knowledge of moral evil, not any truly desirable wisdom. They did gain the capacity to decide right and wrong for themselves, but they also lost the integrity needed to decide correctly or unselfishly. This choice was obviously an *ethical* rather than an *empirical* mistake, as shown by Adam's earlier, innocent inquiries into the nature of the "creatures, and the imposition of names" on them. That knowledge was also properly godlike, a just reflection of the divine image in Adam (cf. *PL* 4.288–293) rather than an unjust usurpation of divine prerogative. Only the latter act impaired the *imago dei*, right reason, by denying the Creator's rightful position as moral architect and lawgiver. By violating his sole "covenant" or requirement to accept the gift of paradise in return for a single fruit, Adam and Eve nevertheless did more damage to their moral judgment than to their *material* ability to fulfill the original command to inquire into nature and to "dress and keep" their garden.[11] That capacity was clearly retained both by our "Grand Parents" and by all their heirs.

Bacon's careful distinctions not only draw a much thinner line between forbidden and unfallen knowledge than the earlier Christian tradition admitted but makes sin less the result of *what* one knows than of how and why one knows it. While attempting to penetrate the rationale behind God's absolute moral imperatives is always evil, objectively or abstractly knowing anything else—including, as *Areopagitica* argues, the physical nature and consequences of evil—is not. Even human language remained essentially unfallen once Bacon eliminated the ancient platonic divide between philosophy and rhetoric, or true "knowing" and false linguistic embellishment. In his view, *both* philosophy and rhetoric can lead to truth or falsehood because both are forms of verbal experimentation needed to sift true from false knowledge. Thus rhetoric "can be no more charged with the colouring of the worst part, than Logic with Sophistry, or Morality with Vice. For we know the doctrines of contraries are the same, though the use be opposite" (*Works* 3:411). This means, in essence, that not our methods but only their results, the uses to which they are put, determine right or wrong. Milton supports these distinctions when he reveals the cause of Satan's fall into evil, which, as the latter admits, is not the possession of too much or too little knowledge but rather a willful blindness to God's creative capacities and tangible gifts (*PL* 4:3170).. That distinction allows both the unfallen and the fallen Adam to pursue sinless inquiries into matters classified as "forbidden knowledge" as recently as Marlowe's composition of *Doctor Faustus*. In the process, the great Augustinian divide between angelic presence or "fullness of being" and human deficiency or lack is largely overcome.[12] Here, as in *The Advancement of Learning*, the "light whereof man did give names unto other creatures in Paradise" exemplifies the "pure knowledge of nature and universality" God intended for all his creatures, human and angelic alike. Knowledge even constitutes the highest possible form of divine worship (*Works* 3:264, *PL* 3:693–704), for, as Bacon insists, truly to reflect the Creator and the glory of his creation requires an endless and infinite exploration of his kingdom:

> Salomon . . . affirmeth that the eye is never satisfied with seeing, nor the
> ear with hearing; and if there be no fullness, then is the continent greater

than the content: so of knowledge itself and the mind of man, whereto the senses are but reporters . . . not only delighted in beholding the variety of things and vicissitude of times, but raised also to find out and discern the ordinances and decrees which through all these changes are infallibly observed. (*Works* 3:265)

Discerning God's "ordinances and decrees" thus means that "knowledge is power," as Bacon famously proclaimed, but no longer in a sinister sense. Because our understanding is perverted only when we try to do the impossible—to become the boundless godhead himself—"sin" is now limited to violent or deluded usurpations of divine wisdom and moral prerogative. So long as we avoid the delusions of wrongful pride, "sinful" human aspiration ceases to exist. Aspiration in itself can still be evil, good, or neutral, but its evil aspects are largely confined to ethical overreaching. The same applies to the means of gaining knowledge, which are no longer neatly divided on pre- and postlapsarian lines and generally incline more toward the good. Yet, while Bacon thereby expands the realm of innocence, the realm of evil is also expanded once humans gain an inalienable capacity to construct "*authentic*" other selves susceptible to self-worship and idolatry. Satan, Adam, and Eve all suffer from this fate after they seize God's rightful place and materially alter their spiritual and physical condition. Nevertheless, as Bacon teaches, even this alternation is materially reparable. Satan first recognizes this fact on Mount Niphates (*PL* 4.91–94), where he comes close to repentance and (had he succeeded in repenting) redemption. Here, as throughout Milton's epic, God's "permissive will" (*PL* 3.685) makes such "soul-building" choices inevitable as creaturely processes of speech participate in the processes of creation (*PL* 7.178).

Both Bacon and Milton construct this free-will theology on a Hebraic rather than an Augustinian or Greek understanding of sin. No longer a deeply mysterious "lapse" from a passive fullness of being, like both free will and good works, sin is as active and creative as integrity or obedience. Gross traces the Hebraic understanding of sin to the Jewish appraisal of the pagan idols, which Bacon in turn follows in his own theory of the Idols. According to this Hebraic tradition, "The dead or never living idol that is no-thing is also the vessel of the freedom, the violence, and the stress of the human imagination in search of its gods." Although an idol may be simply vacant, as the pagan gods were for Augustine, it may also contain sacred or true images "reduced to mechanism, a mystery become a temporal institution subject to the rule of a selfish priesthood" or narcissistic self.[13] The

New Testament preserves this Hebraic understanding of idolatry, when it explains how temptation allures its victim with "his own lust" that, when fertile, "conceives" and brings forth the actual "body" of sin, which is death (James 1:13–15). If this account is taken literally, lust materially engenders a newly sinful and deadly being, but not automatically. At one point in its evolution, the fallen state remains reversible because being "enticed" is not the same as either "seizing on" or "conceiving" sin or death. Both Milton's "yet sinless" Adam and Eve clearly recognize this fact after Eve dreams a sinfully tempting dream implanted in her vital spirits by Satan. The awakened Adam then comforts her by saying that her very abhorrence of this vision means that it has come and gone "without spot or blame" (*PL* 5.119). Both next call on God to disperse "aught of evil" the dream contained "as now light dispels the dark" (*PL* 5. 207–208), and he graciously responds by sending Raphael, who helps Eve understand (as she later informs Adam) that temptation in itself

> . . . precedes not sin: only our Foe
> Tempting affronts us with his foul esteem
> Of our integrity; his foul esteem
> Sticks no dishonor on our Front, but turns
> Foul on himself; then wherefore shunn'd or fear'd
> By us? (*PL* 9.327–332)

This passage is usually (and rightly) connected to Milton's Areopagitican claim that that "which purifies us is triall, and triall is by what is contrary" to innocence, although, in retrospect, Eve should have been more fearful of the attractions of idolatry. Yet the passage is not correctly connected to the idea that sin is a mere "nothing." Eve rightly rejects "unexercis'd" and spotless notions of purity (*CPW* 2:515) because virtue and vice are interdependent and interactive, not absolute opposites, which means that resisting the latter strengthens the former. The process also works in reverse, so that even after Adam and Eve fall into sin and death, repentance and good works prevent them and their world from declining into absolute perversion. Instead, they are punished with "a long day's dying" into a material dust whose atoms can create renewed life in a restored paradise (*PL* 10.964).[14] In the meantime, the human interaction with nature remains ambiguously susceptible of producing good or evil depending on the motivations behind human invention, as the contrast between the Sons of Seth and Daughters of Cain later shows. Bacon anticipates this allegorical passage by affirming that the lovers of truth command nature by obeying her (*Works* 4:47), while her false philosophers or "lovers" subject her to the status of a concubine or second-class "mate." Like Milton's Sin, these mates at first appear beautiful, but their mistreatment creates an imbalance that ultimately recoils on their masters.[15] For both Milton and Bacon, this potential for corruption cannot be removed from sexual, philosophical, or natural knowledge, from which it may spread into matter's infinitely malleable forms. Originating in the formless Chaos that both adapt from Lucretius and the Greek mythographers, matter is thus not a dead but a living force that never loses its capacity for vital transformation, positive or negative.[16]

BACON'S FABLES AND MILTON'S COSMOS

Bacon's two fables of "Cupid, or the Atom," and of "Coelum, or the Origin of Things" in *The Wisdom of the Ancients* seem most directly to have influenced Milton's rejection of Augustine's ex nihilo creation theory, a philosophical by-product of the platonic view of matter as something inherently unclean, godless, and devoid of spirit (*Timaeus* 30a). Bacon's "demiurge," Cupid, overcomes the isolation of spirit from matter by participating with Coelum, the primordial material principle also known as Ouranos, or the formless heavens, in creating order from chaos. Milton's Son does much the same thing when he creates our universe from the "void and formless" atoms of Chaos (*PL* 3.12), the primal space from which a new cosmos arises on the brink of the same "heav'nly shore" (*PL* 7.210) that expelled Satan. Separating "first" or fully atomic matter from its chaotic substrate, the Son's "great divorcing command" (*CPW* 2: 273) thrusts the "infernal dregs" of preatomic life back into the infinite abyss of Chaos (*PL* 7:225–242). Yet, as in Bacon's fable, these chaotic dregs do not actually dissolve into dungeon-like inactivity but remain in a "place of perturbation" midway between heaven and Earth. Here "fragility or mortality and corruption have their chief cooperation" unless the creator-Cupid reorders them (Bacon, *Works* 6:724). He does this by infusing chaotic particles with the same vital energy that Milton ascribes to "Light/Ethereal, first of things, quintessence pure/Sprung from the Deep" (*PL* 7.243–245). Milton's Light and the Son thus share the creative powers Bacon gives to Cupid, and as in his fables, Chaos remains profoundly ambiguous, at once the "Womb of nature and perhaps her Grave" (*PL* 2.911). Yet in neither case is this ongoing source of both creation and destruction either unclean or innately distinct from "pure" matter.

Milton emphasizes the continuities between Chaos and creation by showing that light itself possesses a "dark Nativity" and malleability not unlike the unformed particles of Chaos (*PL* 6.478–487). Like Bacon's "notable commotions in the heavenly regions," its formless realm is also fruitful because its ambiguity permits "the power of the Sun" (or Son) to restore the order temporarily lost as "inundations, tempests, winds, earthquakes" shake the lower or chaotic levels of the universe. After these periodic but inevitable inundations, Bacon assures his readers that both the higher and lower regions settle into a "more durable state of consent and harmonious operation" (*Works* 6:724). Again, much the same thing occurs in Milton's epic after the War in Heaven: Creative order succeeds destructive strife without completely supplanting it, for, as Bacon explains, cosmic matter was never (as Aristotle falsely taught) innately inclined to "privation" or rest (*Works* 6:729–730). Milton's antiprelatical and divorce tracts earlier endorse similar ideas: Material life demands a "struggle of contrarieties" common to all "elementall and mixt things," which "cannot suffer any change of one kind, or quality into another without" it (*CPW* 1:795). Even heavenly matter undergoes strife, for there as everywhere, life springs from a periodic contest of concord and discord, love and hate (*CPW* 2.272). Thus in heaven, as on Earth, evil is primarily an organic imbalance in the hateful direction, although its periods of perversion at once dissipate and renew all things (*PL* 10.616–640), for, without contraries, nothing exists.

Bacon expands on this cosmic paradigm in his famous fable of Pan, or Nature, commonly regarded as the most important chapter of his hugely popular *Wisdom of the Ancients*. Integrating three different yet equally "true" traditions about Pan's origins, Bacon makes his "all-god" represent the entire span of nature from heavenly balance to destructive strife (*Works* 6:711). His fable opens with the speculation that Pan may be either "the offspring of Mercury—that is of the Divine Word (an opinion which the Scriptures establish beyond question, and which was entertained by all the more divine philosophers); or else of the seeds of things mixed and confused together," as "Virgil sang." Never a slave to either/or logic, Bacon decides that both traditions possess elements of truth, which seems to explain why Milton gives both the Word or Son and Chaos important roles in creation. Bacon then recounts a third or purely postlapsarian interpretation of Pan as "the state of the world, not at its very birth, but as it was after the fall of Adam, subject to death and corruption." He decides that this myth must refer to Pan's tragic rebirth as the joint "offspring of God and Sin"; but, even in that form, he retains his roots in "the Divine Word" that created him "through the medium of confused matter (which is itself God's creature)." Nevertheless, after "sin and corruption enter" into nature (*Works* 6:709), Pan takes on the "new nature" that Milton ascribes to his chief allegorical personae, Sin and her son Death (*PL* 10:706–719), a contaminated nature limited only by the force that Bacon identifies with Pan's sisters, the Fates. By measuring "the births and durations and deaths of all things," they conserve the cosmos by decreeing that it will eventually return to its unfallen state. Milton follows suit when he shows that the God whose "will is Fate" (*PL* 7.173) will never permit natural depravity to become total: Sin and Death will die either temporarily or forever (*Works* 6:709–710, *PL* 10. 616–640).

Bacon mythically associates this divine promise with the image of Pan's horns: "Broad at bottom and narrow at top," they illustrate "the fact that the whole frame of nature rises to a point like a pyramid" eventually touching heaven because "the summits, or universal forms, of nature do in a manner reach up to God" (*Works* 6:710). Pan's horns also symbolize the entire "body of nature," which "is most truly described as biform," for, as Milton says, only God himself is single and "alone/From all Eternity" (*PL* 8.405–406). Bacon locates the difference between nature and God in the "very ingenious allegory involved in that attribute of the goat's feet," its split hoof, which allows the half-animal, half-divine goat-god to represent the paradoxical unity and division of the lower and higher species. The goat also represents the creaturely ability to climb upward toward the stars or downward "to the lower world" like the "body" of nature itself (*Works* 6:710–711). The body of Milton's "one first matter" behaves in precisely the same way, evolving and devolving through an integrated life chain of lower and higher forms. Here "all things proceed" from and return to God "if not deprav'd from good" (*PL* 5. 470–471), as they dynamically climb from matter's dark root to its symbolic "green stalk, from thence the leaves/ More aery, last the bright consummate flow'r/Spirits odorous breathes" (*PL* 5. 479–482). Milton also alludes to Bacon's "primal" Pan as the essence of Eden's unfallen nature: In paradise the "Universal *Pan*/Knit with the *Graces* and *Hours* in dance/Led on th' Eternal Spring" of natural renewal (*PL* 4:266–668). Like Bacon's first state of nature, this one is tragically doomed to destruction yet not beyond the possibility of repair.

The many editions of Bacon's *Wisdom of the Ancients* gloss other closely related myths about nature's "confused" but reparable state, consistently teaching that natural mutability does not indicate an irreversible "Donnean" decline because conflict is inherent in creation. Milton early supported this claim in his Latin poem, *Naturam Non Pati Senium* ("Nature is Not Subject to Old Age"), which describes "decay theory" as one of the persistent "errors by which the wandering mind of man is . . . overwearied" and darkened (1–2, Hughes's translation). While not adopting Bacon's device of using Pan's pipes and sheep-hook or staff as evidence of the divine promise that natural harmony will always triumph over destructive strife, Milton's poem similarly argues that "by founding the stars more strongly" than the shades of "Stygian Dis," the "omnipotent Father . . . has fixed the scales of fate with sure balance and commanded every individual thing in the cosmos to hold to its course forever" (31, 33–36). As in Bacon, there are intermittent "commotions" in the heavens (ll.16–32) that will return at the Last Day; but, in the meantime, "the elements do not vary from their faith" despite the shock of lightening bolts, storms, and harsh seasons (51–55). Bacon finds these natural variations symbolized in Pan's staff, which like "eternal" nature can never be "straightened," for "all the works of Divine Providence in the world are wrought by winding and roundabout ways" that the human race must imitate in order to be repaired. Here Bacon's idiosyncratic synthesis of "straight and crooked" distantly recalls the "mazy error" of Milton's Eden (*PL* 4.239), whose irregularly wandering paths are not only innocent but beneficent.[17] Designed to accommodate curious gardeners who seek winding but sinless knowledge, Eden ironically prepares Adam and Eve for the trackless wilderness they must enter after their fall.

Bacon further strains his allegory to make a similar point about the shepherd-god Pan, who, as the "god of hunters," was the first deity to point the path to recovery. He did this by discovering Proserpina's lost and distraught mother Ceres while out hunting. As in *Naturam Non Pati Senium* (10), Ceres' "all-generating womb" conventionally stands for earthly fertility, so his role in her recovery further explains why Pan is the "all-god." He epitomizes "every natural action, every motion and process of nature, [which] is nothing else than a hunt. For the sciences and arts hunt after their works, human counsels hunt after their ends, and all things in nature hunt either after their food . . . or after their pleasures" (*Works* 6: 711). In Milton's Eden, this hunt may be as playful as the lion's innocent pursuit of the kid (*PL* 4.343–344), as abstract as Adam's inquiry into astronomy, or as practical as his postlapsarian "invention" of fire to repair the defects of Earth's altered climate (*PL* 10.1065–1080). Like Bacon, Milton links the need for this repair to the "rape" of Prosperina or Eve by "Dis" or Satan (*PL* 4.269–270), a mythical allusion pointedly placed next to his reference to the "Universal *Pan*" who once reigned in Eden.

This placement points to both the tragedy of Eden's loss and its potential for recovery, for Milton's Adam will also learn that "very true and wise admonition" Bacon derives from Pan's recovery of Ceres. This is, "namely, that the discovery of things useful to life and the furniture of life, such as corn, is not to be looked for from the abstract philosophies, as it were the greater gods, no not though they devote their whole powers to that special end—but only from Pan; that is from sagacious experience and the universal knowledge of nature, which will often by a kind of accident, as it were while engaged in hunting, stumble upon such discoveries" (*Works* 6:713). The fruits of this empirical "hunt" far exceed the barrenness of scholastic abstraction, methods far too rigid or "straight" to be fertile. Adam proves this truism by accidentally discovering fire and whatever "else may be remedy or cure/To evils which our own misdeeds have wrought" (*PL* 10:1078–1080), while his abstract reasoning fails to reveal the "secrets" of planetary motion. Raphael had already prepared the way for his later success by emphasizing the value of pragmatic observation over barren speculation, a lesson Adam eagerly and innocently embraces (*PL* 8.167–178, 188–197). Thus as Milton's *Of Education* claims, we, too, may "repair the ruins of our first parents by regaining to know God aright, and out of that knowledge to love him, to imitate him, to be like him . . . by orderly conning over the visible and inferior creature" (*CPW* 2: 366–367, 369)

Other aspects of Bacon's fable of Pan vary the "recovery" theme by emphasizing its opposite, the ruin of Pan's promise by false methods or (to use Bacon's metaphor) barren "marriages." Here he focuses on Pan's sterile marriage to Echo, his apparently "perfect" reflection. Admitting that Echo's faithful repetition of nature's sounds (the origin of human words) allowed her "most faithfully [to repeat] the voice of the world itself, . . . being indeed nothing else than the image and reflexion of it," he adds that unfortunately she "only repeats and echoes [it], but adds nothing" of her own. Such a bride may be a fit partner for Nature from the divine perspective; but, from the lower, creaturely perspective, Echo's works in the world are too parrotlike and sterile to bear fruit. Bacon draws a similar conclusion from the fact that Echo's only child with Pan was Iambe, a crooked little woman who delayed

Ceres's search for Proserpina by relating "vain babbling doctrines about the nature of things, . . . doctrines barren in fact, counterfeit in breed, but by reason of their garrulity sometimes entertaining; and sometimes again troublesome and annoying" (*Works* 6:714, 709). Freely inventing this legend out of a quite different story in Apollodorus, Bacon suggests that a better "child" than Iambe would have been born to Pan and Echo if her art and his nature were truly married. He symbolizes this happier union in the "true" marriage of Atalanta or "Art" with her suitor Hippomenes or "Nature." Yet for this union to bear fruit, the old tale must be rewritten: Atalanta must ignore the vain baubles that Hippomenes casts in her path so she can beat her slower suitor in a new and fairer race. No longer subjugated to her "husband," Nature, the swiftness of her Art combined with her newly willing and "free" fidelity to Hippomenes will physically and morally restore the human race. Failing to pursue this course will, on the other hand, condemn the human race to the "crookedness" of Iambe-like "babbling" or false knowledge.

THE BIRTH AND EVOLUTION OF SIN, OR FALSE-CONSCIOUSNESS

Both Bacon's *Advancement of Learning* and his *Novum Organum* additionally embody Iambe's defects in Scylla, the "idol" of his prototypical false philosophers, the Scholastics. Scylla not only closely resembles Milton's Sin but also confirms her very real nature and her material effects on human life. Like Scylla, Bacon's ultimate image of false consciousness, Sin's deceptively seductive face thinly conceals a corrupt body literally capable of "poisoning" and deforming the minds and works of her admirers. Yet their fate is just because, like the Scholastics, they neither admire nor reflect the true body of nature but merely echo each other. By seeking only a straightened repetition of themselves, not a more ambiguous but also more fertile complement, they destroy their procreative powers along with those of their perverted "bride." Bacon's analysis of their self-idolatry is further linked to Milton's epic through Bacon's fable of Dionysus, the ultimate "father" of false knowledge and false worship in *The Wisdom of the Ancients*. An important but overlooked ancestor of Milton's Satan, Dionysus for Bacon represents the "dark side" of desire who, like the sinner of James 1:13–15, "seizes" an attractive but actually self-destructive good that produces no truly viable or useful offspring but Death. In the process, Dionysus predictably destroys his female "Other," although the victim in this case is his mother Semele, not Satan's "daughter," Sin. Yet because Milton's fallen female is also the mother of Death, the parallel is nearly exact. According to Bacon, the perverse relationship between Dionysus and Semele represents overheated passion's ability to seduce and be seduced by the "mother" of all desire, "the appetite and aspiration for apparent good," once "some unlawful wish" is "rashly granted before it has been understood and weighed." This intemperate heat at first warms but soon destroys its source, "the nature of the good" that "perishes in [its] flame" (*Works* 6:741). Fallen desire then recoils not just on its "mother" but also on her child or offspring. Although he is initially beautiful, Dionysus suffers such "prickling, pains, and depressions in the mind, that . . . [his] resolutions and actions labour and limp." He nevertheless disguises this deformity through "indulgence and custom," which allow him either to "assume . . . the mask of some virtue or [to] set . . . infamy itself at defiance" (*Works* 6:741).

Bacon shows that the mask of Dionysus often confounds his actions with those of Jupiter because he likes to assume a chariot of power "and leads the Muses in his train," seducing his followers into worshiping him instead of the true God. As in *Paradise Lost*, this seduction turns his followers into the inventors and founders of all "sacred rites and ceremonies . . . such as were fantastical and full of corruption, and cruel besides." These sacrifices simultaneously reflect Dionysus's "original sin" and its consequences, his "infinite insatiable appetite panting after new triumphs" to impress the pompous crew of "ridiculous demons" gleefully dancing about his chariot. In precisely the same way, Satan's "scoffing" followers dance about his concealed cannon on the penultimate day of Milton's War in Heaven, which darkly foreshadows their equally destructive "success" on Earth. Yet in neither realm can they conceal the true ugliness of uncontrollable passion, which "ever seeks and aspires after that which experience has rejected," ever objectifying repellent "others" who reflect their own deformities (*Works* 6:742). This retelling of the legend of Dionysus treats it primarily as moral or religio-political fable, not as a cautionary tale for empiricists, but Bacon's allegory of Scylla in *The Advancement of Learning* and the *Novum Organum* reveals the close link between the two.

Like Semele, Scylla is at once the "toy" and snare of selfish passions masked with the false face of knowledge, power, and beauty. This hollow idol in turn "mothers" all the sterile arts, sciences, customs, and theology that Milton's *Doctrine and Discipline of Divorce* embodies in its miniallegory of "Error" and her male counterpart, Custome. A similar allegory appears in *Paradise Lost* as the daughters of Cain seduce the "sons" of scientific and ethical knowledge into false worship and meretricious crafts (*PL* 11.576–591). Like Bacon's idols of the Cave, Tribe, Marketplace, and Theater, these *femmes fatales*—"So blithe, so smooth, so gay/Yet empty of all [practical] good" (*PL* 11.615–616) morally and physically corrupt everything they touch. As in Bacon, however, the root cause is the self-serving "abject and servile principles" of their male "victims," at once the inciters, accomplices, and casualties of their crimes. *The Doctrine and Discipline of Divorce* shows how truly reversible this gender blame-game is by depicting male "Custome" as "a meer face, as Eccho is a meere voice," an impotent veneer until he finds his other "self" in Error. She "being a blind and Serpentine body without a head, willingly accepts what he wants," so that this "couple" can conspire to "persecute and chase away all truth and solid wisdome out of humane life" until God calls a halt to their iniquities (*CPW* 2:223). At first confined to the cavelike mind's "tribal" fixations on habitual ideas and customs, their "infections" soon spread to the outward habits of language and action represented by Bacon's idols of the marketplace and theater. Here they subvert natural learning, law (in *The Doctrine and Discipline,* especially marital law), and finally human nature itself. Turning aside from God and true marriage, their victims seek the superficial physical satisfactions offered by Custome, Error, and the daughters of Cain. At first only a "ruin" in the realm of thought, their insidious effects finally inform every aspect of human endeavor. Because their pollution cannot be "purged" by any ritual means, as in *The Advancement of Learning,* nothing less than a sweeping cleansing of the inner and outer idols can holistically restore the true marriage of art and nature required by God's vitalistic continuum.

This Baconian model of redemption materially shapes the "free will defense" of *Paradise Lost* in four fundamental ways: (1) Milton's matter remains divinely "good" but also fully mutable and capable of being "deprav'd from good"; (2) providential time not only permits but requires change, although God's universal natural laws and moral dispensations are eternally preserved, not subject to the "fate" of old age; (3) comprehending and applying his laws free postlapsarian life from tyranny and superstition, the twinned idols everywhere condemned by both Bacon and Milton (*CPW* 4.1:535, *PL* 12.512); and (4) this understanding at least partially repairs or "cures" physical and human nature itself.[18] In this schema all creatures, fallen or unfallen, remain free to perfect or pervert themselves and others through idolatry, which makes anti-idolatry into the simultaneous vehicle of virtue, natural redemption, and human liberation. Bacon's Scylla and Milton's Sin obviously represent the evil potential of this freedom, the fatal fruit of the ruin created by idol-making or "Dionysian" desire. The false lovers or "philosophers" of these idols deform first their own minds and affections and then the feminine fertility of their "brides," who, like Echo, produce not unreal but deformed offspring. Bacon gives many names to these male betrayers—Plato, Aristotle, the alchemists and natural magicians—but the most enduring and pernicious remain the Scholastics who "distempered" human learning through their proud self-absorption and "theatrical" unwillingness to actually encounter rather than merely impersonate nature with their pompous, empty words and speeches. Like Dis or Dionysus, they create "female" victims whom they at once "ravish" and imprison in a bleak netherworld, when (as Bacon's fable of Prosperina reveals) a vital marriage of spirit and matter might have rescued them.

Many qualities embodied in Bacon's Proserpina resurface in Milton's portrait of the unfallen Eve, whose obvious antithesis is the false Athena erupting full-born from Satan's head as Sin. This epic event is substantially clarified by Bacon's nontraditonal retelling of the tale of Athena's birth, which does not associate it with wisdom but rather with narcissistic and criminal cannibalism. By consuming his pregnant wife Metis (whose name means "counsel") lest their "son" displace him, in Bacon's view Zeus deprived himself of the true counsel that Metis would have given him. Similarly sacrificing true negotiation and justice, he then enters the ranks of other selfish male lovers—Dis, Dionysus, Narcissus, and Pygmalion—who embody the intellectual and political tyranny of custom, tradition, and ceremony. By desiring only the apparent—not the real—good, Zeus dooms himself to remain a static and unproductive rather than a progressive or insightful ruler and Athena to become a mere prop or tool for his tyranny. Milton's Satan initially enters his version of this fallen state by seeking the uncritical counsel of the one angel who, aside from Sin herself, best reflects his "perfect image." Beelzebub's soothing echo of exactly what he wants to hear cleverly anticipates the actual birth of Sin by supinely "pleasing" Satan, who once "enamor'd" of Sin's seductively "attractive graces," seals their common fate (*PL* 2:762, 764–765). As when Echo weds Pan or Pygmalion weds Galatea, the result is an abortive repetition of themselves and their works without solid "matter," the inevitable effect of falling "in love with a picture" rather than a reality (Bacon, *Works* 3.284). Pygmalion particularly resembles both the Scholastics and Satan because he creates a subservient concubine to serve his every pleasure but loses the real "wife" whose fruitful "womb" could have borne him viable heirs or "works." The material result is male impotence and female perversion, which, in Scylla's case, is inflicted by her lovers' repetitiously "barking" and self-serving demands. Although she still has the attractive and "flattering . . . head and face of a virgin," these demands have "born" terrible "fruit": Her lower body is covered with "barking monsters, from which she could not be delivered" (*Works* 4:14). Unlike the Ovidian Scylla, whom she superficially resembles, these canine mouths are not the work of a wicked rival but of male betrayers and "fathers," whose pompous and "unprofitable subtility or curiosity" (*Works* 3.286) "sterilizes" her through the poison of false "love," or methods.

Milton's Sin suffers precisely the same fate: Her still attractive face disguises a body grotesquely deformed by the seductions of the original pseudophilosopher, Satan, and his all-too-deadly son, Death. As Sin's "inbred enemy," Death not only repeats but intensifies his father's crime against his mother by forcibly raping her and "ingend'ring" the "yelling Monsters that with ceaseless cry/Surround" her, hounds "hourly conceiv'd/And hourly born, with sorrow infinite"; for "when they list, into the womb/That bred them they return, and howl and gnaw" her "Bowels, their repast." Literally a repetition of a repetition, the "hideous Name" *Death* echoes through all Hell's "Caves" as his "sons" repeat his crime by viciously "hounding" their mother with "gnawing" terrors and vexations (*PL* 2.785, 788–789, 794–801. With "wide *Cerberean* mouths full loud," the "Hell Hounds" from which she cannot be delivered ring "a hideous Peal" as they "kennel" in Sin's womb "if ought disturb'd thir noise." Here they "still bark'd and howl'd/Within unseen," which explains why "Far less abhorr'd than these/Vex'd *Scylla* bathing in the Sea that parts/*Calabria* from the hoarse *Trinacrian shore*." No "uglier" creatures "follow the Night-hag" (*PL* 2: 654–662) who tortures Earth's natural children. Sin and her offspring thus share a modus vivendi far more lastingly detrimental to natural harmony than Ovid's literally sterile Scylla or even Spenser's Errour. With the help of the Redcrosse Knight, the latter simply joins her self-aborting brood and quickly perishes in the light they commonly hate. Yet Errour ironically cherishes her "children" while Sin's sons are abhorrent to the sense, sight, and ear of their parent.[19] They also produce the perpetual dissonance Milton associates with Chaos, although they lack its capacity to "hear" the creative voice of the Son, who like Bacon's Cupid, infuses "vital virtue . . . and vital warmth/Throughout" its "fluid Mass" (*PL* 7:236–237). Sin's children will thus predictably petrify and pervert that mass with their fatal bridge to hell, another illicit but real creation.

Here, as throughout Milton's epic, "barbarous dissonance" describes the deformed material sphere that Bacon associates with destructive "perturbations in the heavens," where art, nature, and "all life dies, death lives, and Nature breeds,/Perverse" (*PL* 2: 624–625). After the human fall, the monstrously material effects of Sin's "Sign/Portentous" (*PL* 2:760–761) are repeated on Earth by the "barbarous dissonance" of "that wild Rout that tore the *Thracian Bard/* in *Rhodope*, where Woods and Rocks had Ears/To rapture," but the worshipers of Dionysus, none. Drowning the divine harmony of Orpheus with their "savage clamor" (*PL* 7:32–36), they tear the poet limb from limb. Satan comes to embody the same savagery and artistic perversion after preferring his own "perfect image" to a real Other, indulging a desire for the "same" ultimately responsible both for Sin's deformity and for the repetitive desires and dissonance of their sons. By crafting a Galatea to fulfill his every narcissistic wish, he also breeds an empty Echo who bears only crippled, babbling, and tormenting children. As with Scylla, Bacon's allegory of false knowledge, and the Error of Milton's *Doctrine and Discipline of Divorce*, Sin's vicious side effects begin at the individual level and soon generate more widespread sociopolitical corruption as the "perfect" concubine wins over even the "most averse" to Satan's program with her "double-formed" charms (*PL* 2:762–763, 741). With her help, his cohort is seduced into thinking that his sophistic questions about right, precedent, and order are beyond real debate, as Satan's cynical evasion of Abdiel's objections shows. This mistake is especially fatal because Satan's only logical excuse for his rebellion is patently false: He claims that he owes no obedience to God because he and his crew are self-created "partners" of nature spontaneously generated from heaven's soil. Unlike Bacon's Lucretian paradigm, this is not a truly evolutionary argument but a baseless "barking" in the dark, a transparently self-contradictory excuse for usurping and hence perverting divine power. For if Satan actually believed that the angels were "born" equally, he could never claim the "natural" priority that he as an Archangel derives from the ancient "Orders and degrees" assigned by God (*PL* 5.792). In arguing that his customary and, from a Baconian perspective, "idolatrous" rights cannot be properly altered by the Son's elevation, he thus implicitly admits that a superior power originally *did* assign the old order.

As a result, satanic misrule is based upon a classical logical error: His major premise flatly contradicts his minor. Yet like Bacon's "barking" Scholastics, his crew finds even this Aristotelian error irrelevant because their motive is not philosophical proof but merely self-promotion.

THE MATERIAL EXPERIENCE OF EVIL

In a sense, then, Satan and his fallen angels *are* self-created by their own mental trickery and deceit, but not from nothing. Because even Milton's God does not create ex nihilo, evil must spring full born from the chaotic "matter" of the satanic mind, where it is first felt in his new sensation, bodily pain (*PL* 2.752). Like the physical wounds inflicted in Satan's "Ethereal substance" (*PL* 6.330) after he and his whole cohort experience pain during the War in Heaven, this laceration can heal but not before further impairing Satan's judgment and management of matter. Just as his body bleeds "a stream of Nectarous humor . . . /Sanguine," which stains "all his Armor . . . erewhile so bright" (*PL* 6.332–334), his rebellion "torments" the very air of heaven into a "Conflicting Fire" first of spears and then of cannons (*PL* 6.244–245, 584–589). The Archangel Michael confirms the fact that the stains suffered by heavenly matter or "Nature" are intolerable precisely because they are *not* unreal as he lectures Satan:

> Author of evil, unknown till thy revolt,
> Unnam'd in Heav'n, now plenteous, as thou seest
> These acts of hateful strife, hateful to all,
> Though heaviest by just measure on thyself
> And thy adherents: how hast thou disturb'd
> Heav'n's blessed peace, and *into Nature brought*
> *Misery, uncreated till the crime*
> *Of thy Rebellion?* How hast thou instill'd
> Thy malice into thousands, once upright
> And faithful, now prov'd false. But think not here
> To trouble Holy Rest; Heav'n casts thee out
> From all her Confines. Heav'n the seat of bliss
> Brooks not the works of violence and War.
> Hence then, and *evil go with thee along,*
> *Thy offspring, to the place of evil,* Hell,

Thou and thy wicked crew
. . . *with augmented pain.* (*PL* 6.262–277, 280, emphasis added)

Despite this dismissal, Michael soon finds (much like Satan after he lands on Earth) that evil is not so easily extinguished. A horrifically portable terror, Satan's inner wounds plunge him from "the lowest deep" to "a lower deep" still opening wide to "devour" its author, his accomplices, and their victims (*PL* 4.76–77). Even in heaven, it causes "such commotion, such as, to set forth/Great things by small, if Nature's concord broke," and "among the Constellations war were sprung" (*PL* 6.310–312). This havoc is soon multiplied by Satan's invention of cannon fire, an unquestionably material (if in heaven, temporary) form of destruction. Literally creating a hell-in-heaven, Satan diverts heaven's unformed rays in their "dark Nativity" from following their natural path into "beauteous, . . . ambient light," the natural source of every "Plant, Fruit, Flow'r Ambrosial, Gems and Gold" adorning the celestial landscape. Far beneath the "Ethereous mould whereon" they bloom, he finds "Deep under ground, materials dark and crude,/Of spiritous and fiery spume" that he can impregnate "with infernal flame" as powerful as the "Thunderer['s] dreaded bolt" (*PL* 6. 473–475, 478–483, 491). These explosive energies prove so effective that only the Chariot of God can quell them, especially because the good angels only worsen heaven's ruin by heaving its lovely hills on their enemies. Creating a still deeper hell-in-heaven, their fight then continues "under ground . . . in dismal shade" and

Infernal noise; War seem'd a civil Game
To this uproar; horrid confusion heapt
Upon confusion rose: and now all Heav'n
Had gone to wrack, with ruin overspread,
Had not th' Almighty Father where he sits
. . .
All power on him [the Son] transferr'd. (*PL* 6.666–671, 678)

It certainly can be no accident that this descent into hell begins at line 6.666 of the poem, the number of the beast who creates such physical havoc at the Last Day when a "new heavens and earth" must be recreated. As in Bacon's fables and Milton's divorce tracts, whenever two nearly equal creative forces contend (nearly equal because "sin hath [but] impair'd . . . / Insensibly" the demons), an entirely new phase of nature unfolds. Hell now appears on the far side of Chaos while heaven's "uprooted Hills" are repaired (*PL* 6.691–692, 781). At that point, the common seductress of the damned is appropriately made hell's portress, where she symbolically rules over an uprooted, smoky terrain further "tortured" by the demons' barking questions about fate and free will—questions that the unfree can never answer (*PL* 2.555–569). Yet they suitably thrive in a corrupted nature which "breeds/ Perverse, all monstrous, all prodigious things,/Abominable, inutterable, and worse/Than Fables yet have feign'd, or fear conceiv'd" (*PL* 2: 624–627).

Eve later exposes her children to this world of sin and death by allowing Satan to delude her with an "apparent" but insufficiently examined "good." Accepting the serpent's specious claim to have ascended the scale of nature by eating the forbidden fruit, she facilely believes that God favors ascent without exception or qualification, and that he will therefore gladly retract his interdiction on the apple. Yet, in an equally important sense, Eve follows the Baconian paradigm of the fall simply by deciding to become a law unto herself. Adam follows suit in claiming that he is literally "bonded" to Eve, idolizing his wife as "Bone of my Bone" and flesh of his flesh, a category error that soon turns her into a tormenting object, a "serpent" with whom he denies any kinship (*PL* 9.914, 10.867). Their rapid descent into delusion immediately brings bestiality and discord into both their marriage and into physical nature: Mother "Earth felt the wound, and Nature from her seat/ sighing through all her Works gave signs of woe" (*PL* 9.782–783). These birth pangs of evil literally "open" their world to the advent of the Infernal Triad: Satan and his offspring, the "Dogs of Hell" (*PL* 10:616), soon bridge the space between hell and Eden's "happier Seat," his gift to "his offspring dear" (*PL* 10:237–238). Yet Sin and Death's work is not commanded by their father, but naturally governed by a "secret amity [of] things of like kind" that spontaneously unites them with Death's sister, Discord, in establishing Bacon's third or fallen state of "Pan" on Earth. Discord sets Earth's creatures against one another while her siblings construct a fit "Monument/Of merit high to all th' infernal Host," the hellish bridge or "pontifex" that spreads their cold, dry repetition of deathlike sameness throughout their evil empire. Their vulturelike "amity" or codependence perverts everything in their path, creating a new hell-in-paradise: "carnage, prey innumerable, and . . . /. . . Death from all things . . . that live" (*PL* 10:258–259, 268–269).

This new creation obviously parodies the first, benign birth of nature or Pan from the Divine Word and the "confused seeds" of things, yet it is not simply a false mirror or illusion. Harkening to the voice of "Satan our great Author," his children "Both from out Hell Gates into the waste/Wide Anarchy of *Chaos* damp and dark/Flew diverse, and with Power (thir Power was great)" hover "upon the Waters" in a malign imitation of God's brooding holy spirit (*PL* 10:236, 282–285, 7.234–235). Here they build a pyramid of decay where spontaneous life once reigned. Spurning the confused yet fertile "pregnant causes mixt" of Chaos, they frigidly cement its lowest life forms together with whatever "they met/Solid or slimy" or "petrific" (*PL* 2. 913, 10:285–286). The great Anarch Chaos protests this perversion, but he is helpless to prevent their conversion of his fluid protoelements into the rigidity of frozen waste. Like "two Polar Winds blowing adverse," Sin and Death drive nature's fertile seeds into "Mountains of Ice," as Death becomes an anti-Neptune. His "Mace petrific, cold and dry, /As with a Trident smote, and fix't as firm/As *Delos* floating once; the rest his look/Bound with *Gorgonian* rigor not to move,/And with *Asphaltic* slime" (*PL* 10:289, 291, 294–298). Their new creation thus embraces every level of life, oceanic, airy, or "animal," because life begins and remains rooted in the sea (*PL* 7.387–398).

Milton grimly puns on these holistic effects by describing Sin and Death's path as a "smooth, easy, inoffensive," an indefensible wound in God's "now fenceless World" (*PL* 10:305, 303). Like Xerxes' attack on the free cities of Greece, Death's unnatural "yoking" of potentially creative waters with "wondrous art/Pontifical" makes his bridge "all fast, too fast. . . . /And durable" (*PL* 10:307, 312–313, 319–320). As ideologically "hard" as the false religion and politics they will promote, their misrule will abandon Pan's benignly "winding and roundabout ways" for the straightness of Dis's "dismal shades." Eden of course first feels the "pangs" that will eventually turn her innocently "serpentine" waters into the great Flood and make the garden a sterile "Island salt and bare" (*PL* 7:302, 11.834). Hence the "grim Feature[s]" of Sin and Death (*PL* 10:279) now "own" all of "Hell and this World, one Realm, one Continent/Of easy thorough-fare (*PL* 10:392–393). Yet they no longer govern (as they seem to assume) the true realm of Pan, because their misrule means that their access to heaven's door is now blocked, a limitation early emphasized as Satan sees Jacob's ladder descending either "to dare/The Fiend by easy ascent, or aggravate/His sad exclusion from the doors of Bliss" (*PL* 3.523–325). This new world's lack of heavenly harmony is also expressed in the noisy, dissonant vaunts of the Infernal Triad and their cohort. Satan's all-too-theatrical empire then erupts into contagious babbling and a "universal hiss" from the "innumerable tongues" of serpents, "the sound/Of public scorn" that supplants the demons' "high applause" and mocks the supplanter's "triumphal" return to hell (*PL* 10:505, 507–509). In the meantime, Earth's unfallen connection to heaven is restored by God's prevenient grace (*PL* 11.3), although maintaining that connection will now require answering work on humankind's part (*PL* 3. 185–197)—but work is the Baconian "cure" for the fall.

Hellish hissing is obviously another version of the "barbarous dissonance" that surrounds both Bacon's Scylla and Milton's Sin, another reminder of the generative limits of illusion and error, which may be fertile without being benignly constructive or enduring. Lacking any harmonious balance, Satan and his pseudophilosophers exemplify a horrifically real but also limited generativity as they turn into fabulous serpents possessing only dubious scientific reality.[20] This liminal status signals their ultimately abortive nature, yet in the short run, their destructive appetites prove as insatiable as Sin and Death, as real as the catalogue of "apostate" demons who will pervert pure worship among the Jews (*PL* 1. 376–521) and as truly detrimental to human productivity as Bacon's Idols of the Cave, Tribe, Marketplace, and Theater. As they are forced to chew delusive fruit resembling the apples of Sodom, Satan and his serpentine crew also predict Sodom's fateful perversions and foreshadow the all-too-enduring appeal of false fruit that "not the touch, but taste/Deceiv'd." Because its empty, ashy substance is fully concealed until it is "tasted," Satan and his demons persist in their "drugg'd" obsession with an object that, like the desires of Dionysus and Bacon's false philosophers, continually attracts though experience teaches otherwise. Consuming "fruits" that cannot quench their thirst or otherwise "deliver" them from evil, the demons appropriately feel the parching and freezing side effects associated with Death's world-bridging "span" and his "dark materials" (*PL* 10:563–564, 568, 556), the dark aspect of nature as we know it.

The epic's penultimate book more realistically depicts Sin and Death's bodily effects on humans in its Lazar House episode, which mainly emphasizes the medical consequences of idolatrous physical cravings. God graciously decrees that this "ruin," too, will be limited by fate, but the final reunion of "Heav'n and Earth renew'd" may be long delayed (*PL* 10: 638–640). In the interim, the idols of false desire, rhetoric, and philosophy can be repaired only as the marriage of Adam and Eve is restored, by regaining the once natural cooperation between "nature" and "art," or male and female. As respective symbols of these aspects of human life, the artful Eve and the naturally observant Adam must cooperatively preside over all God's "works, with good/Still overcoming evil, and by small/Accomplishing great things, by things deem'd weak/Subverting worldly strong, and worldly wise/By simply meek" (*PL* 12:565–569). This ethic demands a strenuously self-denying discourse utterly unlike the noisy barking of Scylla's boastful lovers, the clamorous self-adulation of a Dionysus or Pygmalion, or the babbling of the Babel-ish Iambe. In resisting these discourses, Adam and Eve will continue to discover God's providential "track Divine" in nature, the sure sign of his continuing "goodness and paternal Love" (*PL* 11:353–554). While they cannot escape the sorrows inflicted by murderous sons like Cain or the "wounds" that his idolatrous daughters inflict on Milton's true philosophers, the sons of God (*PL* 11.556–627), they remain free to raise or lower themselves and their environment on Pan's biform scale by producing either useful "fruit" or "furniture" for life, or nothing but crooked, corrupt, and crippled offspring.

In every way, then, Milton abandons the Christian tradition of Augustinian and Pauline dualism and adopts Bacon's monistic explanation of the fall. Although his allegoreisis may (like Bacon's) be somewhat backward looking, it also looks forward to an "enlightened" modernity that will typically identify false knowledge and idolatrous "priestcraft" as the chief culprits in humanity's destructive alienation from God and nature. In this he was joined by his fellow republican James Harrington, who compared false religion to an empty boast not only capable of "scratching and defacing human nature" but also of injuring "the image of God" himself. Harrington described this double offense as a "kind of murder" of the divine image in both humans and their environment.[21] Later in the eighteenth century, commentators as different as Edmund Burke and William Blake would follow Harrington and Milton in simultaneously psychologizing and materializing the effects of sin and death, which they Baconianly imagined as beginning with the rape or seduction of a "mother" and ending with a reign of intellectual and political inequity. In these later versions, a repressed or Dionysian id destroys a stable domestic situation and, by internalizing its master, becomes an "equally repressive version of the same," as Ronald Paulson has shown. As in Milton, the "essential dynamic . . . of energy, . . . contained in and vitalizing the human form" is depicted as fundamentally bipolar. It may give birth to a hell in the shape of "contorted, agonized creatures" Miltonically "associated with flames, flight, vortices, and serpents, . . . awesome and threatening, wonderful and sinister in potential"; yet, once these destructive impulses are mastered, this dynamic may give birth to a renewed Eden. Long after Milton and Bacon, the Idols who distort and thwart human and natural creativity thus continue to be allegorically conceived in physical terms; they are not empty abstractions but realities that threaten to pervert both the redeemed imagination and reformed science in a semi-Manichean contest of equal wills.[22]

Ambiguously plastic, these forces also continue to spring from a Chaos ultimately descended either from Bacon's mutable Coelum, the "night" of the universe, or from Milton's "pregnant causes mixt" in Chaos. Ironically anticipating the black holes discovered by modern science—which at once support nature and seem to threaten it with a final "big bang"—these fictions possess both a quasi-scientific truth and a real moral force because "antimatter" is still appropriately associated with all the evils besetting human life and "Mother" Earth, evils still as concretely real as emotional pain and environmental destruction.

Notes

1. Walter Benjamin, *The Origin of German Tragic Drama,* trans. John Osborne (London: New Left Books, 1977). On Hamlet and transubstantiation, see Catherine Gallagher and Stephen Greenblatt, *Practicing New Historicism* (Chicago: University of Chicago Press, 2000), 136–162.

2. One might argue that Donne's *First Anniversarie* does bridge this divide through the figure of Elizabeth Drury, yet her unattainable perfection actually signifies our far greater distance from Eden. Donne thus belongs to a more fully "ruined" phase of baroque allegory, as I show in "Unmeete Contraryes: The Reformed Subject and the Triangulation of Religious Desire in Donne's *Anniversaries and Holy Sonnets,*" in *John Donne and the Protestant Reformation*, ed Mary A. Papazian (Detroit, MI: Wayne State University Press, 2003), 193–220.

3. The Baconian influences on the young Milton were recorded by his first major biographer, David Masson, and more recently supported by Charles Webster, *The Great Instauration: Science, Medicine, and Reform 1626–1660* (New York: Holmes & Meier, 1976), and Christopher Hill's *The Intellectual Origins of the English* (Oxford, U.K.: Oxford University Press, 1965), 85–130. Unfortunately, Hill's later biography of Milton drops this influence in favor of a much more speculative positioning of the poet among the "radical Puritan underground." See *Milton and the English Revolution* (London: Faber and Faber, 1977). On Milton's skeptical linguistics and treatment of "slippery signifiers" in *Paradise Lost*, see Daniel Fried, "Milton and Empiricist Semiotics," *MQ* 37.3 (October 2003): 117–138.

4. John Milton, *Complete Prose Works*, 8 vols., ed. Don M. Wolfe et al. (New Haven, CT: Yale University Press, 1953–1982), 2:563. Milton's complete prose

works (CPW) will hereafter be cited in the text by volume and page number. On the nonseamless nature of truth, see 2:555. Milton cites Bacon twice in this tract alone.

5. Victoria Kahn, *Machiavellian Rhetoric: From the Counter-Reformation to Milton* (Princeton, NJ: Princeton University Press, 1994), 225. Blair Hoxby firmly anchors *Areopagitica* in Baconian discourse in *Mammon's Music: Literature and Economic in the Age of Milton* (New Haven, CT: Yale University Press, 2002).

6. For a more thorough discussion of this mode, see my *Ruins of Allegory: "Paradise Lost" and the Metamorphosis of Epic Convention* (Durham, NC: Duke University Press, 1998).

7. Stephen Fallon ably focuses on seventeenth-century materialism but follows Anne Ferry's and Maureen Quilligan's traditional opinion that Milton's Sin and Death have no "real" existence. He does recognize that Milton follows "Bacon [in] argu[ing] for the seamless continuity of inanimate and animate spirits" in a cosmos where "inert grosser matter is moved by tenuous pneumatic matter." Yet he primarily associates Milton not with Bacon's but with Anne Conway's materialism, although, as he admits, there are no common sources or any real comparison between Conway's cabbalistic and Milton's antimystical atomism (112–113, 118). For a summary of Ferry et al., see Stephen Fallon, *Milton among the Philosophers: Poetry and Materialism in Seventeenth-Century England* (Ithaca, NY: Cornell University Press, 1991), 183–190.

8. Milton's *Paradise Lost* is cited by abbreviated title (*PL*), book, and line number in Merritt Y. Hughes, *John Milton, Complete Poems and Major Prose* (New York: Odyssey Press, 1957).

9. Some critics, however, have found this teaching in *Paradise Lost*; for a refutation and related bibliography, see my article on "Self-Raised Sinners and the Spirit of Capitalism: *Paradise Lost* and the Critique of Protestant Meliorism." *Milton Studies* 30 (1994): 109–133.

10. Kenneth Gross, *Spenserian Poetics: Idolatry, Iconoclasm, and Magic* (Ithaca, NY: Cornell University Press, 1985), 39–41, 37.

11. Francis Bacon, *The Advancement of Learning*, in *The Works of Francis Bacon*, 14 vols., ed. James Spedding, Robert Leslie Ellis, and Douglas Denon Heath (London: Longman and Co., 1859), 3:296–297. Bacon's *Works* will hereafter be cited in the text by volume and page number.

12. On this aspect of the Baconian and "Miltonic" revolution, see Howard Schultz, *Milton and Forbidden Knowledge* (New York: Modern Language Association of America, 1955).

13. Gross, *Spenserian Poetics*, 27; on narcissism, see 35.

14. On mortalism in Milton's poetry, see Raymond B. Waddington, "Murder One: The Death of Abdiel: Blood, Soil, and Mortalism in *Paradise Lost*," *Milton Studies* 41 (2002): 76–93.

15. For an analysis of this paradigm in both Milton and Bacon, see my book chapter on "The Feminine Birth of the Mind: Regendering the Empirical Subject in Bacon and His Followers," in *Francis Bacon and the Refiguring of Early Modern*

Thought: Essays to Commemorate "The Advancement of Learning" (1605–2005), ed. Julie R. Solomon and Catherine G. Martin (Aldershot, U.K.: Ashgate, 2005), 69–88.

16. As I argue in "Fire, Ice, and Epic Entropy: The Physics and Metaphysics of Milton's Reformed Chaos," *Milton Studies,* ed. Albert C. Labriola. Pittsburgh, PA: University of Pittsburgh Press, vol. 35 (1997), 73–113, Milton's conception of Chaos is also based on original borrowings from Bacon's sources, Hesiod and other major Presocratic creation philosophers.

17. This familiar argument was first advanced by Christopher Ricks in *Milton's Grand Style* (Oxford, U.K.: Clarendon Press, 1963).

18. The term *free will defense* refers to Dennis Danielson's useful discussion of Milton's literary theodicy in *Milton's Good God* (Cambridge, U.K.: Cambridge University Press, 1982). On the political overlap between Bacon and Milton, see Hill, *The Intellectual Origins of the English Revolution,* and Richard Tuck, *Philosophy and Government 1572–1651* (Cambridge, U.K.: Cambridge University Press, 1993), 202–278.

19. For a fuller comparison of the contrasts between Spenser's Errour, Ovid's Scylla, and Milton's Sin (as well as her probable source in Bacon's Scylla), see my essay, "The Sources of Milton's Sin Reconsidered," *Milton Quarterly* 35, 1 (March, 2001): 1–8.

20. See Karen Edwards, *Milton and the Natural World* (Cambridge, U.K.: Cambridge University Press, 1999), 85–98.

21. James Harrington, *The Works of James Harrington,* ed. J. G. A. Pocock (Cambridge, U.K.: Cambridge University Press, 1977), 333.

22. Ronald Paulson, "Burke's Sublime and the Representation of Revolution," in *Culture and Politics: From Puritanism to the Enlightenment,* ed. Perez Zagorin (Berkeley: University of California Press, 1980), 248, 254, 256, 258–259.

PART FOUR

New Dimensions for Allegory

TEN

On Vitality, Figurality, and Orality in Hannah Arendt

KAREN FELDMAN

In *Life of the Mind*, Hannah Arendt offers an account of how abstract concepts and philosophical thought depend on what she initially refers to as "vitally metaphorical" language.[1] In most respects, Arendt follows a conventional explication of literality versus figurality, where figurative formulations pertaining to abstractions and "mental activities" derive from literal formulations pertaining to bodily experience. Nonetheless, a more profound, albeit veiled, role of the literal body—and specifically the mouth—in the activation of thought and the production of figurality emerges in key moments of Arendt's thought where speech is at issue. I will argue in this essay that the significance of speech for Arendt in effect situates the mouth at the center of philosophical thought and genuine politics. I will also suggest that this odd centrality of the corporeal mouth for her vision of political life bespeaks a dimension of figurality unaccounted for in Arendt. That is, although Arendt highlights the significance of "speech and action" in her definition of worldliness and politics, what precisely she means by "speech" and how speech both relates to and is differentiated from action remain ambiguous.

This essay therefore offers a double consideration of the significance of allegory in Arendt's reflections on language, philosophy, and action. On one hand, I will show that Arendt's account of philosophical metaphor in fact implicitly concerns allegory as it is conventionally understood—i.e., as extended metaphor. For insofar as Arendt declares that "*all* philosophical terms are metaphors" (*LM* 104, my emphasis) and extends philosophical metaphor from nouns to verbs and beyond, she implies that philosophical accounts are themselves extended figural representations—i.e., allegories in the textbook sense.

My goal, however, is ultimately to examine Arendt's narrative concerning the origins of philosophical thought as itself an allegory and thus to follow Hayden White, who writes, "A narrative account is always a figurative account, an allegory."[2] That is, I will suggest that Arendt's accounts of taste and speech allegorize—in the sense of actively demonstrate or enact—a general ungovernability in the relation of the body and language. Hence, Arendt's attempt to maintain a strict divide between life processes and the spheres of speech and judgment falters. In this respect, I will argue, Arendt's account of speech and action in *The Human Condition* evokes the difficulty of distinguishing speech from action and also literality from figurality. In other words, Arendt's own formulations concerning speech and action unwittingly allegorize, or dramatize, the difficulty of holding apart her central terms. This second, and more complex, consideration of allegory is therefore less an examination of Arendt's own understanding of metaphor and figurality than an observation of the ungovernable operations of such extended figurality in Arendt's own arguments. I thus attempt here to demonstrate in Arendt precisely what Angus Fletcher refers to in *Allegory: The Theory of a Symbolic Mode* as "our psychological and linguistic uncertainty as to what is going on when language is used figuratively."[3]

I. METAPHOR AND THE MOUTH

In volume one of *Life of the Mind: Volume 1*, entitled *Thinking*, Arendt claims that metaphor is the condition for all philosophical inquiry, insofar as abstract philosophical language borrows from concrete language. She offers as examples of such metaphorical borrowing the nouns *psyche* and *idea* (*LM* 104). Arendt goes on, however, to consider how we describe and account for "mental activities" by means of metaphors: "Mental activities, driven to language as the only medium for their manifestation, each draw their metaphors from a different bodily sense" (*LM* 110). Arendt's reference here to mental activities indicates that philosophical metaphors involve not just nouns but also verbs related to bodily senses; she points to the significance of terms related to the act of seeing in philosophical treatments of cognition, for instance (*LM* 110–112). Arendt's investigations in the same section of figural phrases and sentences in Plato, Aristotle, Nietzsche, and Wittgenstein (*LM* 114–118) indicate that figurality is to be found not only in nouns and verbs but in entire formulations. Such "extended" use of metaphorical language would be precisely associated with allegory in its conventional definition, but Arendt prefers the terminology of metaphor, perhaps because of its closer association with what she calls "poetic thinking."

Borrowing a phrase from Percy Shelley, Arendt explains that poetic language is "vitally metaphorical" insofar as it "'marks the before unapprehended *relations* of things and perpetuates their apprehension'" (*LM* 102). Arendt adds an Aristotelian gloss that a metaphor "discovers an intuitive perception of similarity in dissimilars" (*LM* 103). Expanding on the significance of these characterizations of metaphor for philosophical thought, Arendt then cites Kant to reiterate her point that it is only thanks to metaphorical language, borrowed from the realm of the body, that we are able to engage in "'abstract,' imageless thought" (*LM* 103) and to talk or write about "invisible mental activities" (*LM* 105). Arendt ultimately describes the act of thinking itself as one "whose language is entirely metaphorical and whose conceptual framework depends entirely on the gift of metaphor" (*LM* 123). Thus, in Arendt's explanation, "vitally metaphorical" language turns out to be a condition of thinking abstractly and hence of philosophizing, insofar as these depend on the vocabulary of bodily processes.

Given the importance of metaphor to philosophical inquiry, it is clear that for Arendt "vitally metaphorical" language is epistemologically productive, on one hand, because it discovers conceptual relations or even forms the condition of abstract thought. But on the other hand, "vitally metaphorical" thinking is, according to Arendt, also politically productive; for "[a]nalogies, metaphors and emblems are the threads by which the mind holds onto the world even when, absent-mindedly, it has lost direct contact with it, and they guarantee the *unity* of human experience" (*LM* 109). Metaphors do not just enable us to voluntarily transcend the enclosure of our private minds; rather, they connect us to the world without an act of will on our part. Thus for Arendt metaphorical thinking is a transcendental

condition of the persistence of worldly life beyond our voluntaristic participation in it. In this vein Arendt writes, "The metaphor, bridging the abyss
between inward and invisible mental activities and the world of appearances, was certainly the greatest gift language could bestow on thinking
and hence on philosophy" (*LM* 105).

Arendt's references to "the gift of metaphor" highlight how metaphorical (and, we might add, allegorical) language serves as a reserve or resource
used for thought and philosophy. But Arendt also characterizes metaphor
as a process or activity, one of borrowing, which produces the figurative
resources for "imageless thought". She writes,

> Language, by lending itself to metaphorical usage, enables us to think,
> that is, to have traffic with non-sensory matters, because it permits a
> carrying-over, *metapherein*, of our sensory experiences. There are not two
> worlds because metaphor unites them. (*LM* 102)

Here figurality is conceived as an agency or process that unites the nonsensory world with the world of the senses. In this regard, figurality would
be not only the stock of borrowed vocabulary, but also that which *performs*
the "bridging of the abyss" between bodily and mental activities. We see,
then, that for Arendt metaphor encompasses both the process of bridging nonsensory and sensory worlds *and* it is also the result of this process,
namely the reserve of useful figurative vocabulary for abstractions and mental activities.

Arendt's double portrayal of figurality, namely as both vehicle for and result of transfer from sensory to nonsensory realms, portrays the body as connected to abstract thought only allegorically (i.e., by metaphor). But Arendt
tacitly ascribes to the literal body more radical functions; for she also yokes
speech to thought in such a way as to suggest that thinking itself does not
exist without the literal, speaking mouth. She writes, "Thinking . . . *needs*
speech not only to sound out and become manifest; it needs it to be activated *at all*" (*LM* 121, emphasis added). Here the literal body is not merely
metaphorically connected or transferred to a realm of thought. Instead,
actual speech, which of course occurs with the use of the literal, corporeal
mouth, is deemed necessary for thought to take place "at all." Arendt's vocabulary of "activation" indicates that actual speech here is temporally and
even *causally* prior to thought. Arendt thus obliquely implicates the mouth
and the literal body in the production of thought. This represents a stronger
implicit claim for the role of the body in thinking than does her account of

metaphor, which suggests that the body merely provides a resource for the figurative representation of thought and that the connections between the body and thought are metaphorical connections. Instead, the literal, bodily mouth is here characterized as the *literal* source of thought.

What is more, if speech, and hence the mouth, are at the origin of thought, then the literal body is directly responsible for the production not only of thought but of figurality in general. For if the mouth is the locus of thought's origination in speech, then the mouth is also where "vitally metaphorical" language and thought get formed. In this regard, the literal mouth would constitute the literal locus of passage from literality to figurality— for, according to Arendt, oral speech activates the thought that moves metaphorically from the literal body to abstractions. A more profound and complicated relationship between the body and "mental activities" emerges in this model: The literal, bodily mouth appears as the origin of thought, and thought makes use of the literal body as a resource for figuring mental activities (of which thinking is one) and abstractions (of which figurality is one). In this regard, the mouth is not only a resource for figurative language with which to describe mental activities (as we will see in the next section on "taste"). It is also where thought is catalyzed and where, therefore, figurality is engendered, including the figurality that is both vehicle for and result of transfer from sensory to nonsensory realms.

In sum, in *Life of the Mind* Arendt first asserts in her analysis of metaphor a trajectory away from the literal body toward figurative representations of mental activities and, second, describes metaphor as that which connects the sensory and nonsensory realms. Nonetheless, her claims for the dependence of thinking on speech allegorize, or enact, a relationship between the body and thought that differs from the one she describes in her account of metaphor. Arendt appears to reinstate the body, or at least the speaking mouth, as the mainspring of that figurality and thus of philosophical thought. The mouth is for this reason also a point of literal *and* figurative passage from literality to figurality. Hence if Arendt's claims for the importance of speech to thought are taken seriously, the literal body is not nearly as separable from the production and figuration of mental activities as Arendt claims in her characterization of "vitally metaphorical" language. Or, alternatively, it is conceivable that the vitality of "vitally metaphorical" language requires that the body must be preliminarily or provisionally *presumed* to be separate from the production and figuration of mental activities to produce formulations that indeed evoke the apprehension of relations. In other words, to bring figurality to life, perhaps its aboriginal links to the actual body must be first forgotten.

2. POLITICS AND TASTE

In the *Lectures on Kant's Political Philosophy*, Arendt's discussion of taste appears to allegorically enact the trajectory she describes in *Life of the Mind*, where vocabulary is borrowed from the realm of bodily processes to explain abstract mental processes. Because Kant's *Critique of Judgment* and specifically Kant's judgment of taste are the focus of Arendt's lectures, "taste" is here the central metaphor. Arendt reminds us that for Kant the judgment of taste—the disinterested judgment that an object is beautiful—presumes the possibility of judging in a nonprivate way, i.e., in a way that we could in principle ascribe to anyone and everyone. For Kant, the pleasure we take in observing a beautiful object derives from its effect of quickening our imagination and understanding; and because every creature with these capacities of imagination and understanding is able to have such a feeling of quickening, the judgment of the beautiful in principle presumes the potential agreement of all such creatures as ourselves, although any particular object that provokes such a judgment at any one time is subjectively or privately determined.[4]

For Arendt, the judgment that something is beautiful—the judgment of taste—constitutes the political element of Kant's philosophy. Such a presumption of possible agreement with others is evidence for the possibility of what Arendt, borrowing from Kant, calls an "enlarged mentality," namely the capacity to think outside one's own private point of view. Arendt quotes a letter from Kant to Marcus Herz: "The 'enlargement of the mind' . . . is accomplished by 'comparing our judgment with the possible rather than the actual judgments of others, and by putting ourselves in the place of any other man.'"[5] The judgment of taste, in other words, signals the possibility of thinking beyond the sphere of mere opinion and inclination, beyond the sphere of utter subjectivity. For Arendt, if there is a genuine politics to be lived, it depends on the possibility of such a judgment beyond one's own private sphere. The possibility of such a politics is evidenced by the judgment of taste, which embodies precisely the comparison of our own judgment with the possible judgments of others. For Kant this ability to compare our judgments with "the collective reason of humanity" exemplifies the *sensus communis* or common sense (*LKPP* 71).

Arendt thus finds evidence for a common sense and a genuine politics in the judgment of taste. But *taste*–is this not precisely "vitally metaphorical" language in the Arendtian sense? Taste in Kant's *Critique of Judgment* refers to an abstract process of judgment, and yet its name is borrowed from the realm of the body and specifically from the sense associated with the literal mouth. It is remarkable that taste, based on the literal and individual mouth, comes to refer both to thoroughly private sensation and the "enlarged mentality" that makes us fit for politics. Arendt herself is startled at this association: "The most surprising aspect of this business is that common sense, the faculty of judgment and of discriminating between right and wrong, should be based on the sense of taste" (*LKPP* 64). How can private, bodily taste form the basis for nonprivate judgments and hence politics? As we have already seen, Arendt writes in *Life of the Mind* of the connection between bodily processes and mental activities. She declares, "No language has a ready-made vocabulary for the needs of mental activity; they all borrow their vocabulary from words originally meant to correspond either to sense experience or to other experiences of ordinary life" (*LM* 102). The figuration of the judgment of the beautiful as a judgment of "taste" would seem to be precisely such an instance in which an abstract mental activity is allegorically represented by means of a particular bodily sense. Thus Arendt writes, "Judgment draws . . . , as Kant knew so well, its metaphorical language from the sense of *taste*," and she adds in parentheses, "The *Critique of Judgment* was originally conceived as a 'Critique of Taste'. . . the most intimate, private and idiosyncratic of the senses" (*LM* 111). With regard to the connection between bodily taste and the judgment of taste, vital metaphor explains how this most private sense can come to stand for the basis of politics.

3 . THE SPEAKING MOUTH IN POLITICS

In explaining how metaphor permits a transition from the literal sense of taste in the mouth to the figurative sense of taste in aesthetic judgment, Arendt seems quite easily to leave the physical body behind in referring unproblematically to a "mental activity" of judgment. Her account of the judgment of taste conforms to her claims in *Life of the Mind* for the metaphorical transfer from sense experience to mental activities. But is the body categorically excluded from mental activities and from the political? Can it be left behind so easily with regard to *sensus communis* and political life? The apparent absence of the body in Arendt's understanding of politics is something that feminist and other readers of Arendt have pondered. For instance, Julia Kristeva suggests that Arendt's lack of philosophical interest in the body derives from her conviction that our bodies are what render us the same, whereas it is our actions that make us different, that make us each a "who" instead of a "what."[6] Why for Arendt are nature, the body, and the realm of need apparently opposed to the sphere of action and freedom? I suggest that there *is* a way in which the literal, bodily mouth not only belongs to but defines the sphere of politics—that the mouth is, in fact, the center of politics according to Arendt's own conception of genuine political life.

Let us consider for a moment the literal mouth with regard to Arendt's own definitions of privacy and publicity. On one hand, the mouth is part of the body, and in Arendt's analyses the body as a whole is private insofar as it is involved with metabolism and with life processes—with what she deems the sphere of labor in *The Human Condition*.[7] In this regard Arendt would seem to confine orality to the prepolitical and idiosyncratic sphere of privacy, such that "taste" could come to refer to judgment *only* by way of "vitally metaphorical" language. On the other hand, if any single part of our body is important to Arendt's philosophy of the human condition, insofar as it defines our human and political potentials, would it not *have* to be the mouth? For Arendt writes, "Speech is what makes man a political being" (*HC* 3), and she suggests that human beings can experience meaningfulness "only because they can talk with and make sense to each other and to themselves" (*HC* 4). With regard to public speech, then, the mouth is *not* primarily a bodily passage. Rather it is the site where a body is transformed by the act of speech into what she calls a "who" (*HC* 178–180). The mouth is the *literal* place where speech takes shape, where the bare breath and intonation are shaped into speech that lets us be in a world with other human beings. The mouth is where bodily breath becomes words; it is thus a strange passage both from body to speech *and*, therefore, from privacy to politics. Insofar as the literal mouth is the place of speaking, and hence of speaking together with others, it belongs to the quintessence of political life and is not merely a resource for the allegorical representations of abstractions.

Thus far we have seen that speech is in Arendt's work a passage from imagination to communication, from private to public, from solitude to

Mitsein. We have also seen that, with regard to speech, the literal, corporeal mouth turns out to exceed the trajectory of figuration that Arendt describes in *Life of the Mind.* Not merely a resource for Kant's figurative formulations concerning taste, the mouth as the locus of speech is instead for Arendt the catalyst of thought, the origin of figurality, and the literal passage from privacy to politics, a passage that Arendt's appropriation of Kant offers as the source of hope for a genuine politics and thus a truly human life. These direct connections between the bodily mouth and the quintessence of politics depend, once again, on speech.

But is something strange going on here? By way of this itinerary through "vitally metaphorical" language, judgment, enlarged mentality, taste, and above all speech we arrive at the literal mouth as the source of thought, figurality, and politics. Indeed I would suggest that something about the repeated appearance of the literal mouth here is strange, first of all because thinking is *not* activated only in oral speech. A book, such as *Life of the Mind* or *The Human Condition,* also accomplishes the disclosure of thinking in a public realm. It connects ourselves to the world, and to each other, in the ways that Arendt describes "vitally metaphorical" language as doing. A book is able to perform this quasi-messianic function of opening new ways of thinking because it is something in the world. The very worldliness of the book in which we read about the thinking as one-way figurality, as leading from body to the supersensory, puts the presumed primacy and literality of the body into question. Perhaps the vitality that Arendt ascribes to metaphorical language too hastily presumes that the literal body is indeed the origin of figurality—i.e., presumes that the activity of figuration both is secondary to a securely literal body and also issues from it. But figuration is not at all secondary to even the literal body and the functions that are ascribed to it. For here we might ask, What *is* speech? Could Arendt mean the *act* of speaking with the mouth; or, instead, the less directly corporeal *product* of this act; or is she using *speech* in an extended fashion, for instance to refer to language? And moreover, on what basis could we be certain, and anyway how could we ever define these differences with precision and certainty? How do we know where Arendt is writing literally, metaphorically, or allegorically? Here the uncertainty mentioned in Angus Fletcher's characterization of the "psychological and linguistic uncertainty as to what is going on when language is used figuratively" (*ATSM* 11) is extended to an irresolvable uncertainty as to *whether* language is used figuratively or not in the first place.

4. SPEECH, ACTION, AND THE VITALITY OF UNCERTAIN FIGURALITY

I would suggest that Arendt's conjunction in *The Human Condition* of speech and action allegorize—i.e., demonstrate by way of enactment—the difficulty of locating the literality of the body, and specifically the mouth, in Arendt's references to speech and thus to orality. For the definition of speech with regard to action is no easy matter in *The Human Condition*. Becoming a "who," according to Arendt, is a matter of speech *and* action. She writes, "In acting and speaking men show who they are. . . . this disclosure of 'who' in contradistinction to 'what' somebody is . . . is implicit in everything somebody says and does" (*HC* 179). But the precise relationship between speech and action is not clear, and in this regard the role of the literal mouth might be questioned. Arendt attempts to explain: "Action and speech are so closely related because the primordially and specifically human act must at the same time contain the answer to the question asked of every newcomer: 'Who are you?'" (*HC* 178). Arendt even writes, "[M]any, and even most acts, are performed in the manner of speech" (*HC* 178), and "Speechless action would no longer be action" (*HC* 178). Despite the many and complicated references Arendt makes to speech and action, it remains unclear what the relationship is between them and even what the distinction between them might be. Critics have gone in different directions in surmising whether for Arendt speech is itself action (emphasizing the performative component); whether action requires speech as a supplement (emphasizing Arendt's references to storytelling); or whether there is action at all apart from speech. The text is not at all univocal in this regard, however, and thus enables such divergent interpretations of what precisely "speech and action" means.

Speech and action: Are these two separate terms, or could this phrase be a *hendiadys*, making two of what is really just one? Hendiadys is a figure of elocution, a figure of speech, of division—of one into two, *hen dia duoin*. The classic examples of hendiadys transform a phrase composed of adjective and noun into a pair of nouns—e.g., "We'll come despite the rain and weather" instead of "We'll come despite the rainy weather." An example from the film *The Blues Brothers* depicts the perplexity that hendiadys can engender, namely when the brothers find themselves in a bar proud of its own pluralism in featuring music both country *and* western. Is the phrase "speech and action" a hendiadic reference to something else, for something like speechly action, actionlike speech? And if so, can we know for sure where the literal mouth fits into this conjunction?

The recurring combination of the words *speech* and *action* suggests the *hendiadys*, raises the question as to whether speech and action are one and the same. But the formulation "speech and action" can also be read as *differentiating* them, as distancing the speech of the mouth from action in the world. It can, for that matter, also be read as a statement of *transition* from speech to action, e.g., as speech *becoming* action. Likewise, in different moments Arendt seems to imply different possibilities: speech as distinct from action, speech as a form of action, action as requiring speech, speech that becomes action. How do we know whether this "and" signifies a sameness, a differentiation, or a becoming? Not any help is Arendt's ambiguous statement that "[m]any, and even most acts, are in the form of words" (*HC* 178). What form of words makes a deed? What is a deed without words? How are deeds figured or rendered deeds at all by words?

When Arendt cites Shelley's reference to "vitally metaphorical" language, she defines that figurative vitality as evoking apprehension of relations. But the vitality of figurality, including that of allegory, is not nearly exhausted by its capacity to evoke such apprehension. For the "vitality" of the phrase "speech and action" would be too restricted by Arendt's association of "vital" figurality with "the apprehension of relations." Indeed the phrase *speech and action* is central—even vital—to Arendt's text and to many of her readers *not* because we apprehend the relations between speech and action. Rather the phrase raises the question, What precisely are the relations being marked? Is it even a matter of *relation* at all, which would mean that speech and action are separable, or are speech and action one and the same? If they are one and the same, we are back with the mouth—the literal mouth would be the location of action. But are they one and the same, and how would we ever know, based on their proximity in Arendt's text?

Perhaps the "vitality" of the phrase *speech and action* consists precisely in the fact that we cannot be *sure* whether *speech and action* means "speech *is* action" or means "speech is *not* action"; and thus Arendt unwittingly produces an allegory of uncertainty as to whether *hendiadys* is here in play at all. Figurality is in such an instance vital, but this "vitality" derives at least as much from such uncertainty with regard to the relations it marks as from the relations it discloses. That is, vital figures mark relations, but just what relations are being marked cannot be decided on the basis of the figurative formulation alone. Indeed I would suggest that in this regard Arendt underestimates the vitality that she associates with the metaphorical language on which she claims philosophy is based. Even the "vitality" of "vitally metaphorical" language would, according to Arendt's conventional description of figuration, refer in the first instance to the vitality of the body and only metaphorically to the vitality of language. But does vitality begin with the body or with the figures that ascribe vitality to the body? Where the vitality of vital figures comes from, or whether it comes from the body or conversely moves in the direction of the body, cannot be known for certain from the figure itself; Arendt's eclipse of the bodily mouth in her accounts of speech and taste allegorize precisely this uncertainty. Figures do not testify to their own sources or directionalities; and, if they did, how could we be certain that they would be speaking literally? Open-ended thinking, including Arendt's, depends on the vitality of "vitally metaphorical" language. It lives precisely in an epistemological lacuna, amid uncertainty with regard to the source and direction of figuration and likewise with regard to whether it is ever entirely completed and closed off from the concepts it produces.

Notes

1. Hannah Arendt, *Life of the Mind, Volume 1: Thinking* (New York: Harcourt Brace Jovanovich, 1978), 102. Hereafter referred to as *LM*.

2. Hayden White, *The Content of the Form: Narrative Discourse and Historical Representation* (Baltimore: Johns Hopkins University Press, 1987), 48.

3. Angus Fletcher, *Allegory: The Theory of a Symbolic Mode* (Ithaca, NY: Cornell University Press, 1964), 11. Hereafter referred to as *ATSM*.

4. See Immanuel Kant, *Critique of Judgment*, trans. Werner S. Pluhar (Indianapolis: Hackett, 1987); "quickening [*Belebung*]" is introduced on 88 and the presumption of the assent of others on 89.

5. Hannah Arendt, *Lectures on Kant's Political Philosophy* (Chicago: University of Chicago Press, 1982), 43. Hereafter abbreviated in text as *LKPP*.

6. Julia Kristeva, *Hannah Arendt* (New York: Columbia University Press, 2001), 171–184.

7. See especially Hannah Arendt, *The Human Condition* (Chicago: University of Chicago Press, 1958), 79-93. Hereafter referred to as *HC*. Linda Zerilli notes in her essay on Arendt and the body that the body itself is figured as oral and as ravenous; human *Mitsein* in Arendt *is* hungry, and of course the mouth is the place of literal ingestion (Linda M. G. Zerilli, "The Arendtian Body," in *Feminist Interpretations of Hannah Arendt*. University Park: Pennsylvania State University Press, 1995, 171).

ELEVEN

Allegory and Science

From Euclid to the Search for Fundamental Structures in Modern Physics

JAMES J. PAXSON

Even postmodern philosophy of science often tries to exclude figurality from science and mathematics, in spite of what might now be commonly thought about postmodern thought in the wake of deconstruction and its related disruptive theories and practices. In his 1993 study of Leibniz's monadology and baroque esthetics entitled *The Fold*, philosopher Gilles Deleuze begins with an olympian emphasis: that mathematics is the inscription of the literal, indeed, that mathematics—and science—are *the literal.*[1] It would therefore be counterintuitive at best and erroneous at worst to take science as a discourse or system of semiosis in which the relationships of representation could be corrupted and threatened by figurality—the sort of figurality that constitutes most flamboyantly (and historically) that mode or genre or discourse that we label "allegory." This is the mode that proceeds by "saying other" (as the old Greek expression from classical rhetoric, *allos agoreuein*— "to say other"—means).[2] Allegory, both intuitively and historically, seems to be that discourse that would be most threatening to science.

In this short essay, I shall put forward the radical idea that some of the most important advances in modern science, namely in physics, rely on tacitly allegorical structures. More precisely, the grand narrative containing the succession of scientific models that seek to describe the fundamental structures of matter and energy, of space and time, might just involve an allegory of some prior, even archaic, though holistic form. In the experimental picture of this paper, I will consider the geometry of Euclid. Does the succession or progression of modern physics's search for fundamental structures stand as an "allegory of Euclid"? This elementary *Gedankenexperiment* can begin by acknowledging not the separation of science from figurality but its dependence on figure—simile, metaphor, hyperbole, prosopopeia or personification, paradox, irony, and so on.

Just over a half-century ago (and prior to the more celebrated impact of C. P. Snow), Jacob Bronowski declared that a scientific picture was in fact no more or no better than a metaphorical or analogical system, a marshalling of "likenesses" creatively perceived and manipulated by the scientist.[3] Thomas Kuhn's groundbreaking study of the early 1960s about competing and superseding scientific "paradigms";[4] Gerald Holton's career-long project of charting so-called scientific themata of literary and mythographic quality;[5] or the identifying of programmatic rhetorical figures and tropes used in the initial phases of scientific discovery[6]—all extend Bronowski's persistent and on-target formulation. If Quintilian once declared that the mode we call allegory was a kind of extension of the handy figure known as metaphor, then one might intuit further a link between the constitutive or initiating metaphors or figures of scientific discovery (as per Bronowski's declaration) and the grander mode called allegory.[7]

A more fully fledged literary theory of modern science's inhabitation by allegory, however, has already produced fascinating results. To name the work of one of the most salient of researchers, Bruce Clarke's study of the allegorical discourses inhering in nineteenth-century scientific commonplaces such as entropy, the luminiferous ether and the energy flows in Kelvinian thermodynamic theory, shows an enduring dependence on the mode by both popular and mainstream science writers.[8] I have previously demonstrated allegorical properties of thinking and writing in the mathematical productions of Newton, earlier in the seventeenth century.[9]

The very idea of a bilevel reality that inhabits how we think about allegory may hold promise for better understanding the advancements of modern science. Allegory proceeds by showing how one thing—a sensuous object, a person, a locality—can signify an *other*—an idea, a complex philosophical or theological or historical concept. That is to say, an allegory might present one narrative while that narrative "points" to another. In the history of science we often go forward by showing how new scientific pictures simply abandon or obviate or at best vitiate prior models and pictures, prior narratives. In the sort of conceptual scheme propounded by an older and more traditional historian of science such as E. A. Burtt, a new scientific narrative or model competes with or succeeds a prior one.[10] Such is, of course, even the upshot of Kuhn's own "competitor" or rhetorical persuasion theory of scientific success. Aristotle's theory of gravity (described in the *De Physica*),[11] understood as a natural motion or inclination toward the center of the universe, must expire and give way to Newton's theory of gravitation (in the *Principia*), which must itself finally give way to Einstein's more exotic theory of gravitation as a "curvature" in space-time.[12] I wish to show how one narrative arc in the fundamental structures of physics seems to proceed by producing ever-newer images, metaphors, and models of *geometrical* reality at the nano-scale level. The successionist narrative of better models or pictures obviating and replacing prior ones instead might *itself be obviated by* an "allegorical" system in which the newer model or picture faithfully though furtively incorporates or reproduces a far older scheme by actually instantiating an allegory of that older scheme. Allegories often work by presenting a base level of narrative, of reality, that points to a second, or prior, or higher level—an *allos*, "other."

For the demonstration at the heart of this essay, I choose, as that older or prior scheme, the geometrical system of Euclid in *The Elements*. I argue that allegorically reincorporating some structure of this Euclidian system is the narrative of how modern physics has manifested its ongoing search for fundamental structures. The explicit and overt claims of modern physics have been that it continues to carry the world boldly to ever-newer ontologies and epistemologies of being and knowing. In the least, this catechism might prove ironic (and *ironia* has itself been viewed, not accidentally, as a constituent trope in classical *allegoria*).[13] The advances in modern physics, at least since Einstein and the early quantum theorists, have produced models of matter, energy, and space-time that purportedly are characterized by "post-Euclidian" geometries. These are home to some very difficult mathematics that is imply well beyond the apprehensive faculties of the human sensorium and the practical imagination.

By first reviewing key features of the term *allegory*, I will demonstrate the "stratified" hierarchical quality of certain allegorical systems shared by mathematics and literature. I will then resketch the successionist picture of modern physics's search for fundamental structures as a plausible allegory of the succession of geometrical forms constituting Euclid's *Elements*. The task is not as counterintuitive as it might at first seem. Everyone knows that the *Elements* of Euclid are the source and font of all basic geometrical instruction, even today, and that its many pages proceed from simplest, to more complex, to very complex—that is to say, via the logical representation in visualized and rigorous formulation from zero-dimensional geometrical entities, through one-dimensional entities, through two-dimensional or plane-geometry entities, through three-dimensional or solid-geometry entities.[14]

An allegory is a semiotic system by which one thing can mean or be programmatically structured by something else. Therefore, the most elementary kind of allegory would be bilevel. Allegory involves significational supplementarity: The thing "meant" always exceeds somehow the signifying capacity of the sensuous signs put in its place.[15] Allegory, because its signifier always marks a difference, a distance, from its signified, may perforce involve a sense of *temporal* distantiation.[16] Just about all definitions of allegory through the centuries of Western thought take hold of these spare schemae in some form. In the 1960s, the deconstructionist Paul de Man redefined allegory as the inscription of temporality itself, that is, as the coded language of the "anteriority" exhibited by all sign systems: All signs (the conjunction of the signifier and its deictically realized signified) merely point back to other signs; and all we get in "allegory" is this constitutive and phenomenologically reductive effect. De Man's initial understanding seems to naturally set us up for the all-consuming definition of allegory that marks his later theoretical productions—essays in which all human acts of cognition or at least all acts of reading become "allegories of reading."[17] But the demystifying sense of defining allegory had come earlier, in definitions crafted by the twentieth century's more authoritative literary historians of premodern literature.

A few decades before the archmodernist de Man, C. S. Lewis explained that allegories were workmanlike though nonmystical hierarchical collections of "sacramental" or personificational signs of the sort that made up, say, the poetry of Dante.[18] This dual quality thus takes us back to a point I visited above—back two millennia in Western rhetorical and poetic thought to the most prominent of the Roman lawyer-rhetoricians, Quintilian (more prominent even than Cicero himself on these grounds). In his monumental *Institutio oratoria*, Quintilian defines allegory as an extension, a linear seriation, in a narrative, of a key metaphor.[19] It is a trenchant metaphor to speak of a king as the "captain" of a ship of state; one might produce such a metaphor once and for all and be done with it in a poem, an oration, or an essay. But when one *extends* that sole metaphor, when one elaborates on it—saying that the king is the captain of the ship of state; that the senate or parliament is the rudder of the ship; that the army is the prow of the ship; that the priests and philosophers are the mast of the ship—then one no longer has used an isolated metaphor that works as a "local" rhetorical utterance. One now has an "allegory." A bilevel model such as this Quintilianic procedure, in which one (narrative) layer or level gets adumbrated on a second level, works for literary artifacts and may, I believe, hold promise for the continua of other discourses—namely mathematics and physics.

I have elsewhere rethought the sixteenth-century advent of the logarithm, an invention of Scottish mathematician John Napier through the notion of allegory as a bilevel architecture or, more precisely, as a networked grid of different strata, of linked and parallel signifiers and signifieds.[20] Napier had worked out a system of the logarithm, or progressive exponent, largely by the 1590s, though he'd gone on to publish his results in the 1614 book, *Mirifici logarithmorum canonis descriptio*, "A Description of the Wonderful Rule of the Logarithms." Simply put, Napier's discovery works this way: At the main inscriptional level or stratum, the relation of numbers or values in an equation might be multiplicative; at a second, higher yet linked level, the logarithms of those numbers to be multiplied correspondentially relate in an *additive* way. And that's what we still are taught in a precalculus course (though more so if we were educated back in the days of the slide rule).[21] To save time in multiplying, you find the logarithms of two numbers that you want to multiply, then add the logarithms, and then, using an inverse-log table, find the true product of your original two numbers. Napier asserts this correspondentialist logic himself, and its perfection is emphasized by Morris Kline, in his own monumental history of mathematics.[22] To be sure, the process smacks of a kind of alchemical or magical air. It certainly calls up the dual-leveling of platonism. But I submit that the correspondentialism that intuitively "guided" Napier, to use Kline's words, arose as a rhetorical if not literary idée fixe in an intellectual era permeated by literary and artistic allegory—in the intellectual context of Spenser and of Shakespeare, Napier's contemporaries. The logarithmic system seems "allegorical" because it depends on two systematically layered planes of linked signs, each in a scriptive or graphic continuum.

Let us compare this to Spenser. We can think of the great allegorical decodings of Spenser's *Faerie Queene* by its prominent twentieth-century literary critics—C. S. Lewis again, Edwin Greenlaw, Harry Berger Jr., Rosemond Tuve, John Steadman—who've delineated such equational networks and grids for us.[23] As a model, we have the poem's opening scene of Book 1, Canto 1, in which three closely tied characters—the unnamed Red Cross Knight, a woman all in white named Una, and a lazy Dwarf—enter the so-called Wandering Wood to encounter the serpent-monster named Error. Indisputably the literal level points to another level hovering above it, in which the three characters are personifications: Red Cross Knight is Holiness; Una is Platonic Unity; and the Dwarf is Sloth, the medieval sin of *acedia*. Perhaps at a linked but parallel level beyond that, the three characters respectively become the historical Saint George (patron of the English nation), the historical Anglican or True Church, and the English peasantry. So the lateral relation of embodied historical entities or institutions at one level corresponds to the lateral relation of personified abstractions at the next level. This resembles the logic I propound for Napier's logarithm, with its dually multiplicative-additive sets of operations. Yet the former is a literary effect, the latter a principally scientific or mathematical code, one emerging out of nature itself as the very language of nature, as Galileo would have held.

The apprehending of a master trope on which bi-level allegory gets built bears some more explanation as to how modern philosophy of science has successfully resorted to rhetoric's reservoir of tropes to articulate the processes of scientific discovery in general. Earlier, I mentioned the work of modern historian of rhetoric Jeanne Fahnestock, who has identified some of the master tropes on which the world's greatest scientific discoveries have depended. In her 1999 book, *Rhetorical Figures in Science*, she shows how Newton tacitly prioritized chiasmus or antimetabole, the trope of syntactic reversal. Fahnestock argues that the Third Law of Motion as expressed in the *Principia*—the Law blandly couched in high school physics textbooks as the Law of Equal and Opposite Reactions ("for every action there is an equal and opposite reaction")—really rests on an exciting chiasmus. Few may recall the sage's famous analogy, "If you press a stone with your finger, the finger can be said to be pressed back by the stone." The simple inversion of grammatical cola in the complete sentence, in which subject and object get transposed to produce a clever new result, leads perhaps to the concept of mutual action and perhaps even mutual attraction as well.[24] For the moment, we need only agree with Fahnestock that a localized rhetorical trope can be built up into a complex idea system—one at the heart of a strong and new scientific hypothesis or theory. But we would do well to recall that, in this special instance—the chiasmus of the Third Law of Motion—the inversional logic of chiasmus or antimetabole might just bear a connection to the fact that Quintilian at times named *allegoria* using a Latin expression, *inversio*, and that Newton's economical utterance actually engages the rhetorical figure *prosopopoeia* or personification, allegory's most enduring master trope. (How often do stones press back at my finger—unless motivated in a prosopopoetic or anthropomorphic narrative?)[25]

More to Fahnestock's point, that utterance is a chiasmus or antimetabole, the trope whereby one syntactically inverts a first "colon" (a complete grammatical clause) to produce a second and following colon. The composite effect produces, in an inversely symmetrical, semicolon-spliced new sentence, something that did not exist before. "Ask not what your country can do for you; ask what you can do for your country." This is John F. Kennedy, we all know, an orator who loved the trope chiasmus, as witness his other utterance, "We must put an end to war or war will put an end to us." Fahnestock goes on to show how this simple syntactical trope worked for other great scientists—not in the least being Michael Faraday, who had conceptually inverted the position and the circular motion of his famous electrified-wire-and-magnet experiment of the year 1830 to go on to produce the theory of reciprocal electric-magnetic induction.[26] Without Faraday and his transposed wires and magnets, we would be absent of electric motors and Westinghouse Corporation; nor would we have had a Clerk Maxwell some decades later with his unificational electromagnetic theory—and, in turn, Albert Einstein's Earth-stopping 1905 paper, *"Zur Elektrodynamik bewegter Körper"* ("On the Electrodynamics of Moving Bodies").[27] The inverted and newly complete sentence comprised of its two symmetrical cola works like a "simple machine" to get more work out of a modicum of words. The device moves the reader's or hearer's mind using a simple lever.

It's interesting that the logarithm is a force multiplier—that is, it allows you to do more mathematical work faster, just like Newton's or Leibniz's integrative infinitesimal in the calculus—and that tropes or figures are force multipliers. They are—if I might continue to invoke Archimedes for a moment—like levers or wedges or pulleys. They are simple machines that enable the completion of more work using minimal effort. That's what the chiasmus did conceptually for Newton and for Faraday (and for the industrialist Henry Ford through his ultimate elaboration of that tool called the assembly line in which, to apocryphally quote Ford himself, "You bring the work piece to the man, not the man to the work piece"). The multiplication of energy in work for the classical or medieval or Renaissance rhetorician involves just that—the linguistic freeing and enlivening via another tropological effect, *energia*. Allegory, as theorists such as Bruce Clarke or Angus Fletcher have well noted, is the mode par excellence of the freed or multiplied presence of linguistic and cognitive *energia*, its connection to allegory long essential in rhetorical thought.[28]

Energia so understood takes us to modern physics's allegorical narrative of the successionist model. But let it be said in getting there that, just as Fahnestock discerned rhetorical antimetabole or chiasmus to be at the heart of Newton's or Faraday's discoveries, so she discerns the figure *ploche*—the lateral and multiplied repetition of a word or element in a discourse, even to the extent that the effect creates a kind of "plaiting"[29]—in all sorts of analogically dependent scientific discoveries but especially in biological taxonomy or cladistics. Perhaps we might think of the bilevel or dualistic quality of narrative and logarithmic allegory as hinging on the figure *ploche*—another lever, so to speak, enabling a new system of figural discovery making. The Archimedean notion holds too; allegory works as a massive machine built up out of simple machines, out of levers and their fulcrums, that seek to harness and dispense what Bruce Clarke calls "energy forms." Allegory is the discursive form of energy par excellence; or, as Fletcher well demonstrated, it is the discourse of the *daemon*, the diminutive but energetic being, the very personification of energy of the sort that Maxwell conjured to fantasize about the sorting, in a bicameral and periodically sealed chamber, of hot or cool gases, in his famous *Gedankenexperiment*.

Ever since the thinking of Democritus or Lucretius, we've been attracted to the image of the atom, that which is "indivisible." Again, it was a long-held supposition in the traditional history of science that the indivisible, and perhaps infinitesimally small, status of the atom paralleled Euclid's own opening idea in the *Elements*: The atom must be a *punctus*, a point. That is the very first definition on the first page of Euclid's book: "A point is that which has no parts" (*Punctus est cuius pars non est*, as the medieval Latin had it).[30] From this we proceed to the definitions of lines and rays, and then on to planes, then on to circular and rectilinear figures. Some hundreds of pages later we arrive at the requisite definitions and propositions about solid figures. Euclid's system is ascendatory and hierarchical. Subsequent definitions and propositions build on and contain prior ones. Such organizational logic is the very grammar, if you will, of a Euclidean concept of space (that is, classical space taken as "the set of all points," as first-year geometry students are still taught). Such Euclidean geometrical mapping characterizes and controls not only the earlier astrophysical achievements in revolutionary Western scientific thought—Copernicus' *De revolutionibus* of 1543 or Galileo's *Nuncius siderius* of 1610—but the more revolutionary *De principia* by Newton, for which he could have used his already developed calculus (which he called "fluxions") but preferred instead the more comfortable system of Euclidean geometrical proofs.[31]

When J. J. Thomson theorized the electron in 1897, he was still guided by this ancient understanding of an elementary particle of infinitesimally small size (and puny energy)—perhaps a tiny spheroid, a "corpuscle, though certainly something conforming to a mere geometrical point."[32] The same went for Ernest Rutherford's larger proton of 1918: These too were points, zero-dimensional, effervescent phantoms recalling Euclid's own primordial principles. Electrons flew around the central proton or nucleus—an image long used as a visual logo by the U.S. Atomic Energy Commission well after the demise of the simplified standard model.[33] And the same went for James Chadwick's mediational particle, the so-called neutron theorized by the early 1930s.[34]

But metaphorically, the point-concept, the fundamental metaphor in the so-called standard model of particle physics, gave way in succeeding decades to more complex arrangements. The quantum theorists tried thought experiments about elementary particles existing as point-forms and/or wave forms: we should recall the merely "numberable" electron's status, but not its geometry, in the Bohr atom.[35] We might recall, too, Max Born's image of electrons as analogous to the fixed points on a moving crankshaft, each "stroke" of said shaft enacting a Gaussian curve that signified a wave of probability, to use Bronowski's elegant summary of the theory; or, Louis de Broglie's image of an electron orbit as a fluctuating and nonfixed quasi-geometry—first a trefoil, then a cinquefoil—surrounding an atomic nucleus of protons and neutrons as a closed wave form.[36] As the tide of discovered particles through the 1940s, 1950s, and 1960s swelled—producing bosons, tau mesons, pions, and so forth—the general concept of a little infinitisimality, a puny sphericle or mere point, that was evanescent, perhaps coupled with/as a wave form—continued. However, this was a greatly compromised "geometry" scarcely available to the practical imagination or to the mathematics that most scientists were capable of doing.

And yet the Euclidean analogy—let us call it the Euclidian allegory—takes a more interesting turn with the eventual beginnings of string theory in the 1960s by Yochiro Nambu and Lenny Susskind, and later, in the 1970s and 1980s by Edward Witten.[37] In accord with the requirements of the unification of forces, fundamental physics needed to see a more basic structure behind the four basic forces of nature (electromagnetic, strong nuclear, weak nuclear, and gravity). A more mathematically elegant description of putatively existent "quantum gravity" led to subatomic entities that were no longer following Euclidean conceptions, *zero-dimensional* points but that were *one-dimensional* line-segments or "strings." We can say that the analogy of Euclid, traced in the earliest pages of his *Elements*, has been mapped onto the progressive or successionist history of elementary physics as an "allegory": The passage from geometrical *punctus* to *linea*, a conceptual passage at the headwaters of the most influential scientific text of the Middle Ages, names the metaphorical or allegorical passage from subatomic particle physics to subatomic string (or "superstring") physics.

And yet Witten himself was extending the geometrical metaphoricity of these "stringy" or superstringy models by the 1990s, proffering his so-called M-theory (*M* whimsically standing for "magic" or "matrix" or "mystery" or some other exotic, and requisitely alliterating, term). This led in turn to the ascent up the (meta) geometrical ladder in an era of conceptual schemes that was abandoning the classical stuff of Euclidean objects (at the nano-scale of being). Brane theory replaced for many fundamental physicists those one-dimensional strings with "membranes" in various complex configurations.[38] In sum, and to recapitulate this starkly paraphrased narrative of the history of modern fundamental-structure physics, a 0-brane is a zero-dimensional pointlike particle recalling the entities peopling the standard model; a 1-brane is a string, while a 2-brane is a "membrane." The two-dimensional membrane is of course a metaphorical recasting, perhaps a biological one, of Euclid's planar surfaces, the geometrical objects that in fact occupy most of the *Elements*—the simple planes or polygons (triangles, squares, rectangles, rhomboids, parallelograms, and so forth) comprising simple or two-dimensional Euclidean geometry and trigonometry. To sum up: We have, in physics's (post)modern, post-Euclidean world of fundamental structural thought, traced an allegory of the progressive levels of Euclid's hierarchy in the *Elements*. The move from particles to strings to membranes parallels the move from points to lines to planes in Euclid's great ur-text or, to use another term expressly from the literary history of allegory, his "pre-text," as allegory theorist Maureen Quilligan would define it.[39]

This allegorical logic would dictate that we now move to fundamental structures that are three-dimensional—or beyond. But where could scientists go in contemporary, twenty-first-century fundamental physics from the two-dimensional membrane, modified descendant of the one-dimensional string, modified descendant of the zero-dimensional point-particle, as they craft allegories that are ever stranger and more complex? A lively capsulization in a 2007 issue of *Scientific American* foretells where modern fundamental physics's allegory of ascending Euclidian forms seems to be going. In Mark Alpert's "The Triangular Universe," we have a clear development along the lines I've been discussing. It is a brief essay (really a notice) challengingly subtitled "Instead of String Theory, Four-Dimensional Tetrahedrons." This reference is problematic because the tetrahedron is a *three-dimensional* object. I'd like to see physics have the metaphorological courtesy of comprehending the allegory of Euclid before jumping right to the meta-metaphor of *four-dimensional* objects. Nonetheless, Alpert begins by exhorting that we imagine a landscape composed of microscopic triangular structures that constantly rearrange themselves into new patterns. Seen from afar, the landscape looks perfectly smooth, but up close it is a churning cauldron of strange geometries. This deceptively simple model is at the heart of a new theory called causal dynamical triangulation (CDT), which has emerged as a promising approach to solving the most vexing problem in physics—unifying the laws of gravity with those of quantum mechanics.[40]

The crafters of the theory—Renate Loll of Utrecht University, Jan Ambjørn of Copenhagen University, and Jerzy Jurkiewicz of Jagiellonian University—put it in the service of understanding things like the changing rates of the expanding universe; but, at core, they claim to be extending the discourse of quantum physics in the understanding of the most elementary structures on the scale of nano-reality. Their direct explanation of the concept, aired in a more recent issue of *Scientific American*, demonstrates that the absolutely reduced fabric of matter conforms to the interlocking and pulsing geometry of space-time itself, rather than of matter or energy once thought to "occupy" space-time.[41] If we want a metaphor for the littlest, nano-scaled things that constitute matter, energy, and space-time, we must conceive of a myriad of ultratiny (existing down at the scale of the

Planck scale, or 1.616 × 10^{-35} meters), triangle-shaped or triangle-sided tetrahedral, or rather, tetrahedron-sided hyper-tetrahedra (just as a four-dimensional hypercube is "sided" with three-dimensional cubes and not so much two-dimensional squares that side only a solid cube). These alter and inflate at pico-second rates to weave, moment to moment, the fabric of space-time and the evanescent quanta that are the seeming building blocks of matter. The impeccable visual support of *Scientific American*'s artistic arm aids well in grasping this abstruse hypergeometrical idea, although Loll, Ambjørn, and Jurkiewicz proffer the dense mathematics in other venues.[42] If matter or energy might be said to be constituted by space-time at the smallest of physical scales, then space-time's geometry is not a congeries of amorphous quantum fluctuations (such is the notion of nano-space or nano-gravity as a so-called quantum foam) but a dynamically twisting and flattening, piling and unfolding, ballooning and contracting fretwork of tetrahedra all latticed together on their *triangular* "bottom" surfaces (hence, "causal dynamical triangulation," or CDT).

If allegory has been called the discourse of the ineffable, then *allegory* is an apt term for postmodern physics's most fundamental, tiniest of structures comprising the CDT theory, which certainly constitute a domain of supersensuous, meta-experiential abstractions that seem to violate the quotidian quality required by Bronowski of workable science.[43] And in the case of the progression of the disciplinary narrative that I've traced in this short summation—from Thomson and Rutherford, through Nambu and Witten, and through Loll, Ambjorn, and Jurkiewicz—the meta-metaphorics of one-dimensional to two-dimensional to three-dimensional to four-dimensional objects used in explaining the most fundamental, littlest structures of the universe allegorizes the original progression or hierarchy of geometrical objects organized by Euclid himself. Still, the latest allegorical models of fundamental physics continue to grow more and more abstruse as artifacts of the ineffable, the sheerly indefinable. This is part and parcel of even literary allegory, of allegory construed as an object of interest still alive in the humanities.[44]

We have indeed witnessed a reinscribing, at a historically much later narrative level, of the very hierarchy constituting Euclid's geometry in the *Elements*. And so, mine is a simple thesis, really, about persistent analogization using ascending ladders of key metaphors. The framework of my own analogical narrative underlying this allegory of Euclid has its own tendentious turns, but I think it nicely shows how an older discursive formation gets rendered rhetorically as an imaginative sensuous narrative, even in its sequential entirety, and recast at a subsequent imagistic level, a level that is systematically (and laterally) correspondential. The objects of study in science are real, but we often now know them only as arcane and ineffable mathematical models that sprout fanciful hypergeometries. I hope to have shown what Kuhn or Bronowski or Holton had always continued to assert: The mechanism of discovery and final formulation in mathematics, in science, is rhetorical or tropological and not transparent. And I think there is no device, no mode in literary rhetoric more promising (though more mysterious and exciting) for articulating this mechanism than allegory.

Notes

1. Gilles Deleuze, *The Fold: Leibniz and the Baroque*, trans. Tom Conley (Minneapolis and London: University of Minnesota Press, 1993), 88.
2. The etymological defining of the word *allegory* itself marks what I call the requisitely philological "ground zero." See, for instance, Angus Fletcher, *Allegory: The Theory of a Symbolic Mode* (Ithaca, NY: Cornell University Press, 1964), 2 (note 1), whom I follow in this philological spirit.
3. *Science and Human Values*, rev. ed. (Harper, Row and Publishers, 1965; first pub. 1956), 13–14. Following Bronowski's sudden death in 1974, his posthumously assembled collection, *The Visionary Eye: Essays in the Arts, Literature, and Science*, selected and ed., Piero E. Ariotti and Rita Bronowski (Cambridge, MA, and London: MIT Press, 1978), remained faithful to this early and pioneering, cross-disciplinary, and synthetic formulation (see esp. 20–32) that, according to Rita Bronowski, really "opened the two-cultures debate" ("Introduction," *Visionary Eye*, vii)—an achievement that we now tend to ascribe to Snow (*The Two Cultures and the Scientific Revolution*. New York: Cambridge University Press, 1959).
4. *The Structure of Scientific Revolutions* (Chicago: The University of Chicago Press, 1970).
5. *Thematic Origins of Scientific Thought: Kepler to Einstein*, rev. ed. (Cambridge, MA: Harvard University Press, 1988; first pub. 1973). Just as Bronowski remained faithful to his original vision concerning the metaphoric constitution of scientific thought, so Holton holds faith with his own thematic model; see his more recent *Science and Anti-Science* (Cambridge, MA: Harvard University Press, 1993), in which he develops the concept of imagistic themata into one of "dramatic" personae who flesh out said themes in a paradigmatically new scientific proposition. Brian Rotman has achieved a similar, though more thoroughly "semiotic," version of the dramatic model in his understanding of the variously imaginary entities that could be said to constitute the stages or levels of mathematical production (mathematical "subject," "person," and "agent"—the last of which he actually designates a *daemon*, reminiscent of Fletcher's ubiquitous allegorical

daemon, though without acknowledgement of Fletcher). See *Ad Infinitum: The Ghost in Turing's Machine; Taking God out of Mathematics and Putting the Body Back In* (Stanford, CA: Stanford University Press, 1993), 65–87. I have developed Rotman's model in my reading of Johannes Kepler's division of mathematical or scientific cognition in his final treatise, *Somnium*; see James J. Paxson, "Kepler's Allegory of Containment, the Making of Modern Astronomy, and the Semiotics of Mathematical Thought," *Intertexts* 3 (1999): 105–123.

6. I allude here to the more recent work by Jeanne Fahnestock, who shows, for instance, that Newton, in formulating a theory of gravity, effectively invoked the figure of chiasmus or reversal: *Rhetorical Figures in Science* (New York and Oxford, U.K.: Oxford University Press, 1999), especially Chapter 4, 122–155.

7. Quintilian, *Institutio Oratoria*, trans. and ed. H. E. Butler, Loeb Classical Library (Cambridge, MA: Harvard University Press, 1920), 8.6.44.

8. See Bruce T. Clarke's *Energy Forms: Allegory and Science in the Era of Classical Thermodynamics* (Ann Arbor: University of Michigan Press, 2001); see also his *Allegories of Writing: The Subject of Metamorphosis* (Albany: State University of New York Press, 1995) for precursory formulations that trace the Lucretian scientific attitude through the allegorical and mythographic matrix of Ovidian-styled transformation literature from antiquity to modern science fiction.

9. See my article, "The Allegory of Temporality and the Early Modern Calculus," in a cluster for the journal *Configurations: A Journal of Literature, Science, and Technology* 4.1 (1996), 39–66, guest-edited by Clarke.

10. For instance, see E. A. Burtt, *The Metaphysical Foundations of Modern Science* (1925; New York: Dover Publications, 2003), which posits the "radical break" notion regarding prior and succeeding scientific texts, models, and paradigms.

11. See Aristotle, *The Physics*, trans. P. H. Wicksteed and F. M. Cornford, Loeb Classical Library (Cambridge, MA: Harvard University Press), IV.8–10.

12. *Sir Isaac Newton's Mathematical Principles of Natural Philosophy and His System of the World*, trans. Andrew Motte, 1729, rev. Florian Cajori (Berkeley: University of California Press, 1947), 197–198; the statement is the famous "Proposition 75/Theorem 35." See *Relativity: The Special and General Theory*, trans. Robert W. Lawson (New York: Three Rivers Press, 1961), 108–110.

13. See Quintilian 9.2.45–51 for his full discussion of the trope irony.

14. A complete yet beautiful and well-annotated English-language edition of Euclid is *The Elements*, trans. Sir Thomas L. Health, intro. Andrew Aberdein (New York: Barnes and Noble, 2006; first pub. 1908).

15. The surplus or excess or supplementarity of the allegorical sign seems to be the one feature *all* theories of the mode or effect have in common. The matter thus invokes the supplementarity of all sign-making systems, conceived from Plato through Derrida.

16. The view was made infamous by Paul de Man in his seminal essay, "The Rhetoric of Temporality." See *Blindness and Insight: Essays in the Rhetoric of Contemporary Criticism*, second rev. ed. (Minneapolis: University of Minnesota Press, 1983), 207.

17. De Man, *Allegories of Reading: Figural Language in Rousseau, Nietzsche, Rilke, and Proust* (New Haven, CT: Yale University Press, 1979), 201–202.

18. *The Allegory of Love: A Study in Mediaeval Tradition* (Oxford, U.K.: Oxford University Press, 1936), 45–46.

19. See Quintilian, cf. note 7 above.

20. See my "Allegory of Temporality," 45–46.

21. For a fascinating (and delightful) cultural history of the logarithm and its links to the modern sliderule, see Clyde B. Clason, *Delights of the Slide Rule* (New York: Thomas Crowell Company, 1964).

22. Morris Kline, *Mathematical Thought from Ancient to Modern Times* (New York: Oxford University Press, 1972), 236.

23. Paxson, "Allegory of Temporality," 46–47.

24. Fahnestock, 143.

25. Paxson, "Allegory of Temporality," 44.

26. Fahnestock, 147.

27. *Annalen der Physik* 17 (June 30, 1905): 891–921.

28. For a very interesting study on the discursivization of energy in early modern poetics (and which I take to be a nominal sequel to his 1964 book on allegory), see Fletcher, *Time, Space, and Motion in the Age of Shakespeare* (Cambridge, MA: Harvard University Press, 2007).

29. Fahnestock, 158. I single out Fahnestock's elaborate discussion of *ploche* not to displace or compromise my assertion that allegory serves bilevel, analogical structures; rather, I speculate on what she *might have* suggested concerning what I'm trying to do concerning Euclideanism and physics's search for fundamental structure inasmuch as her splendid book never treats *allegoria* at all—aside from recognizing it in a brief catalog (7), that it was one of the important tropes in the *Rhetorica ad herennium*, the Roman treatise nearly as important as Quintilian's for ancient, medieval, and Renaissance poetics and oratory.

30. *Elements*, 1; and see Jacob Bronowski, *The Ascent of Man* (Toronto and Boston: Little, Brown and Co., 1974), 163.

31. Bronowski, *Ascent of Man*, 233.

32. "On the Structure of the Atom: An Investigation of the Stability and Periods of Oscillation of a Number of Corpuscles Arranged at Equal Intervals around the Circumference of a Circle; with Application of the Results to the Theory of Atomic Structure," *Philosophical Magazine*, Series 6, 7.39 (March 1904): 237–265.

33. See E. N. da C. Andrade, *Rutherford and the Nature of the Atom* (New York: Doubleday, 1964).

34. "The Existence of a Neutron," *Proceedings of the Royal Society* 136 (1932): 692–708.

35. See Niels Bohr, *Atomic Physics and Human Knowledge* (New York: Science Editions, 1961).

36. Bronowski, *Ascent of Man*, 364.

37. See essays in Paul Davies and Julian R. Brown, ed., *Superstrings: A Theory of Everything* (Cambridge, U.K.: Cambridge University Press, 1992) for general

introduction; Brian Greene, *The Elegant Universe: Superstrings, Hidden Dimensions, and the Quest for the Ultimate Theory* (New York: W. W. Norton and Company, 2003) for what is probably the most popular guide to the subject for nonscientists; Edward Witten, "The Universe on a String," *Astronomy Magazine* (June 2002); and Leonard Susskind, *The Cosmic Landscape: String Theory and the Illusion of Intelligent Design* (Little, Brown & Company, 2006).

38. See Michael J. Duff, "M-Theory (the Theory Formerly Known as Strings)," *International Journal of Modern Physics* A, 11 (1996): 5623–5642; and Edward Witten, "Magic, Mystery and Matrix," *Notices of the AMS* (October 1998): 1124–1129.

39. See Maureen Quilligan, *The Language of Allegory: Defining the Genre* (Ithaca, NY: Cornell University Press, 1979), 97–155, for discussion of the essential "pre-text" in the allegorical literature of the Middle Ages and Renaissance. The works of Chaucer, Spenser, and many other writers represent often the rewriting, allegorically, of the ancient world's two most prominent pre-texts needing reappropriation, reinscription—the Bible and Vergil's *Aeneid*. Although Jacob Bronowski nonchalantly records that Euclid's *Elements* was the Middle Ages' most reproduced text after the Bible, its life as a classical pre-text is secured in that, although it is not referred to directly in the most au courant of modern scientific or mathematical studies, it possesses a structure that has been getting allegorically reconfigured as the matrix of our new field's *narrative history*, or rather, the field's successionist historical *narratology* of fundamental structures according to my argument in this essay.

40. Mark Alpert, "The Triangular Universe," *Scientific American* 296, 2 (February 2007): 24.

41. "The Self-Organizing Quantum Universe," *Scientific American* 299, 1 (July 2008): 42–49.

42. See J. Ambjørn, J. Jurkiewicz, and R. Loll, "Quantum Gravity: The Art of Building Spacetime," *Approaches to Quantum Gravity: Toward a New Understanding of Space, Time and Matter*, Daniele Oriti, ed. (Cambridge, U.K.: Cambridge University Press, 2009): 341–359.

43. *Visionary Eye*, 28.

44. Thomas Maresca, "Saying and Meaning: Allegory and the Indefinable," *Bulletin of Research in the Humanities* 83 (1974): 248–261.

INDEX